The Celts

The Celts

History, Life, and Culture

VOLUME 1: A–H

JOHN T. KOCH, GENERAL EDITOR
ANTONE MINARD, EDITOR

Editorial Team: Thomas Owen Clancy, Petra S. Hellmuth,
Anne Holley, Glenys Howells, Marian Beech Hughes, Marion Löffler

 ABC-CLIO

Santa Barbara, California • Denver, Colorado • Oxford, England

Copyright 2012 by ABC-CLIO, LLC

Library of Congress Cataloging-in-Publication Data

The Celts : history, life, and culture / John T. Koch, general editor ; Antone Minard, editor.
   p. cm.
   Includes bibliographical references and index.
   ISBN 978–1–59884–964–6 (cloth : acid-free paper) — ISBN 978–1–59884–965–3 (e-book)
1. Civilization, Celtic—Encyclopedias. 2. Celts—History—Encyclopedias. I. Koch, John T. II. Minard, Antone.
CB206.C48   2012
936.4—dc23   2012005137

ISBN: 978–1–59884–964–6
EISBN: 978–1–59884–965–3

16 15 14 13 12   1 2 3 4 5

This book is also available on the World Wide Web as an eBook.
Visit www.abc-clio.com for details.

ABC-CLIO, LLC
130 Cremona Drive, P.O. Box 1911
Santa Barbara, California 93116-1911

This book is printed on acid-free paper ∞

Manufactured in the United States of America

Contents

Acknowledgments

The University of Wales Centre for Advanced Welsh and Celtic Studies and the Editors wish to acknowledge the sustained support and generosity of ABC-Clio Publishers, which funded several members of the CAWCS Research Team working on this encyclopedia. This partnership between a publisher and an academic research centre was a far-sighted decision that deserves high praise and emulation. The financial support of the University of Wales has also been invaluable. We gratefully acknowledge a British Academy small grant that partially funded the posts of Bibliographer and Illustration Editor. A three-year grant from the Arts and Humanities Research Council funded the research for the Celticity Project's Cesair Database, Proto-Celtic Vocabulary, and Atlas. Although this grant did not directly contribute to this encyclopedia, the beneficial synergy afforded by researchers carrying out these collaborative projects simultaneously was immeasurable.

The Research Team is also deeply grateful for the administrative support received at CAWCS from Vera Bowen, Hawys Bowyer, and Nia Davies. As for the publishers, staunch and encouraging support was forthcoming from Ron Boehm, Simon Mason, Ellen Rasmussen, Donald Schmidt, and Tony Sloggett (2006 edition). In 2011, Mariah Gumpert and John Wagner brought a renewed level of support and dedication to the project.

Introduction

The Celts: History, Life, and Culture is designed for the use of everyone interested in Celtic studies and also for those interested in many related and subsidiary fields, including the individual CELTIC COUNTRIES and their languages, literatures, archaeology, history, folklore, and mythology. In its chronological scope, this encyclopedia covers subjects from the HALLSTATT and LA TÈNE periods of the later pre-Roman Iron Age to the beginning of the 21st century. Geographically, as well as including the Celtic civilizations of Ireland, Britain, and Brittany (ARMORICA) from ancient times to the present, it covers the Continental Celts of ancient GAUL, the Iberian Peninsula, and central and eastern Europe, together with the Galatians of present-day Turkey; it also follows the modern Celtic diaspora into the Americas.

These volumes represent a major, long-term undertaking that synthesizes fresh research in all areas with an authoritative presentation of standard information. The 808 entries, ranging in length from 50 to more than 3,000 words, cover the field in depth; they are fully integrated with a clear system of internal cross-references and are supported by a select list of 160 items for further reading in the Bibliography at the back of Volume 2. The work of the 263 contributors represents the leading edge of research currently being carried out at all centres of Celtic studies around the world. The name of the contributor of each entry appears at the end of the entry.

For several reasons, a project of this scope was felt to be essential at this time. First, as a scholarly, but accessible, comprehensive overview of Celtic studies, this encyclopedia is unique. There is no shortage of popular and semi-popular volumes with 'Celtic' or 'Celts' in their titles, but none aims to encompass the whole field with balance and scholarly reliability. At the same time, there exists a body of specialist publications that sets standards for the small corps of professional Celticists. In this narrow context, Celtic studies often means little more than the historical linguistics of the CELTIC LANGUAGES. The publications in this category are often difficult to read and difficult to find in print or even in general library collections. Most of the handbooks and edited texts that constitute the core works of Celtic philology date from the mid-20th century or earlier, and have not been superseded. Even by their own rigorous and esoteric standards, the expert reference works are a generation or more out of date—a major pitfall requiring of Celtic scholars an almost superhuman 'keeping up with more recent advances' to remain current. To put it metaphorically, the glue holding Celtic studies together as an academic discipline has grown old and brittle.

The situation with regard to books in Celtic studies—in which a qualitative gap looms between specialist and more popular works—mirrors divisions between workers in the field. Small numbers of professional scholars, academic departments, and library collections devoted to Celticity contrast with the vast and growing international cohort of enthusiasts. This latter category includes both amateurs and experts in other fields—modern history, comparative literature, ancient and medieval studies, and many other disciplines—who are self-taught when it comes to Celtic studies, owing to the limited availability of formal instruction in the field. In the light of this background, this encyclopedia recognizes a broad need for full and up-to-date information well beyond the limited institutional bounds of Celtic studies per se. My own experience, for example, of teaching Celtic studies to undergraduates in the United States during the years 1985–1998 was a revelation to me: It showed how little material was available, and how much was needed as essential background for newcomers to this fascinating and rewarding field of study—one so near, yet in many ways so unreachably far, from American civilization.

Like all subjects in this time of exponentially expanding information, Celtic studies has tended to fragment into specialties, and its experts have neither the resources nor the training to move easily between subfields—between languages and periods, for example. Once again, the unsatisfactory links that bind the field together are either outdated and arcane or semi-popularized and intellectually suspect.

Another reason for embarking on a major synthesis at this time is that archaeological Celtic studies in Britain underwent a profound crisis of conscience in the late 20th century, and this debate has continued into the 21st century. The validity of applying the term 'Celtic' to any group of people or culture of any period has been questioned—especially in connection with the cultural history of Ireland and Britain, to which the terms 'Celts' and 'Celtic' were evidently not applied until modern times. On the one hand, in the wake of this episode of 'Celtoscepticism', the relatedness and common origins of the Celtic family of languages remain unchallenged scientific facts, and the name 'Celtic' for this family—given that all such terms are ultimately arbitrary—is no more misleading or historically unjustified than such well-established and undisputed terms as, say, 'Germanic' or 'Semitic'. On the other hand, the idea that certain types of non-linguistic culture—such as artefacts in the LA TÈNE style—can be meaningfully described as 'Celtic' now requires greater circumspection. There are few, if any, types of artwork, weapons, or ritual sites, for example, for which it is likely, or even reasonable, to expect that there would have been a one-to-one correspondence between those who used them and speakers of Celtic languages, or speakers of Celtic languages only, or, conversely, that all speakers of Celtic languages used them. While northwest and central Spain, GALATIA in Asia Minor, and all of Ireland (including Munster) were eminently Celtic linguistically—at least by the Late La Tène period—La Tène objects of the recognized standard forms are thin on the ground in these areas. Thus, while this encyclopedia is not exclusively, or even primarily, about the Celtic languages, the defining criterion of 'peoples and countries that do, or once did, use Celtic languages' and an index of connectedness to the Celtic languages have been borne in mind when branching out into other cultural domains, such as art, history, music, and so on, as well as literature produced in the Celtic countries in English, Latin, and French. For areas without full literary documentation, the presence of Celtic place-names and group names has been a key consideration for determining parts that can be meaningfully considered Celtic. Owing to the importance of the study of names as diagnostic of Celticity, the reader will find numerous discussions of etymology in the entries.

The policy of this encyclopedia is also to give proper names in their forms in the relevant Celtic language, where this is practical. For the modern Celtic countries, Anglicized or French forms of names prevail. It is often difficult even to find out what the Gaelic form of a Scottish place-name is, or the Breton form of one in Brittany, and this issue, in turn, can become a major impediment for those moving on to research sources in the original languages, as they cannot always be certain whether what they are encountering is the same place or person. The fact that we are used to seeing Anglicized (and Frenchified) forms of names on maps—and these versions only, unlike the place-names of more widely spoken languages—is a major contributing factor to the invisibility of the Celtic languages, their apparent nonexistence, and their seamless incorporation into the core Anglophone and Francophone areas. Another reason for supplying Celtic-language forms for names coined in the Celtic languages is that it is these forms that are most informative with regard to etymology, explaining topographical features, genealogical links, dedications to saints, and other factors.

Having thus defined the scope of our subject as the Celtic languages and cultures and the people who used them from the earliest historical records to the present, the content of the encyclopedia has also inevitably been shaped by the history and predominant projects of Celtic studies as a field. Since its dual origins in literary ROMANTICISM and the comparative historical linguistics of the INDO-EUROPEAN languages, the centre of gravity of Celtic studies has recognizably remained in the ancient and early medieval periods, the time of the earliest Celtic texts and history's opening horizon that constitutes the background for traditional heroes and saints of the Celtic countries. It is, of course, common origins in these early times that define the Celtic languages, and their speakers, as a family—once again, the glue holding the Celtic studies together as a discipline. Thus the prominence given to early evidence and sources of tradition continues here. Also under the rubric of Celtic origins, we have given special attention to the Picts, Scots, and Britons of the north in the early Middle Ages, where Celtic studies contributes to our understanding of the emergence of Scotland. In addition, however, Romanticism and historical linguistics have focused attention on modern times and the future by defining present-day national identities and aspirations and throwing into relief the special significance of the Irish, Scottish Gaelic, Manx, Welsh, Breton, and Cornish languages and their uncertain fates. Here Celtic studies is a vital ingredient in such modern political processes as the birth of the Irish Republic, for example, or the currently unfolding and as yet unresolved developments in devolution within the United Kingdom and the integration of states and regions within the European Union. In the middle, between archaic Celtic origins and modern Celtic identity politics, the current generation of Celtic scholars are now turning their attention increasingly to the long-neglected later medieval and early modern periods, including, for example, recent work on classical Irish (or Gaelic) poetry and the Welsh poets of the nobility, the fruits of both areas of research being fully reflected here. Recent Celtic studies has also shared with other humanistic disciplines a growing interest in contemporary literary theory; it is largely thanks to the influence of feminist theoretical perspectives, for example, that many entries on recently discovered or reevaluated women writers will be found in these volumes.

How to Use This Encyclopedia

The Celts: History, Life, and Culture is largely self-contained; in other words, it is not anticipated that a second work will be required to enable the reader to understand the information in the entries. A detailed cross-referencing system allows readers to find relevant information shared between related articles. Cross-references in the text of an entry place the title of a related article (or its first word or words) in SMALL CAPITAL LETTERS.

To find a particular piece of information in the encyclopedia, the best starting point is the unified table of Contents at the beginning of each of the two volumes or the index in Volume 2. For broader categories, the list of Contents gives the titles of the 803 entries in alphabetical order, together with page numbers. The index provides a fuller list of subject items in alphabetical order. Within the index, subjects that are themselves entry names are set in **bold type**.

A number of other symbols and abbreviations are used within the encyclopedia as follows:

/	(General)	Means "or" and is used to indicate variant forms of names (for instance, Brecknock/Brecon) or dates (for instance, AD 829/30) where there is uncertainty between two dates.
/ /	(Linguistics)	A letter or symbol between two slashes indicates a sound (phoneme).
cf.	(General)	Short for *confer,* meaning "compare."
e.g.	(General)	Short for *exempli gratia,* meaning "for example."
i.e.	(General)	Short for *id est,* meaning "it is" or "that is."
no.	(General)	Short for *numero,* meaning "number."
†	(History)	Means "died" and indicates that the number that follows is the date of death.
×	(History)	Used to indicate a range of possible dates. "AD 1000×1100" means "a year between AD 1000 and 1100."
c.	(History)	Short for *circa,* meaning "about," and indicates that the number that follows is an approximate date or date range.
fl.	(History)	Short for *floruit,* meaning "flourished," and indicates the date or date range during which a person was active.
r.	(History)	Short for "reigned" and indicates that the numbers that follow are the beginning and ending dates of the reign.
<	(Linguistics)	Means "is derived from" and indicates that the word that follows is the etymon or ancestral form of the sound or word before the symbol.
>	(Linguistics)	Means "gives" and indicates that the word that follows is the derivative or later form of the sound or word before the symbol.

<>	(Linguistics)	Indicates that the letter(s) between the angle brackets is (are) being discussed as a letter or as letters.
[]	(Linguistics)	Indicates that the letter(s) or symbol(s) between the brackets represent(s) a phonetic transcription.
*	(Linguistics)	Means "reconstructed as" and indicates that the word that follows is reconstructed based on historical linguistic evidence but is not attested in a historical or archaeological context.
**	(Linguistics)	Indicates that the word that follows is a hypothetical form that has never been current in the spoken or written language.
gl.	(Linguistics)	Short for "glossed" and indicates that the word that follows was a translation in the source text of the word that precedes.
pl.	(Linguistics)	Short for "plural."
§	(Text)	Means "section" and indicates the section or chapter within a larger work.
.	(Text)	A period is used to separate sections of ancient and medieval texts; for example, 1.2.3 should be read "book one, chapter two, line three"; 1.2.3–5 should be read "book one, chapter two, lines three through five." Two numbers with one period between refer to book and chapter only: 1.2, "book one, chapter two."
col.	(Text)	Short for "column."
l.	(Text)	Short for "line."
ll.	(Text)	Short for "lines."
p.	(Text)	Short for "page."
pp.	(Text)	Short for "pages."
r.	(Text)	Short for *recto,* meaning "on the right," and indicates the front side of a manuscript page, the one on the right when the book is open flat.
s.v.	(Text)	Short for *sub verbo,* meaning "under the word," and indicates that the word that follows is the headword in a reference work.
v.	(Text)	Short for *verso,* meaning "on the back," and indicates the back side of a manuscript page, the one on the left when the book is open flat.

For students and other readers wishing to pursue any aspect of the subject matter of this encyclopedia in greater depth, a convenient first step is provided by the bibliography in Volume 2. This collection represents the most essential, accessible, and up-to-date publications in Celtic studies, offering a wide entryway onto this fascinating and rewarding field. To go beyond this reading list, readers wishing to pursue serious and original research should first turn to the five-volume *Celtic Culture: A Historical Encyclopedia* (2006, print publication and ebook), of which the present volumes represent a concise and updated version. *Celtic Culture* contains a 10,000-item bibliography in its fifth volume, which include pre-modern texts, publications in languages other than English, and specialist studies.

The Celticity Project and the Research Team

The Celts: History, Life, and Culture forms part of a major research project, entitled 'The Celtic Languages and Cultural Identity: A Multidisciplinary Synthesis', in progress since 1998 at the University of Wales Centre for Advanced Welsh and Celtic Studies (CAWCS), Aberystwyth, under the direction of Dr. John T. Koch. It is one of five major publications of the project, the others being: (1) *Cesair: An English–Early Irish Interactive Database*; (2) *A Proto-Celtic Vocabulary and World View*; (3) *Celtic Culture: A Historical Encyclopedia* (ABC-Clio, 2006), and (4) *An Atlas for Celtic Studies: Archaeology and Names in Ancient Europe and Early Medieval Ireland, Britain, and Brittany* (2007).

Five years after the publication of the five-volume *Historical Encyclopedia*, the CAWCS research team decided to undertake a revised and updated encyclopedia, presenting Celtic archaeology, culture, folklore, history, linguistics, literature, and religion in a format that was more accessible to the general reader. *The Celts: History, Life, and Culture* contains all of the essential information about the field of Celtic studies and these subfields within it while setting aside coverage of the more esoteric facets of the field of interest only to specialists. The bibliography, too, has been customized to exclude works that are difficult for most readers to acquire. In this encyclopedia, we have provided a set of 'further reading' bibliographies, grouped by subject, of readily obtainable works in English. In addition, both in the bibliographies and in the articles commissioned for this encyclopedia, we have included references to websites whose information is accurate and reliable.

The following members of the CAWCS staff participated in the Celticity project and the work of the encyclopedia: CAWCS Director Professor Geraint H. Jenkins; Managing Editor Dr. Marion Löffler; Research Fellows Dr. Graham Jones, Dr. Raimund Karl, Dr. Antone Minard, Simon Ó Faoláin, and Caroline aan de Weil; Research Editor Dr. Peter E. Busse; Editors Marian Beech Hughes and Glenys Howells; Bibliographer Anne Holley; Assistant Bibliographers William Slocombe and Heike Vieth; and Illustration Editor Esther Elin Roberts. Dr. Mary-Ann Constantine of CAWCS assisted with French and Breton references and Robert Lacey of the National Library of Wales with Irish and Scottish Gaelic. All of the research staff of the other projects at CAWCS generously assisted; several contributed entries. Also working closely with the team on the encyclopedia were the Contributing Editor for Ireland and Scotland Dr. Petra S. Hellmuth and the Contributing Editor for Scotland Professor Thomas Owen Clancy. Margaret Wallis Tilsley read the entries in page proof.

The Celticity project has also benefited greatly from the generous participation of members of its Advisory Panel: Professor Barry Cunliffe (Oxford), Professor Wendy Davies (London), Professor William Gillies (Edinburgh), Professor †Gwenaël Le Duc (Rennes), Professor J. P. Mallory (Belfast), Professor Máirín Ní Dhonnchadha (Galway), Professor Pádraig Ó Riain (Cork), Professor Peter Schrijver (Munich), Professor Patrick Sims-Williams (Aberystwyth), Professor Robin Chapman Stacey (Seattle, Washington), Professor Claude Sterckx (Brussels), and Professor Stefan Zimmer (Bonn). For Cesair, the Proto-Celtic Vocabulary, and the Atlas, J. P. Mallory has worked with John Koch as co-director.

Abbreviations

BL	British Library
Bret.	Breton

Corn.	Cornish
DIL	Royal Irish Academy, *Dictionary of the Irish Language*, based mainly on Old and Middle Irish Materials
Early Mod.Bret.	Early Modern Breton
Early Mod.Ir.	Early Modern Irish
Early Mod.W	Early Modern Welsh
GPC	Prifysgol Cymru, *Geiriadur Prifysgol Cymru*
Hib.E.	Hibernian English (the English dialect of Ireland)
IE	Indo-European
Ir.	Irish
MBret.	Middle Breton
ME	Middle English
MIr.	Middle Irish
Mod.Bret.	Modern Breton
Mod.Ir.	Modern Irish
Mod.W	Modern Welsh
MW	Middle Welsh
NLS	National Library of Scotland
NLW	National Library of Wales
OBret.	Old Breton
OCorn.	Old Cornish
OE	Old English
OIr.	Old Irish
OW	Old Welsh
R	Red Book of Hergest
RIB	R. G. Collingwood and R. P. Wright, *The Roman Inscriptions of Britain*
RIG	Michel Lejeune et al., *Recueil des inscriptions gauloises*
ScG	Scottish Gaelic
TYP	Rachel Bromwich, *Trioedd Ynys Prydein*

Celtic Chronology

The following timeline is provided to help contextualize the various strands of archaeology, history, language, and literature within this encyclopedia with a relative chronology of major events. For brevity's sake, many dates from archaeology and those known to be within a two- to five-year period have been approximated to a single year, but especially with early dates these should not be taken as absolute. Less precise dates have been given as *circa* (about), abbreviated *c.*: thus *c.* 500 means 'around the year 500'. For fuller details on any given event, see the relevant entry or entries in the encyclopedia.

The Continental Celts in the Ancient World

Date	Transalpine Gaul and Britain	Italy and Eastern Europe	Iberia	Greece and Rome
3200–2400 BC	Late Neolithic; construction of megalithic stone circles (e.g., STONEHENGE)			Early Minoan civilization on Crete
2400–2000 BC	Beaker Culture			
1200–750 BC (or –800 BC)	HALLSTATT A and B (Urnfield Culture)		'Proto-Celtic' castros	Rome settled
750 BC (or 800 BC)	Hallstatt C begins			Homer and Hesiod first written down
650 BC	Hallstatt D begins		Earlier TARTESSIAN inscriptions	
600 BC	Massalia (Marseilles) founded	Earliest LEPONTIC inscriptions		Latin script developed
475 BC	LA TÈNE A begins			
400 BC	La Tène B begins		'Initial Celtic' castros	
400 BC	Earliest GAULISH inscriptions	Gauls' settlement of Northern Italy		
390 BC				BRENNOS sacks Rome
336 BC				Murder of Philip II of Macedon with Celtic sword
320 BC	Pytheas voyages to Britain		'Final Celtic' oppida (see OPPIDUM) begin to appear	
300 BC		Earliest Celtic COINAGE		
295 BC		Romans defeat Cisalpine Gauls at the Battle of Clusium		
279–278 BC		Gauls cross into GALATIA		BRENNOS attacks Delphi
250 BC	La Tène C begins			
225 BC		Romans defeat Cisalpine Gauls at the Battle of Telamon		
218–201 BC		Cisalpine Gauls aid Hannibal	Second Punic War; Romans defeat Hannibal and conquer much of Iberia	
202–191 BC		Romans conquer CISALPINE GAUL		
175 BC			CELTIBERIAN inscriptions begin	

The Continental Celts in the Ancient World (Continued)

Date	Transalpine Gaul and Britain	Italy and Eastern Europe	Iberia	Greece and Rome
150 BC	La Tène D begins			
143–133 BC			Celtiberian War with Rome	
133 BC			Conquest of Numantia	
85 BC				Works of Posidonius on the Celts
58 BC	Helvetii move west, and are defeated by Caesar and allied Gauls			
54 BC	Caesar's invasion of Britain			
52 BC	Battle of Alesia; defeat of Vercingetorix			
51–50 BC	Conquest of Gaul; End of La Tène D			
c. 50 BC			Latest Celtiberian inscriptions	Diodorus Siculus's Historical Library
				Strabo's Geography
20 BC–23 AD		End of La Tène D; Latest Lepontic inscriptions		
1 BC				
AD 38			Celtiberian poet Martial born in Bilbilis	
AD 41	Death of Cunobelinos			
AD 43	Claudius invades Britain			
AD 58	Death of Caratācos			
AD 60–61	Revolt of Boudica and the Iceni			
AD 61–65				Lucan's Pharsalia
AD 79	Agricola becomes governor of Roman Britain			

(continued)

The Continental Celts in the Ancient World (Continued)

Date	TRANSALPINE GAUL and BRITAIN	Italy and Eastern Europe	Iberia	Greece and ROME
AD 84	Battle of Mons Graupius			
AD 122	HADRIAN's WALL built			
AD 142	Antonine Wall built			
c. AD 150				Ptolemy's Geography
AD 303	St ALBAN martyred			
AD 367	'Barbarian Conspiracy' against Roman Britain			
AD 383	Magnus Maximus (MACSEN WLEDIG) proclaimed Roman Emperor in the West			
c. AD 400	GAULISH and GALATIAN still survive as spoken languages according to St Jerome			
AD 410	Full Roman withdrawal from Britain	Armorican autonomy from Rome		Rome sacked by Visigoths

Cels in the Early Medieval Period, to 1066

Date	Ireland (Ériu)	Great Britain	Brittany (Breizh)
c. 400	Primitive Irish first attested in OGAM		
410		Full Roman withdrawal from Britain	Armorican autonomy from Rome
417			Roman authority re-established in Armorica
c. 425	Dál Riata cross into Alba (North Britain)		
428	Death of Niall Noígiallach		
431	Palladius brings Christianity to Ireland		
441			
c. 450		Anglo-Saxon 'conquest' of Britain; fl. Ambrosius Aurellanus	Heaviest period of Breton migrations begins
469			Rigotamus leads autonomous Brittany
493	Death of St Patrick (latest date)		
c. 500		'Age of Saints' begins; St Ninian founds Whithorn monastery; death of Fergus Mór mac Erca of Dál Riata	'Age of Saints' begins
516		Battle of Badonicus Mons	
525	Death of St Brigit	Battle of Camlan	
537			
c. 540–45		Gildas writes De Excidio Britanniae	
547		Death of Maelgwn Gwynedd	
c. 550	Monasteries begin in Ireland (Bangor, Clonard, Clonfert, Clonmacnoise, Derry, Durrow)	fl. Aneirin	
563		Monastery founded on Eilean Ì; Christianity comes to the Picts	
565	Death of Diarmait mac Cerbaill		

(continued)

Celts in the Early Medieval Period, to 1066 (Continued)

Date	Ireland (Ériu)	Great Britain	Brittany (Breizh)
567			Council of Tours
573		Battle of Arfderydd	
574		Beginning of Aedán mac Gabráin's kingship in Dál Riata	
577		Anglo-Saxons take Bath and region	
597		Death of Colum Cille	
c. 600	Old Irish period; Ireland's literary Golden Age begins		Heaviest period of Breton migrations ends
603		End of Aedán mac Gabráin's kingship	
613		Battle of Caer (Chester)	
619		Anglo-Northumbrians conquer Elfed	
634–36	Battle of Mag Roth	Foundation of Lindisfarne; fall of Gododdin; death of Cadwallon	
c. 650		Angles expand into what is now Scotland	
664		Death of Cadwaladr	
673			
679		Adomnán becomes abbot of Eilean Ì	
692		Life of Saint Columba	
c. 700	Beginning of Eóganacht dominance in Munster (Mumu)		
704		Death of Adomnán	
731		Bede's Historia Ecclesiastica	
786			Charlemagne sends his army into Brittany
793	Viking raids on Britain and Ireland begin with Lindisfarne		
c. 800	End of Ireland's literary Golden Age	Southwest Brythonic (Old Breton/Old Cornish) become distinct from Old Welsh	
807		Notable Viking raid of Eilean Ì (Iona)	

Celts in the Early Medieval Period, to 1066 (Continued)

Date	Ireland (ÉRIU)	Great Britain	Brittany (BREIZH)
829		*Historia Brittonum*	
831			Beginning of Nomenoë's reign
832			Foundation of Abbey of Redon
837	Vikings establish Dublin (BAILE ÁTHA CLIATH)		
843		CINAED MAC AILPÍN conquest of Pictland	Treaty of Verdun
845			Battle of Ballon
846	Beginning of Mael Sechnall's rule over most of Ireland		Charles the Bald recognizes Brittany's autonomy
851			Death of Nomenoë; beginning of Erispoë's reign
857		Death of Cinaed Mac Ailpin	death of Erispoë
858			
878		Death of RHODRI MAWR	
c. 900	Middle Irish begins		
931			Breton uprising against the Norse (Viking) occupation
936		Æthelstan fixes the eastern boundary of Cornwall (KERNOW)	
937		Battle of Brunanburh	ALAN VARVEG drives the Vikings from Brittany
950		Death of HYWEL DDA	
952			Death of Alan Varveg
997	BRIAN BORUMA recognized as king of the southern half of Ireland		
c. 1000			*Life of Saint Uuohednou* (Goueznou)

(continued)

Celts in the Early Medieval Period, to 1066 (Continued)

Date	Ireland (Éʀɪᴜ)	Great Britain	Brittany (Bʀᴇɪᴢʜ)
1002	Brian Bóruma becomes high-king of Ireland		
1014	Battle of Clontarf; death of Brian Bóruma		
1018		Battle of Carham: Scottish and British defeat of Northumbria; death of Owain the Bald and probably the end of the British kingdom of Yꜱᴛʀᴀᴅ Cʟᴜᴅ (Strathclyde)	
1042		Mᴀᴄ Bᴇᴛʜᴀᴅ (Macbeth) takes the throne of Moray	
1057		Death of Macbeth	
1066		Norman invasion of England and Cornwall	

Celtic Countries to the Loss of Independence, 1067–1543

Date	Ireland	Scotland and North Britain	Wales (Cymru)	Cornwall	Isle of Man (Ellan Vannin)	Brittany
1075			Accession of Gruffudd ap Cynan		Tynwald already c. 100 years old	
1079					Invasion of the Isle of Man by King Orry (Godred Crovan); Kingdom of Man and the Isles firmly established	
c. 1100			Middle Welsh			Middle Breton
1113					Accession of Olaf I	
1124		Accession of King David I				
1130		Suppression of Mormaers of Moray				
1137			Death of Gruffudd ap Cynan; reign of Owain Gwynedd begins; earliest Gogynfeirdd			
1139		Cumbria becomes part of the Kingdom of Scots	Geoffrey of Monmouth's *Historia Regum Brittaniae*			
1142	Cistercian house founded at Mellifont					Death of Pierre Abelard
1152	Synod of Kells					
1153		Death of King David I; accession of Malcolm IV			Olaf I murdered; accession of Godred II	
1156					Somerled of the Hebrides invades Isle of Man	

(continued)

Celtic Countries to the Loss of Independence, 1067–1543 (Continued)

Date	Ireland	Scotland and North Britain	Wales (Cymru)	Cornwall	Isle of Man (ELLAN VANNIN)	Brittany
1169	Norman military conquest of Ireland begins					
1170	Richard DE CLARE (Strongbow) arrives in Ireland		Death of Owain Gwynedd			First ARTHURIAN ROMANCE of CHRÉTIEN DE TROYES; BRETON Lays of Marie de France
1171	Strongbow becomes King of Leinster (LAIGIN); Henry II invades					
1176			EISTEDDFOD at Cardigan (Aberteifi)			
1194			Accession of LLYWELYN AB IORWERTH			
c. 1200	Early Modern Irish; beginning of literary Classical Irish period	Earliest divergence of written SCOTTISH GAELIC from Irish				
1240			Death of Llywelyn ab Iorwerth			
c. 1250				Middle Cornish		
1265				Glasney College founded		

Celtic Countries to the Loss of Independence, 1067–1543 (Continued)

Date	Ireland	Scotland and North Britain	Wales (*Cymru*)	Cornwall	Isle of Man (*ELLAN VANNIN*)	Brittany
1266		Hebrides sold to the King of Scots by the King of Norway			Isle of Man sold to the King of Scots by the King of Norway	
1282			Death of LLYWELYN AP GRUFFUDD; loss of independence for Wales			
1284			Statute of Rhuddlan			
1286		Death of King Alexander III				
1290		Death of Margaret, Maid of Norway				
1296		Scottish Wars of Independence begin				
1298		Battle of Falkirk				
1305		Death of William WALLACE				
1307		Robert the Bruce claims Scotland				
1314		Battle of Bannockburn				
1328		England recognizes Scottish independence				
1333					Battle of Halidon Hill: English control Isle of Man	
1337			Earliest CYWYDDWYR	Duchy of Cornwall created		

(continued)

Celtic Countries to the Loss of Independence, 1067–1543 (Continued)

Date	Ireland	Scotland and North Britain	Wales (Cymru)	Cornwall	Isle of Man (ELLAN VANNIN)	Brittany
1341						Death of Duke John III; War of the Breton Succession begins
1348	Bubonic plague in Anglo-Irish towns		Bubonic plague in southeast Wales and Cornwall			Bubonic plague
1349	Bubonic plague reaches most of the British Isles; death of Dafydd ap Gwilym					
1364						War of the Breton Succession ends
1366	Statutes of Kilkenny					
1399					Isle of Man comes under the direct control of the English Crown	
1400			OWAIN GLYNDŴR's revolt begins			
1407					Isle of Man granted to Lord Stanley	
1411		Foundation of the University of Saint Andrews				
1412			End of Owain Glyndŵr's revolt			
1469		Control of the Orkney and Shetland Islands passes from Norway to Scotland				

Celtic Countries to the Loss of Independence, 1067–1543 (Continued)

Date	Ireland	Scotland and North Britain	Wales (Cymru)	Cornwall	Isle of Man (Ellan Vannin)	Brittany
1485	First Tudor (Tudur) monarch, Henry VII					
1493		End of the Lordship of the Isles				
1497				Cornish Rebellion		
1499						*Catholicon* published
c. 1500			Modern Welsh			*Life of Saint Nonn*
1510		*Aberdeen Breviary*, first printed book in Scotland				
1513		Battle of Flodden				
1514						Death of Anna Vreizh
1532	Break with Rome					Acte d'Union
1534			Henry VIII's formal break with the Roman Catholic Church (for England, Wales, and Ireland)			
1536			Act of Union			
1541	Henry VIII declares himself King of Ireland and annexes Ireland to England					
1543			Supplementary Act of Union			

The Modern Celtic Countries

Date	Ireland	Scotland	Wales	Cornwall	Isle of Man	Brittany
c 1550				Late Cornish		
1560		Scotland's formal break with the Roman Catholic Church				
1567		First book in Scottish Gaelic (Classical Irish)				
1588			William Morgan's Welsh BIBLE			
1595	Hugh O'Neill (Aodh Ó Néill) leads a revolt					
1596	Spenser's *A Viewe of the Present State of Ireland*					
c. 1600	Modern Irish	Modern Scottish Gaelic				Early Modern Breton
1601	Battle of Kinsale (Cionn tSáile)					
1602	Complete Irish New Testament					
1603		Union of the Crowns				
1607	Flight of the Earls					
1608	Acceleration of Ulster Plantations					
1609	Irish Book of Common Prayer	Statues of Iona				
1641	Rising of 1641					
1642	'English' Civil War begins					
1649	'English' Civil War ends					

The Modern Celtic Countries (Continued)

Date	Ireland	Scotland	Wales	Cornwall	Isle of Man	Brittany
1689		Battle of Killiecrankie				
1690	Battle of the Boyne					
1695			Death of poet Henry Vaughan			
1707		Union with Scotland creates United Kingdom; Edward Lhuyd's Archaeologia Britannica				
1735			Methodist Revival begins			
1745	Death of Jonathan Swift	Beginning of Jacobite Rebellions				
1746		Battle of Culloden; Dress Act bans tartans				
1752				Last Stannary Parliament		
1758					Methodism arrives on Man	
1760		First Ossian poem of James Macpherson				
1765					Isle of Man sold to the English Crown	
1782	Irish legislative independence					
1789			First modern eisteddfod			French Revolution begins
1790						Last Breton parliament
1791	United Irishmen founded					

(continued)

The Modern Celtic Countries (Continued)

Date	Ireland	Scotland	Wales	Cornwall	Isle of Man	Brittany
1792			Edward WILLIAMS (Iolo Morganwg) founds GORSEDD BEIRDD YNYS PRYDAIN			
1796		Death of Robert BURNS				
1798	Wolfe TONE and United Irishmen in rebellion					
1800	ACT OF UNION; Maria Edgeworth's *Castle Rackrent*				Approximate date of death of Late Cornish	
1819			Eisteddfod linked to Gorsedd Beirdd Ynys Prydain			
1827						Breton New Testament published
1828			Thomas Pritchard's novel *The Adventures of Twm Shôn Catti*			
1829	Emancipation of Irish Catholics					
1830	William Carleton's *Traits and Stories of the Irish Peasantry*					
1832		Death of Walter SCOTT				

The Modern Celtic Countries (Continued)

Date	Ireland	Scotland	Wales	Cornwall	Isle of Man	Brittany
1839			Rebecca Riots begin			Hersart de la Villemarqué's *Barzaz Breiz*
1844						
1845	Potato Famine begins		Rebecca Riots end			
1846			Charlotte Guest's translation of the *Mabinogion*			
1847			Treachery of the Blue Books			
c. 1850	Potato Famine recedes					
1866				Revived Cornish	Greater autonomy via political reforms in Tynwald	Complete Breton *Bible* published
1872			University of Wales founded in Aberystwyth			
1879	Land League founded					
1882		Highland Land League formed				
1884	Gaelic Athletic Association (Cumann Lùthchleas Gael) founded					
1893	Gaelic League (Conradh na Gaeilge) founded; first edition of *The Celtic Twilight* by W. B. Yeats					

(continued)

The Modern Celtic Countries (Continued)

Date	Ireland	Scotland	Wales	Cornwall	Isle of Man	Brittany
1898	First Oireachtas					*Kevredigez Broadus Breiz founded*
1899					Yn Cheshaght Ghailckagh founded	
1900						First Goursez
1902	Lady Gregory's *Cuchulain of Muirthemne*					
1905	Sinn Féin founded					
1907			National Library of Wales founded			
1911						*Unvaniez Arvor founded*
1914	Irish Home Rule Bill		World War I begins			
1915	David Lloyd George becomes Prime Minister					
1916	Easter Rising					
1918	Sinn Féin victory in Irish elections		World War I ends			
1919	Irish War of Independence begins					
1920	Partition of Ireland (Éire)					
1921	War of Independence ends; Northern Ireland's Parliament established in Belfast					

The Modern Celtic Countries (Continued)

Date	Ireland	Scotland	Wales	Cornwall	Isle of Man	Brittany
1922	Irish Civil War begins; Irish Free State (Saorstát na hÉireann); James Joyce's *Ulysses*; death of Art Ó Gríofa					
1923	Irish Civil War ends					
1926	Fianna Fáil founded					
1928					First Gorseth	
1935	Irish Folklore Commission active					
1936	Autobiography of Peig Sayers					
1939	James Joyce's *Finnegan's Wake*; death of Yeats			World War II begins		
1941	Death of author James Joyce					
1945				World War II ends		
1949	Republic of Ireland (Poblacht na hÉireann) established					
1951				Mebyon Kernow formed		
1953			Death of poet Dylan Thomas			
1957						France a founding member of the European Community

(continued)

The Modern Celtic Countries (Continued)

Date	Ireland	Scotland	Wales	Cornwall	Isle of Man	Brittany
1958					British government releases control over Manx finances	
1959						First appearance of ASTERIX
1962			'Tynged yr Iaith' lecture; Cymdeithas yr Iaith founded			
1963					MecVannin founded	
1966			Aberfan Disaster			
1968	Beginning of the 'Troubles'					
1971				Institute for Cornish Studies established		
1972	Bloody Sunday; Direct Rule imposed in Northern Ireland					
1973	Ireland joins the European Community	United Kingdom joins the European Community				
1974				Stannary Parliament re-formed	Death of the last native Manx speaker	
1977						First Diwan
1982			S4C established			
1985	Anglo-Irish Agreement					
1988		Lockerbie bombing				
1993			Welsh Language Board established			

The Modern Celtic Countries (Continued)

Date	Ireland	Scotland	Wales	Cornwall	Isle of Man	Brittany
1998	Good Friday Agreement					
1999		Modern Scottish Parliament established; Scottish Office dissolved	National Assembly for Wales established; Welsh Office dissolved			
2000			Death of poet R. S. Thomas			TV Breizh launched
2001			First recorded increase in the number of Welsh speakers			
2002				Beunans Ke manuscript discovered; United Kingdom recognizes Cornish as a European regional minority language	School offered through the medium of Manx	
2004				Complete Cornish translation of the New Testament		
2011		Scottish National Party wins a majority in the Scottish election				

A

ABERFFRAW

Aberffraw, on the estuary of the river Ffraw in the southwest of the island of Anglesey (Môn), was the royal site of the kings of GWYNEDD until 1282. *Aber* 'river-mouth' (< Celtic *ad-ber-*) is common in coastal place-names originating in the P-CELTIC languages.

Excavations in 1973–74 revealed a Roman fort of the later 1st century, with refortification in the 5th or 6th century. The post-Roman re-defence may reflect the arrival of Gwynedd's first dynasty, who claimed descent from CUNEDDA. That the site was already a royal centre in the 7th century is further indicated by the Latin commemorative inscription to king Cadfan ab Iago († *c*. 625) at the nearby church at Llangadwaladr.

Aberffraw remained a principal seat for Gwynedd's 'second dynasty', which came to power with the accession of Merfyn Frych in 825. Under the patronage of King GRUFFUDD AP CYNAN (r. 1075–1137) or that of his son and successor OWAIN GWYNEDD (r. 1137–70), a stone church was built with Romanesque features similar to 12th-century churches on the pilgrimage route to Santiago de Compostela in Spain. This church's chancel arch, pictured above, possesses the most elaborate stonework of any surviving example of its type from Wales, a reflection of the international importance of Aberffraw. King LLYWELYN AB IORWERTH (r. 1194–1240) used *Tywysog Aberffraw ac Arglwydd* ERYRI 'Leader of Aberffraw and Lord of Snowdonia' as his official title. Only after King Edward I of ENGLAND defeated LLYWELYN AP GRUFFUDD in 1282 was the Aberffraw complex systematically dismantled. In the time of Edward III, *c*. 1340, Aberffraw was recorded as a 'manor' held by the king's surgeon, Roger Hayton.

John T. Koch

ABERYSTWYTH

Aberystwyth is in the Welsh county of Ceredigion. The 2001 Census reported 14,966 inhabitants within 'greater Aberystwyth', including adjacent towns such as Llanbadarn Fawr. There were 6,555 Welsh speakers, representing 43.8 percent of the year-round resident population.

The town is situated at the mouths of the rivers Ystwyth and Rheidol, and has been occupied since approximately 6000 BC. A large hill-fort on Pendinas has yielded a few datable items from the 2nd century BC. The foundation of the nearby monastery of Llanbadarn Fawr is traditionally dated the 6th century AD. Originally a *clas* (a native enclosed monastic community), it later became a Benedictine monastery.

In the course of the Anglo-Norman conquest of Wales, a motte and bailey castle was built at the mouth of the Ystwyth. The present town was officially founded in 1277 by Edmund, brother of the English king Edward I. In 1404 the castle was seized for a short period by Owain Glyndŵr, and in 1649 it was finally destroyed by Oliver Cromwell's troops during the English Civil Wars (1642–9).

In the 19th century, the town was connected to the railway and grew into such a significant seaside resort that it was known as the 'Biarritz of Wales'. In 1872, the first constituent college of the University of Wales was founded here, followed by the Llyfrgell Genedlaethol Cymru (National Library of Wales) in 1907. Aberystwyth has since become the main location for several national Welsh organizations, such as Cymdeithas yr Iaith Gymraeg (Welsh Language Society), Urdd Gobaith Cymru, and Merched y Wawr (the national Welsh women's group). It is widely recognized as an intellectual and cultural centre for Wales as a whole and an urban stronghold of the Welsh language.

Aberystwyth takes its name from the river Ystwyth, mentioned in Ptolemy's *Geography* (2nd century AD). This place-name is probably ultimately the same word as the common Welsh adjective *ystwyth*, meaning 'supple, bendable'.

Peter E. Busse

ACT OF UNION, IRELAND (1800)

The Union between Great Britain and Ireland (Éire) was passed by the Irish parliament in 1800. Several factors were involved: the recent French Revolution (1789–99) and its anticlerical sentiments; the threat of revolutionary measures among both Protestants and Catholics in Ireland (see Christianity, Ireland); and, most of all, the failure of the Irish parliament to secure the interests of the British Crown.

Under the terms of the Union, there were to be 100 Irish Members of Parliament in Westminster, England, with 28 lords temporal and 4 spiritual, and the two military establishments were to merge. The Church of England and that of Ireland were to formally unite as a condition of Union—a move that formally consolidated Protestant privilege. Ireland was to gain some protection for its domestic industry as the price of opening its markets. Tithes would be abolished, the Ulster linen trade protected, and weights and measures standardized. Irish laws would remain, but the UK parliament would henceforth legislate for Ireland without further protection for them (cf. Union with Scotland). Ireland began by paying a smaller proportion of the kingdom's imperial expenses (11¾% from its 40% of the population). Due to the expenses of the French wars, even this proportional contribution had materially increased Ireland's debts by the time of full fiscal union in 1817.

The Union of 1800 came under attack almost as soon as it was passed. Catholic emancipation in 1829 undermined the union of English and Irish Protestant churches, while arriving too late to bring Catholic support to the political union, and the economic disparity between Britain and Ireland contributed to the political friction.

Murray G. H. Pittock

ACTE D'UNION, BRITTANY (1532)

After the death of Anne, duchess of Brittany (Breton *Anna Vreizh*), Brittany passed to her descendants in the French royal family. Her grandson François was established as Duke François III of Brittany in 1532. On that occasion his father, King François I, published the *Édit d'Union* (Act of Union) at Nantes (Naoned). Some important features of an independent Brittany continued until the French Revolution: The Breton parliament, for example, was reorganized, but continued until 1790.

After 1589, the Breton succession nominally went to Isabelle of Brittany, the daughter of Henri III's sister, Elizabeth of Valois, while the French crown was taken by Henri IV of the House of Bourbon, who married another of Henri III's sisters, Margaret of Valois.

Antone Minard

ACTS OF UNION, WALES (1536–43)

The 1536 Acts that 'united and annexed' Wales (CYMRU) to ENGLAND are collectively known as the Act of Union, with details provided in a supplementary piece of legislation in 1543. The year 1536 formally brought an end to many rights of the Marcher lordships, which had arisen shortly after the Norman conquest, and formally integrated Wales into England. The Marches were organized into counties: Dinbych (Denbigh), Trefaldwyn (Montgomery), Maesyfed (Radnor), BRYCHEINIOG (Brecknock/Brecon), and Mynwy (Monmouth). Aberteifi (Cardigan), Caerfyrddin (Carmarthen), MORGANNWG (Glamorgan), and Penfro (Pembroke) were all enlarged, as were the English border counties. Wales was to send 24 representatives to the English Parliament from its 12 counties. Justices of the Peace were to be appointed and conduct all business in English, and the Welsh shires were to be divided into hundreds (see CANTREF). Laws and customs at variance with English law were abolished (see LAW TEXTS, CELTIC, WELSH), and land tenure by gavelkind (equal division between sons) was abolished in favour of primogeniture (inheritance to the first-born son).

The Union with Wales was the most successful of the three unions with England, due in part to the Welsh origins of the Tudors (see TUDUR), the long-standing orientation of the Welsh aristocracy toward England, and the absence of political alternatives. The cult of ARTHUR was used to incorporate the patriotic sentiments of Welsh élites into a fundamentally English polity. The language of most of the people of this hardly urbanized country remained Welsh, undisturbed by English in most contexts until the 19th century.

Murray G. H. Pittock

AEDÁN MAC GABRÁIN

Aedán mac Gabráin was king of Scottish DÁL RIATA (r. 574–c. 603, †17 April 608) and one of the most powerful and best-documented leaders in this period. Adomnán's *Vita Columbae* (Life of COLUM CILLE) of *c.* 692 shows that Aedán was a Christian who had undergone an inauguration ritual on Iona at the hands of Colum Cille himself (Enright, *Iona, Tara, and Soissons*), an early example of the Church endorsing the notion of a Christian kingship in the CELTIC COUNTRIES.

According to the Irish ANNALS, Aedán attacked Arcaibh (the Orkneys, then under Pictish rule) *c.* 579. Then, *c.* 581, he was the victor of *bellum Manonn* 'the battle of Manu', which might mean either ELLAN VANNIN (Isle of Man) or the district known as *Manau Guotodin* (Mod.W *Manaw Gododdin*) in what is now east central Scotland.

The names of both Aedán and his father, Gabrán, are Old Irish and indisputably Celtic. Aedán mac Gabráin figures in several early Irish tales, including *Scéla Cano meic Gartnáin* (Tales of Cano mac Gartnáin). In the story *Compert Mongáin* (Birth of Mongán), he figures as king of ALBA (Scotland) at the right period and is also realistically involved in warfare with the Anglo-Saxons (see ANGLO-SAXON 'CONQUEST'). In *Peiryan Vaban* (Commanding boy), a prophetic poem connected to the cycle of MYRDDIN, Aeddan son of Gafran appears as the enemy of a historical 6th-century King RHYDDERCH HAEL of YSTRAD CLUD. In the Welsh TRIADS, he figures in Triad 29 as leader of one of the 'Three Faithful War-Bands'.

There are several indications that Aedán made an impression on Welsh culture. The death of *Aidan map Gabran* is recorded in *Annales Cambriae*—the only Dál Riatan king mentioned there. OW *Aidan* is one of very few Gaelic names with any currency in Wales in the earlier Middle Ages. *Aedan* occurs as a proper name in the elegies of the GODODDIN, which could possibly be a reference to Aedán mac Gabráin himself.

John T. Koch

AGRICULTURE, GAUL

Gaulish farms can be inferred from the 6th century BC. From the 2nd century BC onward, they appeared in greater density and variety across the northern half of France. Such farms were enclosed settlements located in the centre of the territory that they exploited. The typical farm consisted of a ditch surrounding farm buildings (houses, barns, silos). The social status of these sites varied considerably, ranging from simple family farms to aristocratic residences. The richest sites were distinguished by ostentatious architecture and elaborate furnishing—for example, Mediterranean amphorae (large jars used for wine or olive oil), jewellery, COINAGE, arms and armour, and sets of iron tools. The multiplication of isolated settlements, which precede and anticipate the Gallo-Roman villas (residential farming estates), coincides with other features of rising socioeconomic complexity—the development of artisans' villages and finally with proto-urban oppida (see OPPIDUM).

Stéphane Marion

AGRICULTURE, IRELAND

Early Prehistory

It appears that in Ireland (Ériu), as elsewhere in northwest Europe, farming was from its inception a mixture of crop growing and stock (mostly cattle and swine) rearing. Evidence of agriculture appears in the archaeological record from the early 5th millennium BC, including the cultivation of wheat. Pollen analysis from the 4th millennium BC indicates widespread tree clearance in some areas. The earliest Neolithic (New Stone Age) farming appears to have been mainly of the *landnam* or slash-and-burn type, with small areas of woodland cleared and then abandoned when the soil nutrients were depleted. In the later Neolithic (*c.* 3200–2400 BC), farming became more sedentary.

Later Prehistory

For cattle, meat was the main requirement; milk production was of secondary importance. Sheep were of little importance as a source of food, but the presence of spindle whorls shows that their wool was being exploited. In the Later Bronze Age (*c.* 1400–500 BC), small-scale mixed farms remained the norm, with cattle and swine as the main stock and barley and wheat as the primary crops. Some evidence exists for other agricultural products: Flax was grown as early as *c.* 2000 BC for linen, though the earliest evidence for the fabric is much later.

For most of the Irish Early Iron Age (*c.* 500 BC–AD 400), agriculture was in decline, with wilderness reclaiming territory. Grain production continued to a lesser degree. The dominance of pastoral farming in the Early Medieval period may well have begun at this time.

Early Medieval Period

Highly detailed legal documents (LAW TEXTS) written in the 7th or 8th centuries AD illustrate a highly regulated and complex integration of agriculture within the early Irish social structure. The archaeological and documentary both recognize the central role of cattle in this structure. Dairying was now clearly the prime purpose of cattle rearing. There is strong evidence for transhumance—that is, the practice of seasonal movement of the herds to the uplands in the warmer months. This practice continued in Ireland up until the 18th or 19th centuries and was known as 'booleying' (from Irish *buaile*, a cattle enclosure).

The pig also has a high profile in the written texts, with its flesh being considered better food than other meats. Sheep were primarily important for their wool; they, like cattle, were used as a unit of currency in the law tracts. Wheat was the most highly prized cereal grain, though also the most difficult to grow in Ireland. Barley, rye, and oats were the staple cereals of the majority, being better suited climatically to Ireland's terrain.

Land and stock ownership rested on the twin principles of KINSHIP and clientship. Inheritance was a complex legal issue on which generalization is difficult. In short, land was generally held from the extended kin group or *fine*. In most cases inheritance was restricted to the smallest division of the kin group, the *gelfine*, based on the male line of a common grandfather. The practice of subdivision of land, whereby the father's holding was divided amongst his sons, led to the diminishment in the size of the holding, with the result that holdings eventually became economically unviable. This was one of the contributory factors to the Great FAMINE a millennium later. Clientship was a system whereby a landowner could receive a grant (Irish *rath*) from his chief, usually in the form of cattle, on which a set annual return was due to the grantee for a set length of time, generally seven years. This system supplied the client with capital through which he could, by careful husbandry, increase his holding while the chief gained not only interest, but also prestige and status based on the number of clients he could take on.

The focus of the holding in early medieval Ireland was the *lios* (ring fort), a defended settlement of which many still survive. The *lios* was a home, but also a secure enclosure for the stock at night and other times of danger. Evidence from one excavated example, Deer Park Farms, Co. Antrim (Contae Aontroma), indicates that sheep, cattle, horses, goats and pigs had all been present within the enclosing bank.

Anglo-Norman Influence and Beyond

Even before the Norman military conquest of Ireland began in 1169, the effects of the feudal system of agriculture were being experienced in a limited way through the presence of the Cistercian order a generation prior (see CISTERCIAN ABBEYS IN IRELAND). The Normans introduced many agricultural innovations, including the practice of haymaking and more efficient ploughs with wheels and a mouldboard. The new breeds of stock introduced by the Normans were generally larger, more productive, and well suited to the fertile lowlands where their settlement was concentrated. Manorial records indicate that sheep replaced cattle as the stock of most importance in Norman areas. The picture that emerges involves increasing polarization of the two agrarian systems, Gaelic and Norman. This situation continued for centuries, with much of the Gaelic west and north remaining an essentially cattle-based society up until the 17th century. Following the Geraldine and Nine Year Wars, these areas became integrated into the English feudal system, although some Irish practices lived on for a further century or so.

The Modern Period

The 18th century saw the transformation of the west of the country from a sparsely inhabited landscape into a thickly settled small-farming area. This process was enabled by two major factors. The first was the adoption of the Rundale system of semi-communal land management, with its fields arranged around a central settlement or clachan often occupied by a single extended family group. The characteristic radial field boundaries of the Rundale system are still seen particularly in the landscapes of Co. Donegal (Contae Dhún na nGall) and the barony of Erris, Co.

Mayo (Contae Mhaigh Eo). The second factor was the mass cultivation of the potato, which was nutritious and well adapted to the poor soil and damp climate of the west. The agrarian reforms that followed the devastation of the Great Famine of the 1840s saw the end of the native Rundale and clachan system.

Further famine in 1859–64, and again in 1879–84, steeled the British government's resolve to push ahead with radical long-term land reorganization. Many improvements in farming techniques and land management were wrought, particularly in the west. Recognition of the serious injustice of the Irish land ownership system, coupled with the agrarian agitation of the Land League, led successive British governments to adopt a policy of land redistribution. In conjunction with a series of Land Acts coercing landlords to sell land, this policy resulted in two thirds of Irish tenants owning their own land by 1914.

After Ireland's partition in 1921, this trend continued under the newly formed Land Commission. The effectiveness of the reforms was hampered, however, by the ideological outlook of the Fianna Fáil governments of the 1930s and 1940s, which attempted to create a classless rural Gaelic society, in part by limiting farm sizes to an unviably small size of between 8 and 12 hectares (between 20 and 30 acres).

Irish membership in the European Community from 1973 onward resulted in further evolution of the farming economy. Increased specialization, encouraged by ample grant funding, saw the previous pattern of ubiquitous 'mixed' farms transform into large zones dedicated almost exclusively to one specific activity. The Munster dairying area and east-central dry cattle area are examples of this pattern. European Community grants have disproportionately favoured larger farms over the smaller holdings, located mostly on the poorer land of the west.

Simon Ó Faoláin

AGRICULTURE, ISLE OF MAN

Farming was a dual occupation on the Isle of Man until the mid-19th century, with fishing regarded as the main interest to bring money to the family. Men went to sea between July and October, leaving the women to run the farms. Fields were mostly enclosed by the mid-18th century, but before that main boundaries were only fenced and fields with growing crops had temporary sod hedges to protect them. Grazing livestock animals were also restricted by 'lankets' made of 'suggane' (straw rope), which were tied to their legs. Varieties of oats and barley suited to poor, exposed soils were grown. Rye, once in favour, had gradually declined by the 17th century and wheat, popular by the 18th century, thrived in the productive lowland areas of the northern plain and southern limestone districts. Root crops came late to the island, with potatoes appearing by *c.* 1706 and turnips by the late 18th century. 'Spuds and herring' thus became part of the diet alongside oats.

Celtic farmers in Man (Ellan Vannin) relied upon their livestock, with breeds native to the island dominating until the 19th century. The cattle were similar to the Kerry: small, hardy animals capable of producing good-quality milk. Their horses were again small, approximately 13 hands high, and were used as farm and pack animals. The pigs, known as 'Purrs', were small, multicoloured animals; they became extinct by 1840. Sheep were bred for milk, wool, and meat; the native brown 'Loghtan' breed survives to this day. The Manx economy has changed radically in the modern era: By the last decade of the 20th century, agriculture and fishing on the island produced no more than 2 percent of the national income.

Chris Page

AGRICULTURE, SCOTLAND

Early Prehistory

Evidence for farming in Scotland (Alba) is quite poor before *c.* 3500 BC. As elsewhere throughout Britain and Ireland in prehistoric times, mixed farming was the norm, with barley the main cereal crop; emmer wheat and oats were also grown, and there is some limited evidence of flax cultivation. Cattle, sheep, goats, and pigs were reared from the Neolithic onward, as indicated by the bone assemblages unearthed at excavated sites such as Knap of Howar, Orkney (Arcaibh). Nevertheless, it appears that gathering, hunting, and fishing remained integral parts of the Scottish Neolithic and later for a longer period than elsewhere, especially within the marine-oriented economies of the west and north coast and the islands.

Later Prehistory

Pollen diagrams indicate a sudden rise in agricultural activity around 250 BC, which seems to have been accompanied by population expansion in the Lowlands. It has been suggested that the eastern Scottish ring-ditched houses were over-wintering byres for livestock, a practice considered necessary in the northern climes. Cattle are generally considered the most important stock in the Scottish Iron Age, as indicated by the evidence from many sites, though not all. Special status may have been attached to cattle ownership, as demonstrated by evidence at Cnuip wheelhouse, Lewis, where the terrain was far more suitable for sheep. The bone assemblage from this site indicates that the cattle raised here were stunted.

Medieval Period

In the north and west, the wheelhouses, DUNS, and BROCHS seem to have been the homesteads of single extended families engaged in mixed farming, eked out through the exploitation of marine resources. Later on, some of these settlements expand (e.g., Broch of Gurness) to form small nucleated villages. In the later Middle Ages there was a move away from purely subsistence farming, with cattle and sheep being raised for export, although the farmers themselves lived mainly on a diet of oats and bere (a form of barley), along with some dairy products and a little meat. Bone evidence from the manorial farm at Rattray, Moray (Moireibh), suggests that sheep and goats were the main source of milk, while cattle were raised primarily for meat. Kale (for both humans and stock) was also important; flax and hemp were produced for fabric manufacture. Rural settlement took the form of 'fermtouns', consisting of small, nucleated groups of long-houses or single dwellings of the 'Pitcarmick' type.

Early Modern Times

By *c.* 1700 the HIGHLANDS AND ISLANDS and the Lowlands could be seen to share form and structure with regard to landholdings, land use, and modes of cultivation. Fields and grazing rights were owned or leased by several families rather than individuals. A township—*baile* in GAELIC or *toun* in SCOTS—would typically farm 'infields' and 'outfields'. Infields, with fertile soil improved by the animal manure, would be permanently cropped; outfields, by contrast, were cropped until results fell off and then left to recover for some years. For drainage, the fields would be ploughed into runrigs—that is, ridges into which surplus water drained. Beyond the field systems lay the common grazing lands, by far the greater part of the land. In the summer, cattle and sheep would be driven up to the mountain pastures, known as *áiridh*, *shielings*, or *setter*. Labour and resources would be pooled and land use rotated between families.

The agricultural revolution, which called for 'improvement of the land' to create a profit for its owners, came to the Lowlands in the 17th century. Larger and more profitable holdings were created, often robbing the majority of families in a *toun* of their land and leaving only one or two farmers to cultivate the whole holding. More modern farming methods, such as crop rotation, were developed and new breeds of animals and strains of crops introduced. The mechanization of agriculture set in with the development of agricultural machines in the late 18th and 19th centuries. In the course of the 19th century, the runrigs were replaced by subsoil drainage systems that enabled the draining of marshland. Previously common land was enclosed and planned villages erected so that the industrial revolution of the Lowlands could be fueled, with these efforts primarily devoted to the textile industries and brewing and distilling. A more mixed agriculture developed, with oats and barley being the most common crops.

Highland farms increasingly had to be purchased. Consequently, the relationship between clanspeople and clan chiefs changed into that of tenants and landlords. In the Highlands, 'improving' the lands to maximize profit largely meant creating grazing pasture. Often, the resident population was resettled or evicted in a process known as the CLEARANCES. The potato blight of 1846, which hit Scotland as much as Ireland, resulted in further EMIGRATION. The countryside was depopulated, with people migrating to industrial centres or leaving Scotland altogether. In 1951, approximately 88,000 people worked in Scottish farming full-time; by 1991, their number had fallen to no more than 25,000, with many now engaged in fish farming. Today's empty heather landscape, inhabited mostly by sheep, deer, and grouse, with poor, marginal, or coastal lands given over to crofts, is a product of 18th- and 19th-century 'improvement' (see also LAND AGITATION).

Simon Ó Faoláin and Marion Löffler

AGRICULTURE, WALES

Up to the Norman conquest, there was a continuity of agricultural tradition in Wales (Cymru) from the pre-Roman Iron Age. The arrival of the Norman and Flemish population began in the late 11th century and changed patterns of proprietorship and agricultural techniques considerably. Subsequently, the 'Welshry' of areas under Anglo-Norman lordship was largely confined to land above the 600-foot (about 180 m) contour line. These areas were characterized by a considerable survival of traditional tenurial customs and free population. The 'Englishry', located in the lowland and coastal areas, was strongly influenced by the new settlers; it featured both bond tenants and a manorial system.

The inclement weather and acidic soils meant that the bulk of the agrarian population of medieval Wales lived in tiny, scattered homesteads. Native legal sources (see law texts) describe several types of land found in medieval Wales. The normal tenure was hereditary land (*tir gwelyog*). The rights to this land passed to descendants in equal shares, and after a period of four generations the possession developed into legal proprietorship. This type of tenure finds certain parallels in early Irish institutions; it collapsed after the population decline in the wake of the Black Death (1349).

Barley and oats were cultivated as spring cereals, while rye and wheat were cultivated as winter tilth. Some cereals were less common in some areas of Wales than others. For example, rye was grown less generally than wheat in south Wales. Beans, peas, vetch, and flax were also cultivated.

Two kinds of plough (with wheels and without) were in use, both of them heavy. Oxen were the only plough animals recognized by the law; the horse had no place in the plough team. Giraldus Cambrensis reports that four oxen abreast were the most common in his time.

Horse breeding was generally an important part of the Welsh medieval economy and parts of Wales were famous for their horses. Giraldus reported that 'the horses which are sent out of Powys are greatly prized; they are extremely handsome and nature reproduces in them the same majestic proportion and incomparable speed'. The rearing of sheep, which was greatly encouraged by the Cistercians, represented a major branch of agriculture in several parts of Wales.

The cattle of medieval Wales comprised a variety of breeds. The best descriptions of the cattle come from Welsh poetry. Black cattle that gave rise to the famous Welsh Blacks of modern times became the prevalent breed by the 14th and 15th centuries. Red cattle with white faces, to which the modern Hereford breed is normally traced, were common in southeast Wales.

Following the Acts of Union, greater stability and links to the London market enhanced the prospects of landowners and farmers. Herds of hardy cattle were driven overland by intrepid Welsh drovers to the major fairs and markets of southeast England and were subsequently fattened prior to slaughter. Economic growth was reflected by an increase in the Welsh population: Between the Acts of Union and the first population census of 1801, the population more than doubled to approximately 600,000. Yet farms remained small (the norm was less than 50 acres) and most peasant farmers, lacking capital, remained suspicious of change. From the 1750s, however, the formation of progressive county agricultural societies introduced improvements in the quality of livestock and crop rotation.

Progress was severely curtailed by the French wars (1793–1815). Galloping inflation; high taxes, rents, and tithes; and the enclosure of common land caused the Welsh people enormous distress. In the post-war years an acute agricultural depression accentuated the gulf that had emerged between Nonconformist Welsh-speaking farmers and the landless poor on the one hand, and the wealthy Anglican, non-Welsh-speaking landowners on the other hand. In their frustration, small farmers in southwest Wales launched the Rebecca Riots (1839–44), a protest movement that destroyed the hated toll-gates established by turnpike trusts and thereby drew public attention to their plight.

Economic conditions improved briefly beginning in the mid-19th century. The coming of the railways not only provided farmers with direct access to markets, but also brought about the demise of the drover. By 1914, the coal industry had overtaken agriculture as the largest employer of people in Wales. The numbers engaged in farming had declined from 33 percent in 1851 to 11 percent in 1911. By the 1990s Welsh farmers, as a result of the effects of harsh milk quotas, severe cuts in subsidies, the bovine spongiform encephalopathy (BSE) and foot-and-mouth crises, the outward migration of young people and the inward migration of retired people, and the increasing demands upon them to develop resources and skills that would enable them to diversify, were poorly equipped to meet the challenges of the 21st century. In 2001, slightly more than 56,300 persons were at work on agricultural holdings in Wales.

Alexander Falileyev and Geraint H. Jenkins

AIDED ÉNFIR AÍFE AND OIDHEADH CHONNLAOICH MHEIC CON CULAINN

Aided Énfir Aife and *Oidheadh Chonnlaoich mheic Con Culainn* ('The violent death of Aife's only son' and 'The violent death of Connlaoch son of Cú Chulainn') are two versions of the Irish story of how the central hero of the Ulster Cycle killed his son Connla or Connlaoch, committing the crime of *fingal* 'kinslaying'. The story has analogues in Indo-European tradition, notably in the Persian *Shahnameh* and in Arthurian literature.

See also Heroic ethos; Ulster Cycle.

John T. Koch

AISLING

Aisling (vision) is a type of Irish-language poem recounting the visit of a woman from the Otherworld in a dream. The three principal types are the love-*aisling*, the prophecy-*aisling*, and the allegorical *aisling*, in which the woman usually represents Éire. The allegorical form, which may have roots in French literature, became common in the 18th century. It is the best known of the three forms, popularized by poets performing for an Irish-speaking population hostile to the English occupiers of Ireland.

The allegorical *aisling*'s principal traits are: (1) a localization of the action, often in a mystical place; (2) a formalized description of the woman; (3) a request for her identity, comparing her to classical and Irish beauties; (4) a response in which she rejects these comparisons and identifies herself; and (5) a message of hope for the Irish people (e.g., predicting Ireland's liberation).

The allegorical *aisling*'s master was the Munster (Mumu) poet Eóghan Ruadh Ó Súilleabháin (1748–84). The best-known *aisling*, however, is probably the despairing *Mac an Cheannaí* (The redeemer's son) of Aogán Ó Rathaille (*c.* 1670–*c.* 1726), in which the beauty dies before the poet.

See also Irish literature; sovereignty myth.

Brian Ó Broin

AITHBHREAC NIGHEAN COIRCEADAIL

Aithbhreac nighean Coirceadail (*fl.* 1460) was a Scottish poet and the author of a lament for her husband, Niall mac Néill of the Hebridean island of Giogha (Gigha), preserved in the Book of the Dean of Lismore. The poem, *A Phaidrín do Dhúisg mo Dhéar*, movingly combines both the intimate perspective of the spouse reflecting on her dead husband's rosary and the stately rhetoric of classical Irish elegy. The poem thus is testimony to the practice of classical Irish poetry (see Irish literature) among the middle ranks of the nobility within the Lordship of the Isles, and to the education of women in its arts. Aithbhreac (her name comes from the word for Africa) is the earliest in an impressive sequence of Scottish Gaelic women poets whose work has been preserved from the 15th to the 19th century (see Scottish Gaelic poetry).

Thomas Owen Clancy

ALAN VARVEG

Alan Varveg (Alan the Bearded, r. 937–52), reconquered Brittany (Breizh) after 30 years of Viking rule and established the medieval feudal state. His father was Matbidoe, Count of Poher, and his mother was a daughter of Alan the Great (†907), recognized as king of the Bretons by the Carolingian king Charles the Simple. Alan participated in an unsuccessful Breton uprising against the Norse occupation in 931. In 936, with Æthelstan of England's backing, he returned. His victory at Nantes (Naoned) in 937 drove the Vikings from the Loire, and it was at Nantes that Alan established his capital.

Antone Minard

ALBA (SCOTLAND)

Alba (Scotland) is one of the six European countries in which a Celtic language has been spoken in modern times (see Breizh; Cymru; Éire; Ellan Vannin; Kernow). It is the northernmost part of the United Kingdom, comprising northern Great Britain

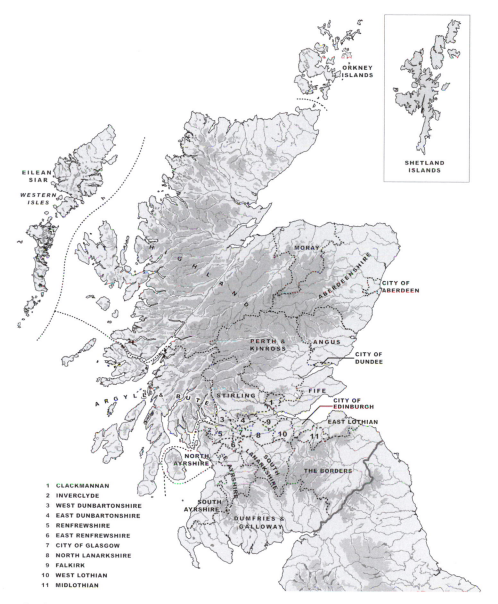

1 CLACKMANNAN
2 INVERCLYDE
3 WEST DUNBARTONSHIRE
4 EAST DUNBARTONSHIRE
5 RENFREWSHIRE
6 EAST RENFREWSHIRE
7 CITY OF GLASGOW
8 NORTH LANARKSHIRE
9 FALKIRK
10 WEST LOTHIAN
11 MIDLOTHIAN

Scotland: post-1966 counties. (Map by Ian Gulley, Antony Smith, and John T. Koch)

and several island archipelagos. Its land mass covers 30,414 square miles (78,772 km^2). At the time of the latest census (2001), Scotland had 5,062,011 residents. Traditionally, the country has been divided into the HIGHLANDS and the Lowlands, with the capital, Edinburgh (DÙN ÈIDEANN), situated in the Lowlands. It is presently divided into 32 council areas. Although Scotland has been part of the United Kingdom since 1707 (see UNION), it has preserved its own legal and educational systems and its own established church (see CHRISTIANITY). The SCOTTISH PARLIAMENT was reestablished in 1999 (see NATIONALISM).

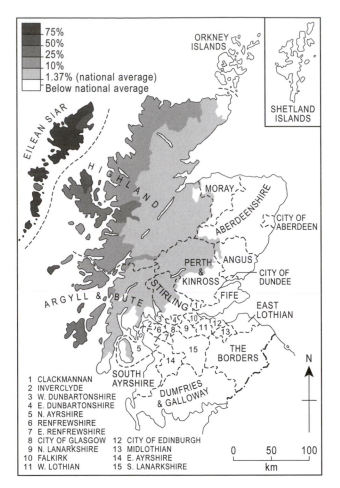

Gaelic speakers in Scotland: 1991 Census figures. (Map by Ian Gulley and Antony Smith)

The present border between Scotland and ENGLAND runs between HADRIAN'S WALL and the Antonine Wall, both of which were constructed by the Romans in the 2nd century AD. Although Scotland had been inhabited since the end of the last ice age 10,000 years ago, today's two indigenous linguistic communities—the Gaels and speakers of English/SCOTS —belong to the post-Roman period, beginning with the GOIDELIC-speaking Scots in the kingdom of DÁL RIATA (roughly presentday Argyllshire), reckoned to have arrived in the 5th century, and the Germanic Angles in Northumbria (see BRYNAICH), who expanded into what is now the territory of Scotland by the mid-7th century. In the early Middle Ages, two additional groups emerged, both P-CELTIC speaking: the PICTS in the north and the BRITONS in the south (see YSTRAD CLUD). Weakened by Viking raids, the northern Pictish kingdom came under the rule of the SCOT CINAED MAC AILPÍN (Kenneth I) in AD 843. This period established the predominance of GOIDELIC speakers in Scotland, and GAELIC became the language of the royal court. Scandinavians settled in the Northern and Western Isles from the 9th century, and a Scandinavian language called Norn survived in Orkney (Arcaibh) and Shetland (Sealtainn) until modern times.

Scotland's status as an independent kingdom was confirmed by the battle of BANNOCKBURN in 1314, which helped to consolidate the royal line later known as the Stuarts. However, once the Tudor dynasty (see TUDUR) gained the English throne in 1485, Scotland's existence as an independent kingdom came under threat once more. A peace treaty of 1503 crumbled after Henry VIII came to power in 1509. His victory over the Scottish army at the battle of Flodden in 1513 was a catastrophe from which Scotland never recovered. Like Anglicization, the Reformation spread from the Lowlands (see Christianity; Bible; Reformation) and prepared the ground for the Union of the Crowns of England and Scotland in 1603. When Elizabeth I of England died, James VI of Scotland—her closest living relative—also became James I of England and Wales. The two kingdoms were formally united through the Act of Union in 1707 (see Union with Scotland) and the new state was named Great Britain. Repeated 18th-century attempts to regain independence by reinstalling the Stuart dynasty failed (see Jacobite rebellions). In their wake, the clan system was destroyed, the Highlanders evicted from their land (see clearances), and an ancient way of living—romantically immortalized in the novels of Sir Walter Scott—was lost forever.

Marion Löffler

ALBA, NAME, DERIVATION, AND USAGE

In the Gaelic languages, (north) Britain is most usually called *Alba* (in early texts, also *Albu*), genitive *Alban*. Although modern translators often lose sight of the fact, when *Alba* occurs in Irish heroic tales looking back to pre-Christian times, the name most often refers to Britain as a whole. The alternative and narrower sense, Pictland (see Picts)—that is, Britain north of the river Forth—is clearly a secondary development. From at least the 9th century onward, *Fir Alban* was regularly used to mean 'Gaels of Scotland, Scots'. *Alba* is the regular outcome in Irish and Scottish Gaelic of the most ancient attested name for Britain, namely **Albiiū* (see Albion).

John T. Koch

ALBAN, ST. (ALBANUS VEROLAMIENSIS)

St. Alban (Albanus Verolamiensis) was a Romano-British martyr, important as evidence for the early spread of Christianity to Britain and the survival of a saint's cult in southeast Britain through the Anglo-Saxon 'conquest'.

Alban is remembered as 'protomartyr of Britain' (the *Martyrology* of Bede, 22 June). First mentioned in the late 5th-century *Vita Germani*, the standard account of Alban is based on Gildas, *De Excidio Britanniae* 10–11.

According to Gildas, during the Emperor Diocletian's persecution of Christians, AD 302–305, the pagan Roman soldier Alban encountered a Christian on the point of arrest who would not worship the pagan gods. Alban was converted and swapped places with him. At the execution, the executioner charged with beheading Alban suddenly converted. Alban's burial place became a place of cult. This was the site visited by the Gallo-Roman bishops Germanus and Lupus after winning a public debate against the followers of Pelagius in AD 429.

Thomas O'Loughlin

ALBION, ALBIONES

Albion is the earliest attested name for the island of Britain. According to Pliny's *Natural History* (4.16), written in the first century AD, *Albion* was already obsolete by his time. Britain is called *insula Albionum* (island of the Albiones) in the *Ora Maritima* (Maritime itinerary) of Avienus (line 112), a late text that is, however, likely to be based the much earlier 'Massaliote Periplus' of the 6th or 5th century BC.

Newer terms for Britain based on the stem *Prettan-/Brettan-* began to replace the older name *Albion* at an early date, probably by *c.* 325 BC, which is when Pytheas of Massalia is said by the Greek historian Strabo to have sailed around Britain (2.4.1, 2.5.8, &c.). *Albion* survived as an archaic usage throughout classical literature, and it is given as the former name of Britain in BEDE's *Historia Ecclesiastica* in AD 731.

Derivation

Albion corresponds to the Gaelic place-name ALBA and the Old Welsh common noun *elbid*, all from Celtic **Albiiū,* which in turn derives from Indo-European **albho-* 'white'. *Elbid* occurs in the Old Welsh *englynion* (see ENGLYN) in the Cambridge Juvencus manuscript of *c.* 900. *Elbid*, Middle Welsh *elfyd,* has a general meaning 'world, earth, land, country, district'. The GAULISH divine epithet and GALATIAN personal name *Albio-rīx* would mean 'king of the world' (cf. Gaulish *Dumno-rīx* 'earth king' and BITURĪGES 'world kings') and proves **albiio-* to be common to the vocabulary of both Gaulish and BRYTHONIC. There is no corresponding common noun *albu, alba* in Old Irish. The Galatian name rules out the possibility that the name had first designated 'Britain'.

The exact meaning of **Albiiū* > Middle Welsh *eluyd* > Modern Welsh *elfydd* is revealed in early poetry as 'the habitable surface of the world': cf. *yn Annwfyn is eluyd, yn awyr uch eluyd* 'in the Un-world (ANNWN) below *elfydd*, in the air above *elfydd*' (LLYFR TALIESIN 20.8–9) and *tra barhao nef uch eluit lawr* 'so long as heaven may endure above the ground of *elfydd*'.

Philip Freeman and John T. Koch

AMAIRGEN MAC MÍLED

Amairgen mac Míled figures in Irish LEGENDARY HISTORY as the poet, judge, sage, and magician (see DRUIDS) of the sons of MÍL ESPÁINE, the first Gaels to take Ireland (ÉRIU). A full account of his rôle is given in the Middle Irish LEBAR GABÁLA ÉRENN ('The Book of Invasions'). The verses attributed to Amairgen in this story have been drawn into discussions of pre-Christian Celtic beliefs, especially those concerning REINCARNATION and shapeshifting; comparisons have often been drawn with the so-called mythological Welsh poetry of LLYFR TALIESIN.

The name *Amairgen* is a compound of Old Irish *amar* 'wonder, song, singing' and the root *gen-* 'to be born'; hence 'he who is born of (wondrous) song'.

John T. Koch

AMBROSIUS AURELIANUS (EMRYS WLEDIG)

Ambrosius Aurelianus (Emrys Wledig; *fl.* 5th century AD) was a military leader in post-Roman BRITAIN who subsequently developed into a figure in Welsh LEGENDARY HISTORY and ARTHURIAN LITERATURE. The only historical evidence for his existence is the account of 5th-century history in the *De Excidio Britanniae* (On the destruction of Britain) of GILDAS, who lived approximately fifty years after Ambrosius' heyday, toward the end of the 5th century AD. Gildas mentions 'Agitius thrice consul', who is usually thought to be the Roman general Aëtius who was consul for the third time in AD 446–54. Gildas calls Ambrosius the last of the Romans in Britain. For him, contemporary inhabitants of Britain were *Britanni*, not *Romani*. Ambrosius Aurelianus led a campaign against the Anglo-Saxons that climaxed in the siege of BADONICUS MONS (Mount Baddon), where the Britons were victorious (see ANGLO-SAXON 'CONQUEST').

In the Welsh Latin *Historia Brittonum* (AD 829/30), Ambrosius appears as a visionary youth who interprets the supernatural impediments that prevented the construction of a stronghold in Snowdonia (ERYRI) for the evil ruler Guorthigirn (Modern Welsh GWRTHEYRN). The ensuing vision involves the oldest literary appearance of the emblematic Red Dragon (DRAIG GOCH) of the Britons. Ambrosius explains that he, rather than Gwrtheyrn, is destined to rally the Britons against the Saxons. In *Historia Brittonum* §48, Ambrosius is called 'king among [i.e., over] all the kings of the British people'.

In his HISTORIA REGUM BRITANNIAE (History of the kings of Britain, *c.* 1139), GEOFFREY OF MONMOUTH envisioned 'Aurelius Ambrosius' (the name of the father of St Ambrose of Milan) as a major British leader and hero, the brother of King UTHR BENDRAGON, and hence Arthur's paternal uncle. Geoffrey effectively split the character that he had found in Gildas and *Historia Brittonum*, calling the prophet of Vortigern's stronghold and the wonder of the dragons 'Merlinus', thus identifying him with MYRDDIN, the prophetic poet and WILD MAN of early Welsh tradition.

John T. Koch

ANAON

Anaon is the name of the community of the souls of the dead in Breton tradition. These souls are generally understood to be in purgatory, doing penance on earth. Interaction with these entities is usually fatal in Breton folk tradition. Activities such as whistling after dark could also attract the wrath of the Anaon. The dead are cold, so they seek out the warmth of the living, returning to their former homes after dark; hell itself is referred to as *an ifern yen* 'cold hell' in Breton tradition. The Anaon is understood to be quiescent by day but virtually omnipresent at night, with lonely places being especially dangerous.

The Middle Breton form is *Anaffoun*. It is the cognate of Old Irish *anmin* 'souls' < Celtic **anamones,* itself cognate to Latin *animus* 'soul, spirit'.

See also BREIZH; OTHERWORLD; REINCARNATION; SAMAIN.

Antone Minard

ANDRASTE/ANDRASTA

Andraste/Andrasta was a Celtic goddess worshipped in Britain. According to Cassius Dio (*Roman History* 62), she was invoked by Queen Boudīca of the Iceni tribe, for help during the uprising against the Romans in AD 61:

> Boudīca said: 'I thank you, Andrasta, and call out to you as one woman to another . . . I implore and pray to you for victory and to maintain life and freedom against arrogant, unjust, insatiable, and profane men.'

Cassius Dio provides the only surviving record of Andraste. He also explains that *Andraste* meant 'victory'. Some scholars have equated Andraste with Andarte, a goddess worshipped by the southern Gaulish tribe of the Vocontii in present-day Provence.

Peter E. Busse and John T. Koch

ANEIRIN

Aneirin fab Dwywai is one of the earliest Welsh-language poets (see Cynfeirdd) to whom surviving texts are attributed—namely, the heroic elegies known as the Gododdin. He is regarded as a historical court poet of post-Roman north Britain (see Hen Ogledd) between the mid-6th century and the early 7th century. The correct Old Welsh form is probably *Neirin*. One possible derivation is from Late Latin *Nigrinus* 'dark one'.

'Neirin' and Historia Brittonum

The earliest surviving record of the poet's existence is included in §62 of the Welsh Latin Historia Brittonum (AD 829/30), where the poet *Neirin* is said to have been a contemporary of Maelgwn Gwynedd (†547) and Ida of Northumbria (r. 547–59).

Aneirin and the Gododdin

The oldest physical copy of the *Gododdin*—the Llyfr Aneirin ('The Book of Aneirin')—is a late 13th-century manuscript. Despite its relatively late date, there is general agreement that the poetry within this volume goes back well into the early Middle Ages, with many scholars agreeing that much of the poem was composed in the era of Aneirin himself.

Aneirin is mentioned four times as the poet of the *Gododdin*. The first is in the opening prose rubric, in the hand of scribe A: *Hwn yw e gododin. aneirin ae cant* 'This is the *Gododdin*. Aneirin sang it'. Within the poetry itself, Aneirin appears, for example, in this verse:

> *Gododin, go·mynnaf o-th blegyt—*
> *yg gwyd cant en aryal en emwyt,*
> *a guarchan mab Dwywei da wrhyt.*
> *Poet gno, en vn tyno treissyt!*

Er pan want maws mvr trin,
er pan aeth daear ar Aneirin,
nu neut ysgaras nat a·Gododin.

Gododdin man, I seek to entertain you—
here in the warband's presence, exuberantly in the court—
with the transmitted poetry from Dwywai's son, a man of high valour.
Let it be made known; and thereby, it will prevail!
Since the refined one, the rampart of battle, was slain,
since earth was pushed over Aneirin,
parted are muse and the Gododdin tribe.

This 'reciter's prologue' is in the hand of scribe B, where it correctly precedes the series of elegies of the Gododdin heroes themselves. If we take the prologue literally, the killing of Aneirin and the end of BRYTHONIC court poetry in the kingdom of Gododdin were simultaneous, which may mean that Aneirin himself was killed when that court fell, possibly in the year 636.

Aneirin in Middle Welsh Sources

About 1230–40, Dafydd Benfras, a poet of the GOGYNFEIRDD, composed an *awdl* to LLYWELYN AB IORWERTH of GWYNEDD containing the following reference: *i ganu moliant mal Aneirin gynt/dydd y cant 'Ododdin'* 'to sing praise like Aneirin of yore the day he sang *Y Gododdin*'.

In the GENEALOGIES of the Welsh saints, a Dwywei is said to have been the daughter of a Lleennawc (probably the 6th-century ruler of the north British kingdom of ELFED of that name). This woman would have lived at approximately the right time to have been Aneirin's mother. If this individual is the same Dwywai, Aneirin would be the brother of St Deiniol. The uncommon name Dwywai always seems to be a woman's name; it is unusual that the poet is known by his matronym rather than his patronym.

Aneirin's killing figures in two of the Welsh TRIADS. In *Trioedd Ynys Prydein* (TYP) no. 33, his slaying is listed as one of the 'Three Unfortunate Assassinations'. The same event is probably noted in TYP no. 34, 'The Three Unfortunate Axe-Blows'.

John T. Koch

ANGLO-IRISH LITERATURE

Anglo-Irish literature refers to literature in the English language by Irish men and women. Historically, much of that writing was produced by the English-speaking descendants of 17th-century English settlers and colonists in Ireland (ÉIRE) who came to be known as the Anglo-Irish; this group includes figures such as Jonathan Swift, Oliver Goldsmith, Maria Edgeworth, Charles Maturin, William Butler YEATS, and Lady Augusta Gregory. In the 20th century, the term gained general currency in relation to Irish writing in English, although less precise terms such as 'Irish Literature' are also used.

In the late 19th century, the waning Protestant Ascendancy caste found itself frequently referred to as the Anglo-Irish and began to accept such usage. As a young man in the 1880s and 1890s, Yeats laboured assiduously to establish that a tradition of Irish writing in English did, in fact, exist (he anthologized and edited with great energy)—a tradition he sought to extend in his own poetry. Lady Gregory, in her book *Cuchulain of Muirthemne* (1902), cast ancient Celtic saga material from the Ulster Cycle into a dialect version of the English spoken in Ireland to make such authentically Irish matter available in the language of the majority. In the early decades of the 20th century, the international reputation of Yeats gave credibility to the claim that an Irish literature in English that expressed the life of the Irish people had not only existed in the past but also could be built on in the present to the future benefit of the country. The creation, of a modern literature in English, therefore, was represented by Yeats and his confederates as a renaissance or Irish Literary Revival.

When the government of the Irish Free State (Saorstát na hÉireann) at the end of the first decade of independence issued an Official State Handbook, it included a chapter entitled 'Anglo-Irish Literature' that announced the country possessed 'a great and distinctive national literature' in the English language, notwithstanding criticism the year before from Daniel Corkery, an influential critic and university professor of English. The literature around which this controversy had gathered was deemed to have had its origins in the 18th century with Jonathan Swift (1667–1745). A substantial body of literature, certainly, had been composed in English in Ireland from well before Swift's birth, dating back to a 14th-century manuscript that includes the fantasy 'The Land of Cockayne'. Other notable early writers include Oliver Goldsmith (1728–74), George Berkeley (1685–1753), and Edmund Burke (1729–97).

The rise of English-language literature in Ireland occurred in a period of European cultural history that saw the construction of the idea of 'the Celt', to which the Ossian fervour of the late 18th century (see Macpherson; Oisín) gave a powerful impetus. The Romantic Movement furthered the glamour or exoticism of difference. Celticism and Romanticism often combined to make Ireland, like Wales (Cymru), Scotland (Alba), and Brittany (Breizh), the site of imagined otherness. Ireland in the immensely popular *Irish Melodies* of Thomas Moore (1779–1852) became the home of poignant lost causes; in Maria Edgeworth's *Castle Rackrent* (1800) or William Carleton's *Traits and Stories of the Irish Peasantry*, (1830, 33), it was the object of amused or anthropological report. By the end of the century, however, in the work of W. B. Yeats (1865–1939) and other poets and dramatists of the Irish Literary Revival, the country was represented as a zone of Celtic spirituality, a territory of the imagination, scenic in the Romantic fashion: rural, primitive, wild, and exotic.

The 'Celtic' dimension of the Irish Literary Revival had its most searching critic in James Joyce (1882–1941), who in his experimental fiction spared neither the rural idylls and Romantic nostalgia of Anglo-Irish poetry nor the narrow nationalism of

Irish Ireland. He assumed that his medium was the English spoken in Ireland (Hiberno-English) and that his artistic destiny was to write in the European tradition of the novel.

Sheridan le Fanu (1914–73), author of *Uncle Silas* (1864), and Bram Stoker (1847–1911), author of *Dracula* (1897), had seemed to register the anxieties of the age more tellingly than those writers such as William Carleton (1794–1869), who sought to represent the country in terms of a more conventional realism. Realism of limited scope found its genre in 20th-century Ireland in the short-story form. George Moore (1852–1933) demonstrated in *The Untilled Field* (1903) that rural and provincial life could be the basis of short, episodic narratives. Moreover, in the early decades of Irish independence (which was won in 1922), writers such as Seán O'Faolain (1900–91), Frank O'Connor (1903–66), and Liam O'Flaherty (Ó Flaithearta, 1896–1984) made the Irish short story—anecdotal, orally based, lyrical in expression—a recognizable literary kind. Realism also affected the dramatic vision of Sean O'Casey (1880–1964), whose *Plough and the Stars* (1926) subjected the foundational event of the new Irish state to a withering critique.

In the 20th century and since, writing in the English language has flourished in drama, poetry, and the novel, while writing in Irish has maintained a visible and distinctive presence in cultural life.

Terence Brown

ANGLO-SAXON "CONQUEST"

The Invasion Hypothesis and the Anglicization of Britain

In the traditional history of BRITAIN, the coming of English-speakers to the southeast is depicted as a forceful invasion. Warlike Angles, Saxons, Jutes, and other Germanic tribes are said to have come across from the European mainland in the two centuries after Roman rule ended in Britain in AD 409/10.

Historical Evidence

Although few contemporary written records deal with the Anglicization of post-Roman Britain, two 5th-/6th-century historical witnesses support this picture. The *Chronica Gallica ad annum CCCCLII* (Gallic chronicle to AD 452) states at the year corresponding to 441: 'The British provinces having up to this time suffered various defeats and calamities were reduced to Saxon rule'. Scholars disagree as to the reliability of this evidence and its date. The second early source is the earlier 6th-century *De Excidio Britanniae* (On the destruction of Britain) of GILDAS, §§23–4. There we are told that the *Saxones* were first recruited to defend Britain from the PICTS. They came at first in three ships from Germany, but their numbers and demands for provisions soon grew unsustainable. They rose in revolt, leading some

Britons to give themselves up as slaves and others to seek refuge in remote places or across the sea (presumably in Armorica). Later, the Britons rallied militarily under Ambrosius Aurelianus, culminating in the battle of Badonicus mons. As Gildas shows no trace of written records regarding the Anglo-Saxon conquest, his account must be based on oral tradition, probably augmented by imagination and moved by a powerful religious sense of the meaning of history. He thus constructed a stirring story to account for Britain's 6th-century present and to explain how different it was from the Roman period. Gildas's account of the conquest served as the basis for the writings of Bede and Historia Brittonum and all subsequent accounts, and has seriously been questioned by historians and archaeologists only in the past 25 years or so.

The End of Roman Britain in Archaeology

The archaeological record for late Roman Britain offers very little confirmation of Gildas's description of burned and looted cities and massacred British civilians; rather, the usual picture for the Romano-British towns is of prosperity into the later 4th century, followed by gradual economic contraction, sometimes followed by abandonment and in other cases by continuity into the early Middle Ages and to the present day.

Archaeological evidence has been taken to suggest that by AD 410 there were already communities of Germanic-speaking settlers from across the North Sea around the Roman towns of East Anglia and the Anglian Kingdom of Lindsey; their presence is revealed by a distinctive type of 'Romano-Saxon' pottery. If this late 4th- to early 5th-century material is correctly dated and forms a continuum with subsequent Anglo-Saxon occupation in the region, then the origins of England would go back before the traditional date of AD 441×456. The clusters of pagan Anglo-Saxon cemeteries around the old Roman towns suggest continuity within the existing late Romano-British landscape at odds with Gildas's account of violent invasion.

Old English and Brythonic

At the close of the Romano-British period in AD 407–10, Brythonic was spoken from the river Forth in the north to the English Channel in the south (see Pictish; Scottish place-names). It is not clear as to when exactly the Germanic speech of the ancestral English first began to eclipse Brythonic Celtic in Britain. Nor is it clear whether this transition was prompted by population replacement, by dislocation or genocide, or by a steady language shift in which the descendants of Romano-Britons came to raise their children as monoglot English speakers. Place-names of Celtic origin in eastern England indicate that a stage of bilingualism preceded the extinction of Brythonic speech. A number of Brythonic names borne by prominent Anglo-Saxons are also consistent with a process of language shift—for example, *Cerdic, Certic* (of Wessex, 495–534) = Old Welsh *Ceretic, Certic; Cædmon* (7th century) = OW *Catman(n)*.

English Political Expansion in the Early Middle Ages

The political expansion of the Anglo-Saxon kingdoms can be traced in the historical record from the mid-6th century. Although the English language generally followed in its wake, the assumption that Brythonic speakers were immediately and violently replaced by English speakers is not guaranteed. The fact that Asser, writing in 893, was able to find Brythonic place-names for many localities that had been under Anglo-Saxon rule for centuries suggests that bilingualism was slow to recede. According to the Anglo-Saxon Chronicle, Gloucester, Cirencester, and BATH were taken into English control in 577. Eadwine of Northumbria occupied the kingdom of ELFED in present-day West Yorkshire and expelled its native king Certic *c.* 619 (*Historia Brittonum* §63). The kingdom of Gododdin fell to the Northumbrians in the 7th century, perhaps in 636. The eastern portion of POWYS, centred about the old Roman town of Wroxeter, probably came under English control in the third quarter of the 7th century. By the later 8th century, lands north of the Bristol Channel under Brythonic rule were virtually limited to present-day Wales and Strathclyde (YSTRAD CLUD) in the north.

John T. Koch

ANGLO-WELSH LITERATURE

The Term and Its Implications

Although a substantial body of distinctively Welsh Anglophone writing emerged only in the 20th century, Welsh and English have coexisted in Wales (CYMRU) since the late Middle Ages. 'Anglo-Welsh literature' was the term commonly used for several decades following its adoption in 1922 to identify an Anglophone literature that recognized the seniority of 'WELSH' (i.e., Welsh-language literature; see WELSH PROSE LITERATURE). This term has now been more or less abandoned in favour of the more unwieldy 'Welsh writing in English'.

The Beginnings of Anglo-Welsh Literature

In 'A hymn to the Virgin' (*c.* 1470), Ieuan ap Hywel Swrdwal used Welsh spelling and native strict metre verse forms as a defiant demonstration of his competence in English. Comparable to postcolonial literature, this cultural hybrid acts as a fitting prologue to the cultural drama of subsequent centuries, from the missionizing work of Morgan Llwyd (1619–59) and William Williams Pantycelyn (1717–91) to the cultural ecumenism practised by T. Gwynn Jones (1871–1949) and other 20th-century writers. It could even be argued that the English language was paradoxically instrumental in the 'recovery' of the very bardic tradition (see BARDIC ORDER) upon which a modern, separatist, Welsh cultural nationalism came to be based: Antiquarians of the late 18th century sought out and translated manuscript material furnishing evidence of Wales's contribution to the broader culture of the United Kingdom.

Welsh Anglophone society was colonial, consisting of four Anglicized, or settler, groupings: the gentry, the Anglican clergy (see CHRISTIANITY), an embryonic professional class, and a tiny urban bourgeoisie. The celebrated collection of metaphysical poetry by the bilingual poet Henry Vaughan (1621–95), *Silex Scintillans* (Latin for 'Sparkling rock', 1650), betrays traces of his cultural situation in its vocabulary, its love of *dyfalu* (definition through conceits; see CYWYDDWYR), and its loving divinization of nature. Almost all the English-language works produced in Wales until the late 19th century were provincial imitations of fashionable English styles and genres, although Thomas Jeffrey Llewelyn Pritchard did draw upon Welsh legend in his picaresque novel, *The Adventures of Twm Shôn Catti* (1828).

The Earlier 20th Century

Modern Welsh writing in English was largely the product of the transformation of south Wales during the second half of the 19th century into a cosmopolitan centre of industrial civilization. This new literature came to public attention with the publication of Caradoc Evans's short-story collection, *My People* (1915), in which the Welsh-speaking author savaged the Nonconformist society (see CHRISTIANITY) of his native Cardiganshire (Ceredigion) by fashioning, through the literal translation of Welsh idiom, a form of speech that turned the rural characters into moral grotesques. Regarded by Welsh-speaking Wales as a violent, humiliating betrayal, Evans's work set the tone for a *kulturkampf* (cultural struggle) between modern Wales's two linguistic communities—a battle that continued for much of the 20th century. In Saunders LEWIS's 1938 pamphlet, *Is There an Anglo-Welsh Literature?*, the author doubted whether Welsh English (as contrasted with Hibernian English; see ANGLO-IRISH LITERATURE) was distinct enough to sustain a culturally distinctive literature.

Even as Evans was setting the two cultures on a fateful collision course, other writers, such as Ernest Rhys (1859–1946), were capitalizing on the fashionable interest in the 'Celtic twilight' (and on the popularity of Lady Charlotte Guest's *Mabinogion*) by adapting forms of WELSH POETRY, as well as legendary and historical materials from Welsh-language culture, to the taste of Anglophone readers.

Dylan Thomas (1914–53)

Although his Welsh-speaking parents named him 'Dylan' from the MABINOGI, like many upwardly mobile Welsh they ensured that their son did not learn Welsh at home. A blend of fascination with and repulsion from his parents' Wales lies at the root of many of Thomas's most powerful works—from the surrealist stories of the 1930s to many of the stories of *Portrait of the Artist as a Young Dog* (1940); and from 'After the Funeral' to 'Fern Hill' and *Under Milk Wood* (1954). While the style of his poetry probably owes more to Gerard Manley Hopkins than tracing directly to the Welsh CYNGHANEDD that Hopkins had absorbed, Thomas did display, from his early period as reporter for the *South Wales Daily Post*, a particular interest in traditional Welsh society.

Both the man and his work elicited strong, open reactions (both positive and negative) from Welsh-language writers. Thomas's antics outraged influential members of a still largely puritan culture, while his individualist stance was radically at odds with the community-centred ethos of Welsh-language literature. Nevertheless, he also inspired Welsh-language writers in new directions. The complex (and incomplete) history of Thomas's reception by Welsh-language culture is a reminder that intercultural influences in modern Wales have all not proceeded in the same direction.

The Mid-20th Century

The great London Welsh poet, David Jones (1895–1974), constructed the most remarkable Christian modernist artefact out of a combination of English and Celtic materials. From *In Parenthesis* (1937) to *The Sleeping Lord* (1974), his works are spectrographs, designed to demonstrate the internal richness of an authentic (as opposed to an Anglo-centric) British culture.

Glyn Jones (1905–95) was the Anglophone Welsh writer of the 'first generation' who most creatively blended elements from Welsh and English to produce, both in poetry and in fiction, a distinctive Welsh modernist text. Jones used the metrics and rhetorical strategies of Welsh-language *barddas* (poetic art) to foreground the linguistic matter of his English texts, and (like his friend Dylan Thomas) used the fantasticating improvisatory rhetoric of oral storytelling to produce remarkable 'magic realist' short stories and novels. His *The Island of Apples* (1965) is loosely but suggestively based on the legend of Afallon (AVALON). Jones's interest in demonstrating creative continuities between the Welsh-speaking and English-speaking cultures of Wales was shared by his friend Idris Davies (1905–53), a native Welsh speaker from the Rhymney valley, whose long poetic sequences (particularly *The Angry Summer* [1943]) capture the community drama of the Depression Years.

R. S. Thomas and Emyr Humphreys

Raised to speak only English, the poet R. S. Thomas (1913–2000) was fascinated early by the Welsh-language culture he saw profiled across Anglesey (MôN) in the craggy outlines of Snowdonia (ERYRI). Although he learned Welsh as an adult, he bitterly resented the fact that he remained insufficiently connected with the language to be able to write poetry in it, and he attributed some of the tense power of his Anglophone writing to his consequent love–hate relationship with the English language.

Emyr Humphreys (1919–) was the premier novelist and man of letters of R. S. Thomas's generation (*Planet* 71.30–6). Humphreys, too, learned Welsh as a young adult, following his conversion to Saunders Lewis's version of NATIONALISM. Unlike his friend Thomas, Humphreys was able not only to produce substantial creative work in Welsh but also to see his Anglophone work as a means of serving the same politico-cultural cause. In particular, he became fascinated by the continuities of Welsh history, from the time of the GODODDIN to the present—a continuity he saw as maintained by the Taliesin tradition of *barddas*, and by the work of the CYFARWYDD (the tribal storyteller and custodian of cultural memory), whose mantle he felt had now fallen on himself as a fiction writer. Most of Humphreys's most ambitious and successful work—from *Outside the House of Baal* (1965) to his seven-novel fictional history of 20th-century Wales titled *The Land of the Living* (1971–91)—constitutes an attempt to introduce the Welsh to their past and recent history in the ideological terms of the nationalist narrative that Humphreys himself has accepted. As a convinced Europhile, he has consistently sought to view Wales in the wider cultural context of European civilization. The inclusion in his *Collected Poems* of poems in Welsh, and of translations from the Welsh, clearly indicates that Humphreys regards his writing as an Anglophone expression of his total identification with Welsh-language culture and his complete devotion to its restoration—like R. S. Thomas, he regards Anglophone Wales as essentially a colonial aberration, and both writers have actively campaigned for official social recognition of Welsh and for the language's full political empowerment.

Harri Webb

One of the gurus of this generation was Harri Webb (1920–94), a sophisticated writer who, having learned Welsh, dedicated himself to producing a populist poetry that would mobilize public opinion on behalf of a radically egalitarian and republican model of Welsh nationalism. A graduate in French, Webb was well read in the early postcolonial theorizing of thinkers such as Frantz Fanon, and was able to see Wales in a European context. Inclined to romanticize Welsh medieval history in some of his poems, Webb was at his most lively and effective when writing verses for popular performance, thereby consciously acting as a kind of *bardd gwlad* (the memorializer in popular verse of the experiences of a locality) to an industrial readership he regarded as linguistically, and thus culturally, disempowered and disenfranchised. Always a strong believer in the Welsh language as the sole guarantor of a strongly distinctive Welsh culture, Webb, in his last years, lived out the extreme logic of his position—a position he shared with R. S. Thomas and Emyr Humphreys—by refusing to write any more poetry in English.

Creative Translators

That this cultural rapprochement involved Anglophone writers other than those who had mastered Welsh was due not only to the changed political climate but also to other factors—including the availability of powerful creative translations of Welsh-language literature (particularly poetry) into English, thanks to the work first of Gwyn Williams (1904–90), from *The Rent That's Due to Love* (1950) to *Presenting Welsh Poetry* (1959), and then of Joseph Clancy (1928–) and Tony Conran (1931–), whose *Penguin Book of Welsh Verse* (1967) served as an introduction for many to the previously 'closed book' of Welsh *barddas*. Even writers such as John Ormond (1923–90), Leslie Norris (1921–2006), and Dannie Abse (1923–)—otherwise not noted for a sympathetic interest in Welsh-language culture—showed signs, in their writings, of exposure to this literature in translation. Conran's own substantial body of original poetry is consequently the most convincing and remarkable instance, in Anglophone writing, of a creative marriage between the two linguistic cultures of Wales. He has developed such influential concepts as 'seepage' between the English- and Welsh-language writing.

Bilingual Literary Culture

Conran is one of an important line of 'brokers' who have attempted to negotiate better terms between Wales's cultures. These individuals include the editors of Anglophone Welsh journals from the *Welsh Outlook* (1914–33), through *The Welsh Review* (1939–48), and *The Anglo-Welsh Review* (1949–88), to *Planet* (1970–) and *The New Welsh Review* (1988–), all of which have commissioned translations from the Welsh, essays in cross-cultural study, and other intercultural materials. Individuals of particular note who have sought to build bridges across the linguistic chasm include Aneirin Talfan Davies (1908–80) and Meic Stephens (1938–), who set about creating an institutional infrastructure with scholarly underpinnings as the founding director of the Literature Department of the newly established Welsh Arts Council (Cyngor y Celfyddydau, 1967–94).

M. Wynn Thomas

ANKOU

Ankou is the name for personified Death in Breton tradition. The figure itself is described in a similar fashion to the Grim Reaper: a tall, thin figure, sometimes a skeleton in a shroud, carrying a scythe. He drives a carriage (*karrigell an Ankou*), which can be heard creaking in the night. The word is cognate with Welsh *angau* and Old Irish *écae* 'death'.

See also ANAON; BRETON LITERATURE; HAGIOGRAPHY.

Antone Minard

ANNALS

Introduction and Overview

The annals provide a contemporary record of history for more than a millennium, beginning in the middle of the 5th century and continuing up to the early 17th century in Ireland. In their genesis, they appear to owe little to the annal writing and chronicling of late antiquity, although at a later stage, the compilers of the Irish annals did borrow from foreign reference works such as BEDE's *Chronica major*.

There is near-consensus that the earliest annals came from a North British context. The core of the early Irish annals is the Iona Chronicle, contemporary from the mid-6th century and compiled in the monastery of Iona (Eilean Ì). Versions of the Iona Chronicle (sometimes drastically abbreviated) are preserved in the extant annals, but no surviving collection of Irish annals contains all of this material: For example, original entries are absent in the Annals of Ulster and present in the Annals of Tigernach, and vice versa. The Iona Chronicle passed to Armagh (Ard Mhacha), and was continued there. From the mid-8th century to the mid-10th century, detailed materials about Meath (Mide) and north Leinster (Laigin) were added from annals recorded at Clonard. The ensuing compilation, sometimes called the 'Chronicle of Ireland', passed in the very early 10th century to Clonmacnoise (Cluan Mhic Nóis) and, with varied additions and omissions, forms the basis of the Clonmacnoise annals down to 911—namely, the Annals of Tigernach, *Chronicum Scottorum*, and the Annals of Clonmacnoise. After 911, the Annals of Ulster and the Clonmacnoise annals diverge. The common exemplar that lies behind the Clonmacnoise group also lies behind the Annals of Inisfallen (which contains very many unique records as well) down to 1065, when the Clonmacnoise group and the Annals of Inisfallen become independent of each other.

Annales Cambriae

Annales Cambriae (The Annals of Wales) are an important primary historical source for events in Wales (Cymru) and north Britain, with entries spanning a period corresponding to *c.* 450–*c.* 955. This work comprises a list of noteworthy events such as battles, plagues, and the deaths of kings and saints, arranged by year, covering a span of several centuries. The language of *Annales Cambriae* is Latin with frequent Celtic proper names, most commonly Old Welsh.

The text of *Annales Cambriae* assumed its current form in the mid-10th century, at which point the entries stop. The text is certainly related to the various surviving versions of the Irish annals, sharing entries with these materials, especially early ones such as the death notices of Saints Patrick, Brigit, and Colum Cille. Two entries in the 1st century covered by *Annales Cambriae* mention Arthur: the battle of Badonicus mons (Baddon) at a year corresponding to AD 516 or 518, and the battle of Camlan (at which Arthur fell) at 537 or 539. It is certain that many entries are near-contemporary. It is unlikely, however, that the entries as early as those citing the death of Patrick or Arthur's battles could derive from contemporary annals, as yearly records of this sort do not appear to have been kept so early in Britain or Ireland (Ériu).

The three principal layers in *Annales Cambriae* are (1) a set of Irish annals, which served as the framework for the years 453 to 613; (2) a north British chronicle, which served as the basis for the entries from 613 to 777, and in which special attention is paid to events in Strathclyde and among the Picts; and (3) Welsh annals kept at Mynyw, now Tyddewi (St David's), continuing from the late 9th century until the mid-10th century. As some or all of the churches of Wales accepted the Roman calculation for the date of Easter in 768, it is possible that the north British annals were brought to Wales at about that time as part of a package of documents to be used for keeping the calendar (see Easter controversy).

Although the entries begin in the 5th century, it is doubtful that any of the Welsh forms in *Annales Cambriae* could be linguistically older than the 8th century, when the prototype of the text arrived in Wales as described previously.

Annals of Ulster (Annála Uladh)

These important annals survive in two manuscripts:

(i)　Dublin, Trinity College 1282, second half of the 15th century/beginning of the 16th century
(ii)　Oxford, Bodleian Library, Rawlinson B 489, first half of the 16th century

It appears that MS (ii) is a fair copy of MS (i), but with supplementary entries; it preserves some text lost by mutilation in MS (i). Later manuscripts also include some important post-12th-century additions and readings.

A remarkable aspect of the Annals of Ulster is the fidelity of the scribes in preserving Old-Irish forms, even archaisms. This practice lends the Annals of Ulster an authority greater than that of any other annals. This reliability does not, however, extend to its chronology, which has been seriously disrupted in the early period. The Annals of Ulster end at 1540 (apart from later additions). See also Ulaid.

Website
www.ucc.ie/celt/published/T100001A.html

Annals of Inisfallen (Annála Inis Faithleann)

These annals are in Oxford, Bodleian Library, Rawlinson B 503 (AD 1092 and later). The early part is a radically abbreviated version of the Iona Chronicle (see Eilean Ì). The same exemplar that lies behind the Clonmacnoise group also lies behind the Annals of Inisfallen down to the year 1065. In addition, the Annals of Inisfallen contain unique material. The annals were continued as a local record, sometimes in a very desultory manner, until the early 14th century.

The so-called Dublin Annals of Inisfallen are an 18th-century compilation made in Paris, and have nothing to do with the Annals of Inisfallen proper.

Website
www.ucc.ie/celt/online/G100004.html

Annals of Tigernach (Annála Thighearnaigh)

These annals survive in two manuscripts. Oxford, Bodleian Library, Rawlinson B 502, folios 1–12 (*c.* 1050×1150), covers the period *c.* 807 BC–AD 160; it is an imperfect copy of a chronicle of the ancient world, much indebted to the chronicles of Eusebius (*c.* AD 260–*c.* 340) and Bede.

The second copy of the Annals of Tigernach is Oxford, Bodleian Library, Rawlinson B 488, fos. 1–26 (second half of the 14th century). The Annals of Tigernach proper occur on folios 7r–26v; they comprise three fragments: (i) AD 489–766, (ii) 973–1003, and (iii) 1018–1178.

Website
www.ucc.ie/celt/online/G100002.html

Chronicum Scottorum

These annals survive in a single manuscript: Dublin, Trinity College 1292 (*c.* 1640×1650). These works span the period from AM (year of the world) 1599 to AD 1135. Further annals for the years 1141–50, of unknown provenance, occupy the last four pages. All later MSS of *Chronicum Scottorum* are modern copies of this manuscript, and have no independent value.

Website
www.ucc.ie/celt/published/T100016.html.

Annals of Clonmacnoise

These annals are preserved, in whole or in part, in nine manuscripts. All of these works derive from a translation of the lost original, completed in 1627, which omitted the traditional dating system. In their order of events, the Annals of Clonmacnoise are closer to the Annals of Tigernach than to *Chronicum Scottorum*, which suggests that these annals' exemplar was close to the Annals of Tigernach. While the Annals of Tigernach break off at 1178 and *Chronicum Scottorum* proper ends at 1135, the Annals of Clonmacnoise deal with prehistory and the coming of Christianity, have annals (with some lacunae) from the 5th to the 12th century, and include pedigrees and detailed late medieval annals from 1200 to 1408. The later annals are very close to the Annals of Connacht, albeit sometimes somewhat abbreviated, and sometimes containing extensive entries absent from the Annals of Connacht.

Annals of Loch Cé

These annals survive in two manuscripts from the second half of the 16th century: Dublin, Trinity College 1293 and London, BL Additional 4792. The first contains the annals from 1014 to 1571, with some lacunae, while the second contains the annals from 1568 to 1590. After 1544, the Annals of Loch Cé serve as a contemporary record of events. From the late 1230s, these annals have detailed narratives of CONNACHT high politics.

Website
www.ucc.ie/celt/published/T100010A.html

Annals of Connacht (Annála Chonnachta)

The Annals of Connacht derive from a compilation made by a member of the learned family of Ó Mael Chonaire in the mid-15th century. They share an origin with the Annals of Loch Cé. The Annals begin in 1224; they are generally fuller than the closely related Annals of Loch Cé. They are preserved in Dublin, Royal Irish Academy MS 1219 (formerly Stowe C iii 1; xvi). The manuscript contains annals from 1224 to 1544, with lacunae. For the greater part of the 16th century, the Annals of Connacht represent a contemporary record.

Website
www.ucc.ie/celt/published/T100011.html

Annals of the Four Masters (Annála Ríoghachta Éireann)

The Annals of the Four Masters represent the endeavour of the Irish Franciscans to gather together and then publish all extant Irish annals they could find as a record of Irish civilization. The work was left ready for press, with a title page and preface, but remained unpublished until the mid-19th century. The text runs from Noah's Flood to 1616. It contains a vast range of historical and legendary materials and is by far the most copious Irish annalistic collection. Among other materials, it contains a copy of the Annals of Ulster, including the 12th-century lacunae in the extant text; a copy of the Annals of Tigernach and at least one lost set of early annals from Leinster (LAIGIN); some four lost books of late medieval annals; lost court annals with a distinctive Renaissance flavour from the O'Brien court in the 16th century; a remarkably detailed contemporary record of Irish history over the period 1589–1616; and early historical verses. For large areas of Irish history, both early and late, these annals are the only authority. The compilers discarded the old chronology in favour of the regnal years of Irish high-kings and an AM (*anno mundi*)/AD dating, and in doing so made many errors that must corrected. They also omitted many entries that reflected ill on the church and modernized the language. Six different manuscripts are housed in Dublin.

Website
www.ucc.ie/celt/online/G100005D.html

Donnchadh Ó Corráin and John T. Koch

ANNWN/ANNWFN

Annwn (earlier Annwfn) designates the OTHERWORLD in Welsh tradition. It is one of the central themes in the medieval Welsh MABINOGI. In the PWYLL, Prince of DYFED, the title character, encounters ARAWN, king of Annwfn. The pair exchange identities for a year, leading to the entanglement of Dyfed's royal house with Annwn's supernatural forces. An early poem entitled PREIDDIAU ANNWFN (The Spoils of Annwn) is found in the Book of TALIESIN (LLYFR TALIESIN). This poem describes a series of mysterious adventures by ARTHUR and his heroes with otherworldly strongholds.

Derivation

Annwfn has more than one possible etymology. The basic root is Welsh *dwfn* < Celtic **dumno-* < **dubno-*, meaning 'deep'. At an early date, it acquired the secondary sense 'world'. The prefix is either Celtic *ande-* 'in', which can have an intensifying force, or else *an-*, a negative prefix (compare English *un-*). Accordingly, varying translations of the sense are possible, including 'very deep', 'the un-world', or 'the world within'.

Gaulish 'Andounnabo'

A probable cognate is attested in Gaulish. ANΔOOYNNABO *andounnabo* 'to the underworld spirits' (see Anaon) is used in an inscription from Collias. The Gaulish spelling best suits the 'un-world' etymology.

John T. Koch

ANU

In Cormac's Glossary (Sanas Chormaic, *c.* AD 900), Anu is 'the mother of the Irish gods' (*mater deorum Hiberniensium*). The goddess Danu is sometimes confused with her. According to *Cóir Anmann* (The appropriateness of names), she was a goddess of prosperity (*bandía in t-shónusa*) associated especially with Munster (Mumu). *Íath nAnann* 'land of Anu' occurs in poetry as an epithet for Ireland (Ériu). Two hills in Co. Kerry (Contae Chiarraí) are called *Dá chích nAnann* 'Anu's breasts' or in English, 'the paps of Anu', underlining her function as a fertility goddess and as a personification of the land. The name *Anu* may be cognate with Doric Greek πάνια (*/pánia/*) 'being filled, especially with food' and Latin *pānis* 'bread'.

Peter E. Busse

ARAN ISLANDS
See Oileáin Árann.

ARAWN

Arawn is a king of the Otherworld (Annwn) in the Welsh tale of Pwyll, prince of Dyfed. While hunting, Arawn finds Pwyll feeding his hounds on a stag killed by Arawn's pack—rude behaviour for a prince. To make amends, Pwyll spends the next year in Annwn. He takes Arawn's form and kills Arawn's enemy Hafgan with a single blow. Meanwhile, disguised as Pwyll, Arawn brings kindness and justice to Dyfed. The identity switch with an otherworldly ruler is found elsewhere in Celtic tradition—for example, in the Irish tale *Compert Mongáin* (Birth of Mongán). Arawn has sometimes been mistakenly labeled as a Celtic god of the dead, but in fact the name may be derived from the Biblical *Aaron*, Moses's brother.

Rhiannon Ifans

ARD MHACHA (ARMAGH)

Ard Mhacha (Armagh), 'high place of [the goddess] MACHA', is the traditional ecclesiastical capital of Ireland (ÉIRE), supposedly founded by St PATRICK. Archaeological evidence of a church foundation at Armagh dates from the 5th or 6th century, with the structure probably being built upon an existing pre-Christian cult site. The ditch surrounding the Cathedral Hill at Armagh has given a radiocarbon date of *c.* AD 290, suggesting that the site was the successor of the nearby prehistoric monument at EMAIN MACHAE.

The *Liber Angeli* has Saint Patrick directed to Armagh by an angelic revelation that declares it to be Ireland's main church, of archiepiscopal status. By the 11th century, its abbacy had become hereditary among the Clann Sínaigh. At the Synod of Ráith Bressail (1111), Armagh was given its modern boundary, while at the Synod of Kells (1152), it was made an archbishopric and given the primacy of Ireland (ÉRIU). Its last Gaelic archbishop was Nicholas Mac Maolíosa (1272–1303), after whose tenure the archbishops lived outside Armagh; of these non-Gaelic archbishops, the most distinguished was Richard Fitzralph (1346–60), the theologian.

Thomas O'Loughlin

ARFDERYDD

Arfderydd is the site of a battle. A full account of this clash does not survive, but like CAMLAN and CATRAETH in Welsh tradition and MAG ROTH in Irish, it drew diverse heroes and dynastic lineages together into a destructive conflict that became the wellspring for epic literature. In the MYRDDIN poetry (*Ymddiddan Myrddin a Thaliesin, Afallennau, Hoianau, Cyfoesi*), Arfderydd is the event at which Myrddin, previously a young noble warrior and follower of the overlord Gwenddolau ap Ceidiaw, was transformed by battle terror and thus received the gift of PROPHECY (see also LLYFR DU CAERFYRDDIN).

The oldest notice of the battle appears in the Annales Cambriae at AD 573 (see ANNALS). Gwenddolau is said to have been defeated and killed at Arfderydd, with the sons of Eliffer, Gwrgi and PEREDUR, being present at the event. In the Myrddin poetry, RHYDDERCH HAEL of Dumbarton (see YSTRAD CLUD)—a friend and contemporary of St COLUM CILLE (*fl.* 563–97)—appears to be involved in the battle and its aftermath.

The battle site was near the present-day western English–Scottish border at Liddel Strength, Arthuret parish (which preserves the old name), near Carwinley (*Kar-Windelhov* 'fort of Gwenddolau' in 1202). *Kar-Windelhov* could, in fact, mean 'fort of the fair dales' and have nothing to do with any historical figure. Although GEOFFREY OF MONMOUTH does not name the battle site, his *Vita Merlini* (*c.* 1150) describes a war between the kings Guennolus (= Gwenddolau), Peredurus, and Rodarchus (= Rhydderch), in which Merlin lost three brothers and went mad.

Arfderydd is mentioned in four TRIADS: no. 29, 'Three Faithful War-bands'; no. 31, 'Three Noble Retinues'; no. 44, the 'Three Horse-Burdens'; and no. 84, 'Three Futile Battles'.

We do not have enough sound early evidence to determine the political reasons for the battle of Arfderydd or its historical consequences. Nevertheless, the facts that all the principals were BRITONS—fighting against each other rather than against SCOTS, PICTS, or Anglo-Saxons—and that the site was near the old Romano-British frontier at HADRIAN'S WALL suggest that the formal division of Britain and its people in Roman times were still determining factors for conflicts in the later 6th century. Of the dynasties involved, only that of Rhydderch surely continued.

John T. Koch

ARIANRHOD FERCH DÔN

Arianrhod ferch Dôn (variant: Aranrhod) is one of the central characters in the Middle Welsh wonder tale MATH FAB MATHONWY, the Fourth Branch of the MABINOGI. In this tale, King Math seeks Arianrhod for an office requiring a virgin. She asserts her virginity, but when she steps over Math's magic wand she gives birth to two beings—Dylan and 'a little thing' that subsequently reappears as LLEU, the tale's protagonist. Resisting her unwanted motherhood, Arianrhod places three supernatural prohibitions (cf. Irish GEIS) upon Lleu:

(1) That he not be named until she names him
(2) That he not take arms until she arms him
(3) That he shall marry a woman from any earthly race

Effectively, these three injunctions deny the child adulthood or, indeed, any social identity at all. They are negative versions of the stock 'rites of passage' that make up the *macgnímartha* (boyhood deeds) of the Irish hero CÚ CHULAINN in the ULSTER CYCLE. The naming episode (1) had a wider Celtic currency, as shown by the tales Irish LUG, the figure corresponding to the Welsh Lleu.

The name Arianrhod probably comes from Celtic *Argantorotā*, 'silver wheel', a name suggestive of the moon. Note that her son Lleu's name means 'light'; cf. also Welsh *lleuad* 'moon' and the proverb *rhod heno, glaw 'fory* 'wheel tonight [i.e., ring of mist around the moon], rain tomorrow'. The name *Caer Arianrhod* refers to a rock visible at low tide near Dinas Dinlle (< *Dinlleu* 'Lleu's fort') in GWYNEDD.

John T. Koch

ARMAGH

See Ard Mhacha.

ARMAGH, BOOK OF

The Book of Armagh ('Canóin Phádraig', Dublin, Trinity College MS 52), is a manuscript made in Armagh (ARD MHACHA) *c.* 807 for Abbot Torbach (†808) by Ferdomnach (†846). It contains: (1) the Vulgate New Testament; (2) an exegetical drawing that interprets the heavenly city of Apocalypse 21–2; (3) elaborations of the 4th-century Christian scholar, Eusebius; (4) *Vita Martini* (Life of St Martin) by Sulpicius Severus; (5) the *Confessio* of St Patrick; (6) *Vita Patricii* by Muirchú; (7) the Patrician *Collectanea* by Tírechán; (8) *Liber Angeli* (The Book of the Angel), which sets out claims for Armagh; (9) six other fragments relating to Saint Patrick including the *Dicta Patricii* (Sayings of Patrick); (10) two liturgical fragments; and finally (11) a note of a gift made to Armagh in 1002 by Irish high-king BRIAN BÓRUMA. It was intended originally as a functional—if elaborate—*vade mecum* for an individual's use, presumably the abbot; it is, in fact, modestly pocket sized. As it gained respect through age, however, the Book of Amagh became a relic whose rightful possessor was the *comarba Pádraig* (Patrick's successor). The book remained with the hereditary stewards of Armagh until the 17th century.

Thomas O'Loughlin

ARMES PRYDEIN

Armes Prydein (The prophecy of Britain) is a 10th-century Welsh political PROPHECY in the LLYFR TALIESIN ('The Book of Taliesin', 13.2–18.26). The 198-line poem envisions a great PAN-CELTIC alliance, including, among others, the *Kymry* 'Welsh'; *Gwydyl Iwerdon, Mon, a Phrydyn* 'Gaels of Ireland, of Mann/ELLAN VANNIN, and Pictland'; *Gwyr Gogled* 'men of the north (HEN OGLEDD)'; and *Llydaw* 'Brittany/BREIZH'. The poem invokes MYRDDIN and *derwydon* 'DRUIDS'. The ANGLO-SAXON 'CONQUEST' is summarized and victory predicted against the English. Kynan and Katwaladr (CADWALADR), heroes from history, are the messianic leaders. *Iwys* 'people of Wessex' are mentioned as enemies, and the defeated foe are predicted to flee to *Caer Wynt* (i.e., Winchester). The poem's vision for the victory is summarized in these final four lines:

> o *Dyuet hyt Danet wy bieiuyd.*
> o *Wawl hyt Weryt hyt eu hebyr.*
> *llettawt eu pennaeth tros yr echwyd.*
> *Attor ar gynhon Saesson ny byd.*

> From DYFED to Thanet they will possess it.
> From (the Roman) Wall to the Forth as far as its estuaries,
> their supremacy will extend over the running waters.
> There will be no returning for the English heathen.

John T. Koch

ARMORICA

In Roman times, *Armorica* referred to the coastal region from the mouth of the river Seine (Sequana) to the Loire (Liger), west of the BELGAE and north of the Aquitani; hence this area was approximately coterminous with Normandy and Brittany combined. The earliest surviving examples of the name appear in Caesar's *De Bello Gallico* (5.53, 7.75). This author uses it to refer to *civitates Armoricae* 'the Armorican tribes'—that is, the Curiosolites, Rēdones, Ambibariī, Caletes, Osismī,

The tribes of Armorica in the Iron Age and Roman period, 1st century BC to 6th century AD. (Map by Ian Gulley and Antony Smith)

Venetī, Lemovīces, and Venellī—elsewhere in *De Bello Gallico* (3.7–11, 16–18). The strongest tribe was the Venetī, whose name survives in Breton Gwened (French Vannes).

Place-name and other fragmentary evidence implies that the GAULISH language survived in parts of Armorica through the Roman period and eventually contributed names, words, and possibly other linguistic features to BRETON. Intermittently from the late 3rd century, Armorica slipped out of Roman control altogether as a result of a series of uprisings by *bacaudae* (rebel bands made of peasants and disaffected soldiers). Concerning the events of AD 409, the Byzantine historian Zosimus (6.5.2) relates:

> [T]he whole of Armorica and other provinces of Gaul, imitating the Britons, freed themselves in the same way, expelling Roman officials and establishing a sovereign constitution on their own authority. (Trans. Thompson, *Britannia* 8.306)

A shaky Roman rule was reestablished in 417, but by the 460s, we find a 'king of the Britons' with the BRYTHONIC name or title RIGOTAMUS 'supreme king'.

The name *Armorica* is Celtic, deriving from the preposition *are* < *ari* 'before, in front of', *mori-* 'sea', and the adjectival suffix *-kā*; thus 'country facing the sea'. Compare Modern Breton *Arvor* 'regions by the sea' and Welsh *arfor-dir* 'coast'. *Armorica* is sometimes used in modern writing as a place-name roughly synonymous with Brittany (BREIZH), in particular with reference to the region in Roman and prehistoric times or geographically without reference to a particular culture;

hence 'the Armorican peninsula'. Beginning with the 6th-century *Historia Francorum* of Gregory of Tours, *Britannia* is the regular name for the peninsula in Latin sources. In present-day discourse, the region is typically called Brittany when referring to both medieval and modern times.

John T. Koch

ARRAS CULTURE

The Arras culture is one of several regional cultures that existed in BRITAIN during the IRON AGE. It is clearly distinguishable from most of its local contemporaries by the culture's uncommon burial rites, which are more reminiscent of Continental European LA TÈNE practices than those of Iron Age Britain. The custom of burying the deceased with their chariots (see CHARIOT; VEHICLE BURIALS) and of burying individuals within square ENCLOSURES (or possibly square barrows with a surrounding ditch) is largely unknown in the rest of the British Iron Age. However, it is noteworthy that the Arras vehicles are usually disassembled, a practice less commonly seen in the Continental chariot burials.

These Arras burials are confined to a restricted area in east Yorkshire (see map). The recently discovered outlying chariot burial from Edinburgh (DÙN ÈIDEANN) appears to correspond more closely to the Continental rite. Chronologically, the Arras burials cover most of the second half of the 1st millennium BC up to the Roman conquest, which reached this area in the AD 70s.

The mixed Continental influences and local traditions, in conjunction with the reference in the *Geography* of Ptolemy (2.3.10) to Parisi on the north bank of the Humber, makes it tempting to draw a connection with the ancient Parisii, the Gaulish tribe who gave their name to the capital of France. The name in both cases is Celtic, 'the commanders'; cf. Welsh *peryf* 'lord'. As yet, however, no solid evidence exists to prove that the British tribe was an offshoot of its namesake in GAUL.

Raimund Karl

ART, CELTIC, PRE-ROMAN

Classification

Celtic art here refers to the symbolic elements of artefacts not strictly necessary for efficient function. An early style of Celtic art is largely

Excavated cart and chariot burials of the Arras culture. (Map by John T. Koch)

Warrior with headgear. Sandstone figure from Hirschlanden *c.* **500 BC. Height: 150 cm. Württembergisches Landesmuseum, Stuttgart, Germany.** (Erich Lessing/Art Resource, New York)

associated with 5th- and 4th-century BC LA TÈNE A burials, and borrowed extensively from contemporary Greek and Etruscan patterns. The following Waldalgesheim Style, named after a La Tène B i grave near Mainz (see CHARIOT; VEHICLE BURIALS), corresponds to the period of Celtic expansion and develops much more individual and free-moving vegetal forms. In the early 3rd century BC and after, La Tène B ii–C contains two overlapping substyles, the earlier Plastic and later Hungarian Sword Styles.

Characteristic Objects and Materials

Generally small-scale, Celtic art is mostly to be found on objects of personal adornment such as fibulae (safety-pin BROOCHES for fastening clothing), neck-rings, arm-rings, and finger-rings for both men and women. It also appears on items of military use such as sword scabbards, knives, spearheads, and shields, as well as objects used for holding wine such as flagons or drinking horns. Sculpture in stone is infrequent, often crude, and rarely representational, while few wooden carvings survive.

Gold and bronze were the favoured metals for personal ornaments and drinking vessels. Much of the individuality of the art is due to the adoption, early in the La Tène period, of lost-wax casting rather than using a two-part mould as in the HALLSTATT period. A model of the desired object was sculpted in wax and then enclosed in clay, leaving a tiny escape hole. The wax was melted and poured out, and molten metal poured in. Wax made detailed modelling possible. Because the mould had to be broken to extract the finished product, no two castings were ever identical. Other methods of decoration were engraving sheet or cast objects with tools similar to those still used today. Colour was added in the form of coral or enamel or vitreous paste, almost always red until late in the La Tène period.

Hallstatt and La Tène Periods

The Hallstatt phase of the European Iron Age, Hallstatt C–D (*c.* 700–500 BC), primarily produced geometric art using straight lines incised or punched on metal and incorporating symbols such as stylized lunar and solar motifs and water birds. Much of the pottery was also painted, often with figural elements. A rare surviving sculpture is the naked figure of a warrior, a displaced grave marker found at the perimeter of a burial mound at Hirschlanden in southwestern Germany.

Most surviving art of the second period, La Tène, comes from burial goods intended to accompany the dead to the next world. La Tène art is primarily curvilinear in character. The use of Baltic amber, coral and cowrie shells in this period indicates long-range trade patterns. Amber, in contrast to coral, was mainly used as necklaces or bracelets rather than inlaid in metal. Coral was used mainly in the 5th and 4th centuries BC, but was gradually replaced by inlaid red 'enamel'. Blue, green, or yellow enamel was rarely used until the 1st century BC.

Stone was also fashioned into full-length statues, which are fairly crude compared with the contemporary metalwork; the only major exception comprises some stone statues, originally painted, found in the south of France. These sculptures show the influence of the nearby Greek colony of Massalia (Marseille). Farther north, La Tène A statues most commonly depict humans, but are generally either rudimentary or so weathered that their details are indecipherable. Several stone heads sport headdresses not unlike modern Mickey Mouse ears. Complete figures are known mainly from western Germany, where one stone figure was found buried with fragmentary stone 'knights' at a site below the GLAUBERG, northeast of Frankfurt. The Glauberg figures are an exception, but most statues are almost impossible to date and similar statues were made in Ireland as late as the 20th century.

Geographical Extent

The earliest La Tène art dates to the 5th century BC. Spectacular material comes from the high ground between the present eastern border of France and the Rhine, from rich burials at sites such as Schwarzenbach, Weiskirchen, Waldalgesheim, and Rodenbach. Increasing contacts with the Mediterranean world correlate with changes in the art—for instance, the adoption of the symposium or FEAST and associated paraphernalia such as wine flagons. At Kleinaspergle, the process of transformation can be clearly seen in the Celtic bronze flagon whose handle attachment echoes faces on the imported stamnoi (a type of earthenware jars) found in the same grave.

In northeastern France, the material is also less exuberant in style. Women were frequently buried wearing a bronze neck-ring and one or more bronze arm-rings, sometimes inlaid with coral; small fibulae were also common. The most distinctive feature of this region is openwork bronze castings associated with harness and chariot fittings with abstract designs. In central Europe, a major area within the eastern Celtic zone is the rich salt-mining centre at the DÜRRNBERG.

Pottery was mostly decorated with simple geometric patterns until the Late La Tène period, except in the Marne region in France. In some areas, simple stamped geometric designs were used, notably in Brittany (BREIZH) and central Europe. In the eastern zone, pottery was frequently stamped, but a few figural designs can also be found—for example, the swans painted in red on the inside of a so-called Braubach bowl from Radovesice in the Czech Republic.

The Vegetal or Waldalgesheim Style

In the 4th to 3rd centuries BC, Celtic groups settled in Italy and along the DANUBE as far east as Romania, while others founded GALATIA. Art of this period is increasingly found on types of objects concerned with war: scabbards, spearheads, shields, and personal ornaments such as neck-rings, worn by women rather than men in this period. Metalwork became less representational, with elusive faces hiding in writhing tendrils, known as the Waldalgesheim Style. The art is also found on new types of brooches: the 'Münsingen' type inset with coral discs and the 'Duchcov' form with a vase-shaped foot. Among the most spectacular is the rich female chariot grave of Waldalgesheim on the Rhine. This grave included a spouted, swollen-bellied, intricately incised flagon with twice the capacity of the earlier beaked flagons. The precision of the engraving suggests that it was created by a highly specialized group of smiths. The flagon was at least a generation earlier than the other material in the grave, dated to the late 4th-century BC. The Waldalgesheim gold arm-rings and ornaments exhibit a continuous writhing pattern, sometimes incorporating chains of triskels (curved-sided triangles). Such new stylistic features are particularly obvious in the Marne region as well as in Italy, where Roman sources record the Celtic Senones tribe. Similar decoration is found on personal and military items. The Vegetal or Waldalgesheim Style, which first developed here or else north of the Alps, allows one to plot the movement of peoples east across Europe. For examples of Late La Téne art, see COINAGE and GUNDESTRUP CAULDRON.

Middle and Late La Tène Art

During the 3rd century BC, even greater changes in Celtic art took place. Cemeteries in central and eastern areas along the Danube, in Austria, Hungary, Slovenia, and Transylvania in northwestern Romania, produced elaborate, flowing, and often asymmetrical tendril designs. Farther west, scabbards were adorned in the rather minimalist Swiss Style, confined to a small area below the scabbard mouth. Confronted 'dragon-pairs' incised immediately below the scabbard mouth were also used across a very wide area of Europe for sufficient time to allow at least three major variations over time.

One new fashion in women's adornment was the wearing of knobbed and hinged ankle-rings, so large and heavy they could scarcely have been used for everyday wear. One pair comes from the Isthmus of Corinth and another off the southwest tip of Turkey, indicating that women took part in the migrations of the 3rd century. Another technique adopted from eastern European traditions for making women's brooches, neck-rings, and arm-rings was the casting of pieces in 'false filigree'—that is, cast imitations of the complex technique of building up patterns with droplets of gold.

A group of cast or repoussé bronze objects, extending from Denmark to Bulgaria, is marked by the highly reductive form of depicting natural forms, including domestic and fantastic animals as well as humans. Less representational than the style seen in Early La Tène, this cartoonish style is dubbed 'Disney' and was likely created in a single workshop. Its most spectacular finds have been collected from burial sites, the most easterly being a chariot grave at Maltepe in northern Bulgaria. The finest examples of this style, however, come from two chariot graves from the region of Paris.

From the 2nd century BC, Celtic society was under increasing pressure from the expansion of the Dacians and the increasing power of the Romans in western Europe. Its response is seen in the growth of oppida (sing. OPPIDUM). These areas contained specialist manufacturing sectors for iron smithing, glass making, bronze casting, wood turning, and the production of wheel-thrown pottery.

As well as a range of standard wheel-turned pottery, rarely decorated with more than simple bands of colour, some spectacular examples of local styles are known. Late in La Tène II in the Massif Central, tall jars were being decorated with 'calligraphic' depictions of deer and horses set against a hatched background.

Insular Early Celtic Art

Apart from a scattering of imported brooches, Britain and Ireland have little La Tène material until after La Tène Bi/Ib, and little sculpture of proven early date. Best known is the carved stone from Turoe, Co. Galway/Contae na Gaillimhe. Most of the Irish material lacks any datable context, as very few burials or settlements have been found. Eight bronze scabbards were found in or near the river Bann/An Bhanna in northern Ireland, produced with the aid of compasses and using hatching to produce interplay between plain and incised areas. These factors are unknown on Continental sheaths, although one or two very minor details can be said to correspond to them. The Northern Irish scabbards resemble a group of scabbards from several graves in Yorkshire. Since their first discovery in the 19th century, the graves have been regarded as showing connections with the Marne (see Arras culture). Neither the Northern Irish art nor the Yorkshire material can be dated before the 3rd century BC.

Weapons are among the earliest La Tène items in Britain and Ireland. Many of the most spectacular, and possibly the earliest, are finds from rivers, presumably votive offerings. These items include the repoussé bronze Battersea and Witham shield covers. Most of these objects have no close parallels on the European Continent. By the 3rd century BC, a group of interrelated workshops in southern and eastern England were producing parade pieces, presumably for a high-status élite.

A series of bronze mirrors has backs incised with looped lyre designs, frequently executed in hatched basketry. These objects come from women's graves in southern England, the majority on a line from Cornwall (Kernow) to the Midlands. Variable in quality, at their best they display a subtle deviation from the symmetrical, a factor of much early Celtic art. A few iron mirrors were found in Humberside and Yorkshire graves.

A contemporary series of new types, found mostly in East Anglia and the south of England, consists of harness and chariot fittings, often decorated with enamel, although chariots were already obsolete on the Continent. One of the richest finds of treasure, which was deliberately buried in several well-concealed hoards at Snettisham, Norfolk, comes from this same period, around the first Roman contact. Discovered by ploughing, it includes 30 kg of gold, silver, and bronze, including 175 torcs, mostly of twisted design. Other deposits of gold torcs come from elsewhere in East Anglia. It is presumed that all were made during the 1st century BC for the Iceni, the tribe over which Queen Boudīca ruled a century later; outliers have been found in the southwest and eastern Scotland (Alba).

The absence of datable contexts for burials or settlements with fine metalwork and of the presumed latest pre-Roman metalwork makes the dating of early Celtic art in the British Isles singularly difficult, but such material is better considered as a prelude to post-Roman Celtic art.

J. V. S. Megaw and M. Ruth Megaw

ART, CELTIC, POST-ROMAN

British and Irish art from the 5th to the 10th centuries AD—known as 'Hiberno-Saxon' or 'insular art'—exhibits two new and lasting external influences: that of Germanic settlers from the Europe and that of CHRISTIANITY.

Antecedents

Elements such as highly complex compass-based designs, broken-backed curves, the pelta or shield-shaped curved-sided triangle, tight 'watch-spring' coils, trumpet junctions, and triskels (triple spirals) clearly continue from pre-Roman Celtic art; for other styles and categories of objects, the evidence regarding their roots is less clear. One may point to the curious bronze 'Petrie crowns' and the disc from Loughan Island in the river Bann/An Bhanna. A common feature of this group is that the ends of spirals take the form of crested water birds. The standing stone of Mullaghmast in Co. Kildare (Contae Chill Dara), dated from no later than the 6th century AD, bears on its side a double spiral within a pointed oval, closely comparable with an unprovenanced latchet or dress fastener, originally with red enamel inlay and incorporating a triple spiral with bird's-head terminals. This latchet is, in fact, a key piece in tracing a transition between pre- and post-Roman Celtic art. Both the Mullaghmast stone and the latchet fit best into a 5th-century context; thus they offer an artistic stepping-stone to some of the key motifs in the gospel books, notably their bird terminals.

The Celtic trumpet spirals, broken-backed curves, and peltas, possibly dating from the 1st century AD, found at Lough Crew, Co. Meath (Contae na Mí), are predecessors of other 'motif pieces', made from an antler tine, discovered in a settlement site of 5th–6th century AD date at Dooey, Co. Donegal (An Dumhaigh, Contae Dhún na nGall). These objects are presumed to be models for metalwork. A bow-shaped brooch, from a crannog or artificial island settlement in Ardakillin Lough, Co. Roscommon (Contae Ros Comáin), shows that these old motifs became intermingled with a new Saxon interlace, while the ridged keel makes a reappearance on the contemporary red leather cover of St Cuthbert's gospel book, the 'Stoneyhurst Gospel'.

Metalwork

The royal burial at Sutton Hoo, Suffolk, England (*c*. AD 625), contains three hanging bowls with decorative escutcheons. These items belong to a class of some 150 examples consisting of hemispherical bowls of very thin bronze, mainly dating to the 6th and 7th centuries AD, the vast majority of which come from the south and west of

Detail of a Celtic hanging bowl from the Anglo-Saxon ship burial at Sutton Hoo, Suffolk, England, from the late 6th or early 7th century CE. This bronze hanging bowl is the largest of three found in 1939 in the richly furnished ship burial, probably of King Raedwald (599–624/ 5). Bronze, enamel, and glass paste. Inv. PY 1939,1010.110. (The Trustees of the British Museum/Art Resource, New York)

ENGLAND. They have been found in several high-status Anglo-Saxon graves. Other comparable pieces were found at an artificial island settlement at Lagore Crannog, Co. Meath (Contae na Mí), Ireland. A large disc brooch and a belt buckle both have fine triskels, while the buckle end with a backward-looking dog's head is very much in the new Germanic manner.

Among fine metalwork, the most common type is the penannular dress brooch (nearly circular with a break in the circuit for pulling the pin through). The most ornate are a splendid series of Irish BROOCHES belonging to the 8th- to 9th-century pinnacle of post-Roman Celtic art; the great silver-gilt 'TARA' BROOCH found on the shore at Bettystown, Co. Meath (Baile an Bhiataigh, Contae na Mí) is one such item (see its entry in this encyclopedia for illustration). Despite its small size, the brooch exhibits every skill the contemporary metal smith knew, applying novel Anglo-Saxon elements to a basically Celtic type. The two plates of silvered bronze on the back of the brooch incorporate the Celtic trumpet spirals, broken-backed curves, and peltas, while other similar brooches exhibit the Germanic-derived tendency to decorate every surface with complex animal interlace, a feature that links this fine metalwork with the earliest of the gospel books. Elements of curvilinear decoration of the 'Tara' brooch and the buckle from Lagore Crannog resemble the Book of DURROW.

The high point of stylistic fusion of post-Roman Irish art can be seen in 8th-century church furniture, particular in two Viking-era hoards. Best known is the chalice found in an earthen ring-fort at Ardagh, Co. Limerick (Ardach, Contae Luimnigh). Running around the communion cup, the names of the Twelve Apostles are incised in a script similar to that seen in the Book of Lindisfarne from Northumbria; other techniques used to construct the chalice parallel those used in creating the 'Tara' brooch.

Human depictions remain rare in post-Roman Celtic art. An 8th-century bronze openwork mount from Rinnagan, Co. Westmeath (Contae na hIarmhí), possibly a book or shrine cover, shows the standard Celtic depiction of the Crucifixion. The general iconography is similar to Mediterranean models, but the detailed patterning with its running scrolls, peltas, and trumpet junctures follows a much older tradition. Christ is shown as a fully clothed Celt. His face (and those of the lesser beings) is depicted full frontal and with stylized, ridged hair, and looks back to the art of the 5th century BC.

Manuscripts

Manuscript production in the post-Roman Celtic world reflects not only its Mediterranean roots in the late antique period, the influence of its Germanic or Saxon neighbours, and a Celtic visual vocabulary. The manuscript conventionally known as the 'Cathach of Colum Cille' (the 'battler' of Columba), possibly early 7th century, is now in the Library of the Royal Irish Academy (Acadamh Ríoga na hÉireann). Initial letters of the Cathach show strong affinities with the Book of DURROW. Durrow is certainly the oldest of the great gospel books to exhibit both 'carpet' pages, whose broad ribbon interlace suggests Coptic models (see DURROW for illustration), and pages that suggest familiarity with contemporary fine metalwork. In addition, Durrow contains pages that depict the Evangelists, again in the Coptic manner, followed by the actual Gospel text. Throughout its entirety, Durrow exhibits an exuberant display of design that is never static and stands in stark contrast to both classical art and the spare products of later pre-Roman Celtic art. Even when animals and human figures are introduced, as in the Evangelist pages, the dominant aim is pattern making rather than representation.

It seems highly likely that, not only during the Roman occupation of Britain but also thereafter, Celtic metalworking styles continued in southern Britain, and much material of that nature could have found its way into Saxon centres. Certainly, there can be no doubt as to the antecedents of many of the triskels, trumpet junctions, and the like found in two other great North British manuscripts—the Lindisfarne Gospels, written by the Saxon Eadfrith of Lindisfarne sometime before AD 721. The Lindisfarne Gospels exhibit more than just the carpet pages, with their combination of complex Celtic scroll work and Germanic-derived interlace and an eclectic nature of other styles.

Later in the 8th century the Lichfield Gospels, 'bought for the price of a good horse', are found in Llandeilo Fawr, Carmarthenshire (sir Gaerfyrddin). The word 'Quoniam' at the opening of Luke's Gospel shows an overflowing nest of crested Celtic waterbirds. Details such as the great initial chi-rho (Christ's monogram in the Greek alphabet) clearly show the influence of Lindisfarne.

A feature of the hybrid art in both Northumbria and Ireland is the figures of birds, animals and humans that appear as incidentals added to the text. Nowhere is this more clearly illustrated than in the most ornate of all the great gospel books, the Book of KELLS (see the article later in this encyclopedia for illustrations). This gospel book was brought from Iona by monks fleeing Viking raids. Along with superb detailing, the full-page illuminations and great chi-rho pages exhibit the continued Celtic propensity for reducing natural forms to stylized pattern. Aspects of Kells recall such fine metalwork as the Dunore handle assemblies and the Ardagh chalice.

The Beginning of the High Cross Tradition

The low-relief Irish crosses of the 8th and 9th centuries are preceded by pillar-stones, usually decorated only with a simple cross, sometimes with an inscription. The basic form of the Irish crosses, with the equal-armed cross set within a wheel, goes back to late antique times and Coptic textiles of the early 6th century.

Some of the two hundred or so crosses known from Ireland and Scotland are decorated almost exclusively with interlace designs, clearly reflecting contemporary metalwork. By the mid-8th century and into the early 10th century, one can observe a flowering of a kind of 'poster art'—readily discernible to the populace at large, and with the Passion, the Eucharist, and the Last Judgement figuring prominently. Among the most impressive of the narrative crosses are those at Monasterboice, Co. Louth, and the 'Cross of the Scriptures' at Clonmacnoise, Co. Offaly (Cluain Mhic Nóis, Contae Uíbh Ghailí).

Beyond Ireland, on Iona and at Kildalton on Islay, high crosses bear testimony to a local school and exhibit links not only with Ireland, but also with contemporary Pictish and Northumbrian sculpture (see HIGH CROSSES). They are again very close to the Book of Kells. Some of the narrative elements were probably inspired by manuscripts and other objects from the Mediterranean and the Carolingian Europe. The tradition of the high crosses continues today.

J. V. S. Megaw and M. Ruth Megaw

ART, CELTIC-INFLUENCED, MODERN, BRITTANY

The volume of Breton BALLADS, BARZAZ-BREIZ (1839), nourished the creativity of many Breton visual artists, as manifested in *Les Lavandières de la nuit* (Washerwomen of the night; 1861) by Yan' Dargent (1824–99). However, it was not until 1884 that the immense canvas *La Fuite du roi Gradlon* (The flight of King Gradlon) by Evariste Luminais (1822–96) was exhibited at the Salon de Paris; this painting was inspired by the legend of the submersion of the town of Ys (see FLOOD LEGENDS).

Whilst Celtic Brittany (Breizh) attracted artists from all over Europe to paint her untamed landscapes and peasant costumes, indigenous artists reacted against these superficial 'bretonneries' imposed from outside. The Fondation de l'Association littéraire et artistique de Bretagne, which was established in 1890, insisted that Brittany had its own creative and progressive style, language, and customs.

During World War I, three young Breton artists—Jeanne Malivel (1895–1926), René-Yves Creston (1898–1964), and Suzanne Creston (1899–1979)—decided to call on Bretons to revitalize their country's art and crafts tradition. Architects, composers, poets and writers also joined their movement, Ar Seiz Breur (The seven brothers), which lasted until World War II.

Robyn Tomos

ART, CELTIC-INFLUENCED, MODERN, IRELAND

In 1785, the Royal Irish Academy (Acadamh Ríoga na hÉireann), the premier learned institution of Ireland, was founded in Baile Átha Cliath (Dublin). It became the repository of a collection of Irish manuscripts and antiquities that provided the nucleus for antiquarian research and examination in the 19th century. By the 1880s, a new visual imagery began to emerge. Like other non-industrialized countries, Ireland sought an evocation of a real and mythical past on which to pin its hopes for future independence. This Romantic nationalism was closely bound to the Celtic revival. New cultural developments flowered as a result of the seminal findings of antiquarians, notably Eugene O'Curry (1796–1862), George Petrie (1790–1866), Henry O'Neill (1798–1880), John O'Donovan (1809–61), and Sir Samuel Ferguson. Their new vision of the past was emotively and accurately evoked in the paintings of Sir Frederick Burton (1816–1900), who accompanied Petrie on ethnographical trips to the west of Ireland and the Aran Islands (Oileáin Árann). Burton's strongest revivalist works are his stirring frontispiece for the Young Ireland anthology, *The Spirit of the Nation* (1845), and his glowingly detailed watercolour, *The Meeting on the Turret Stairs* (1864). *Turret Stairs* was meticulously transcribed from a tragic Danish ballad to suggest early medieval Ireland.

In 1861, the woodcut illustrations by antiquarian Margaret Stokes (1832–1900), created for her popular editions of *Early Christian Architecture in Ireland* (1878) and *Early Christian Art in Ireland* (1887), were widely influential. By this time, images of certain early Christian treasures—the Ardagh chalice, the Tara brooch, the Books of Kells and Durrow, and the shrine of St Patrick's bell—had become predominant motifs in Irish art. They were synthesized with earlier 19th-century emblems such as the harp, the round tower, the rising sun, the wolfhound, personified Hibernia, the ruined abbey, and the shamrock (sorrel). These images became the iconic symbols of Irish nationalism; they were frequently paraphrased, plagiarized, and caricatured, and usually offset with Celtic interlaced, zoomorphic, or Hiberno-Romanesque decoration.

In Dublin, goldsmiths, silversmiths, and jewellers such as Waterhouse & Co. (which bought the 'Tara' brooch from its finder in 1850), West and Son, and the

Goggin firm were among the first to patent, exhibit, and market facsimiles and fancifully named adaptations. Soon there was a proliferation of methirs (ancient Irish drinking vessels), ceremonial drinking horns, bracelets, and penannular BROOCHES. Edmond Johnson (†1900), master of the Dublin Company of Goldsmiths from 1883, was invited by the Royal Irish Academy to clean, restore, and make a detailed study of the craftsmanship of the Academy's 8th-century Ardagh chalice (acquired 1868). Johnson made 182 Celtic facsimiles for display at the 1893 Chicago World Columbian Exposition.

For the next generation emerging in the 1890s, the 'artistic enchantment' of the idealistic two-volume *History of Ireland* (1878–80) by the scholarly classicist Standish O'GRADY (1846–1928) was to draw 'many an ardent spirit to the Romantic age of Ireland'. O'Grady's most accessible book was *Finn and His Companions*, published in a popular children's edition in 1892. The heroic costumed plays written by O'Grady, W. B. YEATS, and others were inspired by the great Ulster and Ossianic cycles (see OISÍN). These dramas were often performed outdoors at FEISEANNA, a series of assemblied fairs revived in 1898. The Royal Irish Academy's 'gold room' offered a hoard of recently discovered treasures to enraptured visitors, until they were moved to the new National Museum of Ireland (Ard-Mhúsaem na hÉireann) in 1891.

During the 1894–1925 period, the Arts and Crafts Movement flourished in Ireland. Continued attempts—focused around the Metropolitan School of Art in Dublin—sought to invest the arts with the spirit of Celtic design, while simultaneously avoiding the 'slavish reversion to ancient forms'. Those who succeeded worked in stained glass, metals, graphics, and textiles, building up individual skills and imaginative expression. Some of these initiatives included An Túr Gloine, the stained glass cooperative workshop set up in 1903 by the Dublin painter Sarah Purser, and the Dun Emer Guild set up in Dublin in 1902 by the carpet designer Evelyn Gleeson with Elizabeth and Lily Yeats, who seceded in 1908 to form the Cuala Industries. Working as individuals, Harry Clarke (1889–1931), Beatrice Elvery (1883–1970), Wilhelmina Geddes (1887–1955), Oswald Reeves (1870–1967), William A. Scott (1871–1921), Oliver Sheppard (1865–1941), and Mia Cranwill (1880–1972) successfully evolved distinctive masterpieces of great skill, beauty, and originality, inspired by the Celtic past but in a modern idiom. Clarke's masterpiece—his eleven stained glass windows for the Honan Chapel in University College, Cork (1915–17)—makes reference to ancient Celtic and early Christian legends. Elvery's painted, sculpted, and graphic personifications of Mother Ireland alternate with early Christian imagery in plaster, silver, and wood. Geddes's monumental stained glass and graphic figures recall Irish Romanesque carving. Reeves's metalwork and enamels reflect the essential spirit of Celtic forms and symbolist imagery. Scott's architecture included public buildings, furniture, and metalwork. Sheppard's sculpted images powerfully portray the heroes and heroines of ancient Gaelic legend. Cranwill's jewellery illustrates contemporary Irish verse using 9th-century iconographical forms.

Nicola Gordon Bowe

ART, CELTIC-INFLUENCED, MODERN, ISLE OF MAN

The most characteristic feature of pre-19th century Celtic-influenced art on the Isle of Man comprises the more than 200 cross-slab Celtic HIGH CROSSES originally found across the island. Like the island's culture generally, they are a complex mix of Celtic and Scandinavian styles and traditions.

The prolific Manx artist and designer Archibald Knox (1864–1933) is most widely known for the designs he produced for the 'Cymric' and 'Tudric' ware of Liberty and Co. between 1895 and 1906. The resulting items reflected the philosophy of the Arts and Craft Movement as well as contemporary interest in the Celtic revival. Knox's designs drew heavily throughout his life on his early fascination for Celtic and Viking decoration and motifs that he encountered on the Isle of Man. His pupils founded the Knox Guild of Design and Craft, which existed from 1912 to 1937, to continue his distinct philosophical approach to design and craft.

Knox's design and illustration centred on the Isle of Man, and steered Manx visual perception of itself away from the English paradigm by referring beautifully and proudly to Man's Celtic origins. His forms of lettering and reinterpretation of ancient interlacing design have been much copied and provide, at the beginning of the 21st century on the Isle of Man, accepted signifiers of 'Manxness'.

R. S. Moroney

ART, CELTIC-INFLUENCED, MODERN, SCOTLAND

Scottish artists have explored and reflected the forms and intelligence of indigenous Celtic culture in their work since the late Victorian period. The systematic recording of some five hundred major PICTISH and other Celtic standing stones by civil engineer and antiquarian John Romilly Allen (1847–1907) for *The Early Christian Monuments of Scotland* (1903) and *Celtic Art in Pagan and Christian Times* (1904) distilled the visual roots of the nation's culture. With Robert Brydall's *History of Art in Scotland* (1889), such research coincided with two collaborative paintings by Glasgow's Edward Atkinson Hornel (1864–1933) and George F. Henry (1858–1943). These works were the first in a modern idiom to reclaim a 'lost' Celtic past. In the large, square gold-decorated canvases of *The Druids: Bringing Home the Mistletoe* (1890, Glasgow Museums) and *The Star in the East* (1891, Glasgow Museums), Hornel and Henry rejected the pastoral tradition, seeking instead to equalize pagan and Christian values and the decorative and fine arts.

Oral traditions—poetry and storytelling, song and pipe music—played a vital part in the formation of the neo-Celtic sensibility. *Carmina Gadelica*, a core of legend and myth deemed central to the GAELIC imagination, was produced by Alexander Carmichael (1832–1912) with historiated initials drawn from authentic manuscripts.

While metalworkers, book designers, and graphic designers might copy design elements, other artists responded to Celtic ideas more intellectually. Subjects such as those seen in the paintings *St Bride* (National Gallery of Scotland; see BRIGIT) and *The Coming of Bride* (Glasgow Museums), the painting *St Columba Bidding Farewell to the White Horse* (Carnegie Dunfermline Trust; see COLUM CILLE), and the drawing *Deirdre of the Sorrows* (National Gallery of Scotland; see Derdriu) linked John Duncan (1866–1945), a leading artist of the Scottish Celtic revival, to a range of literary sources, including the *Carmina Gadelica*.

Duncan directed the Old Edinburgh School of Art for Geddes in the mid-1890s, where students engaged in arts and crafts practice, including the design of modern Celtic ornament for wide application in metalwork, wood, leather, and plaster. The School expressed Celticism as the authentic inherited culture of Scotland (Alba), complementing that of fellow European Celts. Its publication *Lyra Celtica* (1896) included Breton poetry (see Breton literature), underlining Scotland's rôle within Celticism (see Pan-Celticism) and partnered interest in its art in Edinburgh: Mackie had painted in Brittany (Breizh) in the early 1890s, as did other Scots, including future 'Colourists' Samuel John Peploe and John Duncan Fergusson (1874–1961).

A traditional integration of art with life was celebrated in artists' pageants mounted for charity in Glasgow (1905) and Edinburgh (1908) with costumes and props by Duncan, designer Jessie M. King (1875–1949, Mrs E. A. Taylor), and the Irish-born Edinburgh artist Phoebe Traquair (1852–1936). In these displays, historicity was presented as a creative dialogue between Romance and a more linear approach to the historical past.

With its links to the early Christian church and its sheer beauty of natural colour, Iona (Eilean Ì) became an inspiration for its pilgrim landscape artists. Duncan introduced song collector Marjory Kennedy-Fraser to Eriskay (Eirisgeigh) in 1905. In 1946, the poet George Bruce (1909–2002) underlined the Celts' general 'cultivation of intellect' and the interdependency of their arts, aspects reflected in post-war Scottish culture. The Celtic Congress in Glasgow (Glaschu) in 1953 acknowledged the values of Celticism in a city where the arts were dominated by Fergusson's New Scottish Group. Fergusson's ogam-alphabet–infused graphic illustrations created for Hugh MacDiarmid's *In Memoriam James Joyce* (1955) symbolized this synthesis, as did many of his paintings.

Since the 1960s, artists in Scotland have continued to engage strongly with many Celtic philosophical values, particularly in the conceptual arts of installation and land art.

Elizabeth Cumming

ART, CELTIC-INFLUENCED, MODERN, WALES

A sense of Welsh distinctness appears in visual culture dating from the Renaissance. Tapestries illustrating subjects associated with ancient Britain are known to have hung at Raglan Castle, Monmouthshire (sir Fynwy), in the 17th century. In painting, the earliest expressions of ancient British identity are found in representations of landscape: A depiction of Dinefwr Castle, painted *c.* 1670, would resonate strongly as the site of the prophecies of Merlin (Myrddin). The use of landscape in this way persisted into the 20th century. The modern imaging of the Celts, however, came only after the development of antiquarianism. The practical beginning can be traced back to the publication of Henry Rowlands's illustrated *Mona Antiqua Restaurata* (Ancient Anglesey restored) in 1723.

The Last Bard (1774) by Thomas Jones, Pencerrig (oil on canvas). (National Museum Wales (Amgueddfa Cymru)/The Bridgeman Art Library International)

Richard Wilson's *Solitude* (*c.* 1762) seems to be based on a descriptive passage in *Mona Antiqua Restaurata*, and its hooded contemplative figures demonstrate the way in which the development of the image of the druids depended on the conflation of a number of visual ideas, including that of the Christian hermit and the BARD (see also CHRISTIANITY). Gray's poem 'The Bard', published in 1757, resulted in the production of a subgenre of Celticist imagery that projected the 13th-century subject matter back into the imagined world of the pagan Celts. A 1774 painting by Wilson's pupil, Thomas Jones, is the seminal image, drawing together mountain landscape and antiquities.

The 18th-century fashion for WELSH MUSIC was closely linked to visual imagery. William Parry painted a number of pictures of his father, the harper John Parry (see HARP), that were exhibited at the Royal Academy. So many similar images were produced that the landscape alone became an icon of Welsh Celticity for tourists.

In his *Dolbadern Castle* (1800), J. M. W. Turner took a subject from medieval Welsh history and projected it backward into a timeless Celtic mist. As early as 1751, the Banner of the Cymmrodorion Society had symbolized Wales by the pairing of a druid and St David (DEWI SANT). The conflation of pagan and Christian Celtic imagery was exemplified by the brothers John Evan and William Meredith Thomas in their sculpture *The Death of Tewdrig* (1848). In this work, the dying Christian king points a crucifix accusingly at the pagan Saxon invaders, though he is accompanied by a distinctly druidical bard. The Thomas brothers' work emanated from the intellectual circle of Lady Llanofer, who was concurrently engaged on the creation of the national costume (see MATERIAL CULTURE, NATIONAL COSTUME; PAN-CELTICISM).

Although interlaced designs appear in architectural detail and in graphics, they did not generate a craft movement in Wales. Lady Charlotte Guest's translation of *The Mabinogion* (1846; see MABINOGI) did help stimulate art imagery. Clarence Whaite painted *The Archdruid: A Throne in a Grove* in 1898 and Christopher Williams began his trilogy of Ceridwen (see TALIESIN), BRANWEN, and BLODEUWEDD in 1910. In sculpture, William Goscombe John (1860–1952) produced works that drew on Celtic subject matter, most notably through his contributions to the regalia of GORSEDD BEIRDD YNYS PRYDAIN.

Celticist imagery declined in importance after World War I. The most notable exceptions to this tendency were the paintings and calligraphy of David Jones (1895–1974).

Peter Lord

ARTHUR, HISTORICAL EVIDENCE

De Excidio Britanniae

At the beginning of the 21st century, the central question remains, Did Arthur exist at all? The earliest historical source, GILDAS, does not name Arthur, but his work *De Excidio Britanniae*, 'Destruction of Britain', presents several of the leading themes of the LEGENDARY HISTORY of Britain found in later texts. These include the removal of the Roman garrison by the usurper Maximus (see MACSEN WLEDIG), the incursions of the PICTS and SCOTS, the appeal to the Roman consul 'Agitius', the invitation of the Saxons to Britain by the British leader, the Saxon revolt against the BRITONS followed by the rally led by AMBROSIUS AURELIANUS, and eventually the Britons' great victory at BADONICUS MONS (Welsh Baddon), which later sources attributed to Arthur. The same passage says that Gildas was born in the year of the battle, so he would have had the benefit of eyewitness testimony; for the date of the battle, see GILDAS and BADONICUS MONS.

Y Gododdin

The earliest reference to Arthur occurs in the GODODDIN, attributed to the 6th-century north British court poet ANEIRIN. The allusion to Arthur occurs in the following lines, defined by end-rhyme as a distinct section within an elegy of a hero whose name is given as *Guaur[dur]*:

> *Go·chore brein du ar uur*
> *caer—ceni bei ef Arthur—*
> *rug c[um n]erthi ig [cl]isur,*
> *ig kynnor guernor—Guaur(dur).*

He used to bring black crows down in front of the wall of the fortified town—though he was not Arthur—amongst equals in might of feats, in the front of the barrier of alder wood [shields]—Guaurdur.

The idea here is that the hero 'Guaurdur' killed many enemies and thus enticed crows down to feed. To say 'he was not Arthur' is to say that Arthur was an even greater killer of enemies, elsewhere in the *Gododdin* said to be the men of *Lloegr* (ENGLAND). Saying that the hero of the verse was a lesser hero than another is a very unusual comparison for early Welsh praise poetry. The verse also implies that Arthur flourished at a period before Guaurdur. The question, then, is how old is the *verse* and is Arthur really integral to it? Because *Arthur* rhymes and -*ur* is not one of the common end-rhymes in early WELSH POETRY, and is also uncommon as the final syllable of men's names, it is unlikely that *Arthur* has slipped in as a substitute for another hero's name in textual transmission. The outlook of this part of the text is distinctive in that it shows no political interest in the area that became Wales (CYMRU), as opposed to north Britain, and no Christian ideas. Therefore, the Arthur verse is as likely as any in the *Gododdin* to have been composed before *c.* 750, in north Britain rather than in Wales.

The Battle List

The 9th-century Welsh Latin HISTORIA BRITTONUM made use of diverse materials. The Arthurian *mirabilia* are overtly folkloric and nonhistorical in nature, but there is also a list of Arthur's twelve victorious battles. In the broader structure, the list forms a bridge between an account of 5th-century events and a series of Anglo-Saxon royal genealogies down to the 8th century interspersed with memoranda of north British events of the period *c.* 547–687. In the description of Arthur's rôle that precedes the list, it is said that Arthur fought along with the *reges Brittonum* (kings of the BRITONS) as their *dux bellorum* (battle leader).

The battle list seems to derive from a poem in BRYTHONIC that resembles poems surviving in LLYFR TALIESIN ('The Book of Taliesin'). The Old Welsh names of the battles probably preserve the rhyme scheme of the poem: *Dubglas* rhymes with *Bassas*; *Cat Coit Celidon* with *Castell Guinnion*; *Cair Legion* with *Bregion*. Battle 12 is *Badon*. The historicity of the battle list is uncertain. Battle 9 at *urbs Legionis* (the city of the Legion) looks suspiciously like the famous battle of Chester (CAER) fought *c.* 615, which had nothing to do with Arthur. Conversely, the place-name *Linnuis* (Lindsey), a direct survival of Romano-British *Lindenses,* shows how Welsh tradition could remember places that had come under Anglo-Saxon domination hundreds of years before. The oral tradition probably preserves a mix of factual, partly factual, and purely legendary history.

No doubt exists regarding the historicity of other chieftains mentioned in 6th-century poetry. It is plain that the attitude of these poems is contemporary, with their subjects considered to be living. The same attitude in the original vernacular battle list could explain why the battle of CAMLAN in which Arthur fell (see the next section) is not included in the battle list. This detail is consistent with the possibility of very early composition for the poem behind the Arthurian list.

Annales Cambriae

Two Arthurian ANNALS exist. At the year corresponding to 516 or 518 is noted *Bellum Badonis in quo Arthur portauit crucem Domini Nostri Iesu Christi tribus diebus et tribus noctibus in humeros suos et Brittones uictores fuerunt* (the battle of Baddon in which Arthur carried the cross of our Lord Jesus Christ three days and three nights on his shoulders, and the Britons were victors). The second, at 537 (or 539), concerns *Gueith Cam lann in qua Arthur et Medraut corruerunt* (the battle of Camlan in which Arthur and Medrawd fell).

Baddon and Camlan entries do not occur in any extant Irish ANNALS, so it seems likely that these are retrospective insertions after *c.* 613 rather than contemporary entries from Brythonic annals in the first half of the 6th century. Furthermore, if Camlan has been correctly identified with the Roman fort of Camboglanna on HADRIAN's WALL—not an unlikely site for a 6th-century battle—the spelling *Cam lann* (not **Cam glann*) is much later, either a modernization or a later creation.

Arthur carrying the image of the Virgin Mary or the cross most strongly suggests a relationship between *Annales Cambriae*'s Baddon entry and *Historia Brittonum*'s battle list. If there is a confusion of written Old Welsh *scuit* 'shield' and *scuid* 'shoulder' in the battle list, we have the same confusion in the Baddon annal; that error in transmission is unlikely to have come about independently twice. In other words, within the history shared between the two accounts the icon story has mistranslated from Old Welsh into Latin. The Baddon annal is more elaborate than any other entry in *Annales Cambriae*; thus it is possible that an original, more characteristically laconic entry might have undergone expansion in the period 955×1100 under the influence of the battle list. In other words, Arthur might not have been mentioned in the original annal at all. In all details, the Baddon annal is more easily understood as derived from the battle list, in which case it might have been placed with reference to a preexisting Camlan annal in which Arthur's death *was* noted.

The Name "Arthur"

In both *Historia Brittonum* and *Annales Cambriae,* the commander's name is Old Welsh *Arthur*, just as it is (proved by rhyme) in the GODODDIN. It is generally agreed that the name derives from the rather uncommon Latin name *Artōrius*. Thus it does not, as sometimes thought, derive from Celtic **Arto-rīxs* 'bear-king', which gives the rare Welsh name *Erthyr*. It is remarkable that the early Latin sources consistently use uninflected Welsh *Arthur* alongside the Latinized battle name *bellum Badonis*. If *Historia Brittonum* and the *Annales* were drawing on contemporary or near-contemporary 6th-century Latin notices of the battle of Baddon, these sources evidently did not name Arthur as the commander, as the notices would have spelled the name *Artorius* or *Arturius*. The spelling *Arturius* does, however, occur in the late 7th-century Hiberno-Latin of Adomnán for Prince *Artúr* of DÁL RIATA, who died *c.* 580. This Arturius was the son of AEDÁN MAC GABRÁIN of Dál Riata.

Conclusion

The evidence reviewed in this article is broadly consistent with the proposition that the starting point of Arthurian tradition was among the early Brythonic poets and that his reputation was already highly exalted in that context by the very early Middle Ages, before literacy had much impact on the bardic tradition. Further support for this view is found in the ARTHURIAN allusions in the early poems *Pa gur yv y porthaur?* and *Gereint fil. Erbin* (in which Arthur is called *ameraudur* 'emperor'; see GERAINT) and *Englynion y Beddau* ('The Stanzas of the Graves'). From such beginnings the tradition forced its way—by the earlier 9th century, if not before—into an originally distinct tradition of British Christian Latin historical writing founded by Gildas. Such a conclusion does not rule out the possibility that the figure famed among the vernacular poets had existed; however, there is no reason to suppose that the synthetic historians (such as GEOFFREY OF MONMOUTH) or the compiler of *Annales Cambriae* placed the Arthur of oral tradition correctly into the record of written history.

John T. Koch

ARTHUR, IN THE SAINTS' LIVES

Arthur is mentioned in several BRYTHONIC Latin saints' lives—namely, those of Cadoc, Carantoc, Illtud, Padarn, Efflam, GILDAS (by CARADOG OF LLANCARFAN), and Uuohednou (Goueznou). The most important of these sources for the relationship with ARTHURIAN LITERATURE are Lifris of Llancarfan's Life of Cadoc and Caradog of Llancarfan's Life of Gildas. The Breton Latin Life of Uuohednou is important in establishing Arthur's place in the LEGENDARY HISTORY of Britain (see CONAN MERIADOC). All probably predate GEOFFREY OF MONMOUTH's HISTORIA REGUM BRITANNIAE (*c.* 1139). Arthur is generally portrayed in this HAGIOGRAPHY as ruler of BRITAIN. Arthur's rôle in these Lives is as a foil to the saint rather than as a heroic king.

John T. Koch

ARTHURIAN LITERATURE, BRETON

Very little of the Arthurian legend has survived as actual writing. Breton Arthurian material can be glimpsed in a wide variety of texts, from Latin saints' lives (HAGIOGRAPHY) to medieval French Romance, but there are no vernacular sources to compare with Welsh prose texts such as CULHWCH AC OLWEN or the early medieval WELSH POETRY. The widespread reputation of Breton singers and *conteurs* (storytellers) and the Breton names and settings in many French Arthurian works have been taken as strong indications of a flourishing Breton literary and/or storytelling tradition.

In a record of a journey through Cornwall (KERNOW) in 1113, which predates the influence of GEOFFREY OF MONMOUTH, the canon Herman of Tournai noted an encounter with a local man at Bodmin who claimed that ARTHUR was not dead 'just as the Bretons are in the habit of arguing against the French on King Arthur's behalf'. Arthur also appears in his legendary-historical rôle as the victorious leader of the Britons in the Prologue to the Latin Life of St Uuohednou (Goueznou). With Geoffrey of Monmouth's HISTORIA REGUM BRITANNIAE (History of the kings of Britain; *c.* 1139) and the subsequent explosion of literary interest in the *matière de Bretagne* (Matter of Britain), Brittany's reputation as a locus of Arthurian legend spread through Europe. Various BRYTHONIC personal names and place-names appear in the late 12th-century poems and Romances of writers such as Marie de France and CHRÉTIEN DE TROYES, and Marie in particular is keen to stress the 'Breton' source of some of her short narrative *lais*. Much of the story of TRISTAN AND ISOLT, which became attached to the Arthurian cycle, is also set in Brittany, and the Breton forest of Brocéliande appears in the 12th-century works of Chrétien and the Anglo-Norman Wace.

When Arthur does finally appear in a Breton-language text, dated 1450, it is in a relatively colourless rôle. *An Dialog etre Arzur Roue d'an Bretounet ha Guynglaff* puts the king in conversation with a WILD MAN, who prophesies various catastrophic events; Arthur's part is restricted to asking what will happen next. The figure of the prophet Guynglaff (or Gwenc'hlan) is more interesting, as the wild man character-type also evokes associations with the MYRDDIN/LAILOKEN legend.

Later Breton popular tradition also include Arthurian elements. In the drama *Sainte Tryphine et le Roi Arthur*, Arthur is 'king of the Bretons', yet merely a stock husband figure. All other familiar Arthurian characters are absent. A 19th-century version of a long oral ballad about Merlin (see BALLADS) tells the story of a young man who wins a king's daughter by capturing first Merlin's harp, then his ring, and finally Merlin himself. This lovely and un-self-conscious piece is an exceptional case in the Breton ballad tradition, which, though rich and varied, is not a large repository for medieval and Arthurian themes. Analogues to this song exist in the form of several Breton FOLK TALES, where the exact nature of Merlin (sometimes described as 'a Murlu' or 'a Merlik') is ambiguous.

Arthurian material naturally played its part in the 19th-century Breton revival (see LANGUAGE [REVIVAL] MOVEMENTS IN THE CELTIC COUNTRIES), as studies of linguistic Celtic KINSHIP reestablished and reinforced notions of a shared Brythonic culture. One of the key texts of that revival was Hersart de La Villemarqué's collection of supposedly popular ballads, the BARZAZ-BREIZ (1839), which includes the blood-thirsty *Bale Arthur* (The march of Arthur), an 'original' Breton source for Marie de France's *Laustic* (The nightingale), and two poems about Merlin (one of which, based on the text mentioned previousl, would ultimately be vindicated as an 'authentic' part of the tradition). Arthurian themes have remained popular in modern BRETON LITERATURE.

Mary-Ann Constantine

ARTHURIAN LITERATURE, CORNISH

Arthurian episodes are often localized in Cornwall (KERNOW), and Arthuriana figures as a continuing theme in CORNISH LITERATURE. In the Welsh 'Dialogue of Arthur and the Eagle' (*Ymddiddan Arthur a'r Eryr*), Arthur is explicitly identified with Cornwall, while in CULHWCH AC OLWEN (*c.* 1000×1100), Arthur and his men pursue TWRCH TRWYTH to Celliwig (Cornish Kyllywyk; see ARTHURIAN SITES). Perhaps the most important early text, however, is John of Cornwall's *Prophecy of Merlin*. John (†*c.* 1199) was born in St Germans, Cornwall. His surviving Latin text calls upon the 'House of Arthur' to unite against incursions into BRITAIN, in particular Cornwall. John of Cornwall's notes and glosses reveal that his sources were in Old CORNISH, including references to Periron (an earlier name for Tintagel) and Brentigia (Bodmin Moor).

Arthur: A Short Sketch of His Life and History in English Verse by the Marquis of Bath (*c.* 1428) expands on the two core elements: that Arthur died in Cornwall and was later taken to Glastonbury, and that the Cornish and Bretons believed Arthur would return. The Middle Cornish play, Beunans Ke, from *c.* 1500, contains Arthurian material, while Nicholas Roscarrock's Life of St Piran (*c.* 1620) records how Arthur made St Piran the Archbishop of York. A very literary history of Arthurian activity in Cornwall was written by William Hals (1635–*c.* 1737), one of whose sources was the now lost *Book of the Acts of Arthur* written by the medieval Cornish scholar, John Trevisa.

The long-held belief that Arthur's spirit is embodied in the Cornish chough (a large black bird) forms the basis of Robert Morton Nance's allegorical drama *An Balores* (The chough; 1932). The modern Cornish language revival brought about a fashion for Arthurian-based drama in Cornwall, connecting it with the popular theatrical tradition. Within the Cornish Arthurian corpus, the narrative of Tristan and Isolt forms a central strand, as do legends connecting Arthuriana with Lyonesse (see flood legends), and with Joseph of Arimathea, the boy Christ in Cornwall, and the Holy Grail. Renewed interest in the Cornish Arthurian connection emerged in 1998 when a 6th-century inscribed stone—the so-called Arthur Stone—was found on Tintagel Island, with its inscription PATERNIN COLIAVI FICIT ARTOGNOU containing three masculine names: Latin *Paterninus* and Celtic *Col(l)iauos* and *Artognouos*. However, the name *Artognou* 'bear-knowledge', which recurs as Old Breton *Arthnou*, cannot correspond exactly to *Arthur*.

Alan M. Kent

ARTHURIAN LITERATURE, IRISH

Arthur is not a major figure in early Irish literature, but the study of the Irish tales reveals Celtic concepts of the heroic ethos, kingship, and the Otherworld relevant to the Arthurian legend. The tales of the Ulster Cycle, Fiannaíocht, and Kings' Cycles provide illuminating comparisons with stories of Arthur and his heroes, and indicate just how Celtic the content of Arthurian literature remained, even as the tales were reworked outside the Celtic countries (see Arthurian literature, texts in non-Celtic medieval languages).

A Middle Irish translation of Historia Brittonum, known as *Lebor Breatnach* (The Brythonic book), was produced in the 11th century. The earliest literary reflections of Arthur in native Irish literature belong to the 12th century. In the tale *Acallam na Senórach* ('Dialogue of [or with] the Old Men'), an Artú(i)r figures as the son of Béinne Brit, king of the Britons. More complete transfers of Arthurian stories occur later. The Gaelic names and titles used for Arthurian characters point toward their sources: For example, the forms *Cing Artúr* in *Lorgaireacht an tSoidhigh Naomhtha* (Quest for the Holy Grail) and *Ceann Artair, Caoin Artúr* in the later folk material clearly indicate an English source for this content. *Caithréim Chonghail Chláiringnigh* (The martial exploits of Conghal Flat-nail) conflates Arthurian tradition with the native Ulster Cycle, including some direct borrowings from the Middle Irish tale *Fled Dúin na nGéd* (The feast of Dún na nGéd; see SUIBNE GEILT). In it, Artúr Mór mac Iubhair (Arthur the Great, son of Uther) is king of the Britons and faces a Saxon threat. The Early Modern Irish Arthurian Romances have tended to assimilate a Gaelic cultural milieu—for example, king's *geasa* (taboos; see GEIS) and Gawain as Arthur's *dalta* (foster son). The recurrent theme of Arthur and his knights hunting follows the pattern of native *Fiannaíocht* in both Irish and Scottish Gaelic Arthurian tales.

John T. Koch

ARTHURIAN LITERATURE, SCOTTISH GAELIC

Arthurian literature is a trace element in the Scottish Gaelic literary tradition. The two clearest examples are the *Amadan Mòr* tale and BALLAD, in which the 'great fool' derives in some important respects from the figure of Perceval (see PEREDUR); and the waulking song known as *Am Bròn Binn* (The sweet sorrow), which seems to reflect an unknown Arthurian adventure undertaken by Gawain.

The subject of *Am Bròn Binn* is the fateful dream of a king in which he sees a beautiful girl, similar to the Old Irish 'Dream of OENGUS MAC IND ÓC', the Welsh *Breuddwyd* MACSEN WLEDIG, and the Breton Latin Life of IUDIC-HAEL. Although no early manuscript versions exist, the modern oral texts' linguistic features indicate an original written with Gaelic letter forms.

The processes whereby these vernacular Gaelic texts have developed from Early Modern Arthurian literature (whether surviving or not) would have become final in the 18th century when the aristocratic audience for 'high' Gaelic literature disappeared, but would doubtless have begun much earlier through the dissemination of Romance texts read aloud. Some evidence suggests that this literature may have had a heyday in the later 16th century, when printed versions of Arthurian Romances were relatively freely available.

There are also hints of a longer-standing Arthurian presence in Gaelic Scotland (ALBA), especially in connection with the claims of the Clan Campbell to an Arthurian descent. Centuries earlier, the personal name *Artúr* crops up here and there in the early medieval Gaelic record. It is likely that these names either are independent derivatives of Latin *Artorius* or else are derived from the fame of a British Arthur, called 'Artúr son of Iobhar' in Gaelic sources.

William Gillies

ARTHURIAN LITERATURE, TEXTS IN NON-CELTIC MEDIEVAL LANGUAGES

French Literature

The most important French Arthurian writer is CHRÉTIEN DE TROYES. Apart from his other works, he wrote five Arthurian Romances: *Erec et Enide* (6,598 lines, composed *c.* 1170) is the French version of the Welsh GERAINT; the story of *Cligès* (6,784 lines, *c.* 1176) is patterned on the Tristan legend; *Yvain* (6,818 lines, *c.*

King Arthur and his knights around the table—an illustration in a Vulgate cycle text from about 1280–1290, *L'Histoire de Merlin*, Ms Fr 95 f.326. (Art Media/StockphotoPro)

1180) is the French version corresponding to the Welsh OWAIN *neu Iarlles y Ffynnon*; and *Lancelot* (7,134 lines, *c.* 1180) is the earliest Romance mentioning this hero. The last Romance written by Chrétien is *Perceval* (9,234 lines, *c.* 1181), an unfinished work that contains the first reference to the GRAIL legend. It was adapted and completed by many authors. The *Elucidation* (484 lines, beginning of the 13th century) was written as a prologue to it, and tells the story of some maidens who lived in wells until a king named Amangon and his men raped them and stole their golden cups. As a consequence, the land became infertile and the court, which housed the Grail, was lost to those who sought it. Apart from the connection with the stories of fountain FAIRIES of Celtic folklore, this work underlines the fact that the theme of the wasteland has significant parallels in Irish and Welsh texts (for example, in the tale of MANAWYDAN FAB LLŷR). A long section of the First Continuation (also known as the Pseudo Wauchier, 10,100 lines, *c.* 1200) is about a knight named Caradoc (of Welsh origin) and his adventures. The Second Continuation (13,000 lines, *c.* 1200) contains references to a magic castle, an enchanted white stag, and a mysterious lighted tree; they can be compared with similar elements in Celtic folklore and medieval wonder tales. *Perlesvaus* (a prose Romance composed between 1191 and 1212) is an important example of how Celtic motifs were transformed within a Christian context: For example, magic fountains are here connected with magic cups symbolizing the Trinity.

The Vulgate Cycle (1215–30) is a group of five prose Romances: the *Estoire del Saint Graal*, *Merlin*, *Lancelot*, the *Queste del Saint Graal*, and the *Mort Artu*. The first part of the vulgate *Lancelot* tells the story of Lancelot's childhood in a magic lake, after being stolen from his mother by the Dame du Lac (The lady of the lake); this story parallels the numerous Celtic tales about children stolen by fairies and about magic realms under the waters. The narrative context of the vulgate *Mort Artu* is essentially based on the very well-known Arthurian institution of the round table (first mentioned in the *Roman de Brut* by Wace, *c.* 1155, lines 9747–58), a circular dining table where the seats were without difference in rank. A circular table was uncommon in the medieval period, but Celtic traditions give good parallels: There is the account of ancient dining customs by Athenaeus in which he says that Gaulish warriors used to sit in a circle around the main hero to honour him. An alternative theory is the symbolic conception of the table as a cosmic table governed by Arthur, seen as an archetypal emperor of the world; this interpretation has in its favour the fact that, in all the French texts that mention it, *table ronde* rhymes almost exclusively with the word *monde*, world.

In the prose Romance *Artus de Bretaigne* (1296–1312), a dream causes two young people to fall in love with each other without having met. This episode particularly resembles the central theme of the Welsh *Breuddwyd Macsen* (The dream of Maxen; see MACSEN WLEDIG). In the same Romance, the character named Maistre Estienne conjures up an army to advance upon a castle, and the castle disappears when all the enemies have fled. A parallel to this episode is found in the Welsh MATH FAB MATHONWY (Math the son of Mathonwy), when GWYDION conjures up a fleet to surround a castle, then makes it disappear when it has served his purpose. In the Romance *Yder* (6,769 lines, *c.* 1220), the hero rescues Queen Guenevere from a bear and she says that she would have preferred him to Arthur as a lover if she had been given the choice. One could see here a possible reference to the Celtic etymology of the name *Arthur* (which seems to contain the word for 'bear', Welsh *arth*). The name of this hero, well known in Irish and Welsh literature, is also found in the Latin form *Isdernus* in the Arthurian sculpture of Modena (see 'Italian Literature' later in this article). This commonality is also perceptible with reference to the name *Durmart* (the main character of *Durmart le Galois*, 1220–50), recorded as *Durmaltus* in the Italian archivolt. In *Tristan et Lancelot* by Pierre Sala, Tristan loses his way in a forest while trying to hunt a white stag, and following other adventures he meets Lancelot in a marvelous land inside a magic lake.

German Literature

Hartman von Aue's *Erec* (10,192 lines, 1170–85) is an adaptation of Chrétien de Troyes's *Erec et Enide*. It contains several allusions to the symbolism of *Enide*'s horses and her dominion over them: a tract that is absent in the French source, and that could derive from some independent tradition in which Enide had strong equine associations like those of the Gaulish EPONA, Irish MACHA, or Welsh RHIANNON. Hartman's *Erec* also contains the first reference to the character—of a Celtic origin—Morgain la Fée as an evil enchantress. Hartman also adapted Chrétien's *Yvein* (*Owein*): here, the episode of Guenevere's abduction seems to be older than that depicted in the other versions, and to reflect an archaic form of the theme of the marriage between a mortal and an Otherworld woman.

Lanzelet is a poem of more than 9,400 lines composed at the beginning of the 13th century by Ulrich von Zatzikhoven, and mainly based on Chretien's *Lancelot* and the vulgate *Lancelot*. It contains episodes and themes that can be seen as originating in the mythological period of the Arthurian legend, but did not survive in French texts. For example, the Land of the Maidens, where Lanzelet receives his education, reminds us of the Land of the Women of the Irish IMMRAM BRAIN, and the deathlike sleep of the captives in King Verlein's castle is similar to the state described in the Irish *Compert Con Culainn* (see CÚ CHULAINN).

Wolfram von Eschenbach's *Parzival* (24,810 lines, first decade of the 13th century) is an adaptation of Chrétien's *Perceval*. Its importance for the studies of the origins of the GRAIL legend lies in the fact that here the Grail is not a dish or a chalice, as in the other traditions, but rather a stone that provides food and drink, and preserves from death those who see it. Although an Oriental origin has been proposed for this conception, references to similar powerful stones exist in Celtic folklore, particularly in Ireland (ÉRIU) and Cornwall (KERNOW).

The *Tristrant* by Eilhart von Oberg (1170–90) is considered a translation of a French source that has not survived. Eilhart was followed by Gottfried von Strassburg, who adapted Thomas's version of the legend in his *Tristan* (*c.* 1210); in this text, one can find references to a magic and 'joyful' (*vröudebære*) landscape, an image that belongs both to the rhetorical topos of *locus amoenus* (nature idyll) and to the Celtic conception of the OTHERWORLD. Other Tristan narratives include Ulrich von Türheim's *Tristan* (*c.* 1240), the anonymous *Tristan als Mönch* (*c.* 1250), and Heinrich von Freiberg's *Tristan* (*c.* 1285), and Wirnt von Grafenberg's *Wigalois* (1310s).

Dutch Literature

The *Historie van den Grale* (History of the Grail) and the *Boek van Merline* (Book of Merlin) by Jacob van Maerlant, written around 1261, form a unity of 10,100 lines. Although both are adaptations of the Old French *Joseph d'Arimathie* by Robert de Boron (*c.* 1202) and the vulgate *Merlin*, they contain different details—for example, an allusion to the episode of Arthur pulling the sword from the stone, which is absent in the French sources. Lodewijk van Velthem's *Merlijn* (26,000 lines, 1326) is a translation of the Old French and the vulgate *Merlin*, but the author must have used another source for the episode—unknown to the other versions of the history of Merlin—of the young Arthur who, assisted by a magical power, subdues the rebellious noblemen in a sort of Otherworld.

Lantsloot van der Haghedochte (Lancelot of the cave; *c.* 1260) is the oldest Middle Dutch translation of the Lancelot tale in prose. In this text, the fairy who kidnaps Lancelot does not live in a lake, but rather in a cave that cannot be found unless she wishes it; one may compare this element with Celtic legends (mostly Irish) where FAIRIES live inside a mountain. In the short text *Lanceloet en het hert met de witte voet* (Lancelot and the stag with the white foot, 850 lines, *c.* 1289), a powerful queen announces at Arthur's court that she will marry the knight who will bring her the white foot of a stag that is guarded by lions; a similar scene can be read in the Old French *Lai de Tyolet* (end of the 12th century), and it is possible that both texts derive from an unpreserved source.

Many episodes narrated in *Torec* (a text of 4,000 lines that is probably a translation from a lost Old French text) and in *Walewein* (written around the middle of the 13th century by Penninc and Pieter Vostaert) can be compared with Celtic material—for example, the magical ship that takes the hero to a Castle of Wisdom, the battle against a creature of the Otherworld to save an abducted princess, and the fight with dragons. The fountain with healing powers described in *Walewein ende Keye* (Gauwain and Kay, 3,700 lines, second half of the 13th century) can be compared with the numerous magic wells of Celtic folklore.

English Literature

The first English-language work to feature King Arthur is Layamon's *Brut*, composed in the late 12th or early 13th cenutry. More than 16,000 lines interpret Wace's Anglo-Norman version of Geoffrey of Monmouth's Latin language Arthurian history. Three later romances—*Sir Landevale*, *Sir Launfal*, and *Sir Lambewell* (1st half of the 14th century)—are adaptations of Marie de France's *Lai of Lanval* (646 lines, 12th century). These works develop the folk-tale theme of the young man helped by a magical being typical of Celtic narrative, and contains allusions to a beautiful enchanted territory similar to the Celtic OTHERWORLD.

Sir Gawain and the Green Knight (2,530 lines, composed in alliterative stanzas around 1375) is considered the masterpiece of English medieval literature. It tells the story of an unknown knight who arrives at Arthur's court during the New Year's feast and challenges the knights to the 'beheading game', in which the knight who cuts off the Green Knight's head must meet him at the Green Chapel in a year's time to have his own head cut off. The Green Knight survives the beheading. The game has several parallels in Celtic tales, notably in the Irish FLED BRICRENN. Gawain's horse has the same name (*Gryngolet*) as Gwalchmai's horse in the Welsh MABINOGI. The beheading game is one of the main subjects of *The Carle* (500 lines, late 14th century).

The Awntyrs off Arthure (715 lines, composed in Scotland [ALBA] *c.* 1425) contains references to motifs such as the presence of ghosts who interfere with humans, generating misfortunes. In *The Turke and Gowin* (a fragmentary Romance [355 lines] composed in northwest ENGLAND *c.* 1500), a magical realm is described, situated on an unknown island and inhabited by giants and figures that have been identified with Manx folklore (see MANX LITERATURE). *The Marriage of Sir Gawain* (a ballad of 852 lines) and Chaucer's *Wife of Bath's Tale* (408 lines, late 15th century) develop the theme of the loathly lady, a beautiful woman in the shape of a loathsome hag, which has an analogue in the Irish *Echtra Mac nEchach Muig-medóin* (The adventure of the sons of Eochaid Mugmedón). The method of narrating the childhood of the hero in *Sir Percyvell of Gales* (2,288 lines, 14th century) has correspondences with the Irish Cycle of FINN MAC CUMAILL and *Macgnímrada Con Culainn* ('The Boyhood Deeds of Cú Chulainn') that are not found in Chrétien's *Perceval*—for example, Perceval's ability to catch wild animals.

Iberian Literature

Generally, Arthurian texts written in the Iberian Peninsula follow the French sources, and the new episodes inserted are not relevant in a Celtic context. A few exceptions can be cited: In a love poem included in his Galician-Portuguese *Cancioneiro de Lisboa*, and in other *Cantigas* (Songs), Alfonso X (1221–84) refers to an Arthurian tradition in Catalonia, which is now lost. The Spanish *Libro del Caballero Zifar* (The book of the knight Zifar, *c.* 1300) refers to Arthur's combat with the Cath Palug; more than a translation from the vulgate *Merlin*, this work seems to be taken from the indigenous folk-tale about a monster who lived in the Lake of Lusanne.

Italian Literature

Arthurian references occur in a few poems of the 12th and 13th centuries (for example, in lyrics written by Arrigo da Settimello, Giacomo da Lentini, Guittone d'Arezzo, Boncompagno da Signa). In the *Inferno* (canto V), Dante Alighieri alludes to Tristan and Lancelot. Several Arthurian allusions are found in Giovanni Boccaccio's works. Adaptations of the French Romances (for example, the *Tavola Ritonda*, the *Tristano Riccardiano*, the *Tristano Veneto*, and the *Cantari*) do not introduce significant elements for a possible Celtic connection, with the exception of the Romance *Tristano e Lancillotto* by Niccolò degli Agostini (*c.* 1515), which is probably based on a lost French version of the Tristan legend that elaborates the theme of the submerged Otherworld.

An Arthurian scene is depicted in stone on an archivolt of Modena cathedral in northern Italy. In this sculpture, which can be dated between 1120 and 1130, King Arthur and five other knights approach a stronghold to rescue a woman named *Winlogee*. The personal names of this scene are very precious, because they are signals of Welsh and Breton stages in the development of the Arthurian legend on the Continent. For example, the name *Winlogee* preserves a Breton form, and one of the knights (named *Galvariun*), has been identified with *Gwalhafed*, the brother of *Gwalchmei* in the Welsh CULHWCH AC OLWEN.

Francesco Benozzo

ARTHURIAN LITERATURE, WELSH

ARTHUR appears in the earliest stratum of narrative in Wales (CYMRU). In the 9th-century HISTORIA BRITTONUM (§56), he is given a historical context as the leader of the kings of the BRITISH in their resistance to the English settlers. The *Historia* adds comments on two of these battles: that Arthur carried the image of the Virgin on his shoulders to great effect at the battle *Guinnion* and that 960 men fell at his onrush at Mount Baddon. The gloss in *Annales Cambriae* (see ANNALS) for that battle (AD 516 or 518) says that Arthur carried the cross on his shoulders for three days. Collectively, these variations suggest a fluid tradition related to Arthur's military successes.

The *mirabilia* (marvels) section of the *Historia* contains popular elements. *Carn Cabal* in Builth (Buellt), mid-Wales, bears the imprint of Arthur's hound's 'footprint', made when the boar *Troit* was being hunted by Arthur the soldier, while the tomb of his son Amr is in Ergyng (English Archenfield). The features are evidence of Arthur's prominent place in folklore by the early 9th century as soldier and hunter (cf. the Irish DINDSHENCHAS tradition).

The Black Book of Carmarthen (LLYFR DU CAERFYRDDIN) contains several Arthurian poems. In a poem to the hero GERAINT, Arthur and his men are praised in the conventional rhetorical phrases of WELSH heroic poetry. A stanza from *Englynion y Beddau* suggests that there is no earthly grave for this undying hero. In a fragmentary dialogue poem (*Pa gur yv y porthaur?* 'Who is the gatekeeper?'), Arthur describes his men and lists their exploits in battles with human and supernatural foes, giving a prominent place to CAI and BEDWYR. Arthur's world is more fully portrayed in the prose tale 'How Culhwch married Olwen' (CULHWCH AC OLWEN, *c.* 1100).

PREIDDIAU ANNWFN, an 8th- to 10th-century poem in the Book of Taliesin (LLYFR TALIESIN), is another indication of 'conventional' Arthurian adventures. It describes an expedition made by Arthur and his men to ANNWN to free a prisoner and win one of its treasures. In some saints' lives, Arthur is an arrogant tyrant humbled by the saint's superior powers, rebuked for denying his own code of social behaviour (see HAGIOGRAPHY).

The portrayal of ARTHUR IN THE SAINTS' lives and in one poem, 'The Dialogue of Arthur and the Eagle' (perhaps 12th century), is the negative side of his presentation in the other Welsh texts. These references predate GEOFFREY OF MONMOUTH's influential HISTORIA REGUM BRITANNIAE. Welsh narrative was inevitably influenced by foreign models—indirectly in the case of the Welsh 'ROMANCES' OWAIN *neu Iarlles y Ffynnon*, GERAINT *fab Erbin*, and PEREDUR *fab Efrawg*, and directly in the translations of French prose Romances in *Ystorya Seint Greal* (see GRAIL). In native literature, BREUDDWYD RHONABWY (Rhonabwy's dream) shows how the heroic figure could be used to comment satirically on his own tradition (see also WELSH PROSE LITERATURE).

Allusions in texts such as *Englynion y Beddau* and the TRIADS serve as evidence of lost tales and of the vitality of the native Arthurian tradition in Wales to the early modern period. Medieval Welsh Arthurian literature reveals Arthur as a hero whose name was potent enough to attract the names, and sometimes the stories, of other heroes. He also had his own legend with close comrades Cai, Bedwyr, and Gwalchmai, as well as an established court and some specific adventures, such as the freeing of a notable prisoner, an attack on the OTHERWORLD, the abduction of Gwenhwyfar, the final disastrous battle at CAMLAN, and his mysterious end and prophesied return.

Brynley F. Roberts

ARTHURIAN SITES

Arthurian sites is a term that, in its most general sense, refers to places connected with the historical ARTHUR, ARTHURIAN LITERATURE, Arthurian folklore, and the LEGENDARY HISTORY of BRITAIN. Since the 1960s, the narrower and more important focus has been on a number of archaeological sites that have produced, on excavation, evidence for intensive and high-status occupation during the historical period assigned to Arthur, namely the 5th–6th centuries AD. After the Devil and Robin Hood, Arthur and Arthurian figures are associated with more natural features and prehistoric antiquities in the landscape of ENGLAND than are any other characters in folklore; therefore, the likelihood of finding an Arthurian association for any given picturesque archaeological site is fairly high. Important post-Roman sites with Arthurian associations include the massively refortified IRON AGE hill-fort of SOUTH CADBURY CASTLE in Somerset, England, and the small, naturally defended, peninsula of TINTAGEL, CORNWALL (KERNOW), where a vast quantity of post-Roman imported pottery has been uncovered, which suggests a place of great economic importance in the 'Arthurian period'. South Cadbury has been identified as King Arthur's Camelot only since the 16th century. The name *Camelot* itself does not appear in Arthurian literature until the late 12th century; it is almost certainly derived from the pre-Roman Belgic OPPIDUM of CAMULODŪNON, later a Roman *colonia*, and now modern Colchester, Essex. GLASTONBURY, Somerset, has been identified with the Arthurian AVALON since the 12th century and was the site of both an aristocratic occupation and an early church in post-Roman pre-English times.

For the sites of Arthur's battles as listed in HISTORIA BRITTONUM §56, *Linnuis* is Lindsey, a large region around Lincoln town in present-day Lincolnshire, eastern England. *Urbs Legionis* 'the city of the Legion' most probably means Chester (CAER). *Cat Coit Celidon* 'the battle of the Caledonian forest' would have to be somewhere within a large region of what is now central Scotland (ALBA). Old Welsh *Breuoin*, if this is the correct reading, could continue the Old Romano-British name for a fort north of HADRIAN'S WALL, *Bremēnium*. CAMLAN, for the battle site where Arthur is said to have fallen in 537–39, according to *Annales Cambriae*, can be derived from the ancient Celtic name of a fort on Hadrian's Wall *Camboglanna*. Although sometimes identified with the fort at Birdoswald, Romano-British *Camboglanna* has more recently been equated with Castlesteads (CUMBRIA) on the river Cam Beck, which possibly has a related name; Birdoswald was probably Romano-British *Banna* (Rivet & Smith, *Place-Names of Roman Britain* 261–2, 293–4).

In the case of the post-Roman fortifications at DINAS EMRYS in Snowdonia (ERYRI) in north Wales, the legendary link is not to Arthur himself, but rather to *Historia Brittonum*'s tale of GWRTHEYRN, Emrys or AMBROSIUS, and the white and red dragons (DRAIG GOCH); later, the prophetic figure of Emrys came to be identified with the Arthurian wizard Merlin, the Welsh MYRDDIN. Similarly, the sites named in the tangentially Arthurian tales of the tragic lovers TRISTAN AND ISOLT (DRYSTAN AC ESYLLT) have been drawn into the study of the Arthurian sites. The 12th-century Anglo-Norman poet Béroul, for example, presented detailed Tristan geography in Cornwall, but recent research has now shown that Castle Dore (Béroul's Lantien) was, in fact, a pre-Roman Iron Age site; thus it could not possibly have been the stronghold of the historical 6th-century ruler Marc Cunomor, the prototype of Béroul's King Mark.

Arthurian sites also include places named in Arthurian sources that are probably real places, but whose identification remains uncertain—for example, the site of the famous battle of BADONICUS MONS and Arthur's court in the oldest Arthurian tale

CULHWCH AC OLWEN at Celliwig in Cernyw (KERNOW/Cornwall). The latter name appears to be a combination of *celli* 'wood' and *gwig*, probably meaning 'settlement' < Latin *vīcus*. Various attempts at identifying the place have been made, including proposals for Calliwith near Bodmin, the hill-fort at Castle Killibury, the hill-fort near Domellick (GEOFFREY OF MONMOUTH's *Dimilioc*), and a place in Cornwall called *Cællincg* and also *Cællwic* in Anglo-Saxon sources (possibly modern Callington). In 1302, two men were accused of murdering a Thomas de Kellewik in west Cornwall, but this is the only occurrence of this Cornish name that seems to correspond exactly to the Welsh *Celli Wig*. In considering this unresolved question, it is important to remember that the region named Cernyw in *Culhwch*, and in early Welsh tradition in general, was more extensive than the modern county. It is also possible that early Welsh sources might sometimes mean the old tribal lands of the Romano-British *civitas* of the Cornovii in what is now Shropshire (Welsh swydd Amwythig) and POWYS, though a conclusive example of such a meaning for Cernyw has yet to be found. A suitably important sub-Roman place with a philologically workable name would be Calleva (Silchester), the fortified centre of the *civitas* of the Atrebates, which continued to be occupied and free of Anglo-Saxon settlement into the 5th century; Silchester, however, is nowhere near either Cornwall or the Cornovii. There has been no serious attempt to identify Arthurian Cernyw with Kernev/Cornouaille of Brittany (BREIZH). However, Ashe (*Discovery of King Arthur*) has proposed that the 5th-century 'King of the Britons' RIGOTAMUS who led 12,000 men against the Visigoths in GAUL was the historical basis for Arthur and has drawn attention, in this connection, to a place called *Avallon* in France.

In contrast, the hunt for the supernatural boar TWRCH TRWYTH and other quests of the Arthurian host in *Culhwch ac Olwen* can be located and traced across the map of Wales (CYMRU) in close detail. The 9th-century compiler/author of *Historia Brittonum* knew an earlier version of the story of Arthur's hunt of 'porcum Troit', and he includes three landscape marvels (*mirabilia*) with Arthurian connections. The Old Welsh marvel name *Carn Cabal* in the region of Buellt (now in southern Powys) seems to mean, on the face of it, 'horse's hoof', but it is explained as a cairn (Welsh *carn*) bearing the footprint of Arthur's dog Cafall, impressed into the rock during the great boar hunt. Another of the *mirabilia*, that of *Oper Linn Liuon* on the Severn estuary, though it does not name Arthur or the Twrch Trwyth, describes a climactic episode from the hunt in *Culhwch*: If an army gathers there as the tide comes in (as Arthur's band did in the tale), they will all drown if they face one direction, but be saved if they face another. *Historia Brittonum*'s wonder of *Licat Amr* occurs at a spring at the source of the river Gamber in the region of Ergyng, now Herefordshire (Welsh swydd Henffordd). This location is said to be the site of the strangely size-changing grave of Arthur's son Amr, whom Arthur himself, *Historia Brittonum* tells us, killed. Amhar, son of Arthur, is mentioned in the Welsh Arthurian Romance GERAINT, but the story of his slaying by Arthur does not survive. Conversely, the story that Arthur killed his son named MEDRAWD/Mordred does become one of the central themes of international Arthurian Romance in the High Middle Ages.

Geoffrey of Monmouth and Welsh material showing Geoffrey's influence, such as the 'Three Romances' (TAIR RHAMANT), place an important court of Arthur's at the site of the old Roman legionary fortress of Isca Silurum, now Caerllion-ar-Wysg in Gwent, a major ruin still impressively visible today. This idea does not seem to pre-date Geoffrey, and Caerllion has not produced evidence for itself as an important centre in the sub-Roman period.

John T. Koch

ASTERIX

Asterix is the creation of Albert Uderzo (1927–) and René Goscinny (1926–77). The cartoon character first appeared in 1959, and the first book, *Asterix le Gaulois* (Asterix the Gaul), in 1961. The premise is that in 50 BC a few Gaulish villages in ARMORICA still hold out against the Roman conquest, thanks in part to a magic druidi-cal potion that gives them super strength (see DRUIDS). The common GAULISH personal-name element *-rīx,* 'king', as in VERCINGETORIX, was the inspiration for Uderzo and Goscinny's ubiquitous *-ix,* used to denote Gaulish names, usually humorous puns. For example, the hero is Asterix and his companion is Obelix.

Uderzo is the illustrator and, since Goscinny's death in 1977, the author. The books have been translated into a number of languages, including BRETON, SCOTTISH GAELIC, and WELSH. Asterix, though fictional, attempts to depict Gaulish life as realistically as possible within the storylines.

Antone Minard

AUDACHT MORAINN

Audacht Morainn (The testament of Morann) is a 7th-century text in Old IRISH that consists of advice doled out by the legendary judge Morann to a young king, Feradach Find Fechtnach (Fair Feradach the Battler).

The main concern of the text, widespread in early IRISH LITERATURE, is the importance of justice (*fír flathemon,* 'true ruling'). This justice not only guarantees peace and stability, but also is expected to bring about abundance of food, fertility of women, and protection from plagues, lightning, and enemy attacks.

Morann stresses the interdependence of a king and his people, and advises: 'Let him care for his subjects (*túatha*), they will care for him.' He compares the king's task with that of a charioteer, who must constantly look to either side as well as in front and behind (see also the CHARIOT article). The king should not let a concern for treasures or rich gifts blind him to the sufferings of the weaker members of society, and he should respect the elderly and regulate commerce.

Fergus Kelly

AURAICEPT NA NÉCES

Auraicept na nÉces ('The Scholars' Primer') is the title of a medieval Irish tract on various linguistic topics, including the origin of the Irish language. The earliest manuscripts date from the 14th century. The canonical part of the *Auraicept*—that is, its original nucleus—has been dated to the late 7th century. It is attributed in the extant recensions to Cenn Faelad mac Ailello (†679), working at the monastery of Doire Luran (now Co. Tyrone/Tír Eoghain), and it includes the idea that the Irish language was created by Fénius Farsaid after the confusion of tongues at Babel. Doctrines discussed in the *Auraicept* are also found in LAW TEXTS and in the Old Irish St Gall glosses on Priscian's Grammar (see GLOSSES, OLD IRISH). A central concern of the compilers of the *Auraicept* was the vindication of a learned interest in the Irish language (Old Irish *Goídelg*; see GAELIC) and its textual heritage.

Erich Poppe

AVALON (YNYS AFALLACH)

Insula Avallonis (the Isle of Avalon) is first mentioned by GEOFFREY OF MONMOUTH in his HISTORIA REGUM BRITANNIAE (*c.* 1139) as the place where ARTHUR's sword Caliburnus (see CALADBOLG) was forged, and then as the place where Arthur was taken after the battle of CAMLAN for his wounds to be tended. In the Welsh versions of *Historia Regum Britanniae* (BRUT Y BRENHINEDD), the place is called *Ynys Afallach*. In Geoffrey's *Vita Merlini* (Life of Merlin; see MYRDDIN), *Insula Avallonis* is explained as *insula pomorum* 'island of apples' (cf. Welsh *afal* 'apple', *afall* 'apple trees'). *Ynys Afallach* thus corresponds closely to the poetic name that occurs in early IRISH LITERATURE for the Isle of Man (ELLAN VANNIN)—namely, *Emain Ablach* 'Emain of the apples', a name applied specifically as the otherworldly domain of the sea divinity MANANNÁN mac Lir. *Vita Merlini*'s *Insula Avallonis* is located vaguely in the west and is inhabited by nine sorceresses, the chief of which is Morgan (Morgain La Fée of later ARTHURIAN LITERATURE). Geoffrey's *Insula Avallonis* may have been based on some very early traditions and/or literary sources.

In medieval Welsh sources, the name Afallach designates an ancestor figure in the remote mythological past of the second dynasty of GWYNEDD, the son of the mythical progenitor BELI MAWR. In the Welsh TRIADS (Bromwich, TYP no. 70 'Three Fair Womb-Burdens of the Island of Britain'), Owain and Morfudd are said to be the children of URIEN fab Cynfarch and the supernatural Modron, daughter of Afallach.

Avalon had come to be identified with GLASTONBURY by 1191, when the Glastonbury monks said that they had exhumed the bodies of Arthur and Guenevere (GWENHWYFAR). A small inscribed lead cross was produced at the time (since lost) and said to have been found under the coffin. The readings vary. That on the drawing from Camden's *Britannia* (1607) is as follows: HIC IACETS | EPULTVS·INCL | ITVS·REX ARTV | RIVS·IN INSV | LA·A | VALO | NIA 'Here lies buried the famous King Arthur in the Isle of Avalon'. The late form *Avalonia* shows that the cross is not from the 6th century; compare the Gaulish place-name *Aballone*, now *Avallon*. Writing a short time after the Glastonbury exhumation, GIRALDUS CAMBRENSIS accepted its authenticity, giving two detailed accounts of it, and the association continues into modern Arthurian literature.

John T. Koch

AWEN

Awen is a Welsh word meaning 'poetic gift, genius or inspiration, the muse'. It is linguistically related to the Old Irish *aí* 'poetic art' and the Welsh *awel* 'breeze' as well as the English *wind*. The etymological sense of *awen* is a 'breathing in' of a gift or genius bestowed by a supernatural source. Thus, for example, Llywarch ap Llywelyn claims that he received inspiration from God, similar to that TALIESIN received from the legendary CAULDRON:

> *Duw Ddofydd dy-m-rhydd rheiddun awen—bêr*
> *Fal o bair Cyridfen.*

> The Lord God gives to me the gift of sweet inspiration
> As from the cauldron of Cyridfen [Ceridwen].

The earliest reference to *awen* occurs in a 6th-century name mentioned in the 9th-century HISTORIA BRITTONUM.

Ann Parry Owen

B

BADONICUS MONS

Badonicus mons (Mount Baddon) was the site of a battle mentioned by Gildas at which the Britons decisively checked the Anglo-Saxon 'conquest'. In *Annales Cambriae* and the battle list in Historia Brittonum, Arthur is said to have been the victorious commander. For Gildas, Baddon was an event of central importance, resulting in a period of cessation of foreign wars and security for the Britons for a generation or more. Gildas places the battle in the year of his own birth, the '44th year with one month now elapsed'. Bede understood the passage to mean that Baddon occurred *c.* AD 493 (*Historia Ecclesiastica* 1.15–16). Most modern writers have taken it to mean *c.* 500. In contrast, Ian Wood interprets the passage to mean that there were 43 years between the early victory of Ambrosius against the Saxons and Baddon, and that Baddon was one month before Gildas's writing, leading to a date range of 485 × 520 for the nearly simultaneous battle and *De Excidio* (*Gildas* 22–3), which accords with the *Annales Cambriae* date for the battle at 516/518.

Location

Given that Gildas calls Baddon an *obsessio* (siege), the hill was probably fortified, but Gildas does not say who was beseiging whom. The site has not been identified with certainty (cf. Arthurian sites). There is no evidence earlier than the 12th century for the idea that Baddon = Bath; Welsh *Baddon* came to be applied to Bath only because of the English word 'bath'. Kenneth Jackson argued that a Brythonic name *Baδon* lay behind the five hills in England with old fortifications now called *Badbury*, Old English *Baddan-byrig*. Of those, the Badburys in Dorset, near Swindon in Wiltshire, and in Oxfordshire above the Vale of the White Horse (see Uffington) have been thought likely for reasons of historical geography.

The Name

Gildas's *Badonicus* and *Badonis* in *Annales Cambriae* and *Historia Brittonum* seem to be early British (i.e., Celtic) names. Whether the identification with one of the places called Old English *Baddanbyrig* is correct or not, Old English *Baddan-* could be borrowed from this British *Badon-*. *Badon-* appears to have the Gallo-Brittonic divine suffix, as seen, for example, in the names of the goddesses Epona and Mātrona (see Matronae). *Badonicus mons* might, therefore, refer to a fortified hill named in the pagan period for a Celtic divinity, although no Badonos or Badona is known from Britain or Gaul.

John T. Koch

BAGPIPE

The bagpipe has often been perceived as the 'national instrument' of Scotland (ALBA), familiar in the form of the Great Highland bagpipe, a powerful wind instrument with unique qualities. Nevertheless, that variant is only one example of an instrument family that has a worldwide distribution. Early identifiable forms include the prehistoric shawms and hornpipes of Near East civilizations, which evolved with bag and 'drones' in classical and early European history. It thrives still in 'Celtic Europe' and particularly in northern Spain, France (including Brittany/BREIZH; see BINIOU; BRETON MUSIC), northern ENGLAND, Ireland (ÉIRE), and Scotland, but also regionally throughout the continent in areas with no Celtic connection.

Specific bagpipes now strongly associated with Celtic culture may be only a late development in bagpipe history. Irish uilleann pipes (*píob uilleann* 'elbow pipe'; see IRISH MUSIC) are not an ancient folk instrument but rather a highly sophisticated modern concert-hall instrument perfected in city workshops in London, Edinburgh (DÙN ÈIDEANN), BAILE ÁTHA CLIATH (Dublin), and Chicago. The breakdown of traditional Gaelic society left the *pìob mhòr* or Great Highland bagpipe as the martial instrument of the armies of the Empire and of Highland Societies in the 19th century. The bagpipe in modern Scotland, therefore, is the product of recent interpretations of 'light' music for entertainment, dancing, and marching; of more exclusive traditions of *piobaireachd* composition and performance; and of competition.

The principal bagpipe element is the melody pipe or 'chanter', made of wood, cane, bone, ivory, or metal, on which the music is played by the fingers covering and uncovering a series of finger-holes. Chanters have been broadly classified as having a cylindrical bore, tending to give a quieter, lower-pitched sound, or a conical or tapered bore, giving a brighter and sharper sound. A typical chanter has eight finger-holes and one thumb hole, achieving a melodic compass of only nine notes. The placing of the holes and their relative sizes have remained unchanged on most bagpipes, thus producing a traditional scale that has remained largely unchanged or modified. This has left significant differences between the scale and the sound of the bagpipe and the musical system of the equal-tempered scale that evolved in Europe from the late medieval period. Some instruments, such as the Irish pipes, responded to changing fashions by adding keys to increase the melodic compass. Another characteristic of the bagpipe is the playing style on the open and unstopped chanter with its continuous sound, with the player separating and accentuating the melody notes by 'gracing' or the playing of rapid embellishments. Supplementary pipes, as part of a typical bagpipe and tied into the bag, provide a continuous and fixed note 'drone' or 'drones'.

Hugh Cheape

BAILE ÁTHA CLIATH (DUBLIN)

Dublin (Irish Baile Átha Cliath) is the capital of the Irish Republic (ÉIRE). The Irish name means 'town of the ford of hurdles'; a 'hurdle' is a rectangular wooden object woven out of willow or hazel, used for temporary fencing or (as here) to ease passage over marshy ground. Its English name contains two elements that are also Irish in origin, *Dubh-linn* 'black pool'.

Dublin was founded by Vikings who arrived in the mid-9th century. The expansion of Scandinavian power in Ireland was curbed by Brian Bóruma at the battle of Clontarf (1014). Following the Anglo-Norman invasion, Henry II (1133–89) of England made Dublin the centre of his government in Ireland. In early modern times, this area was the core of what was known as 'The Pale', the part of Ireland most distinctly English in make-up and character.

In the 18th century, Dublin was considered the second city of the British Empire. However, the Act of Union

Location of Báile Átha Cliath (Dublin) and its environs in east-central Ireland. (Map by John T. Koch)

(1800) diminished the political importance of Dublin.

Present-day Dublin is a major European city, with approximately 953,000 inhabitants in the greater area. It is the seat of the Irish government, the Dáil (the Irish parliament), and also serves as the economic and cultural centre of the Irish Republic. The National Museum (Ard-Mhúsaem na hÉireann) displays high-status metalwork in bronze and gold from the Bronze Age, objects in the insular La Tène style from the Iron Age, and early Christian masterpieces of insular art, such as the Tara brooch. The National Library (Leabharlann Náisiúnta na hÉireann) and the Royal Irish Academy (Acadamh Ríoga na hÉireann) keep major collections of early Irish-language and Hiberno-Latin manuscripts. Dublin is also the home of the oldest university in Ireland, Trinity College (1592), whose library houses many famous Irish manuscripts, among them the Book of Kells. The School of Celtic Studies of the Dublin Institute of Advanced Studies (Institiúid Ard-Léinn) is a dedicated research centre and major publisher of texts and linguistic reference works for IRISH and the other CELTIC LANGUAGES. Dublin is the home of numerous governmental and nongovernmental organizations involved with various aspects of promoting and/or studying the Irish language, including FORAS NA GAEILGE and the Ordnance Survey.

Petra S. Hellmuth

BALLADS AND NARRATIVE SONGS, BRETON

The Breton song tradition is one of the richest and most fascinating aspects of Breton culture. It can be roughly divided into two groups: the lyrical *sôn* (pl. *soniou*) and the narrative *gwerz* (pl. *gwerziou*) or ballad. It is the strength and diversity of this latter type that marks Breton folk-song as distinct from French. Thousands of songs have been recorded since serious collection began in the early decades of the 19th century. The most notable collection, the BARZAZ-BREIZ of 1839, has been dogged by questions of authenticity, which deflected much serious attention from the Breton ballads until the 1990s. The *gwerz* tradition is profoundly concerned with remembering the past: A large proportion of the songs are based on local events, usually tragic, such as shipwrecks or murders, many of which can be traced back two or three hundred years. Studies of individual ballads have shown how surprising details may be preserved over hundreds of years. Thus the *gwerziou* represent a very useful source for the historian of Breton culture. While names, places, and the bare bones of the plot are very conservative, the characters and their motives often adapt the historical facts to the conventions of the genre.

Other kinds of narrative draw on very different sources. Saints' lives offer stories of the miraculous (see HAGIOGRAPHY), and international ballad-types appear in Breton settings. The *gwerz* of *An Aotrou Nann* (Lord Nann) is the best known of these, being a version of the fairy-mistress ballad familiar in Scandanavian traditions as *Sir Olaf*. A small number of songs have notably Celtic themes. For example, the *gwerz* of *Santes Enori* (Saint Enori), which tells the story of a princess who saves her father by sacrificing her breast to a snake, contains elements of a narrative complex identifiable in a Latin saint's life, a Welsh triad (see TRIADS), a Scottish Gaelic folk-tale (see FOLK-TALES), and a medieval French Romance. Another extraordinary piece, collected from a beggar-woman in the early 19th century, tells a Romance-like tale about the capture of Merlin (see MYRDDIN). One of the best-studied and most evocative of all Breton songs is the *gwerz* of *Iannik Skolan*, which recounts, in powerful dialogue, a meeting between a mother and her dead penitent son. This ballad, first collected in the 19th century and still sung widely in the 20th century, is the closest known analogue to an enigmatic medieval Welsh poem preserved in the 13th-century manuscript known as LLYFR DU CAERFYRDDIN ('The Black Book of Carmarthen').

The *gwerziou* are generally composed in rhymed couplets (occasionally triplets), and have the distinctively pared-down style common to many oral ballad traditions.

Dialogue is fundamental, but description and authorial comment minimal. In this sense, the songs contrast with the Breton broadsides, which were also very popular, whose sensational 'news' style is rather more verbose. The language of the *gwerzioù* is vivid and compact:

> *Nin a vele merc'hed Goaien*
> *e tont en aod vras gant licheriou moan*
>
> *Kant intanvez deuz bae Goaien*
> *a gasas ganto kant licher venn*
>
> *Int a c'houlas an eil d'eben:*
> *—Na peus ket gwelet korf ma den?*
>
> We saw the women of Audierne
> coming to the great beach with fine sheets:
>
> A hundred widows from Audierne Bay
> bearing a hundred white sheets.
>
> They asked each other:
> Have you not seen my husband's body?

Folk music in general has played a crucial part in the Breton cultural revivals of the 19th and 20th centuries (see BRETON MUSIC), and the songs remain a key marker of Breton identity. They continue to be sung traditionally, and are also adapted to new contexts and technologies.

Mary-Ann Constantine

BALLADS AND NARRATIVE SONGS, IRISH

The term 'ballad' was unknown in Ireland (ÉIRE) until the English and Scottish plantations of the 17th century. Consequently, most ballads found in Ireland and fitting the English definition of a narrative solo song are of English or British origin, including the broadsheet ballad tradition. The earlier Irish *laoithe* (lays), sometimes also translated as 'ballads', began to be composed around the 12th century and continued to be popular until the 18th. Prosodically, they are composed in *óglachas*, relaxed forms of the strict syllabic metres, such as *rannaigheacht* and *deibhidhe*, favoured by the professional poets of the Middle Ages (see METRICS), and heroically recount various episodes of the lives of the FIANNAÍOCHT, a mythical band of professional soldiers. They describe various exploits and are closely related to the prose tales that were the most popular entertainment in the Gaelic world in this period. Lays are also extant from the Isle of Man (ELLAN VANNIN) and have survived most strongly in Gaelic Scotland (ALBA), where some thirty examples have been recorded from oral tradition as sung pieces. Musical examples have also been recorded from Ireland, although recitation seems to have predominated. It was upon such texts that James MACPHERSON based his 'epics', creating a literary sensation across Europe in the mid-18th century. A comprehensive manuscript collection of these lays, *Duanaire Finn*, was compiled in Ostend in the early 17th century.

Only four older songs in the Irish language have been explicitly linked to the canon established by the folklorist Francis Child. They are *Cá rabhais ar feadh an lae uaim* (Where have you been all day from me? corresponding to 'Lord Randal', Child 12), *Peigín is Peadar* (Peggy and Peter: 'Our Goodman', Child 274), *Hymn Dhomhnach Cásca* (The hymn of Easter Sunday: 'The Cherry Tree Carol', Child 54), and *A Bhean Udaí Thall* (O woman yonder: 'The Twa Sisters', Child 10). In every case, they are accompanied by explanatory prose narrative. Emphasis on a dialogue format is retained in the Irish versions, and it may be this feature that led to their adoption by Gaelic singers. Other Irish songs recall ballads without being direct borrowing, such as *Táim Sínte ar do Thuama* (I am stretched on your grave), also called *Ceaití an Chúil Chraobhaigh* (Katy of the branching tresses), which bears similarities to 'The Unquiet Grave' (Child 78). The motif of separated lovers who recognize each other by a ring they had exchanged is also common, especially in *An Droighneán Donn* (The brown thorn bush).

Lillis Ó Laoire

BALLADS AND NARRATIVE SONGS, SCOTTISH GAELIC

SCOTTISH GAELIC heroic songs developed from the classical bardic tradition of the Gaelic world. As a narrative verse genre, these heroic songs enjoyed great popularity in Gaelic Scotland (ALBA). Many texts were transmitted through the vernacular oral environment. The protagonists belong mostly to the context of Fionn (FINN MAC CUMAILL; see also FIANNAÍOCHT), and many are narrated by his son Oisean (Irish OISÍN). A few texts deal with material relating to the ULSTER CYCLE and have CÚ CHULAINN as their protagonist, such as *Bàs Chonlaoich* (The death of Connla), which tells how Cú Chulainn killed his own son.

Warrior elegies assume a prominent place in the tradition. Three different songs deal with the death of Fionn's grandson, Oscar; the death of Fionn's nephew Diarmaid is narrated in *Laoidh Dhiarmaid* (The lay of Diarmaid), localized in various districts in the HIGHLANDS. *Laoidh Fhraoich* (The lay of Fraoch), a text with loose Ulster Cycle connections, tells of the demise of Fraoch in a fight with a lake-dwelling monster, following the machinations of queen Meadhbh (MEDB) of CONNACHT; no Irish versions of this text survive. The repulsion of would-be invaders, often described as Norsemen, is another favourite subject. Some songs tell of expeditions by Fionn and his companions into enemy territory, such as *Duan na Ceàrdaich* (The song of the smithy). The Norse element in the Fionn tradition is anachronistic, considering that his supposed *floruit* was in the 3rd century AD; these texts, however, are well-constructed narratives and enjoyed great popularity for that reason. Another common theme is the enmity between Fionn's comrades and a rival warrior group led by Goll mac Morna; this hostility forms the backdrop to *Bàs Chairill* (The death of Cairill) and *Bàs Gharaidh* (The death of Garadh).

Most songs of which versions from the bardic period are extant are composed in *óglachas*, loose forms of the strict syllabic metres, and the requirements of metre become attenuated in the processes of vernacularization and oral transmission. The number of syllables demanded by the original metre becomes variable, and poetic devices such as alliteration and assonance may disappear, although rhyming words generally possess a high degree of stability. The most common metres are *deibhidhe* and the *rannaigheacht* types, although other metres, such as *ae fhreislighe* and *rion-naird*, make an occasional appearance.

The earliest extant texts of Scottish provenance are found in the Book of the DEAN OF LISMORE; many parallel versions appear in later tradition. The 18th century saw a flurry of collecting activity in the wake of James MACPHERSON's publication of 'Ossian', including both the recording of texts from reciters and the collecting of old manuscripts. The collecting aspect of this effort concentrated mainly on the Perthshire–Argyll area. Some collecting was conducted under the auspices of the Highland Society of Scotland in connection with its investigation into the authenticity of Macpherson's works—for example, the taking down of the repertoire of Archibald Fletcher (NLS Adv. MS 73.1.24). Occasionally, genuine ballad material was adapted to resemble Macpherson's style, for instance, by the Reverend John Smith, who published his compositions under the title of *Sean-Dàna, le Oisian, Orran, Ullan, etc.*

In the 19th century, the focus of collecting switched to the Hebrides, and aimed at recording texts that were beginning to lose ground in the oral tradition. The most prolific collectors were John Francis Campbell, who published both manuscript material and texts collected from oral tradition in *Leabhar na Féinne* (The book of the Fianna), and Alexander Carmichael (author of *Carmina Gadelica*), most of whose collected ballad material in the Carmichael Watson Collection remains unpublished. Both collectors provided valuable information about the reciters who provided texts. Some narrative songs survived into 20th-century tradition, both in the islands and on the mainland, although some were preserved as texts without tunes.

Anja Gunderloch

BALLADS AND NARRATIVE SONGS, WELSH

The first Welsh ballads appear in the 16th century, in all likelihood based on orally transmitted narrative poems now lost. The earliest example to survive, written in 1586, celebrates the failure of the Babington Plot to assassinate Elizabeth I (see TUDOR). Although printed ballads in ENGLAND can be traced to the early 16th century, all of the early Welsh examples survive in manuscript form alone. The Welshman Thomas Jones (1648–1713) opened a printing press in Shrewsbury (Welsh Amwythig) in 1695, opening the floodgates for the Welsh ballad-monger.

Well in excess of seven hundred 18th-century ballads have survived. They were printed in pamphlet form, with three or four separate poems appearing on pages stitched together; the title page would usually indicate the titles of the individual ballads and the air to which they could be sung. As to Welsh broadside ballads, only a few have survived.

The subject matter of the ballads encompassed all the circumstances and experiences of life. The vast majority were concerned with religious topics, often urging their listeners or readers to adopt a higher morality and to decry swearing, blaspheming, drunkenness, Sabbath-breaking, and miserliness toward the poor. All aspects of love and marriage are exhaustively covered. Current events, and particularly disasters such as wars, plagues, and earthquakes, were recorded in verse, as were sensational events such as murders and loss of life in accidents or shipwrecks.

The pattern of ballad production and distribution remained essentially the same in the 19th century, although all aspects of the activity occurred on a larger scale, and industrialized south Wales became an increasingly important market. Examples of more than 1,700 of these 19th-century Welsh ballads have survived.

The basic subject matter of 19th-century ballads continued the tradition of the preceding century, but their numerous authors also embraced new subjects and topics that reflected contemporary society. Industrial developments and innovations gave rise to ballads that rejoice in the coming of the railway, while the darker side of industrialization was represented by the ballads that recorded the frequent and heavy loss of life in industrial accidents. Ballads declined from *c.* 1870. New and more 'refined' forms of popular entertainments such as the public concert and penny readings gained ground, while the ballad-monger's traditional outlet, the fair, was increasingly frowned upon, and current events were detailed in Welsh-language press from the 1850s.

Tegwyn Jones

BALOR

Balor is a mythological Irish figure. A key early account is his confrontation with his grandson Lug and the Tuath Dé in Cath Maige Tuired ('The [Second] Battle of Mag Tuired'), where he is a leader of the Fomoiri (see Mythological Cycle). Balor is described as having an eye whose lid is so heavy that it takes four men to lift it. When Lug sends a stone through the eye, its fatal power is turned upon the Fomoiri. In modern narratives, Balor becomes less a warrior-leader and more a folk-tale villain with monstrous characteristics. His evil eye echoes the single eye of Cú Chulainn in battle frenzy, and Lug's chanting a spell with one eye shut in *Cath Maige Tuired* itself. The theme of the malevolent giant with an eyelid so heavy that servants must lift it recurs in a Welsh tale, Culhwch ac Olwen.

Victoria Simmons

BANNOCKBURN, BATTLE OF

Bannockburn was the high point of Scottish resistance to the English Crown, deciding the fate of medieval Scotland (Alba) as an independent nation. Following the death of four-year-old Margaret in 1290, the claim to the throne passed to her distant cousins, including the de Baliol family and the de Bruce family. After the defeat of William WALLACE in 1305, Robert de Bruce took the kingship and organized a campaign that climaxed with the battle of Bannockburn.

On 23 and 24 June 1314, no more than 8,000 Scottish soldiers led by Robert de Bruce faced in excess of 20,000 English soldiers led by Edward II of ENGLAND. The site of the battle was 6 km south of Stirling. Edward II was thoroughly beaten, although a final truce was not agreed until 1323. This Scottish victory had far-reaching consequences, including the Declaration of Arbroath (1320) and the Treaty of Edinburgh (1328).

The name *Bannockburn* signifies the stream (burn) that flows from the hilly country near Stirling. The old BRYTHONIC name *Bannauc* 'Hilly land' occurs in the GODODDIN as the frontier zone between the BRITONS and the PICTS.

Marion Löffler

BARD, IN CLASSICAL ACCOUNTS

Bards—the professional praise poets—appear in GREEK AND ROMAN ACCOUNTS of ancient GAUL. The principal classical authority on the bard is the lost History of Posidonius (1st century BC), based on first-hand experience in southern Gaul. For instance, Athenaeus says:

> Posidonius, in the twenty-third book of his *Histories*, says that the Celts have with them, even in war, companions whom they call parasites ['those who dine at another's table']. These poets recite their praises in large companies and crowds, and before each of the listeners according to rank. Their tales are recounted by those called bards, poets who recite praises in song. (*Deipnosophistae* 6.49)

Bards are discussed together with the DRUIDS and the 'seers' (*vātes* in Strabo) as related learned professions with comparable social status. The same root as in *vātes* appears in several INDO-EUROPEAN languages: Old Norse *ōðr* 'poetry', Old Irish *fáth* 'prophecy', and Welsh *gwawd*, which now means 'SATIRE' but once meant 'inspired verse, song, song of praise'.

The Celtic FEAST is the setting for the spontaneous praise poetry in the account (again via Athenaeus) of the great banquet of Lovernios:

> Posidonius, describing the great wealth of Lovernios, . . . [describes how] a Celtic poet arrived too late for the feast. He composed a song for Lovernios praising his greatness and lamenting his own tardy arrival. Lovernios was so pleased with this poem that he called for a bag of gold and tossed it to the poet as he ran beside his chariot. The bard picked up the bag and sang a new song, proclaiming that even his chariot-tracks gave gold and benefits to his people. (*Deipnosophistae* 4.37)

It is remarkable that the praiseworthy attributes of the patron—and, by implication, the relationship of poet and patron—are essentially the same as those found in the praise poetry of Ireland (ÉIRE), Wales (CYMRU), and the Scottish HIGHLANDS (see IRISH LITERATURE; SCOTTISH GAELIC POETRY; WELSH POETRY) in the Middle Ages and early modern times.

Julius Caesar provides a great deal of detail on the druids; his Gaulish ethnography owes little to Posidonius, but rather has the value of an independent witness.

The Proto-Celtic word for a person filling this social function was *bardos*, giving Goidelic *bard* and Welsh *bardd*; it was taken into Greek as βάρδος and into Latin as *bardus*. *Bardos* is derived from the Indo-European root *g^wer(ə)-*, which meant 'to raise the voice, to praise'.

J. E. Caerwyn Williams and John T. Koch

BARD, COMPARISON OF THE PROFESSIONAL POET IN EARLY WALES AND IRELAND

Introduction

The term 'bard' (Welsh *bardd*, Irish *bard*) survived in the medieval languages of both Ireland (Ériu) and Wales (Cymru), albeit with somewhat different meanings, and the praise and satire of rulers continued to be central to the rôle of the professional poet in these societies.

Wales

The poetry attributed to Aneirin and Taliesin, which is generally believed to date from the 6th century, is eulogistic and elegiac. The tradition of praise poetry in Wales (Cymru) and in Celtic Britain was thus already ancient when the 12th-century Gogynfeirdd poems were created. Several make reference to the prince's need for the poet, as, for example, when Cynddelw tells Rhys ap Gruffudd that 'without me, no speech would be yours'; in other words, it is the poet who, in his verse, gives substance to the prince's deeds and makes enduring fame possible.

After the fall of Llywelyn ap Gruffudd in 1282, Welsh poets continued to compose eulogy and elegy in honour of the gentry (see Cywyddwyr), but the sense of the vital importance of the bard to the social fabric faded.

There is less evidence of a tradition of bardic satire in medieval Wales. However, a 14th-century tract on poetry insists that to 'malign and discredit and satirize' are appropriate to a lesser grade of entertainer, the *clerwr*, and not to the true poet. These stipulations suggest that there may have been a tradition of poetic satire. No clear evidence of such a tradition in the earlier Middle Ages exists, but poems of the *Gogynfeirdd* known as *bygythion* (sing. *bygwth*) imply a power inherent in the poet to cause harm to a patron who treats him unjustly.

In Welsh, *bardd* is to this day the most common term for any poet, and the *Gogynfeirdd* often use it when referring to themselves. They also call themselves *prydydd* (literally 'shaper'), but seem to make no distinction of function or value between that word and *bardd*.

Ireland

Medieval Irish treated the terminology of poets and poetry somewhat differently, calling the poet *file* (pl. *filid*) for the most part, as does Modern Irish, while reserving *bard* (pl. *baird*) for an inferior grade of poet. However, bardic poetry—eulogy, elegy, and, in all likelihood, SATIRE—was an important institution, and one that endured to the 17th century.

Poets in medieval Ireland appear to have had a considerable degree of professional organization, and seven grades of poet, parallel to the seven ecclesiastical grades, had been established by the 8th century (see BARDIC ORDER). Much of the education of the *filid* in the earlier Middle Ages took place within Christian MONASTERIES (see also MONASTICISM). By the 14th century, however, schools of poetry had been established. Irish bardic poets of the 13th to the 17th centuries composed in highly regulated and complex syllabic metres, in this case called *dán díreach*, and this practice also marked them as an élite fraternity (see METRICS).

Like Welsh, Irish has preserved very little verse that can actually be described as satire. Nevertheless, there are a great many references, especially in narrative literature from the 8th century onward, to the power of poets to cause great harm with censorious verse, and these references can be found well into the Early Modern period.

Catherine McKenna

BARD, ROMANTIC PERCEPTION

Unlike his heroes—kings and warriors who can die young and glorious—the poet must survive to tell the tale. When the heroic age has passed, the bard and his poetry take on an elegiac, nostalgic note. In different ways, the poetry ascribed to ANEIRIN, TALIESIN, MYRDDIN, and Llywarch Hen, and SUIBNE GEILT, the Hag of Beare (CAILLEACH BHÉIRRE), and Oisín contribute to a homegrown literary image of the poet as a melancholy survivor.

The figure of the Celtic bard had certain recurrent characteristics that survived the transitions from Myrddin and Oisín to GEOFFREY OF MONMOUTH's Merlin and James MACPHERSON's Ossian and passed into European art and literature. His age made him a figure of wisdom, to which was added a visionary quality sometimes involving magical or occult powers. That basic image generated many reflexes. There was always a tension between the reverential treatment of the bard and the earlier, more pragmatic view of him as a whipper-up of Celtic insurgency. The bard has been a subject of dispute between literary critics, who have either praised or demonized him for his conservatism and loyalty to an old order. The visionary and 'druidic' traits of the Celtic bard have proved notably resilient, however, resurfacing even in the most recent manifestations of Celticism. They also survive powerfully in in modern popular fantasy writing and contemporary film.

William Gillies

BARDIC ORDER, IN IRELAND

In contemporary usage, the term 'bardic order' is used somewhat confusingly for a group whose members comprised both the ranks of the *file* (poet, pl. *filid*), and the ranks of the *bard* (bard, pl. *baird*). The first term etymologically means 'seer', cf. Welsh *gweled* 'to see'. In the interest of clarity, GAELIC terms will be preferred here.

From the earliest times, Irish sources evidence a tension between the *filid* and the *baird*, with the *filid* consistently marking themselves off from the *baird* on the basis of their greater learning. The spread of LITERACY underlay the first reorganization of the ranks of the *filid* that is clearly discernible in Irish sources. The form that this reorganization took was inspired by the successful establishment of a seven-grade scheme for the ranking of the clergy; this scheme became fixed by the 8th century and is described in various law tracts (see LAW TEXTS), including BRETHA NEMED and *Uraicecht na Ríar* (The primer of the stipulations). The names of the seven grades, in order form highest to lowest, were *ollam, ánruth, clí, cano, dos, mac fhuirmid*, and (again) *cano*. These grades represent the successive stages through which a *file* might progress in the course of his career. *Ollam*, present-day Irish *ollamh*, has come to mean 'professor'.

In the law tracts mentioned previously, the *baird* are largely distinguished from the *filid* in not having a scholarly training: Instead, their reputation is said to rest on an innate talent for poetry. They are portrayed as belonging to a separate caste from that of the upwardly mobile *filid*. *Uraicecht na Ríar* states that an *ollam* will know 350 tales and be competent in all historical science (*coimgne*) and Irish jurisprudence (*brithemnacht fhénechais*).

The persistent efforts of the *filid* to enhance their own status at the expense of the *baird* eventually resulted in the primary meaning of *bard*—namely, 'panegyric/lyric poet'—being expanded to accommodate the meanings 'illiterate poet' and 'oral-performance poet'.

By the Early Modern period (*c.* 1200–*c.* 1600), the term *bard* is used more often when speaking of the lowest-ranking members of the professional poet's retinue than of the gifted high-class amateur. This development is evidenced in both English-language and Irish-language sources. The rich detail found in Old and Middle Irish metrical and legal tracts on the individual grades of the *filid* and the *baird* is not replicated in Modern Irish sources. Some of the distinctions must have been obliterated in the sweeping changes that occurred in the wake of the 11th- and 12th-century church reforms and of the coming of the Normans.

Máirín Ní Dhonnchadha

BARDIC ORDER, IN WALES

The bardic order in Wales (CYMRU) lasted until its gradual decline and disintegration in the late 16th and early 17th centuries. For hundreds of years, bards who were attached to the courts of independent Welsh kings and princes sang eulogies and elegies in which they praised the leadership, martial prowess, courage, and generosity of their patrons. The bards were highly trained professional craftsmen, who had a function as clearly recognized as that of the physician, the smith, the cleric, or the man of law, and they were accorded a status and dignity commensurate with their responsibilities.

The Pencerdd

The duties and privileges of the bards are defined in the Laws of Hywel Dda, which refer to three distinct classes of bards. Highest in status was the *pencerdd* ('chief poet'), who was the head of the bardic community within a geographical area. He had his own chair, won by competition, which gave him the right to instruct young bardic novitiates. He sat next to the *edling* (heir-apparent) in the royal hall. When the king desired to hear a song, it was the duty of the *pencerdd* to sing first. However, he was not assigned a place among the twenty-four officers of the court, although he was to receive the gift of a HARP from the king and to obtain his land for free. The *pencerdd* was also entitled to the marriage-fee (or maiden-fee) of the daughters of the poets who were subject to him, and he was to receive a nuptial gift of twenty-four pieces of silver when they married.

The Bardd Teulu

The second class of poet mentioned in the law books is the *bardd teulu* ('household bard', 'bard of the retinue'). The Latin texts assign him eleventh place among the twenty-four officers of the court. After the *pencerdd* had fulfilled the king's wish by singing two songs in the upper section of the hall, it was the duty of the *bardd teulu* to sing a third song in the lower part. In time of conflict, this individual was to sing *Unbeiniaeth Prydain* (The sovereignty [or monarchy] of BRITAIN) to the royal retinue before going into battle. This traditional song, which probably emphasized the Welsh claim to sovereignty over the whole island of Britain, was singularly appropriate when military campaigns were being conducted against the English. Like the *pencerdd*, the *bardd teulu* enjoyed certain privileges and received various perquisites that were connected with his status. For example, upon taking office, he was entitled to a harp from the king and a ring from the queen. He was entitled to his land for free, a horse, linen from the queen, and cloth from the king. The rôles of *pencerdd* and of *bardd teulu* could, on occasion, be assumed by the same person.

The Cerddorion

The third class of poets referred to in the law books comprised the *cerddorion* (minstrels, Latin *joculatores*), equivalent to French *jongleurs*. They provided a less refined type of entertainment, one that was possibly of a humorous or satirical nature.

Bard and Cyfarwydd

Some evidence indicates that bards could also be accomplished storytellers (*cyfarwyddiaid*, sing. CYFARWYDD), whose medium was either prose or combination of prose and verse. Their repertoire included many complicated saga-cycles, in which prose was generally the medium of narrative and description, while verse was employed for dialogue. These tales were delivered orally, and they incorporated a rich and colourful variety of traditional material, sometimes derived from a remote and inaccessible past.

Changing Practice

By the Age of the Princes (from the 11th century to the 13th), three significant developments had occurred in the history of the Welsh bardic order (see

GOGYNFEIRDD). The earlier distinction between the *pencerdd* and the *bardd teulu* had begun to break down such that eventually the former could, on occasion, act as a *bardd teulu*. The corpus of CYNDDELW Brydydd Mawr (*fl. c.* 1155–*c.* 1195), the leading and the most prolific court poet of the 12th century, suggests he held both roles. His work also shows that by that period a bard could be associated with more than one court, and that bards began to address men of noble birth, not just people of royal lineage.

Developments after the Edwardian Conquest

By destroying the old political order with which bardism had been so long and so closely connected, the Edwardian conquest created an opportunity for changes in both the craft and practice of the poets. In the 14th-century bardic grammar that has been associated with the names of Einion Offeiriad and Dafydd Ddu of Hiraddug, the *pencerdd* is replaced by the *prydydd*, the *bardd teulu* by the *teuluwr*, and the *cerddor* by the *clerwr*. In the works composed by the poets of the post-Conquest period, a new metre emerged, the CYWYDD *deuair hirion*, which became the predominant medium for Welsh verse for two and a half centuries.

In general, two distinct types of bards can be detected from the 14th century onward: a professional bard who was heavily dependent on the patronage of the nobility, and a talented member of the *uchelwyr* (noblemen) who had acquired a mastery of the intricate bardic craft. Among those who belonged to this latter class were DAFYDD AP GWILYM (*c.* 1315–*c.* 1350), who skilfully introduced elements from the European concepts of courtly love into the native bardic tradition. The bards who sang during this period composed panegyric and elegiac verses, poems to solicit gifts of various kinds and to express gratitude to the individual donors, love-songs, and flyting (ritualized insult) poems (see also CYWYDDWYR).

The 15th century witnessed the emergence of a new category of verse, the *cywydd brud* or prophetic poem, foretelling the advent of a great national deliverer. The authors of these poems frequently alluded to prominent contemporary figures by using the names of various animals, and these cryptic references present difficulties for the modern reader. During the 16th century, heraldic bards emerged. Nevertheless, although the range of bardic poetry was unquestionably enlarged, the centuries-old bardic tradition proved to be extremely tenacious: Eulogy and elegy for noble patrons still predominated, and both metre and style continued to be subject to a strict discipline.

Instruction of the Bard

The process of mastering the art of poetry was both long and arduous. The foundation was the medieval *trivium* of grammar, rhetoric, and logic. Much emphasis was placed on mastering the *cynganeddion* (sing. CYNGHANEDD) and strict poetic metres, the old poetry, archaic vocabulary, the contents of the bardic grammar, royal and aristocratic genealogies, the history of the nation, and its lore and legends. Instruction was imparted orally by recognized masters of the bardic craft. The full course of instruction lasted for nine years, and those disciples who aspired to attain to the highest rank passed through the following grades: licensed disciple without a degree, licensed disciple with a degree, disciplined disciple, disciple of the degree of *pencerdd*, *pencerdd*, and teacher (*athro*). This probably presents an ideal picture rather than an accurate description of day-to-day practice.

Orality and Literacy

Only a comparatively small part of the detailed oral instruction imparted to bardic pupils was committed to writing. The earliest extant example of this material is a 14th-century bardic grammar. This work, which was an adaptation of Latin grammars, discusses letters of the alphabet, syllables, parts of speech, syntax, prosody (but not the *cynganeddion*), the twenty-four strict metres, and the prohibited faults.

The professional poets kept the details of their esoteric art a secret from all, with the notable exception of those clerics and members of the nobility who had manifested a genuine desire to study and master the bardic craft. In addition, they were extremely reluctant to use the printing press as an effective means of disseminating their compositions and teaching. Naturally, the professional poets were constantly anxious to safeguard their status and livelihood by preventing inferior, unskilled rhymesters from encroaching in increasing numbers on bardic itineraries and thereby arousing the displeasure of patrons who would otherwise be well disposed and supportive. This guarding of the craft was one of the primary concerns of the bardic *eisteddfodau*, which sought to regulate the activities of the poets by establishing strict metrical rules and by granting licences to those who had successfully completed the prescribed stages of their training, thereby preventing a disturbing and unwarranted proliferation of lesser-skilled bards. The most important of these bardic congresses of which we have any knowledge were those held in Cardigan Castle (Castell Aberteifi) in 1176, under the patronage of RHYS AP GRUFFUDD (Lord Rhys, 1132–97), in Carmarthen (Caerfyrddin) *c.* 1451, and the two *eisteddfodau* held at Caerwys in 1523 and 1567, the second of which was convened under a commission granted by Queen Elizabeth I herself.

Decline of the Bardic Order

The decline of bards' popularity can be attributed to the powerful interaction of a variety of factors: the generally stagnant conservatism of the strict-metre bards and the advanced age of the tradition they represented; the increasing Anglicization of the gentry following the ACTS OF UNION of 1536 and 1543; the dissolution of the monasteries, at which the professional poets had been generously patronized for centuries; the rise in popularity, from the mid-16th century onwards, of verse composed in the free accentual metres; and the whole intellectual and social ethos of the early modern period, with its emphasis on unbridled individualism and private enterprise, which ran counter to the bardic tradition, whose work emphasized the social function of poetry.

The bardic tradition was still uncommonly tenacious, however, and the end itself came only between approximately 1550 and 1650. By the second half of the 17th century, the bardic order, unable to survive the ravages of the Civil Wars (1642–48) and the ensuing political upheavals, no longer functioned as a viable professional and social organization.

Ceri W. Lewis

BARZAZ-BREIZ

Hersart de La Villemarqué's *Barzaz-Breiz: Chants populaires de la Bretagne* appeared in 1839. The author was a young aristocrat from Kemperle (Quimperlé), Brittany (Breizh). Lacking medieval manuscripts containing the literature and history of the Bretons, La Villemarqué turned to oral tradition and began collecting songs from his native region. This raw material was then worked into 53 pieces, beginning with a 'fifth or sixth century' prophecy attributed to the bard Gwenc'hlan.

In 1845, La Villemarqué published an expanded version with 33 new pieces; in 1867, he added three more. The collection includes religious songs and *chansons de fête* (feast-day songs), but the bulk of the work is 'historical' narrative ballads.

Tunes to the pieces appear in an appendix, but these 'popular songs of Brittany' are overwhelming presented as texts. It is clear from the introduction and notes how much La Villemarqué was influenced by Welsh antiquarian Edward Williams (Iolo Morganwg), whose vision of a bardic past was widely accepted as authentic at the time. La Villemarqué's claims for his own material were unequivocal: The Breton peasantry had preserved their language uncorrupted since the 'time of Taliesin', and were still singing ballads about Arthur and Merlin (Myrddin). By the late 1860s, as other collectors began to publish their versions of the Breton ballads, his claims were treated with increasing scepticism. The debate about the 'authenticity' of the *Barzaz-Breiz* remained an issue until the final decades of the 20th century, partly because La Villemarqué never discussed his sources or methods. Not until Donatien Laurent retrieved and partially published his field notebooks in 1989 did any objective discussion become possible. *Barzaz-Breiz* now has little worth as a work of scholarship or a reflection of the Breton ballad tradition, but it remains a milestone in the history of Breton cultural identity as a book that inspired poets, scholars, and folklorists to discover and describe Brittany's past.

Mary-Ann Constantine

BATH

The Roman settlement at Bath, now in the west of England, was known as *Aquae Sulis* 'the waters of [the deity] Sūlis'. Sūlis was conflated in the Roman period with Minerva (see interpretatio romana). Bath is situated on the river Avon and is renowned for three remarkable hot-water springs there. Excavations in the King's Bath spring have recovered a small number of Late Iron Age coins, together with evidence of a rubble causeway built out through the marsh to the spring head (see coinage; watery depositions).

Head of a god or other supernatural being, showing an amalgamation of Classical and Celtic iconography, from the pediment of the temple of Sūlis Minerva at Bath, England. (Charlotte Lake)

Following the Roman conquest of AD 43, Bath developed as a civil settlement. The road crossing became the focus of the urban development, while the springs to the south became the centre of a healing sanctuary dedicated to Sūlis Minerva.

The early religious complex, dating to the Flavian period (AD 69–96), comprised a tetra-style temple in Corinthian style fronted by a paved court containing the sacrificial altar. Immediately south lay the sacred spring (later, the King's Bath), at this time open to the sky, with a suite of baths just beyond, dominated by a large swimming bath filled with a constant flow of hot mineral water. The most notable later modifications were the extension of the temple, the enclosure of the spring in a massive vaulted chamber, and the building of a tholos (a circular temple) to the east of the main temple during the Hadrianic period (AD 117–38).

The most dramatic feature of the religious complex is the highly decorated pediment of the main temple, dominated by a moustached head with attributes of Minerva, an owl, and a Corinthian helmet. The head has similarities to depictions of river gods and Oceanus.

The sacred spring was the place where suppliants could communicate with the deity by throwing offerings into the water, some of which were recovered during excavations. The most prolific offerings were coins, but there were a range of other small offerings and *defixiones* (curse tablets) inscribed on sheets of pewter. Most of the personal names on these objects are Roman, but there is also a significant proportion of Romanized Celtic names.

In the Anglo-Saxon Chronicle, the Saxons of Wessex are reported to have taken the old Roman towns of Gloucester, Cirencester, and Bath in 577. In sources from pre-Norman England, Bath is called Latin *civitas Aquamania*, *urbs Achumanensis*, Old English *æt Baðum* ('at the baths'), and *Acemannes ceaster* (ultimately giving the local Akeman Street).

Barry Cunliffe

BEAN SÍ/BANSHEE

The banshee of folk tradition has essentially become a foreboder of death in certain families. Throughout Ireland (ÉIRE), she is said to perform that function by crying and lamenting, although in the southeast her sound can also have frightening and threatening qualities (see LAIGIN). Her most common name is 'banshee', Irish *bean sí* (earlier *ben síde*), 'woman of the OTHERWORLD', although she is also known by other names. Her cry or *olagón* is plaintive in the extreme, and represents family and community grief.

In folk tradition, a variety of criteria (loudness, repetition, movement, the effect on hearers) serve to distinguish the cry of the banshee from human or animal sounds. It is most strongly associated with the old family or ancestral home and land, even when a family member dies abroad. Such a cry is said to be experienced by family members and the local community rather than by the dying person. Death is considered inevitable once the cry is acknowledged.

The banshee is generally imagined as a solitary old woman with long white hair. Traits in the modern traditions of the banshee suggest an analogy with goddess-figures in medieval Irish literature who conferred SOVEREIGNTY on the rulers of their particular areas. In Co. Galway (Contae na Gaillimhe) and border regions of neighbouring counties, the banshee is said to be washing a garment in a stream, thus paralleling the washing activity of the death-foreboding *bean-nighe* in Gaelic Scotland (ALBA), the *kannerezed noz* in Brittany (BREIZH), and Otherworld women in Irish literature. In a number of IRISH-language texts, the *badhbh* forebodes violent death in battle by washing the blood-stained garments of those who are fated to die.

At the battle of Clontarf in 1014, according to the traditions surrounding BRIAN BÓRUMA, high-king of Ireland, the sovereignty figure Aoibheall of Craglea, Co. Clare (Crag Liath, Contae an Chláir), patroness of the DÁL GCAIS sept, foretold that he would be killed in that conflict and indicated who would succeed him as king. Earlier still, in the 8th-century tale *Táin Bó Fraích* (see ULSTER CYCLE), the hero's death is foretold by the cries of Otherworld women, especially his mother, the divine *Bé Find* 'the white woman', sister of BÓAND.

Patricia Lysaght

BEDE

Bede, the monk of Jarrow and Wearmouth in northern ENGLAND, is Britain's most famous scholar of the early Middle Ages, and his influence on the intellectuals of the period can hardly be overestimated. His name is variously given as *Bede* or

Bæda in contemporary sources, and as *Bede* in modern English. Bede's intellectual horizon was exceptionally wide, and he excelled in almost every aspect of early medieval thought.

This author finished the *Historia Ecclesiastica*—the most important source on early medieval BRITAIN and the first comprehensive work on the history of Britain after GILDAS—in 731. The work includes important information on the peoples of Britain—divided, on linguistic basis (*Historia Ecclesiastica* 1.1), into PICTS (*Picti*), Scots (*Scotti* = Irish, Gaels), Anglo-Saxons (*Angli*), and BRITONS (*Brettones*).

Bede's perspective, and the information he gives, has influenced modern ideas on the period to a high degree, as can be exemplified by the notorious *bretwalda* concept. From Bede's comment on the *imperium*-wielders of Britain (*Historia Ecclesiastica* 2.5), later glossed in Anglo-Saxon as *bretwalda*, translated as 'powerful ruler', modern historians have inferred a formal institution overlordship in early medieval Britain, possibly influenced by the Celtic ideas of a high-king or overking. Among these possible Celtic forebears for an ideology of high-kingship, Adomnán wrote in the 690s of Oswald of Northumbria (†642) as *imperator totius Britanniae a deo ordinatus* 'emperor of all Britain ordained by God' (*Vita Columbae* 1.1). Adomnán accorded a similar dignity to his kinsman, the Irish king Diarmait mac Cerbaill (†565; *Vita Columbae* 1.14). Some writers have also seen far-reaching authority—whether real or wished for—as being implicit in the office, and perhaps the title, of GWRTHEYRN of Britain (the *superbus tyrannus* of Gildas), who is said to have settled Anglo-Saxon mercenary troops in areas of Britain that he did not rule directly. Because Bede is the only source for this *bretwalda* concept on the Anglo-Saxon side, however, it has been treated with scepticism.

Bede's relation to the Celtic peoples appears foremost in his historical works. Bede gives little information about the Picts, but seems rather well inclined toward them. Notably, he blames the Northumbrian king Ecgfrith for the battle at Nechtanesmere (685) against his fellow Christian Picts and elaborates on the efforts of the Pictish king Nechton son of Derelei to submit to the correct Easter date.

Bede's attitude toward the Britons (i.e., the Welsh) is far more antagonistic. He adopted the negative characteristics he found in Gildas, and additionally reproached these peoples for allegedly not trying to convert the Anglo-Saxons to Christianity.

Bede's attitude toward the Irish is ambiguous. On the one hand, he thinks very highly of them, their piety, and their missionary efforts, especially those emanating from Iona (EILEAN Ì) to Bede's native Northumbria. In this respect, his account on the Irish missionaries and holy men is an important addition to the information about Roman-influenced missions derived from other sources. On the other hand, there can be no doubt that Bede disagreed with the Irish clerics of Iona, especially on the question of the correct Easter date.

Alheydis Plassmann

BEDWYR

Bedwyr fab Pedrawg is one of the earliest Arthurian heroes. His name is probably a derivative of *bedw* 'birch trees'. Bedwyr is mentioned in the poems *Pa Gur yv y*

Porthaur? and *Englynion y Beddau* ('The Stanzas of the Graves'), in the Welsh Triads, in the Life of Saint Cadoc, and in the Welsh Arthurian tale Culhwch ac Olwen. He is described as one of the three fairest men in Britain, with a magic spear whose head can leave the shaft, draw blood from the wind, and return. He is involved in the rescue of Mabon son of Modron and the killing of Dillus the Bearded. In Geoffrey of Monmouth's Historia Regum Britanniae ('The History of the Kings of Britain'), Arthur's *pincernus* (butler or cupbearer), Beduer, is given Neustria (northern France) by Arthur as a reward. Bedwyr survives the translation into European Arthurian literature as Sir Bedevere.

Antone Minard

BELENOS/BELINOS

Belenos/Belinos is a Celtic deity whose name is often connected with the Graeco-Roman god Apollo (see interpretatio romana). The Romano-Celtic name *Belenus* or *Belinus* occurs in 51 inscriptions dedicated to the god, most of them in Aquileia, northern Italy, the site of his main sanctuary. To this day, part of the town is known as Beligna. At the siege of Aquileia by Maximinus (AD 238), the god was seen floating in the air, battling and defending his town. Belenus was seen as a typical oracle- and health-giving deity, one of the Celtic gods whose tradition was primary and thus widespread.

This etymologically difficult name, often interpreted as 'the bright one', has also been connected with Gaulish *belenuntia*, Spanish *beleno*, the hallucinogenic henbane, whose stems and leaves are covered in fine white hair and whose Latin name is *Apollinaris*. Gallo-Roman *belisa* 'henbane' (> German *Bilsenkraut*) seems to appear in the personal name *Belisamarus* (*Corpus Inscriptionum Latinum* 13.11224) 'great in henbane'.

The name also appears in Brythonic—for instance, on the coins of the Welsh leader Belyn o Leyn († AD 627), the inspiration for Geoffrey of Monmouth's Belinus (Historia Regum Britanniae 2.17). The mythical Belinus builds an exemplary and peaceful realm. The name of this divine king has been preserved in the personal names Cunobelinos > Welsh *Cynfelyn* (the ultimate source of Shakespeare's *Cymbeline*) and **Lugubelinos* > *Llywelyn* (cf. Llefelys).

Helmut Birkhan

BELGAE

The Belgae were a subgroup of the Gauls whose territory extended from the Seine (Gaulish Sequana) to the Rhine in what is now Belgium, northern France, the Rhineland in Germany, Luxembourg, and the southern Netherlands. The Belgae were subdivided into various tribes (see 'The Celticity of the Belgae' later in this article). Strabo wrote that in pre-Roman times the Belgae had once had approximately 300,000 arms-bearing men (*Geography* 4.4.3).

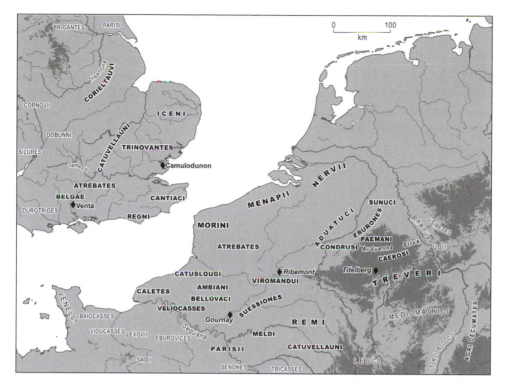

Tribes in the Belgic areas of Gaul and Britain are shown in bold type. (Map by Ian Gulley, Antony Smith, and John T. Koch)

Belgae and Germani

Around 50 BC, Julius Caesar wrote:

> [M]ost of the Belgae descend from the Germani and had crossed the Rhine in ancient times because of the fertility of the soil and expelled the Gauls who had inhabited this place. (*De Bello Gallico* 2.4.1)

Despite Caesar's use of 'Germani', which may have been meant geographically, the territory of these tribes seems to have been predominantly Celtic-speaking, even if some of the minor tribal names are possibly Germanic (*Sunuci, Cugerni*) or of obscure origins (*Segni, Tungri*). Some tribes may have been of heterogeneous origin; for example, the Aduatuci were a remnant of the CIMBRI AND TEUTONES according to Caesar (*De Bello Gallico* 2.29). These tribes are usually regarded as Germanic, although the name *Teutones* is Celtic (see also TUATH; TEUTATES). Most of the ancient place-names throughout Belgic Gaul are Celtic (e.g., names in -*ācon* 'settlement, estate', -*dūnon* 'fort', -*magos* 'plain', and -*bonā* 'settlement'). Traces of Celtic have also been identified in the modern languages spoken in the former territory of the Belgae, Walloon (French) and Flemish/Dutch.

Archaeology

Archaeological evidence shows that the Belgae of Caesar's time had a Late LA TÈNE culture. Recent archaeological research has provided important evidence about the trade relations, material culture, religio,n and political organization of the Belgae. The principal trade route linked the Belgic tribes to the south by way of the Rhône valley. Recently excavated Belgic ritual sites, including Ribemont-sur-Ancre and Gournay-sur-Aronde, have shed light on religious customs from the 2nd century BC down to Roman times. Classic examples of proto-urban fortified sites (OPPIDA) in Belgic Gaul, which include Fécamp and Titelberg, indicate the elaborate social organization of the Belgic tribes.

The Belgae in Britain

The Belgae were a highly expansionist group in the last centuries BC. Caesar noted their presence in BRITAIN, and British tribes sharing names with Gaulish Belgae include the Catuvellauni and the Atrebates. The Belgic migrations into Britain are our only instance of a historically documented movement of a Celtic-speaking people from mainland Europe to the British Isles.

‘Gallo-Belgic’ gold coins began to enter southeast Britain by about 150 BC (see COINAGE). Other features of material culture that indicate Belgic presence or influence in southeast Britain include pottery, *oppida* (for example, CAMULODŪNON), wrought-iron andirons, late La Tène style ART, and cremation burials.

The Celticity of the Belgae

The name *Belgae* derives from Celtic **belgo-*. A variant occurs for the people called the FIR BOLG in Irish LEGENDARY HISTORY (see LEBAR GABÁLA ÉRENN). These tribal names belong to the same root as the Celtic words OIr. *bolg* ‘bag, sack; belly, stomach; bellows’, MW *boly*, Mod. W *bol(a)* ‘belly; swelling; bag (of leather)’, Bret. *bolc'h* ‘husk (of flax)’, and Gallo-Latin *bulga* ‘leather sack’, all of which derive from the Celtic **bolgo-*. The root is also found in English ‘bag’. Thus *Belgae* should be translated as ‘the people who swell (particularly with anger/battle fury)’.

This name is probably also the source of the early Welsh male personal name *Beli*, which occurs in the name BELI MAWR. The modern national name *Belgique* (Belgium) comes from the ancient *Gallia Belgica*, revived in 1831.

An etymological survey of the other Belgic group names follows, including the modern city names that retain them.

- *Ambiani* ‘the people around [the two banks of the Somme]’, modern *Amiens* (Somme, Picardy, France)
- *Atrebates* ‘the dwellers’ < Celtic **ad-treb-a-t-,* cf. Early Ir. *attreb* ‘dwelling-place, possession’ and MW *athref* ‘dwelling-place’—modern *Arras* (Pas-de-Calais, Artois, France) and *Artois*
- *Caletes* ‘the hard people’, cf. OIr. *calad*, W *caled* ‘hard’; modern *Calais* (Pas-de-Calais, Artois, France)
- *Catuvellauni* ‘better battlers’

- *Eburones* 'the yew people', cf. OIr. *ibar* 'yew', W *efwr* 'cow-parsnip, hogweed', from Celtic **eburo-*; cf. the city of *York* (*Eburācon*) in ENGLAND
- *Menapii*—a name preserved in Irish *Fir Manach*, giving the modern county name *Fermanagh*
- *Morini* 'the sea people', cf. W, Cornish, Bret. *mor* 'sea' < Celtic **mori*; see ARMORICA
- *Parisii* 'the makers' or 'commanders', cf. W *paraf: peri* 'to make, to produce, to command to be done', hence W *peryf* 'lord, commander' < **kwar-is-io*—the city of *Paris*
- *Rēmi* 'the first ones, chieftains', (cf. OIr. *rem-* 'in front of', also W *rhwyf* 'king, leader'—modern *Reims* (Marne, Champagne, France)
- *Suessiones*, cf. Gaulish *suexos* 'sixth' < Celtic **suexs-o-*, Ir. *sé*, W *chwech*—Modern *Soissons* (Aisne, Île-de-France)
- *Trēveri,* 'guides', cf. OIr. *treóir* 'guidance, direction, course', with the Celtic preposition **trei-* 'through' (Ir. *tre, tré,* W *trwy*)—*Trier* (Germany; *Trèves* in French)
- *Veliocasses*—contains Celtic **weljo-* 'better' (cf. W *gwell* 'better') + *-casses,* an element common in proper names
- *ViRomandui* '[men] virile in owning ponies' or 'male ponies' < Celtic **viro-* 'man', cf. OIr. *fer*, W *gŵr* + **mandu-* 'pony', MIr. *menn* 'kid, young animal', MW *mynn* 'kid', Bret. *menn* 'young animal'; modern *Vermandois* (a former county now in Picardy)

Belgic group names of possibly Celtic origin include the following:

- *Caeroesi*, either Celtic (cf. OIr *cáera* 'sheep' or *cáera* 'berry', with an unexplained suffix) or Germanic (Proto-Germanic **haira-* 'worthy, exalted, **grey-haired*', cf. German *hehr* 'noble').
- *Atuatuci/Aduatuci:* no known etymology.
- *Bellovaci*, ?**bello-* possibly 'roar/speaking' + **uako-* 'curved'; modern *Beauvais* (Oise, Picardy, France).
- *Condrusi*, modern *pays de Condroz* between Namur and Liège, France. The underlying Celtic **kondrust-* seems to contain the preposition **kon-/kom-* 'with, together' (OIr. *con-, com-*,W *cyn-, cyf-*) and **drust-,* a name element found in DRVSTANVS, from a 6th-century inscription from Cornwall (KERNOW), and in the common Pictish names *Drost, Drust,* and *Drostan* (see DRYSTAN AC ESYLLT).
- *Caemanes/Paemanes* is a tribal name from the Ardennes. A modern form may survive as modern *Famenne* (a region between the rivers Lesse and Ourthe in the Ardennes). The variation between *p-* and *c-* can be explained as Celtic (see P-CELTIC). Alternatively, *Caemanes* has been taken as containing Germanic **haima* 'home'; if this were so the attested spelling, however, *Paemanes* would be unexplained.
- *Nervii* probably belongs to the Western Indo-European **hner-* 'man', known in Celtic from MW *ner* 'lord, chief'. It could also be a Germanic name with the same root.

Peter E. Busse and John T. Koch

BELI MAWR

Beli Mawr (Beli the Great), son of Manogan/Mynogan, appears in early Welsh GENEALOGIES as a legendary ancestor, at or near the prehistoric opening of several royal pedigrees. Beli also appears in the Old Breton genealogy of St Gurthiern.

In CYFRANC LLUDD A LLEFELYS (The adventure of Lludd and LLEFELYS), Beli Mawr is identified as the father of Lludd (see NŌDONS) and Caswallon. The latter corresponds to Julius Caesar's opponent, the historical King Cassivellaunos (*fl.* 54 BC). In Historia Brittonum (§19), the British king who fought against Caesar has a name and patronym unmistakably similar to Beli's—*Bellinus filius Minocanni*. The form in *Historia Brittonum* has been traced to a scribal error referring to Cunobelinos, king of the Britons. However, the name *Beli* is widespread in other contexts.

In historical times, *Beli* is attested as the name of a king in early medieval Wales (Cymru), Strathclyde (Ystrad Clud), and amongst the Picts, where the variant *Bili* is more usual. *Bili*, the common Old Breton name and name element, is probably the same. *Beli* may derive from the Old Celtic name, which is attested as both *Bolgios* and *Belgius*, and was borne by the chieftain who led the Gauls' invasion of Macedonia in 280–279 BC (see also Brennos of the Prausi; Galatia).

John T. Koch

BELTAINE

Beltaine or Bealtaine (1 May) and Samain (Modern Irish Samhain) are the two most significant dates in the Celtic calendar. In the Brythonic languages, Beltaine is referred to as the Calends of May (Welsh *Calan Mai*, Breton *Kalan Mae*). Cormac ua Cuilennáin etymologized the word as the fire (*teine*) of Bel:

> Beltaine, that is Bel's-fire . . . two auspicious fires the druids made with great spells and each year they brought the cattle between them against pestilence.

One of the editions of Tochmarc Emire ('The Wooing of Emer') mentions cattle (*díne*) destined for Bel, explaining, 'They assigned the young of all cattle as the property of Bel. Bel's-cattle then, that is, Beltaine'. Bel was once equated with the biblical Baal, but now it is understood to be the root in the divine names Belenos and Belisama, possibly meaning 'shining'.

Fire continues to be an important aspect of May Day ritual. Bonfires were kindled on hilltops in the Isle of Man (Ellan Vannin), and their smoke was considered beneficial for the health of cattle, crops, and people. May Day beliefs are associated with health, beauty, and protection. Fairies and witches were particularly likely to be abroad on May Day, as were the dead; thus many beliefs and customs were aimed at preventing harm from supernatural sources. Dairy products were especially vulnerable to tampering on May Day.

Magical events associated with May Day in medieval Welsh literature include the colt of Teyrnon Twrf Liant in the tale of Pwyll and the battle between Gwyn ap Nudd and Gwythyr in the tale of Culhwch ac Olwen. In Irish literature, Ailill is killed by Conall Cernach on Beltaine.

May Day was also an important day for legal contracts. Rents were due and workers would hire themselves out 'from May Day to May Day'. May Day was also the time when pastoralists moved from winter quarters to summer quarters. As with Samain, animals increased in value on May Day. For example, bees that swarmed after August (see Lugnasad) would not increase in value until May Day. In Padstow, Cornwall (Kernow), the Obby Oss (hobby horse) festival is celebrated (see also Mari Lwyd).

The ultimate origin of the European celebration of the first of May is not known, though it is likely to date to pre-Celtic times. The celebration of May Day as a labour day is due to a historical coincidence, but has grown in importance while traditional May Day celebrations have waned. The day also continues to be marked as a neo-pagan holiday.

Antone Minard

BERNICIA
See Brynaich.

BEUNANS KE

Beunans Ke (The Life of St Ke or Kea) is a saint's play in Middle Cornish, probably originally written *c.* 1500. It survives in a single manuscript discovered in 2002. The beginning and end are missing, as are several internal folios. The work includes a life of the saint (pp. 1–8) and an Arthurian section that does not mention the saint (pp. 9–20), but is closely related to Geoffrey of Monmouth's Historia Regum Britanniae. The major evidence for St Ke's life is found in Albert Le Grand's *La Vie, gestes, mort, et miracles des saincts de la Bretagne armorique*, which includes a French translation of the now lost, possibly 12th-century, Latin life, which similarly appends an Arthurian passage to the life.

The large parish of Kea in Cornwall (Kernow) near Truro (and possibly once including Truro itself) is the setting for the Cornish part of the play. St Ke is referred to as Ke in the Cornish of the manuscript and as Keladocus in the Latin, as reflected in the various references to the church and parish (parochia Sancte Kycladoce [1390], Sancto Kekeladoco [1517]) and the Breton Ke Colodoc.

The following summary relies on the French life to fill in gaps in the Cornish material. The first five folios are lost, presumably recounting Ke's early life and his promotion to the episcopacy. Ke then restores a shepherd to life and travels to Cornwall, where he is found by the tyrant Teudar's forester in Rosewa Forest (Roseland), taking him to Teudar at Goodern; Teudar and Ke have a theological dispute and Teudar orders Ke's imprisonment; further conflict between the saint and Teudar ensues; Teudar asks the sorceress Owbra to produce a potion, which causes Teudar to get stuck in his bath; Arthur receives various kings and knights; and conflict occurs between Arthur and the Roman Emperor Lucius, as in the work by Geoffrey of Monmouth. The rest is missing.

The play is written in good Middle Cornish, comparable to that of Beunans Meriasek, and is rather more idiomatic and dramatic in the first part than in the rather stolid Arthurian section. It is similar in many respects to *Beunans Meriasek*, although the metrical arrangement in *Beunans Ke* is somewhat more elaborate, and almost certainly both plays share the same provenance—namely, Glasney College at Penryn, which was dissolved in 1545. Teudar and his court at Goodern in Kea parish are referred to in that play (*Beunans Meriasek* 2289, *goddren*), and Glasney also held the great tithes of the parish. A round called Playing Place in a village of the same name still exists partially in the parish and could be where the play was performed, probably over a period of two days. There is a considerable admixture of Anglo-Norman French, Middle English, and Latin in the text, especially in the Arthurian episode, with one stanza containing two lines each of Cornish, French, and English. Nearly all of the stage directions are in Latin, but a few (possibly later additions in the original) are in English, together with several in Cornish, representing some of the earliest surviving Cornish prose (see CORNISH LITERATURE).

Andrew Hawke

BEUNANS MERIASEK

Beunans Meriasek ('The Life of St Meriasek') is a miracle play in Middle CORNISH, written in 1504. Along with BEUNANS KE, it is the only surviving vernacular play in Britain dealing with the lives of saints. The 4,568 lines, organized in seven- and four-syllable verses, weave together historical and legendary characters from different centuries with strong undertones of contemporary Cornish politics. *Beunans Meriasek* was probably written at Glasney College by 'Rad[olphus] Ton'. The work was performed over two days, in the round, offering the twin themes of conversion and healing through miracles involving Meriasek, Sylvester, and the Virgin Mary. According to tradition, St Meriasek lived in Brittany (BREIZH) in the 7th century and is one of the patron saints of Camborne (Kammbron).

In the play, Meriasek comes into conflict with a pagan king, the tyrant Teudar (possibly a satirical interpretation of Henry VII; see TUDUR). The figure of Breton LEGENDARY HISTORY, CONAN MERIADOC, shares a name with St Meriasek, but their traditions otherwise have little in common.

Alan M. Kent

BIBLE, IN BRETON AND CORNISH

Brittany

No published translation of the Bible into BRETON appeared before the 19th century. Brittany owes its Bible translation to the grammarian and lexicographer Jean-François Le Gonidec (1775–1838) and his Welsh supporter Thomas Price ('Carnhuanawc'). In 1819, Price began to collect money for a Breton Bible and contacted the British and Foreign Bible Society (BFBS) in search of support. The BFBS commissioned Le Gonidec to translate the New Testament, which appeared in 1827 as *Testament Nevez Hon Aotrou Jezuz-Krist* in an edition of 1,000 copies. More copies of this edition are said to have been sold in Wales than in Brittany, and because of poor sales the BFBS refused to sponsor an edition of the Old Testament or the whole Bible. As a consequence, the complete Bible was not published in Le Gonidec's lifetime, although he had continued working on the Old Testament and finished its translation by 1835. In fact, the full *Bibl Santel* did not appear until 1866. By then, a revised edition of Le Gonidec's New Testament by a Welsh missionary, John Jenkins

(1807–72), aided by Guillaume Ricou (1778–1848), using simplified spelling and style, had been published (in 1847) and been well received.

Cornwall

The Bible has not yet been fully translated into CORNISH, and the complete New Testament appeared only in 2004, translated under the auspices of the Cornish Language Board. Cornish was a language of religion in medieval and early modern Cornwall (KERNOW), attested by the ORDINALIA. When Henry VIII introduced English as the language of religious services in 1549, the Cornish rose in what became known as the 'Prayer-Book Rebellion'. As a consequence, suggestions that the Book of Common Prayer and the Bible should be translated into Cornish were ignored.

Marion Löffler

BIBLE, IN IRISH AND SCOTTISH GAELIC

The vernacular Bible appeared earliest in Wales (CYMRU). The majority of the populations of Ireland (ÉIRE) and Brittany (BREIZH) remained Catholic, and the Latin Bible predominated until recent times; Bible translations, where they existed, did not gain wide currency. Church and state in Scotland (ALBA) actively discouraged the use of SCOTTISH GAELIC Bibles in the HIGHLANDS. A complete MANX Bible was not published until 1775, too late to replace English as the accepted language of Anglican church services, and the Cornish had accepted English as the language of religion by the 17th century.

Ireland

Although PRINTING and the Protestant Reformation were introduced to Ireland (ÉIRE) at the beginning of the 16th century, the Reformation did not succeed outside the Pale, the region in which the English-speaking population was dominant. The bulk of the native Irish population rejected Protestantism as the religion of the English conqueror. In turn, the relatively early Bible translation was never widely used in Ireland.

From the beginning of her reign, Elizabeth I supported the translation of the New Testament into Irish and donated, in 1571, a set of Irish types for the printing of the Bible. The translation of the New Testament, overseen and completed by Uilliam Ó Domhnaill, was completed in 1602. In the following year, 500 copies of *Tiomna Nuadha* (The New Testament). In 1609, Ó Domhnaill published his translation of the Book of Common Prayer, *Leabhar na nUrnaightheadh gComhcoidchiond*. Both translations continued to be used in Ireland and Scotland for a long time. William Bedell (1571–1642), Church of Ireland bishop of Kilmore, was responsible for 'Bedell's Bible', published in 1685. Although this text is considered inferior to Ó Domhnaill's translation, 'Bedell's Bible' was used in Ireland and Scotland until the 1970s.

Financed by Robert Boyle, both the Old and the New Testaments were published together, using Roman typeface, in 1690. This edition, known as *An Bíobla Naomhtha* (The Holy Bible), was seen through the press by the Reverend Robert Kirk (1644–92), minister of Balquhidder and Aberfoyle, and was largely intended for use in Gaelic Scotland. Parts of the Bible were reprinted in 1754, 1799, and 1806. A new translation of the Bible, under way since the end of World War II, was finally brought to fruition with the publication of *An Bíobla Naofa* (The Holy Bible) in 1981.

Scotland

Foirm na n-Urrnuidheadh, a translation of the *Book of Common Order* by Seon Carsuel (John Carswell, †1572), bishop of the Isles, published in Edinburgh (Dùn Èideann) in 1567, is considered the first book to be printed in Scottish Gaelic, although the language is classical Irish. Efforts to produce religious literature were thwarted by the apathy of the clergy and the suspicion with which the Presbyterian Church viewed the largely Catholic and Episcopalian Highlands. By 1673, the Reverend Dugald Campbell of Knapdale had produced a translation of the Old Testament, but it was never published.

Despite the continued efforts of the Reverend James Kirkwood (1650–1709), a supporter of Gaelic-medium education who made several attempts to supply Highland parishes with 'Bedell's Bible' (see the earlier discussion), the hostility of the religious establishment prevented the majority of those Bibles from reaching their destination.

The New Testament was translated by the Reverend James Stuart of Killin, the Reverend James Fraser of Alness, and the Reverend Dùghall Bochanan (Dugald Buchanan, 1716–68), a licensed preacher and outstanding poet. Ten thousand copies of *Tiomnadh Nuadh arn Tighearna* were printed in 1766. However, this version was more an adaptation of the Irish Bible than a new translation into Scottish Gaelic. The translation of the entire Bible was completed in 1801, when it appeared under the title *Leabhraiche an t-Seann Tiomnaidh* with a total print run of 5,000 copies. In 1807, the British and Foreign Bible Society published the Reverend John Smith (1743–1821) of Kilbrandon and Kilchattan's version of the Old Testament together with the New Testament as *Leabhraichan an t-Seann Tiomnaidh agus an Tiomnaidh Nuadh*, also with a print run of 20,000 copies. This version was to exert considerable influence on the development of Scottish Gaelic literacy in the 19th century. Between the beginning of the 19th century and the foundation of the National Bible Society of Scotland (NBSS) in 1861, various slightly different editions were in circulation. In 1911, the NBSS published the first Gaelic Pocket Bible, which became the basis of the most recent revised Scottish Gaelic Bible, published in 1988.

Marion Löffler

BIBLE, ISLE OF MAN
See Manx literature.

BIBLE, IN WELSH

The earliest extant translations of parts of the Bible into Welsh are the medieval texts *Y Bibyl Ynghymraec* and *Gwassanaeth Meir*, which survive in several manuscripts. When English Prayer Books replaced Latin as the language of public worship beginning in 1549, some debate arose over the rôle of Welsh: Some pundits believed the Welsh would be compelled to learn English, and others that the Welsh people would be an easy prey to resurgent Catholicism and a likely source of rebellion. As a result, in 1563 a momentous statute was passed that declared the Bible and Prayer Book should be translated into Welsh and be used thereafter in public worship. This mandate meant that Welsh became the language of religion in Wales (Cymru).

The greatest part of *Y Testament Newydd* (The New Testament) was translated by William Salesbury. Published in 1567, the New Testament fell short of expectations, largely because Salesbury insisted on inflicting on the unsuspecting Welsh his own peculiar brand of orthography. Poorly educated clergymen were hard put to make sense of his bizarre 'Latinisms', and it was left to William Morgan, vicar of Llanrhaeadr-ym-Mochnant, to produce a much more readable and popular version of the whole Bible in 1588. Had not this work been completed, it is unlikely that the Welsh language could have survived.

Morgan's Welsh Bible was a bulky tome, designed to be used in the pulpit. The revised edition prepared by Bishop Richard Parry (1560–1623) and his brother-in-law, Dr John Davies (*c.* 1567–1644) of Mallwyd—the Welsh counterpart of the Authorized Version of the English Bible (1611)—became the basis for the standard literary language of the native tongue.

The most remarkable progress in Bible-reading in the vernacular occurred when the 18th-century evangelists Griffith Jones (1684–1761) of Llanddowror and Thomas Charles (1755–1814) of Bala founded hundreds of Welsh-medium CIRCULATING SCHOOLS and Sunday schools throughout the land in which humble and underprivileged children and adults made considerable sacrifices to learn to read the Scriptures. As a result of these initiatives, Welsh fared much better than Breton, Scottish Gaelic, Irish, and Manx, and the combination of the availability of Welsh Bibles and widespread literacy provided a robust foundation for the golden age of Welsh publishing in the 19th century. The 400th anniversary of the translation of the Bible into Welsh was marked by a successful new translation—*Y Beibl Cymraeg Newydd*—which was published as a companion volume to the 1588 Bible.

Geraint H. Jenkins

BIBRACTE

Bibracte was a Gaulish OPPIDUM that, according to Julius Caesar's *De Bello Gallico* ('Gallic War') 1.23, served as the capital of the Gaulish tribe known as the Aedui. It is located on Mont-Beuvray, which continues to bear the ancient name, near Autun (Romano-Celtic Augustodunum) in Burgundy, southeast France. The name *Bibracte* is a Celtic collective noun based on the root *bibr-* 'beaver'; hence 'place of beavers'.

The oppidum covers 2 km². The northeastern gate is the largest example of a gate in any Celtic oppidum yet excavated. Bibracte was subdivided into several areas given over to specific activities. The northeast and southwest were reserved for artisans and commerce, respectively. The artisans' quarters show evidence of elaborate metallurgy. The internal street plan was dominated by a south-to-west axis oriented toward the summer and winter solstices. The central residential quarter contained many elaborate houses partly imitating the Roman urban house-type, replete with a central open area (*atrium*) and a garden enclosed by a small colonnade. Each quarter seems to have had a cult site or a temple.

Three wells were located within the fortified perimeter of Bibracte. Evidence indicates that they were used for ritual depositions, which implies the presence of the commonly occurring Celtic cult of spring deities (see WATERY DEPOSITIONS).

Pre-Roman COINAGE was found inside the walls. Bibracte was a mint, and a coin mould for casting 25 blanks was found on the site. The name DUMNORIX, which is mentioned in Caesar's *De Bello Gallico,* has been found on one of the coins from Bibracte.

Peter E. Busse

BINIOU AND BOMBARD

Biniou and *bombard* (French *bombarde*) are wind instruments traditionally played together in Breton dance music (see BRETON MUSIC; DANCES). The style of playing is very much like *kan ha diskan* (call-and-response singing), with the biniou sounding continually and the bombard rotating out every second or fourth line.

The bombard is essentially a shawm or oboe—that is, a pipe with a conical bore, a double reed, and finger-holes for changing pitch. Traditional Breton *bombardoù* are probably very close to the original progenitor of the oboe family.

The biniou is the most common Breton BAGPIPE. It is made up of a bag (usually constructed from leather or sheepskin), a drone of cylindrical bore bearing a single reed, and a chanter of conical bore bearing a double reed and finger-holes for playing the melody. The biniou seems to be descended from the medieval bagpipe, but the chanter is very small and produces an extremely high pitch. Iconographic studies suggest that this instrument was adapted to its current form in the 18th or 19th century.

Stephen D. Winick

BITURĪGES

Biturīges was the name of a Gaulish tribe in the vicinity of Berry, France, a region to which they gave their name. Their capital also takes its name from the tribe: Avaricum Biturigum, modern Bourges. The name is composed of *bitu-* 'world' (cf. W. *byd*, OIr. *bith*) and *rīges* 'kings' (cf. OIr. *ríg*); hence 'kings of the world'. According to Livy (*Ab Urbe Condita* 5.34), the Biturīges were the most powerful tribe in Gaul in the 6th century BC. The tribe was subdivided into two groups, the Biturīges Cubi south of the central Loire, and the Biturīges Vivisci around modern

Bordeaux. Their king Ambigatus (Ambicatus) was said to have triggered the Gaulish invasion of Italy. In the 1st century BC, the Biturīges Cubi belonged to the confederation headed by the Aedui, but supported the Arverni in their fight against Julius Caesar.

Peter E. Busse and John T. Koch

BLODEUWEDD

Blodeuwedd (also Blodeuedd) is one of the central characters in the Middle Welsh tale, MATH FAB MATHONWY, also known as the Fourth Branch of the MABINOGI. In this tale, Blodeu(w)edd is created by the magicians GWYDION and Math out of the catkins (Welsh *blodeu*, 'flowers') of the oak and flowers of the broom and meadowsweet to get around the destiny (*tynged*) imposed by ARIANRHOD on her son LLEU Llaw Gyffes—'that he shall never have a wife of the race that is now on this earth'. Blodeu(w)edd's name means either 'flowers' (*blodeu-edd*) or 'flower-features' (*blodeu+ wedd*) and occurs in the extant text in both spellings.

Blodeu(w)edd deceives Lleu into telling her how he might be killed. She passes this information on to her paramour, who succeeds in killing him. As punishment, Blodeu(w)edd is eventually turned into an owl by Gwydion.

The name Blodeu(w)edd is not found in the early WELSH POETRY, although reference is made to Gwydion and Math creating a person from flowers and trees in the poem *Cad Goddau* (The battle of the trees), one of the mythological poems of LLYFR TALIESIN (36.3–7). However, the name is mentioned in a poem entitled *Tydi, dylluan tudwyll* ('You owl, a land's apparition'). In the poem, the poet is speaking to an owl who was once the daughter of a lord of MÔN (Anglesey), but was changed into an owl by Gwydion because of her affair; there is no mention of Lleu.

The story of Blodeuwedd's creation, treachery, and punishment has captured the creative imagination since the rediscovery of the *Mabinogi* in the 19th century. Saunders LEWIS's Welsh-language play *Blodeuwedd* is one important example of the reworking of this theme in recent times; another is Alan Garner's *The Owl Service* in English.

Ian Hughes

BÓAND/BÓINN/BOYNE

Bóand/Bóinn/Boyne is the name of a goddess and of the river that flows from the northern part of Co. Kildare (Contae Chill Dara) into the Irish Sea east of Drogheda, Co. Meath (Droichead Átha, Contae na Mí). The river-name Βουουινδα *Buvinda* is listed in the *Geography* of Ptolemy of Alexandria (*c*. AD 150) and is a Celtic compound, meaning '[she who has] white cow(s)'.

The source of the river Boyne, the Well of Segais, is close to Carbury Hill, Co. Kildare. It was renowned as a font of supernatural knowledge that could be acquired by eating salmon from the river or nuts from the nine hazels surrounding the well. One DINDSHENCHAS tale explains the origins of the river: Segais could be approached only by Nechtan and his three cupbearers. Bóand approached despite this taboo

(GEIS), and three waves burst from the well and disfigured her foot, eye, and hand. She drowned while fleeing toward the sea.

Three burial sites on the summit of Carbury Hill yielded cremations and inhumations along with grave goods dating from as early as the IRON AGE (*c.* 600 BC to *c.* AD 400). Carbury Hill appears in mythology as SÍD NECHTAIN, the otherworldly residence of Bóand's consort Nechtan. Bóand's own dwelling was BRUG NA BÓINNE, the archaeological complex that includes the megalithic tombs of Newgrange, Knowth, and Dowth (DUBHADH).

The river Boyne was a significant feature in a highly fertile region of the Irish landscape, particularly in relation to the east midland kingdom of Brega. Notes in the 9th-century Book of ARMAGH suggest that the Boyne was navigable to Áth Truimm (Trim, Co. Meath). An early poem proclaims, 'woe to the ULAID if they be beyond the Boyne', suggesting that the Boyne figured as the southern limit of Ulster until the 7th century.

Edel Bhreathnach

BODB

Bodb (later Badb, pl. Badba), 'scald-crow', was a designation for a supernatural female being associated with battle and slaughter in early IRISH LITERATURE. There are references to the Badb, a *badb,* and several *badba*; thus the designation may be both a proper name and a generic term for a supernatural battle creature. The Badb is sometimes identified with other supernatural women from early Irish narratives—the MORRÍGAN, (the) Nemain, Bé Néit (Woman of battle), or MACHA. At other times she is mentioned together with one or more of them as separate personalities.

The Badb appears in different forms in the tales, as both human and animal. Her figure may be marked by asymmetry, the colours associated with her being red and pallor. The battle creatures called *badba* are likewise often described as being pale and their mouths as red. They are said to hover above a battlefield, where their shouts either incite or terrify the warriors. Bleeding *badba* with ropes around their necks are described in TOGAIL BRUIDNE DA DERGA (in the version in LEBOR NA HUIDRE). The Badb often functions as a harbinger of death by battle; thus she may appear as a so-called 'washer at the ford' or as an ominous visitor to a BRUIDEN (hostel), where she prophesies evil (*Bruiden Da Choga*). She may incite people to fight or terrify them, in her appearance as a single woman, in the company of her 'sisters' Bé Néit and Nemain, and as a group (*badba*) together with similar battle creatures. The incitement is done in two ways: either by nonverbal cries or by a verbal message. When the aim is to inspire fear, nonverbal shrieks are uttered. The Badb (equated with the Morrígan) announces the victory in battle and prophesies the end of the world (CATH MAIGE TUIRED §§166–7). In general, the appearance of the Badb is an evil omen.

Bodb is also the name of a male supernatural being: Bodb Derg from Síd ar Femin, king of the *síde* of Munster (MUMU), who is famous for his knowledge (*Aislinge Oengusa*). Bodb Derg is, moreover, a supernatural protector of Ireland (ÉRIU), together with the Morrígan, Midir, and OENGUS MAC IND ÓC (*Airne Fíngein* §9).

Brythonic includes numerous examples of the cognate word, Welsh *boddw* < Celtic **bodwo-*, as a high-status name element. The earliest occurs on coinage of the British Iron Age with the legend BODVOC[- < Celtic **Boduācos*. Early medieval examples include Archaic Welsh *Boduan* in the 7th- or early-8th-century charters appended to the Life of St Cadoc, corresponding to Old Breton *Boduuan/Bodguan* in the Cartulary of Redon, and St *Elbodug* (Elfoddw) mentioned in *Annales Cambriae* at years 768 and 809. Note that Bran/Brân 'crow' also occurs as a man's name in mythological tales in both Irish and Welsh. Such names probably imply Brythonic traditions not merely of naming men after the crow, but rather wider supernatural associations along the lines of those better attested in Irish literature as described earlier.

Jacqueline Borsje

BODHRÁN

Bodhrán designates a frame-drum that is approximately 60 cm (2 feet) in diameter and constructed of a cured and scraped goatskin stretched over a wooden rim, played with a wooden stick. In the south and west of Ireland (Éire), the *bodhrán* was particularly associated with the 'wren-boys' on St Stephen's day. It was especially popular as part of traditional dance music in north Connacht. Largely due to Seán Ó Riada and the Ceoltóirí Chualann (1959–69), the *bodhrán* was adopted as the percussion instrument of the traditional music revival of the 1960s and 1970s (see dances; Irish music).

William J. Mahon

BONONIA/BOLOGNA

Celtic-speaking groups predominated in the north Italian town of Bononia (modern Bologna) in the later pre-Roman period. Literary sources are limited to a few lines from Livy (33.37.4, 37.57.7, 39.2.5–6), Velleius Paterculus (1.15.2), and Servius (*Ad Aeneid* 10.198.5). The earlier, Etruscan name of the settlement was *Felsina*; it was still used during the period of the supremacy of the Celtic tribe the Boii. *Bononia* became the Roman name of the colony after its conquest. The latter is possibly a Celtic name, related to the second element of *Vindobonā* (modern Vienna).

The urban archaeology of Bononia during the Celtic period is limited to funerary artefacts. Bononia's Celtic tombs were uncovered during the 1800s in the western part of the city, a single necropolis whose full size is unknown. Seventy-seven graves in Bononia are datable to the period of the dominance of the Boii. Further inhumation tombs lacked any surviving artefacts and, therefore, are not easily assigned to a particular culture.

Inhumation was the most common type of burial in the Boian period. Late Hallstatt and Early La Tène material, dating from the 5th century BC, was found in three excavated areas of the Certosa necropolis and in two Arnoaldi tombs. This material includes several iron short swords with antenna-type hilts of the typical western Hallstatt C type traceable to the end of the 7th century BC (see sword).

These finds indicate contacts with the transalpine world in the era preceding the historically attested migrations of Gauls into northern Italy in the 4th century BC (see TRANSALPINE GAUL). The tombs with antenna-type swords indicate the presence of transalpine warriors in the 7th to 6th centuries BC at Felsina. Fourteen of the seventy-seven 'Boian' graves are identifiable as those of warriors on the basis of iron swords of La Tène type. Several particularly rich sets of burial goods, including bronze helmets and gold crowns, indicate the presence of a military élite. The Felsina/Bologna burials include tombs of both male and female natives of Etruscan-Italic origin. A dual ethnicity, made up of Etruscans and Celts, is apparent.

On the whole, the burial grounds of the Gaulish period do not give the impression of an extensive urban settlement by the Boii, as might have been expected given the historical importance of this group. Excavations indicate the existence of a territory structured around agricultural or commercially orientated centres and of power based on control of routes. The culturally mixed communities' materials imply the presence of linguistically distinct Etruscans, Ligurians, Umbrians, and Celts coexisting together.

Daniele Vitali

BOTORRITA

Botorrita is significant as the site where the longest texts in any ancient Celtic language yet discovered were located. These INSCRIPTIONS, which are found on bronze tablets, are known as Botorrita I, II, and III. Botorrita I and III are in the CELTIBERIAN language. Botorrita II is written in Latin and uses the Roman alphabet.

The present-day town of Botorrita is approximately 20 km southwest of the city of Zaragoza in northern Spain. In Roman times, the nearby Celtiberian town was called Contrebia Belaisca. Coins with legends in the Iberian script reading *PelaisKom* /belaiskom/ were minted there (the capital P represents a symbol that represents two distinct sounds, /p/ or /b/; K represents /k/ or /g/).

Botorrita I

The Botorrita I inscription is in the Celtiberian language, written in the Iberian SCRIPT on both sides of a bronze tablet (*c.* 40 × 10 cm). It is considered the most important document in Celtiberian.

The text on side A fills eleven lines. In nine lines, side B lists fourteen men designated by the repeated word *Pintis* (possibly 'binder'), who may be acting as officials or witnesses. The text is thought to be legal in character, but has not been fully interpreted. *ToKoiT-* and *sarniKio-*, key words that appear in the first line, have been understood as divine names, as well as words denoting a locality.

There is no secure dating for Botorrita I, but sometime early in the 1st century BC would seem likely in view of the secure dating established for Botorrita II (discussed next). A date of the early or mid-1st century BC is also consistent with the fact the Contrebia Belaisca was destroyed about the middle of that century.

Botorrita II

This Latin inscription discusses the rights of various localities over the building of a canal through the land of the Sosinestani; the neighbouring Allauonenses seem to have objected. In addition to the indigenous names of the Celtiberian magistrates and the Iberian representatives, the inscription contains the names of Roman officials, through which it can be securely dated to mid-May 87 BC.

Botorrita III

On display in the museum in Zaragoza, this Celtiberian inscription is the longest extant inscription in any ancient Celtic language, written in the Iberian script on one side of a bronze tablet (c. 73 × 52 cm). Due to encrustation by oxidized bronze, the greater part of the text can now be read only with the help of X-rays.

Botorrita III has two 'headlines' set apart in larger writing, under which a long list of personal names is arranged in four columns. The title lines have not yet been interpreted. The list itself gives the names of men and women, predominantly in Celtiberian name formulae—that is, an individual name and a family name, sometimes followed by the father's or mother's name. Some persons, however, have Roman, Greek, or Iberian names, which, like the names of Botorrita II, point to the mixed population of Contrebia Belaisca in Roman times. The list also uses the kinship terms *Kentis /gentis/* 'son' or 'child', and *TuaTer- /duater/* 'daughter'.

Botorrita III has confirmed and complemented our understanding of some features of the Celtiberian language—for example, verbal endings that derive from the Indo-European 'middle' or 'mediopassive' voice. Neither active nor passive, in these forms the subject underwent the action of the verb. One such form is the third person plural past tense ending in *auzanto*. The same verb occurs with its third person singular active present tense ending as *auzeti* in Botorrita I.

Dagmar Wodtko

BOUDĪCA

Boudīca or Boudicca († AD 60/61) was queen of the ICENI in what is now East Anglia, ENGLAND. She succeeded her husband Prāstotagos (variant Prasutagos) and led a highly destructive, but ultimately unsuccessful, war of resistance against the Roman occupation.

Under heavy taxation during the transitional period between independence and integration into the empire, the Iceni destroyed Colchester, London, and Verulamion, with great slaughters of the Romano-British civilian population. Afterward, Roman forces regrouped and devastated Boudīca's numerically superior army in a single battle. Boudīca died soon thereafter. A harsh punitive campaign directed at both rebel and neutral tribes resulted in famine in this area.

The Roman documentary evidence for Boudīca is relatively plentiful. The most valuable author on the subject is Tacitus, writing about two generations later. His information is probably derived from his father-in-law Agricola, who had been governor of Britain in the period AD 78–85. The figure of the Amazonian barbarian queen, fearsome yet vulnerable, captured the Roman imagination. Their accounts of Boudīca are some of the most vivid ancient descriptions of people from the Celtic world. Cassius Dio (*Roman History* 62) wrote dramatically of her:

> [A] British woman of royal lineage and an uncommonly intelligent woman was the person who was most instrumental in inciting the natives and convincing them to fight the Romans, who was thought fit to be their commander, and who directed the campaigns of the entire war . . .
>
> She was huge of body, with a horrific expression and a harsh voice. A huge mass of bright red hair descended to the swell of her hips; she wore a large torc of twisted gold, and a tunic of many colours over which there was a thick cape fastened by a brooch. Then she grasped a spear to strike fear into all who watched her.
>
> . . . After that, she used a type of augury, releasing a hare from the folds of her garment. Because it ran off in what [the Britons] considered to be the auspicious direction, the whole horde roared its approval. Raising her hand to the sky, Boudīca said: 'I thank you, [goddess] ANDRASTA, and call out to you as one woman to another . . . I implore and pray to you for victory and to maintain life and freedom against arrogant, unjust, insatiable, and profane men.

The post-Roman writer Gildas viewed Boudīca's revolt negatively, not even using her name. She is not mentioned in later medieval histories. Since the 19th century she has been anachronistically identified as English on a geographic basis.

The name *Boudīca* is Celtic and means 'victorious woman'. There is no authoritative basis for the common modern variant spelling *Boadicea*. *Boudīca* corresponds to the Old Breton man's name *Budic*, the Welsh name *Buddug*, the Middle Welsh adjective *buδic,* and the Old Irish *buadach* 'triumphant'.

John T. Koch

BRÂN FAB LLŶR/BENDIGEIDFRAN

Brân fab Llŷr/Bendigeidfran (Brân the Blessed) is the central character of the Second Branch of the MABINOGI, which traditionally bears the name of his sister, BRANWEN ferch Lŷr.

Bendigeidfran in the Mabinogi

In the tale, the giant Brân is king of BRITAIN, holding the crown of London (Welsh Llundain) in the remote mythological past. Brân's behaviour throughout *Branwen* is consistently honourable and heroic but invariably reactive. Brân is approached unexpectedly by Matholwch, king of Ireland (ÉRIU), who seeks to marry Branwen, but mistreats her after the marriage. Brân reacts by mustering an expedition to Ireland. We are told that the Irish Sea was not yet a sea, but two rivers that Brân waded across. He also serves as a bridge across the river 'Llinon' (Shannon or Liffey).

The battle with the Irish is cataclysmic; Brân succeeds in annihilating them and rescuing his sister. He tells his surviving followers to decapitate him and after a time to bury his head in London. The following eighty-seven-year otherworldly FEAST is referred to in the tale by the peculiar traditional name *yspyδawt urδawl benn* (hospitality of the noble head), during which Brân's head remains uncorrupted and as good a companion as ever. At the opening of the Third Branch (MANAWYDAN), Brân's head is interred as a talisman against the incursion of a foreign *gormes* (oppressor, invader, plague).

In *Branwen*, TALIESIN is named as one of the seven who returned from Ireland with Brân's head. In the poem *Kadeir Talyessin* (Taliesin's [bardic] chair) in LLYFR TALIESIN, allusions are made to two episodes in Brân's story that interestingly use unusual key words also found in *Branwen*.

Bendigeidfran in the Triads

Trioedd Ynys Prydein (TYP) no. 37, *Tri Matkuð Ynys Prydein* (Three auspicious concealments of the Island of Britain), refers to the burial of Brân's head. This triad brackets Brân's interment with the similar account (which occurs in HISTORIA BRITTONUM §44) of the talismanic burial of the 5th-century military leader Gwerthefyr, whose coastal burial had the power of preventing the return of the Saxons to Britain. The 3rd-century fort of Brancaster on the coast of Norfolk, ENGLAND, bore the ancient name *Branodūnum,* meaning 'the fort of Brân'.

Other Associations

The name *Brân* is found a number of times elsewhere in Welsh and Celtic tradition, and it is not always clear to what extent these characters are related. For example, Bran mac Febail, the protagonist of the Old Irish tale IMMRAM BRAIN, shares a number of similarities with the Welsh Brân that may betoken a common source—the two are closely connected to the similarly named figures Manawydan and MANANNÁN, but the surviving stories are quite different.

In his HISTORIA REGUM BRITANNIAE (3.1–10), GEOFFREY OF MONMOUTH conflated the historical BRENNOS OF THE SENONES, conqueror of ROME, with Brân Hen map Dumngual Moilmut of the Old Welsh GENEALOGIES to create an ancient king, Brennius son of Dumwallus Molmutius. BRENNOS OF THE PRAUSI bears a greater resemblance to Brân. As well as having a similar name, he led a massive foreign invasion (into Greece) in which almost all of his followers were killed; was wounded there, and then (according to Diodorus Siculus 22.9) asked his men to kill him; his body was believed to be the source of a talismanic deposition that protected Tolosa (Toulouse) in southwest GAUL from foreign invaders (Strabo 5.1.12–13).

The Name

Welsh *brân* means 'crow', deriving from PROTO-CELTIC **branos*. Crows have numerous poetic and supernatural associations throughout Celtic tradition. For example, the crow is frequently found in descriptions of battlefield carnage; the mention of crows is enough to imply fallen warriors without any explanation. Moreover, and no doubt linked to the first tradition, the Irish war-goddess BODB often appears as a crow.

John T. Koch

BRANWEN FERCH LŶR

Branwen ferch Lŷr (Branwen daughter of Llŷr) is the name commonly given to the second branch of the MABINOGI since Lady Charlotte Guest's 19th-century translation. In this story, the giant Bendigeidfran (or BRÂN) is king of BRITAIN. His sister, Branwen (a corruption, perhaps, of Bronwen, 'fair or white breast', influenced by the name of her brother Brân), marries Matholwch, king of Ireland (ÉRIU). Following the birth of a son, Gwern, Branwen is punished by the Irish because of her brother Efnisien's insult to Matholwch—she is forced to cook in the kitchen and to accept being hit by the butcher each day. She sends a starling with a letter to her brother Bendigeidfran, who crosses to Ireland to rescue her. In the ensuing battle, the boy Gwern is thrown into the fire by Efnisien and all are destroyed apart from Branwen and seven of her compatriots. Branwen's heart breaks, and she is buried beside the river Alaw in Anglesey (MÔN).

An Irish influence on this branch is evident. It has also been suggested that the tale may represent a version of a raid on the OTHERWORLD (see also ANNWN), comparable to that described in the poem PREIDDIAU ANNWFN (The spoils of Annwfn) in the Book of Taliesin (LLYFR TALIESIN). The nature of insult and compensation is a central theme, and we are shown how revenge leads to destruction.

Sioned Davies

BREIZH (BRITTANY)

Breizh (English Brittany, French Bretagne, Welsh Llydaw) is a Celtic country within present-day France. The name *Brittany* is derived from Romano-British *Brit(t)annia* (see BRITAIN). Welsh *Llydaw* is cognate with Old Breton *Letau*, Latinized as *Letavia*, meaning 'broad land, continent'. Its area is 34,140 km^2 (slightly larger than the state of Maryland), and its population in 2009 was 4,578,197. There are no official statistics regarding the BRETON-speaking population in Brittany. Just before World War I, approximately 1,300,000 people used Breton regularly; today, a general figure of 250,000 habitual users of Breton is widely accepted.

The historical province of Brittany is divided into five modern *départements*. Four of these form the modern *région* of Bretagne: Aodoù-an-Arvor (Côtes-d'Armor), Il-ha-Gwilen (Ille-et-Vilaine), Morbihan, and Penn-ar-Bed (Finistère). The fifth, Liger-Atlantel (Loire Atlantique), is in the *région* of Pays-de-la-Loire. The eleven medieval dioceses of Brittany also remain significant. The five French-speaking dioceses are Naoned (Pays de Nantes), Roazhon (Pays de Rennes), Sant-Brieg (Pays de Saint-Brieuc), Sant Malo (Pays de Saint-Malo), and Dol (Pays de Dol). Some Breton is also spoken in Sant-Brieg. The four Breton-speaking dioceses are Kernev (Cornouaille), Gwened (Vannes), Leon (Léon), and Treger (French Trégor). The Breton-speaking area in the west is known as Breizh-Izel (French Basse-Bretagne, English Lower Brittany), and the Galo-speaking area in the east is called Breizh-Uhel (French Haute-Bretagne, English Upper Brittany).

Although overlaying a GAULISH substrate, the distinct Celtic character of Brittany originated on the island of Britain. Distinctive features of the language and culture of Brittany (part of the region of ARMORICA in the IRON AGE and Roman times) were

Départements and principal towns of present-day Brittany. (Map by Antone Minard)

brought across the channel in the early Middle Ages (see BRETON MIGRATIONS). The peninsula experienced political independence or autonomy from the 840s, when NOMINOË broke away from the Frankish Empire, until the French Revolution in 1789, even though Brittany was formally incorporated into France in 1536.

In 1341, a civil war broke out between the heirs of Duke John III (r. 1312–41). This War of the Breton Succession became a part of the larger Hundred Years' War between ENGLAND and France, with England on the winning side. The last ruler of an independent Brittany was Anna Vreizh (r. 1488–1514).

Brittany has historically been an important centre of fishing. Nantes was the centre of the French maritime empire, and Bretons made up a substantial proportion of French sailors. Brittany is also an important dairy region, famous for its butter since the Middle Ages.

The coming of the railroads and modern transportation decreased Brittany's relative isolation, which ultimately had a negative effect on the language and culture of Lower Brittany. With increased communication, it became easier for the authorities to enforce laws against the use of Breton, which was seen as dangerous and potentially seditious. Consequently, the use of the language was suppressed (see EDUCATION). Until recently, it was believed that Bretons collaborated disproportionately with the Nazi occupiers in World War II. This belief, based on the mistaken assumption that Breton separatists and autonomists were willing to use any means to secure an independent Brittany, is unfounded.

Contemporary Brittany is experiencing a revival of its culture and language, although the negative attitudes displayed toward Bretons in the 20th century also persist strongly (see LANGUAGE [REVIVAL]; BRETON MUSIC).

Antone Minard

BRENDAN, ST

St Brendan (Old Irish Brénann) is the name of two recorded early Irish saints.

1. Brendan of Cluain Ferta (Clonfert, Co. Galway/Contae na Gaillimhe), toward the middle of the 6th century, was active as a monastic founder in eastern CONNACHT. Later in the 8th century he became the eponymous traveller in the monastic allegory the NAVIGATIO SANCTI BRENDANI; based on this source, he has remained in memory as 'Brendan the navigator' (see also VOYAGE LITERATURE).
2. Brendan of Birr (Co. Offaly/Contae Uíbh Fhailí) was a monk and founder of the monastery of Birr, probably prior to the end of the 6th century.

Thomas O'Loughlin

BRENNOS (OF THE PRAUSI OR TOLISTOBOGII)

Brennos (of the Prausi or Tolistobogii) led an army of Gauls against Macedonia and Greece in 280–79 BC. Some sources report that he was the leader of the Tolistobogii, a tribe that later crossed over into Asia Minor (see GALATIA). According to Strabo, however, Brennos belonged to the Prausi. The Balkan offensives of two other bands of Celts occurred simultaneously. That led by Kerethrios was directed in the east against the territory of the Triballi and Thrace. That of Bolgios/Belgios (see BELGAE) burst out into Illyria in the west and Macedonia (Pausanias 10.19.5–12). At the beginning of 279 BC, Bolgios's army annihilated the detachment of the young Macedonian ruler Ptolemy Keraunos (r. 281–79 BC), opening the way into Greece for Brennos. According to Pausanias, the army Brennos had assembled to invade Greece comprised 152,000 infantry and 20,400 cavalry.

In the autumn of 279 BC, Brennos reached and passed the strategic defile at Thermopylae, overcoming the defensive stand of the Greeks. Backed by a force of 65,000 men, he attacked Delphi (Justin, *Epitome of the Philippic Histories* 24.7.9). According to classical sources, the Delphic sanctuary was saved by Apollo.

See also BRÂN FAB LLŶR.

Monica Chiabà

BRENNOS (OF THE SENONES)

Brennos (of the Senones) was a Gaulish leader who marched at the head of assembled Celtic warbands *c.* 390 BC, first against the Etruscan city of Clusium (modern Chiusi), and then against ROME. Brennos was known as the *regulus* (prince) of the Gaulish tribe Senones, the last Celtic tribe to arrive in what is now Italy. He routed the Roman army eleven miles from Rome, near the confluence of the river Allia and the Tiber, and occupied the city. After a seven-month siege, the Romans and the Gauls reached an agreement. In a meeting with the military tribune Quintus Sulpicius, the leader of the Gauls set a ransom that the Romans were obliged to pay to free the city. When the gold was weighed, the tribune Quintus Sulpicius accused the Gauls of using counterfeit weights. Brennos, with a disdainful gesture, threw his own sword on the scale together with the 'rigged' weights, declaiming the now proverbial phrase, *vae victis* 'woe to the vanquished'.

Regarding the name Brennos, GEOFFREY OF MONMOUTH makes the conqueror of Rome a Briton named *Brennius*. In the Welsh versions of Geoffrey's Latin HISTORIA REGUM BRITANNIAE ('The History of the Kings of Britain'), the name is BRÂN. Welsh *Brân* could be related to Gaulish *Brennos*, but not its exact equivalent.

Monica Chiabà

BRETHA NEMED

Bretha Nemed (Judgements of privileged persons) is an 8th-century Irish collection of LAW TEXTS from Munster (MUMU) known from other sources that quote them. The *Bretha Nemed* collection appears to be a Munster law-book comparable to the *Senchas Már*, a law-book compiled in the part of Ireland (ÉRIU) ruled by the Uí NÉILL and their allies, the Connachta and the Airgialla. It would, however, be premature to claim that the *Bretha Nemed* is simply the Munster counterpart of the *Senchas Már*. Although further texts have been ascribed to the *Bretha Nemed*, notably *Cóic Conara Fugill* and *Cáin Fhuithirbe*, the evidence so far advanced is slender. There is nothing corresponding to the Introduction to the *Senchas Már* to show that this work is a deliberate compilation of a law-book rather than an accumulation of texts belonging to the same tradition and perhaps the same legal school. Glosses to the *Senchas Már* have been used to show which tracts—both surviving and lost texts—belonged to the law-book, but nothing similar is available for the *Bretha Nemed*. It is unlikely that the *Bretha Nemed* ever attained the same width of coverage as the *Senchas Már*. On the contrary, much of what survives suggests that the two collections are characterized by considerable differences.

Regarding the text's name, the second element *nemed* (gen. pl.) is the same as the Celtic word NEMETON, which is found in Old Celtic place-names in BRITAIN and on the Continent for pre-Christian ritual sites, these having been places of special status and privilege.

T. M. Charles-Edwards

BRETON DIALECTS

Breton Dialects or Breton Languages?

One of the distinctive features of the BRETON language has been a fairly extreme differentiation into dialects, although the Breton-speaking zone of Lower Brittany

The chief Breton dialect areas and their boundaries, the eastern limit of Breton speech, and the Kemper–Gwengamp Corridor. (Map by Antone Minard)

(Breizh-Izel) is not broken up into detached pockets, as is the case with Irish. No major linguistic frontier can be identified in vocabulary or grammar. Breton is, therefore, identified as a single unified language.

The four Breton-speaking bishoprics still represent the main recognizable dialects. The dialectal variety is most prominent on the phonological level—in other words, how the regional varieties of the language sound. It is difficult for untrained speakers from Kernev, Leon, and Treger in the northwest (KLT for short) to understand speakers of Gwened (Vannes) in the southeast, where words are accented on the final syllable rather than the second-to-last syllable (as in Welsh).

Linguistic Geography: Dialect Boundaries and Continua

At opposite ends of Brittany, in Leon in the northwest and eastern Bro-Wened in the east, the language has remained markedly old-fashioned. In the central dialect corridor, spoken Breton has undergone innovations leading to an accelerated evolution overall. Sounds or whole syllables have been weakened and lost, and simplification of the grammar has occurred.

Breton has borrowed words on a large scale, mainly from French. The vocabulary (lexicon) does not differ greatly from one dialect to the other, but it is convenient to remember that the four traditional dialects of the northwest differ by the way one asks 'when?': *peur* in Leon, *pegoulz* in Treger, *pevare* and its variants in Kernev, and *pedamzer* in the sub-dialect of Goueloù (Goëlo, east of Treger in the north).

A Shared Grammar with Variations in Pronunciation

In many instances, what appear on the surface to be grammatical differences are essentially differences in pronunciation. For example, the first and third person plural of the present tense of the verb are -*amp* and -*ant* in Gwenedeg (vannetais), but -*omp* and -*ont* elsewhere: *skrivomp / skrivamp,* 'we write'. The archaic conditional (subjunctive) in -*h*- is maintained in Gwenedeg, but is pronounced -*f*- elsewhere: *vefe / vehe* 'she/he would be'. The third person plural of the conjugated prepositions ends in -*o* in the west and -*e* in the east (*ganto/gante* 'with them'). *Ma* 'my' occurs with its first consonant mutated in Leon, pronounced *va*.

Syntax and the Verb "To Be"

The complicated paradigm of the verb 'to be' differs fundamentally between dialects. For example, the locative form 'to be (at)' is fully conjugated in the west in the present tense, whereas the dialects of the east employ it only in the third person (sing. *emañ*, pl. *emaout*). In the imperfect tense (used for statements of habitual states or actions in the past, like English 'used to be'), special place forms of 'be' occur only in Leon: *e gêr edo* 'she/he was at home'.

One of the characteristic features of Breton syntax is that the affirmative sentence may be reworded so as to begin with any of the principal elements—subject or object, adverb, or verb, as in *hiziv eo glas an oabl* 'today the sky is blue', *bez' eo glas an oabl hiziv* 'the sky is blue today'.

Dialect Variation in Breton Vowels

A common plural ending -*ion* (often used for words denoting groups of people) is -*ien* in KLT and -*ion* in Gwenedeg. The reduction of diphthongs to simple vowels is a characteristic of the central dialects (Kernev and Treger). Middle Breton *ae* is preserved as [ea] in Leon: *leaz* 'milk', elsewhere pronounced as the open simple vowel [ɛ] (similar to English *says* [sɛːz]); thus *laezh* [lɛːz], Leon *er meaz* versus *ar maez* [ar mɛːz] 'outside'. In these words, Bro-Wened has a closed [ia]: *liah, er miaz*.

The diphthong spelled *ao* is in the same way a full diphthong to [aw] (as in English *cow*) in Leon and [ow] in Gwened, as found in the word *taol* 'table'. The dominant pronunciation of this group elsewhere is [ʌ] (similar to British English *law*), although the diphthong is retained in final position in monosyllables: *glav* [glaw] 'rain'. In all regional varieties of Breton, unaccented vowels are often neutralized, turned into the schwa [ə]. The contraction of common prepositions and adverbs also occurs regularly in these regions: *e-barzh* becomes *ba* 'in', *abalamour* becomes *blam* 'because of'.

Dialect Variation in Breton Consonants

The Old Breton dental fricative [θ] (as in English *thin*) has resulted in a [z] in KLT but an [h] (stronger than the English sound) in Gwenedeg. The spelling *zh* is used for a unified orthography: Thus *kazh* 'cat' is never pronounced [kaž] (like the *s* in *measure*), but rather [kaz] or [kah] depending on the dialect.

Old Breton [ð] (as in English *then*) survives only in Leon, preserved as [z]: *menez* 'mountain' (Welsh *mynydd*). Old Breton [w] has also developed in several different ways. In the west of the Breton-speaking area, this phoneme has turned into [v] in the initial position or between vowels: *avel* [a:vəl] 'wind'. The dialects of Treger and Gwened have kept [w] (the latter using its front variant [y]): *awel* /awe:l/.

Palatalization of consonants is another feature that makes the dialects sound strikingly different. In the northwestern area, west of a line from Kemper to Gwengamp, consonants are very rarely palatalized, but in the southeast it constitutes a relevant feature, particularly in central Bro-Wened. This phenomenon affects [k] and [g], which evolve before close vowels to [tʃ] (as in English *church*) and [dž] (as English George). In Bro-Wened, *s* is replaced by a [ʃ] (as in English *shade*) when it precedes a group of consonants. Spelling does not reflect this tendency.

A secondary lenition affects the fricative sounds /s, ʃ, f/, changing them to /z, ž, v/. These sounds did not mutate in Old and Middle Breton, but by analogy have come to show variation in the same situations where the other consonants undergo lenition—for example, *sac'h, ar zac'h* 'bag', 'the bag'; *chadenn* /ʃa:dən/, *da jadenn* / də ža:dən/ 'chain, your chain'; *fest, ur vest* 'party, a party'. The phenomenon is found only in the westernmost parts of Bro-Wened.

Spelling

Owing to the divergence of pronunciation, Breton has encountered difficulty in establishing a unified orthography after that of Middle Breton was abandoned in the mid-17th century, following the publication of the grammar of Père Maunoir in 1659. Consequently, two primary written standards have coexisted—one based on the Leon dialect, the other based on Gwenedeg.

Lukian Kergoat

BRETON LANGUAGE

Brittany (Breizh) has been home to a distinctive Celtic language since ancient times. Gaulish was supplanted by Breton in the early Middle Ages. The successively more ancient ancestors of Breton are discussed in the Brythonic, Celtic languages, and Indo-European entries. See also Breton migrations and Armorica.

Old Breton

It becomes possible to distinguish Breton and Cornish from Welsh in the 8th century, when innovations arise in Welsh to differentiate it from the other two languages. For example, the Old Breton name *Conoc* (< Celtic *Kunākos* 'hound-like'),

Upper and Lower Brittany and the eastern limit of Breton-speaking areas in recent times. (Map by Antone Minard)

pronounced /konōg/, is identical in spelling in Wales in the 8th century. By *c.* 800, the vowel *o* had become /ə/ in Welsh (schwa, now spelled *y*) when unstressed and *au* when stressed, and a distinctively Old Welsh spelling *Cinauc* (/kənaug/, Modern *Cynog*) arose. Breton glosses (see Breton literature, beginnings to *c.* 1900) and proper names survive from the Old Breton period, up to *c.* 1100.

Sources for proper names comprise mainly saints' lives, inscriptions, and charters (see charter tradition). As seen from the charters, personal names in use in Brittany included Biblical Frankish (Germanic) and Latin names; most, however, are Celtic in origin and can be compared with Welsh, Cornish, and even Gaulish and Gaelic forms—for example, *Cunuual* [cf. Welsh *Cynwal*, Irish *Conall*] and *Uuethenoc* [cf. Welsh *gweithenog*, Old Irish *fechtnach* 'bellicose']. Old Breton Iudic-hael survives as the surname spelled variously *Yezekel* and *Gicquel*, the source of the English *Jekyll*.

Middle Breton

Before 1400, the evidence for the Breton language is limited to isolated proper names. Literary Middle Breton is distinct from Old Breton in having sustained substantial influence from French in vocabulary, spelling, and the sound system. A standardized language appears in the 14th and 15th centuries, and more completely in the 16th century (see Breton literature, beginnings to *c.* 1900).

Books were printed in Middle Breton in the 16th and 17th centuries, showing that the standard language was accepted and understood by a significant literate minority. Verse regularly shows internal rhymes in schemes comparable to the *llusg* subtype of Welsh CYNGHANEDD. These features always occur together and must reflect the system of learning writing and poetic composition in Breton at the time. Texts survive with internal rhymes and in popular songs down into the 20th century.

Initial mutations, which had been an essential grammatical feature of all the Celtic languages from at least as early as the 6th century, were not revealed in Middle Breton spelling as they are in the modern language. The final nasal labial spirant (pronounced like strongly nasal /v/) was spelled *-ff*, as in 'first': Old Breton *cintam*, Middle Breton *quentaff*, Modern *kentañ* (cf. Welsh *cyntaf*).

Early Modern Breton

After 1659, the initial lenition or soft mutation (*t* > *d*, for example) comes to be written. Formerly medieval and standardized, the language became dialectal, written according to general principles rather than by following detailed rules. No longer used in an official or administrative capacity, Breton was restricted primarily to the community level.

Modern Breton

For details of regional varieties of spoken Breton in recent times, see BRETON DIALECTS.

The literature of the period from the 19th to the 21st centuries dwarfs the entire Old and Middle Breton corpus, despite the fact that the use of Breton was often strongly discouraged. The social stigma attached to Breton persists. Even today, Breton is alone among the living Celtic languages in that it has no official status.

To date, four main writing systems have been proposed, all of which are in use today to one degree or another. KLT, which stands for Kernev–Leon–Treger (1908), was the first of these, representing the three closest dialects. A Gwenedeg writer, Xavier de Langlais, proposed some emendations in 1936 to include Gwenedeg in the KLT system—most notably the digraph <zh>, which represented the /z/ sound in KLT and the /h/ sound in Gwenedeg. The *Peurunvan* or 'Unified' system followed in 1941, sometimes known as 'Zedachek' (*zh*-ish), as it kept the <zh> character. A written distinction was created between the homophonous nouns and adjectives, where the voiced consonants would be used for nouns, and the unvoiced consonants for adjectives; thus *mad*, '(the) good' (n.) versus *mat* 'good' (adj.). Both variants would be pronounced /mat/ alone, and /mad/ before a following vowel within a phrase. In 1955, the KLT system was modified again to create the *Orthographe Universitaire* 'University Orthography'. An *etrerannyezel* 'interdialectal' system was also proposed, but a separate system continues to be used for Gwenedeg.

Nearly all of today's approximately 250,000 Breton speakers are bilingual in French (see BREIZH). The median age of Breton speakers is relatively high; fewer people are learning the language as children now than in previous generations, though efforts are being made to reinvigorate the language (see LANGUAGE [REVIVAL] MOVEMENTS IN THE CELTIC COUNTRIES).

†Gwenaël Le Duc, Antone Minard, and John T. Koch

BRETON LAYS

The word 'lay' (French and Old French *lai*) has come to be virtually synonymous with 'ballad' (see BALLADS), but in the context of medieval literature it refers to a verse narrative with strong roots in oral tradition. The word itself is presumed to be of Breton origin, although no such Breton word is attested; compare Old Irish *laíd*, f., 'poem, lay, metrical composition, song'.

The best-known composer of these *lais* is Marie de France, a 12th-century Anglo-Norman writer. Little is known about Marie. She states that her sources were Breton and that she merely translated and rhymed them. Whether or not Marie herself spoke Breton, her debt to Breton sources is clear. One lay, *Laustic*, takes its name from the French definite article *l'* 'the' plus the Breton *eostig* 'nightingale', which Marie herself translates as *russignol* (Modern French *rossignol* 'nightingale') and *nihtegale*.

The lays themselves survive in several manuscripts. Their subjects include a mixture of themes dealing with courtly love, folk-tales, and ARTHURIAN Romance. Marie's work does not show any influence from her near-contemporary CHRÉTIEN DE TROYES. Marie wrote one Arthurian lay, *Lanval*, as well as *Chevrefoil* (Honeysuckle), in which Tristram and the wife of King Mark of Cornwall (KERNOW) arrange a tryst (see TRISTAN AND ISOLT). Many other lays incorporate motifs and themes that have close parallels in early Irish or Welsh literature; compare, for example, the chess game in *Eliduc* with the FIDCHELL games in IRISH LITERATURE and the *gwyddbwyll* games in Welsh (see WELSH PROSE LITERATURE).

A number of other lays of uncertain authorship survive from the 12th and 13th centuries. Many of these works have at times been attributed to Marie de France. The anonymous *lai* of *Graelent*, although not explicitly Arthurian, treats a similar subject to Marie de France's *Lanval*, and is explicitly stated to be *lai en firent li Breton* 'a lay composed by the Bretons'.

Antone Minard

BRETON LITERATURE, BEGINNINGS TO C. 1900

Within the historical period, Brittany (BREIZH) has been home to four languages, each of which is essential to understanding the contexts of BRETON-LANGUAGE literature. The other three include (1) GAULISH, the earliest attested language of the Armorican peninsula, which is known from proper names, a few INSCRIPTIONS, and coin legends. It became extinct in the early Middle Ages, leaving only traces. (2) Latin was introduced with the conquest of ARMORICA under Julius Caesar; it continued to be a highly productive literary language throughout the Middle Ages. (3) Gallo-Romance evolved from Latin, eventually becoming French.

A large amount of ARTHURIAN LITERATURE is set in Brittany, which probably played an important rôle in the formation and early transmission of tales featuring ARTHUR, MYRDDIN (Merlin), and DRYSTAN AC ESYLLT (TRISTAN AND ISOLT). Without surviving Breton texts, the precise nature of Brittany's Arthurian literature remains uncertain (see also BRETON LAYS).

Old Breton Literature

No prose tales or poetry survives from the Old Breton period, *c*. 800–*c*. 1100. Nevertheless, the tradition is partly accessible through Latin translations, in particular saints' lives. The Breton character of this material may be gauged from features not usually found in saints' lives elsewhere on the Continent and not derived directly from the Bible. Close correspondences can also be seen between these works and literary texts that survive in the other Celtic literatures. For example, the story of the severing of the arm and head of St Melor closely resembles the Irish story of Nuadu (see Nōdons) and his silver arm, as well as the story of Brân in the Mabinogi.

Until *c*. 800, there was essentially one Brythonic language shared between Britain and Armorica. It would be artificial and anachronistic to view the three traditions (Breton, Welsh, and Cornish) as having completely separate identities at this stage, although Old Breton and Old Welsh can be distinguished by a handful of dialect features. Thus we can assume that Breton literature featured the same genres as Welsh and Cornish literature. For example, the 11th-century Breton Latin Life of Iudic-hael contains a legend of a hero's conception comparable to the Irish *Echtra Mac nEchach Mug-medóin* ('The Adventures of the Sons of Eochaid Mugmedón'), the Welsh Pwyll, and Geoffrey of Monmouth's account of the conception of Arthur. The same Life also contains poetic praise for the martial prowess of its subject, sharing many themes with the heroic elegies of the Welsh *Gododdin*.

We can deduce that poetry was based on schemes of approximately regular numbers of syllables per line bound to a precise number of stresses, that final and internal rhyme was known but not systematic, and that alliteration between initial consonants was common.

Glosses written to elucidate a main text are a common feature of medieval manuscripts. Some 2,000 glosses are available in Old Breton. Most consist of one or two words, but there are some fifty short sentences or phrases. Their interest is more linguistic than literary, as they indicate that a native vocabulary existed for grammar, astronomy, and medicine. Two of the main manuscript sources for Old Breton glosses also contain glosses in Old Welsh, evidence of a rich learned culture in which manuscripts and/or scholars moved between Celtic countries, and in which learning was disseminated in both Latin and Celtic.

Early Breton Literature in Latin

Approximately forty separate saints' lives survive, representing the lives of some sixty saints—a minority of the Breton saints (see hagiography). These texts were composed before the 14th century, although some are known only from later copies, and some now exist only as French translations.

Earlier generations of scholars viewed the Breton saints' lives as historical documents, but their historicity is elusive. Research is currently focusing on the literary qualities of these works and their implications. Badly needed new editions are being undertaken.

Legal texts

A collection of laws, sometimes called the *Kanones Wallici* ('Welsh' canon laws), constitutes one of the earliest textual sources of information that survives from any Celtic country regarding law. This text may have been compiled as early as the 6th century, but it survives in a 9th-century edition. Charters in Latin contain place-names and witnesses' names in Breton. The Scandinavian invasions swept away Brittany's distinctively insular legal culture. From the 11th century onward, the texts no longer show close similarities to patterns maintained in Wales. Additional incidental information concerning early Breton legal culture can be gleaned from episodes in the saints' lives.

Breton Latin literature in the later Middle Ages

After the Viking invasions, there were Bretons writing outside Brittany and foreigners writing in Brittany. Bretons working in medieval France included Pierre Abelard (1079–1142), whose name is clearly a Breton patronymic, 'son of Elard'. He is famous both for his philosophy and his love affair with Héloïse.

Medieval Literature in Breton

An extensive literary record in the Breton language survives from *c.* 1500, along with earlier fragments. Nearly all Middle Breton texts known today are from copies preserved outside Brittany. The destruction of all nonreligious Breton books was an avowed policy of missionaries in the 17th century. The language in what survives is standardized with accepted and universal spelling practices, even for proper names.

Middle Breton Literary Genres

Didactic works

The oldest and most important work is the *Catholicon* of 1499, a Breton–Latin–French dictionary. The so-called colloquies are phrase books for the use of learners of Breton, French, or Latin, but often with a wider readership. Some seventy-three editions are known, many of them made outside Brittany; they date to 1626 and 1656. Older editions also contain elements of grammar, pronunciation, and prayers. The first one was compiled by Quiquer in Rosko (Roscoff) and printed in Montroulez (Morlaix) in 1626 (Breton–French), and much expanded and reprinted in 1632 (Breton–French–Latin). There is no modern edition of these colloquies.

Popular lore

Only fragments of songs scribbled in margins and popular songs included in plays have survived from the Middle Breton period. All of these remnants are short, often trite, and sometimes bawdy. The prophetic verse *Dialog etre Arzur Roue d'an Bretounet ha Guynglaff* (The dialogue between Arthur king of the Bretons, and Guynglaff) is probably the most important piece of literature in this group.

The Christmas carols (*Nouelou ancien ha deuot*) published in 1650 were intended to be sung before mass. Other carols are known in the Gwenedeg (Vannetais) dialect, but only from a late manuscript (see BRETON DIALECTS). This last group occasionally retains internal rhymes characteristic of formal Middle Breton verse, and show that this traditional style of verse-making had a popular audience.

Religious works

The earliest work in this category is *Le mirouer de la mort*, printed in Montroulez in 1575. This long poem (3,600 lines) deals with death and the four possible Christian afterlives facing humanity—hence it is a lengthy methodical reflection about Death, Judgement, Paradise, and Hell. Many other works have no aesthetic ambition and are often direct translations or adaptations of works in Latin, French, or Italian. The oldest of this type is the *Heuryou Brezonec*, a book for private devotion. It was followed by the *Vie de sainte Catherine*, printed in 1576, a translation of the *Legenda Aurea* ('The Golden Legend') by Jacobus Voraginae.

The *Sacré college de Jésus* by Père Julien Maunoir, published in 1659, is a handbook for Jesuits intending to preach in Brittany without prior knowledge of the language. Maunoir proposed a new spelling, based on French principles. This is the end of Middle Breton spelling.

Drama

These texts have considerable aesthetic value, but have been studied mostly as specimens of the medieval Breton language. The Middle Breton religious dramas closely resemble the Middle Cornish miracle plays, and direct cultural influence between the two traditions is very likely (see CORNISH LITERATURE). Some of the Breton dramas are now lost, and are known only from the excerpts quoted by Dom Le Pelletier, a lexicographer working in the abbey of Landevenneg.

The oldest text is the *Vie de sainte Nonne* (2100 lines), known from a *c.* 1500 manuscript. Its subject is primarily the life of Saint Dewy (see DEWI SANT), Saint Nonn's son. The *Passion and the Resurrection* is known from three printings (Paris 1530, Sant-Maloù [Saint-Malo] 1536, and Montroulez 1609). The play was rewritten as a tragedy toward the end of the 17th century, and was performed and read until the 19th century. It was 'revived' in the late 20th century as *Ar Basion Vras*, which contains approximately 4,700 lines.

The *Life of St Gwennolé Abbot* has 1,278 lines. The legendary town of Ys (see FLOOD LEGENDS) appears in the Middle Breton play for the first time. The *Life of St Barbe* (*c.* 5000 lines) was printed in Paris (1557), and reprinted in Montroulez nearly a century later (1647).

The play *The Love of an Old Man Aged 80 for a 16-Year-Old Girl*, was printed in Montroulez in 1647. It is now lost, but the play is known through Le Pelletier's quotations, retaining only what he could not understand. Some of the 300 lines contain risqué or obscene material.

Poetry

Breton poetry shows affinity with other Celtic literatures, a specialized teaching that has left no other trace. The metrical patterns remain constant down to 1651. The exclusive use of this verse to this date, and its complete disappearance afterward, has not yet been satisfactorily explained. Although no type of formal teaching or guild with professional standards is documented, Middle Breton poetry obviously implies their existence.

Middle Breton poetry had five-, eight-, ten-, or twelve-syllable lines most frequently, and documentary evidence indicates that the poems were set to music. Each line has a compulsory final rhyme and a compulsory internal rhyme between the last syllable of the first half-line and the penultimate syllable of the line as a whole. Often, metrical ornamentation in the form of noncompulsory internal rhymes occurs in addition to the compulsory rhymes. Consonantal alliteration can occur.

Rhyme is more complicated than in English. The basis of the rhyme is the vowel: Vowel length, nasality, and stress seem not to matter, and rhymes are possible between similar sounds—for example, *n/m; o/u; eu/y*. Thus *oar an bugalez* contains three rhymes (. . . *ar an al*).

Many composers turned to clichés (also known as chevilles) to fulfil the metrical requirements. As in any tradition based on strict metres, the result is often lines with weak sense. The more complex poetry is mostly to be found in the plays, but some of the religious verse also shows great artistry:

> **An** traou m**an** h**an**u**et** so tremen**et** sed**er**
> Drez trem**en** dre**'n** pas**aig** an p**aig** p**en** mess **ag**er
> Pe evel lestr dre**'n** m**or**, ag**or** na e**or**er
> Ha na gall**er** caff**out** h**e r**out ne gouz**out** sci**er**.

> These things [I've] named have quietly passed (away)
> By passing through the passage of the page or the messenger,
>   [i.e., following his steps]
> Or like boats over the sea, in a fleet, unanchored
> And no one can find their route or know it clearly.

The final rhyme (*-er*) and a rhyme between the sixth and eleventh syllables (here *et | ag | or | out |*) are compulsory, and an intermediary rhyme (relay rhyme) between these is optional. Furthermore, this verse includes internal rhymes in other places and consonantal assonance—here 1 *an*, 2 *re, en*, 3 *el, er*, 4 *el, er—(e)r, (e)l, (e)n* can rhyme together. As for alliteration, note *tr(aou), tr(emenet) | dr(e) dr(emen) dr (en) | p(asage) p(age) p(en)*. The density of words rhyming together or echoing one another is high, which proclaims the mastery of the poet/craftsman.

The aesthetic quality of a work of Middle Breton verse can be judged in the relationship between the meaning and sound correspondences, and how these two combine to enhance expressiveness. Words contain both sound and meaning, and are linked together on both levels. In the example, *tremenet* means 'passed' but also 'passed away': The concept of death is not directly evoked, but rather alluded to. The word (and the concept) is announced by *traou/trau* 'things', relayed in the internal rhyme by *seder* /sedɛr/ (which contains the same sounds, but in a different order). This is carried over to the next line (*dre dremen dren*), while slightly changing the form (*tre/der/dre*). It is then relayed by *passage* (another word; not the same sounds, but the same meaning). The word's literal meaning is 'passage', but because of the words linked to it by internal rhymes, it assumes a secondary sense of 'death', although this meaning is objectively absent if we read the lines as prose. This extended sense is thus moved forward by way of sound—*passage, page, mesager*. The initial *p-* provides a further linking device. Consequently, 'page' and 'messenger' are connected with death. The result cannot be translated explicitly, or imitated in another language, which might explain why it has received so little attention.

Bardic Orders in Brittany?

We have evidence for teaching and transmission of an ancient way of verse-making, but no direct historical evidence for bardic schools or teaching. The word *barz* (< Old Breton *bard*) is indirect evidence; TALIESIN is referred to as *bardus* in the 11th-century Latin Life of St IUDIC-HAEL. In the 18th century, *barz* referred to some sort of clown or singer. Its popular use (meaning 'singer') in the 19th century is known, but it is only later that it was adopted and revived by the literary language (under the influence of Welsh *bardd* and Gaulish *bardos*) to mean 'poet'.

†Gwenaël Le Duc

BRETON LITERATURE, 20TH CENTURY

The corpus of Breton literature written in the 20th century outweighs the combined corpus of previous centuries. In this section, priority is given to writers who owe their prominence to works published in BRETON, as opposed to writers who wrote both in French and in Breton. The three most influential writers—Añjela DUVAL, and Per-Jakez HÉLIAS, and Jakez RIOU—are covered separately.

World War I was a turning point in the history of Brittany (BREIZH). Prior to this time, traditional Breton civilization had not experienced such drastic cultural shifts since the medieval period.

The poet Yann-Ber Kalloc'h (1888–1917) was born on the island of Groix, and died fighting in World War I. His major work is *Ar en deulin* (On our knees). He used his pen name 'Bleimor' for poems such as *Dihunamb* (Let us awake), a long politico-cultural appeal. Some of his simple, but compelling lines were set to music, and are among the most widely quoted of the century: *Me zo ganet é kreiz er mor* 'I was born in the middle of the sea' (*Ar en deulin*; 1960). Shorter, poignant pieces describe the horror and futility of war: 'How long, my God, will this cruel war continue to sever the roots in the woods, the homesteads, everywhere?'

Tangi Malmanche (1875–1953) spent his childhood near Brest. In the early years of the 20th century, he produced an important body of theatrical work in Breton. These dramas include *Marvaill ann ene naounek* (The tale of the hungry soul), *An intanvez Arzhur* (Arthur the widower), *An Antekrist* (The Antichrist), and *Gurvan ar marc'heg estranjour* (Gurvan, the foreign knight). His works entered their widest public arena during the early 1940s when they were broadcast on Radio Roazhon–Breizh (see MASS MEDIA). Malmanche dramatized themes and motifs from medieval Celtic and Breton literature, providing a bridge between traditional and revived Breton Celtic traditions.

Gwalarn (Northwest) was a literary review, published in 1925–44, that espoused the most influential school of thought in 20th-century Breton literature. The father figure of this *Gwalarn* movement was Roparz Hemon. He and the creators of 20th-century Breton literature pursued a twofold objective: to devise and promote a standard literary language and to produce a sophisticated corpus of literature—a matter of both form and content. The million Breton speakers were largely illiterate in that language, so standard Breton remained the language of specialized journals. Other than Añjela Duval, few women's voices are recognized in 20th-century Breton literature.

While standardizing the Breton language, the Gwalarnists stressed its Celticity (see PAN-CELTICISM). Not since a thousand years before, when the BRYTHONIC languages were still mutually intelligible, had Breton been as oriented toward other CELTIC COUNTRIES.

An important figure among the early Gwalarnists was Fañch Eliès (1896–1963), who wrote under the name Abeozen. His *Istor lennegezh vrezhonek an amzer-vremañ* (The history of contemporary Breton literature; 1957) is the most detailed and well-informed account of Breton literature in that period. Foremost among Abeozen's creative works is the short story collection *Pirc'hirin kala-goañv* (All Saints' Day pilgrim). The stories are set before and during World War II.

Many 20th-century prose works are autobiographical to varying degrees. One example is *E skeud tour bras Sant Jermen* (In the shadow of Saint Germain's great tower) by Yeun ar Gow (1897–1966). His book is a valuable social document that avoids nostalgia.

Charles Joseph Marie Tremel (1885–1965), who used the pen name Jarl Priel, wrote *Va zammig buhez* (A small part of my life) describing life in Russia. His travels also moved him to write *An teirgwern 'Pembroke'* (The three-master *Pembroke*), a novel.

Youenn Drezen's (1899–1972) *An dour en-dro d'an inizi* (The water around the islands; 1931) is a racy novelette that spills sensuously off the page as Herri Maheo, an artist, and Anna Bodri, daughter of a successful Douarnenez entrepreneur, flirt with romance. A pragmatic arranged marriage forces them apart, leaving Maheo devastated. The work remains the tour de force of a modern, outward-looking native Breton speaker.

The poet Maodez Glanndour (Loeiz ar Floc'h, 1909–86) was born in Pontrev (Pontrieux) in northern Brittany. His *Komzoù bev* (Lively conversations), published in 1985, is one of Breton literature's most important publications. This compilation includes poems written at different periods of his life. Rhythmic, polished pieces are presented in cycles. Glanndour creates moments of lyric beauty: *N'eo ket elerc'h an erc'h a zo kouezhet askellek en enezeg. N'eus en aber met rec'hier a huñvre kuñv dindan o fluñv* (Not swans . . . winged snow is falling on the island, and at the river mouth there are only rocks dreaming softly beneath their feathers, 78).

Youenn Gwernig (1925–2006) is one of many Bretons who spent time in New York. The emigrants established themselves there in the mid-20th century, working in the catering industry and forming a Breton-speaking community (see EMIGRATION). Gwernig wrote of life in New York in the 1960s, as an emigrant coming to terms with a new environment while pining for the familiarity and simplicity of his distant homeland. Two of his volumes are *An diri dir* (The steel stairs), a trilingual work that embraces French and English, and *An toull en nor* (The hole in the door; i.e., The keyhole).

The two world wars dominated Breton literature as subjects in the early and middle of the 20th century. In the latter decades of the century, industrialization and rural depopulation provided the context. A flame of revival burned in the 1970s, but Breton literature in the 5th French Republic (1959–) is a literature in crisis.

Mikael Madeg (1950–) has emerged as a prolific and confident writer. Collections of his short stories include *Ar seiz posubl* (Level best, 1987) and *Pemp troad ar maout* (The five-legged ram, 1987). Two of his novels are *Tra ma vo mor* (While there is a sea, 1989) and *Gweltaz an inizi* (Gildas of the islands, 1990). Madeg is firmly rooted in the northwestern region of Leon, but his work transcends local boundaries.

Goulc'han Kervella (1951–) is an important dramatist who has also directed spectacular and successful productions by the Strollad Bro Bagan company. Yann-Ber Pirioù (1937–) has published two collections of poetry: *Défense de cracher par terre et de parler breton: poèmes de combat (1950–1970): anthologie bilingue* (No spitting on the ground or speaking Breton: combat poetry [1950–1970]: a bilingual anthology; 1971, and *Ar mallozhioù ruz: komzoù plaen* (The red curses; 1974). Books by Per Denez (1921–2011), a teacher and activist, include *Hiroc'h an amzer eget ar vuhez* (Time is longer than life; 1981) and *Evit an eil gwech* (For the second time; 1982).

Diarmuid Johnson

BRETON MIGRATIONS

BRETON language and culture owe their distinctive origins to BRITAIN, with especially close affinities to the pre-English groups of southwest Britain (see KERNOW). Settlers brought BRYTHONIC speech and culture to Brittany (BREIZH) in a series of migrations from the 3rd to 9th centuries AD, most extensively *c*. 450–*c*. 600, moving into ARMORICA, GAUL. It is likely that Gaulish survived to contribute to Brythonic and possibly even influence its grammar.

Two 6th-century historians, the Byzantine Procopius and the Gallo-Roman Gregory of Tours, both demonstrate that Brythonic Brittany was an accomplished fact. The latter gives a detailed account of a peninsula ruled by chieftains with Brythonic names, effectively independent sovereigns. Nevertheless, only one near contemporary source describes the migrations themselves—the *De Excidio Britanniae* of GILDAS. Writing nearly a century after the event, Gildas gives a melodramatic account of an ANGLO- SAXON 'CONQUEST' from which the Britons had to flee, either to Wales (CYMRU) and Cornwall, or overseas to Brittany.

The spread of languages with the decline and collapse of the Western Roman Empire tends to be understood as *Volkerwanderung* (migration of peoples). The Breton migrations have been seen as a 'knock-on' effect, with Celtic migrants set in motion by earlier Anglo-Saxon movements. In addition, the Armorican peninsula had close and bidirectional relations with Britain from prehistory through the Middle Ages; therefore, the real processes behind cultural and linguistic Bretonization are undoubtedly more complex.

Early Christian communities were clearly a factor in the Breton migrations. In a letter written between 509 and 521, the bishops of Tours, Angers, and Rennes (Roazhon) threatened to excommunicate two priests in Armorica with the Brythonic names Louocatus and Catihernus for their unorthodox practices. Traditional history has long held that the saints were leaders in the journey to Brittany. The study of Breton place-names suggests settlement by British early Christians in the peninsula, especially given the numerous archaic names (often those of parishes and towns and villages of local importance) that comprise the element *Plou-* (< Latin *plēb-em*) + the name of an early Brythonic saint or an obscure element popularly understood as a saint's name. In many instances, the same saints' names are found in parish names in Wales and Cornwall.

From the standpoint of social history, the model of colonization is probably appropriate for the Breton migrations: The movements seem to have been largely voluntary, conducted by family groups and small religious communities, rather than endeavors compelled by conquest. The prior inhabitants of Armorica were probably gradually incorporated into the new society.

Whatever the circumstances of the original impulse to settle Brittany from Britain, it is certain that the connections between Brittany, Cornwall, and Wales were maintained for centuries. Subsequent settlement from Brittany to Britain, and vice versa, occurred throughout the Middle Ages, both in the context of the Norman invasion of Britain and independently.

Antone Minard and John T. Koch

BRETON MUSIC

Brittany (BREIZH) has one of the strongest regional musical cultures in Europe. A well organized folk-music collecting agency, Dastum, sends fieldworkers all over the province to ensure an archive with both breadth and depth.

Vocal Folk Music

The traditional folksongs of Breton-speaking Brittany are divided into the categories of *gwerz* (narrative song; see BALLADS), *sôn* (lyric song), and hymns, *kantikoù*. The traditional style of singing for all these categories of song is unaccompanied. In more recent times, singers have begun to accompany themselves on guitars and other instruments.

The most characteristically Breton style of singing is *kan ha diskan* (roughly 'call-and-response' singing). The first singer begins with the opening line of the song. A few notes before he finishes it, the second singer joins in, in unison. When the first singer reaches the end of the line, he pauses while the second singer repeats the line. Once again, the first singer chimes in for the last few notes before beginning the second line. The two singers continue this way for the entire song. Indeed, sometimes they string two or three songs together to keep dances going for ten to twelve minutes. This pattern differs from that observed in most western European folk-singing, which is generally solo or in unison. *Kan ha diskan* singing is one of the most popular forms of music for Breton dancing (see DANCES).

Instrumental Folk Music

The instrumental folk music of Brittany is mostly played for dancing or for processions at weddings and other community events. One of the older styles still in use is *sonner par couple* (piping in pairs), in which a BINIOU (bagpipe) player and a *bombard* (shawm) player perform together. The dance music they produce is very similar in its overall structure to *kan ha diskan* singing. Another BAGPIPE is also native to Brittany—the *veuze*, which is similar to the western European medieval bagpipe.

Another bagpipe was imported to Brittany in the 1920s, and is now one of the most popular instruments there: the Scottish highland pipes. This instrument is played mostly in the context of the *bagad*, or pipe band.

The other most prominent instruments for traditional music in Brittany include the clarinet, violin, diatonic accordion, and hurdy-gurdy, all of which have been popular instruments in the folk tradition. The violin (see FIDDLE) and accordion gained popularity among the younger generation as a result of the influence of IRISH MUSIC, which became very popular in Brittany during the 1960s and 1970s.

The most dramatic revival of a Breton musical instrument also owed a great deal to Irish music—namely, the recreation of the Breton HARP. Although harps had been common in Brittany during the Middle Ages, the instrument had died out by the 19th century. In the 1940s, a group of cultural activists set out to revive it, creating a new-style Celtic harp on the model of Irish harps. The instrument made its debut in 1952, played by a nine-year-old boy named Alan Cochevelou (later Alan Stivell).

Musical Groups

Alan Stivell and others have combined acoustic Breton music with Irish and Scottish styles. Instrumental bands such as Ar Re Youank and Skolvan have been formed specifically to play at a type of dance called a FEST-NOZ, the most common type of event for folk music in Brittany. Outside the 'Celtic' realm, Tri Yann was put together by Breton cultural activists from Nantes (Naoned), and includes traditional Breton music in its repertoire.

Stephen D. Winick

BREUDDWYD RHONABWY

Breuddwyd Rhonabwy (Rhonabwy's dream) is a medieval Welsh prose-tale. The traditional hero OWAIN AB URIEN appears as ARTHUR's antagonist in a central dream episode set in the heroic past. A fantastic game of *gwyddbwyll* (a board game) between Arthur and Owain figures as a sustained surreal image within the dream's irrational events. The frame tale—that is, the story within which the main story (i.e., the dream) takes place—is set in the reign of Madog son of Maredudd of Powys (1130–60).

A literary tale that is often cited as similar (i.e., a topical SATIRE whose centrepiece is an AISLING, a fantastic dream vision) is the Middle Irish *Aislinge Meic Con Glinne* (The dream of Mac Con Glinne). Celtic affinities have been recognized in a pivotal episode in which Rhonabwy sleeps on an animal skin as a prelude to gaining otherworldly wisdom. Other medieval European dream poems, particularly *Roman de la Rose*, are also comparable in this regard.

John T. Koch

BRIAN BÓRUMA/ BRIAN BORÚ

Brian Bóruma/Brian Ború (941–1014) was overking of Munster (MUMU) and high-king of Ireland (ÉRIU). He belonged to DÁL GCAIS, a dynasty that had attained prominence in northern Munster by the 10th century.

Brian Ború was killed during the Battle of Clontarf (Cath Chluain Tarbh) in AD 1014. (Hulton Archive/Getty Images)

Brian's achievement is magnified by the 12th-century propaganda tract *Cogadh Gaedhel re Gallaibh* (War of the Irish with the foreigners), which alleges that Dál gCais reversed a Viking repression of Ireland. This claim is not supported by contemporary sources, which show how Dál gCais manipulated divisions among the native ÉOGANACHT dynasties of Munster and exploited Norse settlements on the lower Shannon, culminating in the sack of Limerick (Luimneach) by Brian and his brother in 967. Later, as king, Brian allied with a Hebridean–Norse dynasty in 984. Warfare escalated between Brian and Mael Sechnaill II, king of Tara (TEAMHAIR), forcing a partition of Ireland by agreement at Clonfert (Co. Galway/Contae na Gaillimhe) in 997. Following a revolt against his overlordship in 999, Brian crushed LAIGIN and Norse forces at Glenn Máma, thereby gaining tighter control of BAILE ÁTHA CLIATH (Dublin). He finally secured Mael Sechnaill's submission in 1002.

Brian reigned for twelve years (1002–14) as high-king. The political order that he had established unraveled from 1013 onward. Later tradition credited his ex-wife Gormfhlaith with having incited her Leinster and Norse connections to rebel against

Munster overlordship. In any event, the conflict culminated in the battle of Clontarf. Dál gCais were victors, but at great cost—Brian and his son Murchad were among the casualties. Brian's successors included his son Donnchad and grandson Tairdelbach, ancestor of the Ua Briain kings (the O'Briens). Brian did break the Uí Néill supremacy and shaped the course of Irish history for two centuries by creating a precedent whereby any powerful and ambitious dynasty could aspire to a high-kingship of Ireland.

Ailbhe MacShamhráin

BRICRIU MAC CARBAID

Bricriu mac Carbaid, sometimes with the epithet Nemthenga (Poison-tongue), is a troublemaker figure in the medieval Irish ULSTER CYCLE. He appears in FLED BRICRENN ('Bricriu's Feast') and in MESCA ULAD ('The Intoxication of the Ulstermen'); more briefly in TOCHMARC EMIRE ('The Wooing of Emer'), *Echtrae Nera* ('The Adventure of Nera'), and *Táin Bó Flidais* (The cattle raid of Flidas); and once in SCÉLA MUCCE MEIC DÁ THÓ ('The Story of Mac Dá Tho's Pig'). The byform of *Bricriu*, *Bricne*, is a common noun meaning 'freckling, variegation'; *Bricriu* may derive from the same root.

John T. Koch

BRICTA

Bricta /brixta/ 'magical spell(s)' is an element of COMMON CELTIC vocabulary attested from Gaulish. The word occurs in the set phrase *bnanom bricto-* 'women's magical spell' in the inscription from Larzac, which closely parallels the Irish *brichtu ban*. The preservation of the set phrase in Irish is evidence that pre-Christian magico-religious ideas persisted in the Christian period, at least in literature. Both Larzac and CHAMALIÈRES also pair the word with *andern-* 'underworld', corresponding to Latin 'infernus'; see ANNWN.

John T. Koch

BRIGANTES

Brigantes (Βριγαντες) was the name of Celtic tribes attested in the later IRON AGE and Roman period in Ireland (ÉRIU) and BRITAIN. Settlements with the name *Brigantium* in the extreme northwest of Spain (GALICIA) and in the Alpine region (modern Bregenz) indicate that similarly named tribal groups had resided there as well. A cultural link between the Irish and British Brigantes is implied by the presence of a shared cult of St BRIGIT, whose early cult was rooted in Leinster/LAIGIN and whose name derives from Celtic **Brigantī*, and the *Dea Brigantia,* whose cult was strong in northern Roman Britain.

Location and Extent of the Brigantes

The 2nd-century Greek geographer Ptolemy places the Brigantes in the southeast of Ireland. The name of a medieval Irish septs, the Uí Brigte (Descendants of Brigit) has

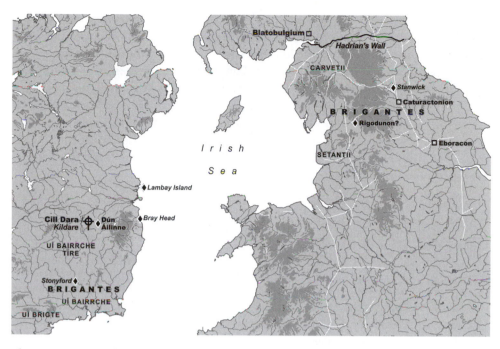

The Brigantes in Ireland and Britain. Roman roads are shown in white. (Map by John T. Koch)

also been seen as a possible survival of the Brigantes. Ptolemy's British Brigantes stretched from the North Sea to the Irish Sea, including Κατουραχτονιον Caturactonion (Catterick/CATRAETH) and Εβορακον Eborācon (York). Dedications to the goddess Brigantia are thick in the region of HADRIAN'S WALL. The presence of smaller tribes within this same region suggests that the British Brigantes were a confederacy of several tribes.

Archaeology

The region of Ptolemy's Irish Brigantes, like the south of Ireland generally, experienced an Iron Age characterized negatively by the absence of material in the LA TÈNE style. The Brigantes of Britain fall outside the 'Iron Age C' zone, characterized by Gallicized Late La Tène metalwork and pottery, COINAGE, and the OPPIDUM, and associated with southeastern tribal groups known as BELGAE. Many archaeologists have described British Brigantia as an area of cultural continuity from the Bronze Age. Hill-forts are less numerous and less densely sited in Brigantian territory than in south-central and southwest ENGLAND or Wales and the Marches.

History and Continuity

In Britain, the Brigantes are quite well documented for the period covered by Tacitus, AD 43–85. The primary focus of Tacitus's attention is the turbulent reign of Queen Cartimandua and the civil war between her first husband, Venutius, and her second husband, Vellocatus. The fact that the Brigantes were ruled by a woman is noteworthy but not unique. After the 1st century, Roman histories tend to deal with Brigantia only as part of Roman Britain in general. This region was one of the most important and heavily militarized frontier zones within the Empire and repeatedly came into play in internal struggles for imperial power as well as in the protection of the northwest frontier. It is unclear how the *civitas Brigantum* related to this northern military zone or even to what extent civilian provincial government functioned there. Nonetheless, a Roman inscription exists in which an individual is named as a *Brigans* (sing. of *Brigantes*) by nationality and a dedication to a *deus Bregans*, as well as seven dedications to *dea Brigantia*, all of which point to the vigorous survival of tribal identity with Roman sanction.

A territorial name *Brigantī* or *Brigantia* would give Early Welsh *Breint*. An occurrence of *breint* appears in the GODODDIN that could, therefore, mean either 'privilege' or 'land of the Brigantes'. There are also a number of rivers with this name, probably all once regarded as goddesses.

The Name

The literal meaning of Brigantes is 'the elevated ones' < INDO-EUROPEAN *$b^h\underset{.}{r}\hat{g}^h\underset{.}{n}tes$. Although this definition could be purely metaphorical or ideologically bound up with the tribal goddess *Brigantī* (BRIGIT), all the tribes so named did have spectacular heights within their territories—the Wicklow Mountains in Ireland, the Cumbrian massif and Pennines in Britain, the steep Galician headlands, and the central Alps. The same root is found in the very common Continental Celtic place-name element –*brigā*, which means 'hill' or 'hill-fort' (cf. Welsh *bre* 'hill'). See also the BRIGIT (GODDESS) article.

John T. Koch

BRIGIT (GODDESS)

The Irish goddess Brigit was honoured as the goddess of poetry and prophecy, and as the patron deity of the *filid* (see BARDIC ORDER). Her name, meaning 'the exalted one' (< COMMON CELTIC *Brigantī*), has related forms across the INDO-EUROPEAN languages, with cognates in the Sanskrit feminine divine epithet *brhatī* and tribal names such as the Celtic BRIGANTES and the Germanic Burgundians. The name may have been more of a title than a personal name. In the SANAS CHORMAIC ('Cormac's Glossary') attributed to CORMAC UA CUILEANNÁIN (†908), Brigit is identified as the DAGDA's daughter and her two sisters, also named Brigit, as the patrons of smiths and healers. In the mythological tale CATH MAIGE TUIRED ('The [Second] Battle of Mag Tuired'), Brigit or Bríg of the Tuath Dé appears as the wife of the Fomorian king, Bres. Their son Ruadán is killed when he tries to murder the divine smith, GOIBNIU. Bríg's lament over her dead son was the first keening.

Brigit is also equivalent to the Romano-Celtic Brigantia, the tribal goddess of the Brigantes of Britain. Dedications to Brigantia are numerous near HADRIAN'S WALL. Julius Caesar equated a native Gaulish deity with the Roman goddess Minerva, also a patron of crafts; elsewhere, Minerva was identified with Brigantia (see BATH; INTERPRETATIO ROMANA). Brigit gives her name to the river Brent in ENGLAND, the Braint in Wales, and the Brighid in Ireland. In the fragmentary early Welsh poem *Gofara*

Braint, the river Braint in Anglesey (Môn) overflows in response to the death of King Cadwallon, here reflecting the goddess as the ruler's consort (see SOVEREIGNTY MYTH). The festival of IMBOLC, 1 February, is associated with Brigit as a Goddess of fertility. She has also been linked to a fire cult.

Brigit was the tutelary goddess of the LAIGIN (Leinstermen), the region of Ireland in which Ptolemy placed the *Brigantes*. She has been linked to the Christian Saint BRIGIT, the patron saint of Laigin, who has acquired several of the goddess's attributes: They share a name, feast-day, and many functions. Both are celebrated as patrons of poets, smiths, and healers and connected with fertility, AGRICULTURE, and images of fire.

Dorothy Bray

BRIGIT (SAINT)

St Brigit flourished in the late 5th to early 6th centuries AD. Her death is set *c.* 525 according to the ANNALS of Ulster. She is considered one of the three preeminent saints of Ireland (ÉRIU), along with PATRICK and COLUM CILLE (Columba). Her Latin Life by Cogitosus, a monk of Kildare (Cill Dara), was composed in the mid-7th century; this work and the anonymous *Vita Prima* (first life) are the earliest examples of Irish HAGIOGRAPHY. A 9th-century Life in Old Irish is known as *Bethu Brigte*. Cogitosus relates that Brigit was born of Christian parents and founded Kildare. The *Vita Prima* states that she sold to a druid and set to work in the dairy. She rejected the druid's food, accepting only the milk of a pure white cow. In versions of a story in the *Bethu Brigte* (§15) and the *Vita Prima* (§19), Brigit puts off a suitor when she plucks out her eye. In the *Bethu Brigte* version, this disfigurement is miraculously followed by a spring bursting forth before her. The saint is often thought of as one-eyed in modern Irish folklore.

St Brigit's connection with cattle continued in later iconography, in which she is often depicted with a cow. She became the patron of women in childbirth, and a late legend from the Hebrides (Innse Gall) makes her the midwife to the Virgin Mary and second mother to Christ, supporting her reputation as 'the Mary of the Gael'.

St Brigit's feast-day is 1 February, coinciding with the pagan celebration of IMBOLC. GIRALDUS CAMBRENSIS described a perpetual fire in the saint's shrine, surrounded by a hedge which no man was allowed to cross, suggesting a connection with a pre-Christian cult. Another anecdote claims that, at her ordination, the presiding bishop read the orders of a bishop over Brigit by mistake.

The cult of St Brigit became widespread in ENGLAND, Scotland (ALBA), and Wales (CYMRU), where she appears as St Bride and Welsh Sanffraid. St Bride's Day continues to be celebrated in Ireland and Scotland. In Modern Irish, the spelling is *Bríd*.

Dorothy Bray

BRITAIN

Britain is the everyday term for the island of Great Britain, comprising the countries of ENGLAND, Scotland (ALBA), and Wales (CYMRU) except for their smaller islands. Britain also refers to the political state (the United Kingdom) created by the UNION of England and Wales with Scotland in 1707. The term 'England' does not refer to the whole island.

Aspects of the name Britain and of its specialist usage in the field of Celtic studies are discussed in the articles on Breizh; British; Britons; and Brythonic. The English proper name *Britain* is easily traced back through written records to Latin *Brit(t)annia,* which was used in ancient times to refer to the whole island or, after the Roman invasion of AD 43, the Roman province of Britannia. The ultimate source is a Celtic group name, *Pritanī* 'the Britons'—literally, 'people of the forms' / 'shapely people'. The Welsh reflex of *Pritanī, Prydain,* means 'Britain'.

John T. Koch

BRITISH

As a geographic term, 'British' pertains to the island of Britain. As a political and cultural term, 'British' is less straightforward and has changed its meaning over time. The oldest sense of 'British' refers to the inhabitants of Britain before the settlements of the Anglo-Saxons (see Anglo-Saxon 'conquest') and Gaelic Scots; in other words, 'British' designated the ancient Brythonic population and their descendants (the Welsh, Cornish, and Bretons). As such, 'British' was also an alternative name for the Welsh, Cornish, and Breton languages. This older sense of a non-English Britain became increasingly confusing and incongruous as the newer sense 'of the island of Britain' (regardless of language or ethnicity) took hold after the Act of Union of England and Scotland in 1707. 'British' had generally ceased to be a synonym for 'Welsh' by the mid-19th century. At that point, the term 'ancient Britons' came to be used to distinguish Britain's pre-Roman, pre-Anglo-Saxon inhabitants in the modern sense.

In Celtic studies and historical linguistics, 'British' means the oldest attested stage of the Celtic speech of Britain. 'British' is used in this sense in this encyclopedia. In the narrow specialist sense as the ancient Celtic language of Britain, a sizeable body of proper names in British survives from the time of Caesar's expeditions (55 and 54 BC) onward. The language of this period agreed quite closely with the contemporary speech of Ireland, termed Primitive Irish, but also has affinities with Continental Celtic. Many of the first attested tribal and personal names in British—known from legends on coinage and Graeco-Roman writers—occur on both sides of the Channel.

Polysyllabic words in British speech weakened and grew indistinct by the 6th century. For example, British Cunobelinos would become Late British *Cunəbelinəh,* then Early Welsh *Cun'belin'* (Modern *Cynfelyn*). The Roman spelling *Cunobelinus* continued as long as the Roman educational system persisted, even though British speakers had probably tended to pronounce the same name as /kunvelʋn/ for a long time.

John T. Koch

BRITONS

Definitions

The term 'Briton' can be defined in the following ways:

1. In nonspecialist English with reference to the period since the Union of England and Wales (Cymru) with Scotland (Alba) in 1707, 'Briton' usually means an inhabitant of the island of Great Britain. With reference to native-born inhabitants of Ireland

(ÉIRE), the term 'Briton' or 'West Briton' has sometimes been used, mostly limited to self-consciously Unionist discourse (see ACT OF UNION).

2. A fairly widespread usage is for 'Britons' to refer to the ancient and early medieval pre-Anglo-Saxon inhabitants of Britain, including those who migrated to Brittany (BREIZH) during the 4th to 7th centuries AD.

The meanings in use in CELTIC STUDIES and related disciplines are all based on the second definition. For such specialist purposes, 'Briton' may be defined as 'a native speaker of BRYTHONIC (the P-CELTIC language of Britain and, later, Brittany), during the period from the first evidence of such speech in the pre-Roman IRON AGE until the central Middle Ages'. After the Norman conquest of England (1066), it is more usual to speak of the Welsh, Bretons, and Cornish separately, as these groups have separate histories. In the contemporary Latin sources of the pre-Norman period, it is more common not to make such a distinction on a geographical basis; instead, the terms *Brittones*, *Britanni*, and *Brettones* occur, to be translated as 'Britons' in the second meaning given previously. The corresponding Old English word was *Bryttas* or *Brettas*, and Old English *Wealas* 'Welsh' has the same meaning—'Brythonic P-Celts'—not limited to the people of the territory that is now Wales.

Derivation

Phonologically, the modern forms English 'Briton' and French *Breton* require a pre-form with an old double *-tt-*. Welsh *Brython* and Irish *Bretain* likewise imply an Old Celtic *Brittones*. The modern English spelling with a single *t* has probably been influenced by the incorrect medieval Latin spelling *Britones*. *Brittones* appears in Latin texts from the 1st century AD onward.

The underlying tribal name, *Pritanī*, means 'people of the forms' / 'shapely people'; compare Old Irish *cruth* and Welsh *pryd* 'form', from COMMON CELTIC *k^writu-*.

John T. Koch

BRITTANY
See Breizh.

BROCHS

Brochs—IRON AGE dry-stone built circular tower-houses—are primarily distributed throughout the north of Scotland, in Caithness (Gallaibh) and the Orkney (Arcaibh) and Shetland (Sealtainn) archipelagos, with lesser concentrations in the Outer Hebrides (Innse Gall). Many of them still survive almost to their original height (e.g., the Broch of Mousa on Shetland is some 13 m high). They appear to span the last century or two BC and the first two or three centuries AD.

The intricate layout of brochs, with their two concentric layers of walling, intermural galleries, and rows of 'voids', was probably developed as a means of insulation. Current archaeological consensus views these structures as functioning farmsteads, a complex variation on the round house. As many as three floors of living space may have been utilized, although the lowest level may have served as a storage space.

Simon Ó Faoláin

BROOCHES AND FIBULAE

Fibulae—safety-pin brooches for fastening clothing—are important in Celtic culture from the HALLSTATT period. Cloaks usually had one fibula at the shoulder. Fibulae with enamel or pseudo-filigreed ornamentation are among artefacts typically produced by eastern Celts—for example, those found at Novo Mesto, Slovenia. Because of their use on clothing, fibulae are good examples of CELTIC ART. Changes in design help date the archaeological contexts in which they are found. A bronze cauldron containing hundreds of fibulae was discovered at Duchcov in the Czech Republic. Most

Fibulae and rings from Lahošt' in the Czech Republic. Celtic Museum, Teplice, Czech Republic. (Erich Lessing/Art Resource, New York)

of these finds date to the late 4th and 3rd centuries BC, the LA TÈNE B period, with their back-bent feet representing a development from the wire fibulae of the La Tène A period.

A later example from Ireland is the Bettystown brooch. The form, a pseudo-penannular type, was developed in the 7th century. Despite its small size, the brooch exhibits every skill the contemporary metalsmith knew, applying novel Anglo-Saxon elements to a basically Celtic type. The plates of silvered bronze on the back of the brooch incorporate Celtic trumpet spirals and broken-backed curves.

Antone Minard

BRUCE, ROBERT DE

'The Bruce' (1274–1329) was Earl of Carrick and, from 1306, King Robert I of Scotland (ALBA). Robert de Bruce was a native speaker of GAELIC, an excellent soldier, and an inspiring leader.

The career of Robert de Bruce resolved the struggle for the Scottish crown following the untimely deaths of King Alexander III in 1286 and his only surviving heir in 1290. He continued the military campaign against English occupation begun by William WALLACE. In 1306, he was crowned king of Scotland in defiance of Edward I, and led a ten-year campaign of guerrilla warfare against the occupying English troops. He was victorious at the battle of BANNOCKBURN, triumphing over King Edward II. In 1324, he was formally recognized as king of Scotland by Pope John XXII; with the 1328 'Treaty of Edinburgh', he won formal recognition of Scottish sovereignty from Edward III. The latter, especially, had far-reaching historical consequences (see SCOTTISH PARLIAMENT; NATIONALISM).

Marion Löffler

BRUG NA BÓINNE

Brug na Bóinne (the hostel of the Boyne, Newgrange) is usually identified with the important archaeological complex on the bend of the river Boyne (BÓAND), most importantly the great passage tombs of Newgrange, County Meath (Contae na Mí), and possibly also including the tombs of Knowth and Dowth (DUBHADH). The Brug is the otherwordly residence of Bóand, the Dagda, and most importantly their son OENGUS MAC IND ÓC. It is also reputed to be the burial-place of the god LUG. Brug na Bóinne provides the setting for *Aislinge Oengusa* ('The Dream of Oengus') in the MYTHOLOGICAL CYCLE.

The archaeological complex to which Brug na Bóinne belongs is one of the most important in Ireland (ÉRIU). The megalithic passage tombs were built by Neolithic farming communities between 3260 and 3080 BC. The main 4th-millennium burial passage incorporates a remarkable solar alignment, by which a slender ray of light illuminates the back wall of the central burial chamber at the sunrise of the winter solstice. It is clear that this landscape was the focus of intense ritual activities, probably including seasonal communal assemblies and inauguration ceremonies. Newgrange, in particular, became the focus of Romano-British/Celtic cultic activity during the 3rd and 4th centuries AD.

Edel Bhreathnach

BRUIDEN

Bruiden (pl. *bruidnea*) was the term normally applied to a hostel or large banqueting hall in early Ireland (ÉRIU), but might also simply mean a large house. *Bruiden* was also used to denote the festive hall of eternal feasting in the OTHERWORLD. Being a *briugu* or hospitaller was a highly respected profession; according to the early Irish LAW TEXTS, a chief hospitaller would be of equal status to a chief poet or the lowest grade of king.

The importance of hostels within early Irish society is reflected in the literature, and several tales are set in a *bruiden*, the most famous of which is TOGAIL BRUIDNE DA DERGA ('The Destruction of Da Derga's Hostel'). The literary descriptions illustrate the abundant hospitality provided by such hostels: Seven doors would lead into the premises, seven ways would go through it, and seven hearths would maintain seven cauldrons, each containing a whole ox with a flitch of bacon.

Petra S. Hellmuth

BRUT Y BRENHINEDD

Brut y Brenhinedd (*Brut*, roughly 'British chronicle', of the kings) is the name given to Welsh translations of GEOFFREY OF MONMOUTH's HISTORIA REGUM BRITANNIAE. The *Historia*, carrying the implicit authority of a Latin text and the explicit claim of being based on a 'BRITISH' book, was accepted wholeheartedly in Wales (CYMRU) by both the native and Latinate learned classes as an authentic account of British/Welsh history. It reflected some of the traditional LEGENDARY HISTORY in its assignment of origins for the Britons (see Trojan legends), its emphasis on a single British crown, and its claim that British hegemony would be restored in the fullness of time. The book provided the first continuous narrative of Welsh history and of Arthur.

The *Historia* quickly became canonical and was absorbed into native *cyfarwyddyd* ('vernacular tradition'; see cyfarwydd) by means of a number of translations that began to appear in the 13th century. Cyfranc Lludd a Llefelys, a tale from Welsh tradition, is inserted into the *Historia*.

In the 14th century, one version incorporates elements from other texts, including Wace's French Arthurian Chronicle based on Geoffrey, *Roman de Brut,* and material taken from a Latin chronology. It was used in a compilation of Welsh history attributed to the 15th-century poet Gutun Owain and was the main source of the so-called *Brut Tysilio.* All versions follow the *Historia* quite closely, and the translators and scribes felt little need to change or comment on the text—a sign of the distance, generally, between the *Historia* and the native *cyfarwyddyd*. The only major omission is that the translator (or perhaps the scribe) of Peniarth 44 does not include Merlin's prophecy 'since people find them difficult to believe'. Other translators sometimes make a comment, such as that Arthur's slayer is not named or that the 'book' is ambiguous about Arthur's end (both in *Brut Dingestow*), and there are a few glosses. The translators add traditional epithets to personal names where possible, and an occasional reference to a Welsh source, such as a triad (see triads), a proverb or *vita sancti*, or an attempt to iron out an inconsistency provides other links with native history.

The production of many separate translations and 'editions' from the 13th to the 15th centuries and the continued copying of these texts or of amalgams of them down to the 18th century testify to the importance of the *Brut*, or of the *Historia*, for Welsh historians and readers from its first appearance and for long after it had lost its authority among English antiquaries and historians (cf. Renaissance).

Brynley F. Roberts

BRUT Y TYWYSOGYON

Brut y Tywysogyon ('The Chronicle of the Princes') is the name that, by the 17th century, came to be used to describe the medieval chronicle of the history of Wales (Cymru) under its kings and princes. It exists in two main versions—the NLW Peniarth MS 20 version and the Red Book of Hergest (Llyfr Coch Hergest)—which are independent translations of a lost Latin text. These translations were probably made between the last years of the 13th century and *c.* 1330, following the death of Llywelyn ap Gruffudd in 1282.

The chronicle begins in 682 with the death of Cadwaladr Fendigaid (the Blessed), the point at which the Historia Regum Britanniae by Geoffrey of Monmouth comes to an end. Thus it is likely that the Latin original of the *Brut* was conceived as a continuation of the *Historia* and designed to extend from the demise of the last of the kings of the Britons to the death of the last of the princes of Wales. This text was based upon ANNALS. The annals are characteristically brief and terse, but many of the entries in the *Brut* in the period *c*. 1100–75, such as those that describe the attack on ABERYSTWYTH Castle in 1116 or the death of Rhun ab OWAIN GWYNEDD in 1146, are greatly elaborated in a rhetorical style, but contain no additional factual material.

Brenhinedd y Saesson ('Kings of the English') is another version of *Brut y Tywysogyon*, also derived from an original Latin text, in which material from English chronicle sources is combined with that from the original text of the *Brut* to give a composite chronicle of the history of Wales and ENGLAND extending, in the BL Cotton Cleopatra B.v manuscript, from 682 to 1188, with a composition in WELSH in the Black Book of Basingwerk extending the narrative to 1461. Between them, *Brut y Tywysogyon* and *Brenhinedd y Saesson* provide a historical source in which the factual record is blended with a sympathetic account of the endeavours and tribulations of the princes.

J. Beverley Smith

BRYCHAN BRYCHEINIOG

Brychan Brycheiniog was a 5th-century Welsh saint and king of Brecheniauc, Modern BRYCHEINIOG (Breconshire). Brychan is a legendary figure, and most facts about him are doubtful. Brychan seems to have been of Irish descent, and a possibly cognate Old Irish man's name *Broccán* is known, a diminutive of *brocc* 'badger'. Irish settlements in Brycheiniog (now southern POWYS) are demonstrated by the presence of six ogam-inscribed stones in the area, dating roughly from the 5th and 6th centuries. Irish influence is also evident in the remains of Brycheiniog's 9th- and 10th-century royal site at Llan-gors.

According to tradition, Brychan fathered a number of children who became saints. This tradition appears to have grown over time, such that more than 70 different children eventually became attributed to him in Breton, Cornish, Irish, and Welsh sources, including Saints Cynon, Dyfrig, Dwynwen, Eluned, Gwen, and Mabon. According to the evidence of places named after Brychan, there seems to have been a missionary movement in the 5th and 6th centuries along a Roman road in Brycheiniog.

Peter E. Busse and John T. Koch

BRYCHEINIOG

Brycheiniog was the name of an early medieval kingdom in what became the southern part of the historic county of Breconshire, Wales (CYMRU). Medieval Brycheiniog is south of Mynydd Epynt and chiefly drained by the river Usk. Several mid 8th-century kings of *Brecheiniauc* are mentioned in the Book of Llandaf.

The Welshman Asser reported that King Elise of Brycheiniog, in company with other southern kings, had been under threat from the kingdom of GWYNEDD and asked for protection from Alfred the Great of Wessex. This dependency is suspected to have led, in 916, to an attack by Alfred's daughter Aethelflaed on the royal centre at *Brecananmere* (probably the excavated island crannog on Llan-gors lake) in which Brycheiniog's queen was captured. Elise's son Tewdwr was described in charter witness lists as *subregulus*, presumably in subordination to Wessex, and kings of Brycheiniog were still attending the court of ENGLAND in 934. The last king of Brycheiniog mentioned in the genealogies was the grandson of Elise. Thereafter Brycheiniog appears to have been subsumed into Deheubarth, the southern kingdom of Wales.

J. Graham Jones

BRYNAICH (BERNICIA)

Brynaich (Old Welsh *Bernech*, Old English *Beornice*, Latin *Bernicia*) was a dominant and expansionist kingdom in northeast BRITAIN in the 7th and 8th centuries. Although Brynaich was ruled by an Anglian dynasty for most of its recorded history, it is important to CELTIC STUDIES because it was probably a British kingdom before the time of the Angles, in the 5th and early 6th centuries; this view is confirmed by a reference to the 5th-century north Brythonic chieftain CUNEDDA 'leading men of Brynaich' in *Marwnad Cunedda* and by a reference to *beδin Odoδin a Breen[e]ych* 'the army of GODODDIN and Brynaich' in the *Gododdin*, as though the two kingdoms had been allies or even united at the time of the battle of CATRAETH. The fact that several of the great secular and religious sites of post-Roman Brynaich had Celtic names—for example, Yeavering, Dunbar, Doon Hill, and Melrose—supports this interpretation, as does the archaeological evidence for the pre-Anglian origins of most of these sites.

Further, King CADWALLON (†634) of GWYNEDD had a claim on the kingship of Brynaich, probably on the basis of descent from Cunedda, which is articulated in the panegyric *Moliant Cadwallon*. He conquered and ruled Brynaich for a year. A later Anglian king, Oswald (†642), and his brother and successor Oswydd (†671) spent 18 years of their early lives (617–34) in exile among the Irish; they were, as described by BEDE, fluent speakers of Irish and ardent devotees of the Irish churches founded by COLUM CILLE of Iona (EILEAN Ì) and his successors.

Northumbria's 'Golden Age' is understood largely as a vigorous fusion of Celtic traditions and learning with the Anglo-Saxon culture, the fruit of which can be seen in the intricately illuminated Lindisfarne Gospels of the late 7th century (see ART, CELTIC) and the extensive learning of the scientific and historical works of BEDE with their evident debt to Adomnán and other Irish authors. After Brynaich had ceased to exist as a kingdom, the name continued to be used as a general term for English enemies in the Welsh court poetry of the GOGYNFEIRDD.

Brynaich's boundaries no doubt fluctuated, but in Anglo-Saxon times the region's southern border was the river Tees. Brynaich probably extended its northern frontier to the Forth (Foirthe) under King Oswald by conquest in 638, at the time of the *obsesio Etin* (siege of Edinburgh/Dùn Èideann), noted in the Annals of Ulster at 638. Then, or at about this time, with the annexation of Lothian in the present-day Lowlands of Scotland (Alba), Brynaich had become more or less coterminous with the old Brythonic kingdom of Gododdin. Modern Scotland now includes the lands between the Tweed and Forth that had once been part of Brynaich and entertained designs on the whole of it in the Middle Ages.

John T. Koch

BRYTHONIC

Brythonic, as a specialist linguistic term, refers to a closely related subfamily within the Celtic languages. Two Brythonic languages have survived continuously to the present day, Breton and Welsh. Cornish, which also belongs to this group, died out toward the late 18th century or early 19th century, but was soon after revived. Cumbric refers to one or more Brythonic dialects spoken in early medieval north Britain; these died out and were replaced by Scottish Gaelic and English in the central Middle Ages.

Following the four peoples and four languages scheme of Bede (*linguae Anglorum, Scottorum, Brettonum et Pictorum*), the Pictish language is treated by many writers in Celtic studies as distinct from Brythonic. However, the actual surviving linguistic evidence for Pictish overwhelmingly supports its categorization within the Brythonic group (see also Scottish place-names).

Some writers in Celtic studies use the term British in the sense used for 'Brythonic' here; therefore, in that usage 'British' can include medieval and modern Breton, Cornish, and Welsh. This meaning of 'British' is found, for example, in the *Concise Comparative Celtic Grammar* of Lewis and Pedersen, which remains one of the standard handbooks.

In early Welsh Latin texts such as Historia Brittonum and Asser's Life of Alfred, *lingua Britannica* and *sermo Britannicus* are used for 'the Welsh/Brythonic language' and *Britannice* for 'in Welsh/ Brythonic'; cf. Bede's *lingua Brettonum* (*Historia Ecclesiastica* 1.4.). At this period, these terms apply equally well to Cornish and Breton. This usage points to an Old Welsh/Old Cornish/Old Breton *Brithonec,* the source of Middle Breton *Brezonec* 'Breton' < British and British Latin **Brittonica.* The Welsh word *Brythoneg* 'Brythonic, Welsh language' does not appear until early Modern Welsh.

Arthur—celebrated in the literature and folklore of Wales, Brittany, and Cornwall—can meaningfully be called 'a Brythonic hero'. The political alliance envisioned in the 10th-century prophetic poem Armes Prydein—including Wales, Cornwall, Brittany, and Strathclyde, as well as the Vikings and Irish—can be concisely encapsulated as a 'Brythonic-Gaelic-Norse coalition'.

John T. Koch

Robert Burns, Scotland's national poet. (Perry-Castaneda Library)

BURNS, ROBERT

Robert Burns (1759–1796), from Alloway, Ayrshire (Allmhaigh, Siorrachd Àir), is the national poet of Scotland, although he wrote in a mixture of Scots and Standard English rather than SCOTTISH GAELIC. Burns was a contemporary of James MACPHERSON, and shares some themes of ROMANTICISM and NATIONALISM with him. Indeed, 'The Vision' (1786) was directly inspired by *Ossian*, and, as celebrated in 'The Twa Dogs' (1786), he named his own dog Luath (Gaelic for 'swift') after CÙ CHULAINN's dog in Macpherson's *Fingal*. It is his close relationship with the landscape and themes inspired by local folklore, however, that make Burns a poet of interest for CELTIC STUDIES. His 'Halloween' (1780) and the more famous 'Tam O'Shanter' (1791), for instance, recall the Gaelic SAMAIN, and a great many of his poems celebrate HIGHLAND culture and Scottish history.

Antone Minard

CADWALADR AP CADWALLON

Cadwaladr ap Cadwallon (Old Welsh Catgualart map Catgollaun) was king of Gwynedd. He died in a plague, probably in AD 664. Cadwaladr likely founded the church at Llangadwaladr, where an inscription commemorating his grandfather, Cadfan ab Iago, was found. In the 10th-century Armes Prydein, Cadwaladr figures as one of two messianic leaders who were expected to restore the Britons to the sovereignty of Britain and expel the Anglo-Saxons. It is not clear how he achieved this reputation, but one possibility is that, during his own lifetime, Cadwaladr was expected to avenge the death of his father Cadwallon against the Northumbrians, thereby restoring Gwynedd's short-lived hegemony over the leading English kingdom (then Northumbria). The name *Cadwaladr* is Celtic < British * *Catu-walatros* 'battle-leader'.

John T. Koch

CADWALLON AP CADFAN

Cadwallon ap Cadfan, king of Gwynedd (625–34/5) and Northumbria (633–34/5), was the last Brythonic-speaking ruler to hold sway over much of eastern Britain until Henry VII (Harri Tudur) secured the throne of England 800 years later. He claimed direct descent from Cunedda through Maelgwn Gwynedd. A panegyric in his honour (*Moliant Cadwallon*) seems to be the first surviving poem from Gwynedd. Several early medieval Latin sources mention Cadwallon. Bede's *Historia Ecclesiastica* demonized Cadwallon, a step essential to Bede's moral message justifying the Anglo-Saxon domination of Britain.

According to Bede, Cadwallon defeated and killed Eadwine at the battle of Hatfield (Old English Haethfelth) on 12 October 633 (*Historia Ecclesiastica* 2.20). In *Annales Cambriae* (631), Cadwallon is said to have overthrown Eadwine in *Gueith Meicen*. In this campaign, Cadwallon was supported by the pagan Anglo-Saxon king, Penda of Mercia. A further cause for scepticism about Bede's account is the fact that Cædualla of Wessex (†689) was born and given his unusual name, adapted from Brythonic *Cadwallon*, a generation after Cadwallon ap Cadfan's death; this could hardly have happened if Bede's thoughts on Cadwallon had been shared by the Saxons of Wessex.

After a year or two spent mainly in continued fighting to consolidate his power, Cadwallon fell in 634 or 635 against the Bernician prince Oswald, who had lived in exile among the Irish since his father Æthelfrith had been defeated and killed by Eadwine in 617. This battle occurred at a place called *Cantscaul* or *Catscaul* in the Welsh Latin sources (*Historia Brittonum* §64; *Annales Cambriae* 631) and *Hefenfelth* (Heavenly field, *Caelestis campus*) by Bede (*Historia Ecclesiastica* 2.2). The site was eight miles northeast of Hexham, near HADRIAN'S WALL. Writing in the 690s, Adomnán (*Vita Columbae* 1.1) ascribes Oswald's victory against *Catlōn Brittonum rex fortissimus* (Cadwallon strongest king of the Britons) to the miraculous posthumous intercession of St COLUM CILLE of Iona (EILEAN Ì), who appeared to Oswald in a dream on the eve of the battle.

The name *Cadwallon*, Old Welsh *Catguollaun*, is Celtic and corresponds to the British and Gaulish tribal name *Catuvellauni*, which means something like 'excelling in battle'. The name is attested also as Old Breton *Catuuallon* and *Catguallon* in the witness lists of the charters of Redon and LANDEVENNEG.

John T. Koch

CAER (CHESTER), BATTLE OF

The battle of Chester, Welsh Caer, (*c.* 613 × 616), pitted the Anglo-Saxon dynasty of Bernicia (BRYNAICH) against the principal dynasty of early POWYS, the Cadelling. The BRITONS were crushingly defeated, and a major atrocity was perpetrated by the pagan English king, Æthelfrith, against the monks of Bangor Is-coed. This battle has long been understood as a decisive event in British history, and more particularly the history of the Celts in BRITAIN. The circumstances of the battle illuminate the reasons why the Britons and the Anglo-Saxons tended to polarize into antithetical identities rather than coalesce into a single hybrid people and church establishment. From the standpoint of the history of Welsh language and literature, Chester presents the fusion of the interests of the dynastic war leaders and the church of the Britons in such a way as to make intelligible how, from this period onward, the study and transmission of vernacular heroic verse was a suitable activity for monastic scholars.

The Site

The Old Welsh name for the place was *Cair Legion* 'city of the legion', medieval Latin *urbs Legionis*; it had been a place of pivotal military importance in Roman Britain until the late 4th century. The Romano-British place-name had been Celtic *Dēva* 'goddess', a transference of the ancient name of the nearby river Dee.

Early Records of the Battle of Chester

The entry in *Annales Cambriae* for the year corresponding to 613 or 615 AD records *Gueith Cair Legion* (battle of the city of the legion [i.e., Chester]) 'in which *Selim filii Cinan* [Selyf son of Cynan] fell'. The Irish ANNALS also record the event and Selyf's death.

In BEDE'S longer account, some details have been suppressed and there has been a radical reinterpretation. The English king, Æthelfrith fights against the monastic community at Bangor, guarded by a man named Brocmail, who had been praying against him. There is no mention of Selyf.

Bede's spellings of the names *Carlegion*, *Bancor*, and *Brocmail* in this passage show standard Brythonic orthography of the 7th or 8th centuries. Elsewhere, he uses the

Old English *Bancornaburg* for the monastery; therefore, he had a Brythonic Latin written source for the battle.

Given that Bede was well informed about the battle, it is remarkable that he omits mention of Æthelfrith's most important enemy, Selyf. As the name occurs in several of the brief accounts mentioned previously, the erudite Bede had probably seen it, which is confirmed indirectly by his bizarre likening of Selyf's killer, the pagan Æthelfrith, to the biblical King Saul, differing only in the detail that the English king did not believe in the true God (*Historia Ecclesiastica* 1.34). The allegory of Æthelfrith as Saul is intelligible if we understand that both Bede and his intended readers knew the derivation of Selyf's name (Old Welsh *Selim*) from the Biblical Solomon. The name of the loser at Chester, 'King Solomon', carried Old Testament associations of anointed, God-guided kingship, as well as proverbial wisdom. Saul was likewise an anointed warrior king of Israel (I Samuel 10). To call Æthelfrith 'Saul' thus challenged what Bede probably saw as the presumptuous name of the Britons' king.

John T. Koch

CAI FAB CYNYR

Cai fab Cynyr, Sir Kay in English, is one of the core figures of early Welsh Arthurian tradition and continued in ARTHURIAN LITERATURE throughout the Middle Ages. The usual Middle Welsh spelling is *Kei*, possibly from Latin *Caius* (although *Cynyr* is securely Celtic), which occurs in conjunction with the epithets *(g)wyn* 'fair' and *hir* 'tall'. Like a mere handful of Arthurian figures—Cai's comrade BEDWYR, ARTHUR's wife GWENHWYFAR (Guenevere), and his rival MEDRAWD—Cai survives more or less intact from the earliest Arthurian tradition, in contrast to such figures as MYRDDIN/Merlin, OWAIN AB URIEN, and PEREDUR, who originated in other early Welsh traditions.

Cai fab Cynyr is not mentioned in either the early historical sources or the WELSH POETRY; thus there is no evidence of him as a historical figure. He first appears in two highly fantastic pieces of literature—the poem *Pa Gur yv y Porthaur?* (Who is the gatekeeper?) and the closely related earliest Arthurian prose tale CULHWCH AC OLWEN.

In the fragmentary *Pa Gur*, Kei is as prominent as Arthur and far more active:

> [Arthur:] When he [= Cai] went to battle,
> he would slay them by hundreds.
> Unless it were God who worked it,
> Cai's death could not be achieved.

> Fair Cai slew nine witches.
> Fair Cai went to Anglesey
> to destroy lions.
> His shield was polished
> against Cath Palug

Pa Gur's Cai is an exaggeration of the idealized warrior; like the Irish CÚ CHULAINN, his superlative nature extends the hero to supernatural limits with the slaying of witches and monsters and the claim that he could not be killed without God's intervention. The nine witches slain by Cai in *Pa Gur* recall the Nine Witches of Gloucester (Welsh Caerloyw) in *Peredur* and the Breton Latin Life of St SAMSON.

In *Culhwch ac Olwen*, Cai is named first among the worthies of Arthur's court. He takes an active part in the adventures, and his supernatural attributes are described in a way that has led many modern scholars to view him as a mythological figure: among other attributes, he could breathe underwater and forgo sleep for nine days; no doctor could heal a sword wound from him; he could grow to the height of a tall tree.

In the French Arthurian Romances from CHRÉTIEN DE TROYES onward, Ké figures as Arthur's steward. He sometimes shows a surly or churlish character in these later sources.

John T. Koch

CAILLEACH BHÉIRRE

Cailleach Bhéirre (The old woman of Beare), one of the finest examples of early Irish verse, probably dates from the late 9th century and consists of 34 quatrains, plus one interpolated quatrain (§27 of the editions), in which an old woman contrasts the loneliness and privations of her old age with the joy and pleasures of her youth.

The best manuscript copy of the elegy is preceded by a prose introduction, in origin presumably extraneous to the poem, which summarizes the tradition surrounding the Old Woman of Beare and explains that the *Cailleach Bhéirre* was one of the revenants of Irish tradition who enjoyed extraordinary longevity, having lived for several mortal lifetimes. Nonetheless, the poet indicates that even the Old Woman of Beare has at last become an ordinary mortal who cannot postpone death.

The anonymous poet lays heavy stress on the contrast between the human condition, subject to ageing and decay, and the continuous renewal evident in nature, whether in the form of the sea flooding always after ebb, or the land reproducing a crop each year.

There is evidently some Christian influence on the text, but scholars have seen echoes of the pre-Christian worldview in the poem as well, and the *Cailleach Bhéirre* may, like the heroes of *Acallam na Senórach* ('Dialogue of [or with] the Old Men'), represent an attempt to bridge the two traditions.

Donncha Ó hAodha

CAISEL MUMAN

Caisel Muman (Cashel, Co. Tipperary) was a centre of secular power in Early Christian Ireland (ÉRIU), seat of the ÉOGANACHT dynasties of Munster (MUMU, Modern An Mhumhain), second in significance as an early medieval royal site only to Tara (TEAMHAIR). During the early Middle Ages, Caisel developed a dual rôle, becoming the seat of a bishop as well. In the early 12th century Caisel became an archdiocese, second in status only to Armagh (ARD MHACHA) in Ireland.

Derivation

CASHEL (Irish *Caiseal*) 'fort, castle, fortified settlement' is a borrowing from Latin *castellum*. It is also used by Irish archaeologists to designate a stone-built ring-fort, of which many thousand dot the Irish landscape.

Caisel and the Éoganacht Kings

Caisel Muman (Cashel of Munster) is the name of an important early secular centre of power dominated by the Éoganacht dynasty and founded on 'the Rock of Cashel', a natural outcropping that dominates the surrounding plain, Old Irish *Mag Femin*. According to the 7th-century account of Tírechan (§51), St Patrick baptized the sons of Nie Froích at Petra Coithrigi ('Patrick's Rock') in Cashel; this name probably refers to the Rock of Cashel itself. In the 9th- or 10th-century foundation legend *Senchas Fagbála Caisil* ('The Tradition of the Finding of Cashel'), the site was discovered by two swineherds who had fallen into an enchanted slumber. In it, they saw an angel and an ancestral founder—an account interesting and atypical in that the TUATH DÉ and typical Irish OTHERWORLD figures are absent.

Generally speaking, the kings of Caisel were seldom strong enough to challenge the powerful Uí Néill dynasties. One exception was the king/bishop CORMAC UA CUILENNÁIN (r. 902–8).

The Church at Caisel

In 1101, the high-king of Ireland, Muirchertach Ua Briain, gave the Rock of Cashel to the church. In 1111, the Synod of Ráith Bressail determined that Caisel was to be the seat of an archbishop second to Armagh in its ranking among the Irish archdioceses, and in the same century an important Benedictine monastery was founded at Cashel (see MONASTERIES). The king of Munster, Cormac Mac Cárrthaig (†1138), sponsored the building of a Romanesque church (Cormac's Chapel) for the monastery. This small but highly ornamented church remains well preserved and shows similarities to Romanesque churches in western Germany, France, and western Britain.

Since Irish Catholic emancipation (1829), the cathedral town of the archdiocese of Caiseal and Emly (Imleach) has been at Thurles, Co. Tipperary (Durlas, Contae Thiobraid Árainn), 20 km north of Caiseal. The architectural remains on the rock are a major tourist attraction.

John T. Koch

CALADBOLG/CALEDFWLCH/EXCALIBUR

The early Irish ULSTER CYCLE shares this name for a marvellous sword with Welsh and international ARTHURIAN LITERATURE.

Fergus's Sword

Toward the end of TÁIN BÓ CUAILNGE, King Ailill of Connacht returns the sword of the Ulster hero FERGUS MAC RÓICH. Fergus chants a formal verse over the sword, calling it *Caladbolg* according to the LEBOR LAIGNECH text or, in later manuscripts, *Caladcholg* 'hard sword'. He then wields this weapon with both hands to cut a gap (*berna*) of a hundred men through the host of ULAID. As he is about to strike the Ulster king, CONCHOBAR, Fergus is deterred and vents his fury instead by striking the top off three hills, thus creating the three bald hills of Meath (*teóra maele Midi*; see MIDE).

The sword Excalibur drawn from the stone—a stock motif of Arthurian literature not found in the Celtic-language sources. Manuscript illustration from the 'Romance of the Saint Graal' by Robert de Borron, France, 1300–*c*.1315. Roy 14 E, III, folio 91 (detail). (The British Library/StockphotoPro)

Arthur's Sword

Early in the action of the prose tale CULHWCH AC OLWEN, Arthur refers to his sword by name, *Caledfwlch*. He does not actually use the sword in *Culhwch*, but one of his heroes, Llenlleawc Wyδel (Llenlleawc the Irishman), uses it to slay Diwrnach Wyδel. In the HISTORIA REGUM BRITANNIAE of GEOFFREY OF MONMOUTH, Arthur's sword is named *Caliburnus*, a Latinization probably influenced by *chalybs* 'steel'. *Calibor(e)* and *Escalibor(e)* also occur for Arthur's sword in medieval French sources. In the Cornish play BEUNANS KE, the corresponding Cornish *Calesvol* is used.

Derivation

Irish *Caladbolg* and Welsh *Caledfwlch* are both composed of elements meaning 'hard' + 'gap, notch': Irish *calad* and *bolg*, Welsh *caled* and *bwlch*. The compound would thus mean 'hard cleft' or 'cleaving what is hard'. However, it is less clear whether we are dealing with a COMMON CELTIC inheritance or a borrowing between CELTIC LANGUAGES. The fact that Caledfwlch comes into the action in *Culhwch* only in connection with characters called *Gwyddel* may point to an Irish source. Conversely, the names *Kleδyf Kyuwlch* 'perfect sword' and *Cleδyf Diuwlch* 'sword with no gap' elsewhere in *Culhwch* suggest that the element *bwlch* was productively applied to swords specifically in Welsh.

John T. Koch

CALENDAR, CELTIC

Although distinctive festivals and seasonal traditions are found in the folklore and literature of the CELTIC COUNTRIES (see BELTAINE; IMBOLC; LUGNASAD; SAMAIN), it would be misleading to suppose that a pre-Christian Celtic calendar had survived and remained in use in medieval or modern times. What calendars survive—for example, the Gaulish lunar Calendar of COLIGNY—reveal a debt to the classical traditions of marking time.

The Day

The most important division of the day was into day and night. The evidence indicates that the Celtic day formerly began and ended at dusk or sunset, as did the Athenian, Hebrew, and other ancient calendars. The GAULISH word *trinox*[B] 'three night[s], three-night [festival]', attested on the Calendar of Coligny, probably refers to a three-day period; compare modern Welsh *wythnos* 'week', literally 'eight nights'.

The INDO-EUROPEAN words for 'day' and 'night' are preserved in all the Celtic languages: 'day' is Old Irish *dia* in compounds, Welsh *dydd*, Breton *deiz*; 'night' is Old Irish *nocht* in compounds, Welsh *nos*, Breton *noz*.

The Week

The names of the days of the week are all either borrowings from Latin or based on the medieval Christian calendar. The modern BRYTHONIC languages are unique in preserving all of the Latin names for the days of the week: *dies Sōlis* 'the day of the sun, Sunday' became Welsh *dydd Sul*, Breton *ar sul*.

Some of the GOIDELIC names for the days of the week are based on the Roman system—for instance, Tuesday (Irish *Márt*, Scottish Gaelic *Dimàirt*, Manx *Jemayrt*)—but several describe the weekly fasts of the medieval church. The Old Irish for Wednesday is *cétaín* 'first fast', which gives Irish *An Chéadaoin*, Manx *Jecrean*.

The Month

Although the Julian and Gregorian calendars have been used throughout the Celtic countries, some evidence indicates that at least some of the month words found in Old Irish were applied to periods at variance with the ordinary calendar. In Scottish Gaelic, *Faoilleach* 'January' and *Iuchar* 'July' can refer to either the calendar months or the periods from a fortnight before to a fortnight after 1 February and 1 August, respectively. Contemporary use conforms to the standard Gregorian calendar, and the Celtic months are primarily of interest for their names.

The Roman calendar has had a significant influence on the names. 'March' is universally a Latin borrowing, and in the Brythonic languages the words for January through May are taken from Latin. Native names are either descriptive (e.g., Welsh *medi* 'harvest, September') or based on the seasons: Early Modern Welsh *Cyntefin* 'May', Old Irish *céitemain* 'May', Scottish Gaelic *Cèitean* from the words for 'first' and 'summer'.

The Seasons

The most notable distinction between the Celtic seasons and the conventional understanding of their function is the time at which they occur. Meteorologists understand spring as beginning at the equinox, whereas the agricultural calendar of the British Isles considered it to be the midpoint of spring. Likewise, Midsummer's Day falls near the beginning of summer meteorologically, but was the midpoint of summer in the traditional calendar. Although Midsummer's Day celebrations are common in the modern Celtic countries, there is no evidence that the ancient Celts celebrated either the solstices or the equinoctes.

Quarter Days and Festivals

The year is traditionally divided not only into four seasons, but also into four quarters, which do not necessarily coincide with the seasons as they are now marked. In ENGLAND, these quarter days are Lady Day (25 March), Midsummer's Day (24 June), Michaelmas (29 September), and Christmas (25 December). Lady Day, also known as the Feast of the Annunciation, was officially designated as New Year's Day until 1752 in England and the territories it administered.

In Scotland (ALBA), the quarter days are Candlemas (2 February), Whitsuntide (15 May), Lammas (1 August), and Martinmas (11 November). In Ireland (ÉIRE), they are Lá Fhéile Bríde (St BRIGIT's Day, 1 February), a continuation of Old Irish IMBOLC; Lá Bealtaine (May Day, 1 May), a continuation of Old Irish BELTAINE; Lá Lúnasa (Lammas, 1 August), a continuation of Old Irish LUGNASAD; and Lá Samhain (All Saints' Day, 1 November), a continuation of Old Irish SAMAIN.

Care must be taken with fixed dates. The Gregorian calendar used today was proposed as a replacement for the Julian calendar in 1582, but its adoption occurred at different times and with different levels of success in the Celtic countries. France, including Brittany (BREIZH), adopted the reform in the 1580s, Scotland in 1600, England (and thence Cornwall [KERNOW], Ireland, and Wales [CYMRU]) in 1752, and the Isle of Man (ELLAN VANNIN) in 1753. As a consequence, a ten- or eleven-day discrepancy between the calendars used by England and Scotland persisted for more than 100 years. Many festivals are still celebrated according to the 'old calendar', so that, for example, Samain customs sometimes take place on 1 November, but these may have become Martinmas customs.

Antone Minard

CALIDONES

The Calidones were a major tribe in ancient BRITAIN who resided beyond the Roman frontier. The name was in use by the 1st century AD and, therefore, the group predates the PICTS, whose range overlaps. The corresponding place-name *Caledonia* occurs in the Agricola of Tacitus and other sources, and is used in modern times as a poetic name for Scotland (ALBA). The Celtic spelling *Calidū* occurs on the COINAGE of the Caletes and Arverni of GAUL. It is nonetheless uncertain whether the name *Calidones* is related to *Caletes* or PROTO-CELTIC *kalet-* 'hard'.

The *Geography* of Ptolemy (2nd century AD) places the καληδονιοι (Caledonioi) in the vicinity of the Great Glen and Loch Ness. The name survives in three GAELIC place-names from Perthshire (Gaelic Siorrachd Pheairt): *Dùn Chaillean*/Dunkeld 'Fort of the Calidones', nearby *Ro-hallion* 'Rath of the Calidones', and *Sìdh Chaillean*/Schiehallion 'SíD of the Calidones'.

Silva Calidonia 'the Caledonian forest' is mentioned by Pliny (*Natural History* 4.102) and others. Old Welsh *cat Coit Celidon* 'battle of the forest of the Calidones' occurs in the 9th-century Historia Brittonum (§56) as Arthur's seventh battle. In the early Welsh poetry connected with Myrddin, Coed Celyddon is the place where he flees for refuge after the battle of Arfderydd.

John T. Koch

CAMLAN

Camlan is the name of the battle in which Arthur and Medrawd fell, possibly at the Roman fort of Camboglanna (now Castlesteads, Cumbria). See also Arthur, the historical evidence; annals; Arthurian sites.

Camlan figures twice in the great catalogue of Arthurian heroes in the early Welsh prose tale Culhwch ac Olwen. *Gwynn Hyuar maer Kernyw a Dyfneint* 'Gwynn the ready to anger, overseer of Cornwall and Dumnonia' is noted as one of the nine men who 'wove' or plotted the battle of Camlan. In the Welsh Arthurian tale Breuddwyd Rhonabwy, the battle is blamed on another troublemaker, Iddawg the 'Churn of Britain'. We lack a coherent story, but these allusions suggest that there was a tradition of a complicated background, with numerous characters interacting to seal the fate of Arthur.

Camlan is named in five of Welsh Triads. No. 51 ('The Three Dishonoured Men') closely follows Geoffrey of Monmouth's account in Historia Regum Britanniae: While Arthur was campaigning against the Romans, Medrawd instigated the rebellion. Arthur returned and killed Medrawd at Camlan; he himself was taken mortally wounded to Ynys Afallach (see Avalon). No. 53 ('The Three Harmful Blows') says that the battle was caused by Gwenhwyfach striking her sister, Arthur's wife Gwenhwyfar. The Welsh law texts direct that 'a song of Camlan' be sung to the queen.

According to Geoffrey, who serves as the basis for subsequent texts, Arthur's nephew 'Modred' treacherously married Arthur's wife 'Guanhumara' while Arthur was in Gaul. The battle was then fought on the river Camblana (i.e., the Camel) in Cornwall. Geoffrey's spelling suggests a written source whose first element was still written as Romano-British *Camb(o)-*, rather than Old Welsh *Cam(m)-*.

John T. Koch

CAMMA

Camma (*fl.* 2nd century BC) was a Galatian high priestess of the goddess identified with Artemis (see interpretatio romana). Two versions of her story appear in the *Moralia* of Plutarch ('On the Bravery of Women' 257; 'The Dialogue on Love' 768). Another version is provided by Polyaenus (*History* 8.39); it tells the story of two men, Sinātos and Sinorīx of the Tolistobogii tribe. Camma was a young, beautiful, virtuous priestess of Artemis, 'the goddess whom the Galatae [Galatians] most revere'. She was also, in contrast to priestesses of the Greek Artemis, a married woman, to Sinātos. Sinorīx, whose name means 'old king,' fell in love with her. To obtain her, he treacherously murdered her husband and pursued her. At last she agreed, but poisoned both herself and him at the altar, declaring to Artemis that since her husband's death she had lived only for revenge.

The Celtic names of the three characters suggest that the details took shape as a Galatian legend. As a tragic love triangle, the Camma story has parallels in Celtic materials: ARTHURIAN LITERATURE, TRISTAN AND ISOLT, early Irish stories. In FIANNAÍOCHT, for example, the tale TÓRUIGHEACHT DHIARMADA AGUS GHRÁINNE also hinges on a poisoned drink given treacherously by the unwilling bride to the powerful would-be groom in the wedding ritual. The Camma story is also the subject of a large baroque painting by Eustache Le Sueur (1616–55), *Camma Offers the Poisoned Wedding Cup to Synorix in the Temple of Diana, c.* 1644, now in the Museum of Fine Arts, Boston.

John T. Koch and Antone Minard

CAMULODŪNON AND CAMELOT

Camulodūnon (present-day Colchester, ENGLAND) was the largest OPPIDUM in Britain and probably anywhere in the Celtic world. It became the Romano-British *civitas* of the Trinovantes. The original site was just south of modern Colchester. Around the year AD 5, Camulodūnon was conquered by CUNOBELINOS, head of the Catuvellauni, who built a new capital north of the old centre.

After the Roman invasion under the Emperor Claudius in AD 43, this tribal settlement became the administrative centre of the Roman province of Britannia, which initially consisted of only southeastern Britain. This site was destroyed and its inhabitants massacred during the revolt of BOUDĪCA in AD 60/1. Camulodūnon recovered slowly, and London subsequently became the capital of the province.

The name Camulodūnon comes from the Celtic god Camulos, known extensively from Iberia (see also GALICIA) to GALATIA, in INSCRIPTIONS as well as place-names. It is most probably the source of Camelot, which figures prominently in ARTHURIAN LITERATURE from the late 12th century onward. The first mention of Camelot occurs in the Old French poem *Lancelot* of CHRÉTIEN DE TROYES. Therefore, some connection between post-Roman Camulodūnum and a historical ARTHUR would not be impossible, but it is most likely that Chrétien or one of his sources simply came across the name as an important ancient town in Britain.

John T. Koch and Peter E. Busse

CANTREF

Cantref comes from Welsh *can(t)* 'hundred' + *tref* 'holding' (modern 'town'). The *cantref* was the largest administrative unit in medieval Wales (CYMRU) and generally consisted of two or three *cymydau* (commotes; sing. *cwmwd*).

The earliest usage in Wales is found in the Book of Llandaf (*Liber Landavensis*). No complete list of the *cantrefi* exists prior to the 15th century. The Four Branches of the MABINOGI refer to several *cantrefi* in parts of Wales, and the prologue of the Cyfnerth texts of the Welsh laws refers to others, but it is difficult to know how much credence to place in these groupings.

The *cantrefi* were divided into a number of *trefi* (not necessarily one hundred in number), which were economic units providing renders for the king. The royal court—which consisted of the *llys*, a collection of buildings that constituted the king's palace; his *maenol*, where his cattle were pastured; and his *maerdref*, where the Welsh bondmen lived—formed its centre.

The *cantref* also functioned as a judicial unit and had its own court, which was an assembly of the *uchelwyr* (noblemen) of the *cantref*. These courts would have been presided over by professional judges in north Wales, but by local landowners in the south.

Morfydd E. Owen

CARADOG OF LLANCARFAN

According to a Latin couplet at the end of the Life of St Cadoc and the Life of St GILDAS, the 12th-century Welsh hagiographer Caradog of Llancarfan wrote both Lives (see also HAGIOGRAPHY). In the former case, he appears to have been revising the work of a hagiographer called Lifris. Both Lives include narratives involving ARTHUR that go beyond simple demonstration of saintly over secular authority. In Cadoc's Life, Arthur helps the future saint's father carry off his future mother. The Life of Gildas contains the earliest reference to conflict between Arthur and Gildas's brother Hueil as well as the earliest abduction tale involving Arthur's wife GWENHWYFAR. (Gildas negotiates between Arthur and Melwas, who is holding the queen in Glastonbury.) Caradog may have assembled the Book of Llandaf (*Liber Landavensis*).

The common Welsh man's name Caradog is derived from the attested Old Celtic CARATĀCOS. Caradog's usual epithet Llancarfan is the name of a monastery, situated in Bro MORGANNWG in south Wales (CYMRU).

Elissa R. Henken

CARATĀCOS

Caratācos, son of CUNOBELINOS, the king of the Catuvellauni and the Trinovantes, was a British prince and a key figure the British struggle against the Roman invasion in the period AD 43–51. After the death of Cunobelinos in *c.* AD 41, Caratācos reconsolidated his father's hegemony in southeast BRITAIN. His main adversary was the Roman governor Publius Ostorius Scapula. The British forces lost, but Caratācos escaped to stir up anti-Roman action among the free tribes of what is now Wales (CYMRU) and northern ENGLAND, including the Silures and Ordovices. In AD 51, Queen CARTIMANDUA took Caratācos into custody and handed him over to the Romans. He was taken in chains to Rome where, in a celebrated speech, he chastised the Emperor Claudius for the oppressive greed of his kinsmen.

The name *Caratācos* (the common *Caractacus* is a late corruption) is Celtic, an adjectival formation based on Celtic *kara-* 'love'. The early medieval name is Old Breton *Caratoc* and Old Irish *Carthach*. In Old Welsh, *Caratauc map Cinbelin map Teuhant* recollects the historical Caratācos († AD 58) son of Cunobelinos († *c.* AD 41) son of Tasciovanos († *c.* AD 10).

Peter E. Busse and John T. Koch

CARNYX

Carnyx is a term applied to an animal-headed trumpet once common across Celtic-speaking Europe in the period *c.* 300 BC–*c.* AD 300. The GUNDESTRUP CAULDRON depicts the carnyx in use—a long segmented metal tube, held vertically, with an animal-head terminal. There are five surviving examples, and further evidence from depictions on COINAGE, statues, and bronzes. Although it is often seen as a Celtic instrument, it is clear that the carnyx was also used outside the Celtic world.

The finest surviving fragment is the boar's head from Deskford, northeast Scotland (ALBA), in sheet bronze and brass. This is a late example, dating from *c.* AD 80–200×300, and was buried as a votive offering in a peat bog (see WATERY DEPOSITIONS).

Fraser Hunter

CARTIMANDUA

Cartimandua (r. pre AD 43–*c.* 75) was queen of the BRIGANTES of north BRITAIN. Information about her turbulent reign is preserved in Tacitus. Cartimandua's story serves as evidence for the rôle of women in political leadership among ancient Celtic groups; thus, as Tacitus wrote (with reference to BOUDĪCA), 'The Britons do not discriminate by gender in selecting war leaders' (*Agricola* 16).

Under Cartimandua, the Brigantian territory was a Roman client kingdom beyond the frontier of the province of Britannia. Such divide-and-conquer arrangements were vital to the early phases of Roman expansion in Britain. In AD 51, Cartimandua turned CARATĀCOS son of CUNOBELINOS of the Catuvellauni over to the Romans. Subsequently, according to Tacitus, she abadoned her husband Venutius in favour of Vellocatus, his armour-bearer.

'This huge scandal rocked her household to its foundation. The tribe's sentiments favoured her rightful husband [Venutius]. Favouring the illegitimate husband were the queen's libido and her ferocious temper. In response to her rejection, Venutius mustered some war-bands and was helped at that same time by an uprising among this tribe, the Brigantes. He succeeded in putting Cartimandua into an extremely desperate position. She requested Roman forces. 'Some of our infantry and cavalry auxiliary units, after fighting for a time with mixed results, rescued the queen from this dangerous crisis' (*Historiae* 3.45).

The name *Cartimandua* is Celtic. The second element of the compound probably means 'pony' or 'small horse' (cf. *Catumandus*; *Mandubracios*). The meaning of the first element is uncertain.

John T. Koch

CASHEL

Cashel is a term that refers to the stone version of an Irish earthen ring-fort or 'rath'; see also CAISEL. Several thousand of these structures have been identified in the Irish landscape. They occur most often in the west of Ireland (ÉIRE), where stony terrain is prevalent, and consist of a stone wall or rampart enclosing a roughly circular area averaging 15–25 m in diameter, smaller than typical earthen ring-forts.

Mural chambers—small rooms and/or passages built within the thickness of the rampart—and souterrains (underground chambers) are found within cashels. At Leacanabuaile, Co. Kerry (Contae Chiarraí), the souterrain was accessed via a hole in the floor of a mural chamber.

A number of structures usually existed within the walls of a cashel: dwellings, workshops, and agricultural buildings. Stone huts or clocháns were unmortared and most often circular.

Cashels were often situated adjacent to viable agricultural land in prominent positions that provided good views of the surrounding countryside. Some may have controlled important routeways and associated trade. Excavation, however, suggests that cashels functioned primarily as enclosed farmsteads.

The term 'cashel' is generally applied to stone enclosures associated with the early historic period, the pre-Norman Middle Ages (5th–12th century AD). Prehistoric native enclosures such as those on Aughinish Island (Co. Clare/Contae an Chláir) and at Carrigillihy (Co. Cork/Contae Chorcaí) may reveal the origins of the cashel. A small number of cashels saw continued use into the modern period; Cahermacnaghten (Co. Clare), for example, was used as a law school by the O'Davorens in the 17th century.

Michelle Comber

CASSIVELLAUNOS/CASWALLON

Cassivellaunos (Welsh *Caswallon*) was the war leader chosen by the assembled British tribes to oppose Caesar during his second expedition to BRITAIN in the summer of 54 BC. Caesar does not tell us to which tribe his opponent belonged, but the Catuvellauni seem the most likely, based in part on the fact that Cassivellaunos's lands were separated from Kent (*Cantium*) by the river THAMES (*flumen Tamesis*).

Cassivellaunos engaged in strategic warfare against the Romans with tactics that included ambushes from concealed locations, rapid mobility relying on a core force of 4,000 chariots (*esseda*, see CHARIOT), tactical retreat over difficult country unknown to the Romans, and the driving off of livestock and civilian population to deny the enemy food and reconnaissance. Caesar admits to having some difficulty in finding and coming to grips with the BRITONS. He countered his foes' actions by destroying the Britons' crops. It was another century before the Claudian invasion broke the anti-Roman power of the Catuvellauni and Roman Britain began in earnest.

In medieval Welsh and Welsh Latin literature (HISTORIA BRITTONUM, HISTORIA REGUM BRITANNIAE, BRUT Y BRENHINEDD), this story is colourfully woven into LEGENDARY HISTORY: Cassibellaunus, Welsh Caswallon, is portrayed as a national hero. For this group of sources, some information independent of Caesar seems to have been available. Caswallon son of BELI MAWR is also a figure of mythologized Welsh legend. As such, he is the only known historical figure in the Four Branches of the MABINOGI, where he appears as a sinister magician who usurps the crown of London by donning a cloak of invisibility and surprising his enemies by cutting them down with a sword.

Several mentions of Caswallon in the T<small>RIADS</small> suggest that he had once been the subject of extensive and complicated narratives (cf. also C<small>YFRANC</small> L<small>LUDD A</small> L<small>LEFELYS</small>). In TYP no. 35, he is said to have led an army, who never returned, to the Continent in pursuit of Caesar's men. Caswallon's horse Meinlas (slender grey) is mentioned in TYP nos. 38 and 59.

The name *Cassivellaunos* is a Celtic compound that may be compared with the Continental Belgic tribal name *Veliocasses* (see B<small>ELGAE</small>). Vercassivellaunos was a general of the Arverni and involved at Caesar's siege of Alesia in 52 BC (*De Bello Gallico* 7.76); the name is the same with the Celtic prefix *wer-* 'super'.

John T. Koch

CATH MAIGE TUIRED

Cath Maige Tuired ('The [Second] Battle of Mag Tuired') is the central work in the Irish M<small>YTHOLOGICAL</small> C<small>YCLE</small>. The story survives in two versions: the better-known medieval saga and the 16th-century *Cath Muighe Tuireadh*. This tale is an important source of information on the T<small>UATH</small> D<small>É</small>, including L<small>UG</small>, D<small>AGDA</small>, O<small>ENGUS MAC IND</small> Ó<small>C</small>, Nuadu (see N<small>ŌDONS</small>), Badb (B<small>ODB</small>), G<small>OIBNIU</small> the smith, Bríg (also known as B<small>RIGIT</small>), M<small>ACHA</small>, and Ogma (see O<small>GMIOS</small>). The central theme of the tale is the conflict between the Tuath Dé and the demonic overseas race known as the F<small>OMOIRI</small>.

John T. Koch

CATHBAD

Cathbad is the name of a prominent *drui* (<small>DRUID</small>) in the Irish U<small>LSTER</small> C<small>YCLE</small> of tales. In the 'Boyhood Deeds of C<small>Ú</small> C<small>HULAINN</small>', contained in T<small>ÁIN</small> B<small>Ó</small> C<small>UAILNGE</small>, it is Cathbad who inspires the hero's taking of arms. In L<small>ONGAS MAC N</small>U<small>ISLENN</small>, Cathbad foretells D<small>ERDRIU'S</small> birth and the impending tragedy that she will bring. Cathbad is also present in M<small>ESCA</small> U<small>LAD</small> and F<small>LED</small> B<small>RICRENN</small>. In a version of the conception tale of King C<small>ONCHOBAR</small> (*Compert Conchobuir*), Cathbad is described as a *fénnid* (tribeless warrior; see F<small>ÍAN</small>) as well as a druid; he forces Nes, mother of the future king, into marriage. The Old Irish name *Cathbad* is clearly Celtic—a compound whose first element is the very common P<small>ROTO</small>-C<small>ELTIC</small> **katu-* 'battle'.

John T. Koch

CATRAETH

Catraeth, identified with modern Catterick, Yorkshire, E<small>NGLAND</small>, was the site of military action celebrated in the heroic poetry attributed to the earliest Welsh poets or C<small>YNFEIRDD</small>. There is no mention of this battle elsewhere in any period sources, such as A<small>NNALS</small> or H<small>ISTORIA</small> B<small>RITTONUM</small>. Nevertheless, it is clear from the last source that Catterick (*vicus Cataracta*) was a place of central importance for 7th-century Northumbria and its fledgling church. Archaeological evidence—though not showing evidence for a battle—does indicate that the important Roman fortified town of Cataracta (Ptolemy's κατουραχτονιον *Caturactonion*), situated at a hub in the north–south Roman road network, continued to be occupied by people who coexisted with incoming Germanic groups by the later 6th century.

Catraeth and the Gododdin

A battle fought at Catraeth is repeatedly mentioned in the heroic elegies known collectively as the GODODDIN, where the name of the battle site is given 23 times. The host gathered at Din Eidyn (Edinburgh/DÙN ÈIDEANN) and included heroes from various regions. The idea that the Gododdin forces lost and were annihilated, or nearly so, at Catraeth is present in later texts, but not the most archaic (B2).

Catraeth and Urien Rheged

In the panegyric *awdlau* addressed to the 6th-century Brythonic military leader URIEN of RHEGED, Catraeth is mentioned twice. In a poem celebrating the victory of *Gweith Gwen Ystrat* (The battle of the white/blessed valley), Urien is portrayed as mustering *gwyr Katraeth* (men of Catraeth) at dawn and leading them against mounted attackers at a ford. The battle is prolonged and bloody. A final decisive charge by Urien is anticipated at the end of the poem. These details are broadly consistent with what can be gleaned of the battle of Catraeth from the *Gododdin*, assuming that we are now looking at things from the side of the defenders. There is also a political correspondence in that Text A of the *Gododdin* once refers to the enemy at Catraeth as *meibyon Godebawc*—that is, the Coeling, progeny of Coel Hen Godebog, and Urien's dynasty.

In the poem *Yspeil Taliessin, Kanu Vryen* (Taliesin's spoils, Urien poetry), the reference to Urien at Catraeth occurs in the following lines:

> On Easter, I saw the great light and the abundant fruits. . . .
> And I have seen the ruler whose decrees are most generous:
> I saw Catraeth's leader over the plains.

The praise of an early martial hero in connection with a lyrical celebration of Easter is remarkable. The poet is clearly expressing the Christian concept of the day on which light triumphs over darkness and life triumphs over death. The reference is intelligible as an allegory in the context of 7th-century Christian Northumbria, in which the EASTER CONTROVERSY was the central theological dispute and Catterick had special claims as a high-status site connected with England's Christian origins.

A reference to a warrior called Gwallawg at Catraeth occurs in *Moliant Cadwallon* (Praise of CADWALLON). Urien and Gwallawg were collateral kinsmen within the Coeling dynasty, as shown in the Old Welsh Harleian GENEALOGIES §§8–9. According to *Historia Brittonum* §63, the two kings were allies at the time of Urien's death at the siege of LINDISFARNE.

Vicus Cataracta and Northumbria's Conversion

The Anglo-Saxon material begins in the Catterick area shows both intrusive Germanic features and a continuation of local features from the Roman period. The baptism of thousands conducted by Paulinus near Catterick in the river Swale in 627 is described by Bede; *Historia Brittonum* §63 tells us that it was Rhun ap Urien who directed the mass baptism. Catterick remained a Northumbrian royal residence 'suitable for large ceremonial occasions', such as royal weddings, until the late 8th century.

John T. Koch

CAULDRONS

Metal cauldrons were widely used for cooking, storing, and serving food, as well as for ceremonial and ritual purposes, in both Continental and insular Celtic society from the Late Bronze Age to early medieval times. Archaeological finds and literary references confirm that the cauldron was a status symbol whose possession and use was probably restricted to the more privileged members of society and, perhaps, formal festive occasions. As a symbol of plenty and, perhaps, power, the cauldron was important enough to be depicted on Celtic COINAGE, as examples found in ARMORICA show.

The numerous archaeological sites at which cauldrons have been found stretch from Norway in the north to Bosnia-Herzegovina and southern Italy in the south, and from Ireland (ÉRIU) in the west to Rumania in the east. Cauldrons were found among the grave goods at many burial sites of the western HALLSTATT area. At numerous other later prehistoric sites, they were deposited as votive gifts, sometimes filled with other metalware (see WATERY DEPOSITIONS). This latter group also includes the famous GUNDESTRUP CAULDRON.

In Irish and Welsh literature, cauldrons are highly treasured possessions whose gain or loss is worth mentioning. The numerous literary references highlight the cauldron's importance in Celtic culture, especially as a symbol of inexhaustible plenty. Mighty rulers of the OTHERWORLD, as in the early Welsh ARTHURIAN poem PREIDDIAU ANNWFN, and the DAGDA, senior

A bronze cauldron wagon with figures suggesting a mythic or heroic narrative, found in a Hallstatt princely grave at Strettweg near Judenberg, Austria. The tall female figure in the centre is perhaps a goddess to whom the stag is being sacrificed by the naked man with the axe. Bronze, 33 cm in height. Landesmuseum Joanneum, Graz, Austria. (Erich Lessing/Art Resource, New York)

deity of the Tuath Dé, owned marvellous cauldrons. The cauldron welded by the Irish smith-god Goibniu provided all the food at Otherworld feasts. A connected symbolism is that of resurrection of the dead, as in the tale of Branwen in the Mabinogi, where Irish warriors are revived by being thrown into the *peir dadeni* (cauldron of rebirth). Cauldrons were also connected with wisdom, prophecy, and truth. In *Chwedl Taliesin* (The tale of Taliesin), Gwion gains the supernatural knowledge that helps him become Taliesin when he tastes three drops from the magic potion boiling in Ceridwen's cauldron (see also Llyfr Taliesin).

The Celtic languages include several words for cauldrons and similar large vessels for food and drink. The most widespread inherited form is Proto-Celtic *k^war-io-*, the common source of Irish and Scottish Gaelic *coire*, Middle Welsh *peir*, Old Cornish *per* glossed 'lebes' (kettle), and Breton *per*.

Marion Löffler

CÉITINN, SEATHRÚN (GEOFFREY KEATING)

Seathrún Céitinn (usually Anglicized Geoffrey Keating, *c.* 1580–1644) was an Irish Catholic priest and historian. He is best remembered for his Irish-language history of Ireland (Ériu), *Foras feasa ar Éirinn* (Compendium of wisdom about Ireland, *c.* 1634), the story of Ireland from Creation to the coming of the Normans in the 12th century. Céitinn's stylish use of Irish helped ensure its lasting popularity. His work circulated widely in manuscript form in Irish, English, and Latin in the 17th century, and was first issued in print in English in 1723.

Céitinn's ancestry was Anglo-Norman. Educated in a bardic school, Céitinn pursued his education in France, where he gained a doctorate in divinity from the University of Rheims. Céitinn became a renowned preacher in the diocese of Lismore (Lios Mór). In addition to his history, he wrote bardic poetry and two theological tracts in Irish, one on the Mass and one on sin and death.

Bernadette Cunningham

CELTIBERIA

Celtiberia refers to the upper Ebro valley and eastern Meseta in Spain, comprising roughly the modern provinces of Soria, Zaragoza, Guadalajara, and Cuenca. The Celtiberians, who were famous for their martial ability, fought a long and bitter war against Rome known as the Celtiberian war (*Bellum Celtibericum*, 153–33 bc). Rome eventually conquered and absorbed Celtiberia and the Celtiberians.

Catullus (*c.* 84–54 bc), addressing a Celtiberian named Egnatius in a humorous poem, wrote:

> Egnatius, son of rabbity Celtibēria, Whom a dark beard makes good, And [who has] teeth scrubbed with Iberian urine. (37.18–20)

This habit of brushing teeth and washing with stale urine was widely remarked upon by classical commentators (Strabo, *Geography* 3.4.16; Diodorus Siculus, *Historical Library* 5.33). Stale urine is sterile and decomposes into ammonia, which was used for laundry well into the modern period, so this process is neither as implausible nor as unsanitary as it sounds.

Although Celtiberia, strictly speaking, formed a compact area (here ringed in white), Celtic tribal and place-names (such as forms in *-briga* 'hill, hill-fort') occurred widely through the Iberian Peninsula. Names of non-Celtic peoples appear in italics. (Map by Antone Minard, Raimund Karl, and John T. Koch)

The Roman poet Martial (AD 38–103) was a Celtiberian from Bilbilis (now Catalayud, Zaragoza, Spain). He mentions his Celtiberian origins several times (*Epigrams*, 4.55, 7.52, 10.65), and contrasts his physical qualities as a Celtiberian with a Roman from farther east: hairy rather than shaven legs and cheeks and a loud rather than a 'feeble and lisping' voice.

The CELTIBERIAN language was probably spoken into the 2nd century AD, and several important INSCRIPTIONS have survived in it.

Philip Freeman and Antone Minard

CELTIBERIAN LANGUAGE

Introduction

Celtiberian is the CONTINENTAL CELTIC dialect for which we have written evidence from eastern central Spain *c.* 179–50 BC. Sometimes called Hispano-Celtic, it is attested in a few major INSCRIPTIONS (e.g., BOTORRITA, Luzaga, and Peñalba de Villastar) and in numerous legends on COINAGE. The SCRIPTS used are the Iberian semi-syllabary and, in the later inscriptions, the Latin alphabet. The Iberian script

causes difficulties of interpretation because many characters represent a consonant followed by a vowel; therefore, clusters of consonants must often be written as though they were a series of syllables. Most often, Celtiberian script did not differentiate between voiced and unvoiced stops, with the same character used for the sound pairs /b, p/ /d, t/ /g, k/, even though the sounds themselves were distinct for Celtiberian speakers. In modern transcription, the sounds are sometimes represented by the capital letters *P*, *T*, and *K*, respectively. For example, the name written *PeliKios* is to be pronounced /beligios/. The nasals /m, n, ŋ/ at the end of a syllable are not always indicated. *TirTanos* is to be read /tridanos/.

Morphology and Syntax

Although Celtiberian is a 'fragmentarily attested language', its longer inscriptions tell the linguist much about Old Celtic phonology, morphology, and syntax. Case forms have been preserved that are not known from Gaulish or Insular Celtic evidence— for example, the locative case in -*ei*: *KorTonei* 'at Cortonos' and the dative plural in -*Pos* /-bos/ instead of the *-*Piś* /-bis/ expected from the Old Irish dative plural -(*a*) *ib*. The vocabulary, where understood, differs somewhat from the other Celtic languages and, in part, shows more similarities with other old Indo-European languages such as Sanskrit or Hittite: Celtiberian *VTA* /uta/, Sanskrit *utá* 'and'.

The Indo-European pronouns **so-* (the demonstrative pronoun 'this', 'that') and **io-* (the relative pronoun 'who', 'which', 'that') have fully inflected forms (*so, soð, somui, somei, soisum*), whereas in Insular Celtic these are found only as enclitics, unstressed words attached to another word.

Within the attested Celtic languages, Celtiberian syntax shows the most archaic features. An example is SOV (subject–object–verb) order in the unmarked sentence. Another feature is the repetition of enclitic *-kue* 'and' (< Proto-Indo-European **kʷe* 'and'). All of this evidence points to the fact that Celtiberian is by far the most archaic Celtic language known to us. Many of the longer texts still await a satisfactory translation.

Peter E. Busse

CELTIC COUNTRIES AND CHARACTERISTICS OF THE CELTIC TERRITORIES

Definition

As a conventional term, 'the Celtic countries' means Ireland (ÉIRE), Scotland (ALBA), Wales (CYMRU), Brittany (BREIZH), the Isle of Man (ELLAN VANNIN), and Cornwall (KERNOW). The first four of these regions have an unofficial primary status, largely due to their historical importance as politically and culturally distinct areas, and also as possessing CELTIC LANGUAGES that have survived continuously to the present. The Isle of Man's cultural, linguistic, and political history is closely allied with that of Scotland. Cornwall, too, is thoroughly recognized within Celtic studies, as it is a territory that was home to a Celtic language into modern times and generated a sizeable body of literature (see CORNISH LITERATURE). Indeed, literature continues to be

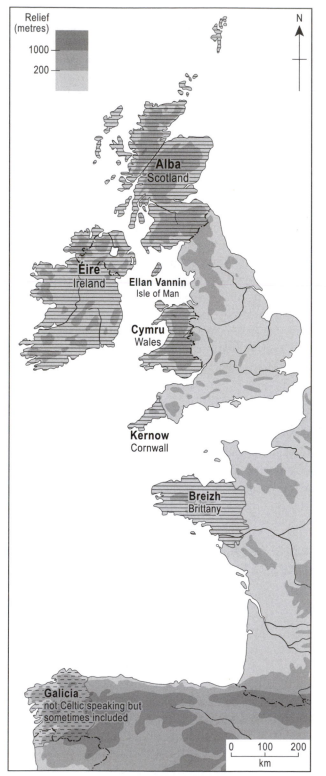

(Map by Ian Gulley and Antony Smith)

produced in both MANX and CORNISH. GALICIA is often considered a Celtic country, particularly with regard to its music, although no Celtic language has been spoken there since the very early Middle Ages.

The idea of Celtic countries is a modern one, growing out of the development of philological science from the RENAISSANCE onward, leading to the recognition of the six languages as forming a closely related family. The term *Celtic* was first applied to non-English languages in BRITAIN and Ireland by George Buchanan (1506–82). The language family was later defined systematically, with supporting evidence, by Edward LHUYD (1660–1709). The extension of the term into non-linguistic matters of culture, such as costume, music, and national identity, gained impetus through PAN-CELTICISM and related intellectual movements in the 19th and 20th centuries. 'Celtic countries' remains a useful concept, in part justifiable by the stability of the geographic limits of Celtic-speaking territory between the mid-7th century AD and early modern times.

In light of these understandings, in the present article 'Celtic territories' or 'countries' will not mean ENGLAND and western Europe—areas where Celtic languages were undoubtedly spoken in late prehistory, in the Roman period, and here and there in the early Middle Ages. Also omitted are those parts of the world, such as the Americas and Australasia, where Celtic languages have been spoken and literature written only following recent EMIGRATION.

Essential Geography

The Celtic territories exhibit a variety of geographical characteristics. Much of Scotland and a significant part of northwest Wales are mountainous. Much of Wales, some of Cornwall, and most of western Brittany are exposed plateaux. Parts of Ireland have extensive peat bogs. While such descriptions do not have to mean that those areas were totally deserted, they certainly did not lend themselves to settlement and AGRICULTURE. Given that life was not easy to support in these regions, people on the whole lived elsewhere. Consequently, population distribution was noticeably coastal in western Scotland, Wales, Cornwall and Brittany; and was much denser in Fife (Fìobha) and eastern Scotland, in Anglesey (Môn), the extreme southwest and the southeast of Wales, and in eastern Brittany. In Ireland, by contrast, as in the Isle of Man, settlement was much more widely distributed.

Vegetation was much more mixed in earlier times: deciduous woodland (oak, alder, birch) up to 610 m (2,000 ft); broom, furze (gorse), and bracken (fern) on the southern plateaux. 'Dense forest'—a recurrent image in the literature—was not extensive outside Scotland; light woodland, in contrast, was common. Extensive hedge planting was a development of the late Middle Ages and the early modern period.

Given the terrain, communications were slow in many parts. Wales and Scotland were difficult to cross except through a few narrow corridors; even today one cannot travel quickly across country north to south from Bangor (GWYNEDD) to Cardiff (Caerdydd), Wales, or in Scotland. Inland Brittany was served by a group of Roman arterial roads from the 1st century, some of which has survived (see ROADS). Ireland, by contrast, was better served by its inland waterways.

Political geography was also significant for medieval development. Major differences separated Celtic areas with a relationship to the Roman Empire, whatever the levels of acculturation (Brittany, Cornwall, Wales, and for a period the Scottish Lowlands), from those areas outside them (Isle of Man, Ireland, and central/northern Scotland).

Migration and Populations

In the late and immediate post-Roman period, Germanic groups (Angles, Saxons, Frisians, and others; see ANGLO-SAXON 'CONQUEST') came from northern Germany and southern Scandinavia to settle in eastern Britain, thereby introducing the English language. They also introduced an alien aristocracy, wiping out many recently established British kingdoms, especially in the course of the late 6th and 7th centuries. The ensuing political upheaval left its mark on Brythonic literature, with heroic defeat emerging as a major theme of the early poetry (see GODODDIN).

(Map by John T. Koch)

There were also Irish raids on western Britain in the late and immediate post-Roman period, with smaller-scale settlement, most notably the Dál Riata. These movements are reflected in the literature in different ways. Subsequent to the raids there was an enforced Christian mission to Ireland, mostly by British Christians such as St Patrick, and a trail of British Christians can be traced through early Irish literature. At the same time, the political movement reinforced and extended the use of Gaelic in what is now Scotland.

Some of the British (that is, the Celtic Britons) remained living in eastern England, and some migrated south, to the Continent. By the mid-5th century British groups could be found in the middle Loire area, and by the late 6th century the name of the northwestern peninsula of Gaul (modern France) had changed to *Britannia Minor*, 'Little Britain', roughly equivalent to the former French province of Brittany (see Breton migrations).

A few centuries later came Viking raids, beginning in Scotland and Ireland in the very late 8th century and lasting (in various forms) into the 12th century in Ireland and the Scottish Isles. Raiding touched Cornwall in the early 9th century, Brittany from the early 9th to early 10th centuries, and Wales intermittently from mid-9th to late 11th century. The Isle of Man became a major Scandinavian political base during the 10th century. In many of these areas, raiding gave way to settlement, notably at Dublin/Baile Átha Cliath). Scandinavian settlement occasioned major linguistic change in northern Scotland and the Isles, and had a significant linguistic influence in the Isle of Man.

Peasant Proprietors and Lordly Estates

In all Celtic territories, an estate owner, who may or may not have laboured himself, took rent in one form or other. In some areas, notably medieval Brittany, good evidence supports the presence of free peasant proprietors—that is, peasants who worked their own private smallholdings. The continuing prevalence of slavery was much more common than in Germanic and Latin Europe.

Specialization and Exchange

Production in the early Middle Ages was overwhelmingly agricultural. Salt was a notable commodity, as was pottery. Craft workers proliferated during this era; Irish texts are especially detailed in this respect, distinguishing those of high and low status (goldsmiths and fine metalworkers as against cart makers, for example). Elsewhere, the variety of those concerned with food provision (cooks, bakers, butchers)—for example, in monasteries—is more often noted, but there were always some clergy, along with the servants and agents of aristocrats.

During this period in European history, evidence of merchants and markets is plentiful. Such evidence can be found in Brittany, whereas before the 9th century it is difficult to find evidence of either in Wales and Ireland. However, during the 10th century, Irish evidence of markets and market activity increases. Conversely, there are no such references in Wales, a remarkable comparison with English and other European developments of the period.

Celtic areas were under-urbanized by comparison with England and the Continent. There were a few towns in east Brittany throughout the early Middle Ages, but not much development until new foundations were made in the 11th century. In Wales and Ireland, there is no good evidence for urbanization prior to Viking and Norman settlement, and such developments occur later still in Scotland.

Wendy Davies

CELTIC LANGUAGES

The Celtic languages form a subgroup of the Indo-European family that can be defined by a special combination of changes that affected the inherited sound system. This article discusses general problems of terminology and the internal structure of the group.

Ancient Names for Celtic-Speaking Peoples on the Continent

Celti (κελτοι), *Galatae* (Γαλαται), *Celtae*, and *Galli* are names used by Greek and Latin authors for the Celtic-speaking tribes in northern Italy and west-central Europe, north of the Alps, and later also in Anatolia (present-day Turkey). The name *Celtiberi* (Greek κελτιβηρες) was used for those in central Spain (see CELTIBERIA; CELTIBERIAN; GREEK AND ROMAN ACCOUNTS). No generally agreed etymology exists for these names. Possible roots include IE **kel-*'to hide' **kel-* 'to heat' or **kel-*'to impel' for **kelt-*, and, more securely, IE **gelh₂-* 'power' (also in OIr. and Welsh *gâl* 'a warlike blow') for *Galatae* and maybe also *Galli*.

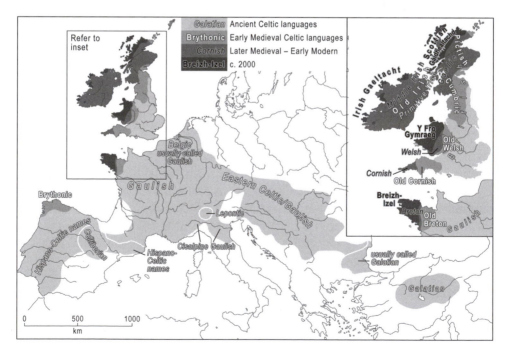

(Map by Ian Gulley and Antony Smith)

Recognizing the Celtic Languages as a Unity

Caesar states that the Belgae, Aquitani, and Galli had different languages, but gives no details. He remarked that the language of the Britons was very similar to the language of Gaul. The use of 'Celtic' for the whole family of languages is modern, going back to George Buchanan in 1587. The first scientific description of the Celtic group, based on fieldwork, is Edward Lhuyd's *Archaeologia Britannica* (1707). Franz Bopp (1839) proved that the Celtic family was a branch of Indo-European, and *Grammatica Celtica* (1853) by J. K. Zeuss was the first comprehensive comparative grammar.

Continental Celtic

All of the Continental Celtic languages—that is, all of the languages attested in antiquity on the European mainland—have died out, replaced by spoken Latin, Greek, or Germanic, probably also Slavic, mostly before the middle of the 1st millennium AD. Their exact relationship to the Insular Celtic languages is not yet certain.

Inscriptions discovered in Spain (Botorrita), Italy, and France (e.g., Larzac, Chamalières) have yielded evidence suggesting that Common Celtic must have been developed into at least two distinct languages by the time of Roman invasions into Hispania and Gallia.

The following terms are used to designate distinct varieties of Continental Celtic:

- Lepontic is attested in approximately 140 short inscriptions around Lugano in northern Italy, dated 6th to 1st century BC.
- Celtiberian differs markedly from Gaulish in its handling of the Proto-Celtic sound system and its syntax, dated 3rd to 1st century BC.
- Gaulish is known from roughly 600 inscriptions. Thousands of Gaulish proper names and occasional words are also found in Greek and Roman texts, dating from the 3rd century BC until the 4th AD. Two inscriptions from northern Italy are bilingual (Latin and Gaulish). Nothing, except a few glosses in Greek authors and roughly a hundred proper names (persons, tribes, and places), is known about the Galatian language. St Jerome states that it is 'very similar to [the language of] the Treveri', the Gaulish tribe who gave their name to Trier, Germany.

Evidence has been adduced for a Celtic language in the 'Tartessian' inscriptions of south Portugal and southwest Spain (dating 7th–5th centuries BC).

P-Celtic and Q-Celtic on the Continent

Continental Celtic is divided linguistically according to 'isoglosses'—that is, specific mappable dialect differences, including the well-known p/q- isogloss. This dual treatment reflects the fate of Proto-Celtic k^w (< PIE k^w and $\overset{\smile}{k}u$). The Q-Celtic languages preserved k^w. P-Celtic has changed k^w into p (the old PIE *p having already been lost) before the earliest attestations. Celtiberian is Q-Celtic throughout its history, and Gaulish has a few Q-forms (Sequana 'Seine'). These examples show that the change Proto-Celtic *k^w > Gualish *p had not yet operated in all parts of Gaul at the time of the Roman conquest. By comparison, Lepontic (which is attested several centuries earlier) has only p. The change IE *k^w > p is not confined to the Celtic languages.

The Insular Celtic Languages

Insular Celtic has two main divisions: BRYTHONIC (also called BRITISH or Brittonic), attested in Britain and Brittany; and GOIDELIC (more commonly called GAELIC), found in Ireland, Scotland, and the Isle of Man.

The oldest forms of Gaelic or Goidelic. The OGAM inscriptions in 'Primitive Irish' still have a q /k^w/ distinct from c /k/ (as in MAQQI 'of the son', later *mic*). In the earliest loanwords into Gaelic from Latin, q has been substituted for p. By the Old Irish period (*c.* 600–*c.* 900), q is generally no longer used. Inherited Proto-Celtic k^w and k have fallen together in c /k/.

The discovery of additional inscriptions or other types of ancient and early medieval texts from Gaul, Britain, and Ireland might shed more light on the prehistory of the extant Celtic languages and permit the reconstruction of intermediate stages between Proto-Celtic on the one side, and Proto-Goidelic and Proto-Brythonic on the other.

Stefan Zimmer

CELTIC LANGUAGES IN NORTH AMERICA, BRETON

Evidence indicates that Bretons were familiar with the fishing grounds off Canada from as early as 1500. Modern immigration of Breton speakers to North America, however, dates from the last two decades of the 19th century. The beginning of this movement is generally attributed to the tailor Nicolas Le Grand, who, along with two companions, travelled from the port of Morlaix (Montroulez) to Canada in the early 1880s. Soon, mass migration from his Roudouallec-Gourin region was under way. In 1901, the French tyre company Michelin opened a factory in Milltown, New Jersey, which employed 500 workers, many of whom were Bretons from the company's factory in Clermont-Ferrand, France. By 1911, Milltown had a colony of approximately 3,000 Bretons, mostly Breton-speaking individuals from the Gourin region. The Michelin factory in Milltown continued operating until 1930, when the Great Depression forced its closure. During those years, parts of Milltown were largely Breton speaking. Breton was spoken on the job, in the streets, and in the houses of the local population.

Another North American destination for Breton emigrants was Canada. This migration started in the early years of the 20th century, for economic and religious reasons. The most notable of these migrations occurred in 1904, when several hundred Bretons, many of them Breton speakers, left under the direction of Father Paul Le Floc'h. They settled in Saskatchewan and named their settlement Saint Brieux, after Saint Brieuc (Sant Brieg) in Brittany. Between 1904 and 1908, 110 Bretons, mainly from north Finistère, settled in Saint Laurent at Lac Manitoba.

After World War II, large numbers of Breton speakers emigrated to New York City and Montreal, and many of these immigrants became established in the restaurant trade. Youenn Gwernig's novel *La Grande Tribu* depicts New York's Breton community of the 1960s. It is estimated that more than 20,000 Breton speakers resided in the greater New York area during the last decades of the 20th century. In spite of the large number of Breton speakers in New York, Breton language classes do not form part of the curriculum of any school or university in the New York area. Breton is taught occasionally at Harvard University and at the University of California at Berkeley. At least two major Breton writers live in the United States— René Galand (Reun ar C'halan), for many years a professor of French at Wellesley College, and Paol Keineg, currently a professor of French at Duke University in North Carolina. The American branch of the International Committee for the Defence of the Breton Language has done much to inform Americans about the Breton language.

In Montreal, as in New York, many Bretons entered the restaurant trade. Indeed, in the 1960s–1980s many of Montreal's crêperies were Breton owned and staffed. It is estimated that more than 10,000 Bretons live in Montreal. Breton courses have been offered occasionally at l'Université de Montréal and at the University of Ottawa.

Kenneth E. Nilsen

CELTIC LANGUAGES IN NORTH AMERICA, IRISH

Natives of Ireland (Éire) formed part of the Spanish colony in Florida in the mid-1560s as well as the early English colonies, such as those on the Amazon, in Newfoundland, and in Virginia. At least some of these early Irish adventurers were Irish speakers. One of them was Francis Maguire, who accompanied the English on an expedition to Virginia.

During the mid-17th century, thousands of Irish were forcibly transported under Cromwellian rule to the islands of the West Indies, many of them Irish speakers. Goody Glover, who was shipped to Barbados and later settled in New England, was hanged as a witch in 1688 in Boston.

In the 18th century, one of the most popular destinations for the Irish of the counties of Cork, Waterford, Tipperary, and Kilkenny was Newfoundland, known in Irish as Talamh an Éisc (Land of the fish). Letters referring to the Catholic Church in Newfoundland point out repeatedly the need for priests to have a knowledge of the Irish language. Although considerable evidence supports the presence of Irish in Newfoundland from the mid-1700s to the mid-1800s, the language seems to have died out as a spoken language there around the turn of the 19th/20th century.

In colonial America, many of the indentured servants were Irish speakers. States with large concentrations of Irish speakers included Maryland, Pennsylvania,

New York, and, to a lesser extent, Massachusetts. The first Catholic prelate in New York City was Father Charles Whelan (1740–1806), who was said to be more fluent in GAELIC and French than in English.

Large numbers of Irish immigrants, among them many Irish speakers, arrived in the United States at the beginning of the 19th century. The majority were poor, illiterate labourers who could be found on building sites in the new national capital in Washington, D.C., and on the Erie Canal (1817–26). Patrick Condon, the only pre-FAMINE Irish poet in the United States whose work is known to us, emigrated to Utica, New York, in 1826, following in the footsteps of relatives who had been working on the Erie Canal. Also in the 1820s, large numbers of Irish emigrated to Canada—specifically, Nova Scotia, New Brunswick, Quebec, and Ontario.

During the years of the Great Irish Famine, the rate of EMIGRATION skyrocketed. The monthly reports of Irish-speaking colporteurs who peddled religious literature in New York, Boston, and Philadelphia indicate how widely Irish was spoken among Irish immigrants in the 1840s and 1850s. One of these reports estimates that five-eighths of the Irish-born population of New York was Irish speaking. In the 1850s in Pennsylvania, so many Irish speakers resided in the area that the Czech-born bishop of Philadelphia, John Neumann, learned Irish so that he could hear the confessions of his parishioners. Estimates suggest that between 1851 and 1855 more than 200,000 Irish speakers came to the United States and between 20,000 and 30,000 Irish speakers entered Canada. In the years 1891–1900, an esti-mated 24 percent of emigrants from Ireland were Irish speakers, which suggests that more 100,000 speakers of the language came to the United States and 2,500 came to Canada in those years.

John O'Mahony (1819–77) arrived in Brooklyn in 1853, and in 1856 published his translation of Keating's *Foras Feasa ar Éirinn* (see CÉITINN) in New York. His Gaelic column in the New York weekly *Irish-American* marked the first appearance of Irish in print in North America; O'Mahoney's column continued sporadically until the newspaper ceased publication in 1915.

Also in the 1850s, the first attempts were made at forming Irish-language soci-eties in the United States. Probably the very first of these organizations was estab-lished in the Wilkes-Barre region of Pennsylvania in 1853. In the late 1850s and early 1860s, an Irish class was established in New York City under the auspices of the New York branch of the Ossianic Society.

In 1881, Michael Logan started publication in Brooklyn of a bilingual monthly *An Gaodhal* (The Gael), one year before the Dublin-based *Gaelic Journal* was founded. In the 1880s and 1890s the bilingual *Irish Echo* was published in Boston, and in the 1880s Irish-language columns also appeared in O'Donovan Rossa's *United Irishman* (New York), the *Chicago Citizen,* and the *San Francisco Monitor.*

Today, Irish is taught at a number of universities across North America, from Saint Francis Xavier University in Antigonish, Nova Scotia, to the University of California at Berkeley. A new language organization, Daltaí na Gaeilge (Students of Irish), has enjoyed unprecedented success in helping North Americans attain fluency in Irish by conducting classes and language immersion programs throughout the continent. Numerous websites, including live and archived broadcasts of Radio na Gaeltachta (see MASS MEDIA), enable North Americans to keep in daily contact with the language.

Kenneth E. Nilsen

CELTIC LANGUAGES IN NORTH AMERICA, SCOTTISH GAELIC

The first major wave of Highland EMIGRATION to North America occurred in the late 1640s and early 1650s, when Highland soldiers of the defeated Scottish forces were sent as prisoners to the West Indies, Virginia, and New England by the victorious Cromwellians. Major Highland emigration to British North America (Canada after 1867) subsequently occurred in every decade from the 1770s to the 1920s.

In the 1730s, James Oglethorpe, a Lowlander, brought Highlanders, all GAELIC speakers, to Georgia to act as a buffer to the Spanish colony to the south in Florida; he named the settlement Darien after an earlier failed Panama endeavour. By 1735, this colony had acquired the services of a Gaelic-speaking minister.

The tale of *Soitheach nan Daoine* (The ship of the people also dates from this time. This ship purportedly carried a cargo of abducted Hebrideans who were to be sold into slavery in America.

Some Highlanders had settled in North Carolina as early as the 1720s, but it was in 1739 and thereafter that they started to arrive in large numbers. Thousands of Gaelic speakers settled in the upper Cape Fear region, and smaller groups moved farther south across the border into South Carolina. Several songs composed by John MacRae of Kintail (*fl.* mid-18th century) during his years in North Carolina have been preserved in oral tradition in Scotland (ALBA) and Nova Scotia. By the time of the American Revolution, there may have been as many as 20,000 Highlanders in North Carolina. After the war, some of them left for Canada. However, Highlanders continued to arrive in the state until the first decade of the 19th century, and Gaelic continued to be spoken and used in church services at least until the Civil-War (1861–65). The first item printed in Gaelic in North America is a sermon by the Reverend Dugald Crawford published in Fayetteville, North Carolina, in 1791.

Much of the 18th-century emigration was led by tacksmen—lower-ranking Highland nobility who were being squeezed out by the Highland CLEARANCES and other economic factors. In 1801, such a clearance in Strathglass prompted hundreds of tenants to make the voyage to Nova Scotia, where they settled in Antigonish County and where their descendants remain.

Gaelic publishing in British North America began in 1832 with Donald Matheson's *Laoidhean Spioradail* (Spiritual hymns) in Pictou, Nova Scotia, and a Gaelic translation of William Dyer's 'Christ's Famous Titles' (*Ainmeanna Cliuiteach Chriosd*) in Charlottetown, Prince Edward Island.

Large-scale Highland immigration to Cape Breton began around 1800. Inverness County, Cape Breton, was settled largely by people from Lochaber, Moidart, Morar, Eigg, Canna, and South Uist, along with some immigrants from Skye, Harris, and Lewis. The North Shore area of Victoria County received settlers from Lewis and Harris. Barra people took up holdings around the shores of Bras D'Or Lakes. North Uist settlers went to Richmond County and Cape Breton County. Immigration to Cape Breton continued into the 1840s when it came to a virtual halt, due in part to the potato blight on the island. In fact, during this era some Cape Breton Gaels from Inverness County crossed over to Newfoundland, where they settled in the Codroy Valley and where Gaelic continued to be spoken well into the second half of the 20th century. It is estimated that between 30,000 and 50,000 Highlanders emigrated to Cape Breton in the first half of the 19th century. It became the most thoroughly Gaelic region outside of Scotland and the language and culture continued intact until well into the 20th century. In 1931, the Canadian census listed 24,000 Gaelic speakers in Nova Scotia, most of whom resided in Cape Breton. Today, several hundred Gaelic speakers are left in the island, many of whom have a wealth of Gaelic folk material.

In the early 1900s, the Canadian government published *Machraichean Móra Chanada* (The great prairies of Canada), an immigrant's guide to the region. The last major Gaelic settlements in North America at Red Deer, Alberta (1924), and Clandonald, Alberta (1926), met with mixed success.

Today, SCOTTISH GAELIC is taught at a number of North American universities. At Saint Francis Xavier University in Antigonish, Nova Scotia, Gaelic is not only the major focus of the Celtic Studies department, but also the working language of the department. Students at Saint Francis Xavier have a weekly Gaelic radio programme during the academic year, which can also be heard on the Internet. Several organizations throughout the continent are working for the promotion of Gaelic and, especially in Nova Scotia, serious efforts are being made to ensure the survival of the language (see LANGUAGE [REVIVAL] MOVEMENTS IN THE CELTIC COUNTRIES).

Kenneth E. Nilsen

CELTIC LANGUAGES IN NORTH AMERICA, WELSH

The publication of Welsh books in the United States dates back to the earlier part of the 18th century with Ellis Pugh's *Annerch i'r Cymry* (Salutation to the Welsh), which appeared in 1721 and, incidentally, predates the country's first German books by approximately seven years. While some of the texts were translations (most often from English) into Welsh or republications of what was previously available in Wales (CYMRU), most were the original work of immigrants. Utica, New York, was a major centre of Welsh-language culture in the 19th and earlier 20th century. As in Wales, the biographies of renowned preachers were popular among the 19th-century American Welsh. Approximately 40 such volumes were published in the United States.

Overall, more than 300 Welsh books and pamphlets were published in the United States. A relatively wide range of material found its way into print: Works were mostly religious, but other publications of note include the *Meddyg Teuluaidd* (Family doctor) and the 1862 *Cyfansoddiad Talaethau Unedig America* (The Constitution of the United States of America).

Reflecting the Welsh poetic tradition, about 30 volumes of verse appeared from U.S. presses. One collection of verse, published in Chicago in 1877 and called *Blodau'r Gorllewin* (Flowers of the West), contained a detailed treatise on the traditional Welsh system of metrical ornamentation (known as CYNGHANEDD) found in verse in the strict metres (see CYWYDD, ENGLYN). As well as being remarkable as a Welsh metrical treatise from America, *Blodau'r Gorllewin* is of literary importance in predating and anticipating the still unsuperseded standard work on the subject, *Cerdd Dafod* (Tongue craft; 1925) of Sir John Morris-Jones. Another volume, *Gweddillion y Gorlifiad* (Remnants of the flood), recalls in its title the great flood of Johnstown, Pennsylvania.

Though less popular, other literary forms are represented in the Welsh American corpus, including at least one published novel and several plays. Newspapers and journals were also established in the 19th century, but few of them survived for a substantial period of time. One notable exception was *Y Drych*, founded in 1851 in New York and still in production until 1975, although its content was by then written in English. It was replaced by *Ninnau*.

Eirug Davies

CELTIC LANGUAGES, ONLINE LEARNING RESOURCES

The Internet has been a boon to minority languages, allowing geographically isolated speakers and learners to share information and communicate in ways that were not possible before the 1990s. In addition to helping maintain the Celtic languages in their communities, online tools are allowing new learners to connect with Celtic speakers.

The most effective way to begin learning a Celtic language is within a Celtic-speaking household and/or community, ideally in conjunction with some sort of formal educational program. Outside of the CELTIC COUNTRIES, however, this is not always feasible. Umbrella organization such as Mercator, the European Research Centre on Multilingualism and Language Learning (www.mercator-research.eu/), and the European Union's Multilingualism Commission (http://ec.europa.eu/education/languages/languages-of-Europe/doc139_en.htm) provide background information on the languages and contact information for organizations promoting minority languages. In a North American context, some resources are available from the North American Association for Celtic Language Teachers (www.naaclt.org) and on Wikipedia, whose articles on the phonology and grammar of the Celtic languages are generally good. Eric Armstrong of York University has provided an interactive chart of the IPA (International Phonetic Alphabet) symbols used by linguists to describe the sounds of a language at http://www.yorku.ca/earmstro/ipa/.

While many works in and about the Celtic languages are available online, including dictionaries, grammars, translators, and entire scholarly works now in the public domain, it can be difficult to find an authoritative place to begin. The following is a selection of websites that offer solid introductory material for learning the six modern Celtic languages; Proto-Celtic and Continental Celtic resources exist as well, but due to the fragmentary or hypothetical status of the these languages, learners' materials are not listed here. As with any online resource, content is changeable. The following lists are not complete, but include stable sites whose content is both authoritative and geared toward beginning learners.

Irish

The government of Ireland (Éire) offers resources to Irish learners through An Comhairle um Oideachtas Gaeltachta & Gaelscolaíochta ('The Council for the Gaeltacht and Irish-medium Schools', www.cogg.ie), including links to resources in Northern Ireland, though these materials are primarily aimed at learners living on the island of Ireland. For worldwide learners, a number of introductory courses are available. A radio course from 2008 from the BBC begins at http://www.bbc.co.uk/northernireland/Irish/blas/index.shtml. Many Irish classes have been filmed—for example, one introducing the language to an American audience at http://www.youtube.com/watch?v=f7nyXgtuis0, with handouts online at http://www.hofshi.net/Ceachtanna_BunRang_E07/BunRang_E07.htm. Erin's Web (http://www.erinsweb.com/gae_index.html) has 128 lessons from pronunciation to advanced syntax. Grammatical explanation is kept to a minimum and few sound files are included, but there is a message board for help with translation and pronunciation and general comments. Seventy-two lessons, most five to ten minutes long, are available as .mp3 files from the Philo-Celtic Society at http://www.philo-Celtic.com/PII/Progress.htm.

Scottish Gaelic

The primary Scottish Gaelic resource online is Sabhal Mòr Ostaig ('The Big Barn of Ostaig'). It has compiled a list of online resources, both internal and external, at http://www.smo.uhi.ac.uk/gaidhlig/ionnsachadh/, including lessons with descriptions of Scottish Gaelic spelling, sound files, and grammatical resources.

Manx

Yn Cheshaght Ghailckagh ('The [Manx] Gaelic Society') has links to a number of learners' resources at http://www.ycg.iofm.net/, and the website www.learnmanx.com has a complete range of lessons with .mp3 sound files available. Although the government website does not included any direct lessons, some further information about Manx on Man is available through Eiraght Ashoonaght Vannin ('Manx National Heritage', http://www.gov.im/mnh/heritage/about/manxlanguage.xml).

Welsh

The Welsh Language Board has a number of resources for learners at http://www.byig-wlb.org.uk/english/learning/Pages/index.aspx. In addition, BBC Wales provides places to start with Welsh, including video lessons: http://www.bbc.co.uk/

wales/learning/learnwelsh/. Another general resource, with links to further information, can be found at www.welshforadults.org, a Welsh government website. S4C, the Welsh-language television network, has a section on its website geared toward learners: http://www.s4c.co.uk/dysgwyr/. Mark Nodine's site (http://www.cs.cf.ac.uk/fun/welsh/) is written with the North American learner in mind, and includes links to other resources as well as some information on the medieval language.

Breton

Most of the online learning materials for Breton are presented through the medium of French, but a few sites—notably Kervarker (http://www.kervarker.org/) and a short introduction at Sabhal Mòr Ostaig (http://www.smo.uhi.ac.uk/saoghal/mion -chanain/brezhoneg/)—are in English. Both include sound files. A number of English lessons, again with sound files, can be found at Wikiversity (http:// en.wikiversity.org/wiki/Topic:Breton).

Cornish

Cornish is the most difficult of the modern Celtic languages for which to provide resources; several distinct versions of the revived CORNISH LANGUAGE exist, each with its own orthography. Maga (http://www.magakernow.org.uk/) maintains a detailed list of language learning resources, including distance-learning courses.

Antone Minard

CELTIC STUDIES, EARLY HISTORY OF THE FIELD

Beginnings to the Mid-19th Century

As an interdisciplinary field, Celtic studies includes linguistics, literature, history, archaeology, and ART history. Although the study of Celts began in classical antiquity, the modern field has its origins in the 16th and 17th centuries. This period saw the rediscovery, publication, and translation of GREEK AND ROMAN ACCOUNTS. Despite their biases and occasional inaccuracies, these classical texts have formed a foundation of the modern discipline since the 1500s.

As study continued into the 18th century, linguists began to make progress in the CELTIC LANGUAGES. The first major milestone came in 1707 with the publication of Edward LHUYD's *Archaeologia Britannica*, which established the existence of a Celtic language family consisting of BRITISH, GAULISH, and IRISH. The next advancement came almost 80 years later when another Welshman, Sir William Jones, first proposed the classification known as INDO-EUROPEAN. Little real progress was made until 1856, when Johann Kaspar Zeuss published his comparative *Grammatica Celtica*.

Celtomania in the 18th and 19th Centuries

The 18th and 19th centuries also saw the rise of NATIONALISM in the CELTIC COUNTRIES and 'CELTOMANIA', as well as imaginitive, romantic views presented as scholarship.

William Stukeley (1687–1765) published two volumes of a history of the ancient Celts: *Stonehenge, a Temple Restor'd to the British Druids* (1740) and *Abury, a Temple of the British Druids, with Some Others, Described* (1743). His idea, now discredited, was that Stonehenge and other sites were temples of British DRUIDS.

Known collectively as the *Poems of Ossian*, James MACPHERSON's three works—*Fragments of Ancient Poetry* (1760), *Fingal* (1762), and *Temora* (1763)—were presented as a translation of a genuine GAELIC epic. *Poems of Ossian* found a wide readership, and Macpherson also indirectly stimulated sound Scottish Gaelic scholarship for generations.

A more successful creative re-inventor of ancient traditions was Iolo Morganwg (Edward WILLIAMS), a Welsh stonemason. His notion was that Welsh bards 'had preserved, virtually intact, a continuous tradition of lore and wisdom going back to the original prehistoric Druids'. In 1792, Iolo began publicizing a bardic ceremony called *Maen Gorsedd*, an institution that he successfully yoked to the Welsh EISTEDDFOD in 1819, thereby contributing to the national institutions of WELSH POETRY down to the present (see also GORSEDD BEIRDD YNYS PRYDAIN).

One major project of subsequent Celtic studies has been to purge the field of fantasies, fabrications, and forgeries. Literary ROMANTICISM has proved persistent, especially in popular material about the ancient Celts.

The Mid-19th to the Mid-20th Century

In the 1840s, archaeologists began to correlate the remains of IRON AGE sites and classical textual sources. A major breakthrough came in 1846, when Johann Ramsauer began his investigation of a cemetery at HALLSTATT, Austria; he eventually concluded that the graves were Celtic. Today the Hallstatt finds are divided into a number of separate chronological phases, not all considered Celtic.

Less than a decade later, archaeologists made another major discovery at LA TÈNE on the northern shores of Lake Neuchâtel in Switzerland. These artefacts were later than the Hallstatt materials and characterized by a form of curvilinear ornamentation. Artefacts of this distinctive 'La Tène style' were found elsewhere in Europe, particularly in places where Celts lived and CELTIC LANGUAGES were attested. As a result, these items quickly became strongly associated with the Celts. Scholars are today more wary of making simplistic equations between linguistic groups and material culture. Despite such reservations, the terms 'Celtic archaeology' and 'Celtic art' are by now well established and can be retained because they are not drastically out of step with the linguistic and historical uses of the term 'Celtic'.

The field of Celtic art history began in earnest with the publication of Paul Jacobsthal's *Early Celtic Art* in 1944. His classification of Celtic art based on stylistic criteria provided a secure, if imperfect, foundation for future research in the field.

Dan Wiley

CELTIC STUDIES, ONLINE RESOURCES

As with language resources, a number of websites have come online in the last ten years to provide access to otherwise rare resources, notably primary texts. Even more than language resources, this area continues to grow and change. Thus the following is not intended to be a complete list; notably, it excludes scanned texts of books in online libraries.

General

The Celtic Studies Association of North American maintains an online searchable bibliography of academic references in Celtic studies at http://www.humnet.ucla.edu/humnet/Celtic/csanabib.html. The Digital Medievalist, a site maintained by Lisa Spangenberg, is another general resource for Celtic studies: http://digitalmedievalist.com/. The Internet Sacred Text Archive (http://www.sacred-texts.com/neu/celt/index.htm) offers a number of primary texts, although many of the translations of medieval texts are public-domain works no longer considered authoritative. More recent translations and classical texts pertaining to Celtic studies can be found on a website maintained by Mary Jones: http://www.maryjones.us/ctexts/index.html.

Goidelic

The premier source for texts relating to Ireland is CELT (http://www.ucc.ie/celt/), 'a searchable online corpus of multilingual texts of Irish literature and history with over 14 million words available'. Old and Middle Irish texts not found at CELT can usually be found at TITUS 'Thesaurus Indogermanischer Text- und Sprachmaterialien' ('Thesaurus of Indo-European Texts and Components of Language', http://titus.uni-frankfurt.de/indexe.htm), which also contains LEPONTIC and other texts. The Dictionary of the Irish Language—the main dictionary of Old and Middle Irish—is online at www.dil.ie. Many individual manuscripts have their own dedicated sites, such as the Book of DEER: http://bookofdeer.co.uk/. A variety of information pertaining to Manx studies is maintained by the North American Manx Association at http://northamericanmanx.org/nama/nama_links.php.

Brythonic

In addition to the Welsh, Cornish, and Breton texts on the sites mentioned previously, a nearly complete collection of Middle Welsh prose, including the entire MABINOGION, is available at a site maintained by the University of Wales, Cardiff: http://www.rhyddiaithganoloesol.caerdydd.ac.uk/en/. The Digital Mirror at the National Library of Wales site (http://www.llgc.org.uk/index.php?id=122) provides access to a large number of collections, including collections of poetry, laws, and the Cornish manuscript BEUNANS KE. The works of DAFYDD AP GWILYM, including sounds files, have been put online at http://www.dafyddapgwilym.net.

Antone Minard

CELTIC TIGER

'Celtic Tiger' was a label applied to Ireland (ÉIRE) around the turn of the 21st century, when its economy was growing at a much faster rate than those of other

Western countries. This phase of prosperity reversed a centuries-long trend of EMIGRATION. The term was first used in the mid-1990s and continued to be applied until the worldwide economic downturn that began in 2008. In 1999, for example, Ireland's gross domestic product (GDP) growth was 10.4 percent, compared with 2.1 percent in the United Kingdom and 2–4 percent elsewhere in the industrialized West. The average growth from 1995 to 2007 was 6 percent.

The phrase was coined by analogy with the 'Asian Tiger economies,' referring to the high-growth economies of smaller nations in Asia (e.g., Hong Kong and Singapore). Each of these nations, most of which were former colonies of Britain, experienced an economic transformation resulting in a sustained period of high growth. Ireland had a similar pattern of growth as well as a similar history of British colonial infrastructure. Despite the name, Ireland's economic success in this period cannot be attributed to its Celtic culture. In fact, the IRISH LANGUAGE may have suffered as a result of this surge, as part of Ireland's appeal lay in its ability to provide an English-speaking work environment for North American companies seeking a European hub.

The Irish economy prior to independence can only be viewed in a colonial context, as part of the broader economy of the United Kingdom. After independence, Ireland experienced a trade war with Britain in the 1930s due to its protectionist policies, followed by hardship after World War II; although Ireland remained neutral during the war and suffered little direct damage, the indirect consequences of neutrality were resentment from Allied nations and exclusion from Marshall Plan aid.

The United Kingdom remained Ireland's chief trading partner into the 1950s, and the country's economy was beset by multiple detrimental factors: debt, emigration, and political unrest. The situation stabilized only in the early 1990s, owing to a host of factors ranging from national policy to judicious use of Ireland's European Union (EU) membership and the growth of the technology sector. Additionally, intangible factors such as the fading of colonial stereotypes of the Irish worker and the prominence of Irish-American businesspeople contributed to Ireland's success.

As elsewhere, the end of the high-growth period was attributable partly to a housing bubble (inflated real estate prices), and partly to governmental assumptions about continued future growth.

Antone Minard

CELTOMANIA

Enthusiasm and admiration for Celtic civilizations and languages reached new heights in 19th-century France. Commonly referred to as the Celtic revival, the fashion for all things Celtic swept through Europe in tandem with ROMANTICISM. Against a backdrop of Chateaubriand's druidic adventures in *Les Martyrs* (1809), Walter SCOTT's Romantic Celtophilia, and Ossian (see MACPHERSON; OISÍN), and diffused and remodulated by Goethe's *Werther* (1774), linguists and historians began investigating the history and development of Celtic literature, language, and civilization in unprecedented detail. The work of historians popularized the idea that the Gauls were the true ancestors of the French (see GAUL), whereas the Franks were the ancestors of the aristocracy overthrown in the Revolution of 1789. During Romanticism, attention turned from 'Gaulish' to 'Celtic', and thus to Brittany (BREIZH), thanks to the popular equation of the modern Breton with the ancient Celt.

'Celtomanie' was a retrospective and pejorative label, coined around 1838, showing its heyday had already passed. The Académie celtique was founded in 1805 under Napoleon with the purpose of elevating the study of France's own past, only to be completely revamped and given the safer title Societé royale des Antiquaires de France in 1814.

The climate of suspicion that followed, but also overlapped with the fashion for Celtic themes, explains why both positive and negative clichés of Brittany are found at the same date in 19th-century French culture—see, for instance, Balzac's overwhelmingly negative portrayal in *Les Chouans* (1828, 1834) and Brizeux's idyllic Brittany in *Marie* (1831). This climate also explains why the portraits of Brittany that were most successful in their day are insipid, as 'difference' was tolerated by mainstream French culture only if it was unthreatening, apolitical, and preferably restricted to the level of the picturesque. Many would argue that the same is true today, and that both Celtoscepticism and Celtomania are alive and well.

Heather Williams

CELTS IN CENTRAL AND EASTERN EUROPE

The important archaeological sites of HALLSTATT and LA TÈNE are found in Central Europe, and evidence suggests that the cradle of the Celtic languages and culture began in what is now the southern portion of Germanic-speaking Europe. Early expansions brought the Celts into Gaul, Iberia, and northern Italy, where the LEPONTIC inscriptions in CISALPINE GAUL provide the earliest records of the CELTIC LANGUAGES.

The Celts in Bohemia

The region of Bohemia, in the present-day Czech Republic, takes its name from the Boii, one of the most important peoples in the eastern Celtic area. Their name in turn probably derives from PROTO-CELTIC *bouios, 'a man who possesses cows'. The main territory occupied by the northeastern Boii consisted not only of Bohemia, but also of much of modern Moravia, northeastern Austria, western Slovakia, and western Hungary.

Between the 8th and 5th centuries BC, Bohemia was part of the wider Hallstatt zone. Evidence of characteristic burial practices such as wagon graves is found in Bohemia, as are other typical finds. Because these societies were preliterate, it is impossible to state beyond doubt whether the inhabitants of Late Hallstatt Bohemia actually spoke a Celtic language. Nevertheless, the strong cultural links documented in the archaeological record at least make it reasonable to see them as parts of a wider cultural continuum where Celtic speech was documented in succeeding centuries.

In the later Early and Middle La Tène phases, the Boii become more visible archaeologically. Similar forms of material culture stretch from Bohemia over northeastern Austria, Moravia, and southwest Slovakia into the Hungarian plains southwest and north of the Danube. Strabo's *Geography* (7.2.2) reports from Posidonius that the Boii had lived in the Hercynian forest (Hercynia silva) before 113 BC, and various historical sources place them in northern Italy. The place-name *Boioduron* 'fortified settlement of the Boii', modern Passau, is at the confluence of the rivers Inn and Danube.

Pliny (*Natural History* 3.147) records the Hungarian plains southwest of the Danube as the *deserta Boiorum* (the Boian waste), a region depopulated after the defeat of the Boii at the hands of the Dacians. This desertion coincides with the discontinuation of a type of Hungarian Celtic coinage, the 'Velem'-type, in the area that became the *deserta Boiorum*.

The Celts in East-Central Europe

According to written evidence, the Celts first appeared in the western part of the Carpathian Basin in the 4th century BC. In Justin's abridgement of the lost works of Trogus Pompeius, a historian of Celtic origin living in the later 1st century BC, it is stated that Italy and Pannonia were occupied at roughly the same time.

It seems likely that the Celts reached the north–south section of the Danube and crossed the river in the earlier 4th century BC, as evidenced by several La Tène B cemeteries in the Danube Bend and northeastern Hungary. Transylvania, too, came under Celtic rule during this era. The sudden and conspicuous increase in the number of sites in southern Transdanubia, northeastern Hungary, and the Great Hungarian Plain imply that these areas came under Celtic control in the late 4th–early 3rd century BC as well. Celtic graves appear in the cemeteries of the Iranian-speaking Scythians in the Great Hungarian Plain from the mid-3rd century BC, roughly the same time as settlements yielding distinctively Celtic finds, suggesting that the Celtic expansion was relatively peaceful. Although affected by gradual Romanization after the conquest of the last 1st century BC, the Celts of Pannonia preserved their lifeways, workshop traditions, religion, and names for many hundreds of years.

Several new cemeteries were established from the mid-6th century BC, and their founding was accompanied by the transformation of burial practices and the spread of inhumation. The first burials in the early cemeteries can be assigned to the later part of the Hallstatt D period and the latest ones to the early La Tène B period, although some communities used the same burial ground down to the 2nd century BC. It seems likely that, concurrently with the appearance of flat cemeteries containing inhumation burials throughout Europe, the custom of inhumation spread in northern Transdanubia, and that cremation burials reflect the survival of earlier traditions. Both inhumation and cremation burials were covered with stones or marked with a single stone; in some cases, a ditch was dug around the grave. The majority of the inhumation burials have the deceased laid to rest in an extended position, sometimes with an arm folded across the chest. Scattered cremation and urn burials occur until the very end of the La Tène period, often within the same cemetery.

Many male burials contained weapons. The sword and its fittings were always laid on the right side, and spears were found on both sides of the body, usually beside the head. Early graves often lacked a sword. Helmets are extremely rare finds, which suggests that only warriors with outstanding prowess were deemed worthy to wear one; helmets also likely signalled higher status. The finds from women's burials indicate that they wore two to three or more fibulae (BROOCHES) as well as arm-rings and anklets. The TORC was apparently linked to social rank or status within the family. Sets of arm-rings and anklets as well as belts were the most characteristic pieces of jewellery worn by Celtic women. Grave goods from female burials also included tools and implements, especially spindle whorls (loom weights).

The sunken oblong houses, measuring 2–3 m by 4–6 m, had a pitched roof resting on timbers aligned along the shorter side of the house. Smaller huts were probably roofed with thatch or wattling; the post holes and the daub fragments with twig impressions suggest that the walls were of the wattle-and-daub type. Benches, smaller pits, fireplaces, and the occasional oven made up the interior furnishings. Houses were ringed by external pits, some of which were used for the extraction of clay, while others functioned as storage bins or refuse pits. Animal bone samples indicate that the culture consumed a wide range of domestic animals and hunted animals, aurochs, deer, and boar. Springs, bogs, mountain-tops, and caves were also used for ritual activities.

The Celts in the Balkans

For the earliest elements of Celtic culture in the hinterlands of the eastern Adriatic coast, one must go back to the late 5th and early 4th centuries, when the earliest imported finds from Celtic-speaking west central Europe begin to appear in areas south of the Alpine area and in the western Balkans.

The Celts of the Adriatic region are mentioned most often in connection with the famous rulers of Hellenistic Macedonia. The earliest Celtic grave finds from the Balkans belong to the period after 300 BC, and it is impossible to speak of a large density of Celtic settlement before the first half of the 3rd century BC. The Celtic tribes migrated into the hinterlands of the eastern Adriatic coast in two major distinct waves. The Taurisci settled in hilly eastern Slovenia and northeastern Croatia, while the greater and lesser branches of the Scordisci settled on the southern Pannonian plains between the Sava and the Danube. At the confluence of these two rivers they founded their centre, ancient Singidūnon (now Belgrade, Serbia). Other Celtic groups continued northward, and eventually mingled with Celts who had previously settled in Transylvania in present-day Romania.

Interactions between the Hellenic world and Celtic migratory war bands and mercenaries are well described in historic sources. According to the Ptolemaic history of Alexander the Great, Alexander hosted a Celtic delegation from the Adriatic region during his expedition against the Triballi in 335 BC. The so-called Danubian Celts appeared in Greece in larger numbers just after Alexander's death.

In approximately 310 BC, Casandrus defeated them in the area around Haemus (Mount Balkan). After defeating the Macedonian king Ptolemy Keraunos, the Celtic army, led by BRENNOS OF THE PRAUSI, crossed Thessaly and headed for Delphi. Some 30,000 Celtic warriors and their families crossed at Thermopylae in 279 BC and defeated the Greeks at Marathon. At Delphi that winter, the Greeks attacked and defeated the Celts, and the survivors retreated northward.

According to Strabo, the Tectosages collected a large amount of booty from Greece and subsequently settled around Tolosa (modern Toulouse, southwest France). Other tribes, including the Tolistobogii and Trocmi and others of the Tectosages, crossed the Dardanelles and penetrated further into Asia Minor as the Galatae (see GALATIA).

Celtic influence in Thrace (roughly modern Bulgaria and European Turkey) is very modest, but these groups established a kingdom known as Tylis or Tyle on the Thracian coast of the Black Sea. This kingdom persisted until the later 3rd century BC, when its last ruler, Kauaros (cf. Welsh *cawr* 'giant'), minted coins and imposed tribute on the nearby Greek city of Byzantion. The grave of a warrior from CIUMEŞTI, Romania, which contains a helmet decorated with a huge bird, can certainly be connected with these early Celts. Helmets with reinforced crests are typical for these eastern Celts. One feature of Thracian-influenced Celtic style was the production of oversize ornamental objects, particularly apparent in some well-known pieces from western Europe—for example, at Trichtingen, where a silver torc weighing more than six kg was found, and probably at Gundestrup, Denmark, where the famous giant silver cauldron, about 80 cm in diameter, decorated with motives and cult scenes paralleled elsewhere in Celtic contexts, was found (see CAULDRONS; GUNDESTRUP CAULDRON).

With the increasing influence of Rome in the 2nd century BC, the significance of Celts on the extreme eastern edge of Europe began to decrease rapidly. Their independence was slowly lost in a series of battles with the Roman legions, and one of the last of these Celtic tribes to submit to Rome were the Scordisci.

Mitja Guštin, Elizabeth Jerem, and Antone Minard

CERDD DAFOD

Cerdd dafod (literally 'tongue craft') is the Welsh term for poetic composition in strict metres. The traditional system of poetic ornamentation in the WELSH language is remarkable for its use of intensive phonetic correspondences; comparable features can be identified in Irish systems (see IRISH LITERATURE; METRICS), which supports the idea that this is a Celtic cultural inheritance.

The basic discipline of *cerdd dafod* is the mastery of CYNGHANEDD, a strict system of alliteration and internal rhyme. Einion Offeiriad (*fl. c.* 1320–*c.* 1349) is credited with the authorship of the earliest book on the topic to survive; it lists twenty-four canonical metres. In the EISTEDDFOD held at Carmarthen (Caerfyrddin) *c.* 1450, Dafydd ab Edmwnd replaced two of these metres with two highly complicated ones that he himself had devised, and these were subsequently accepted as the traditional twenty-four metres.

At the beginning of the 20th century, the Celtic linguist, poet, and literary critic Sir John Morris-Jones classified the *cynganeddion* ('patterns of *cynghanedd*') and published his findings in a book, *Cerdd Dafod* (1925), which remains the definitive work on the subject.

Dafydd Islwyn

CERNUNNOS

Cernunnos was a Gaulish god whose distinctive representative features are thought to include antlers or horns on his head, multiple torcs (neck-rings), accompanying stags, and sometimes ram-horned snakes. The distinctive iconography of 'Cernunnos' depicts the god sitting cross-legged, most famously on the GUNDESTRUP CAULDRON. These patterns of representations, which recur fairly consistently, such as at Val Camonica, have been understood by modern writers as reflecting 'the lord of the animals'. The most important representation of the god and the lone instance of his name appears on the monument of the Nautae Parisiaci ('the sailors of the [Gaulish] Parisi'). Antlered goddesses are observed at Clermont-Ferrand and Besançon, and the antlered god is also known from Britain on the relief from the Romano-British town of Corinium (modern Cirencester) and appears on one coin from Petersfield, Hampshire (see COINAGE).

The etymology is usually traced to INDO-EUROPEAN **ker-n-* 'horn'. The epithet *cernach* (angular; victorious) of CONALL CERNACH of the Irish ULSTER CYCLE may derive from the same root, and it has been suggested that Conall Cernach and Cernunnos are ultimately the same figure.

Peter E. Busse

CHAMALIÈRES, INSCRIPTION

The inscription from the Chamalières site in the GAULISH language is written in Roman cursive script, similar to that of many of the ROMANO-BRITISH curse tablets from BATH, on a lead tablet roughly 6 × 4 cm, and probably dates from the first half of the 1st century AD. Along with the texts from Larzac and Chateaubleau, it is one of the longest-surviving Gaulish texts. It contains Gaulish religious vocabulary and provides invaluable insight into pagan Celtic ideas. This inscription thus illuminates the history of the CELTIC LANGUAGES, with numerous points of comparison in its vocabulary, grammar, and syntax to the better attested medieval and modern INSULAR CELTIC languages.

The verb of the first sentence is *uediiu-mi* 'I beseech, pray'; cf. Old Irish *guidiu*, Welsh *gweddïaf*. It then invokes *Mapon Aruerniiatin*, probably meaning '[the god] MAPONOS of the Arverni tribe'. The third line includes the phrase *brictia anderon* 'by a magical spell of underworld beings' (see BRICTA). There follows a list of men's names. Between lines 7 and 8 is the phrase *toncnaman tonsciiontio*, which has been compared with the formulaic oaths, Old Irish *tongu do dia toinges mo thuath* 'I swear to the god by whom my tribe swears' and Welsh *tyghaf tyghet* 'I swear a destiny' (CULHWCH AC OLWEN 50). The text culminates with the repeated formula: *Luge dessu-mmi-iis* (repeated thrice); *Luxe*, probably invoking the chief god Lugus, 'By Lugus I prepare them (set them right), by Lugus'.

John T. Koch

CHAMALIÈRES, SANCTUARY

A sanctuary excavated in Chamalières, Puy-de-Dôme, produced 1,500 sculptures and 8,500 fragments, representing body parts and also full-length dressed figures. Collectively, this find constitutes the most important series of wooden votive figures (see ritual) known in France. Most of the objects can be dated to *c.* AD 1–*c.* 50. They are displayed in the Musée Bargoin at Clermont-Ferrand.

Also discovered at the site were remains of pitchers and cups, some Roman coins, numerous small knobs, and a leaden tablet engraved with a magical inscription written in GAULISH (see below). In the middle of the 1st century AD, the site, which was probably situated within the tribal *civitas* of the Arverni, was abandoned after only a few decades of use.

M. Lévery

CHAMPION'S PORTION

'Champion's portion' is a term that refers to the choice portion (usually a cut of meat) that the hero receives at a public FEAST as a token of his honour. In early IRISH LITERATURE, the champion's portion is a way of setting up the competition for hierarchical status. The term for the champion's portion is *curadmír* or *mír curad*; *mír* means 'portion' and *curad* is the genitive of *caur* or *cor*, 'hero'.

This concept was by no means confined to Celtic cultures, as was already recognized in the GREEK AND ROMAN ACCOUNTS of the ancient Gauls. Diodorus Siculus, quoting Posidonius, wrote (*Historical Library* §28):

> While dining [the Gauls] are served by adolescents, both male and female. Nearby are blazing hearths and CAULDRONS with spits of meat. They honour the brave warriors with the choicest portion, just as Homer says that the chieftains honoured Ajax when he returned having defeated Hector in single combat [*Iliad* 7.320–1].

Again quoting Posidonius, Athenaeus adds that two Gaulish heroes might duel to the death over the champion's portion.

The conjunction of these two themes—violent contention at feasts and the champion's portion—is similarly the pivot for the narrative of two of the best-known sagas of the early Irish ULSTER CYCLE of tales, *Fled Bricrenn* and SCÉLA MUCCE MEIC DÁ THÓ. In 'Bricriu's Feast', the supreme hero CÚ CHULAINN repeatedly proves himself worthy of the *curadmír*.

Although Posidonius represents the champion's portion as a reality, it is clear from the account of Athenaeus that Posidonius relied on oral accounts of what had been done in ancient times. Therefore the traditions record the deeds of legendary heroes—possibly reflecting actual social institutions, but possibly not—in all instances, and the comparison with Ajax suggests that the Greeks understood this practice.

John T. Koch

CHARIOT AND WAGON

The chariot, or more generally the high-status wheeled vehicle, is considered to be one of the characteristic features of Celtic aristocratic display. First appearing as a four-wheeled wagon in HALLSTATT aristocratic tombs, it was largely replaced by the two-wheeled chariot at the beginning of the LA TÈNE period.

Archaeological Sources

The earliest wheeled vehicles that can be more or less certainly assigned to ancient peoples known to have spoken CELTIC LANGUAGES are the four-wheeled examples found in Hallstatt period burials in central Europe (for example, HOCHDORF; see VEHICLE BURIALS), often interpreted as ceremonial and funeral procession vehicles (see ritual). They were replaced at the end of the Hallstatt period or at the very beginning of the La Tène period by lighter, faster, and more versatile two-wheeled chariots. In fact, the transition from the four-wheeled wagon to the two-wheeled chariot may be viewed as an important diagnostic of the Hallstatt–LaTène transition.

Early chariots appeared in great numbers in burials in central Germany, Belgium, and the Champagne region of France from about 500/450 BC onward. More isolated finds are known across Celtic Europe. Their greatest technological advantage was the flexible spring suspension on which the chariot platform was mounted. The chariots were approximately 4–4.5 m in length, had an overall width of around 1.6–2.0 m, and relied onn an average wheel-gauge of around 1.35–1.45 m.

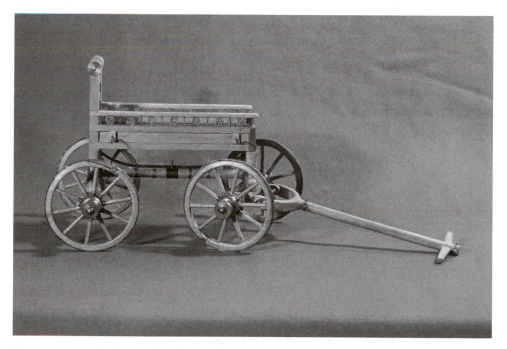

Reconstruction of a chariot found at the tomb of a high-status burial at Vix, France (wood, 6th century BC). (Musee Archeologique, Chatillon Sur Seine, France/Giraudon/The Bridgeman Art Library International)

The spoked wheels had iron tyres with an average diameter of approximately 0.95 m. They were usually drawn by two yoked horses.

Iconographic Sources

Soon after their first appearance in burial contexts, wagons and chariots also appear in the iconographic record. In the early period, four-wheeled wagons and some two-wheeled chariots appeared on decorated sheet metal, especially on situlae (wine buckets), and, for example, on the bronze κλίνη *klīnē* (couch) in the Hochdorf burial. In the La Tène period from the mid-3rd century BC, chariots frequently appear on COINAGE and on burial monuments from CISALPINE GAUL. The inscribed stone from Briona in northern Italy combined a Gaulish text in the alphabet of Lugano (see SCRIPTS) with a relief sculpture of four spoked wheels. Finally, chariots appear on HIGH CROSSES, such as one at Ahenny, Co. Tipperary, Ireland (Contae Thiobraid Árainn, ÉIRE).

Historical Sources

Chariots are also mentioned in the historical sources, and records for the use of chariots by Continental Celts can be found in many places—for example, Appian (*Roman History* 4.12), Athenaeus (*Deipnosophistae* 4.37), Livy (*Ab Urbe Condita* 10.28.9), and Strabo (*Geography* 4.2.3). The most concise summary of chariot use by the ancient Gauls is given by Diodorus Siculus, who wrote: 'In both journeys and battles the Gauls use two-horse chariots which carry both the warrior and charioteer' (*Historical Library* 5.29.1). Caesar records the use of chariots in Britain (*De Bello Gallico* 4.33.1–3), as well as the existence of ROADS on which they are driven (*De Bello Gallico* 5.19.2). Chariots are also mentioned in various types of sources from early medieval Ireland (ÉRIU)—for example, in the ANNALS of Ulster for the year AD 811, in the Life of COLUM CILLE (*Vita Columbae* 2.43), and in legal material such as *Bretha Crólige* (Laws of Sick Maintenance).

Linguistic Sources

Terms for chariots and their parts in the ancient Celtic languages are known mainly from Celtic loanwords in Latin and from place-names. Some words for wheeled vehicles of Celtic origin known from classical sources are *carpentum* (cf. Old Irish *carpat*), *carrus*, and *essedum*. *Carrus* survives in French *char* 'chariot', Spanish *carro* 'cart' ('car' in American Spanish), and English *car*. The most important terms in classical sources seem to have been *carpentum* for the Gaulish chariot and *essedum* (variant *asseda*) for the Belgic and southern British chariot (see BELGAE).

Raimund Karl

CHARTER TRADITION, MEDIEVAL CELTIC

The distinctive charter-writing tradition of Celtic areas in the early Middle Ages is overwhelmingly a Latin practice, although a few translations and equivalents exist in the vernacular languages (see Celtic countries). The charters deal, for the most part, with the transfer of property rights, including the manumission or freeing of slaves (see slavery), in western Britain, Wales (Cymru), Scotland (Alba), Ireland (Ériu), and Brittany (Breizh); they relate to transactions that took place, or were supposed to have taken place, between the 6th and the 12th centuries.

Substance

The Latin charter form from Celtic areas characteristically includes a disposition, witness list, and sanction, and invariably uses the third person and past historic tenses. While many charters also include preambles, narrations, and boundary clauses, they lack formal protocol, such as an initial invocation, formal title and address, and final dating clause and subscriptions. This and the past tense distinguish them from the western European charter tradition of a comparable date, as in England and on the European continent.

The corpus of charters consists of more than 200 complete texts, at least 100 incomplete texts, and a handful of formulae inscribed on stone. Many are written into gospel or liturgical books; some are written into cartularies (and were sometimes edited in the process); a few are recorded in formal extents and surveys; and a few are appended to saints' *Vitae*. More than 200 complete examples exist, most from Wales; most of the fragments and the Celtic-language charters come from Ireland. Recognizable charter language in narrative and other texts adds at least 40 further examples.

Context

The earliest of the indisputable and uncontroversial material is Irish, and belongs to the 8th century; the earliest indisputably Welsh material is of the 9th century. Material from central and western Brittany is notable in the late 9th century.

The bulk of the material dates to the 9th and 10th centuries, as befits a period of growing concern with the security of ecclesiastical property. The latest known southwestern English examples are from the years 1042–66, Breton 1085–1112, Welsh 1132–51, Irish from 1133, and Scottish from the later 12th century, after 1131/2. This recording tradition originated in a variety of ways. The detailed record of witness names has parallels in late Roman and very early medieval contexts elsewhere in Europe. Registration procedures of this kind were clearly known in the Celtic West in the early Middle Ages; for example, the early 8th-century collection of Irish canons reiterates earlier patristic and synodal prescriptions that a sale should be confirmed by witnesses, writing, and sureties. The language of imperial rescripts (replies from the emperor to his subjects) and Continental formularies is echoed in charter formulae from southern Wales and Brittany. The context of this Celtic material is exclusively ecclesiastical. The common features in the Irish and British material indicate the 5th–7th centuries as the period of origin, when British missionaries were working in Ireland before the ecclesiastical traditions of the areas diverged.

The practice of making this kind of record is likely to have developed in episcopal circles in the 5th century in Britain when the bishops met in synods and drew upon the language of the early Church Fathers for their texts. The tradition is, therefore, the fossilized practice of the increasingly isolated bishops of western Britain in the mid-5th century, a practice that was carried to Brittany with the migrants (see BRETON MIGRATIONS), and to Ireland with the early missions. Thereafter, the form tended to be retained while the formulae varied.

Uses

There can be no doubt that some people in Celtic areas considered a written record to be valid proof of ownership, and the evidence shows that records were occasionally used in cases of dispute. In an Irish heptad (meaningful group of seven items) of *c.* 700, 'old writing' is listed alongside valid witnesses, immovable stones, *rath*sureties (a way in which third parties could guarantee a contract), and a bequest, as viable proofs of ownership. From Saint-Pol-de-Léon in Brittany come references, in the later 9th century, to the belief that people should be notified of transactions in writing. In Welsh material of the 9th–11th centuries, a stock phrase occurs that invokes the same respect for the written record: *in sempiterno graphio* (this transaction is recorded 'in an eternal writing'). By implication, writing the record made the recorded action permanent: Writing was a way of making things last. Because people perceived writing as a mechanism for achieving permanence of possession, charters were also written into gospel books and hagiographic texts.

By the 9th century, ecclesiastical charter writing was an aspect of property management: It helped the owner to know which rights he had in landed property and from whom he might expect income. This concern was certainly evident early on in Wales and Brittany, and in Scotland at least by the 12th century. Ecclesiastical charter writing could also make claims to establish proprietary rights. Records could be massaged to support an existing position, or claim a new one, by endorsements on the original or expansion when recopying. This happened all over Celtic areas. The first twenty or so charters of the Landevenneg Cartulary were put together in the mid- to late 10th century to demonstrate the absorption of small monasteries and churches by the larger monastic community of Landevenneg.

In Ireland, by contrast, charter writing does not seem to have been a major protective technique used in the 9th–11th centuries. The influence of charter writing can be seen in other traditions, especially those of central southern Ireland, in Latin hagiographic material from Kinnitty (Ceann Ettaig), Lismore (Liosmór), and Clonfertmulloe (Cluain Fearte Molua). It is likely that some charter writing took place at some centres in Ireland through the 9th–11th centuries, and that the charter tradition influenced the formulation of written property claims both in Latin and the vernacular. Even so, charter writing was clearly not taken up in Ireland in the way that it was in other Celtic areas, and there are alternative influences on some of the 11th-century Middle Irish charters. The Irish habit of citing the names of guarantors rather than of witnesses indicates a significantly different approach to the transfer of property rights as well as a substantial variation in the form of the record.

The Scottish practice reflected the Irish: The distinctive 'Celtic' charter language occurs in the Abernethy material in Paris, Bibliothèque Nationale, Latin MS 4126, clearly implying a knowledge of the Latin tradition in Scotland before the 11th century. The survival of 10th- and 11th-century charters in 12th-century copies indicates the use of charter writing before the impact of the new wave of religious foundations in the 12th century.

Charter writing was about property rights—and was one of the techniques used by churches in the central Middle Ages to maintain and extend them. The language chosen for these records was often decidedly archaic: Old formulations could be repeated for centuries.

Wendy Davies

CHESTER

See Caer.

CHRÉTIEN DE TROYES

Chrétien de Troyes, the most influential author of French Romances, was a court poet active between about 1170 and 1190. His works firmly established the new genre of *Roman* (Romance) and helped to develop ARTHURIAN traditions on the Continent. Chrétien was influenced by classical and scholastic texts and indirectly by GEOFFREY OF MONMOUTH'S HISTORIA REGUM BRITANNIAE, probably as translated into Norman French by Wace in 1155. The relationship between three of his Romances and their Middle Welsh counterparts has been the subject of heated debate since the 19th century; see TAIR RHAMANT for further discussion of the relationship. Chrétien's other verse Romances, written in octosyllabic rhyming couplets, comprise *Lancelot* or *Le Chevalier de la Charrette*, which explores the theme of the eponymous knight's adulterous love for Guenevere, and *Cligès*, which combines Arthurian and classical elements and owes not a little to the TRISTAN AND ISOLT legend that was circulating in French by the mid-12th century.

Chrétien's Romances were initially probably read aloud to an audience at the courts of his patrons, Marie de Champagne and Philippe d'Alsace, count of Flanders. They seem to have met with immediate success. After Chrétien's death, perhaps *c.* 1190, other writers provided *Continuations* of his *Perceval*, which he had left unfinished, and his influence and popularity continued unabated. Later French GRAIL Romances, now composed in the newly fashionable medium of prose, assume familiarity with his work, whilst in other western European countries not only *Perceval* but also his *Erec*, *Yvain*, and *Lancelot* were adapted into other languages or provided the ultimate source for new texts about these knights.

Ceridwen Lloyd-Morgan

CHRISTIANITY, BRITTANY, LATE ANTIQUITY AND THE MIDDLE AGES

Introduction

Christianity played a central rôle in the migration of people to Brittany (Breizh) in late antiquity and the early Middle Ages. The subsequent development of the Breton churches, under the Normans and Angevins in particular, shows that Brittany was increasingly drawn, politically and ecclesiastically, into a wider European world, although some features, such as the abundance of saints, gave the Breton Church a noticeably 'Celtic' appearance (see Christianity, Celtic).

Roman Armorica and the Coming of Christianity

In the Roman period, Armorica (now Brittany) came under the jurisdiction of Tours. By the 5th century, Christianity must have been relatively well established in the area, as it was in other peripheral regions of Gaul. Two reputedly 3rd-century Nantes martyrs, St Donatien and St Rogatien, are attested in 5th- and 6th-century sources. Breton bishops attended provincial councils in the 5th century. Nantes (Naoned), Rennes, and Vannes (itself the site of a council c. 463) are the diocesan seats mentioned by name, but other sees are implied. The council of Tours of 567 asserted the authority of Tours over the 'Romans' and 'Bretons'.

In many ways, early medieval Christianity in Brittany seems to have resembled that of other Celtic regions. The promulgations of the 5th-century Council of Vannes seem to describe monastic practices similar to those found in other Celtic regions. An early 6th-century letter from several bishops, among them the bishop of Rennes and the metropolitan of Tours, to the peripatetic Breton priests Louocatus and Catihernus identifies what could be seen as distinctively 'Celtic' practices—the moving from house to house and the distribution of the sacrament in two kinds, with women (*conhospitae*) administering the chalice to the congregation while the priests administered the host themselves. Wrdisten, the 9th-century author of a Life of St Guénolé (Old Breton Uuinuualoe) and the founder of the abbey of Landevenneg, includes a diploma from the Carolingian emperor Louis the Pious that criticizes the monks' customs and tonsure as 'Irish'.

Another way in which the Christianity of medieval Brittany is visibly similar to that of other 'Celtic' regions is in the cults of its saints. Brittany is very well provided with saints—some of whom are common to other Celtic areas, but many who are unique to Brittany. Some of these saints are the subjects of written Lives (see hagiography); many more are known chiefly or only from church dedications and place-names.

Brittany has a particularly distinctive toponymic usage, directly relevant to the question of the nature of early Breton Christianity and the significance of the migration from Britain at its formative period. This is the place-name element *plou*, which has no real equivalent in other Celtic-speaking areas. The element is derived from the Latin *plēb-*, cognate with Welsh *plwyf* and Cornish *plu*; its broad meaning is 'parish'. Our earliest detailed documentary evidence, in the form of the 9th-century Cartulary of Redon, shows the term *plebs* indicating a distinctive civil and social community and its territory, with a deliberately organized provision of pastoral care. We can broadly assume that the place-name element *plou* denotes a similar unit.

Lives of saints, especially those written a relatively long time after the events they narrate, are very difficult to use as historical sources. These Lives notoriously rely on formulaic events (*topoi*), which give an impression of uniformity. Apart from the Life of St SAMSON of Dol (discussed below), none of the Lives of the Breton saints show significant knowledge of their subjects. Several Lives date from the 9th century, many more from the 11th century, and the rest were composed in the 12th century or later, culminating in a flurry of 'scholarly' activity in the 17th century that saw the invention of several more Lives. The Lives of the Breton saints overwhelmingly describe a period of conversion and foundation of churches from around the 5th to the 7th century. Many show their subjects travelling between one or more of the Celtic regions and meeting other Breton, Brythonic, or Celtic saints. Some show particular affinities with other Lives of Celtic saints in the *topoi* that they employ, which strongly suggests that the Lives of saints from other Celtic regions were a significant source of hagiographic models.

The first Life of St Samson of Dol—the earliest Life of a Brythonic saint—tells of a saint and his companions coming to Brittany, in this case from south Wales via Cornwall. The Life is long and detailed, and seems to be full of useful information about the religious (including pre-Christian), social, and political life of the 6th century, when its subject almost certainly lived. St Samson is thought to be the signatory to the council of Paris of *c.* 562. His Life seems to have been written in Brittany, by a monk of the house the saint founded at Dol. It claims to have oral and written information about the saint's activities on both sides of the Channel, as well as personal experience of the sites it discusses. The portion of the Life concerned with the saint's life in Wales and Cornwall, by far the longest portion of the text, shows the saint as a reluctant participant in coenobitic MONASTICISM, in pursuit of an increasingly eremitical life. The Breton section presents the saint much less as a monastic founder and much more as a diplomat: It describes the founding of two religious houses, Dol and Pental, but climaxes with an account of the saint's intervention with a Frankish emperor on behalf of two princes of DOMNONIA.

The 9th Century and the Carolingian Renaissance

In religious affairs, NOMINOE is most notably associated with the attempt to establish a Breton archbishopric independent of Tours. The defining event of this struggle was the 'synod' of *Coitlouh* (identification uncertain) of 849, at which Nominoe deposed the five existing Breton bishops, effectively putting the Breton dioceses outside Carolingian (and papal) control. One of Nominoe's successors, Salomon, presided over an attempt to the Pope that St Samson had founded a Breton archbishopric not historically subject to Tours. In 1199, the matter was decisively settled by Innocent III in favour of Tours.

The 9th century was a period of visible activity in Breton churches. Lives of saints date from this period onward. While learned culture clearly looked to the Continent, the influence of other Celtic regions is clearly visible, in particular in the evidence of manuscripts: British and Irish texts were copied in Brittany, in a mainly insular version of the Carolingian script, and glossed at times in several CELTIC LANGUAGES.

Karen Jankulak

CHRISTIANITY, BRITTANY, PROTESTANTISM

Protestantism has never been the religion of the majority in Brittany (BREIZH), and it is unlikely that more than about 5,000 adherents lived in the region at any given time from the 17th to the 19th century. Nonetheless, Breton Protestants have had a cultural significance, particularly in the shaping of Modern BRETON LITERATURE and the modern literary BRETON language.

The Breton Huguenots

From the 1530s, Protestantism gained ground among élite social groups in Brittany— that is, cultivated craftsmen, printers, magistrates, mariners, and soldiers. The great families of the Breton nobility were attracted by Calvinism and at the denomination's peak in Brittany (1565) approximately one fourth of the upper class were followers. However, there is little evidence that they attempted to impose their religion on their vassals or serfs. The Breton-speaking countryside in the west remained untouched, as the early Protestants evangelized in French. Nonetheless, the Huguenots (French Protestants) represented an important part of the French-speaking élite, among them mathematician François Viète (1540–1603) and Roch Le Baillif (doctor, alchemist, and advisor to King Henri IV of France). Henri IV had granted some civil rights to Protestants with the Edict of Nantes in 1598, revoked by Louis XIV in 1685. This first phase of Protestantism came to an end with this revocation of religious freedom, and many Protestants fled Brittany.

From Tolerance to Recovery (1787–1850)

When Napoleon Bonaparte pronounced freedom of worship in 1802, Protestantism in France was largely confined to foreigners. Nineteenth-century Breton Protestantism expanded most rapidly in the west of Brittany. The arrival of Welsh missionaries marked a major new direction in Protestant proselytizing in Brittany. With communications reestablished after the end of the Napoleonic wars, the Protestant churches of Wales were able to begin a project that was of concern to them: to spread their reformed creed among the Bretons, whom modern comparative linguistics had recently rediscovered as their 'cousins' (see PAN-CELTICISM). In 1818, the Welsh periodical *Goleuad Gwynedd* (The light of GWYNEDD) published a contribution lamenting the 900,000 Breton speakers in France who languished under the 'iron yoke of Catholicism'. In April 1819, the Anglican minister and linguist Thomas Price (also known as 'Carnhuanawc') noted the fact that the Bretons did not possess a complete translation of the BIBLE, and brought this omission to the attention of the Committee of the British and Foreign Bible Society. His collaborator, the Reverend David Jones, met Jean-François Le Gonidec, one of the founding members of L'Academie Celtique in Paris, who had already published an authoritative Breton dictionary and grammar (see DICTIONARIES AND GRAMMARS, BRETON). Le Gonidec finished the translation of the Bible in 1835, although only the New Testament was published. His highly literary use of language represents a major milestone in the revival of a high-culture written style in Modern Breton. Together, the Welshmen Reverend John Jenkins (1807–72) and the Methodist James Williams revised Le Gonidec's translation of the Bible and published multiple small works in Breton. Using colloquial Breton speech, they succeeded in reaching the rural population, mainly with the aid of itinerant pedlars. Literacy in Breton was key to their efforts, which explains why the first book written in Breton, by Jenkins, was a primer, *An A B K* ('A B C' in the Breton alphabet).

After 1870: A Strong Protestant Proselytism

The foundation of the Third Republic in 1870, during the Franco-Prussian War, opened a new era in Breton Protestantism. The half-century between 1875 and 1925 marked the peak of Protestant missionary activity. The impact on the population of fishermen was remarkable. A new wave of Protestant evangelism in the early 20th century multiplied the number of places of worship on this part of the north coast of Brittany. The Quaker Charles Terell founded a meeting house at Paimpol (Pempoull) in 1906, which was later taken over by the Welsh Baptist minister Caradoc Jones.

In 1905, with the approval of the Reformed Church in Rennes, the Protestants of Saint Brieuc (Sant-Brieg) employed a Methodist minister, Jean Scarabin. Scarabin organized a major missionary drive in the *département* of Côtes-d'Armor (formerly Côtes du Nord, Aodoù-an- Arvor), and particularly on the coast in the region of Perros-Guirec (Perroz-Gireg).

The Protestants denounced the cultural backwardness of the province, starting with the weak local production of newspapers and writings in Breton. They considered this void to be an indictment of Catholicism for having failed in its rôle as a cultural and educational institution.

In the course of the 19th century, the general progress of EDUCATION permitted a growing output of Protestant works in the Breton language. From 1830 to 1930, several million pamphlets, *gwerziwhere* (BALLADS), and gospels; more than 100,000 New Testaments; as many issues of the *Almanach mad ar Vretoned* (The Bretons' good almanack); 20,000 Bibles; and numerous polemical works came off the presses. The Baptist minister Le Coat and his brother-in-law François Le Quéré were admirably equipped to express Protestant ideas in their native Treger dialect (see BRETON DIALECTS), adapting the message to rural Breton sensibilities. Their poems and songs on broadsides mocked the Catholic clergy and became bestsellers. In Breizh-Izel, broadside pedlars served as the spearhead of Protestant proselytism. From the middle of the 19th century, they travelled the Breton countryside, going from market to market selling their popular publications. Those who were not singers themselves worked together with singers, and their evangelical *gwerzioù* sometimes inspired spontaneous public gatherings.

The Breton Bible, a legacy of 19th-century Protestantism, was adopted by the Catholic Church in the later 20th century. It endures as the one great monument of Protestant literary activity in Brittany.

The second characteristic of Protestant strategy in Brittany between 1832 and 1914 was its constant association with anticlerical, republican, and socialist movements. Under the Second Empire (1852–70) in particular, the Protestants formed a lasting alliance with the *Bleus* ('Blues', supporters of a French republican constitution), who, as secularists, were also viewed with hostility by Catholic clergy. The ministers focused their efforts primarily on places that were physically remote from Catholic churches. Almost all of the rural and coastal Protestant foundations in Breizh-Izel belonged to an 'anti-establishment diagonal' running from Trégor in the north via Poher to the Bro-Vigoudenn in the south. These isolated communities tended naturally to form a sense of solidarity, in which the outsider Catholic superintendent came to be distrusted.

Jean-Yves Carluer and Erwan Rihet

CHRISTIANITY, CELTIC

'Celtic Christianity' is a phrase used to designate a complex of features held to have been common to the Celtic-speaking countries in the early Middle Ages. The majority of scholars consider this term to be problematic, however. There are three ways in which 'Celtic Christianity' has been conceived: (1) as a separate institution or denomination within Christianity, meaning a 'Celtic Church' that can be contrasted with the Roman Church or the Orthodox Churches of the East; (2) as a body of distinctive beliefs and practices; and (3) as a more impalpable assemblage of attitudes and values.

"The Celtic Church"

The view that at one time there existed a 'Celtic Church', uniting the Celtic-speaking peoples with one another and dividing them from the rest of Christendom, no longer has a place within serious scholarly discourse. No persuasive evidence can be advanced in support of such a model, whereas evidence is plentiful that Christians within the Celtic countries considered themselves a part of Latin Christendom.

"Celtic" Practices and Beliefs

The churches of the Celtic-speaking countries certainly had much in common with one another, for good historical reasons. All of the Celtic countries derived their Christianity directly or indirectly from Britain (see Patrick; Uinniau). Ireland (Ériu) remained under strong British influence during the 6th century, while Brittany (Breizh), settled from Britain, retained a vivid sense of the British background of its early saints. At a later date, Irish manuscripts found their way to Breton monasteries. As a result of such connections, the same or similar usages can be found in various parts of the medieval Celtic world. Resemblances that are as close, or closer, can also be found in non-Celtic lands that were subject to Gaelic influence (notably in Northumbria; see BRYNAICH), and few, if any, of these 'Celtic' features can be shown to have been present at any given time throughout the Celtic area.

From the 6th century onward, a divergent Easter reckoning has been the 'Celtic' trait that has attracted the most attention (see EASTER CONTROVERSY). The claim that Irish and British clerics used an irregular tonsure is rendered more colourful by the fact that some of its critics associated this tonsure with the wizard Simon Magus: There may be some connection here with traditions in which the DRUIDS had a tonsure of their own. Here, too, however, practice within the Celtic areas (and, indeed, beyond them) was by no means uniform.

While there is considerable evidence for divergent Irish and (to an even greater degree) British practice in matters of liturgy, baptism, and ecclesiastical administration, the usages in question seem to have characterized only specific regions, but not necessarily to have been uniformly present there. Other practices that became current, such as marriage on the part of the higher clergy and hereditary proprietorship of churches, were characteristic of unreformed usage throughout Christendom. The only peculiarly 'Celtic' thing about them is that the reform movement championed by Pope Gregory VII reached the CELTIC COUNTRIES later than it did other parts of Europe.

"Celtic" Attitudes and Values

The characterist attitudes and values are the most difficult aspects of 'Celtic Christianity' to define. The only possible source would be that the pre-Christian cultures and the new religion encountered in the various Celtic countries resembled each other in significant ways, reflecting a shared inheritance, and that this substratum had a formative influence on the nascent churches.

This scenario cannot readily be supported from the existing evidence. There seems to have been no uniformly 'Celtic' attitude toward the old religion. In Ireland, clerical condemnation of paganism existed side by side with a keen curiosity concerning the native past, and with attempts to accommodate aspects of non-Christian belief within a Christian framework. In contrast, there are no persuasive indications of a corresponding mentality in Wales, where much of the earliest surviving evidence for native legend occurs in a context that is outspokenly anti-clerical.

One of the features most frequently claimed for a 'Celtic Christian' mentality is a sense of the natural world as God's handiwork, leading to a spirituality that contemplates and celebrates the creation (see NATURE POETRY). This perspective is certainly striking in some early WELSH POETRY, closely comparable to what we find in Ireland. Other, and more disparaging, attitudes to the material world can also be found in Irish writings, however. Moreover, 'Celtic' enthusiasm for nature should not necessarily be seen as a relic of paganism: The terms in which it is expressed are clearly indebted to such patristic writers as St Augustine of Hippo (†430), and there is no reason not to see much of its inspiration as deriving from the same source.

Motivations for Positing "Celtic Christianity"

A forerunner of the modern idea of a 'Celtic Church' can be found as far back as the 13th century, when the claim that Joseph of Arimathaea founded the church of Glastonbury seemed to give British Christianity an antiquity greater than that of Rome; in his *Discourse on the Religion Anciently Professed by the Irish and the British* (1623), James Ussher (1581–1656) postulated such a church as a predecessor for the Protestant Church of Ireland. A whole series of subsequent writings arguing for the existence of a 'Celtic Church' had the same sectarian agenda. A vision of 'Celtic Christianity' that was not so determined by denominational politics was promulgated by the Breton scholar Ernest Renan (see PAN-CELTICISM) in 1854.

John Carey, with Thomas O'Loughlin

CHRISTIANITY, CORNWALL

Christianity may have reached Cornwall (KERNOW) during the ROMANO-BRITISH period, and was probably a significant force by the 5th century when Christian Latin INSCRIPTIONS begin to survive on tall 'pillar' stones commemorating local aristocracy. Aldhelm, the Anglo-Saxon bishop of Sherborne, visited Cornwall in about 700 and wrote a letter to Gerontius (Gerent), the king of the region, urging him and his clergy to adopt the Roman CALENDAR (see EASTER CONTROVERSY; GERAINT FAB ERBIN). During the 9th century, Cornwall and its Church came under the control of the kings of Wessex.

By the time that Cornwall became a county of ENGLAND in the 10th century, the early monasteries had evolved into minsters staffed by canons, priests, or clerks. Fifteen minsters are recorded in the Domesday Survey of 1086, all of which were also parish churches. By the 10th century, many smaller religious sites had acquired or would acquire graveyards, church buildings, and parishes. These eventually numbered about 155, giving a total of approximately 170 parishes in the county by 1291. Cornish churches were usually named after Brythonic men or women, who came to be regarded as saints and patrons of the churches. More than 100 churches had a unique saint, while another 62 commemorated saints from other Brythonic lands—chiefly from Brittany, but a few from Wales (CYMRU). A series of bishops based at Bodmin and St Germans ruled Cornwall until 1050, when the diocese was merged into that of Exeter in Devon.

Medieval Christianity flourished chiefly in the parish churches and in the collegiate church of Glasney at Penryn, founded in 1265 as a kind of surrogate cathedral. Many parish churches were rebuilt in the 15th and early 16th centuries, housing numerous cults of international saints supported by groups of parishioners. Hundreds of additional chapels were founded in gentry houses and outlying communities, or to promote saint cults, and pilgrimage took place, notably to St Michael's Mount. Religious drama became popular, and plays on Biblical and hagiographical topics survive in the CORNISH language, linked with Camborne, Kea, and possibly Glasney (see BEUNANS KE; BEUNANS MERIASEK; CORNISH LITERATURE; ORDINALIA).

The Reformation of the 1530s and 1540s closed the religious houses, abolished images and pilgrimage, and replaced Latin worship by English. These changes caused discontent, culminating in the so-called Prayer-Book Rebellion of 1549, during which protesters from Cornwall and Devon besieged Exeter, before being routed by royal troops. Under Queen Elizabeth I (1558–1603), Cornwall became nominally Protestant, although the contemporary Cornish writers Richard Carew and Nicholas Roscarrock state that saints' days continued to be celebrated and holy wells visited for cures or divination. In the 17th century, the region was noted for its strong political support for Charles I, and consequently for the Church of England or 'Anglican Church'.

The Anglican dominance was challenged by the rise of Methodism at the end of the 18th century—a development that began as an evangelical movement within the Church of England. At the national English census of attendance at worship in 1851, Methodists and other nonconformists in Cornwall greatly outnumbered Anglicans. A bishop and diocese were reestablished in 1877, centred at Truro. The building of Truro Cathedral (1880–1910) gave Anglicans a major building and powerful symbol.

Nicholas Orme

CHRISTIANITY, IRELAND

Origins

The legendary picture of a sudden and decisive conversion of Ireland to Christianity at the hands of Saint PATRICK at Easter 432 is essentially the dramatic creation of Muirchú's *Vita Patricii* (late 7th century). Christians could have first reached Ireland (ÉRIU) anytime after their establishment in BRITAIN, by the late 2nd century. From this early period we have one enigmatic piece of evidence: the question of the original home of PELAGIUS (*c*. 350–*c*. 425). He is usually said to have come from Roman Britain, but Jerome, a contemporary who is unusually precise with geographical information, held that he belonged to the Irish people (*Scotticae gentis*).

The 5th Century

By the 430s, sizeable communities of Christians in Ireland. It is quite likely that these groups were composed mainly of slaves captured from Britain or their descendants. From elsewhere in the Roman world, we know that communities of Christians continued to concern themselves with the spiritual welfare of their brethren who had been taken into slavery—for example, by supplying them with clergy—and the British church probably continued to minister to Christians in Ireland. Prosper of Aquitaine (*c*. 390–*c*. 463) records that in 431 Pope Celestine sent to those in Ireland 'who believed in Christ' a bishop named PALLADIUS, who is not mentioned in any other insular source until the late 7th century. In Prosper's *De gratia Dei et libero arbitrio contra Collatorem* (written in 434), he tells us that Celestine had sent a bishop to the British Church to free it from 'Pelagianism' and that he had ordained a bishop for the Irish so that 'the barbarian island might be made Christian'. These passages, taken with other references to missionary work beyond the imperial frontiers, point to a Roman mission to Ireland still working 20 years later when Leo the Great was concerned with the state of the Christians in Ireland.

Our most important sources for the 5th century are the two documents written by Patrick. His *Confessio* justifies his mission as a bishop in Ireland against Christian critics either in Ireland or Britain, while his 'Letter to the Soldiers of Coroticus' is a sentence of excommunication aimed at people who were taking Irish Christian converts into slavery. Patrick's dates are probably sometime in the later 5th century; there are no contemporary references to his mission.

The Early Christian Period

By the mid-6th century, when the silence of our sources begins to end, the evidence reveals a well-organized Christianity with important monastic foundations, well-known teachers such as Comgall at Beann Char (Bangor), and a church that is able to see itself as equal to those on the Continent in matters of learning, establishment of doctrine, and pastoral praxis.

From the 7th century onward, much better evidence is available, and contemporary ANNALS provide accurate dates. MONASTERIES grew to become the great centres of learning and economic life, and Christianity emerged as the intellectual form of the society. While the Church incorporated several native features into its law, its canon law was taken over into secular law and became its pattern as a written corpus (see LAW TEXTS). Ireland also emerged as one more region within Latin Christendom, with travel by monks, teachers, and administrators occurring in both directions. By the later 7th century Ireland had a vibrant theological community whose works were having an impact on the rest of the Latin Church. The best examples are in the area of law; for example, *Cáin Adomnáin* (697)—an attempt to limit the effects of warfare—shows the Church seeking to influence society. Likewise, the first systematic canonical collection was compiled in Ireland and was soon copied and imitated abroad—its new directions affected all subsequent western canon law. It is against this background that we should view the Irish clerics active in Charlemagne's kingdoms.

Issues of Perception

Two very different monastic ideals, both well rooted in Ireland, came into conflict at the end of the 8th century: one championed by the ascetic reform movement, the Céili Dé (Fellows of God), and the other touted by the author of the NAVIGATIO SANCTI BRENDANI. Rather than a clash between a 'Celtic MONASTICISM' and some imagined 'normative' or Roman monasticism, however, this battle involved two *Irish* local theologies, both closely related to contemporary monastic disputes elsewhere in the Latin West. At no point did Irish Christians perceive themselves as religiously separate *as Christians* from others in the West. While it is clear that they recognized their cultural separation from Christians elsewhere, in that they prepared lists of 'their saints', meaning those born in Ireland, they were equally conscious that they expressed that cultural distinctiveness in Latin, which was the bond of their Christian solidarity as one *gens christiana* 'Christian nation' among those nations that made up the *gens sancta Dei* 'holy nation of God'. This sense of being one ethnic group within the unity of Latin Christianity is seen in the number of *peregrini* ('pilgrims') who went to the Continent and settled there as monks or teachers; while fully seen as being from a part of the Latin Church, they distinguished themselves with the appellation *Scottus*.

There has been a long-standing desire—going back at least to John Toland's *History of the Druids* (1726)—to find 'pagan' elements mixed with Christianity. It is undoubtedly the case that Ireland experienced syncretism in its religious practices—any religion takes on a different appearance with every new cultural situation it encounters—but no evidence suggests that paganism survived as any sort of cohesive system much beyond the 5th century.

In the 1st millennium, Christianity proved itself remarkably flexible in adapting to various environments and taking on local colour (acculturation), and in this sense it was far more successful than other explaining religions of the late Roman empire (e.g., Mithraism) that presented themselves as exotic. Thus, when Christianity came to Ireland, it came in its late antique Latin dress, and this guise then took on new local hues as it encountered a society that was non-urban, did not have either a Roman imperial background or a Roman legal system, did not perceive Latin to be the prestige language. Christianity also showed from its outset an unwillingness to import elements from other religious systems that it considered 'superstitious', although what constituted 'SUPERSTITIONS' varied with time and place; thus there was an ongoing fear of assimilation. In Ireland, we have no record of resistance to Christianity that would show us directly the nature of the other religion's content, and by Muirchú's time there was no longer any living memory of what the pre-Christian Irish believed. Using Continental parallels—usually from much earlier—carries with it many difficulties of method. The result is that, far from being easily uncovered, reconstructing the pre-Christian religion of Ireland is a most difficult but important academic task, and the absence of such understanding is our single greatest limitation in understanding early Irish Christianity.

The 12th Century

Developments on the Continent seemed to bypass Ireland between the 9th century and later 11th century, especially the new, more codified monasticism that can be traced to Benedict of Aniane (*c.* 750–821) and that resulted in Benedictinism and led to later monastic 'reforms' such as those of Cluny and, later still, the Cistercians. The later 'Gregorian reforms', which entailed developments of new models of church/secular relations linked to Pope Gregory VII (*c.* 1021–85), also seemed to leave Ireland lagging behind. In the 12th century, however, a key running theme in church activities in Ireland was the desire for 'reforms' so that the Irish Church had the same structures as those elsewhere. This perspective is best seen in the various synods, most importantly Ráith Bressail (1111) and Kells (Ceanannas Mór, 1152), which established dioceses and provinces in Ireland and sought to give the same shape to Irish structures as those found elsewhere. Linked to this process are the names of the powerful bishops of the period, such as Cellach, Mael Maedóc, and Lorcan Ua Tuathail (St Laurence O'Toole). This period also saw the introduction of several new orders that brought contemporary ideals of religious life from the Continent and left their mark in many ways in religious writings produced in Irish from the 12th century until the Reformation. The two most important groups were the Cistercians, who arrived in the mid-12th century (see CISTERCIAN ABBEYS IN IRELAND), and the Franciscans, who arrived in the 13th century. Two distinct churches grew up in the wake of the Norman invasions—one in the Norman-controlled areas, the other in the Gaelic areas—and this situation persisted until the 17th century.

The Period of Reformation and Counter-Reformation

The 16th-century revolution within Latin Christianity affected the two churches in Ireland (ÉIRE) differently. The English Reformation directly altered the organization of the *ecclesia inter Anglos* (the English church) while hardly touching that *inter Hibernos* (the Gaelic church). By 1612, however, it was clear that religious and political divisions would not simply follow the old medieval divisions; from that point onward, then on there would be an increasingly close identification of non-English with Catholic. This divergence resulted in the last great flowering of religious writing in Ireland, in Latin and in IRISH. On the one hand, there was a desire to translate materials into Irish to advance the Protestant cause. William Bedell (1571–1642), for example, insisted that clerical graduates of Trinity College Dublin should be able to minister to Irish people in their native language, and oversaw the translation of the Old Testament into Irish (see BIBLE). On the other hand, there was a desire to provide material that would introduce counter-Reformation Catholicism into Ireland and rebut the Protestant advance. Many new devotional works were written in Irish. In this process, the Irish Franciscans had a unique place, for it was their desire to preserve the Catholicism of Ireland and to strengthen it by introducing new works in Irish that placed them at the forefront of the attempts in the 17th century to preserve as much as possible of the inheritance of early Irish history, such as the work of the Franciscan John Colgan (Seán Mac Colgáin, 1592–1658) on Irish HAGIOGRAPHY.

Thomas O'Loughlin

CHRISTIANITY, ISLE OF MAN

The date at which the Isle of Man (ELLAN VANNIN) became Christian is uncertain. The dominant tradition is of conversion by a Patrician mission from Ireland (ÉRIU)—there are four quite standard OGAM inscriptions—while other linguistic evidence links the earliest church on the island with Wales (CYMRU), northwest ENGLAND, and Galloway (Gall Ghàidhil). The multiple dedications of churches to PATRICK, Columba (COLUM CILLE), Cuthbert, and NINIAN seem to reflect this diversity of influence, and the island has no patron saint.

The wealth of cross slabs, INSCRIPTIONS, and chapel sites that date from between AD 600 and 800 suggests a strong and vigorous religious life. Monasteries, such as those established at Maughold and Peel, provided literate, educated foci that were in regular contact with religious communities around the Irish Sea. The Vikings may have brought a brief period of paganism, but the persistence of the local population—evidenced by personal names in runic inscriptions—suggests that Christianity probably survived in some form throughout the Viking Age. Within a generation the Vikings were burying their dead in Manx-style coffins and marking their graves with Christianized forms of contemporary Scandinavian art styles.

The 12th century saw a raft of reforms. King Ólafr I brought in the Savignacs from Furness to found Rushen Abbey in 1134. At the time of his death in 1153, the Pope was in the process of reorganizing the northern European dioceses along 'modern' lines, leading to the creation of a diocese usually dubbed *sodorensis*—of the southern isles, meaning the Scottish Western Isles and Man (see HIGHLANDS)—within the province of Nidaros (modern Trondheim). The other major reform was the creation of parishes, originally 16 in total.

After the sale of the Isle of Man and the Western Isles to the Scots by the Treaty of Perth in 1266, Scottish kings appointed the bishops until 1374, by which time English control of the island had become more secure. Man on its own came within the province of York. In addition to the bishop, the Abbot of Rushen and Prioress of Douglas were significant landowners and barons in their own right and, together with the bishop, in a period of political instability, provided a major source of civil and religious authority.

The influence of the monasteries, especially Rushen, was profound on the development of Manx social, economic, and cultural life. Not only did the Abbey bring from the Continent new agricultural and industrial ideas to Man, but it also maintained its links with Furness and represented a vital element of stability and political continuity.

At the Dissolution, Edward, sixth earl of Derby and 'king' of Man, dissolved the monasteries on the island and eventually paid the proceeds to Henry VIII's exchequer in London. In 1611, Bishop Phillips began the process of a Manx translation of the Prayer Book—the earliest document to survive in the language (see MANX LITERATURE, MANX PRAYER BOOK AND BIBLE). Although parts of the New Testament were translated later in the century, not until the late 18th century was the whole Bible made available in MANX.

The 18th century is dominated by the work of two Anglican bishops—Wilson (r. 1698–1755) and Hildesley (r. 1755–72), and by the arrival of Methodism in 1758—John Wesley himself visited the Isle of Man in 1777 and 1781. In addition to completing the translation of the Bible in 1775, the bishops interested themselves in educational reform, poor relief, and the development of an educated clergy.

Christianity remains a major influence in Manx life. Church attendance has declined less than in neighbouring Britain, and relations between the major traditions are good. The bishop, the one surviving medieval baron, still retains a seat and a vote in the Legislative Council, the upper house of the Manx parliament, TYNWALD. The churches themselves, often working ecumenically, remain significant players in education, welfare, and social life.

P. J. Davey

CHRISTIANITY, SCOTLAND, BEFORE 1100

The Christianization of the BRYTHONIC peoples living in close proximity and contact with northern Roman BRITAIN seems to have begun shortly before the end of direct Roman rule in Britain in AD 409/410 (perhaps somewhat earlier in the north). This process has attracted little comment from scholars, but the Christianization of the PICTS has been the subject of lively ongoing debate. A traditional focus upon proselytizing saints such as NINIAN or COLUM CILLE has given way recently to the growing realization that such individuals did not play the key rôles formerly ascribed to them, and that the Christianization of northern Britain was a longer-drawn-out and more complex process than such saint-focused models have allowed.

Historical, place-name, and archaeological evidence come together to suggest that Christianity was already firmly established among the GAELIC and Pictish peoples by the time that Colum Cille came into contact with them (563–97). His monastery on Iona (EILEAN Ì) was the most influential force in northern ecclesiastical culture until the 8th century. Colum Cille himself seems to have been influential in the politics of DÁL RIATA and Brythonic Alt Clut (Dumbarton; see YSTRAD CLUD), as well as a monastic founder and influence among the Picts. Ionan daughter houses were the dominant ecclesiastical and Christianizing influence in northern ENGLAND until 664 (see EASTER CONTROVERSY), and the monastery retained a degree of influence in Northumbria thereafter. By the end of the century, it was possible for the Columban *familia* to credit itself with the Christianization of the northern Pictish zone and the founder as the father of Pictish monasticism.

Even with its formal interests in Pictland curtailed by royal decree in 717, Iona remained prominent, its influence with regard to monastic practices, ecclesiastical sculpture and ART, historiography, theology, and law transcending even the insular Celtic zone, before repeated attacks on the community by Scandinavian raiders forced a reorganization in the 9th century. Surviving contemporary evidence allows few insights, however, into the range of devotional behaviour that took place at other centres in Celtic-speaking northern Britain or in the areas affiliated with them.

In those regions of Scotland that became occupied by Scandinavians in the Viking Age, it is difficult to ascertain the extent to which Christianity had been established beforehand or, where it had done so, the extent to which the religion endured thereafter. Meanwhile, the Gaelicization of the Pictish peoples during the course of the 9th and subsequent centuries seems to have included an ecclesiastical element. Some kind of formal realignment from Pictish to Gaelic practices took place early in the 10th century, but the details of this adjustment are quite obscure. Certainly, the severe form of Gaelic MONASTICISM practised by the Céili Dé took firm root in the Gaelicized kingdom of ALBA, and prominent Pictish ecclesiastical centres such as Meigle, Portmahomack, and Abernethy seem to have declined as others such as Dunkeld (Dùn Chailleann) and, particularly, St Andrews (Cennrimonad) grew to greater prominence. The impression of moral turpitude and decline in canonicity in the Church of 10th- and 11th-century Alba created by 12th-century reformist commentators is exaggerated, but few scholars would argue that it was entirely without foundation.

James E. Fraser

CHRISTIANITY, SCOTLAND, C. 1100–C. 1560

Traditionally, the 12th century has been regarded as a period of change for the Scottish church. The realm was certainly brought more fully into the mainstream of western Christendom: New monastic orders made an appearance in Scotland (see MONASTICISM), with the Tironensians being introduced to Selkirk (Sailcirc) as early as 1113; a system of territorial dioceses was established; closer links with the papacy were forged. These developments owe much to the influx of settlers of English or northern French origin under the encouragement of King David I (1124–53) and his successors. Evidence indicates that the diocesan system was partly based on ancient provinces dating from Pictish times (see PICTS); bishops with Celtic names in David I's reign point to a line of native prelates, and the diocese of Caithness (Gallaibh) was probably the only new foundation by David. Iona (EILEAN Ì) became a Benedictine abbey, albeit not without resistance.

Little is known about religious observance in medieval Scotland (ALBA); as elsewhere, there was doubtless an attachment to ancient holy sites and saints (see HAGIOGRAPHY). Most parish churches were small, and priests usually poorly educated; there was no university in Scotland until 1410. The Scottish bishops, except the Bishop of Whithorn, were freed from the metropolitan jurisdiction of York by the papal bull *Cum universi* toward the end of the 12th century. Some 13th-century statutes, made in the wake of the Fourth Lateran Council, survive, but evidence from the later Middle Ages suggests that many beneficed clerics were not ordained to the priesthood, and ignored the requirement for celibacy; in GAELIC-speaking areas clerical dynasties can be traced, with churches passing from father to son. These irregularities probably had little effect on pastoral work.

The Reformation came late to Scotland. King James V (1513–42) perceived the material benefits of remaining loyal to Rome, and enacted legislation against Lutheran heresies. The reckless sale of indulgences found in parts of Europe did not engender a parallel in Scotland. Although there had been a growing interest in the cult of native saints such as NINIAN at Whithorn and Duthac at Tain (Baile Dubhthaich), marked by the publication of the Aberdeen Breviary shortly after 1500, evidence for widespread religious change is elusive until the late 1550s, and even then it was connected with fears that the marriage of Queen Mary (1542–67) to the French dauphin might involve Scotland in undesirable Continental entangle-ments. Even after the formal breach with Rome in 1560, much of rural Scotland remained doctrinally conservative.

Andrew D. M. Barrell

CHRISTIANITY, SCOTLAND, AFTER 1560

From its origin in 1560, the reformed Church of Scotland was conciliar in government and hostile to state control, unlike the Church of England. Through the influence of John Knox (1505–72), the Church of Scotland was Calvinistic, but its presbyterian structure was not fully established until 1592. It was later undermined by King James VI (James I of ENGLAND), who, in 1612, managed to secure parliamentary sanction for a mixed Episcopalian-cum-Presbyterian system. Presbyterian resentment led to a revolt in 1637 against a new Anglican-style Prayer Book. A year later, the National Covenant against the King's policies was signed in Edinburgh (DÙN ÈIDEANN), and shortly after the Covenanters seized power and swept away not only the bishops but also royal control of parliament. Reform of the state as well as the church was essential to this movement. The political theories of George Buchanan, the great 16th-century humanist and associate of Knox, strongly influenced the Presbyterians, who rejected the claims of divine right kingship.

In 1641, Charles I was forced to accept the new Scottish constitution in church and state. Nevertheless, a year after the outbreak of the Civil War in England, the Covenanters, fearful of a royal victory, allied with the Parliamentarians under the Solemn League and Covenant. This liaison gave rise to the Westminster Assembly of 1643, which produced its famous Confession of Faith and Catechisms, both markedly Calvinist.

After the restoration of the monarchy in 1660, however, Episcopacy was restored in Scotland, the Westminster standards were dropped, and the constitutional reforms that had been accepted by the Crown in 1641 were jettisoned. The repres-sive Restoration regime failed to overcome Presbyterian resentment. The Scottish Revolution Settlement under William and Mary rejected the Episcopalian regime in 1689, and a year later Presbyterianism and Westminster Standards were reinstated, but without reference to the Covenants.

At the UNION of England and Scotland in 1707, Presbyterian Church government in Scotland was guaranteed. Successive schisms arose over lay patronage, which was allowed by Parliament from 1712 to 1874.

In 1834, after years of struggle, the Evangelical Party gained control of the General Assembly of the Church of Scotland and passed the Veto Act. The resulting bitter 'Ten Years' Conflict' ended with the intervention of the civil courts. This crisis brought on the Disruption in 1843 and the setting up of the Free Church of Scotland, which dealt a serious blow to the established church. The Disruption was the last and greatest rift in Scottish Presbyterianism; from then on, the trend was toward reunion. In 1847, the United Secession Church and the Relief Church joined to form the United Presbyterian Church. In 1900, the United Presbyterian Church merged with the Free Church to form the United Free Church, a majority of which, in 1929, rejoined the Church of Scotland. This organization's spiritual independence was fully recognized in Acts of Parliament of 1921 and 1925.

Other denominations exist in present-day Scotland, two of which have had chequered histories since the Reformation. Roman Catholicism survived, but was steadily worn down. By the mid-18th century, the old faith was mainly confined to a few areas in the HIGHLANDS and Western Isles. Here, all of the competing churches found difficulties owing to remoteness, rugged terrain, and not least a culture clash. Although these bodies lacked adequate resources, they needed to provide a GAELIC-speaking ministry and were hampered by the absence of Christian literature in SCOTTISH GAELIC. Support for the Jacobite cause had worsened the situation of the Roman Catholics since 1688 (see JACOBITE REBELLIONS).

The third largest communion in Scotland today, the Episcopalians, derive from the 17th century when bishops governed the Church of Scotland in 1610–1638 and again in 1661–1689. After the reintroduction of Presbyterian government in 1690, many people in Scotland still adhered to Episcopacy, but their support for the exiled Stuarts led to persecution, and their numbers steadily diminished. From the early 19th century, however, when its loyalty was no longer in question, the Episcopal Church in Scotland, formed in 1804, prospered. It is in full communion with the Church of England, but is autonomous with its own constitution headed by a Primus and with its own Prayer Book.

Baptists and Congregationalists appeared in Scotland in the second half of the 18th century, but like the Methodists their main institutional development came in the 19th century. The outstanding fact, however, is that the main Christian influence in Scotland from the Reformation to the present has been Presbyterian, which has had a marked impact on education and general culture. Today, Christianity in Scotland is no longer the potent force that it was. Secular trends have led to falling church attendances and to church closures, and in varying degrees these developments have affected all denominations.

William Ferguson

CHRISTIANITY, WALES

Christianity first came to what is now Wales (CYMRU) during the Roman occupation. The Christian martyrs Aaron and Julian of Caerllion, mentioned by GILDAS, probably died in the persecution of Emperor Diocletian (AD 303–5). Christianity survived the collapse of Roman rule in Britain (AD 409/10) and underwent a period of consolidation and expansion during the late 5th and 6th centuries, which has become known as the 'Age of the Saints'. During this period, men such as Cybi and Deiniol were active in the north, and Teilo and David (DEWI SANT) in the south. It was not until 768 that the Welsh church came into conformity with the practices of Augustine's successors in ENGLAND by accepting the Roman calculation of the date for Easter (see EASTER CONTROVERSY), but the influence of the Welsh saints had by then left an indelible mark on Welsh culture.

The Welsh Church was deprived of its status as a 'national' church following the Norman Conquest. By the mid-12th century, the Welsh bishops had capitulated;

thus, where previously the Welsh had looked directly to Rome, they now came under the authority of Canterbury.

Uniformity became the order of the day and, as territorial parishes were established, the traditional *clas* of the old Welsh church disappeared. Continental monastic orders were introduced and the Cistercians were regarded with greater favour (see CISTERCIAN ABBEYS IN WALES; MONASTICISM).

As in England, it was politics rather than theology that first instituted change in the Welsh Church. Wales's loyalty to Henry VIII as a descendant of a Welsh dynasty (see TUDUR), coupled with the widespread spiritual lethargy and the disillusionment that was characteristic of the period, ensured that there was little opposition to his reorganization of the Church and his abolition of the monastic orders. By 1540, all 47 of the Welsh religious houses had been dissolved. Protestant theology brought a new vitality; churchmen, eager to ensure that the Welsh accepted the principles of the REFORMATION, gained the authorities' permission to translate both the Book of Common Prayer and the BIBLE into Welsh. Among the positive repercussions of William Morgan's translation of the Bible were the preservation of the Welsh language and the Welsh way of life. Bishop Richard Davies sought to promote the new Anglican way by describing it as a return to the practices and beliefs of the native Celtic Church (see CHRISTIANITY, CELTIC). He claimed that the gospel had been brought to Wales by the preaching of Joseph of Arimathea. It was Augustine of Canterbury who had corrupted this Church with the errors of Rome and, according to Bishop Davies, the Reformation had now purged the Celtic Church and returned it to its former purity.

Toward the middle of the 17th century, nonconformist churches were established in Wales. Under the leadership of Vavasor Powell, Morgan Llwyd, and others, Puritanism achieved a tenuous foothold that allowed the gathering of Congregationalist, Baptist, Presbyterian, and Quaker congregations. Many churches succeeded in maintaining their witness despite sometimes savage persecution. Religious tolerance was partly achieved through the 1689 Toleration Act.

The Methodist Revival began in Wales during the spring of 1735, when Howell Harris (1714–73), a young Anglican from Breconshire (sir Frycheiniog), underwent a conversion experience. Although much was done to prepare the way for an awakening by the CIRCULATING SCHOOLS of Griffith Jones (1684–1761), it was the preaching of men such as Harris, Daniel Rowland (1713–90) of Llangeitho, and Howell Davies of Pembrokeshire (sir Benfro) that truly ignited the spirits of the converts. The hymns, poetry, and prose of William Williams of Pantycelyn then provided them with a means of expressing their newly found faith. The Revival gained its following among ordinary Welsh people by means of the regular *seiat* or 'society meeting', organized in every part of the country. In 1742, the leaders, doctrinally all Calvinists, formed an Association, which assumed control of the Calvinistic Methodist movement throughout Wales. It was not until 1811, long after the first generation had died, that the movement seceded from the Anglican Church to form the Calvinistic Methodist Connexion, later the Presbyterian Church of Wales.

As Dissenters' numbers grew, the Calvinistic and by then Wesleyan Methodists seceded and joined their ranks together under the leadership of men such as

Thomas Charles (1755–1814) of Bala, Thomas Jones (1756–1820) of Denbigh (Dinbych), John Elias (1774–1841), Christmas Evans (1776–1838), and William Williams (1781–1840) of Wern. By 1851, Nonconformists in Wales outnumbered Welsh Anglicans. This prominence led not only to a new vitality in Welsh culture, but also to a desire to see the Church of England disestablished—a goal that was finally achieved in 1920.

The 1904–5 Revival was the last revival to take place on a national scale. Since that time, Welsh Christianity has been in decline. Changes in working practices, the rise of the Labour Movement with its often quasi-religious message of social improvement, greater leisure opportunities, and a wide range of other factors all contributed to the working-class rejection of traditional religious forms. World War I and II also affected attitudes toward the established church. With many new nondenominational, charismatic, and Pentecostal churches thriving, mainly as English-language communities, the traditional denominations continue to decline. Welsh Christianity faces an uncertain future.

The elevation of a Welsh-speaking Welshman Rowan Williams as Augustine's successor as Archbishop of Canterbury in 2002 was accompanied by an immediate swell of national pride in Wales as well as controversy in the British press over the popular perceptions of about his identity as a DRUID of GORSEDD BEIRDD YNYS PRYDAIN.

Geraint Tudur

CHWEDLEU SEITH DOETHON RUFEIN

Chwedleu Seith Doethon Rufein ('Tales of the Seven Sages of Rome') is a Middle Welsh version of the international popular tale 'The Seven Sages of Rome' by Llywelyn Offeiriad (Llywelyn the Priest). The story is structured as a series of brief narratives told by the Emperor of Rome's wife, which she uses in an attempt to convince her husband to kill his son, her stepson. The seven sages save the young man.

R. Iestyn Daniel

CIMBRI AND TEUTONES

Cimbri and Teutones were two tribes located east of the Rhine. They were often assumed to be linguistically Germanic, but the name *Teutones* is most probably Celtic (see also TUATH; TEUTATES). These groups are also significant in CELTIC STUDIES because their movements disrupted core Celtic-speaking areas in central and western Europe, and catalyzed early contacts between the Romans and Celtic groups in and beyond the Alps.

Together with a tribe called the Ambrones, the Cimbri and the Teutones migrated from present-day Himmerland (which preserves the name of the Cimbri) and Thy, Denmark, arriving in Noricum in 120 BC, where they defeated a Roman army that had been driven around central and eastern Europe for two decades. The Romans decimated the Teutones in the battle of Aquae Sextiae, now Aix-en-Provence, in 103 BC. The Cimbri met a similar fate in the battle of Vercelli in 102 BC. An inscription from Miltenberg on the Main indicates that a group called *Toutones*, the same name in a clearly Celtic spelling, lived there in Roman times.

Some early modern writers incorrectly identified the name *Cimbri* with *Cymry*, the Welsh name for the Welsh people (see Cymru), but the preform for *Cymry* is ancient Celtic **Combrogī*.

Peter E. Busse and John T. Koch

CÍN DROMMA SNECHTAI

Cín Dromma Snechtai ('The Book of Druim Snechta') is a famous early Irish manuscript, now lost. Given that the word *cín* is explained in the ancient glossaries as a 'stave of five sheets of vellum', this document was probably smaller than other similar Irish manuscripts. The *Cín Dromma Snechtai* is cited as a source by some of the most important extant Irish manuscripts from the 11th and 12th centuries, among them Lebor na hUidre ('The Book of the Dun Cow'), Lebor Laignech ('The Book of Leinster'), Leabhar Bhaile an Mhóta ('The Book of Ballymote'), *Leabhar Mór Leacáin* ('The Great Book of Lecan'), and Egerton 88. However, the codex was probably lost before the 17th century because Geoffrey Keating (Seathrún Céitinn) does not seem to have had access to it.

On the basis of the scribal annotations in the other manuscripts mentioned previously, the approximate contents of the lost manuscript have been determined. The codex seems to have mainly contained tales on supernatural characters, along with some of the earliest references to Fiannaíocht, as well as genealogies and legendary history. The comparative compactness of the manuscript suggested by its name is also reflected by these texts, both prose and poetry, which tend to be concisely worded and often short, with a large proportion of texts taking the form of prominent verse speeches. Among these texts are Immram Brain ('The Voyage of Bran'), *Echtra Conlai* (Conla's adventure), Togail Bruidne Da Derga ('The Destruction of Da Derga's Hostel'), Tochmarc Étaíne ('The Wooing of Étaín'), *Verba Scáthaige* (The words of Scáthach), and *Forfes Fer Fálchae* (The siege of the men of Fálchae).

Those texts that can be traced back to the *Cín Dromma Snechtai* stand out in the surviving manuscripts containing them. They tend to be significantly more archaic linguistically than other texts in these same manuscripts. In other words, they generally belong to the Old Irish rather than the Middle Irish linguistic horizon.

Petra S. Hellmuth

CINAED MAC AILPÍN

Cinaed mac Ailpín, also known as Kenneth I of Scotland (Alba), was king of the Scots (840–58) and Picts (*rex Pictorum*, 847–58). His father is not well documented, but the name is Pictish, the cognate of the Early Welsh man's name *Elphin*. Cinaed mac Ailpín began his rise to power with the assistance of Norse allies; his daughter married King Ólafr the White of Baile Átha Cliath (Dublin), and he took advantage of a Viking massacre of Dál Riata to seize their kingship. Cinaed died in Fothar Tabaicht (i.e., Forteviot, in modern Perthshire) in 858 and was buried in Iona (Eilean Ì). The name *Cinaed*, common among the early kings of Scotland, is probably

Celtic. It is the source for the English name, *Kenneth*. The second element reflects the Celtic word **aidhu-* 'fire'.

Peter E. Busse

CIRCULATING SCHOOLS AND SUNDAY SCHOOLS, WELSH

The system of circulating schools that existed in Wales (CYMRU) between 1731 and 1779 was essential for the successful development of modern Welsh-medium EDUCATION. As in Scotland (ALBA), the Society for the Promotion of Christian Knowledge (SPCK) had attempted to establish charity schools from the end of the 17th century, but using English as the medium of instruction. Griffith Jones (1684–1761), rector of Llanddowror, founded schools to teach students in WELSH, concentrating on rural areas. His teachers would work in a community for three to six months, teaching children and adults alike, and move on when literacy was established. Jones's annual reports, published under the title *The Welch Piety*, show that 3,750 circulating schools, attended by at least 167,853 people, were held between 1737 and 1761. After his death, Madam Bevan (1698–1779) continued his work.

When the system of circulating schools disintegrated, Thomas Charles of Bala (1755–1814), the famous Methodist preacher, introduced a pattern of Welsh Sunday schools. They provided a system of 'further education' in Welsh for children and adults alike. While the former learned to read Welsh and acquired a basic religious education, the latter would read and analyse complex religious texts and hold formal discussions on secular issues. At a time when what little secular education was available was conducted strictly in English, the 18th-century Welsh circulating schools and the 19th- and 20th-century Welsh Sunday schools ensured that the Welsh learned to read their native language. There is no doubt that such efforts contributed greatly to the strength of the Welsh language and its literature in the 20th century.

Marion Löffler

CISALPINE GAUL

Cisalpine Gaul, Latin *Gallia Cisalpina*, literally 'Gaul on this side of the Alps', was the Roman term for part of northern Italy, stretching from the ALPINE passes in the north and west to the Apennines in the southwest, including the fertile plains along the river Po to the shores of the Adriatic Sea in the east (originally Etruscan territory), along with the lands of the Raeti and Veneti to the nort-east. It became the primary zone of contact between Romans and Celts for much of the 4th, 3rd and 2nd centuries BC, and the first Celtic area under Roman control.

The Arrival of Celts in Italy

INSCRIPTIONS in the LEPONTIC language, the earliest dating from the 6th century BC, prove the presence of significant numbers of speakers of Celtic in parts of Cisalpina around Lake Como, a territory later occupied by the Insubres (coinciding with Livy's account that the first Celtic settlers under their leader Belovesus settled

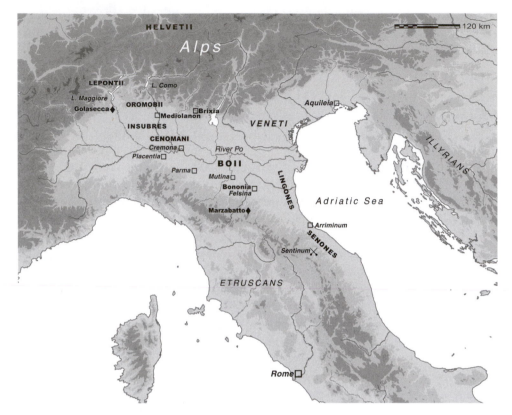

Cisalpine Gaul (Map by John T. Koch)

in the Insubres territory). Large-scale transalpine influences seem to appear only in the Early LA TÈNE period, roughly in the late 5th and 4th centuries BC. As such, a single massive Celtic migration into Cisalpina is far from likely.

Expansion and Consolidation

By the end of the 5th century BC, most of the Gallia Cisalpina north of the Po was subject to significant 'Celtic' influences. La Tène material culture first appears in this period, but only in the first half of the 4th century BC do large amounts of La Tène material culture appear in cemeteries south of the river Po, in the territories associated with the Boii and Senones. By the middle of the 4th century BC, most of Cisalpina seems to have become 'Gaulish', with strong La Tène influences obvious in the material culture. The Etruscan town Felsina was renamed/replaced by Celtic Bononia, the central location of the Cisalpine Boii. For the capture of Rome by the Celts c. 387 BC, see the entries on BRENNOS OF THE SENONES and ROME.

Gaulish Cisalpina in Decline

During the 3rd century BC, the Gaulish Cisalpina slowly declined. Fewer settlements than before can be identified, and the amount of prestige material goods in the archaeological record slowly declined—a trend interpreted as evidence of an economic crisis. During this period, the growing military power of Rome also led to a series of military setbacks and losses of territory. Following the battle of Sentinum in 295 BC, the Senones were quickly subjected under Roman rule, with two colonies founded—Sena Gallica in 280 BC and Arriminum in 268 BC—in their territory.

The Roman Conquest of Cisalpina

The Roman conquest of the Po valley itself began when Roman armies crossed the Apennines into the territory of the Boii in 225 BC, following the defeat of a Celtic force at Telamon earlier the same year. A series of swift campaigns against the Cisalpine Gauls culminated in the defeat of the Insubres at the battle of Clastidium in 222 BC and the capture of Mediolanon (Milan). By 218, the Romans had founded colonies in the central Po valley at Cremona and Placentia. When Hannibal crossed the Alps during the Second Punic War (218–201 BC), he successfully recruited Celts for his armies. Following his defeat, Romans campaigned every year between 201 and 190 BC in Cisalpina to gain control over the area.

Roman Celts

In the years following the conquest, the Romans proceeded with a massive colonization programme. Roads (notably the Via Aemilia and the Via Flamina) were built and colonies founded, including Bononia (Bologna) in 189 BC and Parma in 183 BC. During this period La Tène material slowly disappeared. This may be as much the result of a change in burial practices as anything else, with evidence of burials also disappearing during the 2nd century BC in much of the area north of the Alps. It is likely that a substantial Celtic population continued to occupy much of Cisalpina in the same dispersed pattern in this period as had characterized the previous two centuries, with Roman settlers taking up previously unoccupied land, thereby quickly integrating the local population into their own communities. It was only in 89 BC that the inhabitants of Cisalpina south of the Po became Roman citizens, compared to 42 BC for those north of the Po.

Raimund Karl

CISTERCIAN ABBEYS IN IRELAND

St Bernard of Clairvaux (1090–1153) initiated the Benedictine movement for a more austere monastic life, known as 'the Cistercians'. By his death there were already ten such MONASTERIES in Ireland (ÉRIU), and thirty-six had been established by 1272. They remained an important force in both English and Gaelic Ireland.

The arrival of the Cistercians is usually dated to the journey of Mael Maedóc (Malachy) to visit Innocent II in 1139, when he stayed with Bernard while travelling in both directions. He was so impressed that he left four of his party to train in Clairvaux and later sent others to join them. Then, in 1142, these Irish Cistercians, along with others, arrived to found Mellifont (Co. Louth/Contae Lú), which would become the mother-house of twenty-three other monasteries. The abbot of one of these houses, Congan of Inislounaght, requested that Bernard write the *vita* of Mael Maedóc, who had died in Clairvaux in 1148.

By 1169, twelve monasteries were operating, and the arrival of the Anglo-Normans brought a new pattern of foundations in the territories they acquired. For instance, John de Courcy and his wife founded Inch (1180) and Grey (1193), while William Marshal founded Tintern *minor* (1200) and Graiguenmanagh (1204). These Anglo-Norman–sponsored monasteries, ten in total, brought monks from English or Welsh houses (see CISTERCIAN ABBEYS IN WALES). A clear racial divide separated these organizations from the Irish houses, which looked to Mellifont. The clash between the groupings amounted to a monastic civil war, and it was only in 1228 that some order was brought to the situation.

A combination of reasons can be suggested to explain the amazing popularity of Cistercianism in Ireland. The most significant factor is the absence of Benedictinism there. Because none of the new religious movements arising from the 9th century onward had touched Ireland directly, the coming of the Cistercians marked a new way of life unlike anything found in Ireland, but in tune with the spirituality and theology of the Latin church. Cistercian spirituality was spread by Irish monks to Irish monks; it was not perceived as an import, and its interest in a strict asceticism allowed it to present itself as the authentic successor to the Irish MONASTICISM of an earlier 'golden age'.

The Cistercians also brought a new scale of architecture and, as elsewhere, a revolution in agricultural methods and organization. Their production methods affected the supply of cattle, horses, and wool, while their arrangement of lands into farms ('granges') had a lasting effect on the Irish landscape (see AGRICULTURE).

Thomas O'Loughlin

CISTERCIAN ABBEYS IN WALES

Wales (CYMRU), with its rugged, rural landscape, proved particularly attractive to the Cistercians and their way of life. The first Welsh Cistercian house was Tintern (Tyndyrn), colonized from L'Aumone in 1131, a daughter of Cîteaux. Over the next century, no fewer than eleven Cistercian abbeys were founded in Wales, along with two Savignac houses and two nunneries.

Cistercian MONASTICISM appealed particularly to the native princes of north and west Wales, and the majority of the abbeys were established in these regions. From Clairveaux came the 'family' of Whitland (Hendygwyn; colonized 1140), which included Abbey Cwmhir (original foundation 1143), Strata Florida (YSTRAD-FFLUR, 1164), and Strata Marcella (Ystrad Marchell, 1170). These groups, in their turn, established colonies—Cymer (1198), Llantarnam alias Caerleon (1179), and Aberconwy (1186), all from Strata Florida, and Valle Crucis (1201), from Strata Marcella. The two nunneries can also be included in this 'family'; Llanllugan was founded *c.* 1200 by Maredudd ap Rhotpert, lord of Cydewain, and came under the supervision of Strata Marcella. Llanllŷr (*c.* 1180) was founded by the Lord Rhys (RHYS AP GRUFFUDD), and supervised by Strata Florida.

The Cistercian abbeys of the Whitland 'family' were notably sympathetic to the aspirations of the Welsh princes, and closely identified themselves with the language, literature, and culture of Wales. Indeed, they seem to have figured importantly in the production and copying of manuscripts in the WELSH language. The lists of known abbots of these communities include names that are overwhelmingly Welsh, in marked contrast to the traceable succession in those houses founded on the initiative of Anglo-Norman patrons.

Decline in the strength and economy of the communities before the dissolution of the monasteries in the 1530s, combined with neglect and depredation of the ruins, has taken a heavy toll on these sites. The majestic ruins of Tintern Abbey famously inspired the Romantic poet William Wordsworth. Nothing remains above ground of Strata Marcella (whose church, if completed, would have rivalled St David's cathedral for length; see DEWI SANT), Grace Dieu, or the nunnery at Llanllŷr. A few houses survive as parish churches. Whitland, the mother-house of the Welsh 'family', is little more than foundations, and Abbey Cwm-hir a few shattered walls.

John Morgan-Guy

CIUMEŞTI

Between 1962 and 1965, a cemetery of the LA TÈNE culture of the IRON AGE was excavated at Ciumeşti in northwest Romania (see CELTS IN CENTRAL AND EASTERN EUROPE). Thirty-four graves were excavated, twenty-one simple cremations in pits, six cremations buried in urns, and seven inhumations.

Among the grave goods were bronze and iron objects: personal ornaments including bracelets, anklets, and fibulae (BROOCHES); weapons comprising SWORDS, sword chains, spearheads, daggers, and a shield boss; and tools and utensils including knives, razors, and bones. The burials were often accompanied by animal SACRIFICE. The burials at the Ciumeşti cemetery began at the end of the 4th century BC, and the site remained in use for about two centuries. Many similar cemeteries were also excavated in the Transylvania region of Romania.

A spectacular warrior chieftain grave, probably a cremation burial, contained, in a more or less delicate state of preservation, an iron helmet with a bronze crest, a pair of griffins made of bronze, a spearhead, and a chainmail shirt on which was affixed a bronze rosette with a coat ornament. The helmet, whose top features a bird of prey with outstretched wings made of sheet bronze, is especially important because it is unique among Celtic finds, one of the best-known and most often reproduced pieces of Celtic ART. One of the scenes displayed on the inside of the GUNDESTRUP CAULDRON provides a good parallel to the Ciumeşti bird helmet. The helmet was manufactured in the 4th century BC, but its deposition happened some generations later, in the 3rd century BC.

Lucian Vaida

CLAN

The English word 'clan', now a common term in anthropology, is a loan from SCOTTISH GAELIC and IRISH *clann*, Old Irish *cland*. This GOIDELIC word's original meaning is 'children' or 'descendants', a borrowing from BRYTHONIC or British Latin *planta*, meaning 'children' (cf. Modern Welsh *plant*, 'children'), showing a special insular semantic development of Classical Latin *planta* 'sprout, shoot'.

As a social institution, the clan has a particular association with Celtic cultures, particularly the Scottish HIGHLANDS and Islands. The Highland clans of Scotland (ALBA) were an institution that came into being as kin-based societies were breaking down. The extended kin-groups or lineages (e.g., the Welsh *gwely* or Irish *fine*) had a tendency to grow from shallow or minimal lineages, extended across three or four generations, to deep maximal lineages that extended across as many as ten generations or more. Clans developed out of the latter. While maximal lineages were still bonded by actual kinship (e.g., the *cenedl* of Wales/CYMRU or the *gens* of early Ireland/ÉRIU), clans were as much about assumed ties as real ones. Over time, as the family of this ancestor-founder expanded, it divided into branches or septs (called *sliochd* in the Scottish Highlands). Once a maximal lineage absorbed non-kin as members, it became a clan. This evolution usually occurred when the lineage controlled more land than it could occupy using men from its own ranks. Their absorption of non-kindred groups occurred either by formal alliance, such as with the bonds of friendship used in the Scottish Highlands, or by individuals simply adopting the name of a clan.

Clans in this sense were widely developed in the Highlands and Islands of Scotland and in parts of Ireland, but were not a prominent feature of native Welsh society. They usually emerged in politically volatile areas that lay beyond the bounds of early state systems. In the Scottish Highlands, for instance, clans emerged during the 13th and 14th centuries in the more rugged places that the Scottish Crown regularly threatened but could not subdue. Feuding and rivalry among the clans meant that they were never a stable form of socio-political order. Successful feuds and marriages were occasions for a FEAST that could last for days, its extravagance of consumption making a powerful statement in a poor society.

Robert A. Dodgshon

CLANN MACMHUIRICH

Clann MacMhuirich, the MacMhuirich family of hereditary BARDS and other learned professionals, maintained a prominent rôle in GAELIC learning, and especially Classical Gaelic poetry, in Scotland (ALBA) from the time of their progenitor, Muireadhach Albanach Ó Dálaigh (*fl.* 1200–30), down to the 18th century. Part of the prominence of the Clann MacMhuirich undoubtedly derived from their relationship with the Clann Domhnaill Lords of the Isles (see LORDSHIP OF THE ISLES), to whom they seem frequently to have been court poets as well as occasional lawyers and physicians. Following the downfall of the Lordship, patronage of the family seems to have shifted to the Clann Raghnaill (Clanranald). The earliest of their poets was probably Niall Mór Mac-Mhuirich (*c.* 1550–*c.* 1613), author of the superb and intimately enticing love lyric, *Soraidh slán don oidhch' areir* (Farewell forever to last night). It is a MacMhuirich *seanchaidh* (tradition-bearer/genealogist) who gave the Clann Domhnaill their most coherent Gaelic narrative history, in the Books of CLANRANALD. Cathal MacMhuirich (*fl.* 1625) and Niall MacMhuirich (*c.* 1637–1726) continued the tradition into the period of the Jacobite rebellions. The last Scottish practitioner of Classical Gaelic poetry, Domhnall MacMhuirich, was a tenant on Clanranald lands in South Uist in the 18th century, and his descendants were both book-learned and tradition-bearers.

Thomas Owen Clancy

CLANRANALD, BOOKS OF

The Books of Clanranald are two manuscripts of the late 17th/early 18th century. They are best known on account of their Gaelic history of the MacDonalds. The Red Book was written by Niall MacMhuirich of South Uist (Uibhist mu Dheas), hereditary poet historian to Clanranald (see Clann MacMhuirich). The manuscript may have been one of those removed by James Macpherson to London at the time of the Ossianic controversy. The so-called Black Book is a more miscellaneous compilation, containing a mass of historical, literary, and other material with a clear Antrim provenance.

The Clanranald History is a valuable document, both as a source with a Highland perspective on Highland history and as an example of a Scottish family history written in Scottish Gaelic. Its account begins with the coming of the Sons of Míl Espáine to Ireland (Ériu). The next section deals with the rise of the House of Somerled and the Lordship of the Isles, and draws on other lost historical sources. Following the forfeiture of the Lordship of the Isles in 1493, the narrative focuses on the Clanranald branch. The quality of the Clanranald History becomes increasingly detailed in the 1640s. The narrative reverts to chronicle mode and a Hebridean focus for its last section, which includes the period up to the death of Charles II in 1689 (*sic*).

William Gillies

CLAWDD OFFA (OFFA'S DYKE)

Clawdd Offa (Offa's Dyke) is a linear earthwork built in the late 8th century at the direction of the Anglo-Saxon king Offa of Mercia (r. 757–96) to separate his territory from that of independent Welsh rulers to the west. Running near the line of the present border of England and Wales (Cymru), it remains visible over many long stretches as a bank with a defensive ditch on its west. Its original course has been projected to fill gaps between a northern terminus near Prestatyn and a southern one west of the lower Wye (afon Gwy) near Chepstow (Cas-gwent), a distance of some 190 km (120 miles). It is the longest linear defence in Britain and on a scale comparable to that of Hadrian's Wall.

The historical situation had clearly changed by the later 8th century, such that four battles are reported between Mercia and Welsh kingdoms in *Annales Cambriae* in the period 760–96. The fact that a Welsh language, showing linguistic features distinct from the cognate Old Breton and Old Cornish, does not emerge until *c*. ad 800, also means that the building of Offa's Dyke is a useful milestone at which point it becomes unproblematical to speak of Wales, the Welsh people, and the Welsh language meaning much what they do today.

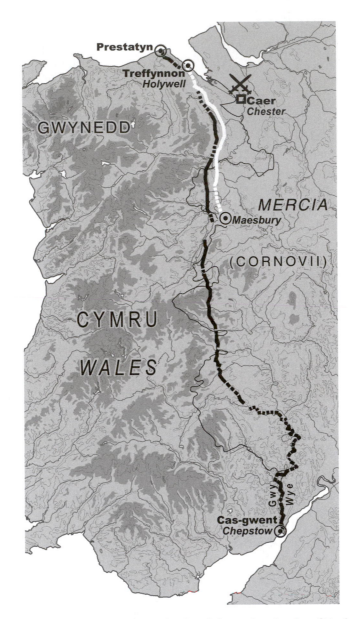

Offa's Dyke (in black) and Wat's Dyke (in white) and the modern border of England and Wales (thin black line). Projected courses of the dykes are shown as broken lines. (Map by John T. Koch)

A similar ditch-and-bank structure about 55 km (35 miles) long, known as Clawdd Wad or Wat's Dyke, runs parallel to Offa's Dyke a few miles to the east. A comparable long east–west linear earthwork in southwest England known as the Wansdyke appears to be a work of 5th- or 6th-century Britons.

John T. Koch

CLEARANCES

'Clearances' are generally understood to be evictions in the HIGHLANDS and Islands of Scotland (ALBA) that took place between the 1780s and the 1850s to make way for sheep and, later, deer runs. The wholesale eviction of communities contributed greatly to the destruction of the ancient CLAN system and the decline of the SCOTTISH GAELIC language.

From about 1760 landowners began to introduce sheep to their estates to maximize income derived from the land and thus 'improve' it. The communities that lived there were driven out and their members scattered—either to emigrate or to be resettled. Resettlement most often took place on poor coastal crofts, where fishing and kelping (collecting seaweed, which would be processed to make fertilizer) became the main means of making a living. Most of those evicted, however, were forced to emigrate. Between 1762 and 1886, the first and the last clearances, an estimated 100,000 Highlanders emigrated to Scottish towns, to Canada, the United States, and Australia.

It is now acknowledged that, as in ÉIRE, AGRICULTURE in the Highlands might not have been capable of supporting the growing population throughout the 19th century (see FAMINE), so that the emigration of a proportion of the population was unavoidable. Nevertheless, the brutality and harshness with which many Highland clearances were conducted left bitter memories that persist to this day.

Marion Löffler

CÓICED

Cóiced (pl. *cóiceda*) 'a fifth' was the term used for 'province' in early Ireland (ÉRIU). Medieval Ireland had five provinces: ULAID (Ulster), CONNACHT, MUMU (Munster), LAIGIN (Leinster), and MIDE (Meath). Most of what used to be Meath figures as northern Leinster. The Modern Irish form is *cúige*.

The idea of five separate and equal provinces is probably ahistorical. Although Mide clearly constituted an overkingship by the 7th century, its earlier status is uncertain. *Rí chóicid*, equivalent to *rí ruirech* of earlier law tracts, represents the highest order of KINGSHIP—'overking' of several mid-level kings ('mesene kings'), each of whom is the lord of several local kings. Classical Irish polity was seemingly closer to the heptarchy (the five provinces plus the realms of Ailech and Airgialla) reflected in the 12th-century *Lebor na Cert* ('The Book of Rights').

Ailbhe MacShamhráin

COINAGE, CELTIC

Celtic coinage first emerged in the late 4th to the early 3rd century BC (Middle LA TÈNE period). The earliest Celtic coins copied Greek designs, but did not attempt to follow weight and metal purity standards. Moreover, usually remained in the regions where they were issued. Thus it is not immediately clear to what extent the appearance of coinage among Iron Age Celts signals the transition to a true cash

Gold coin of the Ambiani of northern Gaul from the 2nd century BC. The image derives from Classical representations of Apollo. (British Museum/Barbara Heller/StockphotoPro)

economy on the Mediterranean model; it could have been a continuation of earlier patterns of exchange of prestigious gifts between chieftains and followers.

The First Generation of Celtic Coins

Three broad geographical zones are recognized for the Celtic prototypes:

1. An eastern silver belt followed the DANUBE from the southern valley of the upper Elbe to the Black Sea. Most of these coins derived from the Macedonian silver coins of Philip II (359–336 BC) and his successors, Alexander the Great (336–323) and Philip III (323–317).

2. Several southern silver groups copied the coins of three Greek cities: Massalia in GAUL, and Emporiai and Rhoda in Iberia. Another group copied Roman Republican *quinarii* (small silver coins roughly parallel to American nickels or dimes). Celtiberian coins, some inscribed with names in the CELTIBERIAN language in either Celtiberian or Greek SCRIPT, were produced in eastern Spain from the 3rd to earlier 1st century BC.

3. The northern gold belt began to the east of the middle and upper Elbe, curved southwest into south central Germany, and then northeast to the mouth of the Rhine. This zone included ENGLAND from the south of the Humber to the mouth of the Severn (Welsh Hafren), and south to Dorset.

A Graeco/Celtic Synthesis

The prototype of the coins found in the vast majority of regions is the stater of Philip II of Macedon. The obverse of this coin depicts the head of Apollo with short hair, and the reverse a two-horse CHARIOT at full gallop.

Two different styles began to assert themselves and draw away from classicism: Belgic (see BELGAE) and Armorican (see ARMORICA). The Belgic style in the north grew more abstract over time, such that the last coins of the British Durotriges appeared as little more than dots and dashes. Some coins in Germany appear to be original Celtic designs.

Rome and the End of Celtic Coinage

The conquest of Gaul did not bring about an immediate end to Celtic coinage. Legends on coins became more common, both in GAULISH and Latin. The larger wartime coins of Armorica gave way to numbers of very small coins, increasingly debased in value.

In Britain, gold continued to be used until the Claudian conquest, albeit often heavily debased. British coins in the peripheral areas maintained Celtic styles until the end of Celtic coinage. The Celtic Coin Index at the Institute of Archaeology, Oxford, has detailed records and photographs of more than 30,000 coins, and much of this data is freely available on the World Wide Web.

The Linguistic Testimony of Celtic Coinage

Because they are mostly of pre-Roman date, not mediated to us by Greek or Roman authors and copyists, and closely locatable and datable, the evidence of the coin legends is of great value for the early CELTIC LANGUAGES. This evidence is mostly limited to names and titles, all often abbreviated. Forms of interest include the Celtiberian regal name ΡΙΓΑΝΤΙΚΟC *Rigantikos,* which contains the Celtic element 'king' **rīgo-* and king TASCIOVAN[OS] (*c.* 20 BC–*c.* AD 10) of the British Catuvellauni, known to us only through his dynasty's coin legends and his subsequent appearance, as Old Welsh *Teuhuant,* in Welsh GENEALOGIES.

John Hooker

COLIGNY CALENDAR

In 1897, fragments of a large bronze calendar were discovered near Coligny (Ain, Burgundy, France), constituting nearly half of the original calendar. This object is similar in form to other Mediterranean inscribed public calendars, but lunar rather than solar based.

The calendar of Coligny covers a five-year span, including twelve months of 29 or 30 days and two intercalary months inserted over the five-year period to keep calendar in line with the solar year. This still results in a solar year that is 367 days long. Each of the days has a small peg hole for a date marker. The calendar contains many

GAULISH words, written in the Roman script, many abbreviations of uncertain meaning.

Both the year and the months are divided into two halves, divided by the word ATENOUX. This term has traditionally been interpreted as 'returning night'. The month names are preceded on the calendar by M or MID, presumably signifying the Gaulish word for month (cf. Old Irish *mí*, Welsh *mis*).

The translations of several of the month names are secure: SAMONI is cognate with Old Irish SAMAIN, and contains the root for 'summer'. GIAMONI, six months later, contains the word for 'winter'; compare Old Welsh *gaem*. Four quarter days are also marked on the calendar: 4 CANTLOS, 2 RIUROS, 4 CUTIOS, and 2 EQUOS. If SAMONI is November as in Irish, these days would be the autumn equinox, winter solstice, spring equinox, and summer solstice. There is no indication as to whether these days were celebrated or merely marked to calibrate the calendar with the solar year. One possible festival is mentioned, however: TRINOX SAMONI SINDIU 'this/ today [is the] three-night Samhain', presumably marking a festival that lasted for three days.

Antone Minard

COLLINS, MICHAEL

Michael Collins (1890–1922) was one of the most charismatic leaders of the Irish War of Independence and one of the most powerful men in the new Irish Free State (Saorstát na hÉireann). His talent for conspiracy and his assassination in the Irish Civil War made him one of the more romantic figures in 20th-century Irish history (see IRISH INDEPENDENCE MOVEMENT).

Born in 1890 near Clonakilty, Co. Cork (Cloich na Coillte, Contae Chorcaí), Collins emigrated to London in 1906. There he learned IRISH at a branch of CONRADH NA GAEILGE and joined the secret Irish Republican Brotherhood (see IRISH REPUBLICAN ARMY). He returned to Ireland (ÉIRE) in 1914 when threatened with conscription into the British army. For his relatively minor rôle in the Easter Rising, he was interned until December 1916. By 1917 he was a member of the Sinn Féin executive (see NATIONALISM) and Director of Organization of the Irish Volunteers. These posts enabled him to extend his secret intelligence network. Following the arrest of most nationalist Irish leaders in 1918, Collins took control of the revolutionary movement. He became President of the Brotherhood and ensured that the radical wing of Sinn Féin won an overwhelming victory at the general election of 1918. Having organized the escape of Éamonn DE VALERA from Lincoln gaol in February 1919, Collins led the Irish War of Independence, which began on 21 January 1919, as Director of Military Organization, acting as Minister of Finance at the same time. On 6 December 1921, he co-signed the compromise that granted Ireland dominion status, which ultimately led to the Irish Civil War.

Marion Löffler

COLUM CILLE, ST

St Colum Cille (or Colmcille, Latin Columba, *c.* 521/9 to June 597), a descendant of NIALL NOÍGIALLACH (Niall of the Nine Hostages), was the founder and the first abbot of

Iona (Eilean Ì). Our knowledge of him derives almost entirely from the *Vita Columbae* by Adomnán, which was written almost a century after Colum Cille's death. He remains one of the most popular saints of Irish and Scottish tradition.

Colum Cille studied with Finnian of Clonard (see Uinniau), and then founded several monasteries in Ireland before setting out in 563 for Iona, which became the centre for a large *familia* of monasteries in Ireland and Britain. Iona served as a linkpoint between the Irish on both sides of the sea, and also between Ireland and Britain. Being on Iona made Colum Cille 'a pilgrim for Christ' and allowed him to engage in missionary work among the Picts. He established many contacts both with other monasteries (e.g., Beann Char/Bangor) and with rulers such as the Pictish king, Bruide mac Maelcon.

Traditionally, several Latin hymns (e.g., the *Altus prosator*) have been attributed to Colum Cille, and his authorship of these works cannot be excluded. A manuscript of the Psalms, known as the *Cathach*, probably dating from the 7th century but possibly the late 6th, is traditionally regarded as Colum Cille's pen work.

Thomas O'Loughlin

COMMON CELTIC

Common Celtic is a historical linguistic term that is used in this encyclopedia for the oldest form of prehistoric Celtic speech differentiated from the other Indo-European dialects; thus it is essentially synonymous in our usage with Proto-Celtic. As an unattested proto-language, its linguistic reconstructions is cited with asterisks; thus Common Celtic *wiros* 'man, husband, hero'. All of the Celtic languages lose Indo-European *p* in most positions; therefore this is a Common Celtic feature. Traces of it survive (perhaps in some positions as *h*, elsewhere as *w* or w^h) in the Romano-Celtic place-name Hercynia silva and in UVAMO- 'highest' on the Lepontic inscription from Prestino. Thus, although Old Irish *athair* 'father' and Gaulish *atir* have lost Indo-European *p*-, we can reconstruct *ϕatir* to show the likelihood that a weakened initial consonant had been present in the Celtic proto-language.

John T. Koch

COMPUTUS FRAGMENT

The Computus Fragment is an Old Welsh commentary, written on one side of a single leaf of vellum, dating from AD 850 × 910. It concerns a detail in the table (the *pagina regularis*) in Bede's scientific works. The subject is a specific point concerning the calendar and the calculation of the date of Easter (see Easter controversy). The fragment is a uniquely valuable source of linguistic information for aspects of the vocabulary, syntax, and morphology of the Welsh language at an early date. It also reflects the level of learning in early medieval Wales (Cymru) and the adaptability of written Welsh as a medium for technical subjects first described in Latin texts.

John T. Koch

CONALL CERNACH

Conall Cernach, a hero from the early Irish ULSTER CYCLE of tales, is second only to the superhero CÚ CHULAINN in martial prowess. He features in the tales FLED BRICRENN ('Bricriu's Feast') and SCÉLA MUCCE MEIC DÁ THÓ ('The Story of Mac Dá Thó's Pig'). In the latter, Conall displays his supremacy by taking enemy heads as trophies (see HEAD CULT). Conall's father is Amairgen mac Aithirni, the poet of the ULAID. The Irish name *Conall* is very common and is cognate with the Welsh man's name *Cynwal*, both deriving from Old Celtic *Cunovalos*, which means something like 'Hound wielder'. 'Hound' appears in the names of many heroes, most significantly *Cú Chulainn*. The epithet *Cernach* could mean 'prominent, having a prominence' or 'horned'; a connection to the horned god CERNUNNOS has been suggested.

John T. Koch

CONAN MERIADOC

Conan Meriadoc figures as a hero and founder in Breton LEGENDARY HISTORY. Though of doubtful historicity, he has an important rôle in the scheme of ancient British history in the HISTORIA REGUM BRITANNIAE (*c.* 1139) of GEOFFREY OF MONMOUTH.

Conanus Meriadocus in the *Life of Goueznou*

Vita Sancti Uuohednouii (Life of Saint Goueznou) is a Breton Latin text, of which only the prologue survives, recopied in a manuscript of the historian Pierre Le Baud (†1505). The prologue states that it was written in 1019, but that date is not secure. This text gives an account of the origins of Brittany (BREIZH), citing an earlier history, which states that the Christian leader Conan Meriadoc led the Britons to ARMORICA, where they slaughtered the indigenous pagans.

Conanus Meriadocus in *Historia Regum Britanniae*

Set during the historical usurpation of Magnus Maximus (r. AD 383–88; see MACSEN WLEDIG), Geoffrey's account adds the following details: The Brythonic troops had 'Conanus Meriadocus' as their leader; Maximus named Conan king of Armorica, which he conquered by violence after seizing Rennes and having massacred all the men in the region; 30,000 soldiers and 100,000 'civilians' (*plebani*) came from Britain to Conan's land to make 'another Britain' of Armorica.

"Kenan" in the *Life of St Gurthiern*

This *Vita* was compiled in the Kemperle Cartulary (Cartulaire de Quimperlé) between 1118 and 1127 by the monk Gurheden, and begins with a genealogy of the saint, presented as the distant descendant of BELI MAWR, son of Outham Senis (Outham the Old). The latter character corresponds to Eudaf Hen in *Breuddwyd Macsen* and to Octavius in *Historia Regum Britanniae*. Beli is given the brother 'Kenan' (modern *Cynan*), the Middle Welsh name corresponding to Breton *Conan*. Thus this text shows that Conan was known in Breton legendary history some years before Geoffrey's book. Given that many details of St Gurthiern's genealogy can be found again in the Welsh genealogy of St Cadoc, the figure of 'Kenan' is probably a Welsh import.

Meriadoc

The *Castrum Meriadoci* from the *Life of Goueznou* and *Castellum Meriadoci* in the *Livre des faits d'Arthur* should be compared with a reference by Marie de France (*c.* 1170) to a 'strong and brave castle' held by 'a knight whose name was Meriadu' in the *Lai de Guigemar* (lines 691–2; see BRETON LAYS). The Guigemar of this lay was son of the 'Lord of Leon', and his name, Breton *Guyomarc'h*, occurs in the house of the viscount of Leon (northwest Brittany). In the parish of Plougasnou, also in Leon, a place called Traon Meriadec (Meriadoc's valley) was recorded by the 15th century.

Conan Meriadoc and St Meriadec in Later Dynastic Legends

In the 15th century, the House of Rohan sponsored the cult of St Meriadec as a tutelary saint of the family. *The Life of Meriadec,* bishop of Vannes (Gwened), survives in fragments. The Chapel of Stival, dedicated to St Meriadec and built in the second half of the 15th century, is decorated with frescoes showing the career of this patron saint. The caption of the first scene tells of 'St Meriadec, son of the Duke of Brittany, descended from the line of King Conan and closely related to the viscount of Rohan.'

This legend implies that the noble houses of Brittany had chronological precedence over the French monarchy. The legend of Conan Meriadoc fell into disuse after the ACTE D'UNION between Brittany and France in 1532. At the end of the 17th century, the Rohans used it to claim the status of 'foreign princes' at the court of Louis XIV in Versailles, which recognized only lineages of royal descent.

The first volume of the *Histoire ecclésiastique et civile de Bretagne*, published in 1750, made the first effort to reestablish Conan Meriadoc's historical status, but the research of the historian Arthur de la Borderie (†1901) finally exposed the medieval legend.

Bernard Merdrignac

CONCHOBAR MAC NESSA

Conchobar mac Nessa, legendary king of ULAID in the pre-Christian period, is covered most fully in this encyclopedia in the context of the ULSTER CYCLE. For the most part he is a good king (see KINGSHIP), though not a historical one and not an ideal one (see IRISH LITERATURE, EARLY PROSE). As the supreme hero CÚ CHULAINN's nominal superior, he is necessarily regarded unfavourably by comparison, much as Agamemnon falls shourt *vis-à-vis* Achilles in the *Iliad*. Remarkably, Nessa is not a patronym, but rather derived from the name of Conchobar's mother, Nes. In Conchobar's conception tale (*Compert Conchobuir*), Nes is an Amazonian woman warrior; the druid CATHBAD foresees Conchobar's future status and notes that his birth coincides with that of Jesus. The death of Conchobar is likewise simultaneous with the crucifixion in *Aided Conchobair* (The violent death of Conchobar). The modern name Connor derives from Conchobar.

John T. Koch

CONN CÉTCHATHACH

Conn Cétchathach (Conn of the hundred battles) is a legendary Irish king who, according to LEGENDARY HISTORY, would have lived around the 2nd century AD. He was the putative ancestor of several leading dynasties of early medieval Ireland, including the preeminent UÍ NÉILL.

Conn's name was used to explain the names of major territorial divisions and population groups. Thus *Leth Cuinn* 'Conn's half' means the northern half of Ireland. CONNACHT, the name of Ireland's traditional northwestern province, is often understood in traditional literature to mean the 'province of Conn'. It may be the other way around; the name *Conn* is of uncertain origin and may be based on a popular etymology applied to *Leth Cuinn* and *Dál Cuinn*, which had originally meant 'Half of the chief (*cenn*)' and 'Tribe of the chief' rather than 'Half/tribe of Conn'. The original Old Irish genitive form of *cenn* derives from Celtic *$k^w enn\bar{\imath}$, and *cuinn* should have been its Old Irish form.

Conn is more significant as a namesake, founder, ancestor, and granter of authority to historical rulers than as a hero or ideal ruler in his own right. According to the legend, his sons were Conlae (whose story is told in *Echtrae Chonlai*, The adventure of Conlae) and Art (*Echtrae Airt maic Chuinn*, The adventure of Art son of Conn), who himself fathered CORMAC MAC AIRT, the idealized legendary king of Tara (*Echtra Chorbmaic Uí Chuinn*, The adventure of Cormac grandson of Conn).

Possibly of Old Irish date is *Airne Fíngein*, a tale concerning the birth of Conn. A Middle Irish death-tale, *Aided Chuinn*, tells of Conn's killing during preparations for the *Feis Temro* (FEAST of Teamhair).

John T. Koch, Peter Smith, and Peter E. Busse

CONNACHT

Connacht is one of the traditional provinces of Ireland (ÉIRE). Counties Galway, Mayo, Sligo, Leitrim, and Roscommon (Gaillimh, Maigh Eo, Sligeach, Liatroim, and Ros Comáin, respectively) are within its modern borders. During the early medieval period the province also incorporated the northern part of the Burren (Co. Clare/Contae an Chláir) and possibly parts of south Donegal (Contae Dhún na nGall). For more on the name, see CONN. The royal ceremonial complex of the province was CRÚACHU (Rathcroghan, Co. Roscommon) in the centre of Mag nAí. A king had to dominate this part of Connacht to hold the provincial kingship.

Edel Bhreathnach

CONRADH NA GAEILGE

Conradh na Gaeilge (the Gaelic League) was founded in BAILE ÁTHA CLIATH (Dublin) in 1893. Its founding members included David Comyn (Daithí Ó Coimín), Eoin

MacNeill, and Douglas Hyde (Dúbhghlas DE HÍDE). Its aims were as follows: (1) the preservation of IRISH as the national language of Ireland (ÉIRE) and the extension of its use as a spoken tongue, and (2) the study and publication of existing Gaelic literature and the cultivation of a modern literature in the Irish language (see IRISH LITERATURE).

Soon after its founding, the Gaelic League established language classes that drew learners from all socioeconomic classes. At first the teachers were untrained, but language-teaching methods employed in other countries—for example, the Gouin and Berlitz methods—were adopted early on. In 1904, Munster College (Coláiste na Mumhan), the first of six training colleges for Gaelic League teachers, was established in Ballingeary, in the West Cork GAELTACHT.

In 1897, the Gaelic League established the annual Oireachtas competition (see FEISEANNA), based on the Welsh EISTEDDFOD. The first Oireachtas was held in Dublin in 1898 in conjunction with the Feis Ceoil, an annual Irish musical festival. Initially, the competitions included categories in folklore, dramatic sketches, and recitations. Literary categories were subsequently introduced and innovative writing was encouraged. Pádraic Ó Conaire, one of the early prize-winners, and Patrick Pearse (Pádraig Mac Piarais) were instrumental in establishing the short story as a successful literary form in Modern Irish. Many Oireachtas prize-winners had their work published by the Gaelic League's own publishing company, Clódhanna Teoranta, which was founded in 1908.

The Gaelic League ensured that the language was taught in primary schools within normal school hours and that Irish was introduced as a teaching medium in Gaeltacht schools. When the National University was established in 1908, this organization became involved in the highly controversial campaign to make Irish an essential subject for matriculation, achieved from 1913.

The League's policies regarding Irish in the EDUCATION system were adopted by the independent state, founded in 1922. The Oireachtas was revived in 1939 and remains a major annual Irish literary event.

Pádraigín Riggs

CONTINENTAL CELTIC

Introduction

'Continental Celtic' refers to the Celtic languages spoken on the European continent during antiquity. Prior to the Roman and Germanic expansions, they were spoken throughout western and central Europe into the Iberian Peninsula in the southwest, across northern Italy and throughout the Alpine region southeast into the Balkans, and even into Asia Minor; they were also spoken in eastern Europe, although it is difficult to know to what extent. While the attestation of Continental Celtic is fragmentary, the record is significant enough to reveal a great deal about its phonology (system of sounds) and morphology (how words changed form to show grammatical relations) in the regions where the language is more copiously documented, and even some facts about its syntax. Because Continental Celtic inscribed texts are attested from *c.* 575 BC in northern Italy to the 3rd or 4th century AD in TRANSALPINE GAUL, it has become increasingly important for the historical study of the CELTIC LANGUAGES in particular, and the INDO-EUROPEAN languages in general.

The Languages

In the Iberian Peninsula, the principal Celtic linguistic testimony comes from CELTIBERIAN. Other linguistic remains around the peninsula resemble attested forms of Celtic, but their attestation is highly fragmentary (see GALICIA). Lusitanian and TARTESSIAN may contain Celtic elements or even be Celtic. In northern Italy, LEPONTIC was concentrated in the northern Italian lake district, and Cisalpine GAULISH was later spread throughout CISALPINE GAUL. In present-day France and Belgium, various dialects of Gaulish were spoken.

Fragments of Continental Celtic languages are also attested in the Balkans, where the form is sometimes called 'Noric', and in the central portion of present-day Turkey, where it is known as GALATIAN. Most of this eastern Celtic material appears very similar to Gaulish/Transalpine Celtic.

Phonology

The representation of the sounds of the Continental Celtic languages is not straight-forward even within a single language area. The vowel systems of the Continental Celtic languages preserve the late Indo-European five-vowel system /i e a o u/ with a short–long opposition for /i e a u/; inherited /ē/ > Celtic /ī/, though it may be vestigially preserved unchanged in a few tokens in Celtiberian; Celtic /ē/ continued as the Indo-European diphthong /ej/ elsewhere; and IE /ō/ continued as Celtic /ū/ in final syllables and as /ā/ elsewhere. However, we find that a new /o/ arises in later Transalpine Celtic from the simplification of the diphthong /ow/. All six of the Indo-European diphthongs /aj ej oj aw ew ow/ are preserved in the earliest attested records of Continental Celtic, but they later simplify to long vowels (e.g., /ow/ > /ō/).

In the consonantal system, an inherited Indo-European voiceless–voiced opposition is continued, which gives three opposed sets—/ t d, k g, k g^w/. Proto-IE /p/ is generally lost in initial and intervocalic positions (see PROTO-CELTIC). Both of the labial-velars /k^w, g^w/ are attested in Celtiberian, but by and large they appear to be absent in Transalpine Celtic, in which /k^w/ > /p/ (save in some religious terms) and Proto-Celtic /g^w/ > /w/. All of the Continental Celtic languages possess the nasals /m n/; in later Cisalpine Celtic, final /m/ > /n/. The liquids /l r/, the glides /j w/, and the sibilant /s/ are also found in all of the languages. In later Transalpine Celtic and Galatian, /w/ tends to be lost between vowels. The sibilant /s/ is affected in this position as well, and sometimes lost. Cisalpine and Transalpine Celtic also possess a phoneme known as the *tau gallicum* ('Gaulish T') that immediately continues / ^{t}s/ < /st/.

Morphology

There is evidence for all eight Indo-European cases in Continental Celtic and three genders, and there is some evidence for three numbers (singular, dual, and plural).

In Celtiberian, evidence supports the introduction of a feminine nominative singular -*ī*, genitive -*īnos,* on the model of the -*ū*, -*ūnos* paradigm. In earliest attested Cisalpine Celtic, the Indo-European *o*- stem genitive singular in *-*osjo* is continued as -*oiso*, but it gives way to familiar Celtic -*ī* later. Early Cisalpine Celtic also shows the replacement of inherited consonant stem dative singular -*ej* by instrumental singular -*i*.

Transalpine Celtic shows the largest number of innovations—for example, the merging of the dative and instrumental singular in the *o*- stem declension and of the dative and instrumental plural in all declensions.

In the verbal system, there is good evidence for the present, preterite, and future tenses, all in a variety of inherited formations. Both Cisalpine and Transalpine Celtic have also created a new *t*-preterite, in which an inherited perfect verbal ending is affixed to the inherited third person singular imperfect form of the verb. Verbal forms are attested in all six person/number combinations, and in the indicative, subjunctive, and imperative moods.

Syntax

Owing to the fragmentary preservation of the Continental Celtic languages, the picture of syntax is far less complete than our current picture of phonology or morphology. In Celtiberian, the basic, unmarked order of the clause is consistently subject–object–verb, as reconstructed for late proto-Indo-European. The subject–verb–object order is found in later Cisalpine Celtic.

Joseph Eska

CORMAC MAC AIRT

Cormac mac Airt was a legendary Irish king renowned in the Middle Ages for his wisdom. Although his historicity is open to question, Cormac is said to have lived in the 3rd century AD. He played a major rôle in IRISH LITERATURE, both in FIANNAÍOCHT and in the KINGS' CYCLES of tales. Included in the latter category are some fifteen texts in Old and Middle Irish that have been grouped by modern scholars into 'The Cycle of Cormac mac Airt'. These sagas, poems, and anecdotes chronicle the major events in his life, from his conception before the battle of Mag Mucrama to his death. The most famous episode in this cycle centres on his first journey to Tara (TEAMHAIR), where he pronounced a *fírbreth* (true judgement) that at once revealed the falsity of the reigning king, Lugaid Mac Con, and established his own fitness to rule. It was this intimate connection with *fír flathemon* (ruler's truth) that set Cormac apart from other kings (cf. AUDACHT MORAINN; WISDOM LITERATURE).

Dan Wiley

CORMAC UA CUILENNÁIN/CORMAC MAC CUILEANNÁIN

Cormac ua Cuilennáin/Cormac mac Cuileannáin (†908), bishop and king of CAISEL MUMAN from 902 to 908, belonged to one of the lesser branches of the ÉOGANACHT dynasties. The fullest version of his biography is found in the ANNALS of the Four Masters. They record the doom-laden prophecies accompanying Cormac, and his death is described in detail. In the coda of the annal entry, he is described as a scholar, bishop, and high-king of all Munster.

A wide range of works have been attributed to Cormac. They include *Lebor na Cert* ('The Book of Rights'), SANAS CHORMAIC ('Cormac's Glossary'), the manuscript compilation known as *Saltair Chaisil* ('The Psalter of Cashel'), and numerous poems and tales. However, recent scholarship has tended to favour the view that many of these attributions should be treated with scepticism. Many of the poems and tales attributed Cormac him await reevaluation: It seems that there was a tendency to attribute works to him to enhance their status and that of the manuscript in which they were contained.

Paul Russell

CORMAC UA LIATHÁIN

Cormac ua Liatháin was a sixth-century Irish ascetic, a contemporary and follower of St COLUM CILLE/Columba (†597). He is of special interest as a voyager saint whose historical exploits anticipate the more fantastic adventures of St BRENDAN in NAVIGATIO SANCTI BRENDANI, as well as the vernacular Irish VOYAGE LITERATURE or IMMRAMA. Cormac is mentioned in three sections of Adomnán's *Vita Columbae* (Life of Colum Cille). Chapter 1.6 relates that he made three unsuccessful attempts to find an island hermitage on the ocean. In Chapter 2.42, we are told that Cormac and his sailors were blown off course on a northern voyage by south winds and experienced terrifying sea creatures. In Chapter 3.17, Cormac set out to find Colum Cille and locate him on the island of Hinba. In the Old Irish Martyrology of OENGUS CÉILE DÉ, Cormac's feast day is 21 June and he is associated with the important Columban foundation at *Dermag a Mide* (Durrow in Meath). In the strange little tale that follows, Cormac cuts off Colum Cille's finger in a squabble over relics, and Colum Cille responds by prophesying that *coin* (dogs, wolves) will devour Cormac.

John T. Koch

CORNISH LANGUAGE

The Cornish language developed along with BRETON from the southwestern dialect of BRYTHONIC. (1) Old Cornish denotes the phase between about 800 and 1250, when the language was first emerging from its parent. (2) Middle Cornish refers to the language between *c.* 1250 and *c.* 1550. (3) Late Cornish occurs from *c.* 1550 to the decline in the 19th century, while (4) Revived Cornish is applied to the language thereafter.

The most characteristic feature of Old Cornish was the Middle Cornish softening of final dental stops /-d -t/ to s-like sounds (sibilants)—for example, Cornish *bys* /bīz/ < Celtic *bitu-* 'world' (Welsh *byd*, Breton *bed*). Cornish reached its highest development as a literary language in the 15th and 16th centuries, as in the ORDINALIA, BEUNANS KE ('The Life of St Ke'), BEUNANS MERIASEK ('The Life of St Meriasek'), and GWREANS AN BYS (*The Creacion of the Worlde*).

In the early Middle Ages, Old Cornish was spoken in parts of present-day west Devon and Cornwall (Kernow), gradually retreating westward. Cornish was spoken as late as 1595 in St Ewe, near Mevagissey, while monoglot Cornish speakers were found in Feock, near Truro, in 1640. By 1700, Cornish had largely become confined to Penwith and the Lizard. A rapid decline occurred in the early 1700s, and the language was virtually unused by 1800, although fragments continued to be retained and collected. Its decline may be attributed to several historical events, among them the Wars of the Roses and the Reformation, which affected relations with close linguistic neighbours in Brittany (Breizh).

The language was revived by a number of scholars, including Henry Jenner and Robert Morton Nance, during the late 19th and early 20th centuries. Revived Cornish occurs in several different kinds of 'Cornishes'. The 20th century brought a literary revival, including developing MASS MEDIA (see CORNISH LITERATURE).

Alan M. Kent

CORNISH LITERATURE, MEDIEVAL

Medieval Cornish literature is closely bound up with drama, community, and festival. The character of Cornwall's literary continuum is greatly affected by the fact that it was the first of the CELTIC COUNTRIES to be 'accommodated' into the English state.

Literature of the Old Cornish Period

In the early medieval period, the earliest evidence of Old Cornish consists of several glosses from the 10th century, written on Smaragdus's Commentary on the classical grammarian Donatus, on the Book of Tobit found in the manuscript Oxoniensis Posterior (see GLOSSES), and in the manumissions found on the Bodmin Gospels, which record the freeing of 122 slaves, of whom 98 were Cornish. Many had native Cornish names. Evidence during this phase also indicates considerable ARTHURIAN material, now lost.

The longest-surviving piece of early medieval Cornish, however, is the OLD CORNISH VOCABULARY (c. 1100), which provides a long list of Latin words and their Cornish equivalents.

Literature of the Middle Cornish Period

The Charter Endorsement consists of 41 lines of Cornish from c. 1400, written on the back of a land charter from St Stephen-in-Brannel dated 1340. The text's theme is marriage, and it offers the couple advice on how to proceed. The most significant trend during this phase, however, is the development of Cornish-language liturgical and biblical drama, of which the trilogy known as the ORDINALIA is one of the few surviving examples.

Broadly at the same time there emerged the elaborate poem, *Pascon Agan Arluth* or 'The Poem of Mount Calvary', which has many similarities to the Passion play of the *Ordinalia*. Its quatrains are based on the canonical gospels with various apocryphal editions. The post-medieval and Tudor phases, however, curtailed much of this literary activity.

In 2002, a Middle Cornish saint's play was discovered, based on the life of St Kea (see Beunans Ke). The discovery of this play, which includes some Arthurian material, markedly increases the canon of Cornish literature.

Alan M. Kent

CORNISH LITERATURE, POST-MEDIEVAL

The post-medieval phase of Cornish literature contains four core texts. The main texts are the two-day-long saints' plays Beunans Ke (*c.* 1500) and Beunans Meriasek (1504); the Tregear Homilies (*c.* 1558), consisting of thirteen homilies (twelve translated from the work of Bishop Bonner by John Tregear); and Gwreans an Bys (*The Creacion of the Worlde*, 1611).

Other interesting texts of the period include accounts of performances of Cornish drama at various locations from the river Tamar in the east to St Just in the west, showing how widespread the theatrical continuum was in Cornwall (Kernow). References in Launceston to the king and queen of Gall in lost texts indicate the presence of secular drama. The *Green Book of St Columb Major* (1589–95) contains a reference to a Robin Hood drama performed there, while Nicholas Roscarrock (*c.* 1548–1634) draws attention to an 'olde Cornish Rhyme' on the life of St Columb, now lost (see hagiography).

One of the most fascinating surviving texts is *The Fyrst Boke of the Introduction of Knowledge* by the English poet Andrew Boorde, which includes a satire (*c.* 1547) on the English speech of various parts of Britain, including Cornwall, as well as some phrases of remarkably good Cornish—one of the few secular pieces from this phase. A few other short pieces survive.

Alan M. Kent

CORNISH LITERATURE, 17TH AND 18TH CENTURIES

The Reformation is regarded as the main factor responsible for shutting down large-scale Cornish literary production and for destroying many extant texts.

John Boson (1665–*c.* 1720) wrote a poem on the process of pilchard curing, and another poem offering advice to Cornishmen leaving for London's sexual hazards; James Jenkin of Penzance (Pen Sans) wrote *Poems of Advice* on marriage and home-making; William Gwavas (1676–1741) recorded proverbs and sayings and wrote short, pithy poetry (ranging from riddles to accounts of lazy weavers). Thomas Tonkin of St Agnes (Bryanek) collected songs and verse in Cornish, while Nicholas Boson (*c.* 1624–1703) crafted a children's story, in an admixture of English and Cornish, entitled *The Dutchesee of Cornwall's Progresse to See the Land's End and Visit the Mount*. Perhaps the best-known work from this period is the folktale *John of Chyhanor*, a retelling of the international story of the servant's good counsels, written sometime between 1660 and 1700. Boson's other major work on the state of the language was *Nebbaz Gerriau dro tho Cornoack* (A few words about Cornish), which was completed in English.

Numerous other scraps and fragments exist, not to mention some biblical translations. By the middle of the 18th century, however, literary production in Cornish had more or less reached a standstill.

Alan M. Kent

CORNISH LITERATURE, 19TH AND 20TH CENTURIES

Fragments of the Cornish language in Cornwall (Kernow) persisted into the 18th century, and the German Georg Sauerwein wrote two poems in Cornish in 1865. The so-called *Cranken Rhyme* was also offered by John Davey near Penzance in 1891. Early in the 20th century, at the start of the revival, Henry Jenner and Robert Morton Nance composed much explicitly revivalist verse, such as *Can Wlascar Agan Mamvro* (Patriotic song of our motherland) and *Nyns yu Marow Maghtern Arthur* (King Arthur is not dead) respectively.

Other important early writers in Revived Cornish include Edward Chirgwin (1892–1960), famous for diversifying the themes of modern writing in Cornish, and A. S. D. Smith (1883–1950), whose epic poem *Trystan hag Isolt* (1951; see also Tristan and Isolt) remains one of the revival's finest works. Peggy Pollard (1903–96) wrote the agnostic play *Beunans Alysaryn* (1941) in the style of the earlier Cornish mystery dramas. The first full-length novel to be published in Cornish was Melville Bennetto's *An Gurun Wosek a Geltya* (The bloody crown of the Celtic countries; 1984). It was followed by Michael Palmer's *Jory* (1989) and *Dyroans* (1998). An emergent Cornish-language writer of this century is Tim Saunders (1952–).

Amy Hale

CORNWALL

See Kernow.

COURTLY LOVE

Courtly love, or *amour courtois*, is a theme in medieval European poetry whose popularity reached its first peak in Provence (southeastern France). The Provençal court poets—the so-called troubadours ('finders, composers')—were in their prime from the second half of the 11th century. The forms and subject matter of the troubadours' poetry were enthusiastically imitated all over western Europe.

The chief theme expressed in poetry of this kind was that of unfulfilled love for an unattainable person, sublimated into poetic expression. Usually, this took the form of the poet's admiration for his patroness, a married woman. This sublimated love is called *fins amors* in Provençal, and is contrasted with vulgar physical love. Writers of the Matter of Britain, such as Chrétien de Troyes, used the ethic of courtly love to a great extent in their works, and this practice, in turn, influenced Arthurian literature in English, German, and a number of other traditions.

The earliest-known poet was Prince Guillaume IX of Aquitaine (1071–1127), grandfather of Eleanor of Aquitaine. With her marriage to King Henry II Plantagenet of England in 1152, the literary fashion of courtly love was brought to

B̶ritain. Courtly love came to Wales (Cymru) during the course of the Anglo-Norman Marcher Lords' campaign to conquer south Wales. From the 12th century onward, slight traces of this theme have been detected in the work of the Gogynfeirdd. Only after the downfall of the last independent Welsh prince in 1282 (see Llywelyn ap Gruffudd) and the rise of the poets serving the post-conquest nobility (largely synonymous with the Cywyddwyr) in the 14th century can a strong influence be seen, especially in the works of the greatest poet of later medieval Wales, Dafydd ap Gwilym.

Poetry on courtly love must have come to Ireland (Ériu) in the wake of the Norman Conquest in 1152. The dánta grádha, a class of 'love poems' sharing numerous motifs with the Provençal material, appear comparatively late.

Peter E. Busse

CROSÁN

Crosán (pl. *crosáin*), commonly translated as 'buffoon', is a designation in Old, Middle, and Early Modern Irish texts applied to a figure whose entertainment both offends and delights. The term is a derivative of Irish *cros* (cross) with the added diminutive suffix *-án* (little cross). The same semantic development took place in Welsh, where the common word for a 'jester' in the law texts is *croesan* (< W *croes* cross). The semantic development is unclear, but the *crosáin* may have played some rôle in religious festivals.

The earliest reference to the *crosán* occurs in the Old Irish legal tract Bretha Nemed Toísech (*c.* AD 750) and is repeated in a late Old Irish compilation of gnomic material (*Trecheng Breth Féne*) edited under the title 'The Triads of Ireland'. The triad is brief and elusive, but suggests the poses of a ribald jester through a reference to his *tíag* 'bag' (DIL 164, 13), possibly referring either to the inflated bladder brandished by the jester or to testicles. The *crosán* does not figure among the lower grades of poets and entertainers named in other early Irish tracts on status, such as the *fuirsire* (jester), *clesamnach* (juggler), or *oblaire*, a 'buffoon without skill' (*fuirseoir gan dán*) who merely recites memorized disparaging verses. Nevertheless, he may have shared some of their comic attributes. The Welsh law tract *Llyfr Iorwerth* (13th century) offers a later, but similarly mocking, portrait of the *croesan* (jester) who, when presented with a horse by the chief groom, ties the end of the horse's halter to its testicles as he departs from the court of the king (*Llyfr Iorwerth* 9 §11.12).

The lexicon of legal terms compiled by Dubhaltach Mac Fhirbhisigh (1660) identified *crosán* as a skill associated with the *forcetlaid*, the third of seven grades of teachers in an Irish monastic school; this label is also used as a derogatory designation in satiric epigrams. The portraits recall the *clerici vagantes* or goliards, an amorphous class of wandering minstrels in medieval Europe who thrived on the fringes of the Christian church and are repeatedly rebuked in church canons. Irish clerical scholars are among those chastised as *deceptores*, *gyrovagi*, and *cursores* (deceivers, wanderers, and stragglers, respectively). The ribald hero of the medieval Irish tale *Aislinge Meic Con Glinne* (The dream of Mac Con Glinne), who composes satirical verses and performs, *cáintecht 7 bragitóracht 7 duana la filidecht do gabáil* 'satire and farting and singing songs with poetry' (*Aislinge Meic Con Glinne* 18), offers a vivid literary representation of such a figure.

The comic antics and ambiguous status of the *crosán* are a theme in other Middle Irish texts. The three *crossáin* who entertain in the house of the hero FINN MAC CUMAILL are called *Cles* (Trick), *Cinnmear* (Headmad), and *Cuitmhedh* (Mockery) (*Duanaire Finn* 1.27.25). In a poem that parodies the customary distribution of meat to guests at a FEAST according to social status, the *crosán* is served the 'rump' (*crochet*)—a portion traditionally awarded to one of noble status—and the 'fools' receive the 'kidneys'.

Several religious texts portray the *crosán* as a disreputable figure, although their attitudes range from fierce condemnation to distant amusement. 'The Fifteen Tokens of Doomsday' envisioned the final damnation of *na druithi 7 na cainti 7 na crosanaigh* 'the harlots and the satirists and the buffoons'; the arrival of the *crossáin* is ominously predicted in the *Book of Fenagh*; and the grouping *croessan a phuttein* (buffoon and harlot) in the Welsh *Buched Dewi* (Life of St David) is similarly derogatory (*Buched Dewi* 20). The attitude in other Irish texts is more forgiving. The 'openly sinful' *crosán* named in the Life of Brenainn is the last to enter the saint's vessel but the first to win heaven, and is honoured as a 'wonderful martyr'. Similarly, in the late medieval tale *Immram Curaig Ua Corra* (The voyage of the Uí Corra), one member of a band of *crosáin*, called a *fuirseoir* (jester), joins a group of pilgrims seeking salvation. He promises to provide 'entertainment of the mind and spirit' (*airgairdiugud menman 7 aicenta*) that will not lessen their piety, and when he dies on the journey the pilgrims lament the loss of his delightful *airfitiud* (minstrelsy).

The *crosán* is associated with a style of composition known as *crosántacht*. The earliest example (*c.* 1560) occurs in J. Carney's *Poems on the Butlers*, and samples continue through the 17th and 18th centuries. Only a few later poems refer specifically to the *crosán*. The speaker of a *crosántacht* attributed to Tadhg Dall Ó hUiginn announces that he is 'O'Caroll's *crosán*'; Tadhg Mac Dáire Mac Bruaideadha names the *crosán* among the poets who frequent the house of Maol Mordha Mac Suibhne (†1518); and a prose text composed for the same chieftain reprimands the patron for bestowing gifts to the *crosáin* at the expense of more noble poets.

The 17th-century Irish poet Dáibhí Ó Bruadair provides the latest, but arguably the most vivid, portrait of the *crosán*. Ó Bruadair assumes the comic mask of a *crosán* in the wedding *crosántacht*, *Cuirfead cluain ar chrobhaing gheal-Ghall* 'I will trick the cluster of bright foreigners', and brings comic voices rooted in the medieval tradition to a wedding feast celebrated in 1674.

Various strands of the tradition intersect in Ó Bruadair's poem. The poet was probably familiar with the medieval tale *Seanadh Saighre*, and popular performances of mock priests at wakes and masked 'strawboys' at weddings may also have influenced the performance. Ó Bruadair exchanges the mask of a *crosán* with that of a *sagart súgach* (merry priest), who enacts a bawdy marriage, leads the couple to bed, and blesses the union. Ó Bruadair's comic pose joins the medieval to the modern: The bawdy priest and *crosán* of the poem are reminiscent of the *sacard* (priest) and *crosán* juxtaposed in the Middle Irish epigram cited previously. Ó Bruadair's unified performance of verse, nonsense rhymes, and ribaldry gives coherence to the fragmented allusions to the *crosán* and reflects what seems to be

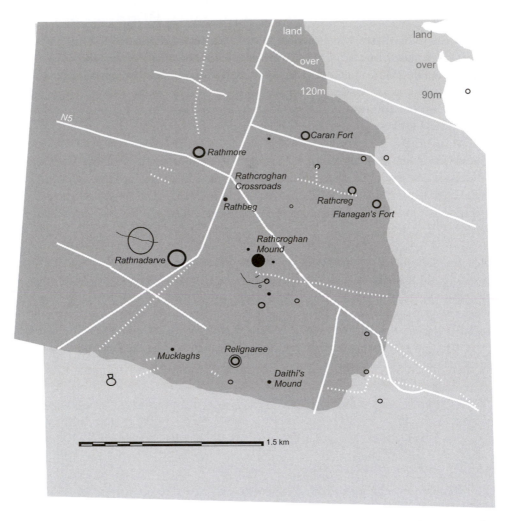

Principal features of the Rathcroghan complex. Mounds are shown as solid circles; ring enclosures are shown as open circles; modern roads appear in white; dashed white lines show trackways or linear earthworks. (Map by John T. Koch)

a strain of licence within the Christian culture of medieval Ireland (Éire), which continued for centuries in vernacular culture.

Margo Griffin-Wilson

CRÚACHU/CRÚACHAIN/RATHCROGHAN

The earthworks at Rathcroghan, near Tulsk, Co. Roscommon, Ireland (Tuilsce, Contae Ros Comáin, Éire), are identified with Crúachu or Crúachain, the legendary seat of the kings of Connacht, including Queen Medb and King Ailill of the Ulster Cycle of tales. The links are further highlighted by an ogam inscription, *vraicci maqi medvvi* 'of Fraích son of Medb', found in a cave popularly seen as an entrance into the Otherworld.

The site itself is a somewhat ill-defined precinct of more than 50 monuments occupying some 800 hectares (approximately 1,900 acres). The complex centres on Rathcroghan Mound, the most spectacular monument of the precinct. Approximately 85 m in diameter at its base and rising about 6 m high, the top of the mound is roughly flat. Geophysical prospection has indicated that the mound covers three circular timber-built structures of imposing size (diameters of 80 m, 35 m, and 20 m), and a series of additional structures has been discerned near the surface of the mound.

In addition to numerous other burial mounds and ENCLOSURES are the Mucklaghs, a paired system of linear earthworks that run for a distance of between 100 m and 200 m; they are formed by upcast earthen banks some 2–3 m high and are presumed to represent a ceremonial function.

J. P. Mallory

CRUITHIN/CRUITHNI

Cruithin/Cruithni are Old Irish ethnonyms (group names) referring to the PICTS in north Britain and to a group in north and east ULAID (Ulster) in the early medieval period. In the PICTISH KING-LIST, *Cruithne filius Cinge pater Pictorum* 'Pict son of Cing father of the Picts' figures as the legendary founder of the Pictish people. In historical times, the most important kingdom of the Irish Cruithin was Dál nAraidi in what is now the south of Aontroim (Co. Antrim). Congal Claen (also known as Congal Caech) was a Cruithnean king of Dál nAraidi who rose to the status of Ulaid's overking in AD 627. He is also listed as a king of TEAMHAIR (Tara) and, therefore, came to be reckoned as an ancient *ardrí* or 'high-king' of Ireland (ÉRIU) by later historians. Congal was killed in the battle of MAG ROTH in 637.

The name *Cruithin* corresponds to Welsh *Prydyn* 'the Picts' < *Pritenī, and is closely related to *Prydain* 'BRITAIN', from Celtic k^writu- 'form, artefact' (OIr. *cruth*, W *pryd*). From a purely linguistic point of view, *Cruithin* could be either the cognate of Welsh *Prydyn* or a borrowing from BRYTHONIC. Recently, some Protestant writers in Northern Ireland have revived the idea of a Cruithnean ethnic identity as an ancient and indigenous, but non-Gaelic, cultural group. The name was also applied to an asteroid in the twentieth century.

John T. Koch

CRWTH

Crwth is a Welsh term for a three- to six-string lyre, originally plucked but from about the 11th century also bowed. The rectangular body and neck are carved from a single block of sycamore. The back and pine soundboard are flat. Set obliquely, the bridge has one foot on the soundboard, while another extends through a sound-hole making contact with the back; it is traditionally tuned in three octave pairs. A flat bridge means that all six strings can be played simultaneously.

The Irish cognate for crwth, *crot*, translates Latin *cithara* (a lute-like instrument) in the 8th-century Old Irish Würzburg glosses. By the 15th century, the *crwth* had become confined to Wales (CYMRU) and the border, where it shared with the HARP recognition as one of the two instruments suitable to accompany the performance of CERDD DAFOD. Essentially a medieval instrument, the *crwth* could not easily adapt to the new fashionable dance music of the Elizabethan court and was gradually displaced by the Italian violin. By the 18th century, this instrument was an object of antiquarian curiosity.

Bethan Miles

CÚ CHULAINN

Cú Chulainn is the principal warrior of the ULSTER CYCLE of early IRISH LITERATURE. Several of the stories in the Cycle are concerned with aspects of his extraordinary life and, in this respect, conform closely to the international heroic biography pattern. The tale *Compert Con Culainn* (The conception of Cú Chulainn) gives multiple conceptions—by a divine father, LUG; the man Sualtaim; and CONCHOBAR mac Nesa of the ULAID, the brother (or father) of his mother Dechtine.

In a section of TÁIN BÓ CUAILNGE ('The Cattle Raid of Cooley') entitled *Macgnímrada Con Culainn* ('The Boyhood Deeds of Cú Chulainn'), Cú Chulainn's precocious exploits as a boy, then called Sétantae, and the manner in which he gained his warrior name (which means 'Culann's hound') are recalled by Ulster warriors. His training abroad in martial arts at the hands of the Amazonian Scáthach is told in TOCHMARC EMIRE ('The Wooing of Emer'). This tale also contains *Verba Scáthaige* (The words of Scáthach), the prophetic poem, also found independently and considered to be one of the oldest compositions of the Cycle. The short tale AIDED ÉNFIR AÍFE (The violent death of Aífe's one 'man' [i.e., son]) tells how Cú Chulainn slew his only son in single combat. This theme is also found in other traditions internationally, including the story of ARTHUR and his son.

Cú Chulainn's own death is related mostly fully and clearly in *Oidheadh Chon Culainn* (The violent death of Cú Chulainn). This source agrees with the earlier account in describing how Cú Chulainn was killed by violating his *gessa* (taboos; see GEIS) and through magic. On being mortally wounded by venomous spears, he ties himself upright to a pillar, and then slays an otter (*dobarchú*, literally 'water-dog') that he sees drinking his blood, ending his warrior career in the same way that it began—by slaying a 'dog'.

Cú Chulainn is the youthful warrior who stands alone against the might of the CONNACHT forces in *Táin Bó Cuailnge*, eventually winning the day for Ulster. In other tales in the Ulster Cycle, however, Cú Chulainn's rôle is muted or he does not appear at all. The meaning of his name 'hound of Culann' is transparently explained in the *macgnímrada*. His boyhood name *Sétantae* may mean 'knower of the roads', but comparison has also been made with the ancient British tribal name *Setantii* in what is now Lancashire.

Ruairí Ó hUiginn

CÚ ROÍ MAC DÁIRI

Cú Roí mac Dáiri was a legendary Irish hero traditionally associated with Cathair Chon Roí (The fortress of Cú Roí), an inland promontory fort on the western edge of the Slieve Mish (Old Irish Slíab Mis) mountain range in Co. Kerry (Contae Chiarraí). He is usually depicted as a warrior king with magical abilities and frequently appears in the shape of an uncouth churl or ogre. Thus standing apart from other Irish heroes—who are more clearly idealized mortal warriors—Cú Roí has often been characterized by modern scholars as a 'demigod'.

Cú Roí plays a rôle in some of the oldest and best-known Irish heroic tales from the Ulster Cycle, among them Mesca Ulad ('The Intoxication of the Ulstermen'), Táin Bó Cuailnge ('The Cattle Raid of Cooley'), and the story of his tragic death, *Aided Chon Roí*.

Cú Roí is an example of an Irish hero whose tradition spread beyond Ireland (Ériu). The episode in Fled Bricrenn ('Bricriu's Feast'), where Cú Roí appears as an ogre challenging the Ulster heroes to a headcutting contest to determine who is Ulster's greatest hero, served as a model for the similar episode in the Middle English Arthurian poetic narrative *Sir Gawain and the Green Knight* (see also Head Cult). The Welsh Book of Taliesin (Llyfr Taliesin) contains an eulogy for Cú Roí, *Marwnat Corroi m. Dayry* (The death-song of Cú Roí mac Dáiri), which is the only literary piece in early Welsh on an Irish subject.

Petra S. Hellmuth

CULHWCH AC OLWEN

Culhwch ac Olwen (Culhwch and Olwen) is the earliest extant Arthurian tale in any language and the most linguistically and stylistically archaic sizeable specimen of Welsh prose. Closely parallel copies of the text survive in the White Book of Rhydderch (Llyfr Gwyn Rhydderch) and the Red Book of Hergest (Llyfr Coch Hergest).

The frame tale involves a hero, Culhwch, who is set a series of tasks by giant Ysbaddaden that he must complete to obtain the giant's daughter Olwen as his wife. Although it provides opportunities for a lyrical description of Olwen's beauty (lines 487–98) and grotesque humour with her father, this story is not central to the Welsh tradition. The plot resembles both the Irish genre of *tochmarc* 'wooing' and a version of the international folk-tale type 'Six Go Through the World'.

Juxtaposed with the isolated story of Ysbaddaden's daughter is the great central hero of Brythonic tradition Arthur. These two strands come together early in the action when Culhwch arrives at his first cousin Arthur's court to ask for his assistance. Arthur's warriors perform many tasks; the longest of these is the hunt of the demon boar, Twrch Trwyth, and his piglets to acquire the razor, scissors, and mirror needed to cut the giant's hair. The tale's exuberant and eclectic character, its great lists of characters and tasks, the numerous naming tales and summarized traditional narratives brought in as asides render it a treasure trove of early Welsh tradition; it is thus of comparable value to the Triads.

As discussed in the article on Arthurian sites, *Culhwch* shows some close points of comparison with Historia Brittonum's topographical *mirabilia*, which include a reference to Arthur's hunt of the boar Troit in connection with the wondrous landmark named Carn Cabal, a name that, on the face of it, means 'horse's hoof ', but is explained as 'the cairn named for Arthur's dog, Cafall'. Clearly, the Twrch Trwyth episode already existed in the 9th century, generating place-name lore, or perhaps affecting extant place-name lore, probably as an oral tale, but there is no hint that it had yet come together with the tale of the Giant's Daughter.

The tale contains a great deal of linguistically and semantically archaic material. Nevertheless, in some ways the language of *Culhwch* agrees with Old Welsh usage, suggesting that the redaction belongs to the Late Old Welsh period, contrasting with the language of the Four Branches, which is so essential to Celtic scholars' description of the Middle Welsh linguistic stage as to be its definition. The tale also shows literary craftsmanship and relationships to other later medieval texts, leading Bromwich and Evans to suggest that the extant version of *Culhwch* was most probably redacted in the last decades of the 11th century.

John T. Koch

CULLODEN, BATTLE OF

Following earlier failed Jacobite rebellions, Charles Edward Stuart—'Bonnie Prince Charlie', 'The Young Chevalier', or 'The Young Pretender'—attempted to regain the throne of Scotland (Alba) and England for his father, James Stuart. Lacking promised French support, Prince Charlie landed on the coast of Scotland with a handful of men in July 1745.

A month later, more than 1,000 men had joined him. His army swiftly proceeded to the Lowlands, triumphantly entering Edinburgh (Dùn Èideann) on 15 September 1745. Prince Charlie proceeded through England, but badly overestimated his support there. His troops then retreated into the Highlands, only to be finally vanquished by a 9,000-strong government army at Culloden Moor (Scottish Gaelic Cùil Lodair) near Inverness on 16 April 1746. Prince Charlie himself escaped only with the help of Lady Flora MacDonald of Uist (dressed as her maidservant Betty Burke) and other supporters.

The ensuing brutal oppression of the Highland people and their culture, the execution of many Jacobite leaders, and the imprisonment or deportation of thousands of their followers and 'Bonnie Prince Charlie' himself became the stuff of national myth. The defeat of 1746 sounded the death-knell for the clan system and the traditional way of living in the Highlands, marking a major milestone in the decline of the Scottish Gaelic language, and setting back dreams of Scottish independence for centuries (see nationalism; Scottish Parliament).

Marion Löffler

CUMBRIA

Cumbria is today the name of the northernmost county on the west coast of England, which overlays the pre-1974 county of Cumberland. The English name is first attested in the Anglo-Saxon Chronicle as *Cumbraland* (945), 'land of the *Cymry*' (i.e., Britons). The first element is etymologically identical to Cymru, the Welsh word for Wales. As the name indicates, this area was one of the last strongholds of Brythonic speech in Britain outside Cornwall (Kernow) and Wales; see Cumbric.

The kingdom of Rheged included part or all of Cumberland, but its boundaries are highly uncertain. This kingdom came under Northumbrian domination in the 7th century. There is no evidence that the Brythonic kingdom centred on Dumbarton extended so far south before 900. In sources of the 10th and 11th centuries, the Latin *Cumbria* is used to signify a kingdom comprising the interior of what is now southwestern Scotland (Alba; see Ystrad Clud) and roughly the northern half of modern Cumbria as far as Penrith. It is not clear whether these references invariably meant one kingdom or one of two.

Only three rulers are specifically referred to as 'kings of the Cumbrians'. Two of these individuals have names that are probably Brythonic: an Owain, who reigned *c*. 915–*c*. 937 and is mentioned by William of Malmesbury and Symeon of Durham, and his son, Dyfnwal ab Owain, who died in Rome in 975. Mael Coluim (Malcolm), probably Dyfnwal's son, is mentioned by Florence of Worcester in 973. It is likely that the Cumbria ruled by these three included Strathclyde and parts of present-day English Cumbria.

Owain the Bald (Owain ap Dyfnwal), Mael Coluim's brother, is called King of Clutenses, and is mentioned by Symeon of Durham as fighting on the side of Mael Coluim mac Cinaeda of Scotland at the battle of Carham in 1018. He is the last known king of Strathclyde–Cumbria. In 1092, William II of England took Carlisle, fixing the English–Scottish border at the Solway Firth, where it remains today.

Antone Minard

CUMBRIC

Cumbric, as a linguistic term, refers to the Brythonic spoken in the early Middle Ages in the area approximately between the line of the river Mersey and the Forth–Clyde isthmus. Evidence for Cumbric consists of the following: (1) proper names and place-names surviving through the medium other languages and in inscriptions; (2) two 11th-century legal terms, *galnes* or *galnys* 'blood-fine' (Welsh *galanas*) and *kelchyn* 'circuit' (Welsh *cylchyn*); and (3) features in the early Welsh poetry of the Cynfeirdd.

A class of Cumbric male names is based on *Gos*, 'servant of', from Celtic **wosto-* (Gallo-Roman *vassus*, Welsh *gwas*): *Gospatric*, *Gos-mungo*, *Gos-oswald*. Possible Cumbric dialect features in the Cynfeirdd poetry include singulative animal names in *penn* 'head' (e.g., *penn ywrch* 'a roebuck' and *penn gwythwch* 'a wild sow'), a feature that survives only in Breton (*pemoc'h*, 'a pig'; *moc'h*, 'pigs').

For the Brythonic place-names of southern Scotland (Alba), see Scottish place-names. *Liscard* on the Wirral peninsula, recorded as *Lisenecark* in 1260, reflects Brythonic **Lis-ən-Carrec* 'the court of the rock' (Welsh *llys y garreg*) with an example of the definite article in its original nasal form. In the northern half of the modern county of Cumbria, which constituted the territory of the kingdom of Cumbria in the 10th and 11th centuries, we find the densest distribution of Brythonic place-names in England outside Cornwall (Kernow) and the Welsh border area, including the names of some of the most important places. For example,

Penrith, the historic capital, means 'the main ford' (*Penred* in 1167, cf. Breton *Perret*, *Pen ret* in 871, and Welsh *Pen-rhyd,* formed from *pen* 'main, chief, head' + *rhyd* 'ford'), and *Carlisle* (Welsh *Caerliwelydd*) is derived from the British place-name *Luguvalion* (*Luguvallo* in the 3rd-century Antonine Itinerary).

The usual pattern in the CELTIC COUNTRIES was for the older language to outlive the loss of sovereignty, sometimes by many centuries. Thus Cumbric may have survived quite late in some areas, and a claim has been made that the 'shepherd's score'—a special method of counting found in Cumbria and other parts of northern England—is one such survivor. In this system some numbers strongly parallel Welsh, such as *pimp* 'five', *dik* 'ten', and *bumfit* 'fifteen' (Welsh *pump, deg, pymtheg*), although several words are clearly later rhyming creations: *yan, tan, tethera, pethera* 'one, two, three, four', cf. Welsh *un, dau, tri, pedwar*. The system is not attested until the 18th century, and its origins may date to any time before that.

Although Cumbric is convenient shorthand for Brythonic evidence falling geographically between Wales and Pictland, it would be misleading to think of it as a distinct language. Written Old WELSH, Old Breton, and Old Cornish of the 9th and 10th centuries are so similar as to be difficult to distinguish, and contemporary sources regard all four as the same language. For BEDE, there was one *lingua Brettonum* (*Historia Ecclesiastica* 1.1). Cumbric is more correctly a geographic rather than a linguistic term. The status of PICTISH as a language distinct from Brythonic remains unresolved.

John T. Koch and Antone Minard

CUNEDDA (WLEDIG) FAB EDERN/CUNEDAG

Cunedda (Wledig) fab Edern/Cunedag was, according to early Welsh sources, a chieftain from north BRITAIN who migrated to what is now Wales (CYMRU) in the 5th century; he was traditionally the father of seven sons who gave their names to territories in Wales, though variation in the tradition has left us with eight different names. Cunedda was the progenitor of the first dynasty of Gwynedd, which continued to dominate the area until Merfyn Frych came to power in 825.

HISTORIA BRITTONUM and the Old Welsh GENEALOGIES describe Cunedda driving out the region's Irish population. Taking literally a 146-year interval mentioned *Historia Brittonum* §62, this gives a date of AD 401 for Cunedda's migration, although other dates are possible. These Irish settlements in late Roman to post-Roman Wales are essentially factual, as shown by OGAM inscriptions in Wales, place-name evidence, and doctrines of Irish dynastic orgins for Dyfed and BRYCHEINIOG. The district names associated with Cunedda's sons are as follows: (1) *Meirion(n)ydd* 'land of Mariānus'; (2) *Osfeiliawn* 'land of Osfael'; (3) *Rhufoniawg* < *Rōmāniācon* 'estate of Rōmānus'; (4) *Dunoding* 'progeny of Dōnātus'; (5) *Ceredigion* 'lands of Ceretic'; (6) *Afloegiawn* 'lands of Afloeg' (possibly signifying an 'ex-layman' who retired to the church); (7) *Dogfeiling* 'progeny of Dogfael'; and (8) *Edeirniawn* 'lands of Aeternus'.

Another strand of evidence is the archaic Welsh elegy known as *Marwnad Cunedda* (Death-song of Cunedda) in LLYFR TALIESIN. This poem is consistent with the Latin sources identified previously in the hero's name (which repeatedly scans as early Brythonic *Cunedag*) and his father's name, *Edern* < Latin *Aeternus*. However, the sons, the migration to Wales, and the war with the Irish do not figure at all in the elegy, raising the possibility that the foundation legend was manufactured by Gwynedd propagandists. Of course, it is also possible that the migration and Irish war did take place, but that these events were of insufficient interest and importance for the north British poet who produced *Marwnad Cunedda*.

It seems likely that Cunedda was an early post-Roman north British leader and a focus of early literary activity. It is also likely that men with Latin and Brythonic names listed as his sons did found small kingdoms in north and west Wales in the early post-Roman period and that these entities displaced Irish lordships. An appropriate historical context for both circumstances can be seen as a struggle for control of the Irish Sea zone in the vacuum created by the withdrawal of Roman forces from Segontium and other bases in west Britain. Nonetheless, the poem *Marwnad Cunedda* leaves room to doubt whether Cunedda ever fought the Irish or migrated to Wales, and the sons need not be his real sons; the subsequent kings of Gwynedd may not, in fact, be descendants of Cunedda.

As a central figure within the scheme of Welsh royal pedigrees, Cunedda also came to figure prominently, by the 11th century and possibly earlier, in the genealogies of saints. In the Triads (No. 81), he is named as the founder of one of the three great kindreds of Welsh saints.

The name *Cunedag* is a Celtic compound. The first element is likely the 6th- or 7th-century spelling of Celtic **cuno-* 'dog'. The name thus means 'having good hounds', with 'hounds' being a common kenning for warriors. The spelling *Cunedda*, although unhistorical, is by now well established.

John T. Koch

CUNOBELINOS

Cunobelinos (r. *c*. AD 10–*c*. 42) was the most powerful king in Britain in the final century of independence before the invasion of the Emperor Claudius in AD 43. His career may be traced through both Roman notices and coinage. On several of his coins, Cunobelinos is said to be the son of Tasciovanos (r. *c*. 15 BC–*c*. AD 10); the same information is preserved independently in the Old Welsh genealogies, where he is identified as *Cinbelin map Teuhant*.

Suetonius (*Caligula* §44) refers to Cunobelinos as *Britannorum rex* (king of the Britons). The distribution of his coinage, however, implies a status of just the most powerful of several pre-Roman rulers, The core area of the coins are the tribal lands of the Catuvellauni and the Trinovantes north of the lower Thames. To the north, this ruler's influence is evidenced by a scatter of his coins in the territory of the Iceni, but their own silver sequence continued. The coins of the Corieltauvi in the north and the Durotriges and Dobunni in the west indicate continued independence. Cunobelinos was succeeded by his sons, first Adminios in AD 39/40 and then Togodumnos and Caratacos, who fought the Roman invaders in the coming years.

The name *Cunobelinos* is Celtic and means 'hound of the god Belenos'. It was a fairly popular name in early Wales (Cymru). Latinizing a Welsh source in Historia

Regum Britanniae, Geoffrey of Monmouth accurately lists Kimbelinus son of Tenvantius (derived from Old Welsh *Cinbelin map Te(u)huant*) as one of the last kings of Britain before the Claudian invasion, a name that ultimately serves as the source of Shakespeare's *Cymbeline*.

John T. Koch

CŴN ANNWN

Cŵn Annwn (the hounds of Annwn) is the Welsh name for the supernatural dogs documented in the folklore of all Celtic countries. The Scottish *cù sìth* (fairy hound) is dark green, the colour of the fairies, and the hounds of Arawn in Pwyll were shining white with red ears, also otherworldly colours; most folk traditions describe them as very large black dogs, sometimes headless or fire breathing. Although their relationships have not been exhaustively catalogued, these creatures are associated with treasure in Ireland (Éire) and Brittany (Breizh), with standing stones in Wales (Cymru) and Cornwall (Kernow), and with other landmarks, such as the Moddey Dhoo (Black dog) of Peel Castle in Man (Ellan Vannin). *Cŵn Annwn* can function like the banshee (bean sí) in Cornish and Scottish tradition. They can also presage storms, as in Brittany, or mark the spot where a disaster occurred, as in Wheal Vor in Cornwall.

Antone Minard

CYDYMDEITHAS AMLYN AC AMIG

Cydymdeithas Amlyn ac Amig (The companionship of Amlyn and Amig) was a popular tale throughout Europe in the Middle Ages. The earliest Welsh version is contained in Llyfr Coch Hergest ('The Red Book of Hergest').

The various texts of the Amlyn and Amig story are traditionally divided into two groups: the Romantic and hagiographic, a somewhat artificial distinction. The Welsh falls into the latter group. The oldest extant version is a Latin poem in hexameter verse composed *c.* 1090 by Radulphus Tortarius, a monk of Fleury, although the evidence of the opening lines suggests that the poet was versifying an international popular tale: *Historiam Gallus, breviter quam replico, novit,/Novit in extremo litore Saxo situs*, 'The Gaul knows the tale, which I am briefly telling, the Saxon in his remote shore knows it'. The immediate source of the hagiographic group is the 12th-century Latin prose tale *Vita Sanctorum Amici et Amelii carissimorum*, but the more distant origins are rooted in folklore. Some of the hagiographic versions, including the Welsh, include an epilogue in which the two friends are killed in action, fighting on the side of Charlemagne against the king of Lombardy, who was in conflict with the Pope. Although they are buried in two separate churches in Mortara in northern Italy, the following morning the bodies are found lying side by side in the same tomb.

The Welsh version is unique in using the order *Aemelius et Amicus* (*Amlyn ac Amic*). The language and orthography suggest an early 14th-century date for the Welsh text; nevertheless, variations of style, syntax, and orthography imply that the epilogue was composed by a different author than the person who wrote the main body of narrative. *Cydymdeithas Amlyn ac Amig* also inspired Saunders LEWIS to write his verse-play *Amlyn ac Amig* (1940), in which the premise that salvation may depend on committing a seemingly irrational and abhorrent act found a powerful expression.

Patricia Williams

CYFARWYDD

Cyfarwydd is a Welsh term connected etymologically with the PROTO-CELTIC root *wēd-/wid-* 'know, see' (cf. also DRUIDS; FEDELM). In the first attestation of the word in Old Welsh, its plural means 'guides'. The *cyfarwydd* was therefore the 'guide', therefore the 'expert', and later the 'storyteller'. The noun *cyfarwyddyd* means 'tale' or 'narrative', originally 'traditional lore'. Two much-quoted sources suggest that poets would narrate *cyfarwyddyd* at court, and the term *cyfarwydd* (storyteller) may well be a functional title rather than a professional class. Some sources suggest that this individual would narrate tales in the king's hall after a FEAST. His repertoire, together with the narrative techniques favoured by him, are reflected in the tales of the MABINOGI. According to GIRALDUS CAMBRENSIS in his DESCRIPTIO KAMBRIAE, one of the most famous storytellers of medieval Wales (CYMRU) was Bleddri.

Sioned Davies

CYFRANC LLUDD A LLEFELYS

Cyfranc Lludd a Llefelys (The adventure or encounter of Lludd and Llefelys) is medieval WELSH PROSE LITERATURE. Lludd, king of BRITAIN, seeks the aid of his brother LLEFELYS to rid his kingdom of three supernatural 'oppressions': the Coraniaid, a frightening cry every May Eve (see CALENDAR), and the disappearance of prepared food and drink. Llefelys's cunning succeeds in eliminating all three problems. The cause of the cry is revealed as two dragons fighting (see DRAIG GOCH). Whether separately from the *Cyfranc* or not, the dragons are obviously related to the account in the 9th-century HISTORIA BRITTONUM §42 relating to GWRTHEYRN (Vortigern) and ultimately brought into ARTHURIAN LITERATURE. The *Cyfranc* first occurs as an insertion into a 13th-century Welsh translation of HISTORIA REGUM BRITANNIAE ('History of the Kings of Britain') of GEOFFREY OF MONMOUTH, where it is introduced as part of the stock in trade of the professional storyteller, the CYFARWYDD, and it is subsequently found in all later Welsh translations of the *Historia*.

Brynley F. Roberts

CYMDEITHAS YR IAITH GYMRAEG

Cymdeithas yr Iaith Gymraeg (The Welsh Language Society) was established as a direct action campaign group in 1962 with the objective of securing official status for WELSH that would place it on an equal footing with English in all spheres of public life in Wales (CYMRU).

The Society was formed as a result of growing concerns about the spiralling decline of Welsh speakers following World War II and frustration with the apathy and inaction of the authorities toward this issue, as expressed in the celebrated radio lecture 'Tynged yr Iaith' by Saunders Lewis. Disillusioned members of Plaid Cymru (The Party of Wales; see NATIONALISM) took up Lewis's challenge of organizing a campaign of civil disobedience on behalf of the language at the party's national conference in 1962.

The Society's principal method of campaigning is nonviolent direct action including protest marches, sit-ins, nonpayment of various taxes and licences, and criminal damage. During the course of its campaign for bilingual road signs, hundreds of Society supporters set upon English-only signs. Despite the fact that the active membership base has been relatively limited, many of the Society's campaigns have attracted widespread—albeit not universal—popular support.

Policies quickly evolved from matters of language equality and increased public status for Welsh to encompass a wide range of issues including EDUCATION and economic development. The Society has developed an increasingly holistic approach to its interests, pursuing bold policies to safeguard Welsh as a living community language. See also LANGUAGE [REVIVAL] MOVEMENTS IN THE CELTIC COUNTRIES).

Dylan Phillips

CYMRU (WALES)

Cymru (Wales) is one of the six modern CELTIC COUNTRIES, regions in which a Celtic language was spoken in modern times. Its only land border, with ENGLAND, roughly follows the 8th-century linear earthwork of Offa's Dyke (CLAWDD OFFA) from the mouth of the river Dee to the Severn estuary. Its landmass covers 8,015 square miles (20,758 km^2). At the time of the 2001 census, Wales counted 2,903,085 residents, who are represented by 40 Members of Parliament in London. The thirteen historic counties are now subdivided into twelve counties and ten county boroughs, with the capital in Cardiff (Caerdydd). In 1999, Wales gained a level of devolved political status within the United Kingdom (see CYNULLIAD CENEDLAETHOL CYMRU; NATIONALISM; SCOTTISH PARLIAMENT).

Wales and the Welsh Language

Due to Wales's early incorporation into the English state and the resulting absence of national institutions, the region's native Celtic language assumed prime importance as the main national symbol in the 19th century. WELSH (Cymraeg) was spoken by 575,604 people (20.5% of the population) at the 2001 census, an increase of nearly 2 percent from the 508,098 speakers counted in 1991. This represents the first increase in the total number of speakers in more than one hundred years. The highest percentages of Welsh speakers are found in the west and north of the country, but the largest numbers of speakers per square mile (i.e., high density) are found in the urban conurbations of south and northeast Wales. Unlike the other Celtic languages (with the possible exception of BRETON), Welsh has succeeded in

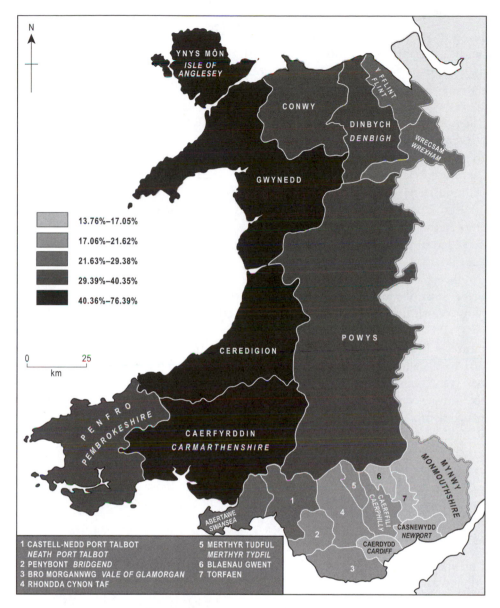

N

	13.76%–17.05%
	17.06%–21.62%
	21.63%–29.38%
	29.39%–40.35%
	40.36%–76.39%

YNYS MÔN
ISLE OF ANGLESEY

CONWY

Y FFLINT
FLINT

DINBYCH
DENBIGH

WRECSAM
WREXHAM

GWYNEDD

POWYS

CEREDIGION

0   25
km

PENFRO
PEMBROKESHIRE

CAERFYRDDIN
CARMARTHENSHIRE

MYNWY
MONMOUTHSHIRE

6

5

CAERFFILI
CAERPHILLY

7

1

4

CASNEWYDD
NEWPORT

ABERTAWE
SWANSEA

2

CAERDYDD
CARDIFF

3

1 CASTELL-NEDD PORT TALBOT
  NEATH PORT TALBOT
2 PENYBONT *BRIDGEND*
3 BRO MORGANNWG *VALE OF GLAMORGAN*
4 RHONDDA CYNON TAF

5 MERTHYR TUDFUL
  MERTHYR TYDFIL
6 BLAENAU GWENT
7 TORFAEN

Contemporary Cymru/Wales: post-1996 counties and the Welsh language in the 2001 census. Percentages signify population older than the age of 3 years with one or more of the following skills: understanding spoken Welsh, speaking Welsh, reading Welsh, or writing Welsh. (Map by Ian Gulley, Antony Smith, and John T. Koch)

developing an urban base: It boasts a lively creative industry unmatched by most of the lesser-used languages of Europe (see WELSH MUSIC; S4C; MASS MEDIA; WELSH POETRY; WELSH PROSE LITERATURE). The main national festival, EISTEDDFOD GENEDLAETHOL CYMRU, held in August, attracts as many as 200,000 people annually.

Early History

The territory of Wales entered history with the Roman conquest of AD 43 and Tacitus's graphic description of the resistance the Romans encountered in this region. Romans fought in what is now Wales, facing the resistance spearheaded by CARATĀCOS (see also BOUDĪCA; CASSIVELLAUNOS; CUNOBELINOS; DRUIDS; MÔN). By the end of the 1st century, the tribes of Wales—the Deceangli, Demetae (see DYFED), Ordovices, and Silures—had been pacified, and Roman control was established within a quadrangle of major forts at Deva (see CAER) in the northeast, Segontium in the northwest, Moridūnum (see Caerfyrddin) in the southwest, and Isca (Caerllion) in the southeast. The period following the collapse of Roman power in Britain in AD 409/10 was marked by the rise of regional kingdoms (see CUNEDDA; GWYNEDD; POWYS) and the (re-)establishment of Christianity during the 'Age of Saints' in the 5th and 6th centuries (see HAGIOGRAPHY). Nevertheless, only a few rulers succeeded in uniting the country under a common overlord (GRUFFUDD AP CYNAN; RHODRI MAWR).

In the century following the Norman Conquest of 1066, Norman lordships penetrated most of south and west Wales, known as the Welsh Marches. The last surviving Welsh kingdom was bloodily subdued by Edward I in 1282, and Prince LLYWELYN AP GRUFFUDD was killed. Edward settled the question of Wales with the Statute of RHUDDLAN (1284) and an extensive programme of castle building. In 1301 he declared his first-born son, Edward II, to be Prince of Wales. Since this event, the English king's first-born has usually been granted this title. A nationwide rebellion against English rule (1400–15), mounted by OWAIN GLYNDŴR, proved unsuccessful. The ACTS OF UNION (1536–43) of Henry VIII integrated Wales into the English state, conferring upon Welshmen the same political rights as available to their English neighbours and evening out the patchwork of native and Anglo-Norman administrative and legal practices that had arisen in post-conquest Wales, albeit at the expense of the Welsh language and cultural instutitions. A new literary standard was created with the late 16th-century BIBLE translations.

Industrial and Post-Industrial Wales

From about 1770 onward, Wales experienced a series of unparalleled demographic and industrial changes. Large numbers of workers migrated from the rural areas into the coalfields of the south and northeast. A golden age of Welsh publishing ensued. However, from the 1880s, immigrants from England by far outnumbered those from Wales itself. Coupled with a hostile state education system from 1870, the linguistic Anglicization of the industrial areas was speedy (see LANGUAGE [REVIVAL] MOVEMENTS IN THE CELTIC COUNTRIES). Welsh was increasingly seen as the language of rural life and a marker of low social status. Even so, the 19th century also saw the rise of NATIONALISM (see also CYMRU FYDD) and national institutions such as EISTEDDFOD GENEDLAETHOL CYMRU and GORSEDD BEIRDD YNYS PRYDAIN, as well as the emergence of political giants such as David LLOYD GEORGE. By the beginning of the 20th century, a national library and museum had been founded (see ABERYSTWYTH).

The south Wales valleys developed a strong tradition of political radicalism that persists today.

Following World War I, the Welsh economy all but collapsed with the decreasing demand for coal and iron. High unemployment well into the 1930s meant high rates of EMIGRATION. Rural areas, although traditionally among the poorest in the United Kingdom, benefited from government subsidies. The country still has a larger than average proportion of the population employed in AGRICULTURE, with sheep and cattle rearing dominant. Large stretches of mountain lands have been given over to timber production. Rural and coastal areas of Wales increasingly exploit their beauty and Celtic connections to promote tourism.

Marion Löffler

CYMRU (WALES), NAME

Cymru 'Wales' is a modern respelling of *Cymry* 'Welsh people', the plural of *Cymro* 'Welshman'. Etymologically, *Cymry* means people of the same *bro*, the latter signifying a compact home region; in BRETON, on much the same scale, *bro* means diocese. In an older Celtic sense, it is **kom-* + *mrugi-* 'persons within common borders'; cf. Old Irish *mruig* 'border'. The term *Cymry* first surfaces in *Moliant Cadwallon*, a poem set about 632/4. From this time onward, the name *Cymry* gained ground at the expense of the term *Brython* 'BRITONS', which continued to be used only in Brittany. By the time the term *Cymry* had gained currency, Anglo-Saxon rulers had already established political control over most of the people and productive land of Britain, and the shift from *Brython* to *Cymry* probably reflects that change. The cognate of *Cymry* has no currency in CORNISH or Breton.

Old English *Wealas* 'Wales, the Welsh' has a general sense of 'foreigners', and was applied by Germanic peoples to Romano-Celtic peoples of the former Roman Empire. The Germanic term seems to have been originally borrowed from the Celtic tribal name *Volcae*, a powerful group with branches in both southern GAUL and central Europe. Celtic *Volcae* had meant 'beasts of prey, wolves' and probably also 'hawks', cf. Welsh *gwalch*.

John T. Koch

CYMRU FYDD

Cymru Fydd, literally 'Wales will be' but known in English as Young Wales, was a patriotic movement formed in London (Welsh Llundain) in 1886 on the model of Young Ireland. It conceived its mission in terms of maintaining Wales's native cultural and linguistic traditions. Its most prominent members included historian John Edward Lloyd, Owen M. Edwards of Oxford, journalist Thomas Edward Ellis (later a Member of Parliament), and barrister W. Llewelyn Williams.

The second branch of the society was formed in Liverpool (Welsh Lerpwl), but the movement was slow to put down roots in Wales (CYMRU) itself. The movement published its own journal, *Cymru Fydd*, from January 1888, and won the backing of the popular press and of David LLOYD GEORGE, Member of Parliament for Caernarfon. Initially a cultural and educational movement, Cymru Fydd evolved into a political campaign. Home rule became central to the Cymru Fydd programme (see NATIONALISM).

The impact of Cymru Fydd became apparent in the appointment of the Royal Commission on Land in Wales in 1892, the grant of a royal charter to a federal University of Wales in 1893, and the introduction of a succession of measures embodying the disestablishment of the Church in Wales (the denomination corresponding to the Church of England).

Although Cymru Fydd branches survived in some towns and cities until World War II, after 1896 the ideal of Cymru Fydd was largely moribund—it became the victim of deep-rooted regional hostility and never succeeded in establishing a broad popular base. The skeleton of a Welsh National Federation survived, but during the early and mid-20th century most Welsh politicians looked for success within the British political system. Welsh sectional, regional, linguistic, and class antagonisms lessened the appeal of a national political autonomy for Wales.

J. Graham Jones

CYNDDELW BRYDYDD MAWR

Cynddelw Brydydd Mawr (*fl. c.* 1155–*c.* 1195) was by far the most prolific of the Welsh court poets (GOGYNFEIRDD) whose work has survived: 3,847 lines of his poetry have been preserved in 48 poems. He sang to the most important princes and noblemen of his age, notably Madog ap Maredudd, prince of POWYS (†1160), OWAIN GWYNEDD (†1170), and Lord RHYS AP GRUFFUDD of Deheubarth (†1197).

Cynddelw's poems contain a wealth of references to characters and incidents in Welsh history and tradition, the TRIADS, the MABINOGI, and legends associated with ARTHUR and Merlin (MYRDDIN). As well as traditional eulogy and elegy to individuals sung on ENGLYN and *awdl* metres, his repertoire included love poems, an ode in praise of Meifod and its patron saint, Tysilio, appeasement poems, poems of thanks, and personal *englynion* eulogizing the death of his son, Dygynnelw.

Cynddelw's work is preserved in four medieval Welsh manuscripts: the Black Book of Carmarthen (LLYFR DU CAERFYRDDIN), the Hendregadredd Manuscript, NLW Peniarth 3, and the Red Book of Hergest (LLYFR COCH HERGEST). Some poems have also been preserved in NLW 4973 in the 17th-century hand of Dr John Davies, Mallwyd.

Little is known of Cynddelw's background. He was probably from Powys. The epithet 'Prydydd Mawr' (great poet) has generally been taken to refer to Cynddelw's genius, but it could refer to his physique.

In the unstable period after Madog ap Maredudd died in 1160, Cynddelw cast his lot with Madog's son Owain Fychan. A short time later, he associated himself with Owain Gwynedd, who died in 1170. Cynddelw emphasizes Owain's superiority as ruler of his kingdom and as an effective battle leader. Cynddelw's longest poem—in which he refers to his patron as *brenin* and *rhi* (both 'king')—was addressed to Owain's son Hywel. After Hywel's death later that same year, he appears to have returned to Powys, where he composed an elegy upon the death of Iorwerth Goch, Madog ap Maredudd's half-brother, in 1172. In 1187, Cynddelw mourned the killing of his former patron, Owain Fychan son of Madog ap Maredudd. During these years Cynddelw also praised Owain Cyfeiliog and his son, Gwenwynwyn. By the early 1190s, however, he was almost certainly in Deheubarth, singing the praises of Lord Rhys ap Gruffudd. As no elegy by him to either Lord Rhys or Owain Cyfeiliog, both of whom died in 1197, has survived, it is presumed that he predeceased them both.

Ann Parry Owen

CYNFEIRDD

Cynfeirdd (sing. *cynfardd*) is a modern Welsh term usually translated as 'first poets' or 'early poets'. On the one hand, the 9th-century Memorandum of the Five Poets is sometimes regarded as defining, as well as dating, the *Cynfeirdd* exactly—five named poets of the 6th century, of which only two, Aneirin and Taliesin, have surviving works attributed to them. On the other hand, in attempting an overall scheme of the history of Welsh poetry, it is conventional to divide the Middle Ages into three sections: (1) *Cynfeirdd*; (2) Gogynfeirdd (rather early poets); and (3) Cywyddwyr. Within such a scheme, a category of the 'later *Cynfeirdd*' emerges, including a diverse mass of anonymous material such as saga *englynion*, secular praise poetry, religious poetry, nature poetry, prophecy—including Armes Prydein—and poems associated with Myrddin, and the so-called mythological poetry of Llyfr Taliesin. For these works of the 'later *Cynfeirdd*', see these articles and Welsh poetry [1]. The core of the corpus is as follows:

1. *Marwnad Cunedda* 'The elegy of Cunedda' [commemorating an occasion of AD 383 × 490]
2. The Llyfr Aneirin corpus [mid-to late 6th century]
3. *Trawsganu Cynan Garwyn* [commemorating events of 575 × 610]
4. *Awdlau* addressed to Urien Rheged [commemorating events of 570 × 595]
5. Enaid Owain ab Urien 'The soul of Owain son of Urien' [commemorating events of 570 × 595]
6. *Awdlau* addressed to Gwallawg fab Lleënnawg of Elfed [commemorating events of 570 × 610]
7. *Moliant Cadwallon* 'The praise of Cadwallon' [commemorating events of 630–34]
8. *Marwnad Cynddylan* 'The elegy of Cynddylan' [commemorating events of 642–655]

John T. Koch

CYNGHANEDD

Cynghanedd, meaning harmony (from the roots *cyf-* 'with' + *can-* 'sing'), is a sophisticated form of strict-metre Welsh poetry with complex alliterative lines, sometimes adding internal rhyme. A rudimentary form of *cynghanedd* is as old as the language itself.

The rules of *cynghanedd*, known as cerdd dafod (poetic art), were fully developed by the Middle Ages. Comparable patterns are found in the other medieval Celtic langauges.

During the 1970s, young poets such as Alan Llwyd and others brought a fresh impetus to the learning of *cynghanedd*. The wide popularity of the radio programme *Talwrn y Beirdd* (Bardic contest), in which teams of poets compete against each other under the chairmanship of Gerallt Lloyd Owen, reflects the revival of interest in *cynghanedd*. The standard reference work remains Sir John Morris-Jones's scholarly volume *Cerdd Dafod*, first published in 1925.

Any student of *cynghanedd* must first be acquainted with the normal accentuation of words. In most words in Welsh, the accent or stress rests on the penultimate syllable (*goben*). A seven-syllable line should have a natural break in the middle of the line, and all consonants before the penultimate accent in the first half of the line should correspond exactly to the consonants before the penultimate accent in the second half. In writing a strict-metre poem, scores of rules must be observed and numerous variations are possible, but the three main types of *cynghanedd* are as follows.

Cynghanedd Gytsain

A line of *Cynghanedd Groes*, a subdivision of this class, reads:

> *Gwaed y groes /a gwyd y graith* (Ioan Madog)
> The blood of the cross removes the scar.

Here the natural break in the line occurs after *groes* and the two main stresses fall on the accented one-syllable words, *groes* and *graith*. The consonants in each half correspond to one another, but those that come after the accented vowels of each half-line (*s* and *th* in this case) do not count. Other subdivisions of *cynghanedd gytsain* are more complex.

Cynghanedd Sain

This form consists of a combination of internal rhyme and alliteration:

> *Cledd*au *digon* <u>br</u>au *o* <u>br</u>en (Lewys Glyn Cothi)
> Flimsy wooden swords.

Note the internal rhyme in *cleddau* and *brau*, and also the alliteration between *brau* and *bren*.

Cynghanedd Lusg

This type of *cynghanedd* consists purely of internal rhyme. Although it is the easiest of the *cynganeddion* to compose, it is very often the most pleasing to the ear:

> *Lle roedd sglein/ar bob* ceiniog (Huw T. Edwards)
> There was a gloss on every copper coin.

Note that the accented *ein* in the monosyllabic *sglein* rhymes with the accented penultimate syllable in *ceiniog*.

Many English-language poets have discovered and written lines using elements of *cynghanedd* (see ANGLO-WELSH LITERATURE), including Dylan Thomas and Wilfred Owen. The first English-language poet to experiment with *cynghanedd* was

William Barnes, who learned both Welsh and the rules of *cerdd dafod*. Gerard Manley Hopkins was by far the most successful user of *cynghanedd* in English-language poetry. While at St Beuno College in St Asaph (Llanelwy) in north Wales, he learned Welsh and studied *cerdd dafod*. The following lines indicate how he introduced *cynghanedd* into his work:

> I wake in the Midsummer not to call night, in the white
> and the walk of the morning … (*Cynghanedd Sain*).

> And fled with a fling (*Cynghanedd Draws*) /of the heart to the
> heart of the host (*Cynghanedd Sain*).

Vernon Jones

CYNULLIAD CENEDLAETHOL CYMRU (NATIONAL ASSEMBLY FOR WALES)

Cynulliad Cenedlaethol Cymru (the National Assembly for Wales) is the elected body that sits in Cardiff (Caerdydd), the capital of Wales (CYMRU). On 1 July 1999, the Cynulliad took over the responsibilities of the Welsh Office for the regional government of Wales within the United Kingdom. Its powers are more restricted than those of the SCOTTISH PARLIAMENT—for example, it lacks the ability to levy taxes—though its function is similar.

Welsh nationalists from CYMRU FYDD to Plaid Cymru (see NATIONALISM) had long campaigned for the devolution of government power to Wales. A referendum was held on 18 September 1997, one week after the Scottish electorate had voted in favour of establishing a Scottish Parliament. In Wales, 50.3 percent of the votes cast were in favour of an elected political body for the country, which was then set up by the Government of Wales Act (1998). The fully bilingual Cynulliad met for the first time on 12 May 1999.

Among the domains in which the Cynulliad exercises power are AGRICULTURE, economic development, EDUCATION, the environment, industry, local government, social security, and the Welsh language. Cynulliad Cenedlaethol Cymru is composed of sixty members, of whom forty are elected directly. The remaining twenty members are elected in five larger regions through the Additional Member System, which allocates four seats per region to depending on the parties' share of the vote.

Elections are held every four years. At the election in 2007, the Labour Party won 26 seats, followed by Plaid Cymru with 15 seats, the Conservative Party with 12 seats, the Liberal Party with six seats, and one seat is held by an independent. Although the first years of Cynulliad Cenedlaethol Cymru—the first Welsh parliament since that of OWAIN GLYNDŴR—have not been easy, it is clear that this body's existence has strengthened Welsh nationhood by providing a focus for its politics.

Marion Löffler

CYWYDD

Cywydd is a Welsh metrical form in use from the 14th century to the present day. The term is cognate with Old Irish *cubaid*, originally meaning 'harmony' or 'song'.

Four types of *cywydd* are listed by Einion Offeiriad in the fourteenth century, but the only one commonly used by bardic poets was the *cywydd deuair hirion*, consisting of seven-syllable couplets with one line rhyming on a stressed syllable and the other on an unstressed one; it is to this metre that the term *cywydd* normally refers. The *cywydd deuair hirion* probably derived from a simpler metre, known as the *traethodl*, which consisted of seven-syllable rhyming couplets and had no CYNGHANEDD. The rhyme pattern may have been influenced by the final couplet of the ENGLYN *unodl union*.

The *cywydd* has no set length, and can range from as few as twelve lines to more than one hundred, although medieval *cywyddau* are usually around sixty lines. DAFYDD AP GWILYM is the first poet known to have made extensive use of the *cywydd*, and it is likely that his love poems popularized the metre.

Dafydd ap Gwilym may also have been responsible for introducing *cynghanedd* into the *cywydd*, although he quite often left the first line of the couplet without *cynghanedd*. By the end of the 14th century, the *cywydd* had become accepted as the standard metre for all kinds of bardic poetry, and it continued to fill this position until the demise of the bardic order in the 17th century. Revived by neo-classical poets in the 18th century, the *cywydd* tradition was maintained by the EISTEDDFOD.

Dafydd Johnston

CYWYDDWYR

The Term

The WELSH plural noun *cywyddwyr* (sing. *cywyddwr*) refers to poets who composed *cywyddau*—that is, poems in the CYWYDD metre—from the 14th to the 16th centuries.

When, in the latter half of the 18th century, the terms CYNFEIRDD, 'early poets', and GOGYNFEIRDD, 'rather early poets', began to be used by Lewis Morris and others to describe Welsh poets up to the 14th century, the medieval term *Cywyddwyr* was added to indicate the third and last chronological stage of strict-metre poetry in Wales (CYMRU), beginning in about 1300 and declining shortly after the ACTS OF UNION of 1536 and 1543. Not all 14th-century poets were *Cywyddwyr*, and the poets of this period are sometimes described collectively as *Beirdd yr Uchelwyr*, or 'Poets of the Nobility'. Thus the terms *Cywyddwyr* and *Beirdd yr Uchelwyr* overlap, being largely but not precisely synonymous.

The *cywydd* was revived by Edward WILLIAMS (Iolo Morganwg) at the end of the 18th century to form a key element in his vision of the modern EISTEDDFOD, and it remains a central feature of *eisteddfod* competitions in Wales to this day. Even so, the term *Cywyddwyr* normally refers exclusively to poets of the central and late Middle Ages who composed in the *cywydd* metre.

The Rise of the Cywyddwyr

Before 1282, court poetry (typically in the *awdl* and *englyn* metres) had been addressed to the ruling dynasties of Wales. Following Edward I's suppression of the Welsh royal dynasties, the social and economic infrastructure of traditional court poetry largely disappeared. What arose in its place was a newly empowered class of patrons, the *uchelwyr*, and a new prestige metre, the *cywydd*. Among the simplest of the twenty-four bardic metres, it was revived in the early 14th century as a useful medium for the new themes of love and nature influenced by English popular song. The *Cywyddwyr* tended to be more mobile than earlier poets, and self-employed. Most of the major artists had multiple patrons, although these individuals were often members of the same extended *uchelwyr* families. More significantly, the *Cywyddwyr* moved freely between the manor houses of their *uchelwyr* patrons and the growing towns of Wales, which provided new audiences among the burgesses and trade-enriched merchants, English as well as Welsh. Poems by DAFYDD AP GWILYM to Newborough and Guto'r Glyn to Oswestry (Welsh Croesoswallt) are among the *cywyddau* that acknowledge the significance of urban life to the status and fortunes of the *Cywyddwyr* from the 14th century onward.

Significant Cywyddwyr

There are no surviving biographies of any of the *Cywyddwyr*, so information about their lives must be inferred from references in the poetry and from what is known of their patrons. It seems fairly clear, however, that many of the *Cywyddwyr* belonged to the same socio-economic class as their patrons, being members of *uchelwyr* families who both supported and produced the professional poets of their age.

The first generation of *Cywyddwyr* included Dafydd ap Gwilym, widely acknowledged as the greatest of the *Cywyddwyr*, but also Iolo Goch, Llywelyn Goch ap Meurig Hen, Gruffudd Gryg, Madog Benfras, and Gruffudd ab Adda, some of the most innovative poets of the medieval period. This generation is credited with turning the *cywydd* into a professional metre, suitable for court poetry, while continuing to compose in the *awdl* and *englyn* metres.

The dominant figure of the first half of the 15th century was SIÔN CENT, whose religious verse is deeply philosophical and didactic. The second half of the 15th century produced some of the most prolific and accomplished praise-poets among the *Cywyddwyr*, including Guto'r Glyn, Gutun Owain, Dafydd Nanmor, Lewys Glyn Cothi, Huw Cae Llwyd, Lewys Môn, and Tudur Aled. The tradition of love poetry established by the earlier generations was also strongly maintained by poets such as Dafydd ab Edmwnd, Bedo Brwynllys, and Bedo Aeddren. Dafydd ab Edmwnd was particularly known for his metrical innovations at the Carmarthen (Caerfyrddin) *eisteddfod* of *c.* 1451, insisting on strict CYNGHANEDD in the *cywydd* metres and increasing the complexity of many of the traditional twenty-four metres that formed the basis of the bardic system of training and grading.

By the end of the 16th century, the tradition of praise poetry was itself in decline, maintained only by a few pupils of Gruffudd Hiraethog. Notably, Siôn Tudur was both a poet and a member of the gentry; his satires draw attention to the gradual decay of the bardic profession. Simwnt Fychan is remembered not only for his poetry but also for his reworking of the bardic regulations, *Pum Llyfr Cerddwriaeth*.

While poetry as a profession was dominated by men in medieval Wales, some surviving *cywyddau* and *englynion* are attributed to a female poet, GWERFUL MECHAIN, who composed in the second half of the 15th century. As the daughter of Hywel Fychan of Powys, and therefore a member of a well-established family of *uchelwyr*, Gwerful belonged to the same social circle as many of the *Cywyddwyr* and their patrons, and was related by marriage to the poet Llywelyn ab y Moel. Among her surviving poems are a number of exchanges with Dafydd Llwyd of Mathafarn and Llywelyn ap Gutun, as well as the raunchy and humorous *cywyddau* for which she is particularly renowned.

Style and Themes

The metre associated most closely with the *Cywyddwyr*, the *cywydd deuair hirion*, determined many of the stylistic possibilities of the poetry. Rhymed as a couplet (with rhyme between an accented and an unaccented final syllable), the metre lends itself to syntactic units of one couplet at a time, a style that became particularly refined in 15th-century praise poetry. Those poets of the 14th century, such as Dafydd ap Gwilym and Llywelyn Goch ap Meurig Hen, who continued to use the *awdl* metre for praise poetry alongside the *cywydd* metre, transferred modes of the *awdl* to the *cywydd*, including single-line sense units, alliteration at the beginning of a series of lines (*cymeriad*), and a series of repeated end-rhymes. In general, the greater flexibility of the *cywydd* metre, compared to the *awdl*, encouraged a lighter and more humorous style of verse expressed through the innovative use of colloquial forms, compound words, and a highly figurative language of extended metaphor and imagery.

The *Cywyddwyr* practised a rhetorical and ornamental style that set their verse clearly apart from prose and from the simpler songs of minstrels and players. Apart from *cymeriad*, the most obvious adornment was *cynghanedd*, the system of consonantal repetition and internal rhyme applied to each line of verse in a number of variant patterns. For their rhetorical ornamentation, the *Cywyddwyr* drew on a common stock of European literary devices derived from Greek and Latin conventions, including metaphor, repetition, oxymoron, and paradox. Two devices particularly associated with the *Cywyddwyr* are *sangiad* and *dyfalu*. *Sangiad* corresponds to the Greek concept of 'parenthesis', and describes the insertion of additional phrases or asides, often in the form of a comment or value judgement, into a syntactic unit, a particularly helpful device in a strict syllabic metre governed by *cynghanedd*. The art of *dyfalu*, meaning 'to describe' or 'to deride', rests in the intricate development of a series of images and extended metaphors that either celebrate or castigate a person, animal or object.

Performance

Medieval *cywyddau* were composed to be performed in public, and to be sung rather than recited. The evidence of the poems suggests that the *Cywyddwyr* normally performed their own work, accompanying themselves on a HARP or CRWTH (a stringed instrument), although the musical accompaniment may have been provided or amplified, at least on some occasions, by professional musicians.

Not all *cywyddau* were necessarily performed by the *Cywyddwyr* themselves, as a class of professional singers known as *datgeiniaid* 'reciters' were active during this era. These singers are mentioned in the earliest versions of the bardic grammar as performers whose rôle is to enhance the songs they perform. The *Cywyddwyr*, then, were often musicians and singers as well as poets, although they might be accompanied by professional musicians and singers, or even replaced by them.

Transmission

The transmission of the poetry of the *Cywyddwyr* seems to have been almost entirely oral until the middle of the 15th century, when secular patrons began to commission manuscripts in significant numbers with the aim of recording what had become the mainstream tradition of bardic poetry. Only two contemporary manuscript sources for any 14th-century *cywyddau* exist: the Hendregadredd Manuscript and the Red Book of Hergest (LLYFR COCH HERGEST).

The main period of manuscript transmission of the work of the *Cywyddwyr* came after 1450 and is notable for the number of versions written by the bards themselves. Sixteenth-century manuscripts containing *cywyddau* were mainly the work of Welsh humanist scholars such as Elis Gruffydd (*c.* 1490–*c.* 1558), Thomas Wiliems (†1622), Humphrey Davies (†1635), and Dr John Davies of Mallwyd (†1644). Many of them are laid out with titles, rubrics, and other indications that the contents were to be read as well as to be preserved for oral performance. By the 17th century, the work of the *Cywyddwyr* was highly regarded among the native Welsh gentry as a mark of social status, and collections were made for the libraries of families such as the Wynns of Gwydir and the Vaughans of Corsygedol. Welsh texts continued to be hand-copied throughout the 18th century.

Major *Cywyddwyr* in Chronological Order

Dates indicate approximate life spans and/or periods of activity as far as they can be documented.

DAFYDD AP GWILYM (*c.* 1315–*c.* 1350)
Madog Benfras (*c.* 1320–60)
Llywelyn Goch ap Meurig Hen (*c.* 1330–90)
Gruffudd ab Adda (*c.* 1340–80)
Iolo Goch (*fl.* 1345–97)
Gruffudd Gryg (*fl.* 1357–70)
Rhys Goch Eryri (*c.* 1365–*c.* 1440)
Gruffudd Llwyd ap Dafydd ab Einion Llygliw (*c.* 1380–1410)
Dafydd Llwyd (of Mathafarn) (*c.* 1395–*c.* 1486)
SIÔN CENT (*fl. c.* 1400–30/45)
Llywelyn ab y Moel (*c.* 1400–40)
Guto'r Glyn (*c.* 1418–*c.* 1493)
Ieuan ap Rhydderch (*c.* 1430–70)
Hywel Swrdwal (*c.* 1430–70)
Huw Cae Llwyd (*c.* 1430–1505)

Bedo Brwynllys (*c.* 1440–80)
Dafydd ap Maredudd ap Tudur (*c.* 1440–80)
Dafydd Epynt (*c.* 1440–80)
Gwilym ab Ieuan Hen (*c.* 1440–80)
Gwilym Tew (*c.* 1440–80)
Hywel Dafi (*c.* 1440–80)
Dafydd Nanmor (*fl.* 1445–90)
Lewys Glyn Cothi (*fl.* 1447–89)
Llawdden (*c.* 1450–80)
Dafydd ab Edmwnd (*fl.* 1450–97)
Gutun Owain (*fl.* 1450–98)
Ieuan Brydydd Hir (*c.* 1450–1500)
Tudur Penllyn (*c.* 1460–85)
Ieuan Deulwyn (*c.* 1460–90)
Llywelyn ap Gutun (*c.* 1460–1500)
Gwerful Mechain (*c.* 1460–*post* 1502)
Bedo Phylip Bach (*c.* 1460–1500)
Tudur Aled (*c.* 1465–*c.* 1525)
Lewys Môn (*c.* 1465–1527)
Bedo Aeddren (*c.* 1480–1520)
Iorwerth Fynglwyd (*c.* 1480–1530)
Gruffudd ab Ieuan ap Llywelyn Fychan (*c.* 1485–1553)
Huw ap Dafydd (*c.* 1500–50)
Gruffudd Hiraethog (*c.* 1510–64)
Lewys Morgannwg (*c.* 1520–50)
Siôn Tudur (*c.* 1522–1602)
Simwnt Fychan (*c.* 1530–1606)
Wiliam Llŷn (*c.* 1535–80)
Edmwnd Prys (1543/4–1623)
Wiliam Cynwal (†1587/8)

Helen Fulton

DAFYDD AP GWILYM

Dafydd ap Gwilym, regarded by his contemporaries as well as by modern critics as the foremost poet among medieval Cywyddwyr, was active in 14th century. There is little documentary evidence for his life, apart from the internal evidence of the poems. He was probably born *c*. 1315, in Brogynin in Ceredigion, Cymru (Wales), and died *c*. 1350, possibly of the plague. Three of his contemporaries—Madog Benfras, Gruffudd Gryg, and Iolo Goch—composed elegies on his death.

Born into a prominent family of *uchelwyr* (noblemen), Dafydd received his training in the art of CERDD DAFOD from his uncle, Llywelyn ap Gwilym, and had formal education at Strata Florida (Ystrad-fflur; see Cistercian abbeys in Wales). Significant patrons include Ifor ap Llywelyn ('Ifor Hael') of Basaleg in Morgannwg, and Ieuan Llwyd of Parcrhydderch in Ceredigion.

The canon of poems established by Thomas Parry in *Gwaith Dafydd ap Gwilym* (1952) numbers around 150. Most are in the cywydd metre, but the collection also includes poems addressed to patrons in the englyn and *awdl* metres. Dafydd is particularly renowned for his courtly love songs and nature poems, often with a deeply religious subtext, but his output also includes humorous narratives about failed love-trysts. Dafydd's contribution to the Welsh poetic tradition resides in his development of the *cywydd* metre as a stylish vehicle for court poetry, his assimilation of native Welsh traditions into the mainstream of European poetry, and the sheer range and quality of his verse. His poetry is characterized by his versatile handling of cynghanedd, verbal wit of puns and metaphors, and imagery of love and nature.

Helen Fulton

DAGDA

Dagda (Dagdae, Dagán) was one of the principal pre-Christian deities of Ireland (Ériu) commemorated in the Mythological Cycle of early Irish literature, figuring in several texts as a leader or the king of the Tuath Dé. His most extensive surviving description is in Cath Maige Tuired ('The [Second] Battle of Mag Tuired').

This deity's name means 'good god' (< Celtic *Dago-dēwos), in the sense of technical competence, and he is often cited 'the Dagda'. He is shown in several tales to possess great sexual potency, mating with many different goddesses, including Bóand and the Morrígan in the *Metrical* Dindshenchas. One of his alternative epithets, Ollathair ('all-father'), invites parallels to the Norse god Òðin (also known as Alfoðr, 'all-father'), who is similarly versatile. The Dagda is the father of Oengus Mac ind Óc, a god excelling in youth and beauty, and the goddess Bríg, also known as Brigit. Other children include Áed Menbhrec, Bodb Derg, Cermat, Mider, and Ainge. The Dagda is described as a great warrior and skilful in magic, but also as gross and uncouth.

The Dagda has two fabulous material attributes, a cauldron of plenty (see CAULDRONS), and a club that can kill the living and raise the dead, inviting comparisons with Heracles and the Gaulish Sucellus. His cauldron, together with his other characteristics, suggests that the Dagda might also have been a Celtic god of the OTHERWORLD, and as such he has been identified with Donn and Dīs PATER.

Victoria Simmons and Tom Sjöblom

DÁL GCAIS

Dál gCais is the name of an Irish kingdom and tribe of the early medieval period. This entity first appears in the early 8th century as a branch of the population group known as Déisi Muman ('Déisi' or 'vassal tribes of Munster/MUMU'), settled on either side of the Shannon estuary. Those tribe members to the south and east of the river were known as the Déis Deiscirt, and those to the north and west as the Déis Tuaiscirt. By the beginning of the 9th century, the lands of the Déis Deiscirt were overrun, leaving the northern sub-kingdom standing alone.

The tribe is first referred to as Dál gCais 'people of Cas' in 934. The name comes from Cormac Cas, brother of the legendary forefather of the ÉOGANACHT tribes who dominated Munster until the 10th century. The 951 death notice of their king Cennétig mac Lorcáin in the ANNALS of Ulster calls him *rí Tuathmuman* 'king of Thomond', approximately coextensive with the modern Co. Clare (Contae an Chláir).

Following the death of BRIAN BÓRUMA at the battle of Clontarf near BAILE ÁTHA CLIATH (Dublin) in 1014, the power of the Dál gCais—or Uí Briain 'O'Briens' as they were henceforth known—fell into eclipse for several decades. Eventually it was revived under Tairdelbach Ua Briain, who, under the patronage of the king of Leinster (LAIGIN), succeeded in wresting control of Munster from his uncle, Donnchad. Tairdelbach subsequently brought Meath (MIDE), Leinster, and Ulster (ULAID) under his lordship. This trend continued under his son Muirchertach, who further expanded this sphere of influence to include CONNACHT.

After the death of Muirchertach in 1118, the supremacy of the Uí Briain came to an end and their lordship shrank back to their hereditary lands in Thomond. Following the Anglo-Norman invasion from 1169, they defended their territory more effectively than most Gaelic lordships and were still a powerful dynasty in the Tudor period (see TUDUR), when they became Earls of Thomond under the English policy of surrender and regrant.

A body of stories concerning the kings of the Dál gCais, the Dalcassian Cycle, is sometimes regarded as part of the KINGS' CYCLES. This material centres on the activities of Brian Bóruma and his son Murchad.

Simon Ó Faoláin

DÁL RIATA

Dál Riata (Dalriada, Early Old Irish Dál Réti) is the term for the GAELIC-speaking kingdom in Argyll (Earra-Ghaidheal) between the 6th and 9th centuries AD.

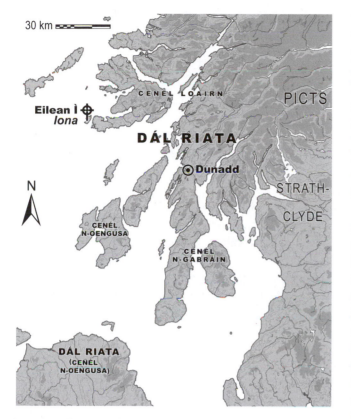

30 km

Eilean Ì
Iona

CENÉL LOAIRN

PICTS

DÁL RIATA

N

Dunadd

STRATH-
CLYDE

CENÉL
N-OENGUSA

CENÉL
N-GABRÁIN

DÁL RIATA
(CENÉL
N-OENGUSA)

(Map by John T. Koch)

Writing *c.* 730, the Nor-thumbrian BEDE ex-plained the presence of Gaelic speakers in Britain as follows: 'These came from Ireland under their leader Reuda, and won lands among the Picts ... They are still called Dalreudini after this leader.'

By the 10th century, the migration had been redated to the time of Fergus Mór mac Eirc (†501). In its intro-ductory passage, the *Senchus Fer n-Alban* (Tradition of the men of North Britain) claims six sons of Erc settled in Scotland (ALBA), prob-ably reflecting six *cenéla* (kindreds) there when the tract was compiled. Later there are three important *cenéla*: Cenél nGabráin (based in Kintyre and Arran), Cenél Loairn (based in Mull and Lorne), and Cenél nOengusa (part of Islay). It is also clear that part of the kingdom of Dál Riata was in Ireland, but whose kingdom and how extensive it was are less clear.

For most of the historical period, from the mid-6th century to the end of the kingdom in the 9th century, the kingship, or overkingship, was held by Cenél nGabráin. In the decades around 700, Cenél Loairn was sometimes able to challenge this monopoly.

Dál Riata is most famous for St Columba (COLUM CILLE) and his foundation of Iona (EILEAN Ì). As a result, we are relatively well informed about the kingdom from the period of Columba's arrival (*c.* 563) through to the mid-8th century. Columba's contemporary AEDÁN MAC GABRÁIN (r. 574–608) is the most famous king, partly because he features significantly in the saint's *Life* but also because he seems to have been the most successfully aggressive of the kings of Dál Riata, campaign-ing widely in northern Britain and establishing a regional hegemony in north-central Ireland.

After the end of the Iona Chronicle coverage in the mid-8th century, our under-standing of the history of Dál Riata is reduced. By the middle of the 9th century, a Cenél nGabráin dynast, CINAED MAC AILPÍN, made himself king of the PICTS and set the stage for the Gaelicization of all northern Britain. Precisely how this was achieved remains far from clear. Likewise, the date of the disappearance of Cenél nGabrain control over parts of Ireland is unknown, although it presumably followed the Vikings' rule in the latter part of the 9th century.

Alex Woolf

DANCES, BRETON

Traditional dance in the Breton-speaking region of Breizh-Izel (Lower Brittany) has retained the oldest types of dance known in Western European culture—namely, round dances formed by a closed chain of an unlimited number of dancers, who circle with a single repeated step. These patterns are still in use and are well represented in the countryside of the modern departments of Aodoùan-Arvor (Côtes d'Armor), Penn-ar-Bed (Finistère), and Morbihan. The name usually given to these dances in Lower Brittany is *an dro* or *dañs-tro,* based on the word *tro* 'turn'. In general, the *dañs-tro* is followed immediately by another dance, the *bal,* which involves changing the arrangement of the dancers between a round and a procession, with additional separation into couples.

With the exception that no one dances during Lent, the *dañs-tro* is not tied to the religious or secular calendar, or even to a seasonal one. Instead, it is closely linked to marriage days and to certain kinds of rural labour. The musical beat may be 8-count or 4-count, less often 3- or 6-count, and the rhythm may change.

Another type of dance, also very old, is performed in a northern zone stretching west to east, from Upper Leon to the north of the Monts d'Arrée, and also at the western edge of Treger that adjoins it. Here the main element of the ensemble is not the closed chain but the double front—one consisting of men, one of women, facing each other. Where the circular disposition of the *dañs-tro* reveals its affiliation with round dances of the greater European tradition, the double front of the *dañs Leon* and the *dañs Treger* marks a radical distinction.

Jean-Marie Guilcher

DANCES, IRISH

Early references to dance in Ireland (Ériu) are rare. Earlier use of words such as *cleasaíocht* (acrobatics) and *léimneach* (jumping) indicate a form of dancing, but the modern Irish words for dance, *dámhsa* and *rince,* are loanwords, appearing in the 16th and 17th centuries, respectively. The Irish word *céilí* means an informal social gathering in a neighbour's house, but since the beginning of the 20th century it has come to be used to describe an organized dancing session.

The jig was well established in Ireland by the 18th century, toward the end of which the reel and the hornpipe also became part of the dance and music repertoires in Ireland. These three are the most frequent dance rhythms of today.

Sets and half-sets were the most popular dances throughout Ireland in the 19th and 20th centuries. They derive from the quadrille, which was very popular during the time of Napoleon, having been imported by the armies of the Duke of Wellington. The set dances contain several figures, and much of the nomenclature and movements recall their military origin.

Solo or step dancing is found in all parts of Ireland (ÉIRE) and allows for a demonstration of the individual's creativity and artistry in footwork. At the same time, modern displays such as 'Riverdance' have drawn on traditional step dance forms.

Ríonach uí Ógáin

DANCES, SCOTTISH

Indigenous Scottish dances include weapon dances, ritualistic dances, dramatic dances, social dances, and solo step dances.

Scottish weapon dances involved step dancing as part of mock battles with dirks or cudgels or dancing over dirks or crossed SWORDS. Ritualistic hilt-and-point sword dances performed in Perth (Peairt) in the 16th century and in Papa Stour in the Shetlands (Sealtainn) until the late 19th century symbolically slayed a hero as a sacrificial victim and then brought him back to life. These dances were related to the guisers' play (in which one character was wounded or slain, and then resurrected by a comic doctor) and morris dances. The death-and-resurrection theme recurs in the widely known dramatic dance *Cailleach an Dùdain* ('The Old Woman of the Mill Dust').

Early social dances were communal ring dances, performed around a venerable object such as a sacred tree, a holy well, or a BELTAINE fire, and accompanied by communal dance-songs, called carols, or by BALLADS. A leader chanted a narrative line of a verse, and those in the ring responded in unison with the chorus as they danced around in a circle holding hands. The vocal solo and response form may derive from the communal work song. The SCOTTISH GAELIC-speaking areas also had ring dances of this type, such as *An Dannsa Mór* ('The Great Dance'), known on the Isle of Skye (An t-Eilean Sgitheanach) and the island of Eigg (Eige).

The *Ruidhleadh Mór* ('The Big Reel') from Skye is similar to a ring dance in which the circling stops as the dancers drop hands and perform setting steps on the spot before continuing around in a circle. This type of dance may have been the progenitor of the uniquely Scottish social dance called the reel. The reel consists of a travelling figure alternating with setting steps danced on the spot and sometimes swinging. Reels also introduced the use of raised arms or arms akimbo during setting or swinging, snapping the fingers, and heuching (giving a sudden yelp of glee). Dances were accompanied by BAGPIPE, FIDDLE, or, in the Highlands, *puirt-a-beul*.

The Scottish tunes and travelling steps used for reels were applied to the English country dances introduced into Scotland (ALBA) after 1700. The unique Scottish contribution to the figures of the country dances was the figure 'set to and turn corners and then reels of three with corners', which derived from the setting, swinging, and travelling patterns of the reel. The rhythmic pattern of the travelling step—step, close, step, hop—is the basis for any step or dance historically referred to as a *Schottische* (German for 'Scottish').

The devising and teaching of setting steps to dance in the reels led to the development of solo dances that emphasized the display of numerous steps choreographed to match a specific tune that gave the dance its name. The earliest of these dances still featured travelling steps in a circle interspersed with setting steps. Each turn of setting steps had a different variation at first and then ended with the same set of movements.

Most of the competitive dances performed at HIGHLAND GAMES are not traditional Highland dances, but rather were devised by Lowland dancing masters in the 1790s and the early 1800s.

Susan Self

DANCES, WELSH

Dances of Wales (CYMRU) were, in the main, connected with the seasons or with annual festivities such as May Day (*Calan Mai*), Midsummer's Day, harvest time, Hallowe'en (*nos Galan Gaeaf*), Christmas, and New Year (see further BELTAINE; CALENDAR; SAMAIN).

With the exception of the clog dancing tradition, which has survived unbroken, dancing all but disappeared in Wales during the religious revivals of the Nonconformist Protestant denominations in the 18th, 19th, and early 20th centuries (see CHRISTIANITY), but regained popularity later in the 20th century. The Welsh Folk Dance Society was formed in 1949, in large part due to the efforts of Lois Blake, who researched and taught dancing after moving to Wales in the 1930s.

Details of the 'Llangadfan dances' were discovered in 1920 among the papers of Edward Jones (*c.* 1729–95). Lady Herbert Lewis provided information on the dance called 'Cadi ha'. Lois Blake also met a remarkable lady by the name of Margretta Thomas, from Nantgarw, southeast Glamorgan (MORGANNWG), who remembered the dances performed at fairs and festivals in that part of Wales.

Glyn T. Jones

DÁNTA GRÁDHA

Dánta Grádha was the title of a 1916 book by Irish scholar T. F. O'Rahilly (Tomás Ó Rathile) on IRISH-language love poetry. Gearóid Iarla (†1398) was the first recorded poet of Norman descent to compose poetry in Irish. Acquainted with both the French tradition of *amour courtois* and the Irish tradition of *bairdne* (bardic poetry), authors such as Gearóid Iarla were admirably placed for introducing COURTLY LOVE into Irish verse. Most foreign influence comes from English rather than French sources. For example, Riocard do Burc's *Fir na Fódla ar ndul d'éag* (The men of Ireland after dying) is a free adaptation of Ovid's *Non ego mendosos ausim defendere mores*, *Amores* 2.4.

Bilingual authors were at a distinct advantage in enriching the Gaelic literary tradition with the current trends in contemporary English verse. Members of the Gaelic aristocracy in both Ireland and Scotland (Alba) also turned their hands to amatory verse, in keeping with the prevailing fashion across western Europe. Understandably, the professional poets did not take kindly to outsiders invading their domain, and responded in kind. When they involved themselves in composing love poetry, however, they did so with a certain sense of irony and wordplay, love for them being much more of a game rather than a matter of life and death. While Eochaidh Ó hEódhasa's *Ionmholta malairt bhisigh* (Change for the better should be praised) is usually interpreted as a light-hearted lament for the decline of classical syllabic poetry, it is equally possible to interpret Ó hEódhasa as claiming that amatory verse was both easier and more profitable than formal eulogy. The poem was composed around the time of the marriage of Rudhraighe Ó Domhnaill to Bridget Fitzgerald in 1603.

Mícheál Mac Craith

DANUBE (DĀNUVIUS)

The Danube (Dānuvius) is the second longest river in Europe, coursing for slightly more than 2,800 km. It rises in the Black Forest in southwest Germany and flows through Austria, Slovakia, Hungary, Croatia, Serbia, Bulgaria, and Romania, where it meets the Black Sea.

Danubia in the Iron Age and Roman Times

The Greek historian Herodotus wrote in the 5th century BC that Danube, which he called the Ister, began in the land of the Celts (κελτοί *Keltoi*, 2.33). In the Iron Age (8th–1st century BC), the Upper Danube region was in the heartland of the Hallstatt and La Tène cultures, and many significant hill-forts and *oppida* (sing. oppidum) have been found on the banks of the river, such as Heuneburg, Manching, and Kelheim. Place-name evidence in the Danube region points to an ancient Celtic-speaking population, with places such as Vienna (*Vindobonā* 'White or fair settlement') and Passau (ancient *Boioduron* 'Oppidum of the Boii tribe)' bearing Celtic names. Most of the river-names in this region are also Celtic, such as the two headwaters Brigach and Breg (see Brigantes), the Inn, the Isar, and the Iller.

The Name

In Roman records, *Dānuvius* at first referred only to the upper course of the river, with *Ister* as the name of the lower Danube. Modern European language forms imply a Proto-Celtic *Dānouîo-, the same as the Welsh river-name *Donwy*. *Danube* is probably derived from the Indo-European word *deh$_2$nu-* 'river', from the root *deh$_2$-* 'flow', cf. Ossetian *don* 'water, river'.

Peter E. Busse and Caroline aan de Weil

DAVID, SAINT
See Dewi Sant.

DE CLARE, RICHARD

Richard De Clare (known as Strongbow, *c.* 1130–76) was a Norman nobleman. Two near-contemporary sources describe his involvement with Ireland (ÉRIU): GIRALDUS CAMBRENSIS wrote a history called *Expugnatio Hibernica* ('The Conquest of Ireland') in the 1180s, and there is an Old French *chanson de geste* entitled 'The Song of Dermot and the Earl', written between 1226 and 1230. According to these sources, De Clare contracted with Diarmait Mac Murchada (Anglicized as Dermot MacMurrough), exiled king of Leinster (LAIGIN), offering military assistance in return for Mac Murchada's daughter Aífe (modern Aoife, sometimes Anglicized as Eve). De Clare and Mac Murchada landed at Wexford in 1170. They managed to reconquer and hold Leinster. When Mac Murchada died the following year, Strongbow used both his marriage and his military might to establish himself as king of Leinster. Henry II, displeased with the *de facto* independent Norman kingdom that resulted, came to Ireland himself. De Clare acknowledged Henry as his overlord. County Clare in Ireland is named after Thomas de Clare, a younger relative.

Antone Minard

DE GABÁIL IN T-SÍDA

De Gabáil in t-Sída (Concerning the taking of the otherworld mound) is a brief Old IRISH text, in the Book of Leinster (LEBOR LAIGNECH). It throws light on the early development of several doctrines that find fuller expression in the longer later texts of the MYTHOLOGICAL CYCLE and Irish LEGENDARY HISTORY, including ideas about Ireland's supernatural race, the TUATH DÉ, the conquest of Ireland (ÉRIU) by the sons of MÍL ESPÁINE, and the nature and origin of the OTHERWORLD of the SÍD mounds.

In *De Gabáil in t-Sída* a flashback deep into the pre-mortal mythological age concerns the control of time by the inhabitants of the *síd* mounds, particularly Síd in Broga (i.e., Newgrange/BRUG NA BÓINNE). This story is intriguing when we consider that many of these prehistoric burial monuments incorporate alignments with astronomical calendar events such as the solstices and equinoxes. The burial shaft at Newgrange, in particular, is illuminated only at daybreak on the shortest day of the year and a few days before and after it. Thus the idea of tricky extension of a single day into eternity at this site had some four millennia of precedent behind it when the tale was written.

Among the medieval Irish literati, *De Gabáil in t-Sída* was counted as one of the *remscéla* (fore-tales) of TÁIN BÓ CUAILNGE.

John Carey and John T. Koch

DE HÍDE, DUBHGHLAS (DOUGLAS HYDE)

Dubhghlas de híde (Douglas Hyde; 1860–1949) was a pioneering scholar of the Irish language, literature, and history, and the first President of Ireland (ÉIRE). Hyde learned IRISH from the farmers in Co. Roscommon (Contae Ros Comáin). He was Professor of Modern Languages at the University of New Brunswick in Canada from 1891 to 1892. On returning to Ireland, he was appointed president of the National Literary Society, and his inaugural speech, 'The Necessity of De-Anglicising Ireland', which was published as a pamphlet, greatly influenced the burgeoning Gaelic movement. Hyde was subsequently appointed president of Conradh na Gaeilge (the Gaelic League) at its founding. Under Hyde's leadership, the League essentially steered Gaelic culture in Ireland for more than two decades.

In 1899, Hyde's very influential *Literary History of Ireland* was published, detailing Gaelic literature from the earliest times to the 18th century. Also in this year, Hyde served as president of the Irish Texts Society (Cumann na Scríbheann nGaedhilge). His play *Casadh an tSúgáin* (translated into English as *The Twisting of the Rope* by Lady Gregory) was performed by the Gaelic League's amateur dramatic society at the Gaiety Theatre, Baile Átha Cliath (Dublin), in 1901. It was the first dramatic work to be produced in Modern Irish (see Irish drama). With the assistance of W. B. Yeats and Lady Gregory, Hyde wrote a number of Irish plays over the next decade, tailoring them for production by activists.

Hyde served as a senator in Seanad Éireann (the Irish senate) from 1925 until 1938. When the redrafted Irish constitution of 1937 created the office of President, Hyde's nomination for the office was unanimously supported. Despite experiencing a stroke in 1940, he remained President until 1945.

Brian Ó Broin

DE VALERA, EAMON

Eamon de Valera (Irish Éamonn; 1882–1975) was, arguably, the most influential politician in 20th-century Ireland. One of the leaders of the Easter Rising and the Irish War of Independence (see Irish independence movement), he became the longest-serving Taoiseach (Prime Minister) of Dáil Éireann, the parliament of Saorstát na hÉireann (Irish Free State), holding office from 1932 until 1948 and again from 1951 to 1954. From 1959 until 1973, he served as Uachtarán na hÉireann, President of the Republic of Ireland. De Valera led Ireland on the road to independence and successfully negotiated its difficult early relationship with the United Kingdom.

Born Edward de Valera in New York on 14 October 1882, he came to Co. Limerick (Contae Luimnigh) in 1885 to be brought up by his grandmother. He changed his name to Éamonn when he joined Conradh na Gaeilge in 1908, marrying one of his Irish teachers, Sinéad Flanagan, in 1910. During the Easter Rising, de Valera was in charge of the third battalion of the Irish Volunteers, the last group to surrender to British troops in 1916. He was sentenced to death along with the other leaders, but not executed, probably because he had been born in the United States. As the only survivor, he quickly gained a prominent place in politics when released from prison in June 1917. De Valera escaped from prison in England, with the help of Michael Collins, to become Príomh Aire (president) of the first Dáil Éireann in April 1919. He spent most of the War of Independence in the United States raising support for the Dáil, but negotiated the truce that ended it on 11 July 1921.

Eamon de Valera served as both *taoiseach* (prime minister) and *uachtarán* (president) of Ireland. (Library of Congress)

De Valera's rise to political power in the Free State began with his resignation in 1926 from Sinn Féin and the foundation of his own party, Fianna Fáil. It won the general election of 1932, ushering in his long term as Taoiseach. De Valera then set about realizing his vision of a truly free Ireland, removing the oath of allegiance (to the English Crown) and the office of (the British) Governor General. In 1937, he introduced a new constitution, Bunreacht na hÉireann, which, among other things, changed the name of the country to Éire, gave both Irish and English official status, claimed jurisdiction over the whole island, and laid the foundations for the Irish Republic, which was declared in 1949. The period after the war saw him hard at work raising Éire's international profile and preparing the ground for the country's entry to the European Economic Council (now the European Union) in 1972.

Marion Löffler

DEAN OF LISMORE, BOOK OF THE

The Book of the Dean of Lismore is the most important manuscript of late medieval Gaelic poetry in Scotland (Alba). Compiled between the years 1512 and 1526, primarily by the brothers Seamus MacGriogair (James MacGregor, the eponymous Dean) and Donnchadh MacGriogair, the work represents an effort of collection begun the generation before by Fionnlagh Mac an Aba. The manuscript contains not only Gaelic poetry, transliterated into an orthography based on Lowland Scots, but also poetry and prose in Scots, and some material in Latin.

The Book is omnivorous in its approach to verse. Alongside classical Irish poetry of the highest order, both from Scotland and Ireland (Éire), we have grimly scatological material, affecting love poetry in the courtly mode, heroic BALLADS, philosophical pieces, and allegories. The Dean's Book also includes poetry by at least four women, which must be balanced by the dedicated misogyny of other items.

Thomas Owen Clancy

DEER, BOOK OF

The Book of Deer is an insular gospel book, probably originally copied and illustrated in the 9th or 10th century, that was present in the religious community of Deer, in Buchan, northeast Scotland (ALBA), by the 11th century. The illustrations are in a calligraphic, cartoon-like style. Other contents beside the incomplete gospels include a liturgy for the anointing of the sick and dying, of a sort found in Ireland (ÉRIU) in the company of gospel books, which has suggested a relationship between these books and aspects of pastoral care. The most discussed aspect of the Book of Deer, however, is its collection of property records, dating from the early 12th century, the latest from *c.* 1150, the earliest set being retrospective, and recording grants dating back to the 10th century. With one exception, these records are in the vernacular, and reveal some emergent signs of a local Scottish dialect of GAELIC.

Thomas Owen Clancy

DERDRIU/DEIRDRE

Derdriu/Deirdre was the focus of the tragic love triangle involving the hero Noísiu mac Uislenn and CONCHOBAR, king of ULAID. The earliest version of this tale is the Old Irish LONGAS MAC NUISLENN ('The Exile of the Sons of Uisliu'), which provides background to the central saga TÁIN BÓ CUAILNGE. Derdriu is discussed in this context in ULSTER CYCLE OF TALES. The tale of Derdriu remained popular in Early Modern Gaelic, which accounts for the popularity of the name Deirdre today. On the 18th-century Irish *Imeacht Dheirdre le Naoise* (The elopement of Deirdre with Noísiu), see IRISH LITERATURE, POST-CLASSICAL. An oral Scottish Gaelic version was collected by Alexander Carmichael. The demythologized *Deirdre of the Sorrows* by the playwright J. M. Synge (1871–1909; see ANGLO-IRISH LITERATURE) was first performed in 1910. The name *Derdriu* is explained in *Longas Mac nUislenn* as the unborn girl is heard crying out from her mother's womb, 'It is well that the child may cry (*ro-derdrestar*)'. This verb is otherwise unattested, but the meaning is clear in context; it is probably related to Old Irish *dord* 'a noise, murmuring'.

John T. Koch

DESCRIPTIO KAMBRIAE

Descriptio Kambriae ('The Description of Wales') is a portrayal of contemporary Welsh social life and mores by Gerald of Wales (GIRALDUS CAMBRENSIS), written in Latin in 1194. Gerald gives a résumé of Welsh history and then portrays the qualities of the Welsh. Although he strives to be objective, his Welsh sympathies are unmistakable.

Given that Gerald set considerable store by the value of political PROPHECY, it is significant that the work ends with the prophecy of 'the old man of Pencader' to Henry II, which claims that the Welsh, and none other, will be answerable for this piece of land on Judgement Day. The *Descriptio* is unique as a consciously written description of contemporary Welsh custom, manners, and society. It reveals Gerald at his disciplined best as a writer. Although he wrote as an experienced observer of Welsh life, however, he sometimes misinterprets what he sees, and the formal, rhetorical pattern that he chose for his book occasionally leads him to overemphasize some features. As a result, his description must be used with care.

Brynley F. Roberts

DEVOLUTION AND THE CELTIC COUNTRIES

Devolution is the term used to describe the decentralization of political powers. The six modern CELTIC COUNTRIES all experienced increasingly centralized control from London or Paris over the course of their history, from the twelfth-century Norman conquest of parts of Ireland (ÉIRE) and Wales (CYMRU) to the dissolution of the Breton parliament in 1789. Within Celtic studies, the term is primarily used in relation to the constituent countries of the United Kingdom.

Calls for some form of home rule began in Ireland almost immediately following the ACT OF UNION (although the term 'home rule' emerged only later), but actual devolution of powers began later in the 19th century. The Scottish Office (1885) was the first new governmental body with a remit specifically for one nation of the United Kingdom. The Partition of Ireland resulted in the creation of a Northern Irish parliament in 1921, and the Welsh Office was created only in 1965. Both the Welsh and Scottish offices were dissolved in 1999, with their powers transferring to the Welsh Assembly (see CYNULLIAD CENEDLAETHOL CYMRU) and the SCOTTISH PARLIAMENT, respectively. The situation continues to evolve both within the context of the United Kingdom and within the European Union.

Antone Minard

DEWI SANT (ST DAVID)

Dewi Sant (St David) is the patron saint of Wales (CYMRU). A Life, composed in Latin by RHYGYFARCH in the late 11th century, has been seen as an apologia for the antiquity, orthodoxy, and independence of the church and cult of Dewi in the face of the advancing Normans. It tells of the conflict and miracle surrounding the birth, youth, and ministry of Dewi. Dewi's education took him to Henfynyw (near Aberaeron in Ceredigion), and then to the teacher Paulinus (probably not the Northumbrian apostle). He and his companions followed a life of extreme austerity, dividing their time between worship, study, and toil, eschewing the use of draught animals to till the fields, and living on a meat-free diet of bread, herbs, and water. Dewi's sobriquet of *Aquaticus* (Welsh Dyfrwr) is probably due not only to his diet but also to his daily habit of standing up to his neck in cold water to subdue the flesh. In company with two companions, Teilo and Padarn, he was urged in a vision to go to Jerusalem, where the Patriarch made him archbishop and bestowed gifts on the three; Dewi's gifts included a tunic, a bell, and a portable altar. After his return he was summoned to Llanddewi Brefi to address a synod of bishops called to defend the church against the Pelagian heresy (see PELAGIUS). Here, the ground is said to have risen under Dewi's feet so that he could be heard by all present, and a dove, the symbol of the Holy Spirit, rested on his shoulder. Dewi died on Tuesday, 1 March, between 588 and 602 AD. The name *Dewi* reflects an early borrowing into Brythonic of the biblical name *David*.

J. Wyn Evans

DIARMAID UA DUIBHNE

Diarmaid ua Duibhne is an Irish legendary figure best known through stories of his elopement with Gráinne, the betrothed of FINN MAC CUMAILL (see FIANNAÍOCHT; TÓRUIGHEACHT DHIARMADA AGUS GHRÁINNE). Diarmaid had a *ball seirce* (love spot) that made him irresistible to women. Gráinne, daughter of CORMAC MAC AIRT, the legendary king of Tara (TEAMHAIR), drugged the celebrants at her wedding to Fionn and put Diarmaid under a GEIS (sworn promise) to elope with her. The enraged Fionn and the Fianna (war-band) pursued the pair for 16 years before making peace. Years later, while hunting with the Fianna, Diarmaid was gored by a boar and left to die by Fionn.

Brian Ó Broin

DICTIONARIES AND GRAMMARS, BRETON

The earliest BRETON lexicography, as in the other CELTIC LANGUAGES, is in the form of occasional Old Breton glosses of Latin words found from the 9th century onward (see BRETON LITERATURE). The function of these glosses, however, was utilitarian rather than systematic, and the first serious attempt to record the Breton language in a form useful for non-Breton speakers was the late medieval *Catholicon*, a trilingual Breton–French–Latin dictionary, first printed at the end of the 15th century. In 1659 Julian Maunoir (1606–83) published a Breton catechism that included a Breton dictionary and grammar. Louis Le Pelletier (1663–1733) and Jean-François Le Gonidec (1775–1838) were important lexicographers of the period; both produced grammars, along with their dictionaries, and Le Gonidec also published Breton manuscripts.

   The codification of Breton has been beset from the beginning by difficulties of orthography, both in representing the sounds of the language where divergent from Latin and French, and in representing the BRETON DIALECTS where divergent from each other. Both Le Pelletier and Le Gonidec used a Breton alphabetical order where the sounds of the letters determined their placement, following the traditional Latin order. As set out in *Yezhadur bras ar brezhoneg* (The big grammar of Breton), it is A B K D E F G H CH C'H I Y J L M N O P R S T U V W Z. This arrangement has largely been superseded by one that conforms more closely to the conventional order of the letters, regardless of sound: A B CH C'H D E F G H I J K L M N O P R S T U V W Y Z. In 1744 Abbé Armeyrie published a Breton dictionary based on the dialect of Vannes. The controversy over which dialect(s) to represent, and which spelling system with which to represent it (them), has not been solved. The best guide to the diversity of Breton is Francis Favereau's 1997 dictionary and grammar, which uses the International Phonetic Alphabet to indicate the pronunciation in various dialects.

Most Breton dictionaries and grammars have been aimed at a French-speaking audience, but as early as 1903 J. Percy Treasure published an English-language grammar of Breton in Wales (Cymru), and many of the publications dealing with Old and Middle Breton have been in English. The most important introduction to Middle Breton, Henry Lewis and J. R. F. Piette's *Llawlyfr Llydaweg Canol* (Handbook of Middle Breton), first published in 1922, has been reprinted in Welsh and translated into German with additions and corrections, but has never been published in English or French. The late 1980s and 1990s saw the beginning of a wider interest in the Breton language, with dictionaries in German, Irish, Spanish, Welsh, and a number in English becoming available. Also in this period, Yann Lagadeg and Martial Ménard published the first monolingual dictionary of modern Breton, *Geriadur brezhoneg gant skoueriou*. This period, too, has witnessed an increase in the user-friendliness of the dictionaries. Keys to pronunciation, usage, and grammar, which were absent or sparse in the early dictionaries designed for people living in Breton-speaking areas, are now becoming standard.

Websites

http://www.lexilogos.com/breton_langue_dictionnaires.htm
http://br.wiktionary.org/wiki/Degemer

Antone Minard

DICTIONARIES AND GRAMMARS, CORNISH

Manuscript Glossaries

The earliest Cornish lexicon is the Old Cornish Vocabularium cornicum, an adaptation of Ælfric's Old English–Latin glossary. It was followed, half a millennium later, by several antiquarian glossaries, including Edward Lhuyd's MS notebook, which accompanied him on his travels to Cornwall (NLW, Llanstephan 84) and which later supplied some of the material for the published vocabulary (1707).

Printed Dictionaries

The earliest printed dictionary of Cornish was compiled by Lhuyd and his team from evidence gathered from his field-trip to Cornwall (Kernow) in 1700 and from copies he had made of several of the Middle Cornish texts. This material was published in Lhuyd's *Archæologia Britannica* in 1707, as 'A Comparative Vocabulary of the Original Languages of Britain and Ireland'.

The first attempt at a historical dictionary of Cornish was the *Lexicon Cornu-Britannicum* of Canon Robert Williams, published in parts between 1861 and 1865. This work cites examples from the Cornish plays, with references and cognates from the other Celtic languages.

Robert Morton Nance, who inherited Henry Jenner's rôle as the leader of the Cornish language revival (see LANGUAGE [REVIVAL] MOVEMENTS IN THE CELTIC COUNTRIES), devoted years of study to the entire known corpus of CORNISH LITERATURE, culminating in his much condensed *Gerlyver Noweth Kernewek ha Sawsnek: A New Cornish–English Dictionary* of 1938, a much more comprehensive counterpart to his earlier *English–Cornish Dictionary* (Nance & Smith, 1934). Although much smaller than Williams's *Lexicon*, the 1938 dictionary remains an indispensable work, marred only by the inclusion of many unmarked conjectural forms based on Welsh or BRETON. Much useful lexical information is contained in Oliver Padel's important *Cornish Place-Name Elements* (1985).

Recent Dictionaries

There has been something of a spate of Cornish dictionaries recently, partly encouraged by the internal divisions within the revival movement that have spawned several orthographical systems, necessitating their respective dictionaries. The proponents of Kernewek Kemmyn (Common Cornish) have produced two new dictionaries based on a reappraisal of the existing texts, but retaining most of the semantic information from Nance's dictionaries. George's 'Gerlyver Meur' Cornish–English version (1993) is the most useful for scholarly purposes, as it gives an indication of attestation and occurrence (see N. J. A. Williams, *Cornish Studies*, 2nd ser. 9.247–311), and his 'Gerlyver Kres' is a condensed two-way version (1998). Richard Gendall has produced a series of dictionaries based exclusively on his extensive study of the evidence of the Modern period of the language and the Cornish survivals in the English dialect of Cornwall, with brief details of attestation. Nicholas Williams (2000) has produced the most comprehensive English–Cornish dictionary published to date (with online addenda, including the new evidence from BEUNANS KE), based on his own 'Unified Cornish Revised' version of the language.

Grammars

Lhuyd was the first to systematically describe the grammar of Cornish in his *Archaeologia Britannica* (pp. 222–53), which forms the basis for a number of subsequent works. Edwin Norris reappraised the grammar in his *Sketch of Cornish Grammar*, which is more commonly found as part of *The Ancient Cornish Drama*, his edition of the ORDINALIA and VOCABULARIUM CORNICUM. Henry Jenner attempted to simplify the grammar of (predominately) Modern Cornish in his *A Handbook of the Cornish Language* for those interested in learning the language in the early days of the revival movement; his effort marked the beginning of a long tradition of revivalist grammatical works, which generally tend to simplify and generalize. Henry Lewis published the standard grammar of Middle Cornish in 1923, with a substantially revised edition appearing in 1946. Smith's *Cornish Simplified* contains much useful information, although primarily intended for learners of Revived Cornish. Wella Brown's *A Grammar of Modern Cornish* is the most comprehensive grammar of the revived language, but Lewis's *Llawlyfr* remains the standard scholarly work.

Andrew Hawke

DICTIONARIES AND GRAMMARS, IRISH

Dictionaries

For approximately a thousand years IRISH lexicographers concerned themselves with the words of their own language, which they explained in monolingual GLOSSARIES, often with etymologies. The earliest of these works is O'Mulconry's Glossary (*Descriptio de Origine Scoticae Linguae*), written between AD 650 and 750. Other early medieval Irish glossaries include the famous SANAS CHORMAIC of *c.* 900.

In the modern period, the Irish Franciscans in Louvain published Micheál Ó Cléirigh's *Foclōir nō Sanasán Nua* (1643), a traditional glossary. In 1662, another Franciscan, Risdeard Pluincéad, completed a large manuscript Latin–Irish dictionary in the friary of Trim (Baile Átha Troim). It was borrowed by the Welsh linguist and scholar Edward LHUYD for use in the first Irish–English dictionary, included in Lhuyd's *Archaeologia Britannica* (1707), and in the 'Comparative Vocabulary' section of the same.

The most notable dictionary of the 19th century was created by Edward O'Reilly and first published in 1817. One of the subsequent editions included a supplement of archaic manuscript words brought out by John O'Donovan in 1877.

The first published dictionary to do justice to the spoken language was that of Fr. Patrick S. Dinneen (Pádraig Ua Duinnín) in 1904; a much-extended version appeared in 1927, published by the Irish Texts Society. This volume remains the most useful dictionary to scholars and readers of 18th- and 19th-century literature. In 1957, An Gúm (the Department of Education) produced an English–Irish dictionary that provided much-required technical vocabulary, but it ignored the existence of dialect and register. This edition has since been supplemented by several technical dictionaries, and work on its replacement has been begun by FORAS NA GAEILGE.

In 1975, the Royal Irish Academy (Acadamh Ríoga na hÉireann) concluded its (*Contributions to a*) *Dictionary of the Irish Language* (DIL), the first volume of which was edited in 1913 by Karl Marstrander. This large historical citation dictionary, which is based mainly on Old and Middle Irish materials, represented a momentous advance in Irish lexicography.

In 1978, work began on a similar project for Modern Irish—*An Foclóir Nua-Ghaeilge*—with Tomás de Bhaldraithe as general editor. The project has been badly under-resourced, and is currently confined to compiling a machine-readable corpus of Modern Irish to be published on CD-ROM.

DIALECT DICTIONARIES. See lists at the following websites:
www.ria.ie/projects/fng/index.html
www.celt.dias.ie/publications/cat/cat_e.html#E.4

Websites
www.focloir.ie
www.ria.ie/projects/fng/index.html
www.celt.dias.ie/publications/cat/cat_e.html#F.4

Grammars

AURAICEPT NA NÉCES ('The Scholars' Primer'), the earliest IRISH grammar, belongs to the Old Irish period, possibly dating back as early as the 7th century. It was later augmented by commentary.

Following earlier efforts, H. Mac Curtin (Aodh Buidhe Mac Cruitín) published an Irish grammar in English in Lovain in 1728. The first really useful grammar for a learner of Irish, it was plagiarized from Froinsias Bhailis, OFM, lexicographer, who had completed it in 1713. This work was republished in 1732.

In 1808, William Neilson published his *Introduction to the Irish Language*, which dealt with Ulster Irish, and William Halliday published his *Uraicecht na Gaedhilge: A Grammar of the Gaelic Language*. These texts were followed in 1809 by the Revd Paul O'Brien's *A Practical Grammar of the Irish Language*. In 1845, John O'Donovan published *A Grammar of the Irish Language*, which attempts to deal with all periods from Middle Irish to modern dialects.

The 20th century saw grammars intended for schools, notably by the Christian Brothers, who first published *Graiméar na Gaedhilge* in 1901. Also of note are the work of Fr. Gerald O'Nolan and the syntactical studies of Cormac Ó Cadhlaigh. In 1945, the spelling of Irish was reformed and the principles published in *Litriú na Gaeilge* by Rannóg an Aistriúcháin. In 1958, a standard grammar, *Gramadach na Gaeilge agus Litriú na Gaeilge: An Caighdeán Oifigiúil*, followed, which was intended to be taught in schools and used in Government publications.

Stair na Gaeilge, edited by K. McCone and others, contains the most useful grammars of Middle, Classical, and Post-classical Irish and modern dialects.

In Early Irish, Johann Kaspar Zeuss extracted from the study of Old Irish and other Celtic GLOSSES his *Grammatica Celtica* (1853). In 1908, J. Vendryès produced *Grammaire du vieil-irlandais*. In 1909, Rudolf Thurneysen published his *Handbuch des Alt-Irischen*, with a revised edition appearing in English in 1944 as *A Grammar of Old Irish*; this work remains the indispensable Old Irish grammar.

Seán Ua Súilleabháin

DICTIONARIES AND GRAMMARS, MANX

Although the MANX Gaelic corpus includes texts dating to the 17th century, the first printed work did not appear until 1707. Given this fact, it is not surprising that the earliest Manx dictionaries and grammars were not published until the beginning of the 19th century. One of the first grammars was produced by John Kelly, whose *A Practical Grammar of the Antient Gael[i]c; or Language of the Isle of Mann, Usually Called Manks* was published in 1804. Kelly's Manx–English dictionary was not published until 1866 in the Manx Society's series of publications, edited by the Reverends Gill and Clarke.

The first half of the 19th century also saw the production of what has become the seminal Manx–English dictionary. Compiled by Archibald Cregeen and published on the Isle of Man (ELLAN VANNIN) in 1835, it was regularly reprinted throughout the 20th century.

With the founding of Yn Cheshaght Ghailckagh, the Manx Language Society, in 1899, antiquarian activity focused once more on Manx Gaelic. Edmund Goodwin's *Lessoonyn ayns Chengey ny Mayrey Ellan Vannin* (1901) was reprinted as *First Lessons in Manx* (1947) and later revised by Thomson. It continues to be regarded as one of the most important primers for the language. Until John Joseph (J. J.) Kneen's *A Grammar of the Manx Language* (1931), written in 1909–10 with the assistance of Professors E. C. Quiggin and Carl Marstrander, Goodwin's slim volume remained the first point of grammatical reference. Kneen's work on the language continued, with this author producing a further volume on Manx Gaelic usage, *Manx Idioms and Phrases* (1938), and, in conjunction with the *Mona's Herald* newspaper, an *English–Manx Pronouncing Dictionary* (1938).

The latter half of the 20th century saw significant developments in the publication of reference books for Manx Gaelic. *Fargher's English–Manx Dictionary* (1979) was originally intended in the 1950s as a Manx–English dictionary combining the work of Kelly and Cregeen with a reverse of Kneen's dictionary.

George Broderick's study of the spoken language of the last native Manx speakers resulted in a three-volume work published by Niemeyer (1984–86), *A Handbook of Late Spoken Manx*. This work comprises a grammar, a dictionary, and phonology.

Phil Kelly, Manx Language Officer for the Department of Education, together with Mike Boulton and F. Craine, produced a reverse of *Fargher's Dictionary* (1991), which was revised and reprinted by Kelly in 1993. It was accompanied by a two-volume *Manx Usage* in 1993.

Website
www.embedded-systems.ltd.uk/ManxStart.html

Breesha Maddrell

DICTIONARIES AND GRAMMARS, SCOTTISH GAELIC

The first major dictionary to mention the SCOTTISH GAELIC language is that of Edward LHUYD, the well-known Celtic polymath. In 1707, when he published *Archaeologia Britannica,* he included an IRISH–English dictionary and, as an Appendix to it, added a number of words from Scottish Gaelic. Robert Kirk published several word lists in 1702, and by so doing provided subsequent dictionary makers with some source materials and effectively founded the history of GAELIC dictionary making.

The first dictionary was published in Edinburgh (DÙN ÈIDEANN) by Alexander McDonald (Alistair MacDomhnuill) as a 'Gaelic and English Vocabulary'. This work appeared in 1741 and was taken from a school dictionary intended to provide instruction in English and Latin. McDonald retained the English and substituted Gaelic for the Latin. The work is organized into sections on general semantic categories, in parallel columns and with no alphabetization of either column, in a total of 161 pages.

A total of nine Gaelic–English dictionaries appeared over the late 18th and 19th centuries, and the culmination of this lexicographical activity was the Gaelic–English dictionary of Edward Dwelly that appeared in 1909. Dwelly's work has served as the reference point for all subsequent smaller dictionaries, as he included materials from most preceding works. It also includes a 'summary of a concise Gaelic grammar'—there have been few published separate grammars until very recently with *Gràmar na Gàidhlig*.

The paucity of new terminology has long been a bane of Gaelic, and several attempts have been made to counter this shortcoming, with the most recent being *Faclair na Pàrlamaid*/Dictionary of Terms (www.scotland.gov.uk/ dictionary/_bin/).

Website
www.scotland.gov.uk/dictionary/_bin/

Cathair Ó Dochartaigh

DICTIONARIES AND GRAMMARS, WELSH

The first printed Welsh dictionary was a Welsh–English dictionary, *A Dictionary in Englyshe and Welshe* (1547), by William Salesbury. Three grammars were published during the 16th century, two of which were written in Latin.

The greatest Welsh scholar until modern days was John Davies (*c.* 1567–1644) of Mallwyd, editor of the 1620 Bible, whose grammar (in Latin) (1621) and Welsh–Latin Latin–Welsh dictionary (1632) are among the most influential works of Welsh scholarship. John Roderick (Siôn Rhydderch, 1673–1735), the almanac-maker, published the first English–Welsh dictionary (1725), along with a grammar written in Welsh (1728). William Gambold (1672–1728) published the first Welsh grammar written in English in 1727; an unpublished English–Welsh dictionary was used by John Walters (1721–97) in the compilation of his comprehensive English–Welsh dictionary (1770–94), which, directly or indirectly, served as a major influence on all subsequent English–Welsh dictionaries.

The greatest influence on 19th-century Welsh was William Owen Pughe (1759–1835), the knowledgeable but incredibly idiosyncratic editor of a Welsh–English dictionary (1793–1803) and grammar (1803). D. Silvan Evans (1818–1903) edited a large two-volume English–Welsh dictionary (1847–58), and a historical Welsh–English dictionary (1887–1906), which, however, reached only the word *ennyd*.

Edward Anwyl (1866–1914) and his brother, J. Bodvan Anwyl (1875–1949), revised William Spurrell's Welsh–English (1848) and English–Welsh dictionaries (1850). These and later revisions were the standard dictionaries of the first half of the 20th century and remain valuable to this day. The work of O. H. Fynes-Clinton (1869–1941) on *The Welsh Vocabulary of the Bangor District* (1913) represented a milestone in the study of Welsh phonetics and lexis.

Grammatical activity flourished during the 20th century. The most important grammar was undoubtedly John Morris-Jones's historical and comparative grammar of 1913, even though it dealt only with phonology and 'accidence' (morphology). The most important subsequent grammars were those of Stephen J. Williams (1896–1992) on standard Modern Welsh and D. Simon Evans (1921–98) on Middle Welsh.

The second half of the century saw the publication of work on previously unstudied topics, covering a broader range of varieties and registers of Welsh, and the use of new methods and models of linguistics. Especially noteworthy among these efforts are *Ieithyddiaeth* (Linguistics, 1961) by T. Arwyn Watkins, and Ceinwen H. Thomas's phonology, grammar, and glossary of her native dialect of Nantgarw in southeast Glamorgan (Morgannwg, 1993), with the glossary bearing comparison with that of Fynes-Clinton.

The last two decades have seen the production of electronic dictionaries and spelling-checkers and the completion of two of the most important and influential projects in the history of the Welsh language: *The Welsh Academy English–Welsh Dictionary* (1995) and *Geiriadur Prifysgol Cymru/A Dictionary of the Welsh Language* ([GPC] 1950–2002), the standard historical Welsh dictionary. In addition, a third standard work published in recent times is Peter Wynn Thomas's Welsh grammar (1996).

Website
www.geiriadur.net

Gareth A. Bevan

DINAS EMRYS

Dinas Emrys is a craggy hilltop with ruined FORTIFICATIONS that rises about 70 m above the Glaslyn valley in north Wales (Cymru), from which forces controlled one of the main routes into Snowdonia (Eryri) from the south. The occupation debris is of mixed date, including late Roman and early post-Roman material.

Giraldus Cambrensis refers to *Dynas Emereis* (Citadel of Ambrosius) in north Wales in his *Itinerarium Kambriae* (1191). In the Middle Welsh mythological tale Cyfranc Lludd a Llefelys, *Dinas Emreis* figures as the place where the slumbering dragons were entombed in Britain's remote pre-Roman past (see also Draig Goch); the earliest surviving variant is in the 9th-century Welsh Latin Historia Brittonum. In this source, the place is said to be in Snowdonia (Old Welsh Heriri).

John T. Koch

DINDSHENCHAS

The Irish term *dindshenchas* (also *dindṡenchas*), later *dinnsheanchas*, means 'lore of high places'. Some of the lore clearly began as mythology—for example, the list of landscape features at the end of Táin Bó Cuailnge ('The Cattle Raid of Cooley'). Many of the stories deal with mythological traditions and the people of the síd (a fairy rath or fort). There are far more allusions to the Ulster Cycle and the Finn mac Cumaill Cycle (Fiannaíocht) than to the Kings' Cycle. However, some saints appear—for example, Colum Cille in the stories of *Coire Breccáin* and *Ailech*, and Patrick in those of *Sliab Fuait*, *Brí Graige*, *Findloch Cera*, and *Tailtiu*. Many of the *dindshenchas* poems also end with religious quatrains praising the coming of Christianity.

After their 8th year of study, Irish poets were expected to be able to narrate all the traditional stories and explain the origin of place-names. An early story tells how Mongán mac Fiachna embarrassed his father's poet, Eochu Rígéigeas, for exclaiming: '*Sochaide lasa ndéntar rátha co nach talla for menmain*', 'So many build castles . . . that they do not all find room in the memory'.

A Mac Liacc († AD 1016) is one of the named authors of *dindshenchas* poems, along with Cinaed ua hArtacáin (†974) and Cúan ua Lothcháin (†1024). A collection made in the 11th century appears in many important Irish manuscripts, and has been edited in five volumes by Edward Gwynn. In addition, anonymous prose pieces are available on many of the names, edited from collections in different manuscripts by Whitley Stokes. It is evident that later recensions were intended to include both verse and prose. Bowen lists articles on 218 different names, some of which are paralleled in surviving tales. The explanations are sometimes stories, sometimes etymological.

Stories based on place-names continued in Irish oral tradition in modern times. An example from Donegal (Tír Chonaill) explains *Loch Finne, Mín-an-áil,* and *Loch Muc* from the hunt for a monster sow, and a story from Co. Down (Contae an Dúin) includes the English house-name Mount Panther among place-names commemorating the chase of a magic cat.

Place-name lore analogous to Irish *dindshenchas* is also a feature of early Welsh literature. Many names are given explanatory stories or etymologies in, for example, the 9th-century Welsh Latin HISTORIA BRITTONUM and the Middle Welsh tales of the MABINOGI.

Kay Muhr

DĪS PATER

Dīs Pater was a Roman god of wealth and the underworld, the realm of the dead, and was identified with Pluto. In *De Bello Gallico* (6.18), Caesar stated that all the Gauls believed that they were descended from Dīs Pater, as was taught to them by the DRUIDS. The Latin word *dīs* has two meanings: 'the rich one' or 'deity'. It is unclear which of the Gaulish gods Caesar meant here. Mythological figures attested in inscriptions who *might* match the identification are Sucellus and Smertrius. In Irish tradition, the supernatural Donn mac Míled, who figures in LEGENDARY HISTORY as the first of the ancestral Gaels to die in Ireland and as the keeper of the house of the dead *Tech Duinn* (Donn's house), is a comparable figure (see also LEBAR GABÁLA; MÍL ESPÁINE).

Peter E. Busse

DOMNONIA

Domnonia is the name of an early Breton polity whose rulers were viewed as kings (*reges*) by some Breton sources, but as counts (*comites*) by the Merovingian Franks. Its best-documented ruler is IUDICHAEL from the first half of the 7th century. Domnonia comprised roughly the northern half of Brittany (BREIZH). The name traces back to the tribe known as *Dumnonii* (< Celtic *dubno-/dumno-* 'deep, the world'), who also gave their name to Devon (Welsh *Dyfnaint*). It is likely that British and Armorican DUMNONIA functioned at times as a single sea-divided sub-Roman *civitas* and then as an early medieval kingdom. Another British tribe and Romano-British *civitas*, the *Cornovii*, gave its name both to southwest Brittany (*Cornouaille*/Kernev) and to the territory west of Devon (Cornwall/Kernow). Domnonia is mentioned in the Life of St UUINUUALOE 1.1 as 'a country notorious for its sacrileges, unlawful feastings and adulteries'. Unlike the long-lived Kernev, Domnonia was not significant in the political or diocesan divisions of Brittany after the early Middle Ages.

Antone Minard

DÔN

Dôn is the ancestor of the central characters in the Middle Welsh tale known as MATH FAB MATHONWY of the MABINOGI, ARIANRHOD, and GWYDION. In the early Welsh ARTHURIAN prose tale CULHWCH AC OLWEN, Dôn is named as the mother of the supernatural ploughman Amaethon mab Don (< *Ambaχtonos* 'ploughman-god') and the supernatural smith Gouannon mab Don (< *Gobannonos* 'smith-god'). In the early 11th-century Breton Latin Life of St IUDIC-HAEL, the legendary poet TALIESIN also figures as the son of Dôn. BELI MAWR had perhaps figured as Dôn's consort.

Dôn is sometimes linked with the goddess of the river DANUBE, but these equations are phonetically unworkable: A cognate of Middle Irish *Danu*, BRITISH **Donū* or **Danū* would necessarily give Welsh ****Dyn* or ***Dein*. The name may mean 'earth'; Welsh *Dôn* occurs only as semantic genitive, mostly preceded immediately by *merch* 'daughter', *mab* 'son', or *plant* 'children'. Thus *Plant Dôn* as 'Children of the Earth' would be parallel to a second great mythological family in the Mabinogi—namely, the children of LLŶR; cf. Old Irish *ler*, genitive *lir* 'sea'. They would also be comparable to the Titans of Hesiod, who were likewise 'children of the earth' and primeval beings of the mythical age. Such a name would originally have resonated meaningfully with the COMMON CELTIC word for 'human being', **(g)donios* (lit. 'earthling'), from whence came Irish *duine*, Welsh *dyn*, and Breton *den*.

John T. Koch

DRAIG GOCH

The Draig Goch (Red Dragon) is the national symbol of Wales (CYMRU). Its four-legged, barb-tailed, winged image is found on the Welsh flag, established as such in 1959. Dragons were already popular Roman military emblems in late antiquity; GILDAS refers to MAELGWN as *insularis draco* (dragon of the isle). Early WELSH POETRY identifies dragons with the virtues of warriors and leaders. The red dragon appears as a symbol of Brythonic identity in the story of GWRTHEYRN'S castle in the early 9th-century HISTORIA BRITTONUM, in which a red dragon defeats a white one. GEOFFREY OF MONMOUTH closely associated ARTHUR with dragons. By the mid-15th century, the sons of Owain Tudor were employing the red dragon as heraldic devices, and Henry Tudor used a red dragon on a green and white field as one of his battle standards at the Battle of Bosworth in 1485 (see TUDUR).

Victoria Simmons

DRUIDS, ACCOUNTS FROM CLASSICAL AUTHORS

Druids as Philosophers

We have no written accounts by the pre-Christian druids describing their own beliefs or system of learning. They figure as one subgroup within a threefold distinction of Celtic men of learning in Diodorus Siculus (5.31), probably deriving from Posidonius:

> They have lyric poets called bards, who, accompanied by instruments resembling lyres, sing both praise and satire. They have highly honoured philosophers and theologians [those who speak about the gods] called druids. They also make use of seers, who are greatly respected.

The druidic role as prophet is also widely attested. Lucan (*Pharsalia* 1.450–58) tells specifically of a druidic doctrine of an afterlife in an OTHERWORLD; see also GREEK AND ROMAN ACCOUNTS.

Druidic Science and Natural Magic

The idea that the druids maintained the Celtic CALENDAR and understood the workings of the cosmos is widespread among the classical writers.

A number of details occur uniquely in the *Natural History* of Pliny—druidical beliefs regarding medicinal plants, their uses, and various harvesting rituals, including the great reverence for mistletoe and the oak trees on which it grew and the elaborate rite in gathering it:

> [T]hey lead forward two white bulls with horns bound for the first time. A priest in white clothing climbs the tree and cuts the mistletoe with a golden sickle, and it is caught in a white cloak. They then sacrifice the bulls while praying that the god will grant the gift of prosperity to those to whom he has given it. They believe that mistletoe, when taken in a drink, will restore fertility to barren animals, and is a remedy for all poisons. (*Natural History* 16.24)

Druids as Judges

Caesar (*De Bello Gallico* 6.16) emphasizes the judicial function of the druids. Interestingly, he states that execution of criminals and sacrifice of captives were functionally interchangeable, in that both practices were believed to please the gods. Dīviciācos of the Aedui was both a *vergobretos* or supreme tribal magistrate and a druid.

Druids as Historians

Regarding the druidic doctrine of the origins of the peoples of Gaul preserved by Ammianus Marcellinus (15.9), see LEGENDARY HISTORY, GAUL (cf. BELGAE; FLOOD

LEGENDS). Another origin legend ascribed to the druids is that the Gauls were all descended from the god corresponding to the Roman DĪS PATER, god of death and the underworld, according to Caesar (*De Bello Gallico* 6.18).

The Status of Druids

According to Caesar, the status of the druids was comparable to that of the *equites* of Gaul—approximately 'the warrior aristocracy'. The picture of an élite status, free from the usual obligations and limitations of a Gaulish tribesman, is further enhanced by Caesar's description of the druids' annual assembly, implying that this group's members represented a learned and judicial class that transcended tribal divisions:

> At a certain time of the year they sit down in a consecrated place in the territory of the Carnutes [around modern Chartres, France], which region is believed to be the centre of all Gaul. To this place all come from everywhere who have disputes and the Druids bring forth their resolutions and decisions. (*De Bello Gallico* 6.13)

Druids in Britain

According to Caesar (*De Bello Gallico* 6.13):

> It is believed the training for druids was discovered in Britain and from there it was transferred into Gaul. And now those who wish to learn the matter carefully depart for Britain for the sake of learning.

In the next century, the British druids of Anglesey (MôN) were perceived by the Romans as an anti-Roman unifying force and were accordingly targeted; cf. also BOUDĪCA; CARATĀCOS. The storming of Anglesey in AD 60 is vividly described by Tacitus (*Annals* 14.30):

> Women in black clothing like that of the Furies ran between the ranks. Wild-haired, they brandished torches. Around them, the druids, lifting their hands upwards towards the sky to make frightening curses, frightened [the Roman] soldiers with this extraordinary sight. And so [the Romans] stood motionless . . . Then their commander exhorted them and they urged one another not to quake before an army of women and fanatics. They carried the ensigns forward, struck down all resistance . . . After that, a garrison was imposed on the vanquished and destroyed their groves, places of savage superstition. For they considered it their duty to spread their altars with the gore of captives and to communicate with their deities through human entrails.

John T. Koch

DRUIDS, ROMANTIC IMAGES OF

Aylett Sammes's *Britannia Antiqua Illustrata, or, The Antiquities of Ancient Britain* (1676) was formed by a process of conflating classical descriptions and archaeological finds with extant iconographies of appropriate other types (such as wild men and holy men) who lent themselves to be reinterpreted as druids. For English speakers, the location of the archetypical druid in Anglesey (MôN), Wales, by Henry

Rowlands in *Mona Antiqua Restaurata* (Ancient Mona restored; 723) had the most important consequences. Rowlands' image, though dependent on that published by Sammes, removed the druid's book with its Christian resonance and replaced it with an oak branch as a symbol of ancient and internalized wisdom.

The work of Iolo Morganwg (Edward Williams) provided the source for the ongoing *gorsedd* pageants of the Celtic nations. The union of Iolo's Gorsedd Beirdd Ynys Prydain with the eisteddfod movement in Wales in 1819 gave permanence to the image, clothed in regalia and robes designed by the Bavarian-born Hubert von Herkomer and the Welsh sculptor William Goscombe John (1860–1952).

Peter Lord

DRUIDS, THE WORD

The oldest attestation of the word 'druids' can be found in Latin *druides* (pl.), probably a loan from Gaulish. It is also found in Old Irish *druí* and early Welsh *dryw* (Llyfr Taliesin). All of these forms are derived from Proto-Celtic *dru-wid-s*, pl. *dru-wides* 'oak-knower', as Pliny the Elder had noted. The Old English word *drŷ* for a magician or wizard is a borrowing from Celtic.

Both Irish *druí* and Welsh *dryw* could also be used to signify the wren. Besides these definitions, we find Breton *drew* 'merry, cheerful' (derived from 'wren') and Middle Irish *dreän* 'wren'.

Middle and Modern Welsh *derwydd* (also attested in texts of Old Welsh date such as Armes Prydein) and Old Breton *dorguid* (or *darguid*) seem to reflect an analogical reformation so that the form was more recognizably based on 'oak' in British, a folk etymology but nevertheless a correct one.

Caroline aan de Weil

DRUNKENNESS

Celts have been stereotyped as excessively prone to drunkenness since classical times. The stereotype is present in Greek and Roman accounts based on ancient perceptions of the Barbarian 'other' (that is, 'people unlike ourselves' from the writers' point of view), and can still be seen in modern times, for example in the popular celebrations of Saint Patrick's Day.

Alcohol was a standard feature of a feast, and many literary narratives were propelled by the excessive consumption of alcohol. The Ulster Cycle tale Mesca Ulad ('The Intoxication of the Ulstermen') recounts Cú Chulainn's journey with his companions across the breadth of Ireland (Ériu) on account of his drunkenness. Although this tale is comic, the magnitude of the journey and the changes wrought on Ireland's topography can also be read as mythic. The figure of Medb may be another aspect of the cosmic importance of drunkenness; her name (Celtic *medwā* 'intoxicating' f.) is cognate with Welsh *meddw* and Breton *mezv*, both of which mean 'drunk, intoxicated' and are also cognate with English *mead*.

The capacity and opportunity to drink large quantities of alcohol are seen as heroic in many sources. For example, much of the Gododdin, an early Welsh poem, is devoted to the glories of the mead-feasts for the year prior to the battle. The chieftain's hospitality and ability to provide his warriors with enough alcohol to keep them pleasantly drunk for a year was seen as a testament to his worthiness as a leader.

Antone Minard

DRYSTAN AC ESYLLT

The famous international tragic medieval love story of Tristan and Isolt is covered in a separate article. This entry treats Welsh versions of the tale, including its Celtic origins and affinities.

Welsh Versions

There is no complete and coherent medieval Celtic version of the Tristan story. The Welsh Tristan fragments comprise the following materials: (1) a poem or fragments of two poems in Llyfr Du Caerfyrddin; (2) allusions in the Welsh triads; (3) allusions by poets to Drystan and Esyllt, beginning with the Gogynfeirdd of the 13th century; and (4) *Ystorya Trystan* (The tale of Tristan), a mixed prose–verse text that occurs only in 16th- to 18th-century manuscripts.

Celtic Origins and Affinities

Celtic origin of the Tristan story is not in doubt, as confirmed by the fact that the principal characters of the love triangle (Drystan, Esyllt, and March, in their Welsh forms) bear names of Brythonic origin. It is possible that the story circulated in the Celtic world and accumulated local elements in Pictland and Cornwall, perhaps assimilating characters to local heroes with similar names. The Pictish/Irish-origin theory rests mainly on the recurrence of the names *Drust(an)* and *Talorg(en)* in the Pictish king-list and the similarity between this love triangle and certain Irish tales, chiefly Tóruigheacht Dhiarmada agus Ghráinne ('The Pursuit of Diarmaid and Gráinne'). The Pictish name *Drust(-)* is the cognate of Welsh *Drystan* (later *Tristan* in the Romances). Pictish *Talorg(-)*, *Talorc-* has been taken as similar to *Tallwch*, Drystan's father's name in the Welsh sources, although the parallel is not exact and not matched in Continental literature.

The Cornish connections of the Tristan story seem to have more in their favour than the Pictish theory. Key points in the case for a Cornish Tristan include the 5th- to 7th-century inscribed memorial to drvsta(n)vs cvnomori filivs 'Drystan son of Cunomor', near the locale of the tale in Béroul's 12th-century French version of the Romance at Castle Dore (cf. Arthurian sites), and the Old Cornish place-name *Hryt Eselt* (Isold's ford) in a 10th- or 11th-century Anglo-Saxon charter, probably reflecting an older form of one of the two episodes set at fords in Béroul's version.

John T. Koch

DUBHADH

Dubhadh (Early Irish Dubad [also Síd mBresail], English Dowth) is an ancient circular mound roughly 85 m (280 feet) in diameter and originally about 16 m (50 feet) high. It lies approximately 2 km east northeast of a similar structure at Newgrange

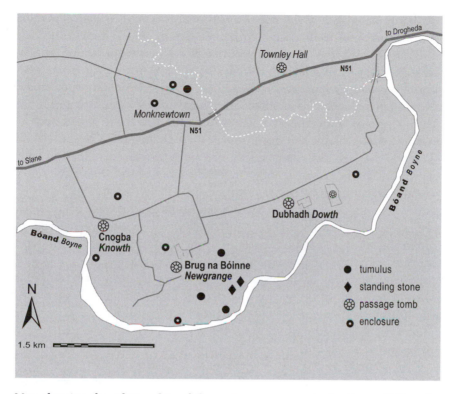

Map showing the relationship of the main monuments in the Boyne Valley, Co. Meath. (Map by John T. Koch)

(Early Irish BRUG NA BÓINNE). Dowth is situated in the valley of the Boyne (see BÓAND); the mound of Dowth, like Newgrange and a third similar tomb nearby at Knowth, is on a hilltop. Two megalithic passage graves have been located in the southwestern sector of the mound. Like its sister tumuli, Dowth is probably a structure of the Neolithic period, dating to *c.* 3000 BC.

Dowth, like Newgrange, is prominent in early IRISH LITERATURE. The two sites are named together in the ULSTER CYCLE tale TOCHMARC EMIRE ('The Wooing of Emer'; §§17, 40), where CÚ CHULAINN's figurative description of a journey 'between the god and his prophet' is later explained as between 'Newgrange and Dowth'—that is, between the residences of the mythological figures OENGUS MAC IND ÓC and Bresal Bófháith.

John T. Koch

DUBLIN

See Baile Átha Cliath.

DUMNONIA

Dumnonia is the Latinized name for a British kingdom that was located in the present English counties of Cornwall (KERNOW), Devon, and part of Somerset. It is named after the P-CELTIC tribe, the Dumnonii. The eastern borders of the kingdom were probably delimited by the river Parret. In the early medieval period, under constant pressure from the English kingdom of Wessex, this eastern border receded westward until the whole of Somerset and Devon was eventually lost by the 9th century (cf. Anglo-Saxon 'conquest').

A number of sites, including Tintagel and Exeter (Isca Dumnoniorum), may have been power centres of the kingdom at one time or other. Archaeological research gives the surprising indication that Dumnonia became more Romanized in the post-Roman period than it had been during the *Pax Romana*. Close trading links with Gaul and the Mediterranean, the use of Latin in inscriptions, and the adoption of Christian burial practice are among cited indications of this influence. The aforementioned trading links are most notably proved by the sites of Tintagel and Bantham, where large quantities of Mediterranean amphorae have been recovered. As in prehistory and the Roman period, it is likely that Cornish tin played an important part in this trade. Several ogam stones in the western part of the kingdom are also indicative of a strong cultural contact with Ireland (Ériu).

Very little is known about the history of Dumnonia. Gildas (*De Excidio Britanniae* §28), writing *c.* ad 550, mentions one Constantine of 'Damnonia' among five British kings of this time, and king-lists for the kingdom that cover the period from the late 5th to about the 9th century survive in some medieval Welsh sources.

Precisely how closely this territory was linked with its namesake in Brittany, Domnonia, is not certain. Linguistic evidence suggests that many or most of the British immigrants of the post-Roman period who crossed south over the Channel were from Dumnonia. The king-lists for the two areas share several names—for example, Cunomor—but it is difficult to assess whether any king held power concurrently in both regions. The language of Dark Age Dumnonia can be called 'Primitive Cornish'.

The name, from whence comes Welsh *Dyfnaint* 'Devon', is Celtic, based on the well-attested Proto-Celtic root *dumno-* reflected in Old Irish *domon* and Welsh *dwfn*, meaning both 'deep' and 'world'. The Fir Domnann, which were prominent in Irish legendary history, share the same name and may reflect an old branch of the same tribal group.

Simon Ó Faoláin

DÚN AILINNE

Dún Ailinne, the modern Knockaulin, Co. Kildare (Cnoc Ailinne, Contae Chill Dara), was the legendary seat of the kings of Leinster (Laigin). It is mentioned as the site of a battle for the Leinster kingship first in 728 and again *c.* 800.

Dún Ailinne occupies a hilltop and shows traces of occupation during the Neolithic (a circular ditched enclosure, Neolithic pottery, flint artefacts) and the Early Bronze Age (a food vessel). The main period of occupation is associated with the later Iron Age occupation, where it is stratified into three main phases. The third, called the Mauve phase, saw a structure with a large (42-m diameter) double-slot outer enclosure that surrounded a middle ring (25-m diameter) of timber uprights and then a central structure that has been interpreted as a tower that may have stood

9 m high. The site is enclosed by an external bank and an internal ditch; the same type of hengiform arrangement is encountered at other 'royal' sites of the period, such as Tara (TEAMHAIR) and Navan (EMAIN MACHAE). Radiocarbon dates suggest that the main period during which the site was occupied spanned from the 5th century BC to the 3rd century AD.

Finds from the site include an iron SWORD and an iron spearhead, bronze fibulae, and glass beads. The faunal remains were primarily of cattle and swine, and their slaughter patterns suggested that they were killed in the spring and autumn, possibly as part of seasonal FEASTS.

J. P. Mallory

DÚN AONGHASA

The great stone enclosure of Dún Aonghasa is located on a cliff 87 m (about 270 feet) above the sea on Inis Mór, the largest of the Aran Islands (OILEÁIN ÁRANN), situated off the west coast of Ireland (Éire). The site comprises an inner stone fort with two outer walls and a *chevaux-de-frise* (a broad band of relatively jagged upright stones placed to hinder access to the inner enclosure). The innermost enclosure is now open to the Atlantic along its southern side. All the ramparts are of dry-stone construction (without mortar), the innermost surviving to 4.9 m in height, more than 5 m thick, and with a slight external batter (that is, a broadening of the

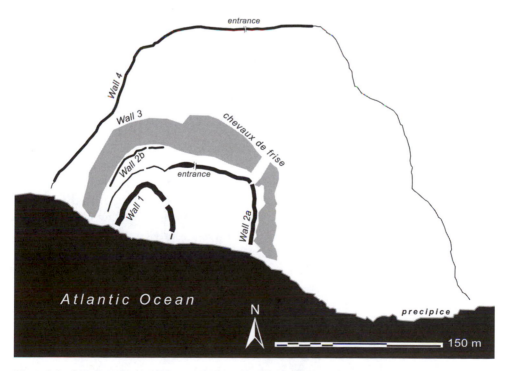

Plan of the fortifications at Dún Aonghasa, Inis Mór. (Map by John T. Koch)

base for increased stability). Access to the interior was provided by a low, narrow, lintelled entrance (that is, with a horizontal stone beam) to the northeast.

Occupation evidence dating from the Irish Middle and Late Bronze Age (*c.* 1400–*c.* 600 BC) was uncovered in the inner and middle ENCLOSURES, and included the remains of circular hut foundations, work areas, and walls. Evidence of habitation included limpet shells, animal bones, sherds of coarse pottery, clay mould fragments, and two clay crucibles for smelting bronze. This material was radiocarbon dated to 1063–924 BC, while earlier occupation material beneath the floor and running beyond the walls was dated *c.* 1300–*c.* 1000 BC.

The excavations also revealed that the economy of the site was based on sheep rearing, with the sheep primarily exploited for their meat rather than their wool. Crucibles and moulds reflected the production of bronze swords, spearheads, rings and bracelets, and pins that reflect the status and importance of the site and its inhabitants.

Today, Dún Aonghasa is a major tourist attraction in an IRISH-speaking (GAELTACHT) area. The site, however, does not figure in the folklore of the island. Thus it is not clear whether the place-name, meaning 'the fort of Aonghus', refers to the early supernatural hero OENGUS MAC IND ÓC of the TUATH DÉ, who is also associated with the great prehistoric monument BRUG NA BÓINNE (Newgrange), or to some other figure with the same common Irish man's name.

Michelle Comber

DÙN ÈIDEANN (EDINBURGH)

Although it has an ancient pedigree, Edinburgh did not become Scotland's leading burgh until the 12th century. At the heart of Edinburgh is the castle, perched upon an extinct volcano and towering over the surrounding settlement. Archaeological excavations have recovered occupation debris dating back to *c.* 800 BC. A range of imported Roman goods dating to the 2nd and 3rd centuries AD are interpreted as an indication that the settlement was economically and politically important, perhaps serving as the regional centre for LOTHIAN.

In the early medieval poetic tradition preserved in the GODODDIN elegies, Din Eidyn is identified as the seat of a great 6th-century king of the north BRITONS. The first secure historical event, however, is a siege of 'Etin' noted in an ANNAL under AD 638. The earliest surviving building in the castle is a chapel dedicated to St Margaret, which has been identified as part of a tower built by David I (1124–53).

The restoration of the castle as a royal palace was undertaken by David II in 1356. The castle remained a major royal residence until the early 16th century, when it was superseded by Holyrood Palace.

Edinburgh developed into the most prosperous burgh in Scotland (ALBA). The castle stood at one end of the long High Street, the Royal Mile, which terminated at Holyrood Abbey. The core of medieval Edinburgh survives intact, thanks to the 18th-century creation of the Georgian new town to the north of the High Street. Midway along the High Street, in the heart of the medieval market, is Parliament Square, where legal buildings surround St Giles, the greatest parish church to be built in medieval Scotland. Throughout the medieval and post-medieval periods, Edinburgh was the acknowledged administrative centre of Scotland.

Stephen Driscoll

DUNS

Duns are a type of Scottish Late IRON AGE defended settlement that appear to have been constructed from the final centuries BC onward. These monuments were used, and in some cases reused, until the beginning of the medieval period. At their most basic, duns consist of small dry-stone built ENCLOSURES, usually with a fairly small internal area (less than 0.3 ha [1 acre]), but occasionally bordering on the size of small hill-forts. They are often subcircular or oval in plan, but vary widely in their range of shapes and situations. The walls tend to be high (up to *c.* 3 m) and quite thick. Duns are most plentifully distributed along the western seaboard from Skye and North and South Uist (Uibhist) in the north to Kintyre (Ceann Tíre) and Arran (Arainn) in the south. Like the BROCHS, with which they partially overlap in both distribution and construction, these settlements are considered to be the defended homesteads of small farming groups, equivalent to the rounds and raths found in the more southerly parts of the Atlantic zone during this period.

Simon Ó Faoláin

DÜRRNBERG BEI HALLEIN

Dürrnberg bei Hallein is an important early centre of salt mining in central Europe that was in use during the pre-Roman IRON AGE; it is the source of numerous and rich finds from graves and settlements dating from the HALLSTATT and early LA TÈNE periods. The Dürrnberg is situated southwest of Salzburg on the border between Germany and Austria over an area of 2 km^2.

Two miners' bodies were discovered in the mines in AD 1577 and 1616, popularly known as the 'men in the salt'. Both a well-known bronze beaked flagon and CHARIOT burials were discovered in the mid-20th century. Recently, in cooperation with several other institutions, the ancient salt mines themselves have been the subject of intensive investigation.

Salt Mining

The salt deposits of the Dürrnberg consist of the so-called *haselgebirge* (hazel mountains), a mixture of 40 to 95 percent pure salt (sodium chloride) together with clay and anhydrite or gypsum. The whole deposit is covered by a layer of 20- to 40-m thick clay, which protects the salt deposit against further leaching by fresh water. At the foot of the Hahnrainkopf (1,026 m) are two brine springs, which were presumably responsible for the discovery of the underground salt deposits by HALLSTATT-period Celtic miners in the 6th century BC. The prehistoric mining areas were mainly distributed around this hilltop because easy access to the salt was possible by shafts cut down diagonally from the slopes. Before commercial mining, the prehistoric miners continuously had to extend the shafts to access new deposits.

Our knowledge about the ancient working areas is, in fact, mainly based on mining in the historic period; mining exploited the salt deposits from the 13th century until 1989.

Iron Age miners formed large working galleries of roughly diagonal chambers in which they retrieved salt by hacking out large lumps. Organic material is preserved in remarkable condition through the saline environment, resulting in a mass of information concerning the tools, the distribution of labour, and the clothes of the miners. Knowledge of these workers' health and diet is based on the analysis of coprolites or paleofaeces (i.e., petrified excrement). On the basis of these data, the mining community is theorized to have consisted of a poorer and socially less favoured stratum of the contemporary Iron Age community. In addition, the small size of some shoes found in the shafts offers evidence for the employment of children in the mines. The working processes and the implements used suggest distinctive and specialized professions evolved among the labourers—hewers, hauliers, carpenters, and the like. Besides natural ventilation, artificial thermal ventilation was implemented in the mines by heating of the air through fire and the hundreds of wooden tapers that provided the main source of illumination below ground.

Settlements

A permanent settlement on the Dürrnberg was established based on the mining of underground salt, albeit no earlier than the late Hallstatt period (Ha D1, earlier 6th century bc). The residences shared close relations with the nearby hill-fort on the Hellbrunnerberg, a rich and therefore presumably chieftainly centre just south of the site of the modern city of Salzburg, especially in the early period. In the latest phase of the Hallstatt Iron Age (D3, c. 500 bc) and at the beginning of La Tène A (the first half of the 5th century bc), several important changes may have led to a regional concentration of the settlement activities on the Dürrnberg. A large trade and crafts settlement was established around the Ramsautal, the hill-fort on the Ramsaukopf and on the Moserstein. At the same time, the rich settlement on the Hellbrunnerberg was abandoned. Subsequently, settlement was concentrated on the Dürrnberg itself. From this time onward, a complex craft and trade centre on the Dürrnberg existed that was linked with the Salzach valley by a settlement located below the modern town of Hallein. In the second part of the 4th century and the beginning of the 3rd century bc, however, this settlement suffered a decline. Mud avalanches in the mine and regular flooding in the Ramsautal may indicate land exhaustion caused by intensive mining and other human activities on the Dürrnberg. In later centuries and into Roman times, we see again a restricted core settlement on the Moserstein. which reveals by then the decreased importance of the Dürrnberg.

Small-scale excavations have also brought to light well-preserved large houses up to 15 m in length in the Dürrnberg area. These houses were constructed on raised areas of dry land and were settled and rebuilt over generations. These more or less dry dwelling areas were secured by drains and wickerwork fences against the permanent moisture of the swampy area. The house constructions and their stratigraphy (i.e., their sequenced layers corresponding to successive time periods) show that living and craft activities were carried out in the same house-units, presumably over several generations, by the same families, or at least by related social groups. Besides bronze casting and ironworking, evidence suggests the presence of meat processing and tanning, glass production, woodworking carpentry, tool making, lathes, pottery, and other crafts. The results of the excavations at the Ramsautal have also provided insights into the complex economic relations between the salt-mining centre of the Dürrnberg and its supporting region. The residents appear to have engaged in economic contacts with the Alpine hinterland, especially with the Fritzens-Sanzeno culture, where pottery and BROOCHES point to a fluctuating exchange of people such as seasonal workers and of trade goods (e.g., sheep) between those regions.

In addition, there are many examples of long-distance trade in rare raw materials such as amber, silk, and coral, as well as luxury goods found in the rich Dürrnberg graves—Etruscan and Greek vessels of pottery and bronze and even wine from south of the Alps. Some graves can be interpreted as being those of traders, one of them presumably having come from the area of the Veneti and the head of the Adriatic.

Late Hallstatt and La Téne Graves

The cemeteries spread over the whole area of the Dürrnberg in the early settlement phases were concentrated especially in three areas: the graves of the Eislfeld (approximately 80–100 graves); the graves of the Simonbauernfeld (a smaller grave group); and a larger group on the Hexenwandfeld. At the beginning of the IRON AGE occupation, one can detect groups of 'founders' graves'. With the changes at the beginning of the 5th century BC, new cemeteries were established, some devoted to warriors or other richer graves. Secondary burials of the Early LA TÈNE period can be observed in older burial mounds first built in the 6th century. In some cases new grave-groups and single graves from the 3rd and 2nd centuries are evident, and sometimes very rich SWORD graves with wagon-fittings or rich women's graves are present, which reveal that some kind of local upper class still existed at that time. The burial rate seems to have been continuously reduced from the 4th century, contrary to what can be deduced from the settlement evidence—the latter shows continual prosperity in the later phases of the Early and especially in the Middle La Tène periods (c. 350–c. 150 BC). Finally, evidence for graves of the latest settlement phases is still lacking, which is not surprising when set against the background of Late La Tène civilization in southern Germany.

Normally, the cemeteries or clusters of graves were situated on steep slopes or on obviously selected and clearly visible sites close to the settlements, especially around the major areas of population such as Moserstein or Ramsautal. Some graves seem to have been constructed with an eye toward being accessible for later ritual practices—perhaps this consideration was also a reason for locating them close to settlements and working areas.

The normal practice for the construction of graves was to build rectangular wooden chambers covered by stones, inside which one or more persons were buried, cremated, or inhumed in an extended position. In some burials, the chambers were used for two individuals, presumably indicating some sort of relationship, such as kinship. These multiple graves, together with gifts of amulets and brooches with elaborate decoration, exhibit a range of fanciful forms of clear symbolic importance and are a prominent feature of the Dürrnberg burials. As many as four distinct layers of burial chambers are known. Secondary burial activities—such as the construction of a new chamber or a succeeding funeral—did not always leave the prior burial undisturbed. Some burial goods were removed, for example, and the earlier skeletons disarticulated. Later disturbance of earlier burial is frequently observed and may have had its origin in robbery or—more likely—in some kind of ritual practice involving two-stage burial.

The dead were normally equipped with drinking vessels and other dishes as well as the remains of joints of meat (pigs, cattle, and sheep/goats). These items indicate that a funerary feast took place as part of the rite of passage into the OTHERWORLD. In addition, single-edged knives, shears, and status symbols such as wagons, weapons, complex belts, and special luxury items have been found in richer and socially higher-ranked graves.

From Hallstatt D (roughly 6th century BC) onward, spears and axes appear in the personal equipment of men's graves, sometimes combined with status weapons such as daggers, helmets, and swords with richly decorated scabbards. Rich costume articles, such as bracelets, anklets, beads, amulets, belts, and a substantial number of brooches, are noticeable in women's graves and also in the richer children's graves, even those of the very young. These sites are present in considerable numbers and include a wide range of grave goods, indicating some sort of local aristocracy. These rich graves of minors stand in contrast to the unaccompanied infants' and neonatal burials close to and even in the floors of houses found in the Ramsautal and other settlement areas.

Other, more outstanding, status symbols are known from rich male or female graves situated in special areas in the cemeteries, such as parts of wagons, a large bronze situla (bucket, probably for wine) of local manufacture and a bronze 'pilgrim flask' copying southern forms, the famous bronze Celtic beaked flagon, a miniature golden boat, splendid axes, and imports from the Mediterranean world. Rings of gold may have been special gifts, as were large dress pins with double spiral heads. Even more exotic are ritual wands or sceptres. Between the working population in the mines on the one hand and what is represented in the graves on the other hand, it is very unlikely that the entire population is represented in the latter sites; that is, the cemeteries appear to represent a cross-section of only the higher-class and more wealthy sections of a settled population. So far we cannot identify miners, seasonal workers, and craftspeople from grave goods or on the basis of pathological evidence.

Cultural Links

Dürrnberg and its northern Alpine extension, the Inn-Salzach region, are closely linked by culture. The interaction between the Hellbrunnerberg and Dürrnberg is clearly demonstrable. We may postulate an important settlement in the Salzach valley that served as trading post, market, and administrative centre.

From the beginning of the 6th century BC, the area was culturally linked with other Eastern Alpine regions within the East Hallstatt province. From the middle of the 6th century BC, however, connections with the West Hallstatt province began to increase, and were marked by changes in dress ornaments, burial rites, and pottery forms. It seems to be a coincidence rather than the result of any direct cultural influence that these changes are contemporary with the establishment of the IRON AGE complex on the Dürrnberg and its flourishing development in the second half of the 6th century BC. From then onward, the area was a closely connected subzone of the West Hallstatt province. Many reasons can be cited for believing that this situation was responsible for the important rôle that Dürrnberg played in the development of LA TÈNE culture at the beginning of the 5th century—a time when Dürrnberg reached its climax. The Celtic migrations in the 4th and 3rd centuries BC also changed the cultural and the basic economic relations of Dürrnberg. Connections with the Carpathian basin and the Alpine hinterland were apparently stronger in the 4th and the 3rd centuries. Late La Tène culture (c. 150–c. 15 BC) was more influenced by the culture of the late Celtic *oppida* in southern Germany than by Noricum in the emerging Roman Empire (see OPPIDUM).

Thomas Stöllner (and thanks to Kurt Zeller)

DURROW, BOOK OF

The Book of Durrow (Dublin, Trinity College MS 57 [A. 4. 5]) is most likely the earliest extant essentially complete illuminated insular gospel book. Besides its text of St Jerome's Latin version of the Gospels and various preliminaries written in a fine Irish majuscule script, the manuscript contains six carpet pages (pages covered with ornament but without text) and five pages displaying symbols of the evangelists. Elaborately decorated initials open each of the four Gospels.

The order of equivalence followed by the individually pictured evangelist symbols is not the canonical Latin order established by St Jerome, but most likely depends on that set out in the 2nd century by St Irenaeus. The symbol type of the four symbols page (fo. 2r) and those separately depicted are also quite unusual. The first is possibly partially inspired by Coptic example, and the second—lacking the usual wings, halos, and attributes—may be related to a type known as 'terrestial' found in the mid-6th century at San Vitale, Ravenna.

Two inscriptions by the scribe of the Book of Durrow appear on fo. 247v, the second of which refers to the writer as St Columba (COLUM CILLE). On fo. 248v, there is an 11th- or 12th-century addition recording a legal transaction concerning the monastery of Durrow, Co. Offaly (Darmhaigh, Contae Uíbh Fhailí). On fo. IIv, there is an inscription, added in the 17th century by the antiquarian Roderick O'Flarety, taken from the *cumdach* (book shrine), now lost, in which the manuscript had been placed at Durrow by Flann mac Mael Sechnaill, king of Ireland (ÉRIU), during the late 9th or early 10th century. Further evidence suggests that the book was at Durrow in the early 17th century, and was still revered as the Book of Colum

Book of Durrow, opening of the Gospel of St Mark, fo. 86r, showing decorated oversize initial (vellum). Dublin Trinity College MS 57. (The Board of Trinity College, Dublin, Ireland/The Bridgeman Art Library International)

Cille. Nevertheless, the character of its script and its repertoire of Celtic, Anglo-Saxon, and Mediterranean ornamental patterns and iconographic formulations connect the book with the monastery of Rath Melsigi in Co. Carlow (Contae Cheatharlaigh), where the Anglo-Saxon missionary Willibrord spent several years before travelling to the Continent in 690. Manuscripts from Echternach associated with Willibrord have scribal similarities with the Book of Durrow, and this and other palaeographic evidence has led to the conclusion that the script developed at Rath Melsigi was employed in the creation of the manuscript at Durrow, probably early in the 8th century.

Martin Werner

DUVAL, AÑJELA

The poet Añjela Duval (1905–81) spent her life on the smallholding where she was born in Traoñ an Dour, Ar C'houerc'had (LeVieux Marché), in northern Brittany (BREIZH). Communion with nature permeates her work.

Añjela Duval turned to poetry at the age of 56: 'My beloved parents died in turn of old age, and one day I found myself alone in my home. And alone in winter by the fire after supper, instead of singing I just pined, my heart full of grief' (*Kan an Douar* 64).

In 1961, she received a valuable gift of books and journals containing most Breton writing since the 1920s. The corpus included creative works, dictionaries, and grammars, largely products of the Gwalarn school whose founder Roparz Hemon was exiled in Ireland. The marriage of popular idiom to the substance of the written word, fuelled by an immense need for personal expression, then resulted in a unique body of work that continues to inspire the Breton language movement.

Twin themes in Duval's poetry are the demise of Breton civilization and the rise of French hegemony. Treatment of the first transports us into a world that has vanished, and the many glimpses afforded of this world ensure the endurance of the work as a social document. Añjela Duval greets the rise of French hegemony with dismay, indignation, outrage, and desperation. The opening poem of *Kan an Douar* makes the point: 'I loathe the sight of my country's old people pining in homes for the toil they once knew, and the young mothers of my country speaking the language of the oppressor to their babies' (*Kan an Douar* 17).

The imminent collapse of the BRETON language casts a long shadow in Duval's work. She writes in strident tones on the subject. French, she says, is 'no more than a corrupt Latin spoken by the soldiers and servants of Caesar' (*Stourm a ran* 61).

Añjela Duval is of unrivalled stature in Breton-language literature in the latter part of the 20th century, although ironically she wrote in an idiom obscure to Breton speakers. Her language incorporated neologisms and archaisms that put her work beyond her fellows and neighbours. It has thus remained inaccessible to 'My brothers in toil: the small farmers' (*Stourm a ran* 59).

Diarmuid Johnson

DYFED

Dyfed is unique among the regions and medieval kingdoms of what is now Wales (CYMRU) in continuing, in name and approximate geographic limits, what was a *civitas* of Roman Britain and a Celtic tribe of the pre-Roman IRON AGE. In this respect, Dyfed is comparable to the post-Roman kingdoms of DUMNONIA in southwest BRITAIN and GODODDIN in the northeast. The tribal name *Demetae*, from which the Welsh *Dyfed* derives, is recorded in the *Geography* of Ptolemy as Δημηται *Dēmētae*.

In Roman times, the tribal *caput* was the town of Moridūnon (Sea-fort), now Carmarthen (Caerfyrddin), preserving the old name with *caer* 'fortified town' prefixed. The post-Roman dynasty of Dyfed arose from an intrusive Irish group known as the Déisi, who probably arrived in the 5th century.

In the 6th century, GILDAS denounced Dyfed's reigning ruler Vorteporius as *tyrannus Demetarum* 'tyrant of the Demetae' (*De Excidio Britanniae* §31). This same man is attested in Welsh GENEALOGIES and on an OGAM stone.

Dyfed figures as the chief setting of the first and third branches of the MABINOGI, PWYLL, and MANAWYDAN. The kingdom is said to have established a main court at Arberth (now Narberth, Pembrokeshire) and comprised seven hundreds (see CANTREF). Pwyll's son and successor Pryderi is said to have added to his legacy seven more. This legendary expansion probably reflects a historical development seen in 11th-century sources, whereby a larger political entity comes to be called Deheubarth 'southern region' with its royal centre at Dinefwr.

Dyfed reemerged with the consolidation of Cardiganshire, Carmarthenshire, and Pembrokeshire (sir Aberteifi, sir Gaerfyrddin, sir Benfro) in the local government reorganization of 1974. These three pre-1974 counties came back into being in 1993.

John T. Koch

E

EASTER CONTROVERSY

Introduction

Perhaps the single most important schismatic issue in insular CHRISTIANITY was the reckoning of Easter—a source of controversy that raged from the late 6th century to the late 8th century. It would be an oversimplification to identify one computus (formula for calculating Easter) as Celtic and the opposing system as Roman/ Anglo-Saxon. The insular reckoning, often termed 'Celtic,' was an 84-year cycle attributed to the 3rd-century Syrian bishop, Anatolius of Laodicaea, in which Easter could not occur before 25 March, reckoned as the spring equinox. Roman practice was a 19-year cycle attributed to Victorius in which Easter could occur as early as the equinox of 21 March. To modern readers, the date of a movable holiday—which often coincided in both systems, anyway—may seem a trivial matter; for medieval cosmology, however, Easter—the resurrection of Christ—was the annual triumph of light over darkness and life over death. To calculate it incorrectly was to misunderstand fundamentally God's creation. It is no coincidence that Bede was simultaneously the leading proponent of the Roman computus (which eventually prevailed) and the greatest historian and scientist of the early Middle Ages, who unreservedly hated the Britons as heretics, and wrote his *Historia Ecclesiastica* with this bias.

Cummian's Letter

During the 6th century and prior to that time, there had been competing systems. Cummian, in his letter arguing for the Roman Easter to Abbot Ségéne of Iona (EILEAN Ì), surveyed several Easter cycles, the first of which he attributed to *sanctus Patricius papa noster* (St Patrick our senior bishop). It was a 19-year cycle of the Alexandrian type sanctioned by the Nicene Council of 325.

Some southern Irish churches had adopted the Roman Easter by 632/3. Following a synod held by this group at Mag Léne, Cummian, one of their leaders, wrote his letter to the abbot of Iona, the intellectual stronghold of the insular Easter. This letter argued for the Roman Easter on the basis of the superior authority of the *tres linguae sacrae*—the three sacred languages of Hebrew, Greek, and Latin—and the intellectual insignificance and geographic marginality of the Irish and Britons. Thus the Easter issue had implicitly spawned an attack on learning in Irish or WELSH.

Streanæshalch and Its Aftermath

In 664, at a council held at Streanæshalch (often called the 'Synod of Whitby'), Northumbria's church—which owed its foundation to Iona—accepted the Roman Easter. Colmán, the Irish abbot of Lindisfarne, withdrew to Ireland (Ériu), by way of Iona. Also present were the noble Anglo-Saxon Bishop Wilfrid, a strong adherent of the Roman side, and his patron, Prince Alchfrith. Presiding was Alchfrith's father, King Oswydd, who, Bede tells us, supported the insular Easter because he had been educated by the Irish and spoke their language perfectly. Bede writes that some British churches adopted the Roman Easter after the battle of Nechtanesmere in 685. Adomnán, the abbot of Iona, accepted the Roman Easter before his death (†704). St Elfoddw was responsible for finally changing the reckoning in Wales (Cymru) in 768, according to *Annales Cambriae*.

John T. Koch

ECHTRAI

Echtrai (sing. *echtrae*, Modern Irish *eachtraí*, *eachtra*), literally 'outing' but usually translated as 'adventures', constitute one of the traditional Irish tale types, usually involving a lone hero encountering supernatural or otherworldly challenges (see Irish literature, early prose). Within the medieval Irish tale lists, there are fourteen *echtrai* in the A list and ten in the B lists, but the lists share only three in common: *Echtrae Nerai*, *Echtra Crimthainn Nia Náir* (The adventure of Crimthann Nia Náir), and *Echtra Con Culainn* (The adventure of Cú Chulainn). The last has not survived, at least not under this name. There is some overlap in genre, especially between *echtrai* and immrama (voyage tales; see also voyage literature). As well as the maritime element, the *immrama* usually include overt Christian themes more so than do *echtrai*. The oldest extant *eachtrae*, *Echtrae Chonlai* (The adventure of Conlae, discussed in voyage literature), is a voyage tale with Christian themes. *Echtra Mac nEchach Muig-medóin* ('The Adventure of the Sons of Eochaid Mugmedón'), an 11th-century foundation legend of the great Uí Néill dynasty, is one of the most famous surviving examples of the Celtic sovereignty myth (see also legendary history, Ireland; cf. Arthurian literature, texts in non-Celtic medieval languages). In it, Níall and his brothers are lost; one brother after another goes out seeking water and confronts a hideous hag who asks each of them for a kiss. Níall at last kisses and lies with her, at which point she is transformed into the beautiful personification of the sovereignty of Ireland (Ériu), conferring the right to rule on Níall and his progeny forever. On *Echtra Fergusa maic Léiti* (The adventure of Fergus son of Léite), see luchorpán.

John T. Koch

EDINBURGH

See Dùn Èideann.

EDUCATION IN THE CELTIC LANGUAGES, BRETON MEDIUM

Despite official French attitudes discouraging continued use of the country's regional languages, there is evidence, as bilingual textbooks testify, that the Breton language was used as the teaching medium in some small private schools during the 19th century. In addition, religious instruction, mainly in the form of catechism, was taught through the medium of Breton in many areas of Lower Brittany (Breizh-Izel) well into the 20th century. With the passing of the Jules Ferry Laws in 1881–89, however, the French government's stance regarding the medium of instruction was hardened to such an extent that users of the Breton language were persecuted in schools.

The 20th century witnessed active campaigning by various associations for Breton to be taught in schools. One of these, ABES (Ar Brezoneg er Skol 'Breton in Schools', founded in 1934), collected votes from more than 200 *communes* in 1936 in support of a motion calling for Breton in schools. Another movement was Ar Falz (The sickle), an association of lay teachers led by Yann Sohier (1901–35) who founded the monthly bulletin of the same name in 1933.

A residential school with nine pupils was founded at Plestin-les-Grèves in 1942. This independent venture, funded entirely by voluntary contributions, taught all subjects through the medium of Breton until its closure in June 1944. The Deixonne Law of 1950–51 authorized the teaching of regional languages in secondary schools.

Breton-medium education truly gained momentum in 1977 when, through the coordinated efforts of parents and teachers, the first Diwan ('germination') school was opened. The number of pupils attending these Breton-medium schools has steadily increased each year. In 1997, the first batch of pupils sat their *baccalauréat* examination, having received all their schooling in Breton.

Children other than Diwan pupils can also receive their education through the medium of Breton, as bilingual schools and bilingual streams can be found within both the public and Catholic (private) education systems.

Gwenno Sven-Myer

EDUCATION IN THE CELTIC LANGUAGES, CORNISH MEDIUM

There is no Cornish Language Act, nor do the Cornish language, literature, and history feature in the National Curriculum of the United Kingdom. Education in Cornish has, therefore, been historically suppressed and underfunded. Provision is piecemeal at best, and nonexistent at worst. Most people learn Cornish as adults at evening classes or by studying independently on their own. Some families speak Cornish exclusively at home, but limited facilities exist for formal education in the language. Movyans-Skolyow-Meythrin ('Nursery Schools Movement') had begun offering Saturday courses as of 2010.

Instruction in Cornish has been dependent upon interested individuals working with the education system, most notably E. G. R. Hooper. Robert Morton Nance's *Cornish for All* (1929) and A. S. D. Smith's *Cornish Simplified* (1939) were the standard textbooks for many years, followed by Richard Gendall's *Kernewek Bew* (Living Cornish, 1972). Secondary provision of Cornish-language education is extremely poor, although some schools do provide limited Cornish studies. Examinations in the Cornish language are held by the Cornish Language Board; Grade Four guarantees bardic acceptance into the Cornish GORSETH.

Alan M. Kent

EDUCATION IN THE CELTIC LANGUAGES, IRISH MEDIUM

Introduction

IRISH-medium education is provided in two jurisdictions: the Republic of Ireland (ÉIRE) and Northern Ireland. In the Republic of Ireland, Irish-medium education takes two forms. In the remaining GAELTACHT (Irish-speaking) regions, Irish-medium education is intended to be L1 (first-language) medium instruction. In contrast, the Gaelscoil (Irish-medium schooling) movement in non-Gaeltacht areas of the Republic of Ireland and in Northern Ireland is following a total immersion model, as the vast majority of students have English as a home language.

Preschool Education

Irish-medium preschools (*naíonraí*, sing. *naíonra*) are part of a national, primarily community and voluntary-based, movement. The first *naíonra* opened in 1968.

Primary-Level Education (Ages 4–12 Years)

Schools in Gaeltacht regions generally teach through the medium of Irish at both the primary and secondary levels. The number of primary-level Gaeltacht schools is 108, with a total number of 7,507 pupils (Department of Education and Science, 1999/2000). Because of the rural nature of the Gaeltacht, the majority of these schools are small.

Table 1   Statistics Relating to Naíonra in 2002–3

	Naíonra Centres	Stiúrthóirí (Naíonra Leaders)	Stiúrthóirí Cúnta (Assistants)	Children
Gaeltachtaí (Irish-speaking regions)	69	70	78	1,152
English-speaking regions	141	156	28	2,348
Republic of Ireland (Total)	**210**	**226**	**106**	**3,500**
Northern Ireland	37	37	76	848
Total	247	263	182	4,348

Source: An Comhchoiste Réamhscolaíochta, Seirbhísí Naíonraí Gaeltachta Teo. & Comhairle na Gaelscolaíochta.

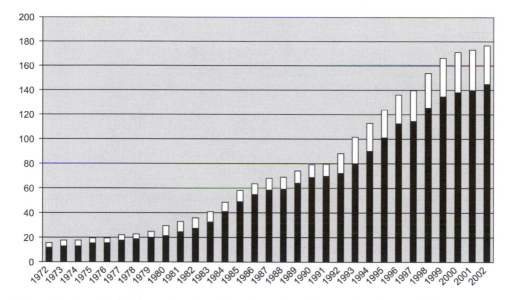

Figure 1   Growth of the number of Irish-medium schools (vertical axis) outside the Gaeltacht regions, 1972–2002. Primary schools are shown in black, secondary in white. (*Source:* Gaelsoileanna.)

From 1972 onward, a parent-based movement led to renewed interest and growth in Irish-medium schooling (see above), known as Gaelscoileanna (Gael-schools) in the Republic of Ireland and Gaeloiliúint (Gael-instruction) in Northern Ireland. Only 6 percent of primary-level students are currently attending Irish-medium schools.

Current challenges facing the sector include the supply of teachers qualified to teach through the medium of Irish, the provision of Irish-medium textbooks and other teaching resources, and planning issues relating to the establishment of new schools. Gaeltacht schools face additional challenges. With the continued shift of language patterns in Gaeltacht areas from Irish to English, Gaeltacht schools must deal with a mixed intake of pupils, some of whom are native speakers of Irish and others of whom are not. A lack of forward language planning has left such schools struggling to deal with a complex linguistic situation without the resources, in terms of personnel and training, to do so.

Table 2   Statistics for Irish-Medium Primary Schools outside the Gaeltacht Regions in 2002–3

	Schools	*Pupils*	*Teachers*	*Families*
Republic of Ireland	119	21,894	1,065	14,920
Northern Ireland	25	1,996	120	1,462
Total	144	23,890	1,185	16,382

Source: Gaelsoileanna.

Table 3   Statistics for Irish-Medium Second-Level Schools outside the Gaeltacht Regions in 2002–3

	Schools	Pupils	Teachers	Families
Republic of Ireland	30	5,213	486 (+45 part-time)	3,796
Northern Ireland	3	427	47	300
Total	33	5,640	533 (+45 part-time)	4,096

Source: Gaelsoileanna.

Secondary-Level Education (Ages 12–18 Years)

In Gaeltacht areas, 20 secondary-level schools currently teach through the medium of Irish, with a total of 3,340 pupils attending them (Department of Education and Science, 1999/2000). In non-Gaeltacht areas, the number of students receiving Irish-medium schooling showed a steady increase from 1972 to 2002 (see Fig. 1).

Where initial numbers are not large enough to justify the establishment of new schools on an independent basis, the model adopted has been to establish semi-independent Irish-medium units within existing English-medium schools. To date, this model has not proved completely satisfactory.

Third-Level Sector

The National University of Ireland, Galway (Ollscoil na hÉireann, Gaillimh), has a legislative responsibility in relation to university education through the medium of Irish, and currently offers a range of courses and modules through the medium of Irish at the diploma, degree, and postgraduate levels. A limited range of options is available through Irish for students at the undergraduate level in several disciplines. Figures for the 2001–2 academic year show that a total of 218 students were following all or some of their studies through the medium of Irish. An Irish-medium academy, Acadamh na hOllscolaíochta Gaeilge, has as its remit the development of Irish-medium teaching and research activities, and Irish-medium degrees are offered in various programmes throughout the country.

Websites

www.gov.ie/oireachtas/frame.htm
www.legislation.hmso.gov.uk/si/si1998/19981759.htm
www1.fa.knaw.nl/mercator/regionale_dossiers/regional_dossier_Irish_in_ireland.htm)
www1.fa.knaw.nl/mercator/regionale_dossiers/regional_dossier_Irish_in_northernireland.htm
www.comhairle.org

Seosamh Mac Donnacha

EDUCATION IN THE CELTIC LANGUAGES, MANX MEDIUM

In 1996, the first regular Manx preschool group was established in Braddan by Mooinjer Veggey ('little people'), with six children learning Manx through play, songs, stories, and activities. MooinjerVeggey expanded rapidly, and by

April 2002 it had four groups with more than 80 children registered. In 1996, following pressure from parents of bilingual (Manx/English) children, the Department of Education agreed on a trial basis to provide a half-day per week language session taught primarily through Manx.

Sheshaght ny Paarantyn (SnyP, Parents for Manx-Medium Education) was formed in 1999 with the specific aim of lobbying the Manx Government. In September 2001, its efforts resulted in the opening of a Manx-medium class in Ballacottier Primary School, Douglas (Doolish), with nine pupils between four and five years old.

Phil Gawne

EDUCATION IN THE CELTIC LANGUAGES, SCOTTISH GAELIC MEDIUM

Education through the medium of SCOTTISH GAELIC was formally introduced into state education in Scotland (ALBA) in 1975. The previous year had seen a major reorganization of local government and the creation of a single local authority for the Outer Hebrides (Innse Gall). The new council, Comhairle nan Eilean, adopted a bilingual policy and initiated a bilingual education project that was partly funded by the central government.

History of Provision

Prior to the introduction of the project, the use of Gaelic as a medium of instruction had been informal, unofficial, and sporadic, and had been tolerated rather than encouraged. No provision was made for Gaelic in the 1872 Education Act, which established state education in Scotland. This omission occurred despite the fact that approximately 250,000 persons in Scotland could speak Gaelic and that the language had been used as a medium of instruction in many of the previously independent schools run by churches and various societies. Official disdain for the language was reflected in the appointment of monoglot English-speaking teachers in Gaelic-speaking areas and the not-infrequent practice of administering corporal punishment to children for speaking Gaelic in school.

Primary Education

Provision for teaching of Scottish Gaelic in the primary sector was instituted in 1985 with the opening of Gaelic-medium units in schools in Glasgow (Glaschu) and Inverness (Inbhir Nis). The success of these units and the spread of Gaelic-medium playgroups fuelled demand for provision in other areas, and by 2003–4 there were 1,972 pupils engaged in Gaelic-medium education in 60 schools. Of these schools, 49 are located in the HIGHLANDS and Islands, and almost all of the schools have parallel Gaelic-medium and English-medium streams. The first all-Gaelic school in Scotland opened in Glasgow in 1999. In addition, five primary schools in the Hebrides, in which the Gaelic-medium stream predominates, have been designated Gaelic schools by the local authority.

Most pupils in Gaelic-medium education in urban areas come from non-Gaelic-speaking homes. A two-year immersion programme in the language is a feature of the curriculum in all Gaelic-medium schools, and Gaelic is the main language of instruction in primaries at ages 3–7, although the balance of language use varies. All schools are bound by the National Curriculum Guidelines for ages 5–14, which specify that Gaelic-medium education should aim 'to bring pupils to the stage of broadly equal competence in Gaelic and English, in all skills, by the end of Primary 7'.

Secondary Education

By 2003–4, there were 15 schools providing some form of Gaelic-medium education to slightly more than 300 pupils in various parts of Scotland. Gaelic-medium education in most secondary schools is limited to two or three school subjects, of which history is the most widely available. The Scottish Qualifications Authority (SQA) offers Gaelic versions of the national Standard Grade examinations in history, geography, and mathematics in the Fourth Year, and it is anticipated that other subjects will be added to those currently available. Gaelic-medium pupils also study the language as a subject, and take the certificate Gàidhlig course designed for fluent speakers.

Tertiary and Higher Education

Some of the colleges of the University of the Highlands and Islands make provision for the Scottish Gaelic language as a medium of instruction. The Gaelic College—Sabhal Mòr Ostaig—on Skye offers a range of certificate, diploma, degree, and postgraduate courses taught through the medium of Gaelic. Lews Castle College also provides some courses in Gaelic at campuses in Stornoway (Steòrnabhaigh) and Benbecula (Beinn nam Faodhla).

Boyd Robertson

EDUCATION IN THE CELTIC LANGUAGES, WELSH MEDIUM

The growth of WELSH-medium education is one of the minor miracles of modern Europe. Education is the chief focus of the language struggle. The Butler Education Act of 1944 permitted Local Education Authorities to establish designated Welsh-medium schools, the first of which opened in Llanelli in 1947. By the early 1950s, there were 15 designated schools, underpinned by a network of voluntary Ysgolion Meithrin (nursery schools), mainly in Anglicized areas. Parental pressure led to the establishment of Welsh-medium secondary schools in Rhyl, Mold/Yr Wyddgrug, and Pontypridd. Subsequently, a wide variation in the national pattern of bilingual teaching emerged, ranging from complete Welsh-medium to differing proportions of Welsh and English within the curriculum and subjects, dependent on both the sociolinguistic context of the catchment area and the Local Education Authority's language policy.

The Conservative Government's creation of a National Curriculum for Wales via the 1988 Education Act resulted in Welsh becoming a core subject, together with English, mathematics, and science, in all schools. The 1988 Act had far-reaching consequences. Welsh-medium education benefited from the additional resources expended on teacher training and the development of teaching materials in the 445 designated Welsh-medium schools (representing 25.9% of Wales's 1,718 schools in 1990). English-medium schools also saw a significant growth in the teaching of Welsh. The Welsh Language Act of December 1993 further strengthened such trends.

Consequent to these legislative reforms, the percentage of primary schoolchildren speaking Welsh fluently increased from 13.1 percent in 1986/7 to 16.0 percent in 1998/9. However, the percentage of primary schoolchildren speaking Welsh at home fell over the same period from 7.3 percent to 6.3 percent. In January 1999, 13.3 percent of secondary school pupils in Years 7 to 11 (the compulsory school age) were taught Welsh as a first language; this percentage has increased virtually every year since 1977/8, when the comparable figure was 9.3 percent. By 1999, 14.6 percent of pupils in Year 7 were being taught Welsh as a first language.

In 2001–2, there were 445 Welsh-medium primary schools, accounting for roughly one fourth of the total number of primary schools. A further 82 schools, representing 5 percent of the total, used Welsh as a teaching medium to some extent. In the remaining schools, Welsh was taught as a second language.

Also in 2001–2, there were 52 Welsh-medium secondary schools, serving 20 percent of the total secondary-level students. The range and quality of bilingual material to sustain the teaching of specialist topics has grown tremendously.

Despite such incremental growth, the lack of continuity of provision at each successive level in the educational system has diminished the effectiveness of national bilingual strategies. At primary-school level, the percentage of children who can speak Welsh fluently continues to rise; when they transfer to high school, however, less than half of the pupils move from a first-language to a second-language category.

By 2003, the educational policy reforms announced by the National Assembly for Wales (CYNULLIAD CENEDLAETHOL CYMRU), together with its adoption of holistic programmes to realize its declared ambition of creating a bilingual Wales (CYMRU), had not yet assuaged the fears of critics who argued that Welsh-medium education was in crisis, especially in the post-16 sector. Because the bilingual infrastructure was so underdeveloped and the vocational element almost nonexistent, many opportunities were being lost for the effective training of a bilingual workforce.

Colin H. Williams

EILEAN Ì (IONA)

Eilean Ì (Iona) is an island of the Inner Hebrides (Innse Gall) in Scotland off of Mull (Muile). The island is approximately 12 km^2 (4.5 mi^2) in area, but was an important religious and cultural focal point during the Middle Ages, being located geographically central between Ireland (ÉRIU) and Gaelic Scotland. Iona was instrumental in

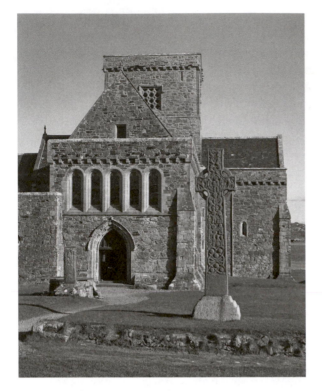

The abbey of Iona with the 9th-century St Martin's Cross (foreground at right). (William McKelvie)

the Christianization of the Picts and Anglo-Saxon Northumbria. In 563, COLUM CILLE (Columba; †597) founded a monastery on the island. Early DÁL RIATA kings, such as AEDÁN MAC GABRÁIN, were buried there.

The monastic scriptorium (manusciptproduction centre) on Iona produced several important documents, among them some of the earliest regular contemporary record keeping in Britain, leading to the Iona Chronicle (c. 686–c. 740).

Iona was an important centre of medieval sculpture, and the island boasts the highest concentration of carved stone monuments anywhere in the Celtic world. Among them are the large, free-standing high crosses, which begin to appear from around AD 800. It is likely that the Iona School is to be credited with having first placed a stone circle around the top part of a stone cross; that design feature is now generally regarded as defining the 'Celtic cross'.

Iona's central (and exposed) maritime position made the island an easy target for numerous attacks by Vikings and Irish kings between the late 8th and 10th centuries. A particularly devastating Viking raid occurred in 807. At the beginning of the 9th century, a new Columban monastery was founded at Kells, Co. Meath (Cenannas, Contae na Mí), Ireland, and Iona gradually lost its position as the main focus of the 'familia' of foundations of Colum Cille and his successors in favour of this new foundation. This shift is illustrated by the moving of the saint's relics to Kells in 877, which may also have been the time when the Book of KELLS arrived on the site from which its name is derived, although the manuscript might have already left Iona in the wake of the raid of 807.

Petra S. Hellmuth

ÉIRE (IRELAND)

Éire (Ireland) is home to the IRISH LANGUAGE and measures 84,429 km² (32,598 mi²) in area.

N

ULAIDH *ULSTER*
Ua Néill *O'Neill*
Tír Eoghain
Tyrone

CONNACHT

The
English
Pale
in
1488

X *Battle of the*
Boyne 1690

○ **Baile Átha**
Cliath
Dublin

Cill Dara
Kildare ○

LAIGHIN

Earldom
of
Ormond LEINSTER

○ Cill
Chainnigh
Kilkenny

Earldom
of
Desmond

MUMHA
MUNSTER

150 km

Contemporary Ireland (Éire) and western Britain, showing the traditional provinces, the border between the Republic and Northern Ireland (black on white), and Gaeltacht (Irish-speaking) areas. (Map by John T. Koch)

Political Division

More than 80 percent of Ireland's land mass is taken up by the Republic of Ireland, Poblacht na hÉireann (Éire for short, although like 'Ireland' it can also mean the whole island). The nation covers 70,285 km^2 (27,137 square miles) and is

Late medieval and early modern Ireland—places mentioned in the text. (Map by John T. Koch)

subdivided into four traditional provinces and twenty-six counties. Its capital is BAILE ÁTHA CLIATH (Dublin). There are slightly more than 4 million inhabitants in the Irish Republic, more than 80 percent of whom identify as Roman Catholics. The six counties in the northeast of the traditional nine-county province of Ulster (ULAID) were partitioned off through the British Government of Ireland Act in 1920. Now known as Northern Ireland, with the capital in Belfast (Béal Feirste), they remain part of the United Kingdom. At the last British census taken in 2001, Northern Ireland had 1,685,267 inhabitants, of whom approximately 40 percent were Roman Catholics and 45 percent belonged to various Protestant denominations. Both the identity politics and census methodology used in this survey have been criticized in the last decade.

The Irish Language

Ireland's Celtic language, Irish, which shares close kinship with SCOTTISH GAELIC and MANX, is spoken as a native language in western parts of the island known as the GAELTACHT areas. In 1996, approximately 30 percent of the population in the Irish Republic—where it is the official language—claimed to be Irish speakers.

In Northern Ireland, 10 percent of the population claimed some knowledge of the Irish language in 2001; see LANGUAGE [REVIVAL] MOVEMENTS IN THE CELTIC COUNTRIES. The continued survival of Irish as a mother tongue cannot be taken for granted.

The breadth of available national symbols and the distinctiveness and worldwide recognition of ANGLO-IRISH LITERATURE may explain why the Irish language and Irish literature are not as important to the Irish as, for instance, WELSH and its literature are for Welsh identity.

The Central and Later Middle Ages

An outline of Ireland's past down to the Anglo-Norman incursions is given in the article on ÉRIU. The Norman Richard de CLARE, 'Strongbow', intervened on the side of the deposed king of Leinster (Laighin < LAIGIN), Diarmait Mac Murchada, in 1169. The English King Henry II landed in October 1171 to reconfirm conquest. Over the next hundred years, Anglo-Norman families built up huge estates. From time to time anti-Irish legislation, such as the Statutes of KILKENNY, was passed to reconfirm the Anglo-Norman aristocracy's originally distinct status.

Plantation and Oppression of the Catholic Population

In the 15th century, the English Crown introduced a policy of 'Surrender and Regrant' of lands by the king. Henry VII's 'Poyning's Law' (1495) provided that future Irish parliaments and legislation had to receive prior approval from the English Privy Council. Having abolished the MONASTERIES and established a Protestant 'Church of Ireland' in 1537, Henry VIII proclaimed himself king of Ireland in 1541 and formally annexed the country to ENGLAND. The majority of the Irish remained Catholic and refused the imposition of Protestantism, often seeking a last resort in rebellion (see BIBLE; CHRISTIANITY; RENAISSANCE).

The Elizabethan plantation of parts of Ireland laid the foundations for the Protestant Ascendancy of the Anglo-Irish landlord class that was to dominate life in Ireland down to the 20th century. Following the Flight of the Earls (1607), when Hugh O'Neill (Aodh Ruadh), earl of Tyrone in Ulster, left Ireland for Spain with a small party of followers, it was clear that the dominant force in future Ireland would be English and Protestant. Under King James VI/I, large parts of Ulster were settled by Scottish and English Protestants. By 1704, the harsh Penal Laws passed against Catholics by the Irish parliament had consolidated and expanded Protestant ownership of land and deprived the Catholic population of any political power they might have had left. Catholics were excluded from parliament; were forbidden to own arms or a horse worth more than £5; and were not allowed to run schools, to vote, to serve in the army, or to engage in commerce or practise law. Classical Gaelic learning and literature, robbed of its patronage and social base, disappeared with the Irish-owned lands.

Union, Famine, and National Reawakening

Although the great 1798 rebellion led by Wolfe TONE was crushed, it resulted in the abolition of the Irish parliament and the full incorporation of Ireland into the

English state by the Act of Union passed in 1800. The new political unit was named the United Kingdom of Great Britain and Ireland, a term that survives in the current name of the United Kingdom of Great Britain and Northern Ireland. Members of Parliament now went to take their seats in London. The emancipation of the Catholic population began in 1829. The Young Ireland movement of the 1840s, led by Thomas Davis through the pages of his paper, *The Nation*, and its unsuccessful rising of 1848, was a first expression of the drive for the repeal of the Union with Britain, which would grow into the independence movement.

Unification with Britain also brought new economic problems, as the value of agricultural produce and real estate plummeted. Too many people relied solely on the potato as their staple crop and diet, with the result that the onset of potato blight led to FAMINE and EMIGRATION on an unprecedented scale. Between 1846 and 1851 almost half the Irish population either starved to death or emigrated.

The 1860s saw a revival of national aspirations with the rise of Fenianism both in Ireland itself and among the Irish diaspora in Britain and the New World. The secret Fenian organization, the Fianna, aimed to secure political independence by injuring English interests, and staged another unsuccessful uprising in 1867. However, with the disestablishment of the Catholic Church in Ireland in 1869 and the 1870 Irish Land Act, the first concessions were made to Irish interests (see LAND AGITATION). The national movement acquired a more constitutional character, with Charles Stewart PARNELL achieving substantial power through the Irish parliamentary party at Westminster, forcing the introduction of Home Rule bills and the passing of further Land Acts in the British parliament between 1880 and 1893. Following a long struggle on both political and cultural fronts, independence was finally achieved in 1921.

The 20th Century: Poblacht na hÉireann

During the Irish War of Independence (1919–21), British forces were fought to a standstill by the guerrilla troops of the IRISH REPUBLICAN ARMY (IRA). The aftermath of this conflict was the partitioning of Northern Ireland and the establishment elsewhere on the island of an independent state. The first name of the Irish state, adopted in 1922 after negotiations with the British government granted independence to Ireland, was Saorstát na hÉireann, or the Irish Free State. However, members of the government still had to swear an oath of allegiance to the British Crown, and the new state, as a dominion, remained part of the British Empire. A short but bloody civil war (1922–23) followed the partitioning, and a new constitution was adopted in 1937 that changed the name of the country to Éire (the ancient Celtic name of the island; see ÉRIU) and asserted its autonomy from the United Kingdom. On 18 April 1949, the country officially became a republic, changing its official name to Poblacht na hÉireann, Republic of Ireland.

Poblacht na hÉireann is a parliamentary republic governed by the Oireachtas, a parliament consisting of the directly elected Dáil Éireann (166 members) and the Seanad (60 members), which is nominated by grand electors. The head of government is the Taoiseach or Prime Minister, and the head of state is the President (Uachtarán), elected directly every 7 years. Poblacht na hÉireann is a member of the United

Nations and the European Union. The first official language of the Republic is Irish (Gaeilge), with English named as a second official language.

Following World War II, with emigration from Ireland again rising, the protectionist high tariff policy pursued by Éire was abandoned and successive programmes of economic expansion put into place. The result has been a mixed-market economy—largely based on AGRICULTURE, chemical industries, high technology, and services—which boomed in the 1990s (see CELTIC TIGER). The country introduced the euro as its currency in 1999, replacing the punt (Irish pound).

The 20th Century: Northern Ireland

The political loyalties within Northern Ireland have historically followed religious lines. The mostly Protestant 'Unionists' campaign for maintaining the union with the United Kingdom and are still in the majority. The 'nationalists' are mostly Catholics, with the political label signifying a preference for the six counties of Northern Ireland to be reunited with the rest of Ireland (see NATIONALISM). The terms 'loyalist' and 'republican', in a Northern Irish context, designate political and paramilitary groups that can be broadly viewed as more extreme unionists and more extreme nationalists, respectively, again tending to follow the Protestant–Catholic divide.

An organization in defence of the Protestant Ascendancy, the Orange Order was founded in 1795, and its annual processions are often the starting point for sectarian violence. Violence between the two factions grew following the partitioning of Ireland, and British troops began to occupy the Northern Ireland region in early 1969. In March 1972, the Northern Irish parliament was suspended, following the escalation of communal violence between Catholics and Protestants, and direct British rule introduced. Following several failed initiatives in the 1970s and 1980s, a ceasefire was agreed between the IRA and the Unionist paramilitary groups in 1994, and discussions involving the Irish Republic were resumed in 1996. On 10 April 1998, the Belfast Agreement, or Good Friday Agreement, established a new 108-member Northern Ireland Assembly in Belfast, which was obliged to include both Protestants and Catholics in its executive branch and pass legislation only if factions of both agreed. Since the Good Friday Agreement, troops have been withdrawn and a new police force—Police Service of Northern Ireland—has been created. Between 1972 and 2000, more than 3,600 people were killed by sectarian violence and/or British troops in Northern Ireland.

Marion Löffler

EISTEDDFOD

An eisteddfod, derived from the Welsh verb *eistedd* 'to sit', was a competitive session of bards and minstrels intent on demonstrating their artistic skills in the presence of a noble patron.

The first recorded eisteddfod took place in Cardigan Castle (Aberteifi) at Christmastide 1176, when Lord RHYS AP GRUFFUDD of Deheubarth presided as bards and minstrels competed for the two prime Chair awards, perhaps influenced by the competitive *puy* (<Latin *podium*) in France.

No more than three eisteddfodau can be verified before the 16th century: Carmarthen (CAER-FYRDDIN) *c.* 1451 and Caerwys, Flintshire (sir y Fflint), in 1523 and 1567, both with royal assent. Their main purpose was to secure the status of the professional bards and minstrels who had been tutored and licenced to practise their art against the trespass of 'rogues and vagabonds'. The forces of social change were to prove irresistible, however, and the bardic tradition petered out in the late 17th century.

In the 18th century, a fistful of devotees kept alive, mainly in north Wales, a wan, tavern-housed eisteddfod culture. But 1789 would change everything. Prompted by Thomas Jones, a Corwen-born exciseman, the London-based Gwyneddigion Society responded to a call for a renewed patronage. In September 1789, a Gwyneddigion-directed eisteddfod at Bala provided a blueprint for the modern institution that would thereafter be at the heart of Welsh culture at both local and national levels.

By 1858, when the Reverend John Williams (Ab Ithel, 1811–62) organized what was to be a fractious but epochal eisteddfod at Llangollen, the country was ripe for a properly constituted National Eisteddfod (see EISTEDDFOD GENEDLAETHOL CYMRU).

†Hywel Teifi Edwards

EISTEDDFOD GENEDLAETHOL CYMRU (NATIONAL EISTEDDFOD OF WALES)

Eisteddfod Genedlaethol Cymru (National Eisteddfod of Wales) made its first appearance in 1861 in Aberdare (Aberdâr). A general meeting of *eisteddfodwyr* at the stormy Llangollen EISTEDDFOD of 1858 decided that the time was ripe for a full-fledged annual national festival, which moved around the country annually until, overcome with debts, 'Yr Eisteddfod' folded in 1868. In 1880, Sir Hugh Owen inspired the creation of the National Eisteddfod Association, and the current ongoing series of 'Nationals' got under way at Merthyr Tudful in 1881.

In 1937, a more amicable relationship between the Eisteddfod Association and the GORSEDD BEIRDD YNYS PRYDAIN (Gorsedd of Bards) resulted in a new constitution and the creation of the National Eisteddfod Council, which in turn gave way in 1952 to the Court of the National Eisteddfod.

A peripatetic institution since its inception, now alternating only between north and south Wales, the location of the 'National' has long been a place of pilgrimage for Welsh people addicted to its mix of culture and *hwyl* (fun).

Today, it is generally accepted that the National Eisteddfod, held regularly during the first full week in August since 1918, exists to celebrate and foster WELSH-language culture, but it was not always so: The 'National' marginalized the Welsh language for the better part of a century. It took the revised constitution of 1937 to turn the tide by making Welsh the official language of its proceedings. Since 1950, when the 'All-Welsh rule' came into force, the 'National' has been true to its commission.

Today, major awards are given for excellence in all the arts. There has been a concerted effort to encourage a greater interest in the sciences as well. Scholarships are awarded to successful young contestants who wish to pursue careers in music and drama, and much more besides (see Welsh music; Welsh drama).

In the past, the 'National' has served Wales well as a forum for debating national concerns, as an arena for protest and dissent, and as a platform for demonstrating a will to prosper. It is now supported by the National Assembly (see Cynulliad Cenedlaethol Cymru).

†Hywel Teifi Edwards

ELFED/ELMET

Elfed/Elmet is the name of an early medieval Brythonic kingdom in what is now southwest Yorkshire, in north-central England. It is particularly noteworthy as a Celtic kingdom situated well outside of Wales (Cymru) and Cornwall (Kernow), and yet surviving quite late. We have three primary sources of evidence for Elfed: (1) place-names, (2) references in early Welsh poetry, and (3) historical notices relevant to the kingdom's annexation by Northumbria following Elfed's last ruler Certic.

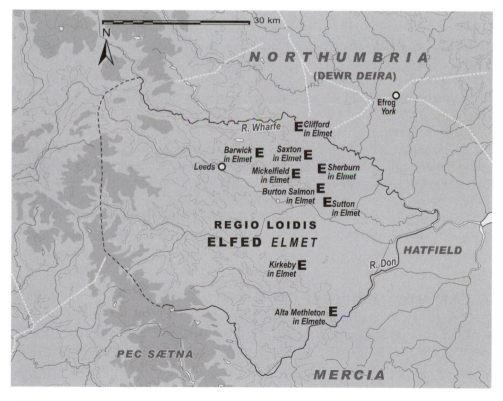

Elfed (elmet) and neighbouring regions. 'In Elmet' place-names are marked with a bold 'E'; the approximate limits of the kingdom before 7th-century annexation by Northumbria are shown in black (less certain western boundaries are indicated with dashed lines); Roman roads appear in white with thin dashed lines. (Map by John T. Koch)

Place-Name Evidence

Elfed is the modern Welsh form; the older form *Elmet* is preserved in several English place-names between the rivers Wharfe and Don in south Yorkshire, including Sherburn in Elmet. A grant of 1361 speaks of 'Kirkeby in Elmet', referring to present-day South Kirkby, south of Leeds. The evidence indicates an extensive land-locked territory astride the strategic frontier of the great kingdoms of Mercia and Northumbria. BEDE mentions the *silva Elmete* (the wood of Elmet; *Historia Ecclesiastica* 2.14). The name is probably Celtic.

Allusions to Elfed in Poetry

Of the praise poems in the *awdl* metre in the Book of Taliesin (LLYFR TALIESIN), two are addressed to a Dark Age north British ruler named Gwallawg. He is described in one as 'magistrate of Elfed'. Madawg Elfed occurs among the heroes of the GODODDIN. As with the style of OWAIN GWYNEDD or URIEN RHEGED, this name can be understood as 'Madawg, ruler of Elfed'. Also in *Llyfr Taliesin* is a 10th-century PROPHECY concerned with the messianic return of CADWALADR, Cadwallon's son, whose anticipated deeds include operations beyond the Solway Firth (Merin Rheged) and ruling Elfed.

John T. Koch

ELISEG'S PILLAR

Eliseg's Pillar is a broken stone pillar, originally about 3.6 m (12 ft) high, located in Llandysilio-yn-Iâl near Llangollen, Denbighshire (sir Ddinbych). It has a lengthy Latin inscription with Old WELSH names dating to the earlier 9th century, which gives the genealogy of the kings of POWYS and a unique version of their origin legend. The inscription commemorates a royal ancestor Elise (ELISEG) who is said to have taken the land from the English by the sword. The genealogical sequence has an exact parallel in the Powys GENEALOGIES in BL MS Harley 3859. It goes on to state that St Germanus blessed the son of Vortigern (see GWRTHEYRN) and the daughter of MACSEN WLEDIG; this seems to be the account of the foundation of the line. The pillar's origin legend is particularly ambitious in claiming descent from two rulers regarded as having held authority over the whole of BRITAIN before the arrival of the Anglo-Saxons.

John T. Koch

ELLAN VANNIN (ISLE OF MAN)

The Isle of Man is neither part of the modern political state of the United Kingdom nor part of Great Britain. Rather, it is a self-governing British Crown dependency and, like Canada and Australia, a member of the Commonwealth of Nations. As sovereign, the British monarch retains the title Lord of Man. Castletown was the ancient capital of this island, but in the 1870s administration moved to Douglas.

The Isle of Man is situated in the centre of the Irish Sea, approximately 26 km from Scotland (ALBA), 43 km from ENGLAND, and 43 km from Ireland (ÉIRE). It is approximately 53 km long and 19 km wide, and its area is 365 km^2.

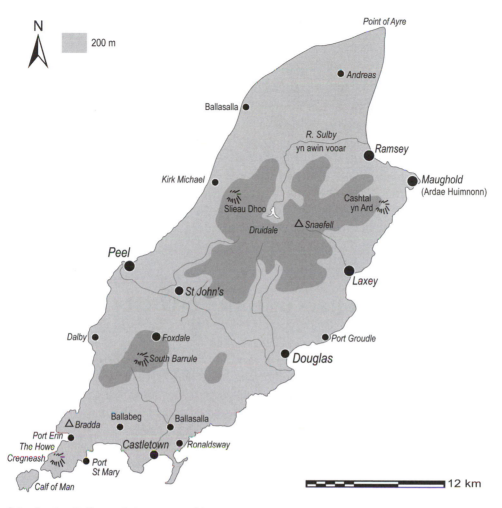

(Map by Ian Gulley and Antony Smith)

A chain of mountains extends from northeast to southwest, the highest of which is Snaefell (620 m). The mountain ranged divides the island into two distinct portions, north and south. Much of the coastline of the Isle of Man is very rugged and steep.

The earliest known inhabitants of the Isle of Man have been identified as Middle Stone Age huntergatherers from *c.* 7000 BC. Dating from the Copper and earlier Bronze Ages, *c.* 2500–*c.* 1500 BC, are the great stone circles such as the Meayl Circle at Cregneash and Cashtal yn Ard at Maughold.

Numerous early medieval monuments are found on the Isle of Man, including early Celtic keeills (small chapels) and sculptured crosses (see HIGH CROSSES). Approximately one fourth of these crosses have inscriptions in early GOIDELIC, written in the OGAM script.

The arrival of the Vikings toward the end of the 8th century had an immense effect on the history and culture of the Isle of Man. Coming from Norway, the Vikings forged links between the two countries that have survived up to the present time in the form of the Isle of Man's parliamentary system, which has existed for more than a thousand years. An annual open-air assembly of all the freemen at some central place where new laws were announced and disputes settled was an essential feature of the Norse system, and such an assembly was called the 'thing'; the Manx Parliament is called TYNWALD, the first part based on this word and the second on the Norse word *vollr,* meaning field or meeting-place. This open-air meeting is still held annually on 5 July on Tynwald Hill at St John's, near the centre of the island.

In Viking times, the coat of arms of the Isle of Man was a ship with sails furled. After the Viking era ended, it was changed to the three legs emblem, the earliest known examples being on the Manx Sword of State (*c.* AD 1230) and the 14th-century Maughold Cross.

Victor Kneale

ELLAN VANNIN (ISLE OF MAN), CELTICITY OF

The date of the arrival of Celtic speech in the Isle of Man is uncertain. Man was never incorporated into the Roman Empire, but the island was noted in GREEK AND ROMAN ACCOUNTS, where it was called variously *Monapia,* Μοναοιδα *Monaoida,* Μοναριvα *Monarina, Manavi,* and *Mevania.* The Old Irish and Old Welsh names for the Isle of Man—*Mano* and *Manau*—also occur for an ancient district in north Britain along the lower river Forth (Foirthe; see GODODDIN). The name is probably connected to the Celtic root reflected in Welsh *mynydd,* Breton *menez,* and Scottish Gaelic *monadh* 'mountain'. Both *Manann* and *Manau* are associated with an early mythological figure associated with seafaring, Irish MANANNÁN and Welsh MANAWYDAN. From the early post-Roman centuries, inscriptional evidence supports the presence of Celtic of both the Goidelic and BRYTHONIC types on the island.

The MANX language is a Celtic language of the Goidelic (GAELIC) type. Although several place-names are clearly of Norse origin, Norse speech failed to survive on the island. The majority of place-names (see ELLAN VANNIN [ISLE OF MAN], PLACE-NAMES OF) and family names of Manxborn families are of Celtic origin. Manx was widely spoken on the island until the later 19th century, but then its use rapidly declined. In recent years efforts have been made to encourage its use, and it is now an optional subject in the schools (see EDUCATION). Since 1977, Yn Chruinnaght (The gathering) has been held annually as a self-consciously Celtic Manx national festival.

Victor Kneale and John T. Koch

ELLAN VANNIN (ISLE OF MAN), IN EARLY IRISH LITERATURE

Although the Isle of Man did not produce any surviving medieval literary texts, it is often mentioned in early Irish texts, in the form of literary place-names such as *Inis*

Falga and *Emain Ablach* (Emain of the apples, cf. Welsh *Ynys Afallach* AVALON). Despite lying within sight of both Ireland and Scotland, the island usually appears as a markedly exotic location in medieval Gaelic literature. A notable feature of its appearance in most of the tales is a lack of detail in the descriptions of the island. While medieval Gaelic literature is rich in onomastics, there is seldom a mention of particular locations on the Isle of Man, and our impressions of the island, based on the tales, are of a dark and misty place, beetling with tall craggy cliffs, and populated by very few and rather strange creatures.

One of its most important and consistent associations in the tales is with the character MANANNÁN mac Lir, the sometime god of the Irish Sea. The Isle of Man, according to the authority of texts such as SANAS CHORMAIC ('Cormac's Glossary') and *Tochmarc Luaine* (The wooing of Luan), is the home of Manannán. In some cases, Manannán even seems to be a personification of the island. There are also connections with Midir, CÚ ROÍ mac Dáiri, and the smith Culann (CÚ CHULAINN's namesake).

One of the most extensive poetic uses of the Isle of Man in all medieval Gaelic literature occurs in a poem in praise of Raghnall, king of Man and the Isles (1187–1229). Raghnall was the great-grandson of Gofraidh Crobh-bhán, or Gofraidh Mérach as he is named in this poem. In 1187, Raghnall took over a kingdom that had been founded by his grandfather on the Isle of Man, but that also, at times, incorporated BAILE ÁTHA CLIATH (Dublin) and some of the Hebrides. Raghnall had strong Norse connections and is noted for his military prowess in *Orkneyinga Saga*.

View from about 1900 of Port Erin, Bradda Head, on the Isle of Man (Kione Vradda, Purt Çhiarn, Ellan Vannin). (Library of Congress)

Other Gaelic poems, including some written in praise of Feargal O'Reilly (†1291) found in the Book of the DEAN OF LISMORE, contain references to Manannán, and by implication to the Isle of Man.

Charles W. MacQuarrie

ELLAN VANNIN (ISLE OF MAN), FISHING AND MINING

The traditional Manx fishery was based on the exploitation of herring and cod spawning and nursery areas of the north Irish Sea on either side of the island. Along with agriculture, fishing was of prime importance in the economy, with the two activities being closely linked. Seventeenth-century fishing regulations indicate the long-established responsibility of quarterland or more substantial farmers to have their boats with stipulated amounts of net in readiness for the annual mustering of the herring fleet. The herring catch was of supreme importance and drift-net fishing continued to be used until the 1930s.

The zenith of Manx fishing was attained in the 1880s. At that time, it was estimated that 13,000 individuals out of a total population of 53,000 were either directly or indirectly dependent on fishing. Many fishermen of this era had an almost year-long commitment to their calling, although this made them more vulnerable than the crofter-fishermen when the shoals were absent, as occurred during much of the 1890s.

The present status of Manx fishing reflects profound changes following an early 20th-century decline in the herring fishery. Beginning in the 1930s traditional drift-net fishing was replaced first by ring-netting and later by trawling. Drastic depletion of fish stocks followed the exploitation of the spawning grounds to the east of the island by pickle curers and Klondykers in the 1970s. Ensuing fishing quotas have severely curtailed herring fishing to the extent that the formerly popular undyed Manx kipper is now difficult to obtain. By the 1990s fishing and farming together produced a mere 2 percent of Manx national income. A new fishing resource discovered close to Port Erin in 1937 in the form of scallops is the target catch of what remains of the Manx fishery. Ninety percent of all fish landed now consist of scallops and queen scallops, which occur over much of the north Irish Sea.

Copper and iron staining on coastal rocks would have encouraged prehistoric mining. The first documented reference is a charter of 1246 authorizing the Cistercian monks of Furness to mine, transport, and sell minerals from the island. In the modern period, Cornish expertise and labour played important rôles in Manx mining, which came to fruition in the period *c.* 1830–90 as sources of lead and zinc.

The Great Laxey Wheel (or Lady Isabella), erected in 1854 to drain the Laxey mine, epitomized the optimism of the period. This remarkable pitch back-shot wheel with a diameter of 22.1 m was the largest to be constructed at that time. Its designer was a local man, Robert Casement. Water from a wide catchment area, collected in a hillside cistern, ascended a stone-built tower to turn the wheel. Power from the wheel was transferred via the crank along the top of a *c.* 410 m stone viaduct by means of a sectional timber beam running on bogies. An inverted T-shaped rocker changed the horizontal movement of the viaduct rod to the vertical movement of the pump rods. The wheel is the island's most famous example of industrial archaeology. Overseas competition and exhaustion of the veins led to rapid decline with little significant production occurring after 1920.

F. J. Radcliffe

ELLAN VANNIN (ISLE OF MAN), MANX CONSTITUTION

The Isle of Man is a dependent territory of the United Kingdom, having full internal self-government. Its constitutional history is unique. Its legislature and customary law can be traced back to the kingdom of Man and the Isles, established by the Norsemen in the 10th century. In consequence, the Isle of Man justifiably claims to have the world's oldest parliament.

The Norse Kingdom

The origins of the Norse KINGDOM OF MAN and the Isles are obscure, but it was well established by the 11th century. This area was not a wholly independent kingdom, as the kings of Man owed allegiance to the kings of Norway, who regarded Man as one of their territories. The kingdom included all of the Hebrides of present-day Scotland until 1156, but thereafter only the Western Isles. An important feature of the Norse kingdom was the annual open-air assembly known as TYNWALD, presided over by the king and attended by his officers, including the two deemsters who were the guardians of the customary law, and representatives of the people. Tynwald was primarily a judicial body, at which the customary law was also proclaimed. The customary law, about which little is known, was probably introduced by the Norse settlers. Elements of Norse feudal tenure survived in Manx customary law to the 20th century.

Scottish Rule

In 1266, by the Treaty of Perth, Magnus, king of Norway, sold Man and the Western Isles to Alexander, king of the Scots, for 4,000 marks and an annual payment of 100 marks. The Treaty provided that the people of Man should be subject 'to the laws and customs' of Scotland. Had the Treaty been fully implemented, Man would have been absorbed into the kingdom of Scotland. Between 1290 and 1333, however, control of Man passed to and fro between the Scots and the English during the Anglo-Scottish wars. Following the battle of Halidon Hill in 1333, English control of Man was finally established, and Edward III then granted to Sir William de Montacute, who claimed Man by right of descent from the Norse kings: 'all the rights and claims which we have, have had, or in any way could have, in the Isle of Man ... so that neither we, nor our heirs, nor any other in our name, shall be able to exact or dispose of any right or claim in the aforesaid Island.' The grant by Edward III effectively restored the Norse kingdom, but without the Western

Isles. Sir William de Montacute, who had been created Earl of Salisbury in 1337, died in 1344 and was succeeded by his son; in 1392, he sold Man to Sir William Le Scroop. In 1399, Le Scroop was beheaded by Henry IV and Man then came into the absolute possession of the English Crown. It has remained a possession of the Crown ever since.

Rule of the Stanleys

In 1406, Man was granted by Henry IV to Sir John Stanley and his heirs, on the service of rendering two falcons on paying homage, and two falcons to all future kings of England on the day of their coronation. Thereafter, for more than 350 years, the descendants of Sir John Stanley were the hereditary kings of Man, or 'Lords' as they were styled after 1504, until, in 1765, the second Duke of Atholl sold Man to the English Crown for £70,000. The Revestment Act 1765 provided that the Isle of Man should be 'unalienably vested' in His Majesty and his heirs.

Throughout the period from 1406 to 1765, the kings or lords of Man rarely visited the island. They ruled through the captains or governors whom they appointed. Although the customary laws were respected and Tynwald continued to meet, English influence was pervasive. English was the language of government, although Manx Gaelic remained the language of the people until the beginning of the 19th century. The Stanleys established courts on the English model, alongside the deemsters' courts in which the customary law was administered. The two systems gradually converged, but were not brought together until 1883.

During the 17th century, Tynwald began to enact legislation in a recognizably modern form. Tynwald comprised the Governor and the principal officers, including the deemsters and the bishop, who formed the Lord's Council, later to become the Legislative Council, together with the twenty-four 'Keys'—originally a kind of jury, but later to be regarded as the representatives of the people, although generally appointed by the Lord. In the 18th century, the Keys became the 'House of Keys' and elected a Speaker, emulating the House of Commons. Bills passed by Tynwald did not become law until approved by the Lord.

After 1765, the British government assumed complete control of the island's finances. The island's revenue, mainly customs duties, was remitted to London and, although it had been intended to manage the Manx revenue as a separate fund, in time it was treated as part of the revenue of the United Kingdom. Public expenditure had to be approved by the Treasury in London. In addition, the Governor was answerable to the Home Secretary, and the Home Office in London thus exerted effective control over the island's affairs. In form and in fact, the Governor—or Lieutenant Governor as he was now styled—was the government. He presided over the Legislative Council and Tynwald, and served as the senior judge of the island's courts. For most of the 19th century, the island was largely governed by a form of direct rule from London, and was, for many purposes, treated as though it were part of the United Kingdom. Although Tynwald continued to enact legislation, increasingly Acts of the Westminster Parliament, which had assumed the power to legislate for the Isle of Man since the 14th century, were applied to the island.

In 1866, the British government agreed to allow Tynwald some control over public expenditure; at the same time, the House of Keys became an elected body and ceased to have judicial functions. In addition, Tynwald began to perform an administrative rôle by creating statutory committees to undertake specific functions. A Committee of Highways had been established in 1776 by Act of Tynwald, but by the end of the 19th century eleven such bodies, which became known as Boards of Tynwald, were in operation. Subsequently, many other boards were formed as government assumed responsibility for new matters. The significance of these boards was that they were a form of local government, largely independent of the Governor. Local authorities were also created for the towns, villages, and parishes in the latter part of the 19th century.

Twentieth Century

In the 20th century, the House of Keys became the dominant element in Tynwald. Starting in 1919, the official members of the Legislative Council were progressively replaced by members elected by the House of Keys, which was itself given power, by Act of Tynwald, to override the Legislative Council. The British government relinquished all control over the island's finances in 1958, leaving Tynwald in control of both taxation and expenditure. Between 1961 and 1992, almost all of the executive functions of the Governor were transferred to other bodies answerable to Tynwald. The Governor retains certain constitutional functions and appoints, or advises on the appointment of, the judiciary, and is the representative of the Crown on the island.

In 1986–87, the Boards of Tynwald were replaced by nine Government Departments, each headed by a Minister nominated by the Chief Minister, who is himself appointed by the Governor on the nomination of Tynwald. The Chief Minister and the Ministers, who must all be members of Tynwald, constitute the Council of Ministers—in effect, the Cabinet of the Manx government. Since 1945, nearly all the functions that had been exercised by the British government in the Isle of Man at one time or another, including those relating to the post office, customs and excise, telecommunications, merchant shipping, minerals, and the territorial sea, have been transferred to the Manx government. The British government is now responsible only for defence and foreign affairs.

In 1972, when the United Kingdom joined the European Economic Community (EEC), the Isle of Man was excluded from the Treaty of Accession, except for free trade in goods and for certain other limited purposes.

T. W. Cain

ELLAN VANNIN (ISLE OF MAN), MATERIAL CULTURE IN THE HIGH MIDDLE AGES

The late 11th-century Norse Kingdom of the Isles created a distinctive Norwegian/Celtic cultural entity in the northern Irish Sea. Medieval settlement was disbursed; there were no villages or urban centres. Land division was based upon a primary unit known as the treen, which was subdivided into quarterlands and progressively grouped upward into parishes and sheadings.

Three high-status sites dominate the archaeological record: Peel Castle, Castle Rushen, and Rushen Abbey. There is no evidence for the nature of settlement or the quality of life beyond these centres of power. None of the 700 or so quarterland farms—the backbone of Manx social and economic life—has been excavated. Medieval iron and glass are rare.

Peel Castle has provided a wide range of information about the exploitation of natural resources, especially animals, birds, and fish. Cattle form by far the largest group of animal bones, followed by sheep and pigs, with a few horse, deer, and dog bones being noted. In contrast, of the forty-five species of birds, only five were domesticated, yet at least thirty-eight of them, mostly seabirds, formed part of the human diet. Fish were also important in the Manx economy, as is clear from the complex system of herring tithes. The twenty-eight species identified at Peel imply both deep-sea and inshore fishing. Shellfish were also consumed in quantity. Manx medieval society not only relied on domesticated animals and birds, but also exploited local populations of wild birds, fish, and shellfish to a high degree.

Locally handmade cooking wares continued in production until late in the 16th century. The island also received considerable quantities of imports from Britain and the Continent. Money was in general use: Tithes, payable by the majority of the farms, were valued in monetary terms, although payments in kind were also acceptable.

Manx Medieval Landscape and Society in an Irish Sea Context

The Isle of Man had neither the open-field systems of northwest England and lowland north Wales nor the planned landscapes of Anglo-Norman Ireland. The beginnings of nucleation around the two medieval castles and at Ballasalla seem to date from the 15th century at the earliest. The parish churches are diminutive affairs—simple, single-celled extensions of preexisting keeills. Only the cathedral of St Germans at Peel Castle is aisled. The island was owned and administered as a single entity by its kings and lords. The lack of moated sites and manors is a clear indication that society was much less vertically structured than, for example, in neighbouring areas of England—a feature of Manx social life that persists today.

The earliest extant Manx statutes from the 15th century allowed the creation of boundaries surrounding landholdings and from late in the next century included regulations—heights and materials—for their construction. These laws demonstrate a preoccupation with controlling the movements of livestock and of preserving crops from animal damage. It is considered probable, however, that enclosure did not become the norm until the 17th century. The characteristic Manx field boundary—a 'sod hedge'—is made from a combination of stone and earth, and could be quite large, but it is noticeable that later boundaries relating to the expansion of landholdings were often insubstantial and more heavily reliant on a vegetative topping of gorse to render them stock-proof. Stone walls were built to enclose new intack (cleared land) during the 19th century, as well as to divide the commons following disafforestation in the 1860s, marking a complete change from the customary indigenous boundary construction.

P. J. Davey and Andrew Johnson

ELLAN VANNIN (ISLE OF MAN), PLACE-NAMES OF

Early Names, General

Only a few names are found in the Isle of Man that definitely predate the arrival of the Scandinavian language (from the 9th century onward). They include the name of the island itself: Man, probably from the Indo-European root **men*-'rise', as Man rises from the water. *Douglas* is Proto-Celtic **duboglassio* 'dark water', Welsh *du*, Irish *dubh* 'black, dark', with Welsh *glais*, Irish *glas*, *glais(e)* 'water, stream'. The name *Rushen*, Irish *roisean*, is a diminutive form of *ros* 'moor, heath, hill, headland, swamp, wood'.

River Names

It is noteworthy that there are no old river names attested in Man of the type found in Britain or Ireland. The longest river in Man, the Sulby river, is some 22 km long and is known in Manx as *yn awin vooar* (Irish *an abhainn mhór*) 'the big river'. There is also the *awin ruy* (Irish *abhainn* + *ruaidh*) 'red river'.

Names of Ancient Monuments

Another category conspicuous by its absence—completely in this case—is meaningful sets of names for prehistoric monuments, such as graves and fortifications.

Goidelic Names

Like the Goidelic names in Galloway (Gall Ghàidhil) in southwest Scotland that contain the place-name elements *sliabh* 'mountain, moor-hill' and *carraig* 'rock', names of this type in Man seem to date from the earliest Goidelic settlements on the island *c.* AD 500 and thereafter: *Slieau Dhoo* 'black mountain' (Irish *sliabh dubh*) and *Carrick* '(the) rock' (Irish *carraig*). Names consisting solely of a noun (without the definite article)—for example, *Rushen*, *Ard*, *Carrick*—represent the oldest names in Man. Names comprising a noun with the definite article, such as *Niarbyl*, from *yn arbyl* (Irish **an earball*) 'the tail' (rock formation—unless this is a prepositional form, *in earball* 'at the tail'), would be the next oldest, but are also seldom attested. Nevertheless, they are pre-Scandinavian. Names such as *Purt ny Hinshey*, *Cashtal yn Ard*, and *Cronk y Voddy* have the form definite noun plus dependent definite noun in the genitive, and are in reality phrasal names. Names of this type, which are also encountered in Ireland and Scotland, are relatively recent creations (12th–13th centuries). They form the overwhelming majority of Gaelic names in Man and in their present form are unlikely to be pre-Scandinavian.

Names in *balla* (Irish *baile*) 'settlement, farm, village, town' are the most common name type in Man. Except for possibly one or two examples, the general distribution of names in *balla-* seems to be post-Scandinavian. In Ireland, it can be shown that such names became much more common after *c.* 1150. In Man, the first attestation of *balla-* is to be found *c.* 1280 in the Limites or Abbeyland Bounds attached to the Chronicles of Man, such as *Balesalach* (*Ballasalla*). However, most of the *balla*-names seem to be quite late. The earliest would be descriptive—*balla* plus adjective, such as *Ballabeg* 'little farm' (Irish *baile beag*); then geographically descriptive, with an attached noun in the genitive, such as *Ballacurree* (nominative *Curragh*) 'marsh farm' (Irish *baile curraigh* [*currach*]); and later with a personal name or surname as the specific, such as *Ballakelly* 'Kelly's farm' (Irish *baile (mh)ic Ceallaigh*), *Ballacorlett* 'Corlett's farm'.

Scandinavian Names

Many of the prominent natural features in Man, including valleys, mountains, and coastal rocks, bear Scandinavian names.

- Valleys: *Cardle* < *kvernárdalr* 'mill river dale', *Eskdale* < *eskedalr* 'ashdale' (the older name for Dhoon Glen), *Groudle* < *grafdalr* 'narrow dale'
- Mountains: *Snaefell* 'snow mountain', *Greeba* < *gnípa* 'summit', *Barrule* < *vörðufjall* 'cairn mountain'

Ramsey < *hrams-á* 'wild garlic river' and *Laxey* < *laxá* 'salmon river' are originally river names transferred to settlements. Many headlands and peninsulas bear Scandinavian names: *The Howe* (< *höfuð* 'hill, headland' or *haugr* 'hill, mound'), *Cregneash* < *krók-nes* 'crooked (indented coastline) promontory'. There are some twenty-eight *vík*-names, such as *Fleshwick* < *flesja(r)-vík* 'green (grassy) spot creek', and twenty-six *by*-names, such as *Dalby* < *dalr-by* 'dale farm' and *Sulby* < *súla-by* 'farm by the cleft fork (in a river)'. The element *staðir* 'farm' also occasionally appears, as in *Leodest* < *Ljótólfsstaðir* 'Ljótólf's farm' and *Aust* < *Auðolfsstaðir* 'Auðolf's (Adolf's) farm'.

'Inversion compounds' are formed from two elements from one language, but set together according to the syntax of another language, and as such are a result of language contact: *Dreemlang* 'long ridge', for example, is Manx *dreeym* (Irish *driom*), with English dialect *lang* 'long', but in Gaelic word-order, viz. 'ridge long'. Scandinavian names of this type are scarce, but one or two examples are attested, including *Toftar Asmund* (*c.* 1280) 'Asmund's hillocks' < Old Norse *toftir* 'hillocks' with the Scandinavian personal name *Ásmundr*.

English Names

Castletown and Peel are English. The name Castletown itself is first attested as *casteltown* in 1511. In the Abbeyland Bounds of *c.* 1280, Castletown appears as *uillam* (accusative case of *villa*) *castelli*, which in all probability is a translation of Irish *baile a' chaistil* (*caisteal*), Manx *balley y chashtal*. Peel is first evidenced in 1595. Prior to that, it was known as *Holmtown* (1417) 'island town' (< Old Norse *holmr* 'island' with Middle English *toun*. The parish names in Man comprise the element *kirk* plus the name of the saint to whom the parish church is dedicated, in Gaelic word-order—Kirk Maughold, Kirk Lonan, Kirk Braddan, and so on (although 'Kirk' falls away in everyday speech). Originally, the element is Old Norse *kirkja* 'church'. The development in Man seems to have taken place around the 13th century.

In Manx, the generic for church is *keeill* (Irish *cill*), which is the normal word for a ruined church or cell of the early Christian period. Many of these *keeills*, however, are of a later date, probably of the late Scandinavian period (13th century). In place-names, the element is used to denote small churches or chapels, such as *Keeill Woirrey* 'St. Mary's Church' (Irish *cill Mhoire*). In the genitive, it is found in such names as *Ballakilley* 'church farm' (Irish *baile cille*) and *Lag ny Killey* 'the church hollow' (Irish *lag na cille*).

George Broderick

ELLAN VANNIN (ISLE OF MAN), PREHISTORY

Evidence for the first Mesolithic (Middle Stone Age) on the Isle of Man consists almost entirely of microlithic flint tools. Between 5000 and 4000 BC, the earliest inhabitants were apparently replaced by groups using much heavier tools and weapons, which represent local developments in both Man and Ulster (ULAID). These peoples were also essentially hunter-gatherers, but pollen evidence shows that they had a greater impact on the landscape. They burned woodland clearings to encourage game, and eventually adopted cereal cultivation.

By around 3000 BC, knowledge of AGRICULTURE, pottery, and polished stone tools—harbingers of the Neolithic (New Stone Age)—had arrived. Manx inhabitants began to construct large megalithic tombs in which to bury their dead. The form and ritual associated with these monuments is so close to that visible on tombs in Ulster and southwest Scotland as to suggest that the island was part of a coherent local socio-economic system.

The Late Neolithic (or 'Ronaldsway neolithic') on Man saw a remarkable set of insular developments, unparalleled elsewhere. Between around 2800 and 2200 BC, distinctive pottery (the Ronaldsway urns), flintwork (the hump-backed scraper and lozenge-shaped arrowhead), incised slate plaques, and local exploitation of a local rock source for the production of the unique 'roughened-butt' axes were all characteristic.

During the earlier Bronze Age (*c.* 2200–1500 BC), the island returned to the mainstream. The specific links are with Ireland (ÉRIU), especially the northeast region of that island. At some time during the Later Bronze Age (*c.* 1500–750 BC), a massive dominant hill-fort was constructed on South Barrule, the highest land in the south of the Isle of Man. Bronze tools and implements were used in greater numbers and appear to show closer relationships with Britain.

The IRON AGE on Man runs from after 750 BC up to the arrival of CHRISTIANITY by around AD 500. During the 1st century, a number of very large circular timber houses were built, especially in the south of the island, that show direct contacts with the Roman Empire, with metal and glass artefacts from far afield.

P. J. Davey

EMAIN MACHAE

Emain Machae—the legendary capital of Ulaid and the court of King Conchobar and the Ulster Cycle heroes in early Irish tradition—is identified with Navan Fort, which is situated 2.6 km west of Armagh (Ard Mhacha). Navan Fort is the most prominent monument in an archaeological complex of sites dating from the Neolithic to the early medieval period. The site has been variously identified with either the Ισαμνιον *Isamnion* or northern ρεγια *Regia* of Ptolemy's 2nd-century map of Ireland (Ériu).

The earliest evidence for settlement within the complex is to be found on the drumlin (glacial oval hill) on which Navan Fort was later constructed. It consisted of a series of pits containing Neolithic pottery and flint tools. At approximately 1000 BC, there is abundant evidence for Later Bronze Age activity within the complex. At Navan a circular enclosure, some 46 m across, was made that consisted of a ring ditch (approximately 5 m across and 1 m deep) and a series of internally erected timber posts.

By *c.* 400 BC, Navan Fort began to see a sequence of major architectural changes. Within the area of the earlier ditched enclosure was erected a series of figure-of-eight structures that consisted of a smaller round house, 10–12 m in diameter, attached to a larger enclosure, 20–25 m across and entered by way of a fenced walkway. Finds associated with these structures, which were regularly renewed, include coarse ceramics, a few bronze objects, and the skull of a Barbary ape—the latter seen as evidence for a distant gift exchange from North Africa along ocean trade routes across Europe's Atlantic Zone.

At approximately 100 BC, Navan underwent two major architectural changes. The occupants of the site surrounded the top of the hill with a hengiform enclosure; that is, they encircled the hill with a large outer bank and an inner ditch. The earlier structures were cleared away and replaced by a single circular building, constructed of approximately 269 upright oak posts, which measured 40 m in diameter. The massive central post has been dated to 95 BC. The entire 'Forty-Metre Structure' was filled with boulders and the timber along the outer edge was burned and capped, forming an earthen mound some 5 m high.

At the foot of Navan Fort lies Loughnashade (Loch na Séad), a small lake. Its boggy shore yielded four large bronze horns (see carnyx), decorated in the La Tène style.

J. P. Mallory

EMIGRATION, BRITTANY

See Celtic Languages in North America, Breton.

EMIGRATION, CORNWALL

Emigration may be seen as part of the ongoing experience of the Cornish people from the earliest times to the present, broadly related to 'push' factors in Cornwall (Kernow), such as famine and economic decline, and 'pull' factors in other territories, such as mineral rewards. The earliest historically documented emigration experience for the Cornish was the number of southwestern Brythonic-speaking peoples who emigrated to Brittany (Breizh), generally explained (dating from the 6th-century account of Gildas) as motivated primarily by the pressure from Saxon invaders from the east (see Breton migrations). This age-old movement of peoples between Cornwall and Brittany continued until the Reformation. Over time, emigration out of Cornwall into the rest of the islands of Britain and Ireland (Éire) also occurred, most often where technical prowess in hard-rock mining was required, as in parts of Ireland and in the coal-mining regions of Wales (Cymru) and England.

On the American continent, the Cornish emigrants mined copper in the Upper Peninsula of Michigan and lead in Wisconsin and Illinois, but then moved westward, into territories such as Montana, Arizona, and New Mexico, eventually making for the 1849 gold rush in California. Twenty-four years before the California gold rush, Cornish miners went to Mexico to open the silver mines of Pachuca and Real del Monte. 'Cousin Jacks and Jennies' also travelled to South Africa to mine copper, diamonds, and gold, playing an active part in the Zulu and Boer wars before the Union of South Africa was formed. Chile, Peru, New Zealand, and Canada were other favourite targets of the Cornish, who often travelled for farming opportunities as well.

Territories such as South Australia, founded in 1836, became important destinations for the Cornish, as, alongside copper mining, they offered religious freedom. The potato blight of 1845–46 had an impact in Cornwall as well, causing massive emigration in the 1840s (see Famine). Approximately one third of the entire population of Cornwall had gone overseas by the end of the 19th century, and by this time the maxim that 'wherever in the world was a hole in the ground one was likely to find a Cornishman' seemed entirely true.

Alan M. Kent

EMIGRATION, IRELAND
See Celtic Languages in North America, Irish.

EMIGRATION, ISLE OF MAN
The 18th century saw the widespread emigration of young adults from the Isle of Man (Ellan Vannin). Beginning in the 1820s, favourable reports from pioneering emigrants lured some Manx individuals to Cleveland, Ohio. In 1845, potato blight affected Manx farming communities, and the total loss of the crop in the following year, coupled with news of gold finds in America and Australia, resulted in a further burst of emigration between 1847 and 1851.

The 20th century witnessed successive waves of emigration due to economic pressures—most notably during the 1950s and 1970s. The almost full labour market provided by the success of the finance sector reduced the need for the young working population to emigrate en masse.

The existence of Manx societies in Cleveland, Queensland, New Zealand, Dubai, and London, for example, shows the continued desire of the Manx diaspora to identify with the Isle of Man.

Breesha Maddrell

EMIGRATION, SCOTLAND

See Celtic Languages in North America, Scottish Gaelic.

EMIGRATION, WALES

The movement of Welsh people to settle overseas has been smaller in scale than the corresponding flows of emigrants from Ireland (Éire) and Scotland (Alba). Moreover, such movement has not been as prominent a feature of the history of Wales (Cymru) as internal migration to England. A period of significant migration during the late 17th and early 18th centuries was followed by a longer, more voluminous, and almost continuous phase between the 1790s and the early 1930s. This outward movement has continued in recent times, albeit on a smaller scale. Welsh emigrants have been notably diverse in terms of their geographical, social and occupational origins, their motives in emigrating, and the destinations they have chosen.

The absence or unreliability of statistical records makes it difficult to accurately assess the number of Welsh emigrants, but it is certain it is higher than the recorded figures suggest. In the 19th century, when systematic records of emigration began to be kept by many countries, the British government did not differentiate between emigrants from England and Wales, and in the receiving countries many Welsh were classified as English. Extant official records state that at the end of the 19th century approximately 100,000 people who had been born in Wales were living in the United States, 13,500 in Canada, and 13,000 in Australia. The majority of Welsh emigrants settled in what became the United States, but in the early 20th century greater numbers of Welsh people began moving within the British Empire, especially to Canada. During the last half-century, Canada and Australia have been the main destinations for Welsh emigrants.

The permanent *Gwladfa* in Patagonia, Argentina, was established in 1865 in the Chubut valley to establish a proto-Welsh-language state free from English incursion. During its years of expansion between 1865 and 1914, the colony attracted between 3,000 and 4,000 Welsh people.

Nonconformist religion, *eisteddfodau* (sing. EISTEDDFOD), and choral societies have played a formative rôle in most Welsh immigrant communities. In the United States and Patagonia, Welsh newspapers were, and remain, important vehicles for maintaining Welsh ethnic networks and promoting activities.

Bill Jones

ENAID OWAIN AB URIEN

Enaid Owain ab Urien (The soul of Owain son of Urien; also known as *Marwnad Owain*) is an early Welsh poem attributed by many modern scholars to the historical 6th-century poet Taliesin in the Llyfr Taliesin manuscript. Owain is identified as lord of Rheged.

The poem's content is essentially a prayer for the hero's soul. The poet does not adopt the explicit attitude of singing on the occasion of Owain's death. Given that Owain is otherwise famous in early Welsh poetry, and eventually became one of the great heroes of international Arthurian literature (cf. tair rhamant), concern for his soul among Christian men of letters might have inspired this polished poem a century or more after his death.

John T. Koch

ENCLOSURES

Enclosures are an archaeological feature of Iron Age settlements, highly characteristic of ancient Celtic-speaking areas. This general term functions as an umbrella to cover several subcategories—*Viereckschanzen* (rectangular enclosures), hill-forts, cattle stockades, and other areas of land delimited by earthworks, most commonly a bank and a ditch.

In the eastern La Tène area, most enclosures were *Viereckschanzen*, whose functions are still unclear. Farther west, in Gaul, alongside other types of enclosures, one finds examples of *Viereckschanzen*, which seem to have counterparts in the south of England. In southern England and the western La Tène zone of the Continent, hill-forts and oppida (sing. oppidum) also occur; these are essentially fortified towns.

Peter E. Busse

ENGLAND (LLOEGR/SASANA)

The Anglo-Saxon 'conquest' resulted in the establishment of several Old English-speaking kingdoms on the island of Britain, composed of several different north Germanic tribes including Angles and Saxons. The latter are the source of the Irish and Scottish Gaelic word *Sasana* and the Welsh ethnonym *Saeson* 'English people', although the Welsh word for England itself is *Lloegr*. The word 'England' comes into general use following Bede's AD 731 Ecclesiastical History of the English People (*gentis Anglorum*), but a united England emerged only in the 10th century.

Cornwall (Kernow), one of the Celtic countries, is considered part of England (though not universally accepted as such; see Nationalism). Many other Brythonic kingdoms were incorporated into England over the course of the the Middle Ages as well, including Brynaich, Rheged, Elfed/ Elmet, Cumbria, and part of Ystrad Clud (Strathclyde). There is no record of how long Celtic speech persisted in these areas, but many important place-names in England are Celtic, such as the river Avon (Welsh *afon*, 'river'). There is further evidence that Celtic speech persisted long after conquest. For instance, Asser's *Life of King Alfred* records distinct Old Welsh place-names in eastern England still known in the late 9th century. Some technically 'English' areas bordering Wales remained linguistically and culturally Welsh into the 19th century.

In addition to assimilating a Celtic substrate, Celtic-speaking immigrants have formed a part of English society from the beginning. Reliable statistical data on Celtic speech in England are not available, but London, in particular, played an important rôle in Celtic-language publishing and in cultural and linguistic revival in the modern period.

Celtic contributions to the English language, culture, and history have typically been underplayed, occasionally for political reasons but by and large due to a lack of recognition.

Antone Minard

ENGLYN

Englyn is a type of Welsh metre. Eight different kinds of *englynion* are listed among the traditional twenty-four strict metres, all with obligatory CYNGHANEDD (systematic line-internal sound correspondences) from the 14th century onward (see CERDD DAFOD; CYWYDD). Two of these metres have only three lines—the *englyn milwr* (lit. 'soldier *englyn*') and the *englyn penfyr* (lit. 'short-end *englyn*'). The following famous example of the *englyn penfyr* (in which medieval spelling is retained) is from the HELEDD cycle:

> *Stauell Gyndylan ys tywyll heno,*
> *Heb dan, heb gannwyll.*
> *Namyn Duw, pwy a'm dyry pwyll?*
>
> Cynddylan's hall is dark tonight,
> Without fire, without candle.
> But for God, who will give me sense?

From the earliest period, *englynion* were normally used in extended series known as *cyngogion*, and later as a *cadwyn* or chain, linked by *cyrch-gymeriad*, repeating a word or sound from the end of one line to the beginning of the next. In the work of the Poets of the Princes of the 12th and 13th centuries (see GOGYNFEIRDD), the *englynion* series seems to have been an alternative form to the *awdl*. Isolated instances of the use of *englynion* within *awdlau* by the Poets of the Princes are known, and this practice spread rapidly in the 14th century to become standard practice in the *awdlau* of the Poets of the Nobility. The *englyn* has remained popular with folk poets from the 18th century until the present day, as many commemorative verses on gravestones throughout Wales (CYMRU) attest, and it is the mainstay of the contemporary flourishing of strict-metre poetry.

Dafydd Johnston

ÉOGANACHT

The Éoganacht were a powerful historic federation of related dynasties who virtually monopolized the KINGSHIP of Munster (MUMU) from the 5th to the 10th centuries, up to the ascendancy of Mathgamain mac Cennétig of the DÁL GCAIS in AD 964. The provincial kingship of Munster, lost to the Dál gCais in the 10th century, was wrested back for several decades in the 12th century.

The actual origins are obscure, but based on a doctrine of common descent from Conall Corc, the legendary founder of the royal seat at CAISEL MUMAN. Corc would have flourished *c*. 400.

The name *Éogan* is associated in early accounts with the Celtic word for the yew tree, Middle Irish *eó*, pointing to an Old Celtic name **Iwogenos* 'Born of the yew' (cf. Gaulish *Ivorīgi* 'Yew-king' [gen.]). The main religious foundation of the Éoganacht at Emly, Co. Limerick (Old Irish Imleach Ibar), derives its name from another Old Irish word for yew (*ibar* < Celtic *eburo-*), and a surviving decorated shrine from this site was made of yew-wood.

The central three septs of the dynasty, which inhabited east and central Munster—Éoganacht Chaisil, Éoganacht Glendamnach, and Éoganacht Áine—formed a core, with the great majority of the kings of Munster coming from these groups.

From the accession of Feidlimid mac Crimthainn in AD 820 until the loss of the crown to the Dál gCais, the Éoganacht Chaisil maintained a monopoly on the Munster kingship. Such new dynastic cohesion at home allowed Feidlimid to become the most formidable rival produced by the Éoganacht to challenge the greatest power of Leth Cuinn (the northern half of Ireland)—namely, the Uí NÉILL overkings of Tara (TEAMHAIR). Feidlimid carried out a long campaign of alternating warfare and political manoeuvring against Niall mac Aedo, the king of Tara at the time. However, his surprise defeat by Niall at Mag nÓchtair in AD 841 put an end to any Éoganacht hopes of attaining real Ireland-wide power.

Simon Ó Faoláin

EPONA

Epona is the most abundantly attested Celtic deity of the Roman Empire. Evidence for her cult is strongest in central and eastern GAUL and in military zones. Epona is mentioned by the Roman author Juvenal (see GREEK AND ROMAN ACCOUNTS OF THE ANCIENT CELTS), but we know of the cult mainly from INSCRIPTIONS, almost all in Latin, and accompanying images, many on Romano-Celtic altars with a *focus* cut into the top for the pouring of libations or the presentation of other offerings.

The Epona cult was richly visual. Relief sculptures often show the deity riding a horse side-saddle, with images of her astride the horse being more common in the territory of the Treveri in northeast Gaul. Epona sometimes appears with a foal, particularly in the territory of the Aedui. The figure of the horse cut into the hill at UFFINGTON may reflect a related cult in pre-Roman Britain.

In CELTIC STUDIES, Epona is often mentioned in connection with supernatural female characters in early Irish and Welsh literature who have strong thematic and narrative associations with horses, such as MACHA and RHIANNON (cf. also SOVEREIGNTY MYTH), as well as the MARI LWYD.

The root of the name *Epona* also occurs in Old Irish *ech* 'horse' and the Gaulish month name EQVOS found on the COLIGNY calendar, both from INDO-EUROPEAN **ek'wos* 'horse'. On this type of divine name-formation, cf. MATRONAE and Nemetona.

Website
www.epona.net

John T. Koch

ÉREMÓN MAC MÍLED

Éremón mac Míled was a major figure in Irish LEGENDARY HISTORY, one of the sons of MÍL ESPÁINE who conquered Ireland. Following the final defeat of the TUATH DÉ by the Milesians at *cath Tailteann* (the battle of Tailtiu), Ireland was divided between Éremón (a name based on Ériu [Ireland]) and his brother Éber in accordance with a judgement pronounced by their brother and lawgiver, Amairgen mac Míled. Éremón was given the northern half and Éber the southern portion in an arrangement that mirrors the (supposedly) later division of Ireland between Mug Nuadat and Conn Cétchathach (cf. Éoganacht). The partition of Ireland by the sons of Míl was probably a creation of 7th- or 8th-century writers to explain and justify the ideological division of that period between the prestigious royal site of Caisel Muman and that of Tara (Teamhair).

Simon Ó Faoláin

ERISPOË

Erispoë was the son of Nominoë and leader of autonomous Brittany (Breizh). He reigned from 851 to 857, but had already taken on a leadership rôle at several points during his father's reign, even as early as 843. At one stage in the conflict with Louis the Pious, king of the Franks, Erispoë was recognized as Louis's vassal, and his lordship over the Breton marches (Frankish–Breton frontier zone) was confirmed. In 857, Erispoë was murdered by his cousin and foster-brother, Salomon.

Antone Minard

ÉRIU

Ériu is the Old Irish name for Ireland, corresponding to Modern Irish *Éire*. Celtic *$\bar{I}$weriū* derives from Indo- European *PiHwerjoHn* 'The Fertile Land' and is the cognate of Greek πίειρα *píeira*, Sanskrit *pīvarī*, feminine adjectives meaning 'fat, rich'. In Lebar Gabála Érenn, Íth, whose name is ultimately from the same linguistic root, was the first of the followers of Míl Espáine to see Ireland from Spain. Later, he is the first ashore and praises the country's abundance, and he is the first Gael to die in Ireland.

When Were the First Irish?

When we ask who were the first Irish, this question can simply mean the first human beings in Ireland—in which case the answer is the fishers and hunter-gatherers of the post-glacial Mesolithic from *c.* 7000 BC. We do not have enough ancient DNA from Ireland to know whether the modern Irish are their biological descendants. From the point of view of Celtic studies, the question of Irish origins usually focuses on the origins of the Gaels, meaning *Gaeilgeoirí*, speakers of the Goidelic Irish language. No certain date can be assigned to the emergence of the Gaels.

Prehistory

Owing to the island's remoteness from the literate civilizations of the Mediterranean and independence from Rome, there are almost no recorded events in Ireland before the 5th century AD.

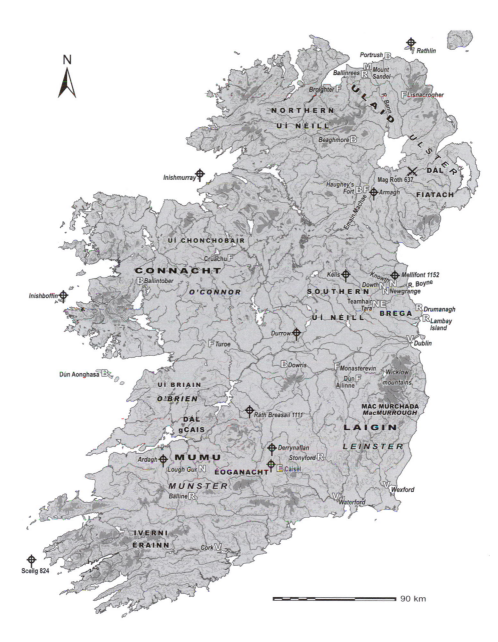

Ériu, pre-Norman Ireland: places and groups mentioned in the article, various periods.
M = Mesolithic site; N = Neolithic site; B = Bronze Age site; F = Iron Age site; R = Roman and/or
Romano-British finds; E = Early Medieval secular site; V = Viking town. (Map by John T. Koch)

The Mesolithic (c. 7000–c. 4000 BC)

Middle Stone Age inhabitants are reflected mainly in distinctive stone tools;
circular huts occupied over several centuries from around 7000 BC have been
found at Mountsandel near Coleraine, Co. Derry (Cúil Raithin, Contae Dhoire).

The Mesolithic inhabitants were not Irish in the ethnolinguistic sense, although their language may have contributed to Irish as a substrate.

The Neolithic (c. 4000–c. 2400 BC)

Handmade decorated pottery of various sizes and shapes appears in the 4th millennium. Small, dispersed domestic settlements, suitable for nuclear or extended families, with various building types are the norm.

The great megalithic tombs of the Neolithic have made an enduring impact on the Irish landscape and tradition. Several subtypes have been identified: Hundreds of 'court tombs' are distributed over Ireland's northern half; 'portal tombs' occur in the north as well as in pockets in the west and southeast; and the distinctively shaped 'wedge tombs' occur mostly in a dense arc from Antrim (Aontroim) in the northeast, over the western half to Co. Cork (Contae Chorcaí). Of the hundreds of passage tombs, distributed mainly over the north and east, the most famous are those of the valley of the Boyne (Old Irish BÓAND), including Newgrange (BRUG NA BÓINNE), Knowth, and Dowth (DUBHADH). These great tombs figure importantly in early Irish mythological literature, in beliefs concerning the OTHERWORLD (see also SÍD), and in modern folk beliefs concerning the FAIRIES.

The Copper Age (c. 2400–c. 2100 BC)

As in Britain and Europe, daggers and other artefacts made of cast copper (sometimes hardened with arsenic) occur together as what has been termed a 'Beaker assemblage'. Overall, the Beaker phenomenon has been seen as the arrival of the metal-using warrior aristocracy who had close cultural connections with the Continent. See also AGRICULTURE.

The Bronze Age (c. 2100 BC–)

Ireland enjoyed a rich Bronze Age as a vital node in trading networks linked to ARMORICA, BRITAIN, the Iberian Peninsula, west-central Europe, and southern Scandinavia. Single (as opposed to collective) graves prevail, comprising both cremations and crouched inhumations; stone cists are common.

By the Middle Bronze Age (from c. 1500 BC), fine metalwork in both bronze and gold comes to be found more commonly in hoards from wet settings—lakes, rivers, and bogs—thus anticipating the WATERY DEPOSITIONS of the Celtic IRON AGE. Conversely, burials become rarer. Cult practices were evidently changing and, arguably, the religious beliefs behind them. From growth in the bronze arsenal we can assume the rising social importance of bronze smiths and their warrior aristocratic patrons through the 2nd millennium.

Neck ornaments are prominent among Bronze Age gold work. Crescent-shaped sheet-gold lunulae with incised geometric design occur in the Early Bronze Age. Bar and ribbon TORCS, usually twisted and with a simple clasp formed by reverse bends at the two ends, become common in the Middle Bronze Age and are found in western GAUL and Britain, as well as in Ireland. These objects can be interpreted as displaying the special status of an emerging élite social group.

The Late Bronze Age (from c. 1150 BC)

The tree-ring sequence reveals a major climatic disaster between 1159 and 1142 BC, which can be attributed to the effects of a massive eruption of Mount Hekla in Iceland. This point also appears to be a significant watershed for several cultural developments—some breaking with the past and others continuing trends noted in the Middle Bronze Age. True swords appear with leaf-shaped blades, effective for slashing as well as stabbing, and parallel central European Late Bronze Age (HALLSTATT B) types. Circular shields occur, such as the large bronze example from Lough Gur, Co. Limerick, decorated and strengthened with concentric circles of repoussé nobs.

In light of the fact that many of the cultural features of Ireland at this period—for example, watery depositions, swords based on Hallstatt A-B models, hill-forts, cauldrons, and gold neck ornaments—can be linked to defining patterns of early Celtic Europe, Koch argues that a recognizably Celtic Ireland emerged in the Late Bronze Age.

Proto-history and the Iron Age

Ireland probably became known to the Greeks with its Celtic name in the 6th century BC. Detailed geographic information comes with Ptolemy (2nd century AD), who includes sixteen tribal names.

Because Ireland, unlike Britain or the Rhineland, has relatively little easily exploited iron ore, it is not surprising that it did not develop as an early centre of iron production. The LA TÈNE style never penetrated southwest Ireland at all, and very little of it found anywhere could possibly predate 200 BC. The great centres of assembly that figure as the most prominent settings for the ULSTER CYCLE and other early IRISH LITERATURE, EARLY PROSE—Tara/TEAMHAIR, EMAIN MACHAE, CRÚACHU, and DÚN AILINNE—have revealed to modern archaeology abundant evidence of varied building and ritualistic high-status activities of Iron Age date.

Because Ireland remained outside the Roman Empire, an 'Ultimate La Tène' was free to develop in the early centuries AD, as evidenced in objects such as the Bann disc and the Monasterevin bowl; see ART, CELTIC. However, several examples of intrusive Roman material have been identified in later Iron Age Ireland, including what seem to be the burials of displaced north Britons on Lambay Island, Co. Dublin.

Christianity and Latin Literacy

From the 4th century, Roman contacts would have carried with them some Christian influence, but well-organized and well-documented Christianization begins with the missions of PALLADIUS and PATRICK in the 5th century. The latter was also the founder of Ireland's Latin literature. In Patrick's writings, we see an Ireland that was still overwhelmingly pagan and dangerous for the fledgling church and its missionaries. By the late 7th century, in Muirchú's Life of Patrick and Adomnán's Life of COLUM CILLE, for example, an ongoing rival pagan establishment seems to have been of no real concern, and the saintly heroes' obstinate pagan rivals in HAGIOGRAPHY are influenced by Old Testament idol worshippers as much as pagan Irish.

Early Literacy and the Church

Irish was written in the OGAM script for short inscriptions on stone. By the end of the 7th century, Old Irish had become the vehicle of major literature in several genres—LAW TEXTS, poetry, religious texts, heroic sagas, science, glossaries and linguistics. It is doubtful whether any extant Old Irish text was committed to writing before 637, with the elegy of Colum Cille (†597) attributed to Dallán Forgaill prominent among a few possible exceptions.

In the early Middle Ages, Irish literature in both Latin and Irish was originated and copied (along with classical and early Christian texts from abroad) primarily in the MONASTERIES. The distribution of more than 40,000 RING-FORTS, dating mostly to this period, over the Irish countryside reflects a continued pattern of dispersed defensible rural settlements in small family and extended-family groups. Thus, unlike in the rest of Europe—where a system of territorial bishops was easily superimposed onto the *civitas* structure of the Roman Empire—the bishops of Ireland were relatively weak and their territorial jurisdictions amorphous; therefore, the monasteries were the leading Christian institutions.

By the later 6th century, a movement known as *peregrinatio*, which meant leaving Ireland forever to pursue a religious life abroad, had begun. The careers of Colum Cille in Britain and Columbanus on the Continent provide early examples. The international impact of Ireland on the early Christian west reflects the confidence that the Irish church had achieved in its faith and scholarship, along with the decline and discontinuity in learning that had affected Britain and Merovingian Gaul following the collapse of the Western Empire and the emergence of the barbarian successor kingdoms, compounded by the conquest of Christian north Africa and Spain by Muslims in the 7th century.

Early Secular Politics

There is no contemporary record of political and military events in Ireland until mid-6th century, at which point two ancient tribal groups of the southeast and northeast, the LAIGIN and the ULAID, emerged within a bewildering pattern of overlapping regional tribes (see TUATH) and hereditary chiefdoms. Two newer dynastic federations were consolidating their strength—the UÍ NÉILL and the ÉOGANACHT. Although not yet a political reality, the idea of a national high-king (*ardrí*), associated with the pre-Christian assembly site of Tara (TEAMHAIR) and monopolized by the Uí Néill, can be seen in written references emanating from Iona (EILEAN Ì). The doctrine of national KINGSHIP contributed to inevitable collisions.

The Viking Impact

In 795, the Vikings attacked four Irish island monasteries. Coastal attacks continued almost every year thereafter, gradually extending the invaders' range. Vikings established a series of permanent bases in the mid-9th century, including the Hiberno-Norse towns of Baile Átha Cliath (Dublin), Waterford (Port Láirge), Wexford (Loch Garman), and Cork (Corcaigh) by the mid-10th century. The Viking towns introduced currency to Ireland.

The Irish monasteries remained the main patrons for learning and the arts, spheres in which major changes took place during the Viking age. Thus Durrow, Kells, and the other great illuminated gospels predate the Vikings, as do the masterpieces of early medieval metalwork (see ART, Celtic). Irish literature continued as an unbroken burgeoning tradition. However, the medium for the literature shifts from Old Irish to the rapidly evolving and somewhat chaotic Middle Irish of the 10th to 12th centuries.

Twelfth-Century Innovations

By the 11th century, Irish abbots had become too powerful, and sexual morality among both laity and clergy did not conform to church doctrine. In response, a series of national synods strengthened and reorganized the diocesan system. The primacy of Armagh (Ard Mhacha) among Irish sees received official papal recognition, with Cashel in second position, and the bishop of Dublin was removed from the jurisdiction of Canterbury. Henceforth, the rôle of the monastic scriptoria waned and Irish literature came increasingly into the keeping of learned families under aristocratic secular patronage.

In 1155, more or less disregarding the reforms that had already taken place, the one and only English pope, Adrian IV, issued a bull authorizing Henry II of England to go to Ireland to reform the church. Henry came instead as a conqueror in 1171, following the intervention by his subject Richard De Clare 'Strongbow' in 1169. Although English political control over Ireland was not to slacken until the 20th century, it is important to note that throughout the later Middle Ages the population remained overwhelmingly Irish-speaking. Many of the native Gaelic aristocratic families retained local power—the O'Briens, O'Connors, and MacMurroughs, for example. The Anglo-Norman élite themselves tended, within a few generations, to adopt the Irish language and customs, and to patronize classical Irish poets, just as the old native families did.

John T. Koch

ERYRI (SNOWDONIA)

Eryri (Snowdonia) is a mountainous region in northwest Wales (Cymru). The first literary mention of Eryri occurs in the 9th-century Historia Brittonum (§40), where an account is given of the downfall of the semi-legendary 5th-century king Gwrtheyrn (Vortigern). Snowdonia National Park (Parc Cenedlaethol Eryri) was established in 1974, in a move that substantially expanded the area of Eryri to the south.

Eryri was an important factor in the strategic security of the kingdom of Gwynedd, forming a formidable barrier between the rest of Britain and Gwynedd's

View of Snowdon (yr Wyddfa) from the Ogwen Valley (Dyffryn Ogwen). (Gail Johnson/ Dreamstime.com)

agricultural heartland. These same factors contributed to the relative ease of contacts between Gwynedd and Ireland (Ériu), whence the peaks of Eryri can be seen.

The place-name *Eryri* has had two Celtic roots proposed to explain it: (1) that it describes a high place (cf. Latin *orior* 'I rise'; GPC s.v. *eryr²*), or (2) that it denotes the abode of eagles (Welsh *eryr* 'eagle', Old Irish *irar*). Many sources record the presence of eagles in the region until modern times.

In Welsh literature, Eryri is associated with suffering and tragedy, and the first reference to the area appears in an *awdl* by Hywel Foel ap Griffri ap Pwyll Wyddel (*fl. c.* 1240–*c.* 1300) from the Hendregadredd Manuscript. The most popular and enduring image of Snowdonia, however, was created by Thomas Gray (1716–71) in his poem *The Bard* (1757), in which the last Welsh poet throws himself from cliffs above the river Conwy into the raging waters. This is one of several places where a young FOLK-TALE hero chances upon the host of ARTHUR'S sleeping knights awaiting the call to battle.

Yr Wyddfa (lit. 'the tumulus', Snowdon) is the highest peak in Wales (1085 m). The first recorded ascent was in 1639 by Thomas Johnson (†1644). The Snowdon Mountain Railway opened in 1896, allowing access to a larger audience.

Paul Joyner

ESUS/AESUS

Esus/Aesus was a Gaulish god. According to Lucan (*Pharsalia* 1.444–6), rites of human SACRIFICE were dedicated to him on altars in GAUL (see further TARANIS;

Teutates). On the Paris stone monument known as the *Nautae Parisiaci* (the sailors of the tribe of the Parisi; 1st century AD), he is depicted as a bearded man wearing the clothes of an artisan, standing beside a tree. Next to the figure of Esus, Tarvos Trigaranus—a bull with three cranes—is depicted.

Peter E. Busse

EVANS, ELLIS HUMPHREY (HEDD WYN)

Ellis Humphrey Evans (Hedd Wyn) was born in 1887 on a farm about a mile from Trawsfynydd in Merioneth (sir Feirionnydd). Hedd Wyn wrote his first correct ENGLYN as a boy and gradually became a master of CYNGHANEDD, often competing in local EISTEDDFODAU and literary meetings. In January 1917, he became a private in the Royal Welch Fusiliers and was sent to the Continent. He completed his *awdl*, *Yr Arwr* (The hero), in the village of Fléchin in France, and the poem was sent from there to the National Eisteddfod office at Birkenhead. A fortnight later, on 31 July, Hedd Wyn died of wounds sustained during the Third Battle of Ypres.

When the Archdruid announced that the author of the prize-winning poem was Hedd Wyn, who had died five weeks prior to the Eisteddfod, the chair was draped in black, and the Eisteddfod became known as *Eisteddfod y Gadair Ddu* (The eisteddfod of the black chair). Hedd Wyn's poetry was posthumously published in 1918 as *Cerddi'r Bugail* (The shepherd's poems), edited by J. J. Williams.

Hedd Wyn was basically a Romantic poet, influenced by Shelley, but some of his last poems display a stark realism as disillusionment with World War I set in. Hedd Wyn's story was eventually made into an Oscar-nominated film, HEDD WYN (1992), directed by Paul Turner and written by Alan Llwyd.

Alan Llwyd

EVANS, GWYNFOR

Gwynfor Evans (1912–2005), was the first U.K. Member of Parliament to be elected for Plaid Cymru (the Party of Wales). Born in Barry (Y Barri) in south Wales, he became active politically in the late 1930s in nationalist and pacifist movements. He was a conscientious objector during World War II and became president of Plaid Genedlaethol Cymru (the national party of Wales) in 1945, a post he held for 36 years.

By the 1960s, Evans had established himself as a national figure, widely respected across the political spectrum. As a long-serving member and alderman of Carmarthenshire County Council and as president of the Congregational Union of Wales, he represented a brand of NATIONALISM that had particular appeal in rural Wales (CYMRU).

The main turning point in his career came in 1966, when the death of Megan Lloyd George led to a by-election in Carmarthen (Caerfyrddin), which Evans won. He lost the seat in 1970, but won it back in 1974, before losing it again in 1979. His impact at Westminster was minimal and Evans was, by his own admission, uncomfortable there. Nevertheless, Plaid Cymru became a major political force in northwest and southwest Wales. During this period Evans's relationship with the more militant language movement often bordered on the ambivalent, and he believed that such campaigns had cost his party valuable votes. In 1980, however, Evans placed himself at the forefront of a protest against a government change of policy with regard to a Welsh-language television channel (see MASS MEDIA) by threatening to embark on a hunger strike unless the decision not to introduce such a channel was reversed. Shortly before his hunger strike was due to begin, the government backed down, and Evans regarded the victory as one of his greatest achievements.

A good starting point for research on the politician is Evans's autobiography, *For the Sake of Wales*, a translation by Meic Stephens of a work originally published in Welsh.

Ioan Matthews

F

FAIRIES

Introduction

Belief in fairies is found throughout the Celtic countries, and a good deal of fairy lore overlaps with traditions regarding other supernatural beings: witches, devils, and even the Tuath Dé of Legendary History and the Mythological cycle of early Irish literature.

Fairies occur in a wide variety of sizes and types, and inhabit a diverse range of landscapes, from underground to outer space. They can have human or animal form, or both (see reincarnation). The fairy tradition includes named individuals such as the *Cailleach Bhéirre* or Cailleach Bheur of Ireland (Éire) and Scotland (Alba), beasts, and types or kinds of fairies such as the Cornish pisky or Irish leprechaun (see luchorpán).

Who or what the fairies are—and where they came from—is accounted for in several different ways in the folk tradition. According to some informants, they are the souls of the dead, who exist in a kind of purgatory on earth, or more specifically the heathen (i.e., pre-Christian) dead, or even the evil dead. According to other accounts, they are fallen angels. Still other sources identify fairies as merely natural phenomena, either material or spirit. These beliefs were held concurrently and varied from individual to individual, rather than being a result of regional or chronological variation.

Fairies were believed to be a source of both good and ill in the Celtic countries, and fairy narratives were used to account for unexplained prosperity, good luck, or wealth, and also for illnesses and deformities. Many families traced their origin to a marriage between a fairy woman and a mortal man, or even a fairy animal (when in human form) such as the Scottish selkie. Musical ability and second sight are common gifts of the fairies, and several traditional tunes are said to have been learned from the fairies—for example, the Manx *Yn Bollan Bane* ('The white herb/mugwort').

Autism, mental illness, nightmares, and strokes were all attributed to the malicious influence of the fairies. A changeling child, where the fairies exchanged a healthy human infant for one of their own kind, may have been a folk explanation for several medical conditions, and allowed the parents some detachment from the situation. Unfortunately, it was believed that cruel or bizarre behaviour toward the child or in the child's presence could induce the fairies to take their changeling back, which had potentially disastrous results for the child. T. Crofton Croker (*Fairy Legends and Traditions of the South of Ireland*) cites a case from Tralee in 1826, in which a mother and grandmother killed a four-year-old child by drowning him. The child could neither walk nor speak, and was thought to be fairy-struck; he was killed during the course of the cure. Fairies could also take their nourishment from common household products such as bread, butter, and cheese, and problems with the production of these items were often attributed either to fairies or to witches.

Because of their potential to cause harm or even death, great care was taken not to offend the fairies. Preventive measures included referring to them by such names as *An Sluagh Maith* or *Na Daoine Maith* (Gaelic for 'The Good People') or *Y Tylwyth Teg* (Welsh for 'The Fair Family'). Green clothing was avoided in some places, because green was the fairies' colour, and this notion has been adapted to a belief that green cars are unlucky.

A sampling of fairy types specific to the individual Celtic countries is presented in the remainder of this article. Many of the fairy traditions are shared between the different countries, or between Celtic and English traditions, or beyond. The English words 'bogey', 'bug', 'puck', and others, are certainly related to such Celtic words as Cornish *bucca* 'hobgoblin, he-goat'; Scottish Gaelic *bòcan* 'hobgoblin'; Irish *púca* 'goblin'; Manx *boag* and *buggane* 'boggle, sprite'; and Welsh *bw(g)* 'ghost, bogey, hobgoblin, scarecrow'. The direction of the borrowings and the relationship to cognates in the Germanic languages are uncertain.

Ireland

While fairies may be designated in various ways in Modern Irish, the core terminology is based on Old Irish síd, 'fairy mound'. Nonetheless, it would probably be misleading to see the *aes síde* 'people of the fairy mounds' of Old and Middle Irish literature as simply and precisely the same phenomenon as the fairies of later Irish tradition. Although the two are generally to be equated, the more complex portrayals in the early literature of individual members of the *aes síde*—who are largely synonymous with the Tuath Dé—function in a different manner to that of folk tradition (see Fomoiri). Other Old Irish or Middle Irish words for fairies exist, notably luchorp(án), and several others with a range of meanings: *abacc, siabair, sirite*.

The fairy tradition of modern Ireland (Éire) is extensive. T. Crofton Croker collected and printed several volumes of fairy lore, under the title *Fairy Legends and Traditions of the South of Ireland*, in the 1820s and 1830s.

Scotland

The queen of the fairies (or witches) in Scotland was Neven or NicNeven, perhaps the Old Irish war-goddess Nemain. Much of the terminology of the fairy tradition in Scottish Gaelic is similar to that of Irish. As elsewhere, fairies and other supernatural afflictions could be kept away with iron, with a pierced stone (i.e., a stone with a hole through it, either natural or bored), with holly, or with rowan.

The Scots-language ballads of 'Thomas Rymer' and 'Tam Lin' describe a journey to and from the Otherworld. Although not current in Gaelic areas, the ballads do show some influence from Celtic tradition—for example, the importance of

Hallowe'en as the time to rescue Tam Lin (see SAMAIN). The association of the colour green with fairies is also very strong in Scotland. Elfland, where Thomas Rymer was taken, is described in opulent terms reminiscent of the Irish otherworld.

Isle of Man

One of the best-known Manx fairies is the *fynnoderee* or *phynodderee*, a helpful brownie-type fairy of the home or farmstead. Like other brownies, he is a small, hairy, helpful being, who can be driven away by a gift of clothing. Other types of fairies include the *buggane* 'elf, goblin' and the *glashtyn* or *glashan*, sometimes used for the water-horse and sometimes for a malevolent but stupid fairy similar to the Scandinavian troll.

Wales

In Wales (CYMRU), the fairies bore several euphemistic names: *Y Tylwyth Teg* throughout the country, but also *Bendith y (eu) Mamau* (the [their] mothers' blessing) in Glamorgan (MORGANNWG) and *Plant Rhys Ddwfn* (the children of Rhys Ddwfn, a figure not otherwise known) in parts of DYFED. An early Welsh fairy abduction narrative is told by Gerald of Wales (GIRALDUS CAMBRENSIS) in *A Journey through Wales*.

The PWCA, a sort of poltergeist, also appears in Welsh folklore, as do other creatures such as the *ŵyll* (sometimes *gŵyll*), roughly 'goblin' in English, and the *ellyll* 'spirit, phantom, ghost, fairy' cognate with the Old Irish personal name *Ailill* (cf. MEDB).

Brittany

In Brittany (BREIZH), the association of supernatural entities with the dead is very strong. Many of these creatures are considered to be part of the ANAON, the community of the souls of the dead. A great many of these revenants (those who come back from the dead) are atoning for sins committed during their lives—priests return to say forgotten masses at midnight, individuals who moved boundary markers return to carry the heavy stones at night, and the drowned lurk where they met their death, hoping to lure someone else to take their place. Souls also return in the form of animals: A thin cow in a field of fat ones indicates the soul of a miser, while a woman who did not want children returns as a sow with as many piglets as the number of children she 'ought' to have had. Standing stones are also sometimes understood to be the souls of the dead undertaking penance. Other creatures, such as the *korrigan* (pl. *korriganed*), are much closer to the traditional dwarf of Anglo-Germanic tradition.

Cornwall

In addition to the piskies and *spriggans*, knockers or Tommyknockers are a prominent feature of Cornish lore. They are similar to German *kobalds*, but benevolent.

They can be annoyed by human activities, especially whistling and swearing, and the presence of the cross. The sound of their knocking indicated a rich vein or lode for mining purposes, and was generally welcomed. The knockers were also called *buccas*, although the *bucca* was encountered outside the mines as well. Robert Hunt mentions the *Bucca Dhu* and the *Bucca Gwiddhen*, Late Cornish for 'black bucca' and 'white bucca', respectively. He says that fishermen would leave an offering of fish on the shore for *Bucca Dhu*, just as miners were said to leave offerings of food for the buccas.

Antone Minard

FAMINE

The Irish Famine (1845–52) ranks as one of the worst disasters in modern European history. An estimated 1 million people died in a population of 8–8.5 million, and as many as 2 million individuals emigrated to escape the devastation. The immediate cause was a blight that devastated Ireland's staple crop, the potato. The potato enabled families to survive on 1–2 acres (0.4–0.8 ha) of land, and these smallholdings under-pinned an agrarian economy that exported livestock, bacon, dairy produce, and grain to Britain. On the eve of the famine, Ireland (ÉIRE) produced sufficient food for 10 million people.

When the potato blight struck, families who had been self-sufficient in food were forced to buy these items, but supplies were scarce and prices soared. A weakened populace and crowding in relief facilities resulted in epidemics of typhus and other fevers. Most deaths were caused by disease, but thousands died of starvation.

The initial response of the British government was to provide relief in the form of public works rather than by providing food. Government soup kitchens opened in the spring of 1847, and were soon feeding as many as 3 million people. In the autumn of 1847, however, the British authorities declared that the famine had ended, and that all further relief should be provided through the poor law.

By the early 1840s, as many as 100,000 people were emigrating each year. Between 1845 and 1855, more than 1.5 million emigrated to the United States, and a further 200,000–300,000 went to Canada (see CELTIC LANGUAGES IN NORTH AMERICA). The influx of famine emigrants placed an enormous strain on health and welfare services in British and American cities, and it is not altogether surprising that it prompted an increase in anti-Irish and anti-Catholic prejudice.

In Ireland, the collapse of the potato-based economy wiped out the agricultural labouring class. The family farm of 20–30 acres (8–12 ha) dominated postfamine Ireland. Farms were no longer subdivided, and later marriages with dowries became the norm. The IRISH language was another major casualty; a disproportionate num-ber of famine victims and subsequent emigrants came from Irish-speaking areas in the west of Ireland.

Mary E. Daly

FANUM AND SANCTUARY

Gaulish sanctuaries often exhibit a long continuity over a period of generations or centuries, into the Roman period (which began shortly after *c.* 50 BC in central and northern Gaul, earlier nearer the Mediterranean). These cult sites were usually enclosed by a small earthen bank accompanied by a ditch of varying length (see Enclosures). In the centre of the enclosure are several structures. The type of buildings found within Gaulish sanctuaries varies over time in the pre-Roman Iron Age. The earliest buildings were constructed of wood, but later buildings were made of stone. Remains of cult practice, offerings, and sacrifice (see also ritual) have been found, mainly in pits and the enclosing ditches. Spectacular quantities of weapons are common, chiefly swords, spears, and shields.

During the Gallo-Roman period, a temple constructed of masonry, the *fanum* 'sanctuary temple', was often added to these sites. This stone building consisted of a central space, the *cella*, and a peripheral part, the gallery. When investigated, sites of this type often reveal that the Roman temple was built on top of a sanctuary of the pre-Roman variety described previously.

Patrice Méniel

FEAST

Introduction

Information on the Celtic feast comes from Iron Age archaeology, Greek and Roman accounts of the ancient Celts, early Irish and Welsh heroic narratives (such as those of the Ulster Cycle and the Mabinogi), and court poetry down to the time of the extinction of the 'Gaelic order' in the 17th century in Ireland (Éire) and the 18th century in the Scottish Highlands. Such a feast was a place for the assembly and reconstitution of the dispersed rural tribal group (tuath), an economic gift exchange between chiefs and followers, the display and consumption of items of élite prestige, the defining and reconfirming—often competitively—of social identity and rank within a hierarchical society, and the confirmation of new social relationships, such as marriage alliances and the elevation of kings.

Archaeological Evidence

During the earlier Iron Age, there is abundant evidence for (sometimes spectacularly) rich drinking vessels, other feasting equipment, and food and drink itself being central features of aristocratic burials in Hallstatt and La Tène periods in Gaul, central Europe, and Britain—for example, at Dürrnberg, Hochdorf, and Vix. In pre-Roman Gaul, evidence indicates that a type of animal sacrifice (see sacrifice, animal) took place at which the flesh of the animal was then consumed. A slaughter pattern suggesting seasonal feasting has been identified in Iron Age Ireland (Ériu) in the faunal remains of the traditional royal centre of Laigin at Dún Ailinne.

The Evidence of the Classical Authors

As the Celtic feast was the primary occasion for assembly, feasts are prominent in most of the Classical accounts of Celtic society. The foundation legend of Massalia involves the arrival of Greek travellers at a royal Gaulish wedding feast. Diodorus

Siculus, drawing on Posidonius, recognized the similarity between accounts of the bestowing of choice cuts of meat on warriors at Gaulish feasts and the deeds of the Greek heroes of Homer; see CHAMPION'S PORTION.

Vocabulary

Several words in the CELTIC LANGUAGES may be translated as 'feast'. The best attested are Old Irish *fled*, Scottish Gaelic *fleadh* 'feast', Modern Irish *fleá*, Old Welsh *guled*, Modern *gwledd*, and Breton *gloé*, all of which derive from PROTO-CELTIC **wlidā*, which is also attested in the Gaulish personal name *Vlido-rīx* 'king of feasts'. Old Irish FEIS is often translated as 'feast', and descriptions in early sources generally involve animal SACRIFICE and feasting; etymologically, however, the word's main sense is 'spending the night' (cf. Old Breton *guest*, Welsh *gwest* 'night's stay'). In 20th-century Ireland, *feis* became a common word for a (GAELIC) cultural festival (see FEISEANNA). More recently, *fleá* has become common in this meaning.

John T. Koch

FEDELM

Fedelm, known as *banfhili* (woman learned poet) and *banfháith* (woman prophet), is best known to modern readers as the striking figure who appears in TÁIN BÓ CUAILNGE ('The Cattle Raid of Cooley'), when she is questioned by Queen MEDB regarding the fate of her vast army in the impending action. Fedelm replies repeatedly, *at.chíu forderg, at.chíu rúad* 'I see it bloody, I see it red', and then goes on to describe poetically the disaster to be inflicted by CÚ CHULAINN's feats. It is likely that the *Táin*'s Fedelm *banfháith* is understood to be the same as the sexually provocative prophetess Fedelm 'of the lovely hair' (*Foltchaín*), who was Cú Chulainn's lover for a year and who caused the mysterious debility of the Ulster warriors (ULAID) through displaying herself naked to them in the brief ULSTER CYCLE tale.

John T. Koch

FEIS

Feis (pl. *feissi*, Modern Irish pl. FEISEANNA) is a term originally used to denote a ceremonial FEAST that had an element of coupling, such as marriages or the confirmation of a rightful king. *Feis Temro* (the feast of Tara) was the inauguration of the kings of Tara (TEAMHAIR). Among the practices associated with the selection rites of Irish sacral KINGSHIP was the *tarbfheis* ('bull-*feis*'). In the early tale TOGAIL BRUIDNE DA DERGA ('The Destruction of Da Derga's Hostel'), the *tarbfheis* is used as the means of recognizing the claims of the legendary Conaire Mór mac Eterscélae as the rightful future king of Tara.

A particularly detailed description of a *tarbfheis* is contained in the tale SERGLIGE CON CULAINN ('The Wasting Sickness of Cú Chulainn'), preserved in LEBOR NA HUIDRE ('The Book of the Dun Cow'; *c.* 1106): A white bull is being slaughtered and a man is chosen to eat and drink his fill of the meat and broth made from it. After that, the man falls asleep, while four DRUIDS are singing the 'Gold of Truth' over him. In his sleep, the future king is revealed to the man, who on waking gives a description of the true king.

Petra S. Hellmuth

FEISEANNA AND THE *OIREACHTAS*

Feiseanna and the *Oireachtas* are festivals organized at the local and national levels in Ireland (ÉIRE) since the 1890s for the promotion of GAELIC language and culture. *Feiseanna* comprise a mix of education and entertainment. In 1898, the first provincial FEIS ('feast', pl. *feiseanna*) was held in Macroom, Co. Cork (Maigh Chromtha, Contae Chorcaí), and similar *feiseanna* were held in the following months all over the country. The Gaelic League's *Ard-Fheis* (national convention) of that year formalized the arrangement, licensing *feiseanna* for the Irish-speaking counties from then on (see CONRADH NA GAEILGE). By 1903, an informal gradation system had been established whereby winners of local and provincial *feiseanna* moved on to higher competitions until they reached the national Oireachtas.

The Oireachtas was consciously modelled on the Welsh EISTEDDFOD and has itself served as a model for all subsequent Oireachtais (pl. of Oireachtas) up to the present day. The first Oireachtas was held in 1897 to coincide with the first day of the second annual *feis ceoil* ('*feis* of music') in BAILE ÁTHA CLIATH (Dublin). The festival was cancelled due to lack of interest in 1925 and not revived until 1939. Interest in the Oireachtas has gradually grown since then. A magnet for language activists, writers, and native speakers, since 1974 the festival has alternated venues between the provinces and Dublin. Its literary competitions have served as launching pads for many new writers in IRISH, and the financial incentives of the prize fund have ensured quality work that has often gone on to publication. Oral-performance competitions (such as those for SEAN-NÓS singing) are broadcast live to large audiences on RaidiÓ na Gaeltachta, the national Irish-language radio service (see MASS MEDIA).

Brian Ó Broin

FERGUS MAC RÓICH

Fergus mac Róich is one of the main characters of the early Irish ULSTER CYCLE of Tales. He appears in a position of prominence as a respected elder warrior. Fergus lost the kingship of ULAID to CONCHOBAR through the wiles of Conchobar's mother Nes in the earlier version of *Compert Conchobuir* (The conception of Conchobar).

Fergus often figures as the spokesman of the Ulaid and the mediator of their oral lore. In *Fallsigud Tána Bó Cuailnge* ('How TÁIN BÓ CUAILNGE Was Found'), Fergus's spirit rises from his grave to recite the *Táin* to the 6th-century poet Senchán Torpéist. Similarly, *Macgnímrada Con Culainn* ('The Boyhood Deeds of Cú Chulainn') occurs as a narrative flashback within the *Táin* related by Fergus to the inquiring Queen MEDB.

Following the tragic contest over DERDRIU related in LONGAS MAC NUISLENN ('The Exile of the Sons of Uisliu'), Fergus led the aggrieved Ulster warriors to their traditional enemies, Medb and Ailill, at CRÚACHU (see further ULSTER CYCLE OF TALES).

This is the situation during the *Táin*, where Fergus often acts as the guide for his new Connacht comrades as they invade Ulster (although his fighting on their behalf is half-hearted), as well as being Medb's lover.

The first element of the common Gaelic name *Fergus* is undoubtedly 'man, hero', Old Irish *fer* < Celtic *wiro-s*. Celtic *Wiro-gustus* might mean either 'chosen man' or 'man force'; Fergus's exceptional virility is mentioned in some of the early texts, has resonances in Irish folk tradition, and has been of understandable interest to modern writers (see Ulster Cycle of Tales). *Fergus* is sometimes confused with a similar Old Irish name, *Forggus*. *Róich*, nominative *Róach*, probably goes back to Celtic **Ro-ekwos* 'great' or 'divine horse, stallion'.

John T. Koch

FEST-NOZ

Fest-noz, literally a 'night party', is an event at which people experience traditional Breton music and dance (see dances). Originally, a *fest-noz* was an event held by the rural agricultural population in a small area of Brittany (Breizh). In the late 1950s, the idea of the *fest-noz* was appropriated by people such as the singer and cultural activist Loeiz Ropars, who saw it as an ideal way to keep Breton dance and music traditions alive. Call-and-response singing (*kan ha diskan*), biniou-bombard duets, and the current Celtic band phenomenon all owe their hardiness as musical traditions to this revival of interest in the *fest-noz*.

The *fest-noz* has also been responsible for the creation of a new genre of music—*fest-noz* music. Stylistically, this genre is instrumental dance music played on some combination of violin, diatonic accordion, bombard, flute, clarinet, bagpipe, guitar, and bouzouki. The influence of Irish folk music and of the hybrid genre of Celtic music on this style is extensive.

Stephen D. Winick

FÍAN

Fían 'warring and hunting band' (pl. *fíana*; *fian, fianna* in later spelling) was a term used in Old Irish texts to designate groups of warriors engaged in expeditions of acquisition, or (more specifically) groups of youths (*óic féne* 'young men of the *fían*') and social misfits bonded together in a formal or even ritualized fashion on the border zones between one tuath and another, and engaged in violent activities. Given the literary evidence, it would appear that the *fían* served a vital function in siphoning off undesirable elements from the social pool, providing an outlet for rambunctious behaviour, and preparing at least some members for regular adult responsibilities through rites of passage. The *fían* way of life (*fíanaigecht* or *féinnidecht*) included hunting, fighting and raiding, martial and athletic games, and even training in poetry. The usefulness of *fénnidi* as mercenaries in a world where standing armies did not yet exist, and of *fían* violence as a way to deal with problems resistant to normal social solutions, contributed to the profoundly ambivalent attitude toward the *fíana* reflected in the literature, perhaps similar to the attitude toward the 'gallowglasses' of a later phase of Irish history. It is now generally agreed that figures designated in early medieval saints' lives as *latrones*, *latrunculi* (robbers), or in Irish *meicc báis* (sons of death, evildoers)—dangerous raiders usually roaming in groups and sometimes characterized by mysterious signs worn on their heads—are, in fact, *fénnidi* (members of a *fian*).

In the literary as well as later Irish and Scottish 'folk' developments of Fionn and his *fian* (in later Irish more often plural, *fianna*), the archaic institution takes on a new life and meaning. Likewise, the heroics of this cycle of story, often designated in English as the 'Fenian', still reflects the original functions and characteristics of the *fian*—in fact, the word 'Fenian' derives from *fian*, genitive *fé(i)ne*.

Joseph Falaky Nagy

FIANNAÍOCHT

Fiannaíocht (earlier spellings *fianaigecht, fiannaigheacht* 'Finn Cycle') is the most enduring narrative cycle in the history of Irish and Scottish Gaelic written and oral tradition. It encompasses smaller cycles having to do with various local heroes that grew out of, or were fitted into, a larger cycle centred on FINN MAC CUMAILL (Fionn mac Cumhaill in later spelling), a mixture of warrior, leader, and poet-seer, and on the institution of the FÍAN (later known in the plural, *fianna*), the hunting-warring band that serves as a showcase for the rise (and sometimes fall) of promising young heroes. This cycle of stories was already attested in early vernacular literature and lived on in the repertories of Irish and Scottish traditional storytellers as late as the 20th century. It is commonly referred to in English as the Fenian or Ossianic cycle—the latter designation derived from James MACPHERSON's rendering of the name of an important figure in the cycle, OISÍN.

Fiannaíocht as Institution and Genre

While the *féinnidi* ('members of the *fian*', sing. *féinnid*) associated with Finn (a figure with deep mythological roots) form what has been the most celebrated *fian* over the last millennium, references can be found to other *fiana*, both historical and fictional, in the early Irish literary corpus, and to other *rígfhéinnidi* ('fiana chiefs'), such as Finn's rival, Fothad Canainne. In some cases, *fian* seems to mean simply 'war-band'; in many others, however, it apparently refers to an institution with parallels in other Indo-European societies that was designed to prepare young men for adulthood (particularly, to acquaint them with the techniques of fighting and hunting, the rules of proper communal behaviour, and perhaps even the tenets of poetic composition). *Fianaigecht* originally denoted the esoteric society, culture, and lore of the *fian*, but by the 12th century it came to refer specifically to Finn's *fian*—that is, to what the members of this group did and experienced, as well as to the stories about them. In some medieval Fenian texts, Finn and other Fenian characters are viewed as the native counterparts to the chivalrous heroes and heroines of Continental Romance.

Early Literature

The earliest surviving IRISH LITERATURE represents only the tip of the iceberg of *fianaigecht*. In the few traces of pre-12th-century Fenian narrative that we do possess,

Finn is more *féinnid* than *rígfhéinnid*, more loner than leader, experiencing adventures beyond the range of the normal human sphere on his own—in particular, hunting down extraordinary wild creatures and supernatural adversaries, winning magical knowledge of, or other valuable commodities from, the síd, and composing poetry that reflects his mantic inspiration, derived from the OTHERWORLD. In the 12th-century text known as the *Macgnímartha Finn* ('The Boyhood Deeds of Finn'), the roughly contemporary text titled *Fotha Catha Cnucha* (The reason for the battle of Cnucha), and the renderings of this strand of the Fenian cycle in DINDSHENCHAS tradition, we have the earliest surviving witnesses to one of the most popular and longest-lived episodes of *fianaigecht*—the story of Finn's conception, birth, and youth.

Later Medieval Literature

In the 12th and following centuries, as literary activity shifted from the ecclesiastical into the secular sphere, the stories about Finn and his men gained in popularity, while the hunting and warring band evolved in the literary imagination into a disciplined (albeit occasionally unruly) organization whose members come together to hunt and fight for the high-king and to protect Ireland (ÉRIU) from invasion. The characters of *fianaigecht* are by this time firmly grounded in the era of the legendary high-king CORMAC MAC AIRT. Finn's rôle as *rígfhénnid* pushes him into the narrative background, his leadership becoming a matter of appointment by the high-king of Ireland to a position that, like the high-kingship itself, was a 'national' institution with its headquarters at Tara (TEAMHAIR). Unless engaged in recreational hunting, the *fían(na)* of late medieval Fenian literature—for instance, the prosimetric *Acallam na Senórach* (Dialogue of [or with] the old men)—spend most of their narrative time responding to the summons of the *rígfhénnid* or the high-king on the occasion of national emergencies, as well as to pleas for help from human and supernatural visitors. In many regards Finn and his men resemble ARTHUR and his 'court' as presented in early Welsh tradition—for instance, in CULHWCH AC OLWEN.

Early Modern Fenian Literature

A staple of *fianaigecht* already attested in the earlier strands of the tradition and, like the story of Finn's youth, still to be found in the repertories of 20th-century oral storytellers in Ireland and Scotland (ALBA), is the tragic tale of the affair between Finn's wife Gráinne, daughter of Cormac, and Finn's beloved kinsman and companion in the fían, Diarmaid ua Duibhne. The Early Modern Irish prose text TÓRUIGHEACHT DHIARMADA AGUS GHRÁINNE ('The Pursuit of Diarmaid and Gráinne') is the literary culmination of the perennial interest in this embarrassing episode of *fían* betrayal, a tale that features a villainously jealous instead of a heroic Finn, a *rígfhénnid* barely in control of his *fían* or his wife. The Diarmaid–Gráinne–Finn triangle is clearly cut from the same narrative cloth as the Noísiu–DERDRIU–CONCHOBAR tale, attested earlier in Irish tradition, and the Drystan–Esyllt–March story in Welsh (see DRYSTAN AC ESYLLT).

Finn and the *fian*'s life beyond the Pale, and the perennial contact with the supernatural that life on the margins provokes, clearly lie behind a popular Fenian story type known as the *bruidhean* ('hostel' or specifically 'supernatural hostel'). The *bruidhead*, which is attested in the earlier strata of *fianaigecht*, grows in importance in the tradition's later literary developments, and survives as part of modern oral Fenian lore. In this kind of tale, Fionn and his men accept an invitation to an otherworldly FEAST, only to find that they have been magically trapped in the hostel by an old enemy seeking revenge. The pattern of an unknown or incognito enemy issuing an invitation or a challenge to the *fian*, and being followed by the Fenian heroes into the Otherworld where various adventures ensue, can be found in many other Fenian tales as well. The same pattern is very much on display in the body of *fianaigecht* that has survived primarily in verse—namely, in the *duan* or *laoidh* style of seminarrative poetic composition sampled in the 16th-century Scottish Book of the DEAN OF LISMORE; the 17th-century Irish *Duanaire Finn* ('The Book of the Lays of Fionn'), an anthology written in Ostend that testifies to the popularity of *Fiannaíocht* among Irishmen both at home and abroad; and other, later Irish and Scottish manuscript collections of this extensive body of material.

Joseph Falaky Nagy

FIDCHELL

Fidchell, literally 'wood-sense' and the Irish cognate of Welsh *gwyddbwyll*, is a board game of medieval Ireland. The object of the game seems to have been to 'slay' the opponent and remove his pieces. The game is sometimes translated as chess (indeed, *ficheall* is 'chess' in Modern Irish), but the game was probably more similar to the Lappish game *tablut* (< Old Norse *tafl* 'table, board'). Fidchell was an important marker of social class and makes frequent and significant appearances in IRISH LITERATURE, sometimes played for high stakes.

Petra S. Hellmuth

FIDDLE

The fiddle is perhaps the most ubiquitous instrument in the regional traditions of the modern CELTIC COUNTRIES. In Ireland (ÉIRE), the fiddle, along with the uilleann pipes (see BAGPIPE), is the only commonly played instrument to have been in use in the native tradition for more than 200 years. Thus it has had a large impact on the traditional Irish repertoire, with many tunes appearing from their style, range, and notation to have been originally written on and/or for the fiddle. A similar situation exists in the Scottish tradition, with most tunes in the repertory being either 'fiddle-tunes' or 'pipe-tunes'. The violin appeared in Scotland (ALBA) in the late 17th century.

The early history of the fiddle in Ireland is more obscure, probably because here it lacked the overlap between traditional and classical styles notable in Scotland. In playing the Irish fiddle, the left hand generally remains in the first position, which essentially means that the matters of tone, attack, volume, and time value are

John Sheahan of The Dubliners performs at De Montfort Hall and Gardens in Leicester, March 2011. (Ollie Millington/Redferns)

controlled primarily by the bowing technique of the right hand. Tuning is generally to concert pitch. Some of the main regional styles and their foremost proponents are Sliabh Luachra (Tom Billy, Patrick O'Keefe), East Clare (Martin Hayes), and Donegal (The Glackins and the Peoples).

The playing of Gaelic-style fiddle music in North America is strongest in the ethnically Scottish areas of Canada, particularly Cape Breton (e.g., Natalie MacMaster).

Simon Ó Faoláin

FINN MAC CUMAILL

Finn mac Cumaill (Modern Irish Fionn mac Cumhaill) is the central figure of the Finn Cycle of Irish and Scottish GAELIC hero tales, FIANNAÍOCHT. In the tales, Finn's primary social function is that of the leader of the renowned war-band, sometimes in service to the legendary king of Tara (TEAMHAIR), CORMAC MAC AIRT, but sometimes as a member of a group of huntsmen outside Irish society altogether; see FÍAN.

Like the boy Setantae (later the hero CÚ CHULAINN), Finn was once called by another name, Demne. As he grew he excelled in hunting and competitive sports. There are repeated episodes explaining how he was renamed Finn: He is once described as *finn* (fair) by youths whom he challenged; later, he is apprenticed to the poet Finn-éces, which accounts for Finn's subsequent fame as a poet. In an episode closely comparable to the transformation of the boy Gwion into the Welsh poet TALIESIN, Finn-éces set the boy to mind the cooking of the salmon of knowledge, a key theme in Irish tradition. Finn accidentally burned himself as he cooked, and in putting his thumb in his mouth received the inspiration himself, becoming a visionary. His son, OISÍN, also has a central rôle in Gaelic tradition.

John T. Koch

FIR BOLG

Fir Bolg figure in Irish LEGENDARY HISTORY among the tribes said to have settled in Ireland (ÉRIU) in the pre-Christian period (cf. also FOMOIRI; TUATH DÉ). As legendary settlers of Ireland, they are first mentioned in the 9th-century HISTORIA BRITTONUM (§14) and in the Old Irish tale CATH MAIGE TUIRED ('The [Second] Battle of Mag Tuired'), where they are credited with dividing the country into *cóicid* (fifths, sing. CÓICED), the provinces of Ireland. The exploits of the Fir Bolg are set out in greater detail in the late 11th-century LEBAR GABÁLA ÉRENN ('The Book of Invasions'), which systematizes waves of settlers in the legendary prehistory of Ireland. Early medieval Irish etymologists had the correct word root with their implausible-sounding *fir i mbalgaib* 'men in bags'—more correctly understood as men who were bag-like when swelled up (i.e., bulging) with heroic valour in battle. See also the cognate group BELGAE.

Petra S. Hellmuth

FIR DOMNANN

Fir Domnann appear in Irish LEGENDARY HISTORY, commonly associated with two closely related or equivalent groupings, LAIGIN and Galeóin. The cognate ancient Celtic tribal name Dumnonii is found in southwest BRITAIN and what is now southwest Scotland (ALBA), preserved in the early medieval kingdom of Domnonia in northern Brittany (BREIZH).

Early written sources provide evidence for the Fir Domnann in Cóice Laigean (Leinster; see also CÓICED), where at least one of their rulers, Mess-Telmann, is credited, in a probably 7th-century Irish poem, with the overkingship of the province and with wielding power from the royal site of Leinster at DÚN ÁILINNE. In this poem the tribal name occurs in its archaic form, sing. *Domnon* < Celtic *Dumnonos*. The area with the strongest place-name associations is in northwest Mayo (Contae Mhaigh Eo), in the barren wastes of Iorrais Domnann (the modern barony of Erris), and nearby Mag Domnann and Dún Domnann. The name is based on the Celtic root *dumno-*, older *dubno-*, which means both 'deep' and 'the world'. Old Irish *fir* 'men' was often prefixed to old tribal names to clarify their meaning (cf. FIR BOLG).

Simon Ó Faoláin

FLED BRICRENN

Fled Bricrenn ('Bricriu's Feast') is one of the early Irish ULSTER CYCLE of tales. For general discussions of *Fled Bricrenn*'s significance within the corpus, see IRISH LITERATURE, EARLY PROSE; ULSTER CYCLE OF TALES.

The story begins with a great and elaborately described feast and fabulous feasting hall; the feast is prepared by the ingeniously malevolent Bricriu with the intention of inciting the status-obsessed heroes and noblewomen of the Ulaid against each other. The action soon settles into a sustained fierce three-way contest between Loegaire Buadach, Conall Cernach, and Cú Chulainn, each seeking explicit recognition as Ulster's greatest hero. The climax is a death-defying beheading game (anticipating by some three or four centuries a very similar episode in the Middle English Arthurian *Sir Gawain and the Green Knight*), in which the three heroes face the disguised axe-wielding Cú Roí; only Cú Chulainn is brave enough to return to face the unkillable giant. *Fled Bricrenn* shares features with the Celtic ethnography of Greek and Roman accounts of the ancient Celts: the themes of status display at the extravagant aristocratic feast; heroic contention at feasts, specifically for the champion's portion (Irish *curadmír*)' the heroic ethos in general; and the so-called Celtic head cult. The extant text is in the main Early Middle Irish, probably dating from the 10th century, although it contains several throwbacks to Old Irish usage, which imply an earlier written version must have existed.

John T. Koch

FLOOD LEGENDS

Origin of Lakes and Rivers

The biblical deluge figures prominently in medieval Celtic attempts to explain their own history and origins. In addition to the great flood, smaller-scale floods are held to have occurred throughout the Celtic countries, accounting for the origin of lakes, rivers, and shallow bays.

Numerous references point to the belief that natural geographical features resulted from the release of pent-up water. Lebar Gabála Érenn ('The Book of Invasions') describes the effect of the biblical flood on Ireland (Ériu), but also recounts several more localized events. Loch Rudraige is said to have burst forth when the grave of Rudraige, Partholón's son, was dug. Geoffrey Keating (Seathrún Céitinn) describes the origin of Lough Foyle, Co. Donegal (Loch Feabhail, Contae Dhún na nGall), in the same terms. This image occurs in Welsh tradition as well; for example, a lake burst traditionally accounts for the origin of Llyn Tegid (Bala Lake). The legendary childhood of Taliesin took place at the bottom of what is now Llyn Tegid, and he subsequently reappears in a basket set adrift in the sea and caught like a salmon in a weir.

Drowned Cities

The legend of a drowned city is by no means unique to Celtic culture; compare, for instance, the Greek story of Atlantis. The Rennes Dindshenchas records a story about the mythological figures Bóand (Boyne) and her husband Nechtan. Bóand opened a well that only Nechtan could safely tap. The unstoppable flow resulted in the river Boyne, pushing Bóand herself to the sea.

The earliest instance of a drowned city in Welsh tradition is a poem in the Black Book of Carmarthen (LLYFR DU CAERFYRDDIN), *Boddi Maes Gwyddneu* ('The drowning of Gwyddno's plain', also known as Cantre'r Gwaelod 'The low CANTREF'). Although the poem obviously alludes to a traditional flood story, it is not itself a narrative poem. The bulk of the poem discusses Mererid, who left a well uncovered after a FEAST, which let in the sea to drown the land. A 19th-century legend from the Iveragh peninsula in Kerry (Ciarraí), Ireland, recounts the origin of Lough Currane (Loch Luíoch) in almost exactly the same way.

Perhaps the most renowned example is the Breton city of Is or Ys (lit. 'lower'). The story first occurs in literature in the 16th-century Breton *Buhez Sant Gwenôle Abat* (Life of St Gwennole abbot; see further UUINUUALOE). The inhabitants of Ys are destroyed through their general wickedness, a fate influenced by the biblical stories of the flood and the destruction of Sodom. Dahut, along with Mererid and Bóand, may be a reflection of a SPRING DEITY.

Antone Minard

FOLK-TALES AND LEGENDS

The two categories of traditional narrative known as folk-tales and legends are found throughout the world. In the academic study of folklore, 'folk-tale' is the name given to those tales that are understood to be fictional, told purely for entertainment. They are characterized by linear plots and the presence of casual magic. The term 'legend' has come to denote a wider variety of tales, from saints' legends (see HAGIOGRAPHY) to urban legends, that are plausible according to the worldview of traditional society, even though they may contain supernatural or magical elements.

Another category of traditional narrative, the 'myth', includes stories of a sacred or cosmically important character. Myths are held to be true, although the setting of a myth is likely to be at an earlier stage of the world where different rules apply, so that otherwise impossible events are taken seriously. In CELTIC STUDIES, mythology (the corpus of myths) usually refers to pre-Christian mythology as recorded in ART and later literature, there being essentially no narrative literature in the CELTIC LANGUAGES from the pre-Christian period. Other narrative genres such as narrative jokes have not been studied in depth in the CELTIC COUNTRIES.

All of these categories are analytical ones imposed by scholars. Native terminology varies from language to language, and does not necessarily maintain the same distinctions (for the native early Irish genres, see TALE LISTS).

Antone Minard

FOLK-TALES AND LEGENDS, BRETON

As in the other Celtic countries, ROMANTICISM played an important part in inspiring the collection of Breton folk narrative. One of the early collectors was Émile Souvestre (1806–54) of Morlaix (Montroulez). Unusually for his time, his two collections *Les derniers Bretons* (1836) and *Le foyer breton* (1844) included some analysis of both text and context as well as a few footnotes providing and explaining the Breton as collected from oral tradition. On the whole, however, the printed versions of the tales were made to conform to French literary standards in both language and structure.

Perhaps the greatest of the Breton folklorists was François-Marie Luzel (1821–95), whose prolific publications include works on legends, folk-tales, and folksongs. Other important 19th- and early 20th-century folklorists include Elvire de Preissac, Countess de Cerny (1818–99), who collected both folk-tales and legendary traditions related to St Brigit in Brittany (Breizh); Anatole Le Braz (1859–1926), who published collections of folk-tales and legends, notably *La légende de la mort chez les Bretons armoricains* (The legend of death among the Armorican Bretons); and François Cadic (1864–1929), author of *Contes et légendes de Bretagne*. Two other collectors, Adolphe Orain (1834–1918) and Paul Sébillot (1846–1918), worked primarily in Upper Brittany (Breizh-Uhel). Sébillot was a significant contributor to folklore studies in France as a whole, coining the term *littérature orale* (oral literature).

Comparatively few folklorists have published folk narratives in Breton. Some collections entirely in Breton have appeared, notably G. Milin's work *Gwechall goz e oa . . .* (Once upon a time there was . . .), which appeared in book form in 1924, and Yann Ar Floc'h's *Koñchennou euz bro ar ster Aon* (Folk-tales from the Aulne river country) in 1950. Per-Jakez Hélias has published several folk narratives in Breton, and in 1984 the publisher Al Liamm produced a five-volume collection of Luzel's folk-tales in Breton from manuscripts housed in the Kemper/Quimper library. Most of these had been published in French translation nearly a century before, in 1887, but had never appeared in Breton.

Lacking a medieval vernacular narrative tradition to inspire collectors, antiquarian interest in Breton folk narrative tradition has focused more on ballads than on folk-tales or legends (see Barzaz-Breiz). More recent scholarship has found roots in Breton oral tradition for the Old French *lais* of Marie de France (see Breton lays), and has brought examples of Merlin to light. The Merlin of Breton folklore is more akin to the Myrddin Wyllt of early Welsh tradition—that is, a wild man and prophet—than to the court wizard of later Arthurian tradition. Jef Phillipe printed some of these tales in his *War roudoù Merlin e Breizh* (On the track of Merlin in Brittany) in 1986.

Many of the classic Breton folk narrative collections, long out of print, are being republished, notably by Terre de Brume in Rennes, which reissues the original text along with an introduction and analysis.

Antone Minard

FOLK-TALES AND LEGENDS, CORNISH

The narrative legacy of Cornwall (Kernow) is complex. Much of the material available today is the product of various initiatives by collectors from the Reformation period onward. Written versions of Cornish epic narratives have not yet been recovered, although the Arthurian and Tristan and Isolt material was probably central to early Cornish narrative traditions. These particular tales or cycles of tales are still important features of Cornish legendary material and have been incorporated into hagiographical and landscape-related legends.

Cornwall has retained a significant body of saints' lore (see HAGIOGRAPHY). In the 17th century, Nicholas Roscarrock compiled the earliest and to date the most comprehensive survey of hagiographical material relating to Cornwall. The legends of St PIRAN, St Petroc, and St Ia are still widely circulated.

The 19th-century collections of Robert Hunt and William Bottrell form the primary corpus of Cornish folk-tales. Although Bottrell collected his material earlier (starting in the 1830s) and his collection arguably contains better narrative quality, Hunt's collection was published first, and is more widely recognized as the standard work on Cornish folklore. Hunt's two-volume collection from 1865 includes tales of giants, FAIRIES, lost cities, fire worship, demons, spectres, King ARTHUR, holy wells, sorcery, witchcraft, miners, and SUPERSTITIONS. William Bottrell's three-volume collection (1870, 1873, 1880) contains longer narratives and covers subjects ranging from witchcraft and changelings to fairies and pixies.

Among the most well known of these narratives are the Mermaid of Zennor, the Tale of Tregeagle, the Wrestlers of Kenidjack, the Legend of Pengersick, Tom and the Giant, Duffy and the Devil, and Madge Figgey and Her Pig. Both Hunt and Bottrell also feature saints' tales associated with landscape features and monuments.

Cornish legends have by now been incorporated into a variety of contemporary ART forms, including film, drama, and poetry (see MASS MEDIA; CORNISH LITERATURE). The poetry of Charles Causley draws on traditional narrative, and folk-tales represent an important part of new community festivals, best seen in Bolster Day at St Agnes, which was inspired by the story of the Giant Bolster and Saint Agnes. Contemporary retellings of the tales collected by Hunt and Bottrell include those by Rawe, Quayle, and Foreman, and dramatized versions by the Bedlam and Kneehigh Theatre Companies. Recently integrated into the corpus is the late 20th-century legend of the Beast of Bodmin Moor.

Amy Hale

FOLK-TALES AND LEGENDS, IRISH

The Irish folk-tale collections, both published and unpublished, are widely acknowledged to be some of the best and richest in Europe—in excess of 43,000 versions of more than 700 tale types were indexed in Ó Súilleabháin and Christiansen's *Types of the Irish Folktale*, which includes only material collected until 1956. Most of these tales are to be found in the archives of the Irish Folklore Commission, which was active from 1935 to 1971. The wealth of documented Irish folk-tales is, in part, due to the efforts of early field collectors. Some of the heroic narratives collected in the 19th and 20th centuries tied into the narratives preserved in Old and Middle Irish—notably the FIANNAÍOCHT, Fenian tales (i.e., those concerning FINN MAC CUMAILL and his comrades.

Thomas Crofton Croker (1798–1854), a native of Cork (Corcaigh), was one of the first persons to collect Irish folklore. He corresponded with the brothers Grimm, who translated his influential *Fairy Legends and Traditions of the South of Ireland* (1825) into German as *Irische Elfenmärchen* in 1826. Many other collectors were active in the 19th century, including the literary figures Lady Wilde (Jane Francesca Elgee Wilde, *c.* 1826–96) and William Butler YEATS (1865–1939).

Jeremiah Curtin (1835–1906) was born to an Irish immigrant family in Detroit, but took his first collecting trip to Ireland (ÉIRE) in 1887. Pádraig Ó Loingsigh explained to the folklorist Séamus Ó Duilearga that it was he who told Curtin the tales in Irish, but his father, Muiris Ó Loingsigh (Maurice Lynch), translated them into English and was listed as the informant. Curtin's wife, Alma M. Cardell Curtin, took them down in shorthand, but, as was the case with many academics' wives of the period, she is usually not credited for her work.

Both Curtin and Wilde were criticized by Douglas Hyde (Dubhghlas DE HÍDE), another early collector, for their lack of fluency in Irish. Hyde's own collection, *Beside the Fire* (1910), was published bilingually. In the 20th century, folklorists placed a greater emphasis on collecting and publishing the Irish texts, although excellent unaccompanied English translations continue to be published, such as *The Folk-Tales of Ireland* (1966) by Sean O'Sullivan (Seán Ó Súilleabháin).

Although the Irish folk-tales are largely the same as other folk-tales throughout the world, the method of narrating them in Ireland became very elaborate over time, through the development of 'runs'—sections of prose text heavily ornamented with alliteration and other poetic devices. The skill involved was recognized beyond the Gaeltacht, such that the Irish word for a professional storyteller—*seanchaí*, or its Scottish Gaelic cognate *seanchaidh*—was borrowed into English as *shannaghes* (plural) as early as 1534; it is now usually spelled *seannachie* or *sennachie*. The word is based on *seanchas* 'lore'. The stories were usually told at night around the fire, beginning with the host (*Ar fhear an tí a théann an chéad scéal*, The man of the house tells the first tale).

Antone Minard

FOLK-TALES AND LEGENDS, MANX

The first collection of Manx folk-tales was compiled by George Waldron in 1726, and was posthumously published in 1731. This collection, with its stories of giants and underground palaces beneath the island's medieval Castle Rushen and the fearsome Moddey Dhoo (black dog) of Peel Castle, has formed the basis for publications of Manx folk-tales ever since.

The folk-tales contain accounts of Manx 'mythology', including creation myths for the island, its people, and 'Themselves' (the FAIRIES). The historical 'mythologies' also seek to place the Isle of Man (ELLAN VANNIN) within a wider cultural framework by identifying it as the Ellan Sheeant (Isle of Peace/Holy Island) of Irish mythology and relating the island's creation to the great battle between Finn Mac Cooil (Middle Irish FINN MAC CUMAILL) and a Scottish giant, when a 'sod of earth' is thrown, thereby creating the Lough Neagh (Loch nEathach) in northern Ireland (ÉRIU) and the Isle of Man. Although the Manx folk-tales were originally peopled with heroes and deities from the early Irish myths and legends, by the 19th century the predominant figure was MANANNÁN MAC LIR. Manannán figured in the early Irish MYTHOLOGICAL CYCLE as god of the sea, but in Manx tales he became the first Manx ruler and was a shapeshifting magician-king (see REINCARNATION) and navigator.

The majority of Manx tales, however, relate to the fairy-folk. Manx fairies are small wingless creatures of supernatural origin who should be called only by euphemistic terms. The stories are primarily cautionary tales that highlight the dangers of associating with 'Themselves', and relate to either concerns over the taking of infants and adults by the fairies or attempts of people to better themselves through 'trading' with the fairies. The need for protection and constant vigilance against the malicious intent of fairies and the fact that no one ever truly profits from dealings with the fairies are constantly emphasized.

Manx folk-tales relate to a whole bestiary of supernatural creatures, ranging from the relatively helpful but cantankerous Fynnoderee (or Phynnodderee) to the dangerous Tarroo-Ushtey (water bull) and the Glashtin (water horse). Of even greater danger was the Tehi Tegi, a beautiful temptress who could lure men to their doom and then revert to being an evil old sorceress, and the Buggane, a malicious hobgoblin.

Although abridged versions of the folk-tales were published in guidebooks and tourist accounts throughout the 19th century, the tales also appear to have remained part of the island's oral tradition until the latter part of that century. In addition, they provided a basis for much of the island's literature of the period, including Hall Caine's novels and T. E. Brown's dialect poetry. The seminal work in this regard is Sophia Morrison's *Manx Fairy Tales* (1911), the last publication to depict folk-tales as examples of Manx folklore (see MANX LITERATURE, MANX FOLKLORE). Successive publications of folk-tales have been abridged and rewritten as collections of 'fairy stories' for a children's audience, with an emphasis on illustration.

Yvonne Cresswell

FOLK-TALES AND LEGENDS, SCOTTISH GAELIC

Folk-tales and legends are well attested in Scottish Gaelic tradition. Tales are scattered throughout some manuscripts from the 17th century onward, although the bulk of the recorded material belongs to the 19th and 20th centuries. The pioneering collector of the mid-19th century was John Francis Campbell, who, with several collaborators (J. Dewar, J. G. Campbell, Alexander Carmichael, and Hector Maclean), tapped into a storytelling tradition that was just beginning to decline as the ceilidh-house lost its importance in the social life of Scottish Gaelic communities.

In the 20th century, the School of Scottish Studies in Edinburgh (DÙN ÈIDEANN) took the leading rôle in collecting tales, much aided by the advent of tape and video recorders. The material has come both from the settled population of the Gaidhealtachd (Gaelic-speaking area) and from Gaelic-speaking travellers. Closely related material was taken by emigrants to Nova Scotia, Canada, and survived there.

A narrative genre specific to Gaelic Scotland (ALBA) is that of CLAN tales, where events purporting to deal with historical characters are narrated in a distinctively terse style. Much attention has focused on the storytellers, their repertoire, and their narrative and memory techniques. Visualization seems to have been an important mnemonic aid. Many storytellers had substantial repertoires (e.g., Duncan

MacDonald and Angus MacLellan), and some tales took several evenings to tell in full.

Anja Gunderloch

FOLK-TALES AND LEGENDS, WELSH

The Mabinogi, a medieval collection of narratives, contain elements from pre-Christian mythology, the international folk-tale, local legend, and individual literary authorship. Retellings of these tales have been prominently featured in popular collections of Welsh folk narrative. Early collectors looked for further information about medieval traditions in Welsh oral tradition and, although there was no additional material on the characters from the *Mabinogi*, traditions were collected relating to Arthur and Merlin (see Myrddin).

Many Arthurian legends in Wales are local aetiological legends, explaining the origin of features such as *coeten Arthur* (Arthur's quoit) and the names of several megalithic monuments (e.g., in Pembrokeshire [sir Benfro] and in Gower [Gŵyr]). The legend of Arthur's Cave has been collected from several localities, in England as well as in Wales (Cymru). W. Jenkyn Thomas's version from *The Welsh Fairybook* (1907) involves a Welshman who comes across a soothsayer (*dyn hysbys*) in London. The soothsayer recognizes the Welshman's hazel staff as having come from outside Arthur's Cave. The two return to Pontneddfechan in Powys and enter the cave, from which they attempt to steal treasure. The soothsayer warns the Welshman not to touch a bell, but he breaks the taboo and the soothsayer has difficulty persuading King Arthur and his knights to go back to sleep. They leave the cave without the treasure and are unable to find it again.

Tales of the *tylwyth teg* (fairies) are an important part of Welsh folk narrative tradition. In the modern period, the most widely known and frequently anthologized legend is that of the fairy bride of Llyn y Fan Fach and the Physicians of Myddvai (Meddygon Myddfai), first printed in 1861. Another well-known tale is the story of Gelert, made famous in English by the poem 'Beth Gêlert' by William Robert Spencer (1769–1834). In this story, Prince Llywelyn ab Iorwerth of Wales returns from the hunt to find his household in disarray. He cannot find his infant son, but he sees his greyhound, Gelert, with blood on his muzzle. Jumping to the logical conclusion, Llywelyn kills the dog. He later finds the child unharmed, along with the body of a wolf, which his own dog had evidently killed to protect the child. Full of remorse, Llywelyn builds a monument for his dog, Bedd Gelert (Gelert's grave). The story of the misunderstood faithful hound is an international migratory legend that became attached to the village of Beddgelert in Caernarfonshire (sir Gaernarfon) as a way of explaining the name.

There is no definitive collection of Welsh folk narrative. Many unpublished orally collected materials are housed in the Museum of Welsh Life at St Fagans (Sain Ffagan), and many of the folk-tales and legends published in Welsh have never been translated into English. Several of the English-language collections have been so heavily adapted that they are literary renderings of folk tradition rather than records of it—for example, Iwan Myles's *Tales from Welsh Traditions* (1923).

Antone Minard

FOMOIRI

Fomoiri is a name that designates a race of hostile beings frequently mentioned in Irish legend; they usually appear to be conceived as supernatural entities, and are often described as being monstrous in appearance. The first element in the name is clearly the preposition *fo* 'under', but the second is more mysterious. Medieval etymologists took it to be *muir* 'sea', with an alternative interpretation of the second syllable as *mór* 'big' reflecting *fomoiri* as a synonym for 'giants'.

The Fomoiri feature in legendary-historical sources as the enemies both of the first settlers of Ireland (ÉRIU) and of some early Irish kings; they also appear as the fierce and sometimes monstrous inhabitants of other islands. In what is probably the earliest reference to them, a possibly 7th-century elegy for Mess-Telmann, a prince of Leinster (LAIGIN), they are spoken of as dwelling 'under the worlds of men'. In CATH MAIGE TUIRED ('The [Second] Battle of Mag Tuired'), the Fomoiri are portrayed as a race opposed to and constrasting with the TUATH DÉ. This dichotomy has been seen as reflecting an Indo-European myth of 'the war of the gods', but seems more likely to be a concept originating with *Cath Maige Tuired* itself, in which the Fomoiri are identified with the Vikings. Other sources indicate an overlap or, indeed, identity between the Fomoiri and Tuath Dé: The Fomoiri are called 'the champions of the síd' and the phrase 'demons and Fomóraig' is glossed 'i.e. Tuath Dé Donann' (*Lebor Gabála Érenn* 32–3). The main distinguishing factor seems to be that the Fomoiri are always portrayed in a negative light, whereas the Tuath Dé are only occasionally cast in this rôle.

The Middle Irish *Sex Aetates Mundi* includes *fomóraig* among the monstrous races descended from Noah's son Ham, in a context that suggests that the word is used as an equivalent of 'giants'.

John Carey

FOODWAYS

'Foodways' is the term given to cultural practices that involve food, including which foods are eaten and the cultural contexts surrounding them (see CHAMPION'S PORTION; FEAST).

Celtic Foodways in Ancient Times

A particular valuable source among the GREEK AND ROMAN ACCOUNTS by Athenaeus is the *Deipnosophistoi*, whose sections on Gaul are heavily indebted to the lost history of Posidonius. Elements of Athenaeus's descriptions of Celtic feasts bear a resemblance to those in the early Irish sagas, particularly FLED BRICRENN ('Bricriu's Feast') in the ULSTER CYCLE of Tales. Other commentaries, such as Caesar's statement in *De Bello Gallico* 5.12 that eating chicken, goose, and hare are taboo, should not be taken at face value.

Cannibalism was alleged by classical authors (see SACRIFICE). Saint Jerome, writing *c.* AD 390–415 (*Adversus Jovinianum* 2.7), says: 'I myself as a young man in Gaul ... [saw] people, feeding on human flesh'. Alleged instances of cannibalism in extreme circumstances, for survival, may have occurred in siege situations, as in

CELTIBERIA at Saguntum and at NUMANTIA, but otherwise archaeological evidence does not support regular cannibalism.

Otherwise, classical writers emphasize only those habits that are different from ordinary Greek or Roman practice, either in kind or in degree: the Celts' (to their minds) excessive fondness for meat, lack of oil (the Celts used butter or lard), and lack of pepper.

Several food words have been reconstructed in PROTO-CELTIC and thus by implication go back to the Iron Age or earlier. Archaeological finds in Gaul and elsewhere confirm the linguistic evidence. The primary domesticated food animals were swine, cattle, and sheep. The pigs were domesticated from the European wild boar. Cattle were small and hardy, and probably largely black in colour, similar to the modern breeds of Kerry and Welsh Black cattle. The sheep were probably similar to the modern Hebridean, Manx Loaghten, and Soay breeds.

Chickens, dogs, ducks, geese, goats, and horses were also raised and eaten, although chickens were rare and dogs may have been restricted to particular medical or ritual contexts. Wild boar, deer, and elk were also sources of food, and the bear, beaver, and hare may have been used as foodstuffs as well. From the seas, seal and fish were harvested. Words have been reconstructed for eels and salmon.

Crops associated with reconstructed Proto-Celtic words include barley, oats, and wheat, along with acorns, apples, berries, blackberries, blackthorn (sloe), wild garlic, hawthorn, hazel nuts, mallow, mast (the fruit of the beech), mulberries, nettles, nuts, tubers, onions, rape (now often called canola), seaweed, strawberries, and watercress.

Many other plant-food sources have been reconstructed from pollen and seeds found in excavations. The grains rye and millet may have been Roman introductions. Other excavated seed evidence shows that peas, a kind of fava beans (*Vicia fabia minor*), and vetch (*Vicia satia*) were grown, probably for livestock—vetch, in particular, is mildly toxic to humans. In addition, several plants now regarded as weeds may have served as food, including lambsquarters (*Chenpodium album*) and orache (*Atriplex patula*).

Honey was the staple sweetener. Fermented grain and honey produced beer, mead, and a wide variety of other alcoholic drinks. Cooking seems to have been done largely on griddles or in metal CAULDRONS over an open fire. Tandoori-like clay ovens are also commonly found on the European continent.

The Medieval Period

Until very recent times, an element of gathering was associated with acquiring the necessities to sustain life—for example, gathering of greens, nuts, and berries; fishing; and small-scale hunting and trapping.

Another important aspect of foodways is *not* eating. Fasting was an important element in the medieval church, but in Ireland (ÉRIU) it had a social function as well. A public fast against someone (*troscad*) was a way of compelling them to do something, discussed in the Brehon laws, and Irish hagiographies show saints using similar actions against God.

Homemade Breton *krampouezh* (crêpes). (Stefan Ataman/Dreamstime.com)

The Norman incursions in the 11th to 13th centuries brought many changes to the diet of the Irish and British Celts. In Ireland, at least, fallow deer (the red deer is native), pheasants, pike, rabbits, and mute swans were introduced. What meat was consumed was largely pork. Prohibitions against consumption of horseflesh are numerous in IRISH LITERATURE, indicating that it was no longer eaten by people of high social status. Apples are mentioned frequently, in both mythological and social contexts.

Modern Celtic Foodways

Following its introduction in the late 17th century, much of Ireland (ÉIRE) and Scotland (ALBA) came to rely on the potato as a dietary staple. The potato FAMINE in the 1840s meant that many wild plants were relied upon to supplement the diet, including berries, charnock (*Raphanus raphanistrum*, a wild relative of the radish), nettles, and sorrel.

Breton cuisine is distinguished by its extensive use of *krampouezh* (crêpes), made of buckwheat or wheat flour, and also by its baking, cider, and seafood.

The Cornish pasty—a pastry dumpling stuffed with a variety of fillings—is the best-known Cornish dish. It was an eminently practical dish for miners, as a pasty baked in the morning would still be warm at mid-day, and was easily portable.

In Ireland, potatoes and cabbage feature in many local dishes—for example, *bacstaí* (boxty) and *cál ceannan* (colcannon). Irish emigrant communities in the Americas have developed the custom of eating a corned beef and cabbage supper on St Patrick's Day, and beer (sometimes dyed green) features in festival contexts throughout the day.

The haggis, a sausage made from rolled oats and sweetbreads, is the stereotypical Scottish dish. Oats and whisky also feature prominently in Scottish cuisine, the latter being used extensively for flavouring as well as being consumed on its own.

Bara brith (speckled bread) is a Welsh currant bread. The dish 'Welsh rabbit', usually but incorrectly spelled 'Welsh rarebit', refers to *caws pobi* (cheese on toast).

Wendy Davies and Antone Minard

FORAS NA GAEILGE

Foras na Gaeilge (Irish Language Agency) was established on 2 December 1999, under the terms of the Belfast (Good Friday) Agreement, with the aim of promoting the Irish language throughout the island of Ireland (Éire). As well as retaining the responsibilities of Bord na Gaeilge (Irish Language Board), Foras na Gaeilge was given a wide range of functions to add to its effectiveness in promoting the Irish language—for example, in education and terminology. The functions previously performed by An Gúm regarding publishing and by the Terminology Committee have also been given to Foras na Gaeilge.

Foras na Gaeilge functions as a partner with Tha Boord o Ulstèr-Scotch to form the Language Body. The Language Body is one of the six North–South Bodies mentioned in Strand 2 of the Good Friday Agreement of 1998 (see Éire).

Foras na Gaeilge has supported worthwhile initiatives on behalf of the Irish language in both North and South, by funding Irish-language organizations, by setting up new partnerships, and through Foras na Gaeilge's own all-island activities.

The Good Friday Agreement also include provisions related to television broadcasting. Two areas in particular are mentioned in the Agreement: expanding TG4's broadcasting signal in Northern Ireland and supporting the establishment and the development of an Irish-language television production sector in the North.

The British government signed the European Charter for Regional and Minority Languages on 2 March 2000. This agreement gave recognition to the Irish language, Scottish Gaelic, Scots, and Ulster Scots in regard to Part II of the Charter. The British government has said that it will specify the Irish language, Welsh, and Scottish Gaelic in regard to Part III.

Websites
www.beo.ie; www.bnag.ie

Éamonn Ó hArgáin

FORTIFICATION, BRITAIN AND IRELAND

Introduction

For their size, Britain and Ireland (Ériu) feature a diverse range of defensive monuments of late prehistoric date, varingy considerably in scale, dating, layout, and construction methods. The construction of many hill-forts occurred in the Late Bronze Age (*c.* 1200–*c.* 700 BC), with ongoing occupation or sporadic reoccupation in the Iron Age and sometimes the early medieval period.

Hill-Forts

The most typical hill-forts are perhaps those that are situated in elevated positions and that consist of one or several rings of defences composed of earthen or composite earth/timber banks with external ditches. This type of site is most common in several areas of Britain, particularly mid-southern ENGLAND, the Welsh Marches, and the Scottish borders; in Ireland, they are most plentiful in the north Munster (MUMU)/mid-Leinster (LAIGIN) area, with further clusters found in the Wicklow Mountains and Co. Sligo. In Ireland, Scotland (ALBA), and northern England, earth is often replaced by stone as the main construction material.

With a few exceptions, the hill-forts of west southern Britain—west Wales and the Devon-Cornwall peninsula—seem to have remained quite modest in size and to have retained fairly simple defensive arrangements. In Scotland, the stone ramparts are often laced with timber, and high-temperature fusion of the stone resulting from the burning of the timber framing in antiquity has been noted at many sites, giving rise to the nomenclature 'VITRIFIED FORTS'.

Oppida

Vast oppida (sing. OPPIDUM)—that is, defended proto-towns of the Continental Final Iron Age—do not occur in Ireland. In Britain, they are essentially restricted to the southeastern part of England, where one also finds COINAGE and the tribal groups identifiable as Belgae. The oppidum seems to have been adopted in the southeast from the 1st century BC, when these large defended sites appear to have been constructed in lowland locations near important river crossings, with the course of the river sometimes forming part of the defensive perimeter of the oppidum. Examples of such 'enclosed oppida' are found at Dyke Hills, Oxfordshire, and at Winchester, Hampshire.

Western and Northern Coastal Zones

The Atlantic-facing areas of Ireland and Britain feature a range of distinctive regional types of late prehistoric defended settlements that are generally on a smaller physical scale than the large hill-forts and oppida of the agriculturally richer lowlands. What most have in common, as indicated by their scale, is a continuing emphasis on the family or extended family as the social unit best suited to exploitation of the resources available in agriculturally marginal areas.

Promontory forts or 'cliff castles' are common along many coastal areas of the Atlantic and Irish Sea, where a cliff-top position is fortified, usually through the erection of a stone or earthen rampart across the landward approach. DUNS and BROCHS are two particularly Scottish types of dry-stone defended sites, most common in the west and north (see HIGHLANDS). Along the west coast of Ireland, particularly in the counties of Clare and Kerry, as well as on the Aran Islands (OILEÁIN ÁRANN), a series of impressive dry-stone built forts are known. These sites, such as DÚN AONGHASA, are often positioned on cliff edges or promontories, and are remarkable for the massive and often complex nature of their defensive architecture. Shared features include terraced ramparts and intramural passages and chambers.

Simon Ó Faoláin

FORTIFICATION, CONTINENTAL

Introduction

IRON AGE fortifications are not merely defenses, but also important cultural statements that define group identity and status. Advanced types of composite ramparts, such as the *murus gallicus* (discussed later in this article), together with their often imposing gateway constructions, must be viewed as monumental elements of the Celtic hill-fort or OPPIDUM.

The majority of fortifications date from the later HALLSTATT period (*c.* 700–*c.* 475 BC) and Earlier and Later LA TÈNE periods (*c.* 475 BC until Romanization). Continuous settlement at such sites was rare, with a hiatus in occupation often being noted during the Middle La Tène period (*c.* 350–*c.* 200 BC). Late Hallstatt and Early La Tène fortifications rarely exceed 30–40 ha (72–100 acres) and are mostly situated on naturally protected high plateaux.

Rampart Types

Besides simple earthen 'dump' ramparts and dry-stone walls, other techniques of defensive construction attested at late prehistoric sites include simple wattle-and-daub structures with palisaded walls and wooden box-type constructions. The main construction methods employed on Continental and southern British hill-forts and oppida are outlined here:

1. The Altkönig-Preist type rampart was constructed of vertical wooden posts inserted in a dry-stone wall. These vertical timbers were exposed in the outer face of the rampart. The posts were earth-bound or supported on stone slabs positioned approximately 1–3 m apart. The thickness of the rampart varied between 3.5 m and 6 m. This type was prevalent in a region stretching approximately from the northern edge of the Alps in the south to Luxembourg in the north.
2. The Kelheim-type rampart was a vertical post and stone panel-work arrangement, similar to the Altkönig-Preist type, but much simplified, with only one layer of horizontal beams anchored into the earthen rampart. In this form of rampart, the inner face was often ramped gradually down to the ground level of the interior. This construction technique was mostly used in the eastern part of the La Téne cultural area.
3. The Ehrang-type rampart was constructed of horizontal beams arranged lengthwise and crosswise and anchored to a stone wall that formed the defensive exterior, with the ends of the beams running crosswise through the rampart, visible in its outer face. The dry-stone facing of the outer walls was generally only a course or two thick and could not have survived any length of time without the timber-laced backing of earth.

4. The *murus gallicus* technique described in Caesar's *De Bello Gallico* ('Gallic War') is a variant of the Ehrang type. In this type, the lengthwise and crosswise beams were fixed together at the point where they passed over one another by using large iron spikes. The bulk of the rampart was filled in with rammed soil and, as with the Kelheim-type rampart, the inner face was often ramped gradually down to the ground level of the interior. This type appears to have been popular in western GAUL. Modern estimates based on excavated examples suggest that as many as 700 man-hours may have been required for the construction of each metre length of such ramparts.

Gateways

Besides simple entrance gaps in the walls accompanied by short passageways, several more elaborate gateway layouts are known. The typical gate was the *zangentor*, the pincer-gate, in which the gate passage narrowed toward the inside. The passageway, which frequently assumed a funnel shape, often had two lanes and was secured by a gatehouse or, rarely, a gate tower. At their entrance point, gates could be as wide as 15 m. At several sites the entrance way featured extra walls or 'hornworks', which extended outward from the main defences at a right angle near the gateway, thereby extending the passageway to the entrance considerably and, as a result, the exposure time of attackers to the efforts of the defenders.

Otto Helmut Urban

FOSTERAGE IN IRELAND AND WALES

Fosterage was a method of childrearing whereby adults, other than the natural parents, were given the charge of raising a child for a particular period of time and under certain specified conditions.

Ireland

The terms applied to the foster-father (*aite*) and the foster-mother (*muime*) are considered terms of affection in Old Irish. The term *dalta* refers to the foster-child.

The medieval Irish legal material notes two types of fosterage: one for payment and one of affection (see LAW TEXTS); three age divisions are identified as well: up to seven years, from seven to twelve years, and from twelve to seventeen years. Fosterage was a formal contract within the Irish tradition. At its core was the education of the child, with a fine of two-thirds of the fosterage fee incurred if one of the required rank-appropriate skills was not taught.

Protesting against a fosterage placement was an important right of the maternal kin, who bore half the cost. If the child was blemished in any way while in fosterage, the foster-father forfeited two-thirds of the fosterage fee. The *sét gertha* (*sét* of maintenance) was an important payment made to the foster-child on completion of fosterage (*c.* 14 years of age for a girl and *c.* 17 for a boy). This payment ensured the maintenance of the foster-parents in later life, illustrating the lifelong commitment involved. Providing foster-parents with refection in poverty and maintenance in old age (*goire*) was an obligatory matter.

Foster-relations were a possible source for military and legal aid in times of need, and a range of shortand long-term benefits to fosterage played a large part in sustaining the power of the institution into the early modern period.

Wales

References within medieval Welsh legal material are concerned with inheritance and property rights, as opposed to the upbringing and education of the child. An important difference between the medieval Irish and Welsh tradition was the possibility of inheriting land through foster-relations in medieval Wales (CYMRU). After a year and a day in certain types of fosterage, the foster-son would have earned the right to inherit land.

Further evidence in the literary sources attests to the existence of the fosterage institution in Wales, particularly within the stories of the MABINOGI. The benefits of being a foster-parent include support from a foster-son in later life, with an intensification in friendship between the foster-parents and natural parents. In both traditions, a fosterage relationship is noted as one that should bring prosperity to the households involved in the process.

Bronagh Ní Chonaill

G

GAELIC

Modern Usage

The word *Gaelic* is a borrowing from Scottish Gaelic *Gàidhlig*. It appears in English in the 16th century referring to Scottish Gaelic, the language of the Scottish Highlanders. By the 18th century, *Gaelic* (alongside *Irish* and *Erse*) and *Gaels* were also sometimes applied to the Irish language and its speakers, supported by the corresponding Irish words *Gaoidhealg* and *Gaoidheal* (in Early Modern Irish spelling). The corresponding Manx word *Gaelg* means the 'Manx language'. Irish and Manx can also be called *Irish Gaelic* and *Manx Gaelic* to avoid confusion with Scottish Gaelic, on the one hand, or with the English speech of Ireland and Man (Ellan Vannin), on the other hand. Simply *Irish*, however, remains the preferred name for Ireland's Celtic language, both as the form established earlier in English and reflecting its status as the national language of Ireland.

Following the Famine of 1845–50, the connotation of *Gaelic* became extended to groups whose cultural identity was defined partly by the Irish language, and also by nationalism and often Roman Catholicism (e.g., the Gaelic Athletic Association). In keeping with these recent meanings, historians now use *Gaelic* to designate the 'native Irish' from the Scandinavians, Anglo-Normans, and the later Elizabethan and Cromwellian incomers. The 'Gaelic Order'—meaning the old system of patronage by Irish-speaking aristocrats for professional poets and scholars—is sometimes said to have ended with the defeat of Hiberno-Spanish forces at Kinsale (Cionn tSáile) in 1601 or some subsequent military milestone in the 17th century.

Derivation

The Old Irish forms *Goídelg* 'Irish language' and *Goídel* 'Irish speaker, Gael' gave rise to the modern linguistic term Goidelic, borrowings from the Brythonic forms that became Middle Welsh *Gŵydel* and *Gŵydelec*. The root corresponds to Old Irish *fíad*, Old Breton *guoid*, and Middle Welsh *gŵyd,* all meaning 'wild, feral, uncultivated'. The original sense of the ethnonym is, therefore, 'forest people'; hence 'wild men, savages'. *Goídel* and *Goídelg* must have been borrowed later than *c.* 600, but the date cannot have been much later, because these words appear in early Old Irish sources such as the archaic Leinster dynastic poem *Mōen ēn*.

The borrowing of the language name and the corresponding group name in the 7th century can be understood in the context of an Irish people—relatively recently Christian, literate, especially in their own vernacular, involved in Britain through colonization (DÁL RIATA; DYFED), centrally involved in the national churches of the PICTS and Northumbria, and engaged in high-level missionary activity (*peregrinatio*) in Frankia and Italy. They were newly aware of themselves as a linguistically defined nation among many, coming into contact with new words and stories with which to express this awareness.

The popular idea that *Gaelic* is related to the names GAUL and GALATIA is incorrect.

John T. Koch

GAELTACHT

The Gaeltacht is the collective name normally ascribed to those districts where the IRISH language is spoken as the main vernacular language or is at least in a strong minority position. At the end of the 17th century, when it first appeared in written form, the word normally meant 'those who spoke Irish' or even 'the Irish heritage' itself, similar to the way *Gàidhealtachd* in SCOTTISH GAELIC normally refers to the HIGHLANDS and Islands—that is, those areas inhabited by the Gaels. It was only with the Irish language and cultural revival (see LANGUAGE [REVIVAL] MOVEMENT IN THE CELTIC COUNTRIES) at the end of the 19th century and the beginning of the 20th century that *Gaeltacht* acquired definite geographical connotations.

History of the Decline of Irish

The Gaeltacht is a collection of scattered districts where Irish has survived. On the eve of the Great FAMINE (1845–52), there were approximately 4 million Irish speakers, many of them monoglots, but the language was already in decline. The Catholic Emancipation Act of 1829 and the establishment of the National School system two years later contributed to this trend in that the former opened up possibilities for adherents of the Catholic religion, the vast majority of the Irish people, to enter professions hitherto barred to them; the latter offered possibilities for obtaining a basic education through the medium of English. The Great Famine accelerated the process of decline. By the end of the 19th century, Irish was in free-fall, used as a community language only in scattered, remote, and underdeveloped areas, mostly on the west and south coasts, known today as the *Gaeltacht*.

State Support in the 20th Century

When the Irish Free State (Saorstát na hÉireann) was established in 1922, the revival of the Irish language became one of the primary objectives of the new state. Thus Irish, alongside English, became an official language. Two main revival strategies were pursued: the inclusion of Irish as an essential subject on the curricula of all schools (see EDUCATION) and the preservation and development of the Gaeltacht. A government-appointed commission, Coimisiún na Gaeltachta, designated two categories of Gaeltacht areas: Fíor-Ghaeltacht (fully Irish-speaking) and Breac-Ghaeltacht (partially Irish-speaking).

At the beginning of the 21st century, Irish-speaking districts are recognized in only seven counties: Donegal (Contae Dhún na nGall), Mayo (Contae Mhaigh Eo),

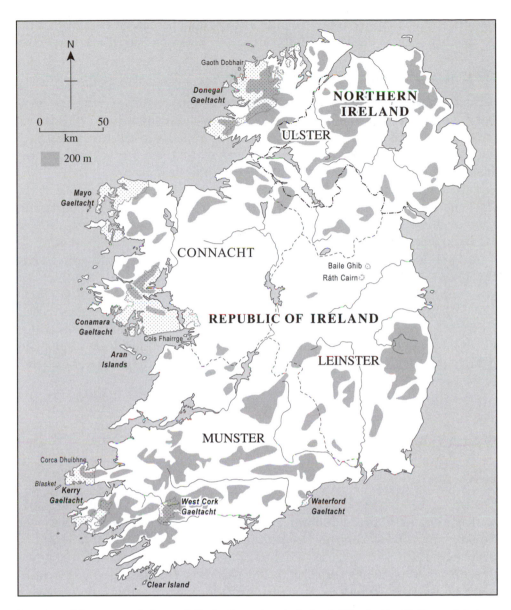

Location of the current designated Gaeltacht regions in Ireland. (Map by Ian Gulley and Antony Smith)

Galway (Contae na Gaillimhe), Kerry (Contae Chiarraí), Cork (Contae Chorcaí), Waterford (Contae Phort Láirge), and Meath (Contae na Mí).

A state scheme of annual grants for Irish-speaking Gaeltacht families was set up and support given for other measures to improve living and working conditions in the Gaeltacht. In 1956, a special government department with responsibility for the Gaeltacht and the Irish language—Roinn na Gaeltachta (Department for the Gaeltacht)—was established. The establishment of industries by foreign investors has proved to be a mixed blessing in the Gaeltacht, as it has tended to strengthen the position and status of English by introducing a new English-speaking management class.

The Current Situation and Prospects

The state language-acquisition policy has succeeded in greatly increasing the number of people able to speak Irish. The 1996 census showed that 1,430,205 claimed to be able to speak Irish, compared with 543,511 in the 1926 census, the first such survey taken after independence. The vast majority of these people have acquired Irish at school, and their knowledge and fluency may be limited.

Irish summer colleges for post-primary school students are supported by the state and the students are normally accommodated with Gaeltacht families. This form of cultural/educational tourism is an important economic activity in most Gaeltacht areas.

In 1971, RaidiÓ na Gaeltachta, an all-Irish radio service for the Gaeltacht, was set up; it was followed in 1996 by a national Irish-medium television service, TG4 (see MASS MEDIA). Although the literary tradition has primarily been oral, many Gaeltacht authors have made valuable contributions to modern literature in the Irish language.

The 1996 census showed that of the 82,715 inhabitants of officially designated Gaeltacht areas, 61,035 claimed to be able to speak Irish. Declining levels of intergenerational transmission continue to be the main threat to the continued existence of the Gaeltacht.

Dónall Ó Riagáin

GALATIA

Introduction

The land in central Anatolia east of the Halys river, around Ankara in present-day Turkey, was settled by Gaulish invaders after 230 BC. The three major tribes—the Τολιστοβογιοι Tolistobogii, Τεκτοσαγες Tectosages, and Τροκμοι Trocmi—maintained their native language (GALATIAN) and many Celtic traditions for centuries under Roman rule. Thus, for example, the Galatians gathered together at a ritual place of assembly known as Δρυνεμετον Drunemeton 'sacred oak wood'; cf. DRUIDS; NEMETON.

Historical Background

Classical sources report that the Gauls crossed into what was then Phrygia in 278 BC, shortly after the death of Alexander III Seleucus, who had conquered the country a generation before. Classical commentators mentioned that they came in families, indicating a genuine migration rather than a gradual settlement. These incomers seem, at least partly, to represent a regrouping of the Celtic forces that had invaded Greece in 280–78 under BRENNOS OF THE PRAUSI. The main military leaders of the Celts entering Asia Minor were Leonorius (Lonnorios) and Luterius (or Lutarius).

Central Asia Minor in Hellenistic times showing Galatian tribes and sites and neighbouring kingdoms. (Map by Antone Minard, Raimund Karl, and John T. Koch)

In the west, the Tolistobogii capital was at Blucium, around modern Ballihisar. To the east of the Tolistobogii, the Tectosages were centred around Ancyra (now Ankara, the capital of Turkey), and the easternmost tribe was the Trocmi, with their capital at Ταυιον Tauion (now Büyüknefes). Another important city in Galatia was the old Phrygian capital, Gordion, renamed *Vindia* by the Galatians, from the Celtic root **windo-s* 'white, fair'. The place of assembly called *Drunemeton* fits with Caesar's account of the Gaulish druids.

The most powerful ruler of the Galatians was Δειοταρος (Deiotaros) of the Tolistobogii, whose reign began in 63 BC. This Galatian dynastic name is clearly

Celtic, deriving from Proto-Celtic *Dēwo-tarwos 'divine bull'. Deiotaros was given the title 'king' by the Roman Senate. He died in 40 BC, and Galatia became a part of the Roman Empire in 25 BC.

Archaeology

To date, archaeological finds that can be attributed to the Galatians in Asia Minor are extremely rare and mostly consist of single finds without detailed context. La Tène material from controlled archaeological contexts in Asiatic Turkey has been found in the excavations of Galatian tombs at Bolu and the excavations at Boğazköy/Hattusa. The finds from Bolu include two gold TORCS, two gold bracelets with dog's-head terminals, a bronze horse bit, and a gold belt buckle with a depiction of a bearded and moustached man's face. Torcs of characteristic La Tène type are clearly represented on the statues of Galatian warriors produced at Pergamon.

Raimund Karl and Antone Minard

GALATIAN LANGUAGE

The Galatian language was a Celtic language first brought to Asia Minor (modern Asiatic Turkey) following the Celtic invasion of Greece in 279/8 BC and was established in GALATIA in north-central Anatolia by 260 BC. Late Classical sources—if they are to be trusted—suggest that it survived at least into the 6th century AD. In a famous passage from his 4th-century Commentary on St Paul's letter to the Galatians (2.3), St Jerome states that Galatian is very similar to the language of the Treveri, a Gaulish tribe who inhabited the Moselle valley along the Rhine.

The attested lexicon of approximately 120 forms is known entirely from citations by Greek authors and from proper names embedded in Greek inscriptions and texts. The confirmed common Galatian words include δυοὺγγος *drungos* 'nose' and τασκός *taskos* (probably 'badger'). Further possible Galatian words include βαρδοί *bardī* (nominative plural) 'poets', κάρνυξ *karnyx* and κάρνον (*karnon*, accusative singular) 'trumpet', μάρκαν *markan* (accusative singular) 'horse', cf. Welsh *march*, and τριμαρκισίαν *trimarkisian* (accusative singular) 'a three-horse battle group', and ἰόρκους *iorkus* (accusative plural) and ἰοκες (nom. pl.) 'wild deer', cf. Welsh *iwrch* 'roebuck'. The famous name of the meeting place of the Galatians, Δρεμετον *Drunemeton* (accusative singular), is evidently composed of *dru-*, a compounding form of 'oak', and NEMETON 'sacred place'. Most of the other attested Galatian place-names and tribal names are obviously Celtic and quite similar to those found in the western ancient Celtic world, particularly GAUL: for example, place-names—Ἀρτικνίακον *Artikniākon* 'holding of the son of Artos, the Bear', Οἰνδία *Vindia* 'Gordion' lit. 'white place'; tribal names—ριγοσαγες *Rīgosages* (containing *rīgo-*, the Celtic word for 'king', nom. *rīχs*), Τεκτοσαγες *Tectosages* ('journey-seekers').

The linguistic analysis of Galatian forms is sometimes impeded by the use of Greek characters (see SCRIPTS), but the very strongly Gaulish appearance of the fragmentary Galatian corpus seems to bear out St Jerome's comparison.

Joseph Eska

GALICIA

Galicia, the northwestern region of present-day Spain, is sometimes counted as one of the CELTIC COUNTRIES, even though its inhabitants have not spoken any Celtic language since the early Middle Ages. The last Celtic language likely to have been spoken in the area was BRYTHONIC in the region known as Britonia, which had received settlers from Brittany or direct from BRITAIN during the post-Roman migration period (see BRETON MIGRATIONS). Prior to that time, ancient Galicia was linguistically Celtic, as was much of the Iberian peninsula.

The modern dialect of Galicia—Galician or Gallego—is a Romance language, related to Portuguese and Spanish. Identification by and of Galicians with the Celtic countries is largely based partly on recognition of their cultural and linguistic distinctiveness from other regions of Spain and Portugal, the region's Atlantic climate, and features shared with contemporary cultures of Atlantic Europe such as the BAGPIPE.

Pre-Roman Galicia

The pre-Roman civilization is commonly called the Castro Culture, after the *castros* (hill-forts) that were especially numerous there. The Celtic element -*brix*, -*briga* means 'hill' or 'hill-fort' (Welsh *bre* 'hill'): for instance, **Uindobriga* (now *Vendabre*) 'white hill-fort', *Segobriga* (now *Segorbe*) 'hill-fort of the victory' or 'the mighty hill-fort', and *Nemetobriga* (now *Mendoya*) 'sacred hill-fort, sanctuary hill-fort' (see NEMETON). Most of the modern Galician place-names ending in -*obre*, -*obe*, -*ove*, -*abre*, -*ebre*, and -*ubre* come from -*brix* or -*briga*, with most occurring in the province of La Coruña, in the old territory of the Arrotrebae. Their chief city was Brigantium, a Celtic name related to the tribal name BRIGANTES/Brigantii.

Roman Gallaecia

During the Roman occupation, Galicia was called Callaecia or Gallaecia, and was divided into three *conventi*—that is, Roman administrative entities, each with a specific territory and capital. These *capitales* were Lucus Augusti (now Lugo, Spain), Bracara Augusta (now Braga, Portugal), and Asturica Augusta (now Astorga in the province of Leon, Spain). Modern Galicia covers only Conventus Lucensis, to which it corresponds almost exactly. A post-Roman layer of place-names commemorates the settlement of *Brittones* 'Britons' in Galicia in the 5th and 6th centuries—for example, one *Bertoña* in the province of La Coruña and another in Pontevedra.

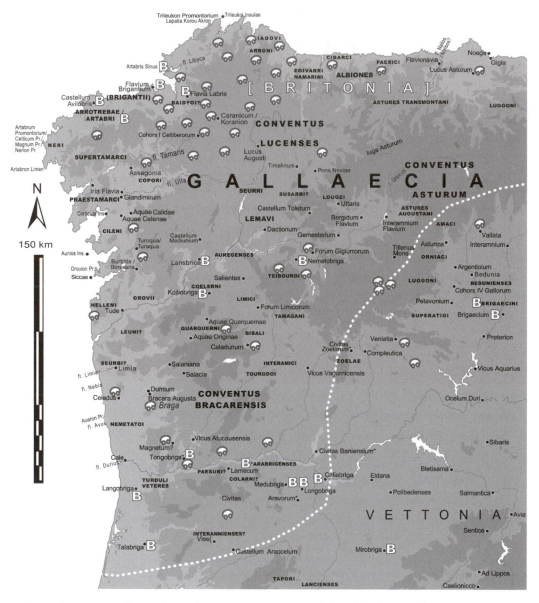

Iron Age and Romano-Celtic Galicia, showing names in *-briga* (B) and find spots of La Tène gold torcs. The zone of hill-forts known as 'castros' is enclosed in the dashed white line. Post-Roman Britonia is labelled in white. (Map by Antone Minard, Raimund Karl, and John T. Koch)

Ancient Personal Names

Latin INSCRIPTIONS give a number of names that can be linked to names known from IRISH, GAULISH, or BRYTHONIC. Recurring names include *Camulus*, attested also in GAUL and Britain, and possibly related to Old Irish *Cumall*, the name of FINN MAC

CUMAILL's father; *Cloutius*, from Common Celtic **klouto-*, meaning 'famous' and related to Old Irish *cloth* and Welsh *clod* 'fame'; *Burrus*, probably meaning 'proud, sturdy, stout'; and *Ambatos*, comparable to Gallo-Latin *Ambactus* 'servant, subordinate' (cf. Welsh *amaeth(wr)* 'farmer').

Gods

Attested names include *Bandua*; *Cosus*, equated with Mars (see INTERPRETATIO ROMANA); *Reua*, whose name may be related etymologically to the name of the Irish demigod CÚ ROÍ; *Bormo*, well attested in the Celtic world and in particular in Gaul; and LUGUS, plural *Lugoues*, well attested in the Celtic world and corresponding to the Irish LUG, Gaulish *Lugus*, and the Welsh LLEU.

José Calvete

GAMES

Celtic games and other traditional pastimes include contests of strength or agility such as the Scottish caber toss and Breton *gouren* (wrestling), and sporting events such as the Irish HURLING or the Welsh *cnapan*, a game similar to football but played with a coated wooden ball. These ball games were often played by a large number of people over an area encompassing several miles, and were often CALENDAR customs as well, played annually as a contest between the young men of neighbouring parishes.

Other sports were played on a smaller scale. For example, in Brittany (BREIZH), *kilhoù* (skittles or ninepins) is a kind of lawn bowling; in *kilhoù kozh*, the pins are of three different heights. Curling remains popular today in Scotland (ALBA). The board game of FIDCHELL (Irish) or *gwyddbwyll* (WELSH) is of great antiquity and high status. *Macgnímrada Con Culainn* ('The Boyhood Deeds of CÚ CHULAINN)' demonstrates the hero's prowess through his ability at games, including *cammán* (hurley) and feats with a *bunsach* (small javelin or dart) and a *líathróit* (ball).

Games were also played in the presence of the dead to pass the time at wakes.

Antone Minard

GAUL

Gaul generally refers in modern usage to *Gallia Transalpina* 'TRANSALPINE GAUL, Gaul beyond the Alps' (from the Roman point of view), a region of ancient Continental Europe bounded by the Rhine on the east, the Alps on the southeast, the Mediterranean on the south, and the Pyrenees on the southwest. Without further qualification, 'Gaul' usually does not include the Celtic-speaking regions of northern Italy, referred to as CISALPINE GAUL ('Gaul on this side of the Alps').

Caesar identified the inhabitants of Gaul as subdivided into BELGAE, Aquitani, and Celtae or Galli (*De Bello Gallico* 1.1). He subdued the Celts of this northern region in a series of campaigns from 58 to 51 BC. This region was inhabited to a large extent by speakers of CELTIC LANGUAGES. Greek writers applied the name Κελτοί *Keltoi* or *Celtae*, namely 'Celts', to people in Gaul and parts of Central Europe and Spain.

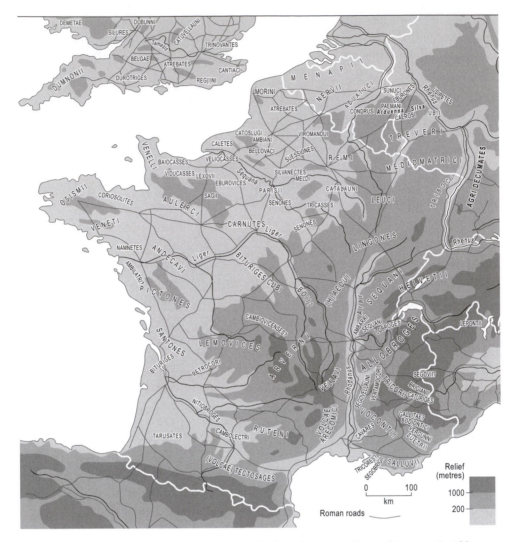

Gaul in the later pre-Roman and Roman periods. (Map by Ian Gulley and Antony Smith)

Many of the same groups on the Continent were also labelled *Gallī* or Γαλάται *Galatae*—that is, 'Gauls' and/or 'Galatians'. The derivation of *Keltī* is unclear, but *Gallī* and *Galatae* most probably go with Old Irish *gal* 'boldness, ferocity' and Welsh *gâl* 'enemy'.

Although a Celtic name, the notion of Gaul has mostly come down to us through GREEK AND ROMAN ACCOUNTS. As to 'Celts', in Roman times *Celtica* was officially an administrative region in what is now central France. The political end of the Roman provinces of Gaul (*Galliae*) came gradually in the 5th century with the foundation of Germanic kingdoms west of the Rhine and the establishment of Breton rule in ARMORICA. The victory of Clovis the Frank in 486 BC marks the end of

Gallo-Roman power in Gaul, and we may speak of 'Frankish' or 'Merovingian Gaul' afterward.

Philip Freeman and John T. Koch

GAULISH

Gaulish is the term given to the ancient Celtic language or languages spoken over a core area that included most of present-day France, Belgium, the Netherlands, and Germany west of the Rhine. Somewhat more loosely, Gaulish often covers the linguistic remains of the western Alpine region (roughly modern Switzerland) and northern Italy, where it is usually more specifically called Cisalpine Gaulish. Gaulish was the most extensive and best attested of the ancient Celtic languages. The main linguistic features of Gaulish, its dialect position, and the surviving evidence for the language are

The Vachères Warrior, a mould of a Gaulish statue from the 1st century BC, wearing a cloak, a belted mail coat, and a torc. The original is in the Musée Calvet, Avignon, France. (Gianni Dagli Orti/The Art Archive at Art Resource, New York)

treated in the articles on CELTIC LANGUAGES and CONTINENTAL CELTIC; see also INSCRIPTIONS.

A synthesis of archaeological and linguistic evidence suggests the following general interpretation concerning the northern part of GAUL. During the late HALLSTATT and early LA TÈNE periods (i.e., from *c.* 800 BC), a material culture and social patterns similar to those observed in the Celtic-speaking core areas of west central Europe gained ground. We might, therefore, suppose that this trend implied a linguistic Celticization. From the late Iron Age to the arrival of Caesar's legions, most of Gaul was Celtic speaking. Thus, for example, the Gaulish place-name *Noviomagos*, 'new [settlement on the] plain', gives modern Nijmegen in the Netherlands, Neumagen-Dhron in Germany, and Noyon in northern France, as well as an earlier name of Saint-Paul-Trois-Châteaux in southern France.

The Gaulish language survived for centuries into, and perhaps even beyond, Roman rule. The 2nd-century AD Greek bishop Iranaeus had to learn a *sermo barbarus* (barbaric tongue), presumably Gaulish, to go about his missionary activities in the upper Rhône valley (*Adversus Haereses* 1). In the next century, the Roman jurist Ulpian records that Gaulish was a perfectly acceptable medium for official contracts, implying that some individuals had need of the Roman legal system in Gaul who did not know Latin (*Digest* 31.1). As the 5th century was beginning, Serverus (*Dialogue* 1.27) records a conversation with two friends in which one of the speakers expresses his inadequacy in Latin and is invited to switch to 'Celtic or Gaulish', which may have been considered two different dialects in Gaul. It is not known how late Gaulish survived—certainly into the 5th century, but perhaps much later in remote or rural areas. It was replaced by Breton in Armorica and elsewhere by Latin or various Germanic languages.

As early as the Late Iron Age (*c.* 150–100 BC), a Germanic language had entered the area of the present-day Netherlands from the northeast. The coastal strip probably remained Celtic speaking well into the post-Roman period, while the northeast came fully under Germanic linguistic influence. When the coastal area later became linguistically Germanic, it kept a strong Celtic 'accent' that gave rise to the dialect phenomenon called 'North Sea Germanic', whereby coastal Dutch dialects, Frisian, and English show some peculiarities distinct from other Germanic languages but are strikingly similar to contemporary developments in Brythonic. North Sea Germanic clearly avoided $\bar{a}$ and had already developed central rounded vowels /ö/ and /ü/ in the 5th century AD. The explanation for these strikingly similar and contemporary developments shared by Brythonic and North Sea Germanic is very probably that the ancestors of speakers of North Sea Germanic had previously spoken a Celtic language closely related to British Celtic. When these people became speakers of Germanic in (approximately) the 5th and 6th centuries AD, they acquired the new language imperfectly—as adult learners of a second language invariably do—which led them to keep their distinctive 'Celtic accent'. The result was that the sound system of the new language became locally distorted in ways resembling that of the older indigenous language. We may thus think of a 'North Sea Celtic' as underlying 'North Sea Germanic' in both Britain (English) and the Low Countries (e.g., Dutch).

The same phenomenon presumably occurred in southern Gaul, now France: Outside of the Basque-speaking areas, a Gaulish substrate contributed to the shape of the local Romance languages, especially the northern *langue d'oïl* (modern French). This effect is obscured by our imperfect knowledge of Gaulish, the passage of time, and the later Germanic invasions, but it is known that a healthy amount of Gaulish vocabulary survives in modern French, both dialectal and standard. Numerous place-names are Celtic. For example, Lugudunum (Lyon, France) 'fortress [of the god] Lugus' often derived from tribal names—*Lutetia Parisiorum* 'Lutetia of the Parisi' became Paris. Other common words from Gaulish include *landa* > Fr. *lande* 'moor, heath' and **molto-* > Fr. *mouton*, 'sheep'. Many were borrowed into Late Latin, where some became international words as well. The best-known example is probably English *car*, French *char*, and Spanish *carro*, from Late Latin *carrus* < Gaulish *carros*.

Lauran Toorians, Antone Minard, and John T. Koch

GEIS

Geis (pl. *gessi;* modern pl. *geasa*) is an Irish word for an important cultural concept that occurs frequently in early IRISH LITERATURE. It may be translated approximately as 'taboo' or 'injunction', although sometimes it functions as a compulsion. *Gessi* are central to early Irish storytelling as a means of motivating apparently irrational actions, either heroic or foolish. As represented in the narratives, legal and political authorities were not responsible for supervising how *gessi* were followed in early Irish society. Rather, they were enforced by culturally postulated powers thought to be responsible for the fates of individuals: gods, the HEROIC ETHOS, unspecified magical or cosmological powers, and/or the even less definable constraints of 'tradition'. Something similar to the Irish *geis*, albeit using a different vocabulary, appears as the swearing of destiny (*tyngu tynged*) in the early Welsh tales MATH FAB MATHONWY and CULHWCH AC OLWEN.

Gessi were usually received at birth or when entering a new rôle in society. They were used to define the essence of human beings and social rôles. Thus violating a taboo amounted to a violation of the essence of one's own nature, or one's social self. For example, in TOGAIL BRUIDNE DA DERGA ('The Destruction of Da Derga's Hostel'), a story dealing with the fate and kingship of the mythical ruler Conaire Mór, Conaire receives his taboos from a supernatural bird-man. These include, among others, a taboo against permitting three red riders to enter the house of the red one before him, a taboo against restraining the quarrel of two of his servants, and a taboo against spending the night in a house from which firelight is visible (*Togail Bruidne Da Derga* §16). The breaking of *gessi* is a standard device for anticipating the imminent downfall of the mortal hero or king. Thus early Irish authors used taboos to define the limits and possibilities of human beings as members of society.

Tom Sjöblom

GENEALOGIES, IRISH

The Irish genealogies, which detail the descent of the principal dynasties and families of GAELIC, and later Anglo-Norman, Ireland (ÉRIU), are an invaluable source for the history of early, medieval, and—to a lesser extent—early modern Ireland (ÉIRE).

The Corpus

The medieval Irish genealogical corpus is the largest of its kind for any country in Europe. The recensions of Irish genealogies preserved in two great 12th-century manuscripts, the Book of Glendalough (*Lebor Glinne Dá Loch*, part of Bodleian MS Rawlinson B 502), and the Book of Leinster (LEBOR LAIGNECH), contain the names of some 12,000 persons (largely men), of whom a large proportion were historical figures who lived at various times between the 6th and 12th centuries. Most of the remaining names are figures from Irish LEGENDARY history and mythology. By the early 10th century, some had begun to bear surnames.

Contents

The genealogies purport to trace the great majority of Irish people back to the family of one Míl Espáine (an Irish rendering of Latin *Miles Hispaniae* 'soldier of Spain'). The genealogical scheme as a whole is made to corroborate a series of origin legends that reach their fullest realization in Lebar Gabála Érenn ('The Book of Invasions'). All are, in turn, tied into, and even modelled on, the genealogical scheme that underlies the Old Testament.

Genealogical texts, in the strict sense, are principally of two types: (1) single-line pedigrees, which trace an individual's ancestry back through paternal male forebears, and (2) *croeba coibnesa* ('branches of relationship' or *croebscaíled* 'ramification'), which detail the side-branches of a family down through the generations and which may enable one to construct a detailed genealogical table for an entire sept or extended family.

Purpose

Genealogies were used from an early period in Ireland to support claims to power and territory. As a consequence, the forging of pedigrees to accord with changing political relationships and circumstances became something of a minor industry, akin to the forging of charters in other countries. Because of this factor, one cannot say that because a pedigree dates from a particular period it is to be deemed either reliable or unreliable; instead, it must first be subjected to a range of critical tests. Whether early or late, it may be a wholly accurate record of a particular line of descent, it may be entirely fabricated, or—as often happens—it may lie somewhere between those two points. A considerable amount of the material can be independently verified, however, and is remarkably accurate.

Women in the Genealogies

The Irish genealogies are almost entirely patrilineal and male dominated; women generally feature only incidentally. The 12th-century *banshenchas* (lore of women) traces the descents and marriage alliances of well-known women from Irish mythology and, following the coming of Christianity, of women belonging to the royal dynasties of Meath (Mide) and Laigin.

Summary

The genealogies represent a most important—and hitherto under-utilized—source for the student of the earlier phases of Ireland's history. Such documents can most effectively be used in tandem with the annals; material in one of these sources can often be used to cross-check, or flesh out, material in the other. The riches of the pre-Norman genealogical recensions have not yet been exhausted, and the later collections—from the 14th century onward—remain largely untapped. An index of this neglect is that only a small proportion of them have yet found their way into print, and still fewer have been subjected even to the most cursory of scholarly examinations.

Nollaig Ó Muraíle

GENEALOGIES, WELSH

GIRALDUS CAMBRENSIS, writing at the end of the 12th century, stated that the Welsh bards had the genealogies of the princes and also retained them in memory from RHODRI MAWR (†878) to the legendary prehistoric patriarch BELI MAWR, and thence to Ascanius and Æneas (see TROJAN LEGENDS), and even on to the Biblical Adam (*Descriptio Kambriae* 1.3). Even the ordinary people could recite their ancestry for as many as six or seven generations (1.17).

The Oldest Genealogies

The oldest pedigrees record the descents of the rulers of Wales (CYMRU) and the BRITISH rulers of what is now southern Scotland (see ALBA; ELFED; GODODDIN; RHEGED) and northern ENGLAND (*Gwŷr y Gogledd* 'the men of the North'; see HEN OGLEDD). The oldest original pedigree that has survived, although much of it is now lost or illegible, is the inscription carved on ELISEG'S PILLAR, near Valle Crucis Abbey in Denbighshire (sir Ddinbych; see CISTERCIAN ABBEYS IN WALES), which was established by Cyngen (Old Welsh Concenn), king of POWYS, in the first half of the 9th century. This inscription traces Cyngen's pedigree back through his great-grandfather Eliseg to GWRTHEYRN (Vortigern, Old Welsh Guarthigirn). An important early collection of pedigrees is contained in the British Library Harley MS 3859, written *c.* 1100 but probably compiled in the mid-10th century in the reign of Owain ap HYWEL DDA (†988).

The Function of Genealogies

Under Welsh law a free man's place in society depended on his pedigree, and a knowledge of this genealogy was a legal necessity (see LAW TEXTS, WELSH). A man's rights and responsibilities were determined by his kinship, which came into play in cases of compensation (e.g., in case of murder), the settlement of disputes, and compurgation of witnesses. Land was not inherited solely by the eldest son but rather by all sons equally, and, in the absence of sons, by nephews or cousins in the male line.

Collection of Pedigrees

The bardic system was in decline from the late 16th century; the last of the traditional herald bards were Rhys Cain (†1618) of Oswestry (Welsh Croesoswallt) and his son, Siôn Cain (†*c.* 1650). During this time, however, the first gentleman antiquarians appeared, and friendly relations between them ensured the survival of many of genealogical manuscripts. The most distinguished of these scholars were

George Owen of Henllys (†1613) in south Wales and Robert Vaughan of Hengwrt (†1667) in north Wales.

With the Acts of Union in 1536–43, Welsh law was abolished, and partible succession along with it. The passion for pedigrees continued, however. During the 17th century, general compilations of pedigrees were made, in which strenuous efforts were made to follow all the descendants of the old tribes. The last great collection, the Golden Grove Book, was compiled in 1765. P. C. Bartrum has compiled the most reliable collection of Welsh medieval pedigrees based on an examination of most of the surviving manuscript sources down to the late 16th century in his *Welsh Genealogies*.

Reliability of Pedigrees

Although the early pedigrees stretched back to legendary heroes such as Brutus, who was believed to have given his name to Britain, and sometimes to Adam, it is generally accepted that some of them are reliable as far back as the 5th century. Where the names of women are given, they are usually genuine in the earlier pedigrees. From the end of the Middle Ages, however, the pedigrees become gradually less reliable for the early period, and 'suitable' wives were supplied where the older pedigrees gave none. In addition, from the Tudor (Tudur) period family pride and the readiness of the bards to provide their patrons with distinguished ancestry led to some faking of pedigrees.

Michael Siddons

GEOFFREY OF MONMOUTH

Geoffrey of Monmouth (Sieffre o Fynwy) was active in Oxford from at least 1129 to 1151. He was ordained priest at Westminster in 1152 and consecrated bishop of St Asaph, Flintshire (Llanelwy, sir y Fflint), shortly afterward, although there is no record of his ever having visited his cathedral or diocese before his death in 1154 or 1155.

Three Latin works bear his name. The Prophecies of Merlin (*Prophetia Merlini*) was later incorporated into his famous Historia Regum Britanniae, which was 'published' about 1139. About 1148–51, Geoffrey 'published' *Vita Merlini* ('The Life of Merlin'), an ostentatiously learned work drawing on Welsh traditions about the poet-seer Myrddin.

The *Historia* became one of the most widely read and influential books produced in medieval western Europe. Geoffrey gives an account of the history of the Britons prior to the Anglo-Saxon 'conquest'. The prologue is an extended narrative of the Trojan settlement of Rome (see Trojan legends). Geoffrey recounts names and exploits of a succession of kings and queens of Britain down to the coming of the Romans. The history of Roman Britain then gives way to the coming of the English. Arthur is the hero of organized and successful British resistance, but he is finally overcome and mortally wounded in the battle of Camlan, caused by the rivalry and disloyalty of his nephew, Mordred (Medrawd). The book closes with an acknowledgement of English sovereignty and a prophecy of the restoration of British rule.

Geoffrey's *Historia* achieved immediate and almost universal popularity. This outcome was in no small measure due to a number of contemporary interests to which Geoffrey responded skilfully: curiosity among his 12th-century Norman audience about pre-Saxon and pre-Roman Britain, as well as concerns about civil war, good government, and the rôle of powerful queens, all allied to current interest in a British hero, Arthur, and in what would now be termed 'Celticity'.

Geoffrey's *Historia* represented his personal response to the English histories being written at the time, as his references to William of Malmesbury and Henry of Huntingdon make clear. The most significant element enhancing the reception of the book, however, was the authority Geoffrey that invested in it, claiming he had been given an ancient British (BRYTHONIC) book. The *Historia*, therefore, could be claimed to be the authentic history of Britain by the Britons themselves. The text contains too many Latin literary borrowings and contemporary influences for this statement to be true as Geoffrey expressed it, but the narrative does include traces of Welsh tradition: Merlin, Maximianus (MACSEN WLEDIG) and his British wife, stories about characters such as Vortigern (GWRTHEYRN), Cassivelaunus (CASSIVELLAUNOS), and some elements in the Arthurian story. Geoffrey appears to have discerned central features of Welsh traditional history—the concepts of Britannia, the Island of Britain, and of a succession of kings bearing a single crown; the loss of British sovereignty; the rôle of messianic prophecy in the Welsh consciousness; and the significance of Rome in the British sense of the past. The lack of any corroborative evidence eventually led to the *Historia*'s rejection by 16th-century humanists. Nevertheless, throughout the Middle Ages, apart from a handful of critics, Geoffrey provided the standard history of early Britain and laid out 'historical' precedents for future rulers, both civil and ecclesiastic. His book was reworked in a variety of forms and languages, and some single episodes became literary themes in their own right, but most importantly Arthur was given a firm historical affirmation and context. In Wales, Geoffrey's influence was both more acute and long-lasting; see BRUT Y BRENHINEDD.

Brynley F. Roberts

GERAINT FAB ERBIN

Geraint fab Erbin was a Welsh legendary hero, probably based on one or more historical figures. The best-documented historical Geraints were (1) Gerontius, the British-born general of Constantine III who was declared emperor by the Romano-British garrison and ruled BRITAIN, GAUL, and Spain from 407 to 411, and (2) the king Gerontius or Geruntius of Dumnonia, to whom a letter was written by Aldhelm in 705. The Arthurian associations of the literary Geraint would better suit a period between these two. Other Geraints are known from Welsh tradition, but the name is not common in Old Welsh, Old Breton, or Old Cornish sources.

The Geraint Englynion

Probably composed *c.* 800–*c.* 1000 is a series of verses in the three-line ENGLYN metre, similar stylistically to the saga *englynion*, concerning *Gereint fil' Erbin* and a battle fought at a place called Llongborth. Geraint was possibly killed there, depending on how the text is interpreted. Arthur is mentioned in the poem as *ameraudur* 'emperor' (< Latin *imperātor*). The location of the battle of Llongborth and its historicity are also in doubt. Rather different and differently arranged versions of the Geraint *englynion* occur in Llyfr Du Caerfyrddin ('The Black Book of Carmarthen') and the closely related Llyfr Gwyn Rhydderch ('The White Book of Rhydderch') and Llyfr Coch Hergest ('The Red Book of Hergest').

The Geraint Tale

Geraint is best known as the central figure of the Arthurian tale *Geraint*, which figures as one of the subgroup known as the Three Romances (Tair Rhamant) within the more broadly defined Mabinogi. See also Arthurian literature; Welsh prose literature.

John T. Koch

GILDAS

Gildas is best known as the author of *De Excidio Britanniae* (On the destruction of Britain), our only contemporary British source for events in Britain in the 5th and earlier 6th century. Effectively, *De Excidio* is the starting point of historical writing in Britain; thus it was highly influential to subsequent writers of both history and legendary history. There is no general agreement among experts concerning the dates at which Gildas was writing, but a common estimate is *c.* AD 500–550.

The testimony of *De Excidio Britanniae* is of central importance as an eyewitness account of the events that brought about the transition from Roman Britain to Anglo-Saxon England and the Celtic-speaking lands of the north and west of Britain (see also Anglo-Saxon 'conquest'). Gildas's *superbus tyrannus* (arrogant tyrant) probably refers to the 5th-century British leader otherwise known as Vortigernus (Gwrtheyrn), literally 'overlord'; the element *super*-is cognate with the element *vor*-.

Gildas was recognized as an authority on Christian doctrine and practice by the Irish churchman and missionary Columbanus (†615). Revered as a saint, his cult is attested by church dedications in Brittany (Breizh), Wales (Cymru), and Cornwall (Kernow). Medieval Lives of Gildas in Latin were created in both Brittany and Wales. Gildas was also prominent in Welsh and Breton vernacular traditions.

Although a foundational work of British history, *De Excidio* was not intended as a chronicle, but rather as a sermon directed at an educated audience of Gildas's contemporaries. It is structured as a short historical introduction (§§1–26), followed by the sermon itself (§§27–110, comprising a complaint against the kings [§§27–65] and a complaint against the clergy [§§66–110]).

The first reference to Gildas and *De Excidio Britanniae* by a second writer occurs in the letter of Columbanus written *c.* 600 to Pope Gregory the Great. AD 547 was the latest possible date of this missive's completion, as deduced from the facts that Maelgwn Gwynedd (Maglocunus in Gildas's spelling) is mentioned and addressed in the work as a living contemporary (§33) and that *Annales Cambriae* give 547 as the date of Maelgwn's death.

De Excidio contains only a few references to place-names, most of which are either unlocated or too widely known to give a clue that might reveal the writer's location. In the Breton and Welsh Lives of Gildas and other medieval sources from Wales, Gildas's origins are associated with Strathclyde (Ystrad Clud) and the Picts. Further points favouring a northern Gildas are that he seems to be well informed about the wars with the Picts and is well aware of both Hadrian's Wall and the Antonine Wall, although his account of their early history is ignorant. Even Bede, who lived near the walls, had little information about them, however (*Historia Ecclesiastica* 1.5.26).

Gildas denounces the following contemporary rulers: Constantius of Dumnonia, a certain Aurelius Caninus (probably in the region of Caerloyw [Gloucester]), Vortiporius of Dyfed, Cuneglasus (very probably in north Wales), and Maglocunus (Maelgwn). The second, fourth, and fifth can be identified with figures in the Old Welsh genealogies in London, BL MS 3859: Guortepir of Dyfed, Mailcun, and Cinglas. Mailcun and Cinglas both figure as great-grandsons of Cunedda, the semilegendary founder of Gwynedd, who is datable to the earlier 5th century.

The process of the separation of the British provinces from the Roman Empire is only briefly described in Gildas's account. He mentions the usurpation of Magnus Maximus (the Macsen Wledig of Welsh tradition), and seems to be responsible for the tradition that blames Maximus for the military weakness of the Britons following his departure.

Years of continuous warfare with the Britons followed the arrival of the Angles and Saxons. The Britons regained their strength under Ambrosius Aurelianus, whom Gildas calls the last of the Romans in Britain to have had ancestors who had 'worn the purple' and, therefore, were of imperial status. The campaign against the Anglo-Saxons climaxed at Badonicus mons, where the Britons were victorious (see annals; Arthurian sites), about a generation before Gildas's time (*De Excidio Britanniae* §26.1). This battle initiated a period of relative peace, which had lasted up to the time of his writing and included the entire living memory of almost everyone alive at the time when Gildas wrote.

Gildas presented historical events to admonish his contemporaries with his relentless message: The continuous sins of the Britons were punished by God. The Britons were *imbellis* 'cowardly, inept at war' and *infidelis* 'disloyal, unfaithful'. Their cowardice is shown in their repeated failure to hold their ground against Romans, Picts, Scots, and Anglo-Saxons. Their infidelity is directed against the Romans and the true Christian faith. Thus God first sends the Picts and the Scots, and then the Anglo-Saxons, as instruments of his wrath. The Britons withstand their adversaries only in exceptional episodes of moral superiority. According to Gildas, the victory of *Badonicus mons* was won because the Britons had placed their faith in God and not in men. As a moral entity tried by history, Gildas's Britons are modelled on God's chosen people of the Old Testament, the Israelites (see also legendary history). Gildas clearly distinguished the Britons from the Romans and did not think of himself and contemporaries as belonging to the Roman Empire any longer.

Gildas was later regarded as a saint (feast day of 29th January). In the 10th- to 11th-century Breton *Vita I S. Gildae,* he appears as the founder of the monastery of Saint-Gildas in Rhuys (Morbihan). The Welsh Latin Life was written by CARADOG OF LLANCARFAN in the early 12th century. The contents of the *Vitae* are legendary and filled with the miracles typical of HAGIOGRAPHY.

Alheydis Plassmann

GIRALDUS CAMBRENSIS

Giraldus Cambrensis (Gerald de Barri/Gerallt Gymro/Gerald of Wales), 1146–1223, was a churchman and writer. He was a highly prolific Latin author who wrote widely about himself and his times, including first-hand accounts of Wales (CYMRU), Ireland (ÉRIU), ENGLAND, France, and Italy.

Born into a family of mixed Welsh and Anglo-Norman nobility, Giraldus was apparently destined from an early stage for an ecclesiastical career. Many of his relatives took part in the military advances in Ireland from 1169 onward. The Geraldines (named after Gerald's grandfather Gerald of Windsor) were to remain prominent in Irish politics for centuries to come.

In 1185, when Prince John was sent to Ireland by his father to superintend English control there, Giraldus was with him—no doubt at least in part due to his relatives' rôle there. Following John's departure, Giraldus stayed on for a year and gathered material for his two books on Ireland: *Topographia Hibernica* ('The Topography of Ireland') and *Expugnatio Hibernica* ('The Conquest of Ireland'), completed around 1189.

Two further works by Giraldus come from his time in Wales: the *Itinerarium Kambriae* ('The Itinerary through Wales') and the Descriptio Kambriae ('The Description of Wales'), completed around 1194. These two books, as well as the two on Ireland, were the most original of his works; they are of lasting importance and provide the foundation of his fame.

It is not clear what Giraldus's mother tongue was.

Illustration of a writing monk from *Topographia Hibernica*, a work by Giraldus Cambrensis (Gerald of Wales). (The British Library/StockphotoPro)

His Latin was fluent, though not brilliant. He must have spoken French fluently, but it is conceivable that his family also spoke English. His writings do not demonstrate an extensive knowledge of Welsh.

Michael Richter

GLASTONBURY, ARCHAEOLOGY

The first evidence of occupation near Glastonbury dates from the Neolithic (New Stone Age). Several timber and brushwood trackways have been discovered, mostly running across the wetlands of the Somerset Levels from the dry-land 'islands'. The oldest and best-known of these trackways is the Sweet Track, constructed in the winter of 3807–6 BC. The vast amount of work required to construct such trackways demonstrates that the Glastonbury area must have been host to a relatively large, well-organized community during this period.

Only a little hard evidence exists in connection with Roman activity at Glastonbury. Excavations on the summit of the Tor have revealed tantalizing evidence of early medieval ('Dark Age') activity at some time in the 5th to 7th centuries, but without yielding a clear account of the nature of this activity. Remains of the foundations of timber structures were accompanied by two partially destroyed graves, an elongated stone cairn, and a metalworking area. Finds recovered included imported goods and a cast copper-alloy miniature head, suggesting that the individuals involved in the metalworking activity enjoyed considerable social status.

A small Anglo-Saxon monastery was certainly in existence on the western shoulder of Glastonbury Tor by the 8th or 9th century. Evidence from this period includes the foundations of a church or communal building, along with several possible monks' cells. The remains of a wheel-headed cross recovered on the summit of the Tor are probably related to this foundation, which may also have been responsible for the establishment of Glastonbury abbey itself.

The origins of the abbey are unknown and a British monastic foundation may well have existed at this site prior to the Anglo-Saxon conquest of the area, as considerable evidence supports the presence of Romano-British Christianity in Somerset from an early date. Subsurface remains of the earliest church mentioned in documentary references to Glastonbury abbey, the *vetusta ecclesia* (old church; Old English *ealderchurche*), have not been uncovered during excavation. This 'old church', which was destroyed by fire in 1184, is referred to as of both wattle-and-daub and timber construction. Its name, its simple construction methods, and the veneration in which it was apparently held all suggest it may have been very early, possibly dating to the 6th or 7th century.

According to the early chroniclers William of Malmesbury (writing in the early 12th century) and William of Worcester (writing *c*. 1480), two tall carved stone monuments described as 'pyramids' and 'crosses' were situated nearby. Descriptions invite comparison to the HIGH CROSSES known in various forms throughout BRITAIN and Ireland (ÉRIU) in the early medieval period, most particularly the Northumbrian variety. Attempts to link these monuments with historical and pseudo-historical figures such as ARTHUR, St PATRICK, and Joseph of Arimathea are not supported by the evidence, such as engravings of Anglo-Saxon names.

St Joseph's Well, situated in an underground chamber attached to the Lady Chapel, was rediscovered in the early 19th century. Its position suggests that it may have been part of the original foundation here, and it has even been surmised that the well could be a Roman construction that later came to form the nucleus of the early medieval abbey.

Simon Ó Faoláin

GLAUBERG

The Glauberg is an archaeological site of the late HALLSTATT and Early LA TÈNE periods located in in Hesse, Germany. This long, narrow plateau rises steeply from the fertile river plains of the Nidder and the Seeme. The hilltop itself was fortified with several walls, the main one enclosing the whole flat summit, which was approxiamtely 600 m in length and 150–200 m wide. On the western edge of the summit, within the area protected by the main summit wall, a small depression approximately 25 m in diameter and 3 m deep contained a small pool. The area defended by the main summit wall and a northwestern annexe wall covers an area of roughly 20 ha (48 acres). The main type of wall construction seems to have been a timber-framed rubble wall with a stone facing. Horizontal timbers were laid at close intervals.

Four entrances into the fortified hilltop have been located. The main one always seems to have been the one oriented toward the northwest, the so-called *Stockheimer Pforte*, where the walls form a narrow passage between inwardly curving walls, in a construction called *Tangentialtor* (tangential gate); this entrance was additionally fortified by a gate tower. Next to nothing is known of the internal structure of the settlement. The identification of the Glauberg as an early La Tène princely seat is based on the finds from the sanctuary/princely tombs located at the foot of its southern slopes.

Walls and ditches on the southern foot of the Glauberg, partially delimiting an area of approximately 1.5 km^2, formed part of what has now been interpreted as a large early La Tène sanctuary. Two tumuli containing tombs have been located. Tomb 1 was found close to the northern edge of Tumulus 1. The floor of the burial chamber had been covered with leather, and each single grave good wrapped in cloth. The whole burial seems to have been covered with a large cloth. The most remarkable finds are a beaked bronze flagon, whose closest parallel is the famous beaked flagon from the DÜRRNBERG. It had originally been filled with mead, and is one of the most impressive examples of early Celtic ART. The flagon is decorated with a group of three figurines at its rim, consisting of a sitting human at the upper end of the handle with one human-headed quadruped on either side. A gold torc was found around the neck of the skeleton, an adult man, 1.69 m tall, who died at around age 30. In addition to the pieces mentioned previously, the man was equipped with an iron sword on his right side, three iron-headed spears at his left, and above them a quiver with three arrows and a wooden bow in a leather cover. A wooden, leather-covered SHIELD with a large iron boss and partial iron rim lay on his chest. Besides the torc, two gold earrings, a gold bracelet on his right wrist, and a gold finger-ring on his right ring finger were found.

Tumulus 2 was significantly smaller than Tumulus 1. While there seems to have been no wooden chamber or box in the case of this burial, a wooden floor was found about 1 m deep, on which the burial rested; this structure may have been covered by leather or cloth, as in Tumulus 1. Like the tombs in Tumulus 1, Tumulus 2 was recovered as a whole block and is currently still being excavated under laboratory conditions. X-rays and preliminary results of the laboratory excavations, however, reveal that the burial, as in Tomb 1, seems to be a flat inhumation, containing at least an iron sword, several bronze rings, a gold bracelet and (probably) a gold finger-ring, a richly decorated bronze fibula, a belt-hook, and a spearhead.

Probably one of the most impressive finds from the Glauberg tombs—perhaps even more so than the grave goods—are the life-sized statues, one almost intact and fragments of three others. Their destruction must have happened sometime after the tombs were built, because the ditches were already partially filled with sediment when they were deposited in them. All four statues were made from local sandstone.

Statue 1, affectionately called 'Glaubi', is complete except for broken-off feet; it is the most detailed depiction of an early Celtic noble. Its remaining height is 1.86 m, and it depicts an adult man, clad in composite armour, with overlapping layers of hide or linen giving a patterned impression at the front, and a large back decorated with leaf ornaments connected to the neck- and shoulder-protection that form part of the armour (see ART, CELTIC for photo). The statue also wears an early La Tène sword at the right hip, and holds a shield with a buckle and strengthened rim in the left hand in front of the torso. He wears a torc, a bracelet on his right wrist, and a finger-ring on his right ring finger, as well as three bracelets on the left upper arm and a 'leaf crown' on his head. This arrangement mirrors the burial in Tumulus 1, Tomb 1 (see the previous description). The other three statues seem to have been very similar.

Raimund Karl

GLOSSARIES

Glossaries form a significant element of the literary remains of early Ireland (ÉRIU). They seem to start life as *glossae collectae* 'collected glosses', an ancillary document collecting glosses originally either interlinear, written between the lines of the main text, or marginal, written in the empty space toward the edge of the page. Such entries typically consist of the lemma (i.e., the word in the text), followed by the comment on the word. The content of these glosses is varied: They consist of grammatical, explanatory, etymological, even explanatory texts.

A crucial step in the move away from a text-based glossary is alphabetization, usually partial, only by the first letter. *O'Davoren's Glossary* is based on a wide range of legal texts and preserves fragments of LAW TEXTS that have not otherwise survived. More general glossaries are *O'Mulconry's Glossary*, *Cormac's Glossary* (SANAS

Chormaic), and *Dúil Drommma Cetta*. While a specialist glossary, such as *O'Davoren's Glossary*, is largely preoccupied with elucidating difficult technical terms and arcane language, the general glossaries contain a vast range of different types of entries, from the single word explanation, rather like a modern dictionary entry, to a more complicated etymological explanation of a word, and even going as far as supplying tales to exemplify the use of a particular word. For their explanations, they often range across several languages, especially Latin, Greek, and Hebrew (regarded as the *tres linguae sacrae* 'three sacred languages' by scholars in the early Middle Ages), but are not averse to using languages closer to home, such as Welsh and even Pictish.

Paul Russell

GLOSSES, OLD IRISH

The stage of the Irish language generally called Old Irish is best preserved in a large number of glosses and marginalia in Latin manuscripts, dating from the 7th century to about 900. The glosses are of special importance in that they are in contemporary manuscripts, rather than surviving only in copies made in later centuries. For modern Celtic studies, the glosses were vital for the establishing of early Irish grammar. The majority of Old Irish glosses are found in manuscripts now kept in Continental libraries, among them Würzburg, Stiftsbibliothek, MS M.th.f.12; Milan, Ambrosian Library, MS C. 301; and St Gallen (St Gall), Stiftsbibliothek, MS 904. The Latin text of the St Paul's epistles form the main text for the 8th-century Würzburg glosses. The Milan glosses are on a Latin commentary on the psalms and are later (9th century) and generally more linguistically evolved than those of Würzburg. The St Gall glosses are on the Latin grammar of Priscian (*fl.* 491–518) and thus have a double linguistic value, revealing both the Old Irish language itself and early Irish scholars' grasp of linguistic matters.

Many glosses illustrate textual or linguistic matters discussed in the manuscripts, and they include direct translations, illustrations, and definitions of linguistic terminology. In the Irish monasteries, the glosses would have been considered an essential part of the text and a vital teaching and learning aid. The glosses can help to determine the extent of knowledge of Latin and grammatical awareness, and they also give some indication to what extent classical traditions and literature were known in Ireland (Ériu) during the early Middle Ages. In many manuscripts, Old Irish and Latin glosses appear intermingled, reflecting a bilingual intellectual milieu.

Petra S. Hellmuth

GLOSSES, OLD WELSH

Marginal and between-line notes in Old Welsh occur in two early medieval manuscripts whose principal language is Latin, now in Oxford. Bodleian The first, MS Auctarium F.4.34, also known as 'St Dunstan's Classbook', is a composite, the *Liber Commonei* (The book of Commoneus of *c.* AD 817), which includes the Alphabet of Nemnivus and the Latin and Old Welsh text on weights and measures.

The second is a mid-10th century copy of Book I of *Ars Amatoria* (The art of love) by the Roman author Ovid (43 BC–AD 17), with contemporary or near-contemporary OW glosses. Given that *Ars Amatoria* was influential for Welsh love poetry in the later Middle Ages, it is significant that Welsh scholars copied and studied this text as early as *c.* 900. Several common Welsh words appear for the first time in the Ovid glosses—for example, *olin* 'wheel' (modern *olwyn*, gl. rota), *lo* (modern *llo*) 'calf', *datl* (modern *dadl*), 'dispute, argument', and *gulan* (modern *gwlan*) 'wool'. The 10th-century Bodleian MS 572, known also as 'Codex Oxoniensis Posterior', contains the mixed Latin and Brythonic text De Raris Fabulis.

John T. Koch

GODODDIN

Gododdin is the name of a tribal kingdom in early north BRITAIN and also the title of a famous body of the earliest Welsh heroic poetry, mostly in the *awdl* metre, which memorializes the heroes of that kingdom, their allies, and their enemies in the 6th century AD.

The Tribe, Its Territory, and Its Name

The tribal name occurs in the *Geography* of Ptolemy as Ωταδινοι *Otadini*, where their territory extends from somewhat north of the Forth in the present-day Scottish Lowlands down to the river Wear, now Co. Durham, ENGLAND. The Anglo-Saxon kingdom of Bernicia (BRYNAICH) succeeded it.

Welsh *Gododdin* (Old Welsh *Guotodin*) implies that the correct ancient form was *Votādīni. Manau Guotodin* occurs in sources of the Old Welsh period as the name of a district on the river Forth that included Stirling (OW Iudeu) and is said to have been the country of the origin of CUNEDDA and his sons, who figure as founders of GWYNEDD's first dynasty.

The Poetry

The verses called *Y Gododdin* are broadly synonymous with the contents of the 13th-century Welsh manuscript known as the Book of ANEIRIN (LLYFR ANEIRIN). Aneirin's historicity and 6th-century date are established by the Memorandum of the Five Poets in HISTORIA BRITTONUM.

Most of the verses are elegies commemorating warriors (individually or collectively) who came from Gododdin and sustained heavy losses in a battle at Catraeth, most probably Catterick, now in North Yorkshire, England. The greatest praise is lavished upon the hero Cynon, who is identified, rather than with Gododdin itself, with what is now southwest Scotland (ALBA). The GENEALOGIES place this Cynon in the Cynwydion dynasty of Strathclyde (YSTRAD CLUD). As well as the repeated allusions to an ill-fated expedition against Catraeth, another pervasive theme is that of a year-long FEAST of wine and mead, which the warriors shared before the battle and which is located repeatedly at Din Eidyn (i.e., Edinburgh [DÙN ÈIDEANN]).

Wider Importance

Although the Gododdin certainly has the status of a literary classic in Wales (Cymru) today, it is unclear how famous it was in medieval Wales. Cynon is among a very few of its heroes who were drawn into Arthurian literature. Connections to the genealogies are rare. There are intentional echoes of the *Gododdin*'s themes and vocabulary in the 12th-century court poetry of the works of Cynddelw of the Gogynfeirdd.

The Gododdin poetry has a central importance in Celtic studies for three reasons: It is a sizeable specimen (more than 1,000 lines) of some of the earliest Welsh language and literature; it deals with important, though otherwise unknown, people and events in the virtually undocumented period of British history following the dissolution of Roman Britain during which England and Wales emerged; and it conveys an absolutely relentless vision of the heroic ethos, in which the hero gives lethal prowess and, ultimately, his own young life, thereby retrospectively 'paying for his mead' (*talu medd*)—that is, for the life of luxury which that lord had provided him—and prospectively earning undying fame in the songs of the bards.

John T. Koch

GOGYNFEIRDD

The *Gogynfeirdd*, or 'rather early poets', as they have been known since the 18th century, comprise all of the poets who composed Welsh poetry in *awdl* and englyn metres between *c.* 1137 and *c.* 1400. Most particularly, they are the Poets of the Princes (*Beirdd y Tywysogion*) of the period *c.* 1137–1282, so called because most were professional court poets for Welsh princes of the last century and a half of Welsh independence (ending in 1282/4). However, several of the poets were not professional court poets—at least one of them was himself a prince, and another was a Franciscan friar—and their poetry includes religious and personal lyrics as well as formal bardic verse. The *Gogynfeirdd* also include the *Beirdd yr Uchelwyr*, or 'Poets of the Nobility', poets who continued to work in the tradition of *awdl* and *englyn* metres after 1282. In the latter group, there is some overlap with the cywyddwyr.

Approximately 12,600 lines of verse have survived that are attributed to thirty-two *Beirdd y Tywysogion*. Poems ascribed to the great 12th-century poet Cynddelw Brydydd Mawr account for 30 percent of the total corpus. The principal medieval manuscript sources of the poetry of the Poets of the Princes are the Red Book of Hergest (Llyfr Coch Hergest), the Hendregadredd Manuscript, and, to a lesser extent, the Black Book of Carmarthen (Llyfr Du Caerfyrddin).

The poetry of *Beirdd y Tywysogion* is most closely associated with north Wales (Cymru). More than a third of the surviving verse praises, laments, threatens, or beseeches one or another of the princes of Gwynedd from Gruffudd ap Cynan (†1137) to Llywelyn ap Gruffudd (†1282), and a third of those poems are directed to Llywelyn ab Iorwerth (Llywelyn Fawr †1240).

Meilyr Brydydd (*fl.* ?1100–post 1137), who celebrated the career of Gruffudd ap Cynan, is generally reckoned to be the first of the Poets of the Princes. At least one of Meilyr's sons and two or three of his grandsons were court poets as well; like the Welsh princes, they are said to be descendants of CUNEDDA Wledig. Thus the genealogies of the poets attest the social status that was associated with their work. Many of the *Beirdd y Tywysogion* associated themselves, exclusively or at least principally, with a single prince, and the association between the princely and the poetic families certainly endured for several generations in the case of Meilyr's family. He sang for Gruffudd ap Cynan, and his son Gwalchmai composed eulogies for Gruffudd's son, OWAIN GWYNEDD, and his grandsons, Dafydd and Rhodri ab Owain.

The terms *pencerdd* (chief of song) and *bardd teulu* (household bard) are used in the LAW TEXTS and elsewhere. Although nowhere precisely defined, they are thought to refer to offices in a prince's court—those of official BARD to the prince himself and of a poet associated with the prince's retinue, respectively. In late 12th- and 13th-century Wales, a *pencerdd* held the highest status and was increasingly, though never entirely, assimilated to the court hierarchy; instead, the *pencerdd* was regarded as an officer of the court. It seems quite likely that Gwalchmai succeeded his father, Meilyr, as *pencerdd* to the Gwynedd princes. The evidence is complicated, however, by the fact that Gwalchmai is also credited with a eulogy and an elegy for Madog ap Maredudd, prince of POWYS from 1132 to 1160. This case exemplifies the difficulty we have in understanding the relationships of poets and patrons during this period.

A poet associated with a particular prince might also serve him in various other capacities. There is firm evidence that Einion ap Gwalchmai was one of Llywelyn ab Iorwerth's ministers, and other poets may have been similarly involved in the legal and administrative affairs of their princes. In general, the poets were closely associated, especially in Gwynedd, with what has been termed the 'ministerial élite' of 12th- and 13th-century Wales, meaning members of a class of learned, privileged, and powerful professionals.

Formally, their poetry employs a dozen or so of the *awdl* and *englyn* measures that would come to be included among the twenty-four 'strict metres' of CERDD DAFOD. *Awdl* measures are often mixed within a single poem, and occasionally different *englyn* forms are combined as well. The poems vary enormously in length, from a few lines to three hundred. In longer *awdlau*, extended passages with a single end-rhyme are very common; the very famous elegy for Llywelyn ap Gruffudd by Gruffudd ab yr Ynad Coch sustains a rhyme on *-aw* throughout its 104 lines. In general, it may be said that the poets make liberal use of alliteration, internal rhyme, and the line- and stanza-linking device known as *cymeriad*, although there are, of course, differences from poet to poet. Both the vocabulary and the syntax of medieval Welsh court poetry are famously difficult; some words, especially compounds, occur only once or twice in the written records of WELSH. The 12th-century verse, in particular, is often characterized by strings of nouns in uncertain and unstable relationship to one another. This syntax is rich in fertile ambiguity, but resistant to paraphrase. The *Gogynfeirdd* of the 13th and 14th centuries make freer use of finite verbs, but their poetry is still rich in epithets that employ a noun plus genitive noun as often as they do a noun plus adjective construction.

The poetry is rooted in earlier Welsh poetry. Nowhere is this more striking than in the *Hirlas* of Owain Cyfeiliog, which not only makes reference to the events commemorated in the GODODDIN of ANEIRIN, but also echoes the earlier work in its structure (i.e., the celebration of many individual warriors), in its imagery of feasting, and even in many of its phrases. Other poets likewise make reference to the legendary *Gwŷr y Gogledd*, or 'Men of the North', to the CYNFEIRDD, and to *Trioedd Ynys Prydein* (see TRIADS), demonstrating that they also value tradition very highly. In this highly conventional poetry, not only metres, themes, and images, but even exact phrases, recur in the work of various poets. In addition, in the qualities that they praise in their princes, *Beirdd y Tywysogion* look back to the heroic age. They celebrate noble lineage, martial prowess and protection of their people, and generosity—especially to poets—above all.

Poetic praise extends to the praise of God in lyrics that combine bardic arrogance with a contrite spirit; praise of saints that focuses on their ecclesiastical foundations; and praise of women that incorporates elements of *amour courtois* (COURTLY LOVE) as it was being elaborated in Provençal poetry of the same period. The continuity of the poetry with some of what precedes it in the Welsh tradition is, therefore, offset by evidence that this poetry represents new literary energies and cultural practices. It is equally possible to read the Poetry of the Princes as a newfangled phenomenon, an aspect of changes in Welsh culture attendant upon the growth of powerful principalities in Wales and the Norman incursions of the 12th century, or as the flowering of an archaic common Celtic institution of bardic poetry.

Catherine McKenna

GOIBNIU

Goibniu, the smith of the TUATH DÉ, has a near-cognate in Welsh Gofannon, with both being based on the common Celtic word for 'smith'. Both craftsmen slay a young kinsman. Gofannon kills his nephew Dylan in MATH FAB MATHONWY, the fourth branch of the MABINOGI. In CATH MAIGE TUIRED §125, Goibniu slays Ruadán of the FOMOIRI; their relationship is not spelled out but both descend through the male line from Goibniu's grandfather Nét. As *an Gobbán Saor* the resourceful mason, the figure of Goibniu has remained popular in modern Irish folklore.

John T. Koch

GOIDELIC

Goidelic, which is essentially synonymous with GAELIC, is the specialist linguistic term for the closely related subfamily of Celtic languages to which Irish, SCOTTISH GAELIC, and MANX belong. In discussing these languages *Goidelic* is preferable to *Gaelic* to avoid some common popular misconceptions, such as the idea that *Gaelic* and *Celtic* are synonymous. Goidelic/Gaelic is, in fact, a smaller subgroup within Celtic.

The oldest attested stage of Goidelic is usually called Primitive Irish, reflected in the ogam inscriptions of the 5th and 6th centuries. Old Irish before *c.* 900 AD is virtually devoid of dialect differences, and its cultural property such as the heroic tales and songs of FIANNAÍOCHT and folk traditions concerning the OTHERWORLD beings of the SÍD may also be accurately labelled 'Goidelic'.

John T. Koch

GOLASECCA CULTURE

Golasecca culture is the term used for an IRON AGE archaeological culture, roughly from the 8th to the 5th centuries BC, located at the southern end of the trade route across the Saint Gotthard pass and probably one of the main connections between the HALLSTATT-culture populations north of the Alps and the Po valley in Italy. The Golasecca culture covers roughly the area between this pass, Lake Maggiore, and Lake Como and the Po valley, and shows some strong links to Hallstatt material. It seems likely that the culture acted as one of the main links for early Etruscan–Celtic trade across the Alps, with influences in both directions. For example, four-wheeled wagons found in Golasecca burials (see VEHICLE BURIALS) show strong links with Hallstatt four-wheeled wagons, but, at the same time, the iron tires, wheel hubs, and other pieces of metalwork demonstrate influences from central Italy.

The Golasecca culture is of special interest because the oldest INSCRIPTIONS in a Celtic language come from it—the LEPONTIC inscriptions, written in the Lugano Alphabet and dating from the 6th to the 1st centuries BC. Roman historian Livy (5.34) says that the first Gauls moved into the Po valley area at that time, but it is far from clear how or when a Celtic language came to be spoken in the Golasecca culture area.

The area occupied by the Golasecca culture is roughly consistent with the Celtic peoples of the Insubres, Oromobii, and Lepontii mentioned in classical literature.

Raimund Karl

GORSEDD BEIRDD YNYS PRYDAIN

Gorsedd Beirdd Ynys Prydain (The assembly of the bards of the Island of Britain) is an association of Welsh poets and musicians allegedly dating from the time of King ARTHUR. The modern incarnation was founded by Iolo Morganwg (Edward WILLIAMS, 1747–1826) in 1792, and linked to the EISTEDDFOD movement in 1819.

Iolo belonged to a coterie of local Welsh-language poets in Glamorgan (MORGANNWG) in the 1770s, who believed strongly in the need for a cultural association to give prestige to neglected areas of Wales (CYMRU) and to raise the standing of Welsh literature in general. During his visits to London (Welsh Llundain), he learned about the Druid Universal Bond, founded by John Toland in 1717, and the Ancient Order of Druids, founded by Henry Hurle in 1781. Iolo expanded his original vision of an association of Morgannwg bards to a much broader institution, claiming a kind of apostolic succession from the ancient DRUIDS. The first modern 'Gorsedd of Bards' was held on Primrose Hill in London in June 1792. The earliest Gorsedd held in Wales itself is recorded for May 1795 in Cowbridge (Y Bont-faen).

In 1819, Iolo persuaded the Cambrian Society of DYFED to hold a Gorsedd at the same time as their EISTEDDFOD, the first such association. Iolo had devised ceremonies and a liturgy and awarded ribbons to each order: green for ovates, blue for bards, and white for druids, today symbolized by gowns.

In 1880, the National Eisteddfod Association was founded to provide a permanent basis for the organization of EISTEDDFOD GENEDLAETHOL CYMRU (the National Eisteddfod of Wales), but it was not until 1888 that a permanent organization was set up, Cymdeithas yr Orsedd (the Gorsedd Society), and that the first archdruid

(Welsh *archdderwydd*), David Griffith 'Clwydfardd', was appointed. The fact that Welsh was declared to be the sole language of the Gorsedd acted as a strong counterpoise to the Anglicizing tendencies within the National Eisteddfod itself in this period. By the end of the 19th century, the regalia with which present-day audiences are familiar were designed by the artists Sir Hubert von Herkomer and T. H. Thomas.

During the 20th century, Gorsedd ceremonies gradually became more solemn. The modern Gorsedd has approximately 1,300 members. It is particularly prominent in the proclamation ceremonies ahead of each National Eisteddfod, as well as in the ceremonies of the crowning of the bard, the chairing of the bard, and, more recently, the ceremony of the award of the prose medal.

From 1896 onward, the very basis of the existence of the Gorsedd came under attack from a new generation of Welsh scholars led by John Morris-Jones, who claimed that it sprang from the overheated imagination of Iolo Morganwg and had no actual basis in Welsh history. By the late 20th century, however, the Gorsedd had been accepted as a Welsh national institution that was a product of the imaginative mythologizing of the late 18th-century Romantic movement (see Romanticism).

Prys Morgan

GORSETH KERNOW (CORNISH GORSEDD)

The Gorseth in Cornwall (Kernow) has been central to the Cornish Celtic language revival. Based on the Welsh ritual (see Gorsedd Beirdd Ynys Prydain), the first Cornish Gorseth was held at Boscawen Un stone circle on 21 September 1928.

In the late 1920s, Henry Jenner, who was a member of the Breton Goursez, and Robert Morton Nance designed the format of the Cornish ceremony, under the direction of the Welsh archdruid. With the support of the Old Cornwall Societies, in 1928 Jenner was made the first Grand Bard or Barth Mur of the Cornish Gorseth. When Jenner died in 1934, Nance succeeded him; he remained Grand Bard until 1958.

The actual ceremony and structure of the Gorseth differs little from its Welsh counterparts. However, there is only one grade, bard, which Jenner and Nance believed would best reflect the Cornish motto of 'One and All'. In the early 1930s, Nance modified the ceremony to symbolize further the relationship between King Arthur and Cornwall; these remain the most distinctive ceremonial elements.

Today, the Gorseth functions as an annual focus of Cornish revivalists, and serves to promote the Cornish language. In recent years, it has also become a way for Cornish activists to secure links with the Cornish diaspora through cultural exchange (see emigration).

Website
www.gorsethkernow.org.uk

Amy Hale

GOURSEZ GOURENEZ BREIZ-IZEL

The creation of the first Breton neo-druidic society is rooted in the assertion of Breton identity at the end of the 19th century. Following the foundation of the

Breton Regionalist Union in 1898, some of its members were invested as bards at the EISTEDDFOD GENEDLAETHOL CYMRU (Wales) in 1899. A Breton society comparable to GORSEDD BEIRDD YNYSPRYDAIN, formally supporting BRETON-medium cultural activities, was founded at Guingamp (Gwengamp) on 1 September 1900 and placed under the patronage of the Archdruid of Wales. This Goursez Gourenez Breiz-Izel (Gorsedd of the peninsula of Lower Brittany) took an active rôle in the Breton LANGUAGE (REVIVAL) movement. The Goursez today is called Breudeuriezh drouized, barzhed, ovizion BREIZH (Brotherhood of druids, bards, and ovates of Brittany). Schisms have given rise to more esoteric societies, such as Kenvreuriezh prederouriel an drouized (The philosophical collegium of druids, 1975).

Philippe Le Stum

GRAIL

The Grail became, in the High Middle Ages, one of the most popular themes of the international literature concerned with the adventures of ARTHUR and his heroes (see ARTHURIAN LITERATURE, TEXTS IN NON-CELTIC MEDIEVAL LANGUAGES). It figures centrally

Galahad, Perceval, and Bohort bring the Holy Grail to cure the beggar in Palestine. Illumination by Evrard d'Espinques from *Queste del Saint Graal, c.* 1470. (Hulton Archive/Getty Images)

in late famous creative works, such as Wagner's opera *Parzifal*, Tennyson's *Idylls of the King*, T. S. Eliot's *Waste Land*, and numerous films, including prominence in the action and titles of *Indiana Jones and the Holy Grail* and the spoof *Monty Python and the Holy Grail*.

The Old French word *graal* (from Late Latin *gradalis*), meaning a kind of serving vessel, was first used in an Arthurian context by CHRÉTIEN DE TROYES in his unfinished *Perceval* or *Conte del Graal* of *c.* 1181, where it is described as golden, of fine workmanship, and covered with rare and costly precious stones. Chrétien's *graal* is part of a mysterious procession, preceded by a bleeding lance and candelabra, and contains a mass wafer, which miraculously sustains the life of an old king as his only sustenance. However, the broader significance and origin of the vessel are not explained in *Perceval*. In the corresponding Welsh tale PEREDUR, there is again a mysterious procession with a bleeding spear and a vessel carried by two maidens, but the word *graal* or Welsh *greal* is not used; rather, the vessel is a great dish, containing a severed head. In *Joseph d'Arimathie* or *Le Roman de l'estoire dou Graal*, written in the period 1191 × 1202 by the Burgundian poet, Robert de Boron, the Grail is explained as the vessel of Christ's Last Supper, later used by his disciple Joseph of Arimathea to collect his blood at the crucifixion, and then brought by Joseph to the 'vales of AVALON' in BRITAIN.

Alongside the undoubted Christian symbolism of Continental litertaure, in CELTIC STUDIES the Grail is of special interest because of possible additional Celtic and pre-Christian resonances, such as the *peir dadeni* (cauldron of rebirth) of BRANWEN or the pre-Christian Celtic HEAD CULT.

John T. Koch

GRANNUS

Grannus, or Apollo Grannus, is a healing god, one of several Gaulish deities equated with Apollo as part of the INTERPRETATIO ROMANA. The etymology of his name is uncertain, but his consort's name, Sirona, means 'divine star' or 'star goddess'. INSCRIPTIONS to Grannus have been found in Celtic territory from DÙN ÈIDEANN, ALBA (Edinburgh, Scotland) to Spain, Sweden, Hungary, and Turkey. The German city of Aachen (French Aix-la-Chapelle) was *Aquis Granni* in Latin, '[at] the waters of Grannus'.

Peter E. Busse

GREEK AND ROMAN ACCOUNTS OF THE ANCIENT CELTS

Introduction

From the fragmentary records of the Greek geographer Hecataeus of Miletus, writing on Mediterranean GAUL just before 500 BC, to the late Latin literature of the collapsing Roman Empire in the early 5th century AD, there is an unbroken, if uneven, account of the Celts in classical literature. Many of the earliest sources are no more than brief notes on Celtic towns and tribal movements, but, beginning with the

4th-century BC Athenian writers, a picture of a people and their way of life slowly begins to emerge. Often, the picture is an unflattering portrayal of war-mad, wine-loving barbarians who delight in burning prisoners alive or, conversely, an appreciative view of a noble, brave, and unspoiled race still possessing the admirable virtues long lost in the Mediterranean world. The point of view of a particular Greek or Roman writer on the Celts may follow either extreme or lie somewhere in the middle, depending on the era, the motivations of the writer, and the particular Celtic group described.

Names and Geography of the Ancient Celts

The people whom we call the Celts were known by a variety of names in the classical world. From the late 6th century BC they were called Κελτοὶ *Keltoi* by the Greeks, but beginning in the late 4th century BC they were more frequently known as Γαλάται *Galatai*, a term that superseded *Keltoi*. The Romans generally called the Celts *Galli* 'Gauls', whether in Gaul or not, but they clearly knew that these tribes were the same as those described by the Greeks as *Keltoi*. Other authors occasionally confuse the Celts and Germans, especially when a Celtic tribe was located east of the Rhine or a German tribe on the western bank. The Irish and BRITONS, most commonly known as *Hiberni* and *Britanni*, respectively, were never called Celts, although the Roman historian Tacitus recognized the close similarity in culture between the British and Gauls (*Agricola* 11), and between the Irish and British (*Agricola* 24).

The most detailed information in antiquity on the Celts of Gaul comes from the ethnographic writings of the Greek scholar Posidonius (*c.* 135–*c.* 50 BC), which describe Celtic geography, warfare, poets, and religion. Unfortunately, his writings survive only in usage by later authors, including Athenaeus (*Deipnosophistae* 4.151–4, 6.246), Diodorus Siculus (*Historical Library* 5.25–32), Strabo (*Geography* 2.5.28, 4.1–4), and Caesar (*De Bello Gallico* 6.11–28), who also drew heavily on his own years among the Gauls.

Britain and Ireland were at the far edge of the Celtic lands, but the classical world knew of both of them centuries before the expansion of Roman power into northern Europe. References to the *Albiones* (see ALBION) and *Hierni*, probably the British and Irish, appear in the late 4th-century AD *Ora Maritima* of Avienus. Julius Caesar's account of his brief expeditions into Britain in 55 and 54 BC provides the first extensive records of the island (*De Bello Gallico* 4.20–38, 5.8–23).

Strabo is the first to describe the Irish people, albeit in unflattering terms as gluttonous, incestuous cannibals (1.4.3–5, 2.1.13, 2.5.8, 4.5.4). The short 1st-century AD passage of Tacitus is the clearest and most informative statement on Ireland in classical literature, revealing that some Romans had military intentions toward Ireland, were familiar with the land and its people, and were actively engaged in trade with the island (*Agricola* 24). Moreover, this document provides the earliest description of an individual Irishman, a petty king who was a camp-follower of Tacitus's father-in-law, Agricola.

In the next century, the Alexandrian geographer Ptolemy wrote an extensive description of Irish tribes, rivers, and towns, and again noted Roman trade with

Ireland (*Geography* 1.11.7, 2.1–2). Fourth-century authors regularly refer to the troublesome Scotti (see Scots), of probable Irish origin.

Languages

Of the generally recognized ancient Celtic languages (Gaulish, Galatian, British, Celtiberian, Lepontic, and Irish), the classical authors provide direct information of varying degrees on only the first four, most notably Gaulish. As early as Caesar, classical authors mention Gaulish literacy, including the fact that the Helvetii of the Lake Geneva region conducted a census using Greek letters in the 1st century bc (*De Bello Gallico* 1.29), and that the druids of Gaul never wrote down any of their sacred teachings, but did use the Greek alphabet for business and personal correspondence (*De Bello Gallico* 6.14). The classical authors record approximately 500 Gaulish vocabulary items, although these are largely rather obscure floral and faunal terms, such as *bricumus* 'wormwood' (Marcellinus 26.41) and *alauda* 'lark' (Pliny, *Natural History* 11.121).

Political Organization

Ancient Celtic society was essentially tribal, although larger units might form temporarily on occasion. Caesar describes 1st-century bc Gaul as rife with political factions and loyalties based on client–patron relationships (*De Bello Gallico* 6.11–13), much like Rome in the same era. He says that the common people were little better than slaves in status, but that the warriors and druidic order shared power, dominating the tribal assemblies that were the centre of Celtic political life in Gaul as well as Galatia. A similarly tribal structure appears to have been in place in Britain and Ireland.

Women

Many classical authors focus on the rôle of women in ancient Celtic society, identifying females as being more independent than their counterparts in Greek and Roman culture. Diodorus notes the physical strength and ability of Gaulish women (5.32), while Ammianus, writing several centuries later, states that Celtic women had a formidable character and would sometimes join their husbands on the battlefield (*History* 15.12). Ancient Celtic women had political power as well, a rare occurrence in the Mediterranean world. Bravery in battle is the one constant and dominant theme in Greek and Roman writings on the ancient Celts.

Religion

Ancient Celtic religion is represented with great diversity in the classical authors, but often suffers from the distorting filter of the interpretatio Romana, which placed native gods in more familiar Roman form. Caesar says that the Gauls worshipped Mercury most of all, as inventor of all the arts and ruler of journeys, trade, and money (*De Bello Gallico* 6.16–17). He adds that they also worshipped Apollo (to drive away diseases), Mars (to control war), Jupiter (to maintain order), and Minerva (to teach skills). In addition, some ancient sources say that the Celts near the ocean honoured the sea-born deities Castor and Pollux above all the gods (Diodorus 4.56). In the first century AD, Lucan lists three native divine names, stating that the Gauls worshipped Teutates, Esus, and Taranis in bloody sacrifices (*Pharsalia* 1.444–6). Juvenal (*Satire* 8.155–6) and others mention the horse-goddess Epona, whose worship spread among the Roman cavalry.

The Druids

According to Caesar, the Gauls greatly honoured the druids, who looked after all divine matters and sacrifices, both public and private (*De Bello Gallico* 6.13–14). He also notes that the druids acted as judges if a crime had been committed or in cases such as inheritance or boundary disputes, and states that ignoring their judgements could result in excommunication from all tribal functions. Caesar continues by explaining that the druids met annually in the centre of Gaul, in the territory of the tribe of the Carnutes (near modern Chartres, 85 km southwest of Paris), and that one chief druid was selected by the vote of his fellow druids at the death of the previous leader. He also states that the druidic order was imported from Britain, where those students desiring the most careful education in druidic lore, which could last as long as 20 years, still travelled. Many authors emphasize the druidic teaching on the immortality of the soul (e.g., Strabo 4.4.4; Caesar, *De Bello Gallico* 6.14; see REINCARNATION), while others note their peculiar rituals, such as augury, sometimes using mistletoe (Pliny, *Natural History* 16.95) or human SACRIFICE (Diodorus 5.31).

Poets and Poetry

The role of Celtic poetry and the poet–patron relationship, so important in later Irish and Welsh tradition, are also noted by the ancient Greek and Roman authors. The writer Lucian visited Gaul, and puzzled over a portrayal of Ogmios, the Gaulish Hercules, as a wrinkled old man leading a crowd by a gold chain through their ears. A Greek-speaking Celt explained to him that they viewed eloquence of speech as the most powerful human ability—hence its association with the withered, yet mighty, Hercules. Posidonius related that Celtic leaders, like later Irish kings, brought well-compensated poets with them to sing their praises, for example. Strabo (4.4.4) and Diodorus (5.31) called the Celtic singers and poets βάρδοι *bardoi* ('bards') and noted that their songs could be either praise or satire, again calling to mind the two-sided power of later Irish and Welsh poetry.

Philip Freeman

GRUFFUDD AP CYNAN

Gruffudd ap Cynan (*c.* 1055–1137), king of Gwynedd, was born and reared in Baile Átha Cliath (Dublin). His father Cynan was the son of Iago ab Idwal, ruler of Gwynedd, and his mother was Rhanillt (Ragnell), daughter of the Norse king of Dublin, Ólafr. Gruffudd ap Cynan ruled Gwynedd from about 1100 until his death.

He is said to have increased peace and prosperity in the region and to have introduced new rules to the BARDIC ORDER in Wales (CYMRU).

The life of Gruffudd ap Cynan is well known to us through the only surviving medieval biography of a Welsh ruler. It was originally composed in Latin, probably in the mid-12th century, but has come down to us in a Middle Welsh translation. The reliability of this document is the subject of much debate; it is clearly designed to legitimize his and his descendants' dynasty.

Paul Russell

GUNDESTRUP CAULDRON

Introduction and Description

The Gundestrup cauldron was found in 1891 during peat cutting in Denmark and deposited at the Danish National Museum. The enigmatic depictions of deities and religious scenes on its 13 silver plates make the cauldron one of the most important works of ART of European prehistory.

The cauldron weighs 8.885 kg, and is made of silver with a purity of 970 per thousand, gilded in places. The bowl-shaped base of this vessel has a depth of 21 cm, a diameter of 69 cm, and a circumference of 216 cm. There are five inner plates and seven outer plates, soldered with tin, all with a height of *c.* 20 cm. One outer plate is missing. The cauldron also has a circular bottom plate, diameter 25.6 cm. The technique used to create this object could be described as fine hammered silverwork, with animal and human figures beaten up in a high repoussé (pressed out from the back) and further decorated with carefully punched patterns. Weapons and ornaments depicted make it reasonable to assume that it was made around 150 BC.

Place of Production

Two areas have been suggested as the geographical origin of the Gundestrup cauldron: Celtic GAUL and areas at the lower DANUBE, Thrace. The motifs and objects demonstrate a certain ambiguity, as objects of Celtic type seem to be depicted alongside objects of non-Celtic type. For instance, some of the torcs shown belong to a normal Celtic type, while two with a conical 'gorget' do not. When it comes to technique and style, convincing parallels are found in Thrace (modern Bulgaria and Romania). Only here do we see animal figures with fur depicted using punch marks and in highly beaten and partially gilded silverwork. Although the cauldron can be perceived as Thracian work on the basis of technique, it carries Celtic motifs and elements—the warriors have Celtic helmets, carnyces (sing. CARNYX), and torcs, and the shape of the cauldron is Celtic. The Celtic tribe could be the Scordisci, settled around Belgrade (Singidūnon), in the territory of the Thracian Triballi.

Motifs and Interpretation

The outer plates depict one human figure or bust surrounded by smaller figures, often antithetically arranged. The inner plates all carry larger and more complicated

Detail of the Gundestrup Cauldron showing a goddess surrounded by exotic animals, including elephants and griffins. (C. M. Dixon/StockphotoPro)

scenes. On one inner plate, a triple bull slaughter or SACRIFICE is seen. A second plate shows a female bust, probably a goddess, surrounded or attacked by animals such as two elephants, two winged griffins, and a wolf. The wheel-bearing bearded male bust on another of the inner plates is also surrounded by wolves and griffins. Another plate depicts a squatting antlered god with a torc and the ram-headed snake in his raised hands.

The plate with a procession of warriors is of particular interest for the archaeologist, as many identifiable objects are shown here. The scene is divided into two panels, lower and upper. The lower panel depicts a procession of warriors facing left: six warriors with a SHIELD and a spear, one with a sword and a helmet carrying a figure of a wild boar, and finally three carnyx players. To the left a large figure dips a person into a cauldron-like object. The uppermost panel shows four horsemen with helmets, seemingly being led by a ram-headed snake. The large man dipping one of the soldiers in the cauldron could be interpreted as a rendering of human sacrifice; however, looking to a Celtic mythological background, we may be dealing with a representation of a mythical Celtic cauldron of revivification. Compare, for example, the tale of BRANWEN in the medieval Welsh MABINOGI, where a 'cauldron of rebirth' (*Peir Dadeni*) revivified warriors slain in battle. It must be stressed that the Celtic texts do not reveal anything that is reminiscent of the rest of the scene on this plate, except the supposed cauldron of immortality.

Some of the figures on the cauldron are known from a Romano-Celtic context, and many symbols and animals depicted make sense in a Celtic context. On the one hand, bulls, boars, and birds of prey are important in the Irish and Welsh tales. On the other hand, neither dolphins nor elephants are mentioned in them, nor are the Celtic stories full of composite fantastic animals. In Thracian iconography, fantastic animals, as well as boars, bulls or heads of bulls, and birds of prey are common. The god with a wheel on one of the plates may be identified as a Romano-Celtic god, a variant of Jupiter; it is commonplace to identify him as the Celtic TARANIS. The identification of the antlered god with torcs and the ram-headed snake as CERNUNNOS seems to be acceptable because of similarities with several Romano-Celtic depictions of such a god. The Gundestrup cauldron displays obvious signs of a culturally mixed origin, and while much of its content seems intelligible as part of Celtic religion, parts of it do not.

Flemming Kaul

GWENHWYFAR

Gwenhwyfar was Arthur's wife; variant name forms in French and English ARTHURIAN LITERATURE include *Guinevere*, Middle English *Gaynore*. She is one of a small core of Arthurian figures and accoutrements—CAI, BEDWYR, MEDRAWD, the sword Caledfwlch—that belonged to the earliest core of Welsh Arthurian literature.

In the earliest Arthurian prose tale, CULHWCH AC OLWEN, Arthur names his wife among his most prized possessions. The recurrent theme of her abduction and rescue is found first in the early 12th-century Life of GILDAS. In *Historia Regum Britanniae*, 'Guanhumara' is forced to marry the usurper Modred (Welsh Medrawd) during Arthur's absence.

Gwenhwyfar is named in five Welsh TRIADS. Two report the tradition that the cataclysmic battle of CAMLAN was caused by a petty quarrel between Gwenhwyfar and her sister. The idea that Gwenhwyfar was responsible for the fall of Arthur and his heroes was thus already present in early Welsh tradition.

The name *Gwenhwyfar* corresponds exactly to Old Irish *Findabair*, the name of the daughter of MEDB and Ailill in the Irish ULSTER CYCLE, a compound of *find* 'white, fair' and *siabair* 'phantom'. Like Gwenhwyfar, Findabair is responsible for the death of many heroes in a calamitous confrontation. Thus it is possible that not only the names but also the characters are of common origin. The forms of the names, *Gwenhwyfar* and *Findabair*, could either be COMMON CELTIC cognates or borrowings in either direction. The parallel is thus exactly comparable with that of Welsh *caledfwlch*: Irish *caladbolg* and TWRCH TRWYTH: *Torc Tríath*. These three form a significant nucleus of old inter-Celtic borrowings or inherited elements in Arthurian tradition generally, and in *Culhwch ac Olwen* specifically.

John T. Koch

GWERFUL MECHAIN

Gwerful Mechain (*c.*1460–*post* 1502) is the only female poet of medieval Wales (CYMRU) from whom a substantial body of poetry has survived. Her subject matter is varied; she was famous for composing some of the most uninhibited and sexually explicit poems in the WELSH language—for example, *Cywydd y Gont* (Poem of the vagina) and *I Wragedd Eiddigus* (To jealous wives). The erotic poems represent only one aspect of her output. Gwerful Mechain also composed religious poetry and prophetic verse (see PROPHECY). In addition, she produced a skilful CYWYDD contemplating Christ's Passion on the cross, while her spirited poem defending women from misogynistic attacks is an important contribution to the fields of social history and feminist literary criticism:

> *'I'w gŵr am ei churo'*
>
> *Dager drwy goler dy galon—ar osgo*
> *I asgwrn dy ddwyfron;*
> *Dy lin a dyr, dy law'n don,*
> *A'th gleddau i'th goluddion.*

'To Gwerful Mechain's husband for beating her'
    May a dagger through your heart's collar slant to the bone of your breast, your knee break, your hand bruise, and your own sword pierce your bowels.

Gwerful Mechain was fully accepted by her contemporaries. Her work reveals that it was possible for a woman in late medieval Wales to absorb the learning required to compose in the strict metres, and also to talk openly about sex.

Nerys Howells

GWREANS AN BYS ("THE CREACION OF THE WORLDE")

Gwreans an Bys ('The Creacion of the Worlde') is a CORNISH-language biblical drama that was probably written for outdoor performance in or near Helston, Cornwall (Henlys, KERNOW). It is similar to the ORDINALIA, and was composed sometime before the date in the manuscript of 1611.

The seven-syllable line is not strictly followed in the text. Kent and Saunders have recently argued that, although it is common to many dramas across Europe, the subtitle 'with Noye's Flood' may have had special significance to Cornish mining communities, where it was believed that their mineral wealth was given to them by the redistribution of the earth's resources in the aftermath of God's cleansing of the world through the Flood. 'The Creacion of the Worlde' has been somewhat neglected in the corpus of CORNISH LITERATURE, and has not been performed in its entirety since the 17th century.

Alan M. Kent

GWRTHEYRN (VORTIGERN)

Gwrtheyrn (Vortigern) was a powerful historical leader in 5th-century BRITAIN and subsequently became a central figure, of generally bad reputation, in LEGENDARY HISTORY and ARTHURIAN literature. In the earlier 9th century, the ruling dynasty of Powys claimed descent from him (as GUARTHIGIRN) on ELISEG'S PILLAR (see also

GENEALOGIES). Beginning with the *De Excidio Britanniae* (On the destruction of Britain) by GILDAS, he is represented as instrumental in bringing the Anglo-Saxons to Britain as mercenaries, with negative results (see ANGLO-SAXON 'CONQUEST'). Gildas's account is credible, and is possibly based on 5th-century written sources. BEDE's *Historia Ecclesiastica* (completed in 731) supplies an exact date, AD 449. For the *Historia Brittonum* of 829, the tragedy of Gwrtheyrn is nearly the overarching central theme; a great deal of information has been added, much of it from legend and HAGIOGRAPHY. Several of these picturesque details were used by GEOFFREY OF MONMOUTH in his HISTORIA REGUM BRITANNIAE ('The History of the Kings of Britain') of *c*. 1139, and thence became established fixtures of the legendary history of Britain—for example, the beguiling of Gwrtheyrn by the beautiful daughter of Hengist, the Saxons' leader, and the 'Treachery of the Long Knives' (*Brad y Cyllyll Hirion*) in which Hengist's men massacred their hosts, the 300 elders of Britain, at a FEAST.

In addition to Eliseg's Pillar, Gwrtheyrn is linked with the area that is now east-central Wales (CYMRU) by the old CANTREF name *Gwrtheyrnion* < British **Wertigerniāna* 'land of Gwrtheyrn'. Gloucester (Welsh Caerloyw) is the place of origin implied by Gwrtheyrn's genealogy (*Historia Brittonum* §49): *Guorthigirn Guortheneu, filius Guitaul, filii Guitolin, filii Gloiu* 'Gwrtheyrn the excessively thin, son of Vitalis, son of Vitalinus, son of Gloucester'. Thus the various territorial connections of the family suggest holdings over a sizeable but coherent area in the southern and central Welsh–English border country.

Gwrtheyrn, Old Welsh *Guorthigirn*, Latinized *Vortigernus*, is not a common name; appropriately, it means 'overlord'. It is possible that it was originally a title or, at least, a meaningful assumed name. A Romano-Briton born in the 4th century, Gwrtheyrn's immediate ancestors were southerners with Roman names.

Website
www.vortigernstudies.org.uk

John T. Koch

GWYDION AP DÔN

Gwydion ap Dôn, like his sister ARIANRHOD and his brother Gilfaethwy, is one of the central characters in the Middle Welsh tale known as MATH FAB MATHONWY, the Fourth Branch of the Mabinogi. He is a magician and, early in the tale, uses his magic powers to instigate a war with Pryderi of DYFED to distract his uncle, King Math, so that lovesick Gilfaethwy can rape Math's virgin footholder, Goewin. Math, also a great magician, then condemns Gwydion and Gilfaethwy to three years as successive pairs of male and female animals who breed with each other (see REINCARNATION). When Math tests Arianrhod as a possible replacement virgin footholder, she gives birth to the aquatic child Dylan and a 'small thing', which is subsequently fostered by Gwydion and later appears as LLEU. With Math he conjures up a woman out of flowers, BLODEUWEDD, as Lleu's wife. After Lleu is wounded by his unfaithful wife's lover Gronw, Gwydion uses a sow to track him, discovers him in the form of an eagle, and restores him to human form.

Allusions in the 'mythological poems' of Llyfr Taliesin imply that versions of Gwydion's story were known outside the *Mabinogi* and at an earlier date. *Caer Wydion* is attested as a Welsh name for the Milky Way.

John T. Koch

GWYNEDD

Gwynedd was a kingdom in north Wales (Cymru) that emerged as the Roman hold on Britain weakened. One of the earliest examples of the name in its familiar Latinized form, *Venedotia*, appears on a 6th-century inscribed stone at Penmachno at the head of the Conwy valley, which commemorates a venedotis cives 'citizen/ tribesman of Gwynedd'. The name is probably Celtic. The kingdom's foundation myth was linked with Cunedda, but its first king for whom we have contemporary documentation was Maelgwn in the mid-6th century, one of the five British rulers denounced by Gildas. The core of the kingdom was the mountain mass of Snowdonia (Eryri); the presence of this landmark made the kingdom easy to defend and contributed to its emergence as the most powerful and successful native Welsh kingdom. In 825, a new dynasty came to power in the shape of Merfyn (Frych) ap Gwriad, and the subsequent political history of independent Wales was to be associated with the descendants of Merfyn. His son Rhodri Mawr (†878) was the first to bring other kingdoms under his rule, albeit only for his lifetime. The kingdom subsequently came under the rule of Hywel Dda of Deheubarth, and in the late 10th and early 11th centuries it may have been under the overlordship of the Norse kingdom of Baile Átha Cliath (Dublin).

An intrusive warlord, Gruffudd ap Llywelyn, brought more of Wales under his rule than any other ruler, before or after. Ultimately, his involvement in English politics at a sensitive time, coupled with his ruthlessness within Wales, led to his downfall and death in 1064. The last quarter of the 11th century saw the return of the line of Merfyn Frych in the shape of Gruffudd ap Cynan. He was able to pass on a stronger kingdom to his son and successor Owain Gwynedd in 1137. Although Owain's death in 1170 was followed by a power struggle among his sons, his grandson, Llywelyn ab Iorwerth, emerged as the dominant ruler in Wales, and *his* grandson, Llywelyn ap Gruffudd, was recognized by the English crown in the Treaty of Montgomery of 1267 as Prince of Wales and overlord of the other Welsh rulers. A succession of crises in Anglo-Welsh relations led to two wars, and Llywelyn's death in action in 1282 and the capture and execution of his brother Dafydd in 1283 meant the end of Welsh political independence. Under the Statute of Wales of 1284 (see Rhuddlan), the region was divided into the three counties of Anglesey (Môn), Caernarfon, and Merioneth (Meirionnydd), amalgamated to reform the county of Gwynedd in 1974; Anglesey (Ynys Môn) separated from Gwynedd in 1995.

A. D. Carr

H

HADRIAN'S WALL

Hadrian's Wall runs some 80 Roman miles (117 km) from the fort at Bowness on the Solway Firth in the west to the fort at Wallsend (Romano-British Segedūnum 'Strong-fort') on the Tyne estuary in the east, crossing and thus bisecting the whole island.

The Building of the Wall

The only Roman reference to the reason behind the wall's construction states that its purpose was 'to separate the Romans from the barbarians' (*Vita Hadriani* 2.2), though it was built within the territory of the Brigantes. The wall would not have served as a convincing defence against large-scale military assault; it is probably better regarded as a means of controlling social traffic and trade. Archaeological investigations indicate that the building of the wall commenced around the time of Hadrian's visit to Britain in AD 122.

The Structure of the Wall and the Hadrianic Frontier

The wall originally varied from 2.2 m to 3.1 m in width and was up to 4.65 m to 6.2 m in height. The western part of the wall—as far east as the crossing of the river Irthing—was built of turf, while the eastern section was made of stone. Most of the length of the wall was accompanied on its northern side by a wide ditch (the *vallum*), and several substantial bridges, such as those at Newcastle (*Pons Aelius*) and Willowford, form part of the overall structure. Small forts or 'mile castles' were constructed up against the southern side of the wall at intervals of roughly a mile, most with gates allowing controlled access to the exterior.

Late Roman and Early Post-Roman Times

The rôle played by Hadrian's Wall in the turbulent final century of Roman rule is unclear. There is no obvious evidence of fighting or destruction, nor is there any archaeological evidence that the wall was overrun around AD 409/10, when centralized Roman government in Britain came to an end. Many of the forts may have been taken over by local Romano-British warlords, and excavations at several of these sites have produced evidence of use and occupation in the subsequent centuries. It is also noteworthy how much of the CYNFEIRDD poetry, such the GODODDIN and *Marwnad* CUNEDDA, point to a tradition of continued hostility in post-Roman times at or near the Hadrianic frontier. Similarly, the early entries in *Annales Cambriae* record battle sites identifiable with places on or near the wall, such as CAMLAN

Hadrian's Wall. (Corel)

(AD 537) and Arfderydd (AD 573). The Old Welsh name for Hadrian's Wall was simply *Guaul*, 'wall' (Historia Brittonum §38).

Simon Ó Faoláin

HAGIOGRAPHY, BRETON

A sizeable and significant body of early medieval Breton saints' lives survives in Latin—the largest such corpus from any of the Celtic countries. General discussions of this material may be found in the articles Breton literature and Christianity in the Celtic countries. Several individual Breton Lives are discussed in entries on particular saints: Gildas; Iudic-hael; Samson; and Uuinuualoe (Gwenole). On St Meriadoc, see Conan Meriadoc.

Early Material

The First Life of St Samson of Dol is one of the earliest of the Celtic *vitae*, possibly predating even the Irish *Lives*. Some Romano-British spellings of proper names in the Breton *vitae* imply the use of older written records, going back to the era of the saints themselves.

Content and Affinities

Several saints are said to have come from Britain, such as Gildas, as already noted, and Samson, whose background is located in Dyfed and Gwent. The Lives may preserve historical recollections of the rôle of missionaries in the Breton migrations. Early Breton and Merovingian Frankish rulers are often mentioned, which is sometimes also of historical value for this poorly documented period (5th–7th century). The Life of Uuohednou (Goueznou) mentions Vortigern (Gwrtheyrn) and Arthur in an introductory section of legendary history. Among the supernatural elements, healing miracles figure prominently, as in hagiography worldwide, but other elements have more specific affinities with the other Celtic literatures. For example, the weird decapitation and revivification of St Melor bears comparison with the manifestations of the head cult elsewhere in the Celtic world. St Malo's voyage to a mysteriously appearing island is similar to episodes in Navigatio Sancti Brendani ('The Voyage of St Brendan') and in immrama (voyage tales) in Old Irish.

John T. Koch

HAGIOGRAPHY, CORNISH

Introduction

Cornwall (Kernow), like other Celtic regions, has a relatively large number of saints. Approximately 140 Cornish saints are known, but they are sparsely represented in hagiographies. Only St Petroc is the subject of a Life entirely composed in Cornwall.

Saints Outside Texts

The bulk of the evidence for Cornish saints consists of place-name evidence and church dedications. There are two particular place-name elements: *lann*, perhaps best translated as 'church-site' (cf. Welsh *llan*, Breton *lann*), and *eglos,* meaning 'church'. It is arguable that these elements are names of people locally commemorated. Almost all of these saints are Celtic, in that they have Brythonic names and are visibly local. Approximately 80 percent are known in Cornwall at one site only; where there is more than one cult site, these are generally fairly widely separated. Moreover, half of these Celtic saints are unknown outside Cornwall and Brittany (Breizh). Most of these church dedications seem to date from before the Norman Conquest.

Medieval Lives

The only extant Lives that seem to have been composed entirely in Cornwall are those that emanated from Bodmin Priory concerning St Petroc. There are two Latin prose Lives, a versified version of one of these accounts, a series of *miracula* (miracles), an account of the theft of the saint's relics in 1177, and a collection of genealogical material. The extraordinarily rich material concerning St Petroc sets him apart from all other Cornish (and many Celtic) saints. It is remarkable, however, that the earlier Life is found only in Breton manuscripts. All the other texts concerning Petroc are found uniquely in the Gotha manuscript of hagiography, a 14th-century manuscript probably assembled at Hartland Abbey in Devon, but now in Germany. This manuscript also contains unique copies of several other west-country texts (including the so-called Life of St PIRAN, the Life of St Rumon, and the Life of St Nectan).

The contrast to the relatively large numbers of Lives of Irish and Breton saints, and to a lesser extent the Lives of Welsh saints, is striking. Cornwall is, however, well supplied with subsidiary hagiographic texts, some of which are pre-Norman in origin. In addition to the invaluable 10th-century list of saints, there are several calendars of saints, liturgical documents, various genealogical tracts (mostly in a Welsh context), lists of resting-places of saints, and charter material. Moreover, various Lives of Cornish saints have been composed and adapted outside Cornwall. For example, the so-called Life of St Piran is more or less a Life of the Irish St Ciarán of Saigir with the ending altered to reflect the saint's death and burial in Cornwall; this would seem to have been accomplished at Exeter in the 13th century. There are medieval Latin Lives of Breton and Welsh saints honoured in Cornwall, but of Breton provenance, as well as Lives of other west-country saints who also have dedications in Cornwall. Some, but not all, of these Lives include Cornish episodes. Not all of these identifications are straightforward.

Also undoubtedly local in origin are the two Lives of saints composed in CORNISH: the early 16th-century dramatized version of the Life of St Meriadoc (BEUNANS MERIASEK), the only extant vernacular Life of a Cornish saint until the discovery in 2002 of BEUNANS KE; and the Cornish verses mentioned by Nicholas Roscarrock as the source of his account of St Columb.

Karen Jankulak

HAGIOGRAPHY, IRISH

Introduction

Hagiography (writings on the saints) survives mainly in the form of accounts of the lives of saints (*vitae sanctorum*), calendars, and martyrologies (lists of saints for every day of the year). Native Irish hagiography was written down over a period of 1,000 years, beginning between 650 and 700 with four Latin Lives (two of PATRICK, plus one each of BRIGIT and COLUM CILLE) and ending in the early 1600s with the Franciscan scheme for the collection of Ireland's ecclesiastical literary remains, which culminated in the publication in Louvain in the 1640s of John Colgan's *Acta Sanctorum* and *Trias Thaumaturga*.

Early Lives

Late 7th-century rivalry between the churches of Armagh (ARD MHACHA), Kildare (Cill Dara), and Iona (EILEAN Ì) led to the composition of Latin Lives for Brigit, Patrick, and Colum Cille. These Lives describe the travels and spiritual power of the three saints, and by extension the territory and prowess of their churches. Between around 800 and 950, one Latin Life (Brigit's *Vita Prima*) and three vernacular Lives—of Brigit, Patrick, and Adomnán—were written at Kildare, Armagh, and

Kells, Iona's successor. A second vernacular Life was composed for Brigit in the 11th century.

Twelfth-Century Lives

There is little or no hagiography in the manuscripts of the period from 1050 to 1150. Paradoxically, Irish hagiography was then being compiled abroad, at Lagny, near Paris, where a Life partly based on Irish oral witness was written for Fursa, and at Clairvaux, where Bernard wrote a Life of Malachy of Armagh (†1148). In ENGLAND, a Life of Brigit was written by Laurence of Durham in the 1140s, while GEOFFREY OF MONMOUTH wrote a Life of Modwenna (MONINNE) in the early 12th century at Burton-on-Trent. After 1170, against the background of the Anglo-Norman invasion, numerous saints' Lives were written in Latin.

Hagiography in the Period 1580–1650

Toward the end of the 16th century, the mainly Jesuit and Franciscan Irish colleges on the Continent initiated a new round of interest in saints' Lives. The Franciscan scheme for the collection of Ireland's ecclesiastical remains, which was based in St Antony's College, Louvain, ensured the survival of numerous texts that would otherwise have perished. At home in Ireland, Anglo-Irish scholar-collectors ensured the survival of the main collections of Latin Lives.

The Liturgical Tradition

Two types of liturgical hagiographical record survive: calendars, which recorded the feasts commemorated in one or very few churches, and martyrologies, which provided much more substantial lists. The earliest surviving record, the *Depositio Martyrum* of AD 354, was a CALENDAR of feasts celebrated in Roman churches.

The earliest martyrology, spuriously named Hieronymian after St Jerome († *c.* 420), was compiled in the late 6th or early 7th century, possibly at Luxeuil. All later martyrologies are based on the bare names of the Hieronymian lists, including the so-called historical versions, inaugurated by the Anglo-Saxon theologian and historian BEDE († *c.* 735), which added biographical details. Historical and Hieronymian martyrologies continued to be copied throughout the Middle Ages.

Two martyrologies—one prose (Martyrology of Tallaght), the other verse (Martyrology of Oengus; see OENGUS CÉILE DÉ)—were compiled at the monastery of Tallaght (Tamhlacht), now south Dublin (BAILE ÁTHA CLIATH), around 830. Many features of the prose martyrology point to a provenance in Northumbria for its exemplar.

Following the revival of learning in the second half of the 14th century, several new copies of the Martyrology of Oengus were made *inter Hibernos* (among the Irish). The latest native martyrology of note was that of Donegal, which the annalist and historian Mícheál Ó Cléirigh (?1590–1643) and at least one other collaborator prepared in the 1620s.

Calendars

The early 9th-century Karlsruhe calendar is the only surviving pre-Anglo-Norman text of this kind. Numerous (mostly unedited) calendars survive from churches in areas under English influence, notably Dublin and Meath (MIDE). The earliest post-Norman calendar from a church *inter Hibernos* forms part of a late 14th-century poem.

Pádraig Ó Riain

HAGIOGRAPHY, SCOTTISH

The Earliest Evidence

The earliest surviving *vita* from what is now Scotland (ALBA) is Adomnán's *Vita Columbae* (Life of COLUM CILLE), written on Iona (EILEAN Ì) *c.* 700 AD, though we know that it is based in part on a book of Columba's virtues written a generation earlier. Many of the stories located in and around Iona itself seem to be based on the eyewitness reminiscences of Columba's monks, probably collected within a generation of his death in AD 597.

No other *vitae* survive from this period. There is an 8th-century Latin poem, *Miracula Nynie Episcopi* ('The Miracles of Bishop Ninian'), written at Whithorn (Taigh Mhàrtainn) during the Anglian occupation of Galloway (Gall-ghaidheil), and a 12th-century *Vita Niniani* attributed to Aelred of Rievaulx. The legends of St Kentigern, which in their present form date from 12th century and later, may contain late 7th- to early 8th-century material embedded within much later texts.

The Middle Ages

The fashion of writing *vitae* underwent a revival in the 10th and 11th centuries, but these were increasingly vernacular or mixed Hiberno-Latin lives. No Scottish example survives. From the same period comes a fantastic version of the foundation legend of Laurencekirk in Mearns, found embedded in the writings of a prolific Canterbury hagiographer. It has probably been preserved because it contains an anecdote about Queen Margaret's pilgrimage to Laurencekirk.

These accounts are not the only Celtic foundation legends for Scottish churches that survived into the High Middle Ages. The foundation legend of St Andrews (Cill Rìmhinn, older Cennrígmonaid) survives in two versions, which describe how the king of the PICTS, Onuist son of Uurguist (*c.* 727–61), founded the church in thanksgiving for victory in battle to house relics brought from Constantinople. The once very important church of Abernethy (Obair Neithich) also had an elaborate foundation legend, which locates its roots in the remote Pictish past and links it with the *familia* of St BRIGIT of Kildare (Cill Dara).

Other *vitae* of the 12th century support the greatness of individual saints whose churches were becoming centres of pilgrimage. Notable among them are the *Vita Niniani* attributed to Aelred of Rievaulx and the two lives of St Kentigern written for the cathedral of Glasgow (Glaschu). Jocelin's *Vita Kentigerni* (*c.* 1180) is of considerable interest because it is possible to disentangle the various threads that went into its makeup.

Another 12th-century *vita* that has survived is the anonymous *Vita Sancti Servani*. Its localized collection of miracles, set mostly in southwest Fife (Fìobha) and the surrounding area, reads like the territorial claims of an early church at Culross (Cùl Rois).

In a different category are a small group of *vitae* of 11th- and 12th-century 'royal saints'. Chief among these materials is the *Vita Margaretae Reginae* by Thurgot, prior of Durham. Aelred of Rievaulx wrote a *Lamentatio* of her brother, King David I, in hagiographic style, datable 1153 × 1154. A third *vita* of a 'royal saint' is Jocelin's *Vita Waldeui*, concerning the life of Abbot Waldef of Melrose (†1159), son of Earl Simon I de Senlis, King David's stepson. A vernacular verse collection survives of saints' lives, mostly drawn from the *Legenda Aurea* and the *Specula* of Vincent of Beauvais, including lives of St Machar of Aberdeen (Obair Dheathain) and St NINIAN of Whithorn.

The Breviarium Aberdonense

Around the year 1500, the task of giving Scotland a large-scale national hagiography was taken in hand by William Elphinstone, bishop of Aberdeen. His *Breviarium Aberdonense* (Aberdeen Breviary), published in Edinburgh (Dùn Èideann) in 1510, is the most important collection of Scottish saints' lives, largely in the form of short lessons for their feast-days. There seems to have been a conscious attempt to spread the net over the whole of Scotland, to include saints from every diocese and to have a sprinkling of obscure and little-known local saints as well as national heroes such as St Ninian and St Margaret. It is not always clear whether the compilers of the Breviary used a well-known existing *vita* of a saint, or a less well-known local legend.

There is a tendency in the Breviary to claim saints as Scots who were, in fact, Irish. Thus St Finnbarr, venerated at Dornoch and Barra (Barraidh), is made son of a Caithness nobleman related to a local king called Tigernach, but the incident described in the readings has been lifted from an Irish Life of St Finbar of Cork (Corcaigh) that locates it, and King Tigernach, in south Munster (MUMU).

The Breviary includes a good deal of local legend and tradition. For example, the lessons for St Patrick allude to his supposed birth at Old Kilpatrick on the Clyde (Cluaidh) near Dumbarton (Dùn Breatann), and also to traditions relating to 'St Patrick's Well' and 'St Patrick's Stone' near the kirkyard. These were important places of pilgrimage in the Middle Ages. For many of its 80-odd Scottish saints, the Aberdeen Breviary provides our only information.

Alan Macquarrie

HAGIOGRAPHY, WELSH

Although Christianized while still a part of the Roman Empire, the 'Age of Saints' in Wales (CYMRU) spanned the 4th to 8th centuries. After the end of Roman rule in 409/10, Romano-British Christianity survived and continued to develop.

The church organization of bishops and dioceses used in Romanized areas did not suit Wales because it lacked towns; instead, in this region, the bishops became associated with particular tribal kingdoms that emerged or, in some cases, re-emerged in the post-Roman period. Most saints were known only in local lore, but a few extended their areas of activity or had more widely spread cults. This is most notably true of saints Beuno, Cadoc, David (DEWI SANT), Deiniol, GILDAS, Illtud, Padarn, SAMSON, and Teilo. Dedications provide a generalized location and degree of relative importance. The saints travelled as missionaries and retreated as hermits, but their most visible activity was in setting up religious communities, the *clasau*, which served as monasteries and centres of learning, and which characterized the Welsh church even long after the Age of Saints.

Traditions about the Welsh saints persisted throughout the centuries, anchored in each one's *clas* and area of activity, but they were not compiled into *Vitae* in Wales until the end of the 11th century when the Norman Conquest led to religious and political change. The Normans aimed to replace the old system of *clasau* with Latin monastic orders such as the Benedictines. The Welsh church was to be brought under the strict control of Canterbury and Rome. In the 12th century in particular, both Welsh and Anglo-Norman clerics employed *Vitae* of the saints to argue the case for their place in the new hierarchy. The most striking examples of this trend are the competition carried out in the apparently answering *Vitae* of Cadoc and David and in the *Liber Landavensis* (Book of Llandaf, *c.* 1130) in which the Norman-created diocese of Llandaf claimed saints Dyfrig and Teilo and all their privileges in an attempt to assert itself as the archiepiscopal seat of Wales (see also CARADOG OF LLANCARFAN; RHYGYFARCH). Medieval Welsh translations exist for only two saints, David and Beuno. Other translations into Welsh appear in later periods for both the Welsh saint Gwenfrewi (late 16th century) and for non-Welsh saints from the broader Catholic tradition.

Traditions of the Welsh saints are recorded not only in the prose Lives but also in medieval poetry, antiquarians' reports, and contemporary folklore. Wherever they appear, they exhibit certain patterns and are expressed largely through shared motifs (though each saint also has distinct traditions). Male saints generally are proclaimed in their saintliness before their births; have a precocious childhood during which they perform wonders; travel, establishing churches and gathering followers; come into conflict with a secular power, either kings or beasts; rule a territory, ensuring peace and prosperity; and finally die and continue performing wonders. The Lives of female saints do not begin until the women reach nubility, when they must earn their sanctity by rejecting the advances of a man; after that event, they do many of the same things as male saints do, albeit often with a more domestic character. Both men and women come of royal blood and are often related to Jesus either through Mary's sister or her cousin Anna.

The Welsh saints were not martyrs like the Continental saints; however, they are notable for their curses and the violence in their lives. Their miracles, which presumably demonstrated their access to God, were more often raw displays of power than of kindness, demonstrated through control of people, animals, or elements. Saints could, for example, create fire, raise wells, and ride rocks across the sea.

Saints continued to play a part in Welsh culture in modern times, mostly in the localities in which they had begun. People living in a saint's territory may point to the saint's well or seat or may tell the legend relating to the saint. Wells, which were used for healing both physical ailments and social ills (e.g., cursing a thief), often served as a focus for a cult and sometimes became the most visible connection with the saint.

David, the patron saint of Wales, is the only canonized Welsh saint. He is celebrated on 1 March with school pageants and concerts, lectures, dinners in social organizations, and the use of national symbols such as wearing leeks or daffodils. Since the opening of the Welsh Assembly (Cynulliad Cenedlaethol Cymru) in 1999, there has been a growing desire to make St David's Day (Gŵyl Ddewi) a legal holiday in Wales.

Elissa R. Henken

HALLSTATT, ARCHAEOLOGICAL SITE

Introduction

Located in the Alpine zone of Upper Austria, the Hallstatt archaeological site consists of several monuments, the most famous being the cemetery in the Salzbergtal on the Hallstatt salt mountain. Remains of settlements of the Hallstatt and La Tène periods and prehistoric mining activity from the Urnfield (Late Bronze Age), Hallstatt (Early Iron Age), and La Tène (Later Iron Age) periods are also known from the site. Today, Hallstatt is a World Heritage Site.

Initial finds of 'men in the salt' were treated according to the standards at that time. One miner discovered in 1734, for instance, was swiftly reburied in a graveyard. Nearly a thousand inhumation burials were excavated by Johann Georg Ramsauer, the chief miner in the Hallstatt salt mines, between 1846 and 1863. More than a hundred futher burials were excavated over the course of the twentieth century.

The archaeological sites of Hallstatt are located on the salt mountain, a steep mountain rising over Lake Hallstatt in the Upper Austrian Alps. The cemetery itself lies at an altitude of 1100–1200 m at the lower end of the Salzbergtal ('salt mountain valley'), approximately 450 m above Lake Hallstatt and directly above the modern village.

The Hallstatt Cemetery

Some 1,270 burials have been recovered during the excavations. Approximately 45 percent of these finds were cremations, and the rest were inhumation burials, mainly dating to the periods of Hallstatt C and Hallstatt D (c. 750–475 BC), with a small number of more recent ones, dating to the Hallstatt/La Tène transition horizon and the earliest La Tène period (5th century BC). These graves are exceptionally rich, containing an extremely large number of large bronze vessels and other metal objects. This pattern indicates not only that the salt mining carried out in the

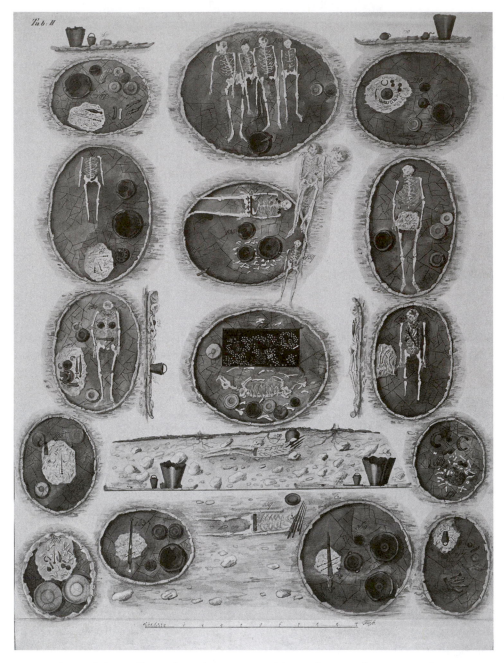

Watercolour of the Hallstatt burial site, painted by Isidor Engel in 1878. Johann Georg Ramsauer began the excavations of the 980 tombs in 1846. Naturhistorisches Museum, Vienna, Austria. (Erich Lessing/Art Resource, New York)

Hallstatt mountain was economically highly profitable, but also that the cemetery was limited to the higher strata of society. New excavations show that a much higher density of burials exists in this area of the cemetery, and estimates run to a total of 5,000 to 8,000 burials.

The Prehistoric Salt Mines

Prehistoric salt-mining activity at Hallstatt began in the Late Bronze Age, in the 12th/11th century BC, with the earliest mining techniques being adapted from earlier copper mines. The greatest known depth reached below the surface by this salt-mining activity is 215 m and the largest known shaft was 17 m wide.

Settlement Activity in Hallstatt–Salzbergtal and Dammwiese

Settlement remains were recovered during several excavations in the Salzbergtal, but these were more extensive on the Dammwiese. Several log buildings have been excavated in the Salzbergtal. During the most recent excavations, since 1994 several buildings for producing salted bacon and settlement layers from the Urnfield period in the 12th/11th century BC have been uncovered.

Raimund Karl

HALLSTATT CULTURE

The Hallstatt Period and Its Chronology

The term 'Hallstatt culture', named after the famous archaeological site in Upper Austria, usually refers to the Early IRON AGE phases of a style known as Hallstatt C and Hallstatt D, and connected elements of social structures, burial rites, and settlement patterns. Hallstatt C and D precede LA TÈNE Iron Age cultures in many areas. On the basis of scientific dating methods and the evidence of the 'southern imports' from the more chronologically secure Mediterranean world, the Hallstatt Iron Age culture has been dated to about 750–475/450 BC. The later Hallstatt culture has been connected with the ethnic label 'Celts'. Caution is advised, however, as equating archaeological material finds and ethnic groupings is problematic, especially because, in the field of prehistoric research, there is as yet no universally accepted definition for 'archaeological culture' or 'ethnic group'. However, the connection between the region of the Hallstatt Iron Age cultures and groups who spoke early CELTIC LANGUAGES is more secure.

Geographical Location and External Contacts

The term 'Hallstatt culture' refers to material found in an area stretching from eastern France to western Hungary, and from southern Germany to Slovenia. To do justice to the many regional variations, reference is often made to multiple Hallstatt cultures, which are then geographically specified—for example, 'inner Alpine Hallstatt culture' or 'southeast Alpine Hallstatt culture'.

The principal division is between an east and a west Hallstatt area. A general border zone can be identified running north–south in the area between the rivers Inn and Enns, and the river Moldau. Hallstatt itself is situated within this zone, as is clearly reflected in the mixed or transitional nature of the material found in its cemeteries. The Czech Republic and Slovakia are often regarded as belonging to the

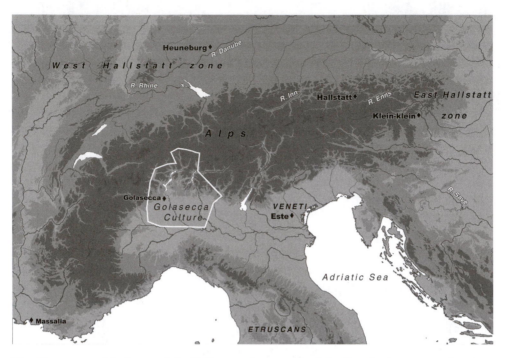

The Alps, geographical core of the Hallstatt culture south of the Danube (western and eastern zones), and its influential neighbours to the south—Massalia (Marseille), the Golasecca culture, the Etruscans, and the Veneti. (Map by John T. Koch)

eastern area, but sometimes this region is viewed as a smaller area, entirely south of the DANUBE. It is generally agreed that the eastern and southern borders are located around the rivers Danube (where it turns south near Budapest), Kulpa, and Save. East Hallstatt contains the cultural areas and groups around Horákov in Moravia, the Kalenderberg in eastern Austria, the Sulmtal in southern Austria, and the various Krainer groups in Slovenia (Slovenian Styria).

The situation in the inner Alpine area, because of its function as a mediator with southern cultures, deserves special attention. The rich grave goods found in Hallstatt graves in the zone that includes eastern France and southwest Germany provide evidence of the trade connections that developed between the Mediterranean and the areas north of the Alps in the Hallstatt D period (c. 600–c. 475/450 BC). The development of the Greek colony of Massalia (Marseille) on the Ligurian coast from c. 600 BC must be seen in this context. Further contacts existed with the Etruscan culture area in and around Tuscany, mediated through the northwest Italian GOLASECCA CULTURE in Lombardy and Tessin and the Este culture of the Veneti of northeast Italy. The latter has especially caught the attention of archaeologists because of the outstanding metalwork in the situla ('wine bucket') style. In addition to contacts with Mediterranean civilizations, a second line of cultural influence was maintained with the Iranian-speaking Scythians and other steppe nomads to the east.

Graves, Settlements, and the Material

The west Hallstatt zone is characterized by relative homogeneity, especially as regards burial customs and gifts: Graves situated in chambers beneath hills were usually richly furnished with weapons, four-wheeled wagons (see CHARIOT), and harnesses for pairs of horses. The main weapon in the earliest period (Hallstatt C, c. 750–600 BC) was the iron sword of the Mindelheim-type, which was replaced in later periods (Hallstatt D) by the dagger. Other material innovations in Hallstatt D included the emergence of different kinds of fibulae. The endowment of graves with sets of pottery (in some cases, rather elaborate) points to the introduction of high-status drinking customs that have been connected with the Greek institution of the *symposium*.

East Hallstatt, apart from the completely different forms of ceramics, is differentiated from west Hallstatt by its different metal forms and burial customs. In contrast to the rather uniform western grave goods, these sites are filled with defensive weapons (SHIELDS, HELMETS, body armour), spear-heads, and axes, as well as riding harnesses. Relief scenes on metal vessels in the situla style show people equipped with military and feasting equipment that corresponds to objects found in the graves.

In contrast with the relatively rich evidence found in Hallstatt graves and cemeteries over the whole area, only a few known settlements have been excavated in modern times. One of the best-known settlements of prehistoric research is the HEUNEBURG on the upper Danube in Baden-Württemberg, Germany.

Jutta Leskovar

HARP, IRISH

The earliest known Irish word for a harp-like instrument is *crott* (< Celtic **kruttā*), which may be compared to *chrotta*, the word used by Venantius Fortunatus (c. 530–c. 600) to describe the type of harp favoured by the BRITONS (the medieval and modern Welsh cognate CRWTH represents a stringed instrument closer to a lute or viola than a harp). While there is no textual evidence for determining precisely the type(s) of 'harp' designated by *crott*, stone carvings suggest that it was some form of quadrangular harp rather than the later triangular frame harp.

While not a 'harp' in the usual sense, the *tiompán* (Old and Middle Irish *timpán*) appears to have been a lyre-like instrument akin to the dulcimer, which was either plucked or played with a mallet or a bow. The lack of technical specificity in the word *crott* (*cruit* in Middle and Modern Irish) and the close connection between the harp-playing and *tiompán*-playing traditions are evident from the interchangeability of the words.

The earliest known Irish depiction of a triangular frame harp is on the 11th-century shrine of St Maedóc. In its classic form, most famously represented by the 14th-century 'Brian Boru' (BRIAN BÓRUMA) harp in Trinity College Library, BAILE ÁTHA CLIATH (Dublin), it was a small, heavy, and low-headed instrument, held on the knees in playing. It may be that *cláirseach*, an alternative term for 'harp' that came into use in the 14th century, originally served to distinguish the newer instrument—with its massive soundboard (*clár*) carved from a single piece of willow—from the older instruments. The metal strings, approximately thirty of them, were plucked with the fingernails, producing a distinctive bell-like tone. The post-medieval development was a larger, floor-standing version, with up to half again as many strings.

Little is known of the kind of music played on the Irish harp in the Middle Ages. The classic source for a description of medieval Irish harp playing is *Topographia Hiberniae* ('Topography of Ireland') by GIRALDUS CAMBRENSIS. He marvelled at harpers' ability to play intricate melodies at a fast tempo while maintaining sweetness of tone and introducing modal and rhythmic variation. The harp was also used to accompany the professional reciter (*reacaire*) of bardic poetry. In return for his services to his patron chief, the medieval Irish harper received gifts of land and stock, and enjoyed a free status and legal privilege unavailable to other entertainers.

It is clear from 18th-century poetry that the harp was an instrument played in taverns as well as large houses. By the last quarter of the century, however, the number of players was in serious decline. In response, James Dungan, a wealthy native of Granard, Co. Longford (Gránard, Contae Longfoirt), financed and organized three competitive 'balls' in Granard during the years 1781–5. These events inspired a 'Harp Festival' in Belfast (Béal Feirste) in 1792. Most of what we know about the tunes, tunings, modes, ornamentations, and terminology of the traditional harpers was garnered by Edward Bunting (1773–1843) at this festival, where he interviewed the ten participating harpers and transcribed their tunes. The oldest of these musicians, Denis Hempson (1695–1807), still played in the old style, plucking the wire strings with his fingernails. The most renowned was Toirdhealbhach Ó Cearbhalláin (1670–1738), whose 200 or so compositions were heavily influenced by Italian baroque art music.

The playing of the harp—the major symbol of Romantic NATIONALISM—was revived in 19th-century Ireland (ÉIRE). The new style of 'Irish harp' introduced for this purpose was merely a small version of the ordinary concert harp, however, and no effort was made to revive traditional styles. Since the 1960s, a new generation has returned to Bunting's manuscripts and conducted experimental research on the old style and repertoire.

The symbolic association of the harp with Ireland has existed since the 14th century, when it featured as a heraldic device. This relationship was formalized by Henry VIII, who had it placed on Irish coinage in 1534. As the symbol par excellence of Romantic nationalism, it has found a permanent place in popular culture as the logo of the Guinness Corporation and the national symbol on Irish coinage and stationery.

William J. Mahon

HARP, WELSH

The Welsh harp (*telyn*) figures within the medieval BARDIC ORDER as described in the laws attributed to the 10th-century king HYWEL DDA (see LAW TEXTS), where it was used as accompaniment to the declamation of the poetry of the bards. The instrument in this period in Wales (Cymru) was about 2 feet (0.6 m) high, and strung with delicate horsehair strings. Welsh harpers shared with the Irish certain techniques in playing the instrument: Nails as well as fingertips were used and, contrary to Continental practice, the harp was placed on the left shoulder.

The use of the medieval instrument gradually ceased during the 16th and 17th centuries, replaced by the triple harp introduced from Italy. By the 19th century, south Wales had become a battleground between the triple harp and the new pedal harp, developed by the Frenchman Sébastien Erard (1752–1831).

In spite of the deep mistrust with which it was viewed during the Methodist revival (see Christianity), the harp has continued to prosper. Both triple and pedal harps—and indeed the small harp—continue to be played. The triple harp survived in the playing of Nansi Richards (1888–1979), and is currently enjoying a revival and a new influx of players. The small harp is played by folk musicians, while the pedal harp is used to accompany *cerdd dant* singers and also serves as a solo instrument in its own right.

Ffion M. Jones

HAY, GEORGE CAMPBELL

George Campbell Hay (Deòrsa Mac Iain Dheòrsa, 1915–84), one of the major Scottish Gaelic poets of the 20th century, was born in Elderslie, Renfrewshire. He spent seven formative childhood years in the fishing community of Tarbert (An Tairbeart), and learned Scottish Gaelic from his relatives. These years established his identification with the Gaelic-speaking, maritime culture of Kintyre (CeannTíre). His earliest poetry (dating from 1932)—consisting mostly of lyrical reflections on his experience—was exquisitely crafted and deeply influenced by traditional and classical Gaelic models. After completing a classics degree at Oxford (1934–8), Hay became active in the Scottish nationalist movement (see nationalism).

Hay published three collections of poetry: *Fuaran Sléibh* (Mountain spring; 1948), *Wind on Loch Fyne* (1948), and *O na Ceithir Airdean* (From the four directions; 1952) in the post-war period. In the 1960s and 1970s, a new generation discovered Hay's work; for him, this era was a very productive period, marked by various publications. As a nationalist, Hay's poetry always reflected his commitment to Scotland and to the Gaelic-speaking community. His most extraordinary work, however, succeeds in relating the difference of Gaelic culture to the corresponding differences of other minority cultures. For example, in *Mochtàr is Dùghall* (Mochtar and Dùghall; 1982), a poem cycle that he had begun writing in North Africa during World War II, the personal and family histories of an Arab and a Scottish soldier—both killed by the same hand grenade—are explored and interrelated with great sensitivity and outrage. It is in work of this sort that Hay earned his recognition as a poet of international stature. He is regarded as one of the pre-eminent 20th-century Scottish Gaelic poets. His complete works have been magnificently edited (with translations, notes, and biographical material) by Michel Byrne and published as *The Collected Poems and Songs of George Campbell Hay*.

William J. Mahon

HEAD CULT

Introduction

There is ample archaeological and artistic evidence of cults of the severed head in Europe from Mesolithic times (Middle Stone Age, *c.* 10,000–*c.* 5000 BC). Decapitation occurs as a prevalent literary theme in several genres within the CELTIC LANGUAGES, as well as in GREEK AND ROMAN ACCOUNTS of the Celtic world and Latin texts by Celtic writers.

The efforts taken to preserve and display heads, and the frequency with which they are depicted, point to their religious importance as symbols of the supernatural, perhaps the seat of the soul, conferring on the keeper the wisdom and energy of the person to whom it once belonged. Judging from classical accounts and archaeological finds, the cult of the head seems to have been most developed in southern GAUL, whereas it may have developed only late in the British Isles. Numerous references in the insular Celtic literatures, especially the Irish tales of the ULSTER CYCLE (cf. IRISH LITERATURE, EARLY PROSE) and FIANNAÍOCHT, reflect ideas in Christian times about head-hunting that are strikingly reminiscent of classical accounts relating to practices and traditions in ancient Gaul—for example, in the account of Athenaeus derived from Posidonius. In the 9th- or 10th-century Irish mythological saga CATH MAIGE TUIRED ('The [Second] Battle of Mag Tuired'), it is said

Portico with skulls from a Gaulish sanctuary, Roquepertuse, France. (C. M. Dixon/ StockphotoPro)

that Dian Cécht, physician of the Tuath Dé, was so skilled that he could heal any wound 'unless his head is cut off, or the membrane of the brain or his spinal cord is severed' (§99); for modern readers—familiar with the idea that brain death equals medical death—this seems normal, but this reference is remarkable considering how few pre-scientific cultures understood the brain and central nervous system as having such preeminent importance.

Surviving Greek and Roman accounts of head-hunting and the severed head in Gaul consistently stress the horrific barbarity of the practices. Diodorus Siculus reports that heads were collected, preserved, and displayed to guests.

Archaeological Evidence

Severed heads are a recurring theme in Continental Celtic sculpture, and severed heads and skulls seem to have been part of the architecture and equipment of sanctuaries and other sacred ENCLOSURES. The Pfalzfeld pillar—one of the earliest and most ornate Celtic sculptures discovered to date—is adorned with carved heads on each side, and must have been crowned by another head, which has now disappeared. Depictions of double- (or Janus-) and triple-headed deities have come to light at many major sites, and are depicted on precious items such as the gold bracelet found at Rodenbach. Important sanctuaries such as CHAMALIÈRES, Gournay-sur-Aronde, and Ribemont-sur-Ancre—the latter two also extremely important in the context of Celtic human sacrifice—have yielded human skulls near the entrance, away from other finds, possibly indicating their display as part of entrance structures.

The most spectacular sites connected with the cult of the severed head are ROQUEPERTUSE and Entremont, both near Marseille (Massalia). The three monolithic pillars found at Roquepertuse featured niches in which human skulls were most probably displayed. Entremont featured a tall stone pillar carved with twelve severed heads, along with human skulls nailed into niches. The severed or disembodied head is also a common artistic motif in the La Tène style.

The cult of the head seems to have experienced a revival in Britain with the coming of CHRISTIANITY when, in connection with the cult of the saints, healing wells were often reinterpreted as holy wells. Saint Gwenfrewi's well was created from her blood after she was beheaded.

References in the Insular Celtic Literatures

Severed heads are an omnipresent feature of the Ulster Cycle tales. In SCÉLA MUCCE MEIC DÁ THÓ ('The Story of Mac DáThó's Pig'), CONALL CERNACH wins the 'CHAMPION'S PORTION' by displaying 'the head of Connacht's most vaunted warrior at his belt'. FLED BRICRENN ('Bricriu's Feast') similarly climaxes with a beheading episode that underscores an unchallengeable claim to the 'champion's portion'. CÚ CHULAINN accepts a challenge by an ugly herdsman to behead him if he were allowed to do the same to Cú Chulainn the following night. When Cú Chulainn takes up the challenge and beheads the giant, he picks up his severed head and walks off, but nonetheless does not shirk his half of the bargain; a similar 'beheading game' episode occurs in ARTHURIAN LITERATURE.

Cú Chulainn, in his rôle as Ulster's single-handed defender throughout most of Táin Bó Cuailnge ('The Cattle Raid of Cooley'), is given to cutting off the heads of his enemies, which he then takes home or displays on the spot.

In the Second Branch of the Mabinogi, the mortally wounded Bendigeidfran (Brân) commands his companions to cut off his head and carry it with them to the White Mount in London, and then to bury it to protect the kingdom against invasion. In the meantime, they spend nearly a century with Bendigeidfran's head, uncorrupted and still pleasant company. See St Melor for an elaborate decapitation legend in Breton hagiography.

Marion Löffler and John T. Koch

HEDD WYN

Hedd Wyn (1992) is a film based on the life of the poet Ellis Humphrey Evans (bardic name Hedd Wyn), who won the chair at the 1917 Birkenhead National Eisteddfod (Eisteddfod Genedlaethol Cymru) a few weeks after dying in World War I. The feature was the first Welsh-language film to be nominated for an Academy Award (1993) in the 'Films in a Foreign Language' category; both the film and its actors won several other prestigious awards in other European film festivals.

Alan Llwyd

HELEDD FERCH CYNDRWYN

Heledd ferch Cyndrwyn has the important distinction of being the first major female character in Welsh literature, perhaps historical and perhaps only literary. A princess from mid-7th-century Shropshire (swydd Amwythig), England, then in Powys, she speaks in a 9th- or 10th-century poetic cycle, *Canu Heledd* ('Heledd's Poetry'), about the death of her brother, the warrior-prince Cynddylan, and the subsequent devastation of their kingdom. *Canu Heledd* is a well-known literary classic in Wales (Cymru) today, which is at least one factor in the continued popularity of the name. It abounds with simple and repeated haunting images, such as the line *Stafell Cynddylan ys tywyll heno* (Cynddylan's hall is dark tonight), which inspired the deeply psychological feminist narrative *Tywyll Heno* (Dark tonight) by Kate Roberts.

In the Welsh triads, Heledd figures as one of the 'Three Unrestricted Guests of Arthur's Court, and Three Wanderers' and also as one of the *Tri Engiryavl*, 'three driven mad by grief'.

John T. Koch

HÉLIAS, PER-JAKEZ

Per-Jakez Hélias (1914–95) was a major figure in Breton literature during the final third of the 20th century. He wrote both in Breton and in French, and his work embraces several genres: journalism, radio drama, creative prose, and verse. *Le cheval d'orgueil* (The horse of pride), the autobiographical French-language text of his best-known work *Marh ar lorh* (1986), met with phenomenal success and gave Hélias celebrity status. Among Helias's principal literary works in Breton are two collections of poetry: *Ar men du* (The black stone; 1974) and *An tremen-buhez* (The pastime; 1979). An important theme in his poetry is the fact of language, and its power to define. His *Marh ar lorh* is rooted in the Bigoudenn region, southwest of Kemper (Quimper), and the work's regionality was central to its success. Hélias also published works on local customs, language, and folklore.

Diarmuid Johnson

HELMETS

Helmets are designed to protect the head. They were used by Celts in a military context from ancient times, as well as for occupational functions such as mining in Cornwall (KERNOW) and Wales (CYMRU). Following from the military use, helmets developed a secondary role as items of costume. In Central and Eastern European Celtic archaeology, helmets are extremely rare finds, which suggests that only warriors with outstanding prowess were deemed worthy to wear one; it is likely that helmets also signalled status.

Helmets occur in many different types. Eastern European Celtic helmets exhibit distinctly eastern Celtic traits: fortified calottes and pseudo-filigreed ornamentation. A helmet of the Berru type with the characteristic high, conical form was found in the context of a two-wheeled CHARIOT burial (see VEHICLE BURIALS) in La Gorge-Meillet, France. In Agris, France, a particularly a richly ornamented helmet from the early LA TÈNE period was discovered in a cave, among the most beautiful expressions of Celtic ART. This object is closely paralleled only by a series of ceremonial helmets from the 4th century BC, which have been found on the fringes of the Celtic world at Amfreville (Normandy), Saint-Jean-Trolimon (Brittany [BREIZH]), Montlaurès (Languedoc), and Canosa (Puglia, Italy). The careful placing of the helmet in a cave is consistent with

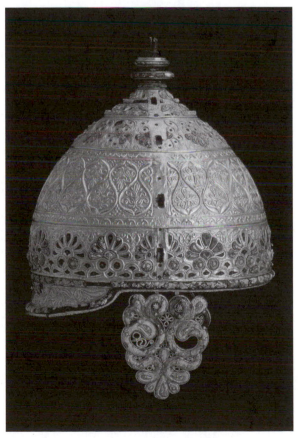

Helmet found at Agris, Charante, France, from the 4th century BC. Iron and bronze, covered with gold and inlaid with coral. (Musee Archeologique et Historique, Angouleme, France/The Bridgeman Art Library International)

ritual deposition (see HOARDS; WATERY DEPOSITIONS), well known in—but not limited to—the ancient Celtic-speaking lands.

Elizabeth Jerem, Thierry Lejars, M. Lévery, and Antone Minard

HELVETII

The Helvetii were a Celtic-speaking tribe or tribal confederation in the western Alpine region around Lake Constance and Lake Geneva. In 58 BC, they attempted to migrate into GAUL (and, according to Caesar, to conquer it) at the instigation of the nobleman Orgetorīx. Caesar defeated them in battle (*De Bello Gallico* 1.24–9), ultimately leading to the Roman subjugation of Gaul. The Germanic Alamanni overran Helvetian territory in AD 259/60.

The Celticity of the Helvetii is demonstrated by their proper names. For example, *Helvetii* itself is probably based on the root seen in Welsh *elw* 'gain, profit' and the Old Irish prefix *il-* 'many, multiple'. *Orgetorīx* is a Celtic compound and means 'leader of killers'. In modern times, *Helvetia* is the Latin name for Switzerland.

Philip Freeman and John T. Koch

HEN OGLEDD

Yr *Hen Ogledd*, 'the Old North', is a term used in the study of early Welsh literature and history signifying the BRYTHONIC-speaking peoples of what are now parts of northern ENGLAND and southern Scotland (ALBA).

Definition

The term 'Old North' is distinct from north Wales (CYMRU). The term focuses on that part of north Britain inhabited by BRITONS, rather than by PICTS, SCOTS, or Anglo-Saxons. This part of Britain formed the northern military zone of the Roman province, whose strong points were the legionary forts of York (Eburācum) and Chester/CAER (Dēva), the numerous lesser forts along HADRIAN'S WALL, and the linking road system.

The geographic term *yr Hen Ogledd* is closely connected with groups called in the 12th century GENEALOGIES *Gwŷr y Gogledd* 'Men of the North'. Hence, Pictland, DÁL RIATA, and Northumbria—once its territory had fallen into English hands—are usually not included in the Old North.

In Welsh literature, *yr Hen Ogledd* was as integral to early Welsh tradition as Wales itself. Works attributed to ANEIRIN, TALIESIN, Myrddin, and anonymous CYNFEIRDD were composed there, and it was home to heroes famous in Wales such as URIEN and his son, OWAIN. In this sense, the Old North contrasts not only with the Pictish, Scottish, and Anglo-Saxon regions of north Britain, but also in another way with Brythonic-speaking Brittany (BREIZH) and Cornwall (KERNOW), which did not figure nearly as importantly in any branch of early Welsh literature.

It is likely that contacts between Wales and the north were simply closer for a longer time, and therefore that the Brythonic dialects WELSH and CUMBRIC remained more similar to each other. It must also be important that both dynasties of independent Wales's most powerful kingdom, Gwynedd, traced back to the Old North.

The old Brythonic north, places mentioned in the article, with Roman roads in white. (Map by John T. Koch)

Divisions of the Old North

Some of the divisions of the Old North are well documented and are covered in their own articles in the encyclopedia: Elfed, Gododdin, Rheged, and Ystrad Clud (Strathclyde, partly synonymous with Cumbria), as well as lesser kingdoms or subkingdoms, such as Aeron, probably in southwest Scotland, Manaw and Lleuddiniawn (Lothian), probably both once subdistricts of northern Gododdin. Given that Bernicia (Brynaich) and Deira (Dewr), the two subkingdoms of Anglo-Saxon Northumbria, both have Brythonic names, it is likely that they had once had Brythonic rulers as well. It is also likely that there were other such kingdoms whose names have not survived or not certainly been identified.

John T. Koch

HEROIC ETHOS IN EARLY CELTIC LITERATURES

Introduction

The hero is a widespread international concept. One of the prevalent themes of Celtic heroic literatures is that the hero himself is short-lived, with his brief life offering a poignant contrast to his everlasting fame. The pre-modern Celtic heroes most often excel in feats of physical force: competitive games, hunting, and, by far the most common, combat. No written descriptions of Celtic warriors have survived that can be proved to be wholly free of the influence of Greek and Roman epic and, therefore, are ultimately indebted to Homer. During the Christian period (including all BRYTHONIC and GOIDELIC literature), the Bible also served as a powerful literary model for numerous heroes.

As well as heroes and warriors, both Goidelic and Brythonic traditions provide many instances of the poet and/or visionary who achieves eternal fame in a struggle against the odds. The pan-Gaelic hero FINN MAC CUMAILL figures as a visionary and poet, as well as a champion and a war leader. The pan-Brythonic TALIESIN, in contrast, is usually presented as a superlative poet and visionary, but rarely as a warrior.

The Celtic Hero in the Ancient World

The heroic behaviour and ideals of Celtic groups can be supported by archaeology, at least in so far as the latter demonstrates the dominant influence of a warrior aristocratic class in the Celtic lands. In numerous rich burials, distributed widely across the Continent and Britain in the HALLSTATT and LA TÈNE periods, one finds sophisticated weaponry, together with fine metal jewellery and feasting equipment, all pointing to a widespread system of shared values in displayed military status and luxury goods. The conjunction of this material in graves implies the belief that the hero's status and fame continued beyond death, through a cult of heroic immortalization.

A few classical heroes achieved fame in the medieval CELTIC COUNTRIES and were drawn into their native genres of heroic tales and praise poems such as Alexander the Great, Hercules, and characters from the TROJAN LEGENDS.

Concepts of the Hero in Early Irish Literature

In Celtic tradition, the 'hero of the tribe', as a champion and defender of his people (CÚ CHULAINN, for example), contrasts with the 'hero outside the tribe', a wanderer and outlaw (Finn mac Cumaill, for example). Rather than two completely separate classes, we should probably think of these depictions as two aspects of a single category.

We can obtain further insight into the dual rôle of the early Irish hero by focusing on the warrior's association with the boundary. The boundary of the *tuath* was of paramount importance in early Irish society. With the exception of certain privileged classes, no one retained his status or legal rights if he left his own *tuath;* in other words, he became an outlaw. The warrior was charged with defending the boundary against attack, or crossing it to conduct raids on neighbouring territories. According to circumstances, therefore, he was either a 'tribal' champion or a lawless marauder. Such opposites appear in the ULSTER CYCLE hero CONALL CERNACH, for example. In the story of Cú Chulainn's taking up arms, Conall Cernach appears guarding the border of the kingdom, ready to extend his protection to any visiting poet, and to challenge any warrior. In SCÉLA MUCCE MEIC DÁ THÓ ('The Story of Mac Dá Thó's Pig'), by contrast, Conall boasts that he kills a man of the province of CONNACHT every day and burns Connacht's settlements every night; the tale as a whole portrays warriors as raiders and cattle rustlers.

The hero's ambivalent character and his association with the concept of the boundary were aptly symbolized by the dog (Irish *cú*). The guard dog is tame in interactions with its own people, but a wild beast when it encounters trespassers from outside. The dog's capacity to be both wild and tame is also reflected in the use of *cú* to mean not only 'dog' but also 'wolf' (often specified as *cú allaid* 'wild dog'). The same word could designate the protector of a settlement and the raider who attacked out of the wilderness. The legal literature displays the same metaphor when it uses the term *cú glas* (grey dog = wolf) for a man wholly without ties, a foreigner from overseas.

The hound's usefulness depends upon its ability to distinguish between friend and foe—that is, 'insider' and 'outsider'. The loss of this ability to distinguish can make the warrior a menace to his own people: Cú Chulainn, returning from a raid beyond the border, threatens to kill everyone in the stronghold until disarmed by a trick.

Cú Chulainn (lit. 'Culann's dog') is the figure in whom this symbolism is most fully expressed. His name is explained with one of his earliest exploits, when he slew and then assumed the duties of the monstrous hound of the blacksmith Culann. This close identification is reflected in his geis against eating dog flesh.

The Heroic Ethos in Early Welsh Poetry

As long as Welsh poets enjoyed the support of a militaristic aristocracy, the traditional heroic value system was very much in evidence in praise poetry. The most intensely heroic piece of Welsh literature is the early Welsh GODODDIN, concerned chiefly with events of 6th-century north BRITAIN.

The cycles of saga *englynion* from the 8th to 10th centuries centred on the figures of Llywarch Hen, HELEDD, and URIEN. They are sometimes termed 'post-heroic', meaning that they focus on the period after the death of the hero(es). The perspective of Llywarch is that of an old noble warrior who has outlived his twenty-four sons, all of whom were killed in battle. The Heledd cycle features a prolonged description of Cynddylan's ruined hall and kingdom, and the Llywarch poetry considers the desolate hearth of RHEGED. Especially in the case of Llywarch, 'post-heroic' can mean not merely set after the idealized heroic age and lamenting its fallen worthies, but also entailing a sober questioning of its values; for example, Llywarch questions himself for exhorting his sons to uphold the code and thus meet their fate in combat. The concept of a post-heroic age is also meaningful as a historical context in that military reversals had brought about the retreat of Brittonic-controlled territory before Anglo-Saxon advance in the centuries immediately before the composition of the *englynion* cycles. It seems more likely, however, that the *englynion*'s view of heroism has more to do with its genre than nascent anti-militarism in Viking Age Wales (CYMRU), when we take into account the continuity of heroic themes, and even the verbal formulae used to express them, from *Y Gododdin* down to the praise poems of the GOGYNFEIRDD to the Welsh princes of the 12th and 13th centuries.

Other Manifestations of the Heroic Ethos in Celtic Literatures

The general conservatism and traditionalism of Celtic-speaking societies is often remarked upon. The consistency of heroic values across time and space in the Celtic world is a fair example of this continuity. One precious indication that the heroic ethos had been celebrated by the poets of medieval Brittany (BREIZH) is the Latin martial eulogy of IUDIC-HAEL, whose themes and images are striking similar to those of *Y Gododdin*.

Although Gaelic FIANNAÍOCHT—as an oral and literary tradition of heroes of old—could continue under centuries of English political and military domination, the praise poetry created for the warrior aristocracy themselves usually came to an abrupt end when a Celtic society suffered conquest by a non-Celtic group. Thus poetry that often echoed the themes and diction of *Y Gododdin* continued in the court poetry composed for Welsh princes by the *Gogynfeirdd* down to the loss of Welsh independence in 1282. This resemblance is especially striking in the works of the greatest *gogynfardd* CYNDDELW and in the *Hirlas* (Long-blue [drinking horn]) attributed to Owain Cyfeiliog. In the Gaelic world, native chiefs continued to lead war-bands and patronize poets until the early 17th century in Ireland (ÉIRE) and until 1746 in Scotland (ALBA). Down to the end of these traditions, the 'panegyric code' of the traditional Gaelic praise poets featured a strongly heroic character, as well as esteeming the illustrious lineage and open-handed generosity of the patron in highly formulaic terms (see SCOTTISH GAELIC POETRY).

John Carey and John T. Koch

HEUNEBURG

Heuneburg was a Celtic aristocratic settlement (*Fürstensitz*) near Hundersingen, Germany, on the upper DANUBE.

The Site and Its General History

The Early IRON AGE hill-fort sits on a triangular hill approximately 60 m above the valley, first fortified during the Late Neolithic period (4th/3rd millennium BC) and subsequently over a span of about five centuries from the Middle Bronze Age. It was fortified again after the Celtic period, in the Middle Ages.

The First Sequence of Iron Age Activity

At the end of the 7th century BC, during the Hallstatt Iron Age, an aristocrat from this region built a fort located on the ruins of the earlier fortifications on the top of the hill, and at the same time founded a much bigger unfortified settlement northwest of its glacis. It is a reasonable conjecture that this leader gained wealth and power by exploiting the rich iron ore layers of the Swabian Alp, a mountainside close to the Heuneburg. It can also be assumed that this person was the prince buried in the central chamber of the 'princely burial mound' (*Fürstengrabhügel*) named Hohmichele, located nearby.

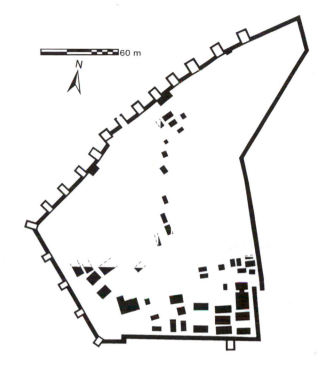

Site plan of the Heuneburg showing late Hallstatt period fortifications, with the bastions on the west, and major excavated internal features. (Map by Egon Gersbach)

The hill-fort covers an area of approximately 3 ha (7.2 acres) and was fortified with a trench and a wall in traditional timber-laced construction. The internal structure of the fort suggests a rural settlement. The construction of the next phase of the fort adopted a radically untraditional design, showing southern influences, unique north of the Alps.

In the southern area, the internal settlement was organized with specialized quarters oriented along the main path leading from the *Donautor* (Danube gate) into the fort. Various craftsmen had their workshops located here. One house covered an area of 130 m^2. The whole built-up area was rebuilt twice without substantial changes to the plan. Later, the gate in the northwest was demolished, a new tower was placed in the western part of the southeastern corner of the wall, and inside the enclosure the structure of the buildings was partly changed. A building located close to the *Donautor*, which was presumably used as an arsenal, is conspicuous in that it covers an area of 202 m^2. Heuneburg's imposing distinctive appearance in the Late Hallstatt period, resembling a Greek town, and the evidence for intensive contact with the western Mediterranean suggest that the hill-fort might be the mysterious Celtic town of Pyrene, located on the upper Danube by Herodotus in the 5th century BC.

The Second Sequence of Iron Age Activity at Heuneburg

A newer Iron Age hill-fort at Heuneburg did not continue the Mediterranean ideas of fortification. In this phase, the enclosure was fortified with a palisade with gaps for two gates, still using a then-1,000-year-old earthen wall that had been built during the Middle Bronze Age.

In this newer phase of building and occupation, the organization of the walled settlement consisted of a loose assembly of houses, storehouses, and workshops in fenced-in ENCLOSURES. During the first three subphases of this period, large three-aisled houses were the predominant structures, along with smaller buildings of other types. These huge buildings covered an area up to 407 m², and were erected in the southern part close to the protecting wall. These aisled halls were rebuilt in the same location at each of the three substages. Over the course of time, the density of buildings within the fort decreased. At the final substage, we can identify traces of what might have been an area of aristocratic occupation, indicated by Greek black-figured pottery.

Egon Gersbach

HIBERNIA

Hibernia is the most common name for Ireland (ÉRIU) in Latin. Caesar gives the first definite Latin reference to Ireland in the first century BC (*De Bello Gallico* 5.13), though the *gens Hiernorum* 'people of Ierne/ Ériu' of Avienus (*Ora Maritima* 111) probably dates to a much earlier Greek ethnic name based on the place-name Iερνη /ˈiernē/ 'Ireland'. Later, in the 2nd century AD, Ptolemy uses ιουερνία /ˈiwernia/. Pomponius Mela (*fl. c.* AD 43) and Juvenal (*fl.* early 2nd century AD) use the form *Iuverna*. Oblique noun cases in the Antonine Itinerary (early 3rd century AD) and St PATRICK's *Confession* (5th century AD) imply the nominatives *Iverio* and *(H) iberio,* respectively, representing spoken Primitive Irish *ˈĪwerijū,* which became Old Irish *Ériu*.

Philip Freeman and John T. Koch

HIGH CROSSES, CELTIC

Celtic high crosses are large, free-standing stone crosses and cross slabs, usually carved in relief with a variety of ornament—figural iconography, animal and occasionally plant motifs, and abstract patterns; some have INSCRIPTIONS. These monuments are found in Ireland (ÉIRE), Scotland (ALBA), Wales (CYMRU), the Isle of Man (ELLAN VANNIN), and Cornwall (KERNOW), and may be dated *c.* AD 750–1150. There is a parallel tradition of similar crosses in Anglo-Saxon and Viking ENGLAND.

Distribution, Context, and Function

Most of the crosses are concentrated on significant ecclesiastical sites of monastic character—for example at Clonmacnoise, Co. Offaly (Cluan Mhic Nóis, Contae Uíbh Fhailí), and Iona, Argyll (EILEAN Ì, Earra-Ghaidheal)—where the foundations had the resources and commanded the patronage to produce them. Some have survived *in situ*, indicating that they stood adjacent to the church or in the cemetery. Others were located at gateways, in the marketplace, on boundaries. and on ecclesiastical land. These monuments were symbols of power, protection, piety, and patronage. They could act as *foci* for graves and, among the Vikings at least, as individual grave-markers.

Form and Manufacture

All of the surviving Celtic crosses and cross slabs are carved from stone. The tallest cross (6.45 m) is at Monasterboice, Co. Louth (Mainistir Buite, Contae Lú). A distinctive feature is the cross head, which usually has the cross arms linked by a ring; the resultant form is considered characteristically Celtic. Geological identification has shown that the stone for most crosses was quarried locally, but was sometimes transported considerable distances by sea. The crosses would have been carved either in monastic workshops or by itinerant sculptors. The more elaborate examples would have taken considerable time and resources to produce. The main carving tools were flat and pointed chisels, and the surfaces were smoothed with abrasives.

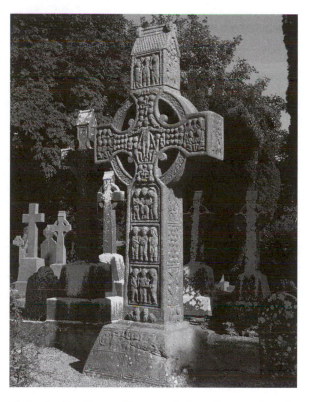

Muiredach's Cross, Monasterboice, County Louth, Ireland/Ardchros Mhuireadhaigh, Mainstir Bhuithe, Contae Lú, Éire. (Martin Mullen/Dreamstime.com)

Iconography

In Ireland, the ornament on many crosses of the 9th and 10th centuries is dominated by Christian iconography, mainly from the Old and New Testaments. For example, on Muiredach's Cross, Monasterboice, the west face is carved with the Crucifixion on the cross head and related scenes on the shaft, while the east face has the Last Judgement on the cross head with other scenes, including the Fall of Adam and Eve and Cain killing Abel, below. It is thought that the main models were Continental, specifically Carolingian, but details of dress, such as BROOCHES, are native, and swords are of Viking type. On 10th-century Manx cross slabs, the Viking patrons chose scenes from pagan Norse mythology—for example, at Andreas, Odin being devoured by the wolf at the battle of Ragnarök—which may be juxtaposed with Christ trampling a serpent on the other face.

Animal Ornament

Celtic crosses have two main types of animal ornament. First, exotic, mythological, and fantastic beasts, such as lions, griffins, and centaurs, are sometimes found in Ireland and Pictland (e.g., Bealin, Co. Westmeath, and Rossie Priory, Perthshire). Second, animals, such as lions, serpents, dragons, birds, and even men, are combined with interlace to produce complex patterns; examples include Killamery Cross, Co. Kilkenny (Contae Chill Chainnigh), and Aberlemno 2. Such motifs on sculpture are often derived from more complex animal ornament in insular illuminated manuscripts, such as The Book of KELLS, and decorated metalwork.

Patterns

Celtic crosses are characterized by a variety of abstract ornament—interlace, spirals, frets, and chequer-board patterns—constructed with the aid of a compass, ruler, and grids. Spirals and frets have their origins in Iron Age LA TÈNE ART, but the origins of the interlace are less clear. The West Cross, Ahenny, Co. Tipperary (Contae Thiobraid Árainn), is carved almost entirely with such ornament, recalling metalwork models.

Pictish Symbols

Cross slabs of the later 8th and 9th centuries in eastern Scotland, such as Rosemarkie (Ros Mhaircnidh), Ross and Cromarty, Meigle 1, Perth, and Kinross (Cinn Rois), are sometimes carved with Pictish symbols. These carvings—for example, a crescent and V rod, mirror and comb, and 'Pictish beast'—are enigmatic (see PICTISH; PICTS).

Inscriptions

A significant number of Celtic crosses and cross slabs are carved with inscriptions. In Wales and Cornwall, Latin was the chosen language; in Ireland and DÁL RIATA, IRISH; in eastern Scotland, Pictish, in either the Roman or OGAM alphabets, or occasionally Latin; and in Viking-settled areas, Old Norse runes. Inscriptions may proclaim the patronage of kings and ecclesiastics and bonds between church and state, such as found on the Cross of Scriptures, Clonmacnoise (Cluan Mhic Nóis). They may record events and entitlement to land, as is the case with ELISEG'S PILLAR, Denbighshire (sir Ddinbych). Some are commemorative, such as Ballaugh, Isle of Man. Exceptionally, two Manx cross slabs name the sculptor, Gaut.

The Celtic Revival

In the second half of the 19th century and the early 20th century, one result of burgeoning antiquarian interest in the early Christian period in Ireland, coupled with nationalist aspirations, was that the carving of Celtic crosses resumed, modelled on their early medieval counterparts. These monuments functioned primarily as grave-markers—for example, in the cemetery of 19th-century Catholic bishops at

Maynooth, Co. Kildare (Má Nuad, Contae Chill Dara). In Scotland, Wales, the Isle of Man, and Cornwall, similar crosses may also be found in graveyards, or occasionally functioning as war memorials. Arthur G. Langdon, author of *Old Cornish Crosses*, was responsible for designing new ones, such as the version found in St Stephen by Launceston churchyard.

Nancy Edwards

HIGHLAND GAMES

The Highland Games can best be defined as a social gathering (whether informal or formal) organized around musical and sporting competition. The origin of the Games remains unclear. There were probably many antecedent forms of sport and cultural practices that existed before their formalization into what can now be recognized as the Highland Games.

The modern idea of the Highland Games began in Braemar, where it can be traced to the Braemar Wright's Society (a charitable organization, later reconstituted as the Braemar Highland Society in 1826), founded in 1816. The patronage of Queen Victoria in 1848 gave the Braemar Highland Games the royal seal of approval, after which they began to mushroom—a development that lasted until the beginning of the 20th century, at which period most of the currently recognized Highland Games were established. The competitions have remained much the same to the present day, and include the following events: athletics—hill races, jumping, pole-vaulting, and sprinting; heavy events—putting the stone, throwing the hammer, tug-of-war, wrestling, and tossing the caber. There are also musical events: Highland dancing (see DANCES), pipe bands, and piping (both *ceòl beag*/light music and *ceòl mòr*/classical music), usually referred to as *pibroch*, a corruption of the Gaelic word *piobaireachd* (see BAGPIPE).

The Highland Games have had a direct influence on international athletics, especially on Canadian and American sport. Some of the influence of ROMANTICISM, which reached its apotheosis with Sir Walter SCOTT (1771–1832), can still be seen at Highland Gatherings today. This can be best summed up as Balmorality ('kitsch' symbols of the Highlands that have since been appropriated by Scotland as a whole as markers of national identity). The modern Highland Games are a major tourist attraction and appear to satisfy the stereotypical image of Scotland to a worldwide audience. This can still be seen at the Braemar Highland Games—the premier World Games—which mark the end of the season.

Andrew Wiseman

HIGHLANDS AND ISLANDS

The Highlands and Islands cover a large area of northern Scotland (ALBA), north of the Highland line, running from Argyll east to Stonehaven near Aberdeen (see map p. 13), which divides the Highlands (A' Ghàidhealtachd) from the Lowlands (A' Ghalltachd). This division, though geographic, can also be compared with a cultural and linguistic divide, with SCOTTISH GAELIC speakers on one side and English speakers on the other.

According to the traditional history of Gaelic Scotland, the Scots began to migrate from Ulster (ULAID), in northeast Ireland (ÉRIU), to Argyll (Earra-Ghaidheal 'the coastland of the Gaels') before AD 500, and established the kingdom of DÁL RIATA, an Irish colony that became the kingdom of the Scots.

Viking invaders began raiding the Hebrides and the Highland seaboards just before AD 800, eventually settling in the Hebrides, Orkney, Shetland, and Caithness. Linguistically, Norse began to predominate in these areas. Norn, a Norse dialect, was spoken here until modern times. The Norse settlements established in the Highlands and Islands during the 9th century owed a nominal allegiance to Norway.

Local Highland rulers eventually began to assert their independence. A powerful Gall-Ghàidheal (i.e., a Gael allied with the Norse), Somerled (Somhairle Mac GillBhrìde †1164) formed the LORDSHIP OF THE ISLES, a semi-autonomous kingdom with its own artistic and literary culture closely linked to Ireland. However, increasing embroilment in Scottish politics caused it to come into conflict with the Scottish Crown as the latter tried to gain influence in the area. The Lordship ended in AD 1493.

Its collapse created a power vacuum that destabilized the Highlands and Islands, leading to the period known as *Linn nan Creach* (the era of plunder). Tribal jealousies and CLAN feuds broke out with renewed vigour as many clans jockeyed for predominance. This conflict aroused the Scottish government to take some sort of action. Through a process of political intrigue and manipulation, the government sought a divide-and-rule policy to exert control over the region. The medieval Scottish kingdom, despite its Gaelic origins, became increasingly hostile toward both Gaelic and the Gaels. Politically, the Statutes of Iona (AD 1609) represented an attempt by the Scottish Crown to Anglicize the leaders and institutions of Gaelic society so that they could gain better control of the area. Soon after, in 1616, an Act was passed to set up parish schools in the Highlands to acculturate the Highlanders and eliminate 'Irish' (i.e., Gaelic) speech, using the stereotype of the Gael as barbaric, backward, bellicose, and alien.

The upheaval of the English and Scottish civil wars during the 1640s further fragmented a politically unstable region. Many Highlanders maintained their loyalty to the exiled Stuarts, supporting armed JACOBITE REBELLIONS with the aim of reinstating the Stuarts, who had been removed during the Glorious Revolution of 1688. The last claimant to the throne, Prince Charles Edward Stuart (1720–88), arrived in Scotland in 1745, and signalled the last Jacobite uprising, known as the '45. The subsequent defeat of the Jacobites by the Hanoverian army at CULLODEN (1746) transformed the Highlands forever. The system of clanship, which had underpinned Gaelic society, was largely dismantled, as the Highlands and Islands became a part of the British state. This process, which was already well under way from the time of the UNION of 1707, was accelerated by the collapse of the Jacobite movement. Chiefs and their subordinates increasingly turned their backs on their Gaelic heritage and culture, and became alienated from their own people.

Conversely, the rehabilitation of the Highlands and the Gaels was supported by the works of James MACPHERSON (1736–96), a key figure in the Romantic movement in European literature and the arts (see also OISÍN; ROMANTICISM). The Gaels were presented as 'noble savages'—a complete reversal of their unqualifiedly negative portrayal by their English and Lowland enemies during the '45. Sir Walter SCOTT (1771–1832) further perfected the ideal and Romantic image of the Gael in his various poems and novels.

Despite the region's status as an international aesthetic touchstone, the Highlands and Islands suffered major depopulation and economic turmoil during the 19th century as the result of large-scale CLEARANCES and emigration. The introduction of large sheep-farms caused enforced displacement of Gaels by landlords who no longer had use for the tenants or their traditional way of life. This trend led to the Gaelic diaspora, in which many Highland residents emigrated to the Lowlands of Scotland or to the New World (see CELTIC LANGUAGES IN NORTH AMERICA).

Up to the period of the clearances and well into the 19th century, the Gaelic-speaking communities can be equated, approximately, with the geographic extent of the Highlands and Islands. At the beginning of the 20th century, there were approximately 200,000 speakers of Gaelic in Scotland. The number of Gaelic speakers in Scotland is now less than 65,000 (see LANGUAGE [REVIVAL] MOVEMENT IN THE CELTIC COUNTRIES).

The history of the Highlands and Islands is inextricably connected with their linguistic and cultural heritage. Whether or not Gaelic and indeed the Highlands and Islands will survive—let alone, flourish—as a distinct region is at present uncertain.

Andrew Wiseman

HISTORIA BRITTONUM

Historia Brittonum (The history of the BRITONS) is a historical work in Latin, with numerous Old Welsh names and some glosses, which was compiled in Wales (CYMRU) in the first half of the 9th century and was popular in Britain and France in the Middle Ages.

The Nature of the Text

Historia Brittonum is an important source for Roman BRITAIN and Wales and the Brythonic north (*yr* HEN OGLEDD) for the 5th to the 7th centuries. While much of the its are picturesque, fantastic, and clearly unhistorical, the reality of most of the individuals named in it can be confirmed from other sources.

The work uses diverse sources: history, HAGIOGRAPHY, GENEALOGIES, native heroic poetry, lore of places and place-names (DINDSHENCHAS), and local historical works. *Historia Brittonum*'s most important single source was the historical material in the 6th-century *De Excidio Britanniae* ('The Destruction of Britain') by GILDAS. *Historia Brittonum* was, in turn, the single most important source used by GEOFFREY OF MONMOUTH in creating his HISTORIA REGUM BRITANNIAE ('History of the Kings of Britain', *c.* 1139). It thus figures as influential in the early formation of ARTHURIAN LITERATURE and the Arthurian framework for Britain's LEGENDARY HISTORY.

Contents

§§1–6 present a scheme of the six ages of the world since the creation, based on the Bible. A description of Britain, derived from Gildas, follows, but introduces other elements—most importantly, Trojan legends of the origins of the Britons and the story of their eponymous founder, Brutus or Britto, with numerous details inspired by Vergil. §12 gives a brief account of the origins of the Picts, ahistorically regarded as arriving after the Britons; §§13–15 describe a series of settlements of Ireland (Ériu); §§19–30 give an account of Roman Britain, including the campaigns of Julius Caesar; §§30–49 concern the unfortunate and infamous King Gwrtheyrn and the coming of the English to Britain, including the tale of the wonder child Ambrosius and the Draig Goch; §§50–5 present a concise Life of Patrick; §56 is the list of Arthur's twelve victorious battles; §§57–65 make up the 'Northern History'; §62 contains the Memorandum of the Five Poets, including the Cynfeirdd, Aneirin and Taliesin. §66 begins with some chronological calculations followed by a list of the Old Welsh names of the 'Twenty-eight Cities of Britain'; as far as these can be identified, most are now in England, and the Welsh names for them are often still in use today—for example, *Cair Ligualid*, Modern *Caerliwelydd* 'Carlisle'. §§67–75 contain the *mirabilia* (wonders) of Britain and Ireland—local legends and remarkable places, often accompanied by place-name tales. The writer knew some of these places first-hand.

Date and Authorship

There are eight recensions (manuscript families) of *Historia Brittonum*, and numerous manuscripts; these vary significantly, and the relationship between them is complex. A rather free Middle Irish translation, the *Lebor Bretnach,* is available. One key manuscript contains a clear reference to the fourth year of the reign of King Merfyn of Gwynedd (r. 825–44), implying writing in that year (i.e., 829/30), which is confirmed in §4, dating its present to 796 years after Christ's Passion. Many modern scholars have believed the recension in which a prologue attributes the text to a 'Ninnius' or 'Nennius'. We know of a Welsh scholar active in the early 9th century with a similar name—the man who created the alphabet of Nemnivus. So widely accepted was the attribution to Nennius that one often sees *Historia Brittonum* referred to as 'Nennius'; however, David Dumville has argued that the Nennian Prologue is a later forgery and was never part of the recensions that now lack it. This question has not yet been settled, and the author is sometimes referred to as 'Pseudo-Nennius' or the text treated as anonymous.

John T. Koch

HISTORIA REGUM BRITANNIAE

Historia Regum Britanniae ('The History of the Kings of Britain') is the common title of a largely fictitious history of pre-Saxon Britain written by Geoffrey of Monmouth, which first appeared *c.* 1139. This work greatly influenced the writing of history and Arthurian literature until the end of the Middle Ages, and continued to influence

Welsh and Breton historiography into early modern times. The author and contents of the *Historia* are discussed at length in the article on Geoffrey.

There is general agreement about the types of pre-Norman Welsh sources to which Geoffrey of Monmouth had access when he wrote the *Historia Regum Britanniae*. These include GILDAS's *De Excidio Britanniae*, HISTORIA BRITTONUM, Old Welsh ANNALS, GENEALOGIES, and HAGIOGRAPHIES. The *Historia* was especially popular in Wales (CYMRU): Welsh translations began to be produced by the earlier 13th century (BRUT Y BRENHINEDD), often containing additional information from Welsh tradition.

John T. Koch

HOARDS AND DEPOSITIONS

Hoards and depositions were relatively common features of religious practice during the late Bronze Age and the IRON AGE within the cultural regions known to have spoken CELTIC LANGUAGES in ancient times. The best attested are WATERY DEPOSITIONS, such as LA TÈNE, Llyn Cerrig Bach, Llyn Fawr, Dowris (Ireland/ÉRIU), Battersea, and Duchov. However, depositions in ditches, pits, caves, and built features such as the earthworks found in various types of FORTIFICATION are also known; depositions in the open air, either in sanctuaries (see FANUM) or in exposed spaces such as mountain passes, have been recorded as well.

Items deposited were often of considerable value: weapons (mainly SWORDS), scabbards, spearheads, SHIELDS, HELMETS, jewellery, TORCS, or bracelets. Less frequently, wagons or CHARIOTS and tools and agricultural implements, as in the Linz-Gründberg hoard (Austria), were deposited. As often as not, items deposited were intentionally damaged (made useless) prior to deposition.

A notable feature of such hoards is that many appear to be associated with liminal space (that is, on the boundary of a region or precinct), and are found either interred in city walls or in gateways or ditches enclosing sites interpreted as sanctuaries. Other examples are depositions in association with bridges across rivers.

While no clear-cut distributional pattern can be established, watery depositions seem to have been the more common practice in BRITAIN and Ireland and in western Continental Europe, while deposition in ditches, pits, and caves are most common in the zone north of the Alps, in eastern France, Germany, the Czech Republic, and northern Austria. In most of the inner Alpine region, deposition in exposed locations or cremation prior to deposition was preferred.

Raimund Karl

HOCHDORF

Eberdingen-Hochdorf is a burial mound in Baden-Württemberg, Germany, associated with the hill-fort of Hohenasperg. It represents the late western HALLSTATT culture, an archaeologically identifiable culture that extended from southwestern Germany and northern and central Switzerland to eastern France in the 6th–5th centuries BC. The aristocratic residences (*Fürstensitze*), such as the one at Hohenasperg, were chiefly

Bronze caryatid from the 6th century BC supporting a bed in a princely grave from Hochdorf, Baden-Württemberg, Germany. Height 30 cm. (Wuerttembergisches Landesmuseum, Stuttgart, Germany/Erich Lessing/Art Resource, New York)

established on prominent hilltops. The pattern of settlement is quite regular, with detached settlements located about 100 km from each other.

Three of the most important graves show the development of aristocratic society during the course of about three or four generations: the tumulus of Hochdorf, dated to *c*. 550 BC; the Grafenbühl, *c*. 500 BC; and the lateral chamber of the Kleinaspergle, *c*. 450 BC, which contains a funeral from the La Tène A period.

Together with the burial at Vix, the tumulus at Hochdorf contains the only undisturbed central grave chamber. For the funeral ceremonies, a platform was banked up in front of the open decorated burial chamber with an entrance way of dressed stone. The outside of the tumulus is enclosed by a stone ring and strong oak posts, which retain the earthen bank. The grave pit in the centre of the tumulus measures 11 m^2 and is 2.5 m deep. The inner burial chamber of 4.7 m^2 is made of oak beams. The gap between the burial chambers and the roof is packed with approximately 50 tons of stone, effectively sealing the tomb in the ground like a bank vault against grave robbers.

A tall man (*c*. 185 cm), approximately 40 years old, was buried in this grave. He wore a flat conical hat made of birch bark, adorned with circle patterns and punched decorations. His characteristic antenna dagger should perhaps be regarded a symbol of social rank rather than a weapon. The golden necklace, like those found in nearly all aristocratic tombs, seems to be another such sign of status. Articles that were used in daily life were also recovered, including a comb, razor, other toiletries, a small iron knife, a quiver with arrows, and a small pouch with three fish-hooks. The deceased was wrapped in finely woven, coloured textiles. The whole chamber was lined with fabrics and decorated with flowers.

Among the equipment typical of such a rich grave were a four-wheeled wagon with harnesses for two horses (typical of Hallstatt wagon burials, the horses themselves were not interred) and a drinking service and dinner set. These items were arranged to serve nine people. Nine drinking horns were suspended from the southern chamber wall, eight of aurochs horn and one five-litre horn of iron. A large three-handled bronze cauldron was found, decorated with three bronze lions on the rim, demonstrating the social position of their owner. It did not contain Greek wine, but rather approximately 400 litres of local honey mead. The dead man was laid out on a couch for a symposium (FEAST). The bed was supported by eight cast bronze female figurines in scanty acrobatic costumes; they stood on small spoked wheels so that the bed could be rolled.

The grave at Hochdorf is a very traditional burial, with only the Greek cauldron definitely imported. Southern influence becomes obvious mainly in the banquet equipment. The grave of the Grafenbühl, in contrast, looks completely different, being more recent by one or two generations. Unfortunately, this grave chamber was looted in antiquity. It is certain that Grafenbühl had been much more richly furnished than Hochdorf.

The development of the aristocratic burial tradition in this region continued up to the tumulus of Kleinaspergle, which dates from about 50 years later (i.e., mid-5th century). The dead woman was cremated, a southern funeral custom.

These three graves demonstrate the development of aristocratic society during the 6th and early 5th centuries. The earliest tombs were enclosed in monumental barrows, with very traditional grave furnishings, and isolated large and very precious imported goods. Imports from the south became more frequent, smaller, and less expensive over time. Attic ceramics figure in the latest graves. Southern ideas and customs were adopted in terms of the artistic style, banquet customs, and burial rites; these were not mindless imports, but rather were imitated and assembled locally. The ornamentation on the handle of the wine flagon from the Kleinaspergle represents the final product of this development.

Compared with the burials, we know very little of the settlements where these sites are found. Excavations show open hamlets of limited size with shifting locations over time. They start at the end of Hallstatt D1 and continue until the beginning of La Tène B (roughly 600–300 BC). Then, a general break in the settlements occurs, as in the burials.

A complete settlement has been uncovered above the village of Hochdorf. It contained large houses (140 m^2), storage pits, granaries, and fenced-in rectangular areas. The settlement seems to have followed a regular plan. A reconstruction of the site shows an open, undefended rectangular hamlet of about ten to twelve homesteads; the plan anticipates the organization of an OPPIDUM of the Late La Tène period. Wheel-turned local pottery is very well represented here in comparison to other sites, implying that the inhabitants enjoyed a position of economic privilege. Blacksmithing, bronze casting, and, above all, textile production are widely attested. The settlement may have been the rough equivalent of a country seat belonging to rulers of the Hohenasperg.

In the course of the 5th century, the principal sites and their surrounding rural villages came to an end. For about 200 years until the formation of the later oppida civilization, a general stagnation can be observed in the region, while the development beyond this region takes a much more dynamic course in such other areas of the La Tène Celtic-speaking world as the central Rhine, Champagne, and Bohemia.

Jörg Biel

HURLING

Hurling or hurley (Irish *iomânaíocht*) is a traditional ball-and-stick game played in Ireland (ÉIRE), broadly comparable to hockey; it should not be confused with a similarly named sport formerly played in Cornwall (KERNOW). The Irish game is recognized in medieval LAW TEXTS and heroic literature—for example, 'The Boyhood Deeds of Cú CHULAINN' in the TÁIN BÓ CUAILNGE ('The Cattle Raid of Cooley'). The Statutes of KILKENNY (1366) forbade the game, but it remained popular into the 18th century. After a period of decline, the Dublin University Hurley Club drew up the first formal rules for the game in 1870. In 1879, a controlling body, the Hurley Union, was formed, and matches were played against English hockey clubs. The Gaelic Athletic Association regulated all-Ireland hurling championships from 1887. The game had achieved its modern form by 1913.

Neal Garnham

HYDE, DOUGLAS

See De hÍde, Dubhghlas.

HYMNS, WELSH

Hymns are songs of praise to God, usually for congregational use. The earliest Welsh religious and scriptural verse that has survived consists of 33 poems composed between the 9th and 12th centuries. The best known of the early hymns and poems is *Gogonedog Arglwydd, henffych well* (Greetings, glorious Lord), recorded in the Black Book of Carmarthen (LLYFR DU CAERFYRDDIN) *c.* 1250 and still in use as late as 1941.

In contrast to psalm singing, Welsh hymns in the modern period are largely a product of the REFORMATION. Rees Pritchard (1579–1644) wrote *Canwyll y Cymru* (Candle of the Welsh, 1646), whose carols *Awn i Fethlem* (Let us go to Bethlehem) and *Rhown Foliant o'r Mwyaf* (Let us give the greatest praise) are still frequently sung in church services. A handful of psalms, hymns, and poems by Morgan Llwyd (1619–59) are the most significant production of this period, aesthetically speaking.

William Williams of Pantycelyn became the epicentre of a truly remarkable upsurge of Calvinist hymn writing in Carmarthenshire (sir Gaerfyrddin) beginning in 1744. Undoubtedly the greatest Welsh-language writer of the 18th century, Williams was not only a hymn writer, but also a writer of epics, elegies, odes, and historical, psychological, and theological prose.

By the beginning of the 19th century, the centre of hymnal gravity had shifted to mid- and north Wales. Edward Jones (1761–1836), of Maes-y-plwm, was the first notable exponent, and the finest of the Denbighshire (sir Ddinbych) hymn-writers: He was the author of *Llond y nefoedd, llond y byd* (He fills the heavens, fills the world) and *Pob seraff, pob sant* (Every seraph, every saint). He was followed by the most remarkable of this mid- and northern Wales group—namely, Ann Griffiths, the passionate scriptural 'mystic', who composed arguably the greatest hymn in the language, *Rhyfedd, rhyfedd gan angylion* (Wonder, wonder of the angels). She is easily second to Pantycelyn in the wonder of her expression, and sometimes exceeds him in the sheer beauty and imaginative energy of her works. The secret of the strength of the southwestern group of hymnists in the second half of the 18th century and of the mighty northern group in the first half of the 19th century was the combination of meaningful doctrinal thought and a sustained emotional dedication.

After this period, hymn writing now veered toward GWYNEDD, and became more classical in tone and polished in craftsmanship. The central tenets of the Christian revelation and biblical faith remained unshaken, however. Robert ap Gwilym Ddu (Robert Williams, 1766–1850) wrote *Mae'r gwaed a redodd ar y groes* (The blood that ran on the cross) and excels in majesty of tone. Pedr Fardd (Peter Jones, 1775–1845) was the third most accomplished hymn-writer produced by Calvinists in Wales. His works included *Daeth ffrydiau melys iawn* (Very sweet streams came) and *Dywedwyd ganwaith na chawn fyw* (It's been said a hundred times that I may not live). A noteworthy successor among the most significant writers of this group was Ieuan Glan Geirionydd (Evan Evans, 1795–1855), an important developer of ROMANTICISM but rather overrated as a hymn-writer. A greater writer generally, however, and a trenchant writer of three heart-wrenching hymns was Eben Fardd (Ebenezer Thomas, 1802–63).

The different demands of modern times are reflected in the content of the recently published collection of Welsh hymns, *Caneuon Ffydd* (2001). On the one hand, there remains the Georgian lyricism (of the great 18th- and early 19th-century hymnists) among emulators of an old tradition; on the other hand, one finds a surfeit of translations of what are usually known as choruses.

R. M. Jones

HYWEL DDA

Hywel Dda († c. 950) ruled over an extensive part of Wales (CYMRU) between AD 943 and 950. He was the grandson of RHODRI MAWR and the son of Cadell, ruler of Seisyllwg. Cadell died in 911 and, in accordance with Welsh custom, the realm was divided between Hywel and his brother Clydog. With the death of his brother in 920, Hywel united the whole of Seisyllwg and Dyfed to form a new kingdom, later called Deheubarth. This kingdom remained in the hands of his descendants for centuries.

Following the death of Edward the Elder, Hywel was among the Welsh princes who paid homage to his successor Æthelstan (king of Wessex, 924–40) in 926/7. Between 928 and 949, Hywel's signature with the title *regulus* 'petty king' appears at the head of those of all other minor Welsh princes as witness to numerous Anglo-Saxon charters.

Idwal ab Anarawd, king of GWYNEDD, and his brother were killed in battle against the English in 942, and Hywel saw his chance to take control over Gwynedd and Powys. In doing so, he extended his power over a large part of Wales.

The most famous and most documented act attributed to Hywel is that of compiling a law-book, but the earliest texts relating his part in this important achievement are at least two centuries later than Hywel's own time. Throughout the Middle Ages, Welsh law was known as the Law of Hywel. According to the LAW TEXTS, he summoned wise men from each hundred (CANTREF) in Wales. The members of the assembly prayed and fasted to warrant the blessing of God on their amendment of the Welsh laws and traditions. This story, in different forms, appears as a prologue or epilogue to most of the Welsh law-books.

Whether or not the story is literally true, such a degree of Welsh political unity was unknown under any other ruler, and there is at least an element of truth in the law-books' account. It has been suggested that Hywel's involvement with the West Saxon kings might have inspired him to revise the native laws, as Alfred and Æthelstan did in ENGLAND. The texts themselves contain traces of Old English words; for example, Welsh *edling* (heir apparent) stems from OE *aetheling*.

Hywel's reign was marked by an outburst of literary activity, perhaps stimulated by the Carolingian renaissance. The poem ARMES PRYDEIN, which possibly reflects the scenario of the battle of Brunanburh, was composed in the first half of the 9th century, and the archetypes of the HISTORIA BRITTONUM and the *Annales Cambriae* originate from the time of Hywel's son, Owain ap Hywel.

The common Welsh man's name *Hywel* (Old Welsh *Higuel, Houel*, Old Breton *Hou(u)el, Hoel*, Anglicized as *Howell*) is a compound of the Celtic affirmative prefix * *su-* and verbal root *wel- 'see'; as an adjective, *hywel* means 'visible' (thus applied to a person probably 'open, forthright', rather than 'good-looking' or 'having good vision').

Gwenno Angharad Elias and Morfydd E. Owen